Public Management Reform

Public Management Reform

A Comparative Analysis—New Public Management, Governance, and the Neo-Weberian State

THIRD EDITION

Christopher Pollitt

and

Geert Bouckaert

OXFORD

UNIVERSITY PRESS

OXFORD
UNIVERSITY PRESS

Great Clarendon Street, Oxford OX2 6DP

Oxford University Press is a department of the University of Oxford.
It furthers the University's objective of excellence in research, scholarship,
and education by publishing worldwide in

Oxford New York

Auckland Cape Town Dar es Salaam Hong Kong Karachi
Kuala Lumpur Madrid Melbourne Mexico City Nairobi
New Delhi Shanghai Taipei Toronto

With offices in

Argentina Austria Brazil Chile Czech Republic France Greece
Guatemala Hungary Italy Japan Poland Portugal Singapore
South Korea Switzerland Thailand Turkey Ukraine Vietnam

Oxford is a registered trade mark of Oxford University Press
in the UK and in certain other countries

Published in the United States
by Oxford University Press Inc., New York

British Library Cataloguing in Publication Data

Data available

Library of Congress Cataloging in Publication Data

Data available

Typeset by SPI Publisher Services, Pondicherry, India
Printed in Great Britain
on acid-free paper by
CPI Group (UK) Ltd, Croydon, CR0 4YY

ISBN 978–0–19–959508–2 (Hbk)
ISBN 978–0–19–959509–9 (Pbk)

1 3 5 7 9 10 8 6 4 2

For our parents,
Freda, John, Leen, and Michel

■ PREFACE TO THE THIRD EDITION

To go into a third edition is quite a serious step. A second edition betokens a modest degree of success in attracting readers who hope to find something useful or interesting between the covers. But a third edition begins to feel like a process of institutionalization—as if one has now become one of the statues in the park of public management and administration.

Unlike statues, however, our book will not stand still. It evolves almost daily, sometimes in accordance with our wishes and at other times in a tiresome or annoying way. In fact this third edition, while inhabiting a similar broad framework of chapters and appendices, is hugely different from the second. Some chapters are completely new, and all the others have undergone extensive rewriting and updating. In the remainder of this preface we would like to explain the logic of this overhaul.

Scope

Our subject—comparative management reform—has grown tremendously over the past couple of decades. It has changed significantly even since the first edition of this book was being written, in 1998–9. The literature has expanded fast and the diversity of perspectives and techniques has also increased. We are delighted that the first two editions of *Public Management Reform: A Comparative Analysis* played their part in this growth. It has been one of the most widely cited publications, and we hope and intend that this very extensively changed third edition will continue to stimulate and inform.

We have stuck to the same twelve countries (plus the EU Commission) as in the second edition. The practical reasons for thus restricting our focus were several. To begin with, a dozen states is already a lot to handle, in the sense of becoming familiar with the details of their reform histories. Further, in order to minimize misunderstandings and superficial interpretations, we took an early decision not to include states which neither of us had recently visited. Additionally, in only two cases were neither of us at least minimally able to understand the mother-tongue: Italy and Sweden. In the case of Italy we were fortunate in obtaining the detailed help of a leading Italian scholar, Eduardo Ongaro (see, for example, Ongaro, 2009). In the case of Sweden, so many documents are published in English as well as Swedish that we felt somewhat reassured. In every country we also contacted resident scholars who generously helped us check our facts and impressions (see Acknowledgements for details). For these various reasons we arrived at our final list of Australia, Belgium, Canada, Finland, France, Germany, Italy, the Netherlands, New Zealand, Sweden, the United Kingdom, the United States of America, and the European Commission. With considerable regret, we resisted the tempting invitations from various parties to add (inter alia) Brazil, Denmark, Estonia, Japan, and Norway to our portfolio.

Choosing a time period also has implications. As in previous editions, we started the clock in 1980. That made reasonable sense, insofar as the first waves of New Public Management-type reforms began to appear internationally in the early and mid 1980s. It does mean, however, that we have a huge additional quantity of more recent material, all to be fitted in to roughly the same number of pages as before. Whereas the second edition covered roughly twenty-three years of reform, this edition covers twenty-nine— and the additional six years have been rather busy! A higher degree of selectivity has been unavoidable.

In a nutshell, therefore, the third edition holds to the same geographical scope as the second edition, but has to cover much more material because of the longer period covered and the marked growth in reform activity during that period.

Changes in chapters

The first chapter is entirely new, and did not exist in the first two editions. Its purpose is twofold. First, it indicates the scope of the book: the nature of the subject matter and how broadly and deeply we will cover it. Second, it introduces readers to some of the main recent debates in the field. These will be summarized here, and then continually picked up in the later chapters, as we proceed. The intention is to give a strong flavour of what our subject is about—what gets scholars (and often practitioners) excited, and where the main arguments and controversies currently lie. It also introduces three major models or visions of what the substance of public management reform has been (or, in some cases, should be). These three models are then picked up at various points throughout the rest of the book.

Chapter 2 introduces a model of the process of public management reform which is basically similar to that in previous editions. However, experiences using the book for teaching students have led us to revise our explanations of what the model does and does not do. Its advantages and limitations should now be significantly clearer. One particularly important development of the original material is the inclusion of a discussion relating what is basically a model of the process of change in *one* country to the increasingly important *international* dimension of management reform.

The revision of Chapter 3 ('Many houses: types of politico-administrative regime') has benefited considerably from the rapid growth in comparative studies over the past decade. Whilst we see no need to alter our list of key factors, there is now much more scholarly and empirical back-up for this general approach, and we cite a good deal of it. Several new sections have also been inserted.

Chapter 4 ('Trajectories of modernization and reform') has been very extensively rewritten. There are two principal reasons for this. First, there is simply an awful lot of new data—recent reform attempts—to be added and considered. Second, the scholarly debate about trajectories, trends, and patterns has become theoretically and conceptually more sophisticated since the previous edition. We have needed to refer to, and engage with, that debate.

Chapter 5 ('Results: through a glass darkly') is another section of the book that has required wholesale revision. Since the first edition was written in the late 1990s there has been an explosion of international indices and 'league tables' pertaining to various aspects of governance (see, e.g. Dixon et al., 2008; Pollitt, 2010b). This growth industry has spawned both new data and new problems and controversies. We try to report some of the most relevant data and (necessarily briefly) comment on some of the controversies.

Chapter 6 ('Politics and management') was also a large-scale rewrite. The last few years have seen a number of illuminating studies of the interface between top public servants and politicians (e.g. Hood and Lodge, 2006; Peters and Pierre, 2004) and we had to catch up on these. The net result has been a refinement and elaboration of the conceptual framework we employed in the earlier editions.

Chapter 7 ('Trade-offs, limits, dilemmas, contradictions, and paradoxes') is largely new. Whilst we have not abandoned the insights in the previous edition, we are now able to set them within a more coherent discussion of developing *patterns over time* (Pollitt, 2008). In doing this we have benefited from another recent academic growth area—the debates around path dependency and cycles.

In Chapter 8 ('Reflections') we take the opportunity to look back at the large canvas constituted by the seven earlier chapters. Like Chapter 1, this is an entirely new chapter, in which we decided to start afresh rather than modify the previous material. Readers will make up their own minds concerning the quality of these reflections, but, for our part, we believe that the mixture or balance, though not utterly transformed since the second edition, does reflect some significant recent learning by us.

In conclusion, we would say that—although this was not our main aim at the start—the changes since the second edition have been sufficiently extensive that scholars who read that earlier work carefully would nevertheless find this third edition of sufficient interest to work through to the end. For most students, of course, it will be first time round, and we hope that we have learned enough from those who worked with previous editions to have further clarified the presentation of some of the key issues, while retaining the overviews and factual summaries that so many readers have told us are useful.

■ ACKNOWLEDGEMENTS

Unsurprisingly, for a book of this scope, now in its third incarnation, our debts are too numerous and go too far back in time for us adequately to acknowledge them all in a small space here. Thus we are, uncomfortably, obliged to be somewhat selective in our expressions of gratitude.

A first acknowledgement must go to our home institution, Katholieke Universiteit Leuven. Over the years it has supported our research efforts and, more specifically, enabled us to spend time together to work on this third edition.

A second acknowledgement is due to our network of colleagues and friends who share an interest in comparative public administration. Our many citations make clear how extensively we have drawn on the work of others, but, in addition to the normal processes of benefiting from each other's publications, we have received a generous portion of informal assistance and comment from a number of individuals during the preparation of this third edition, and its predecessors. Indeed, some of them have helped on a scale way beyond normal professional colleagueship, and we were somewhat embarrassed by the sheer weight of their goodwill. We particularly wish to acknowledge Peter Aucoin, Jonathan Breul, Maurice Demers, Jean-Michel Eymeri-Douzans, Jan-Eric Furubo, Bob Gregory, John Halligan, Sigurdur Helgasson, Jan-Coen Hellendoorn, Ralph Heintzman, Annie Hondeghem, Patricia Ingraham, Werner Jann, Helmut Klages, Walter Kickert, Roger Levy, Elke Löffler, Rudolf Maes, Nick Manning, John Mayne, Nicole de Montricher, Don Moynihan, Johanna Nurmi, Jim Perry, Guy B. Peters, Jon Pierre, Rune Premfors, Isabella Proeller, Beryl Radin, Irene Rubin, Luc Rouban, Fabio Rugge, Donald Savoie, David Shand, Hilkka Summa, Goran Sunström, Colin Talbot, Sandra van Thiel, Nick Thijs, Turo Virtanen, and Petri Uusikylä. We must also thank Elio Borgonovi and Edoardo Ongaro at Università Bocconi in Milan, who produced an excellent Italian translation of the first edition, generously allowed us to draw on their material on recent Italian reforms and, in Edoardo's case, briefed us for this third edition on recent changes.

Third, we have received some special help with this edition. Arianne Sanders and Jesse Stroobants have saved us a lot of time by fishing out needed facts and figures. Inge Vermeulen has worked her magic with diagrams, and Maaike Vandenhaute has tidied up a lot of stuff that badly needed it. Anneke Heylen has performed her usual immaculate job in organizing the final stages before handover to Oxford University Press.

Finally, we would like to acknowledge those organizations which have contributed—indirectly but significantly—to this book by being willing to fund serious empirical research into public management reform. In the age of the 'sound bite' and the 'packaged' management consultancy solution it takes some institutional courage to invest in the kind of time-consuming research which almost always reveals variety and complexity. As this book makes clear, however, if politicians' hopes, public money, and civil servants' time are not to be wasted, such research is desperately needed. We therefore gratefully acknowledge the support we have at various times received from Brunel University, the Canadian Centre for Management Development, Erasmus University Rotterdam, the Finnish Ministry of Finance, the Public Management Institute and the Research Council of the Katholieke Universiteit Leuven, and the UK Economic and Social Research Council.

Christopher Pollitt
Geert Bouckaert

■ CONTENTS

LIST OF FIGURES   xiv
LIST OF TABLES   xv
ABBREVIATIONS   xvi

    1   **Comparative public management reform: an introduction to the key debates**   1

    2   **Problems and responses: a model of public management reform**   31

    3   **Many houses: types of politico-administrative regime**   47

    4   **Trajectories of modernization and reform**   75

    5   **Results: through a glass darkly**   126

    6   **Politics and management**   161

    7   **Trade-offs, balances, limits, dilemmas, contradictions, and paradoxes**   182

    8   **Reflections**   206

APPENDIX A: THE SOCIO-ECONOMIC CONTEXT   222
APPENDIX B: COUNTRY FILES AND TABLES OF EVENTS   231
   AUSTRALIA   231
   BELGIUM   238
   CANADA   247
   THE EUROPEAN COMMISSION   256
   FINLAND   263
   FRANCE   271
   GERMANY   279
   ITALY   285
   THE NETHERLANDS   290
   NEW ZEALAND   298
   SWEDEN   305
   UNITED KINGDOM   313
   UNITED STATES OF AMERICA   321
BIBLIOGRAPHY   332
INDEX   359

■ LIST OF FIGURES

1.1 The focus of this book   3

1.2 Performance: a conceptual framework   16

1.3 *Plats* and paradigms   25

2.1 A model of public management reform   33

4.1 The concept of a trajectory   76

4.2 Extent of use of performance budgeting by central governments, 2007   80

4.3 Some types of public service bargain   96

5.1 Performance: a conceptual framework   133

8.1 Some patterns of reform   211

B.1 Financial implications of further state reform for the Belgian federal system   239

■ LIST OF TABLES

1.1 Three waves of reform thinking 11
1.2 Researching public management reforms 13
1.3 Big models—big claims: the basics 22
1.4 Three approaches to cutbacks 28

3.1 Types of politico-administrative regimes: five key features of public administration systems 50
3.2 Distribution of general government expenditure and employment by level of government 53
3.3 State structure and the nature of executive government 55
3.4 Indicators of different cultural aspects in different countries 65

4.1 Aspects of trajectories: context (what) and process (how) 77
4.2 Accounting trajectories 83
4.3 Strategic choices in decentralization 103

5.1 Government effectiveness scores (World Bank Governance Indicators) 128
5.2 Pisa reading scores, 2006 131
5.3 General government expenditures as a percentage of GDP 137
5.4 Employment in general government as a percentage of the labour force 138
5.5 Social expenditure as a percentage of GDP 139
5.6 Government efficiency 2003 according to the IMD's world competitiveness yearbook 141
5.7 Citizens' assessments of public and private services (Canada) 145
5.8 Confidence in the civil service (World Values Survey) 147
5.9 Trust in the civil service (Eurobarometer surveys) 147

6.1 Roles for politicians and civil servants: three ideal-type models 169
6.2 Weaknesses in the three ideal-type models 170

A.1 Real GDP growth 223
A.2 Changes in real GDP between the first quarter of 2008 and the third quarter of 2009 223
A.3 International trade in goods and services as a percentage of GDP 224
A.4 General government expenditures as a percentage of GDP 224
A.5 General government gross financial liabilities as a percentage of GDP 225
A.6 Population aged 65 and over as a percentage of the total population 227
A.7 Income inequality mid 2000s 228
A.8 Foreign-born populations as a percentage of total populations 228
A.9 Estimated total populations 2010 229

B.1 Cultural differences between the two linguistic communities in Belgium 240
B.2 The development of public sector employment in Belgium 242
B.3 Employment in the core administrations at federal, state, and local levels in Belgium, 2007 242

ABBREVIATIONS

APS	Australian Public Service
BPR	Business Process Re-engineering
CAF	Common Assessment Framework (an EU quality system)
CDR	*Centre de responsabilité* (France)
DEG	Digital-Era Governance
DG	Directorate General (the main organizational division within the EU Commission and in a number of continental European administrations)
EMS	Expenditure Management System
ENA	*Ecole Nationale d'Administration* (France)
EU	European Union
FoI	Freedom of Information
GAO	General Accounting Office (USA – re-named Government Accountability Office in 2004)
GDP	Gross Domestic Product
GEC	Global Economic Crisis (2008)
GPRA	Government Performance and Results Act (USA)
HRM	Human Resource Management
ICT	Information and Communications Technology
KRA	Key Results Area (New Zealand)
LOLF	*Loi Organique relative aux Lois de Finances*
MAF	Management Accountability Framework (Canada)
MAP 2000	Modernizing Administrative and Personnel Policy 2000 (EU Commission)
MbO	Management by Objectives
MP	Member of Parliament
MTM	market-type mechanism
MYOP	Multi-Year Operational Plan
NASA	National Aeronautics and Space Administration (USA)
NHS	National Health Service (UK)
NPG	New Public Governance
NPM	New Public Management
NPR	National Performance Review (USA)
NWS	Neo-Weberian State
OECD	Organization for Economic Cooperation and Development
OFP	Operational Framework Plan (USA)
OMB	Office of Management and Budget (USA)
OPM	Office of Personnel Management (USA)
OSHA	Occupational Safety and Health Administration (USA)
PART	Program Assessment Rating Tool (USA)
PEMS	Policy and Expenditure Management System (Canada)
PI	Performance Indicator

PISA	Programme for International Student Assessment
PM	Prime Minister
PPBS	Planning, Programming, and Budgeting System (USA)
PPP	Public–Private Partnership
PRP	Performance-Related Pay
PSA	Public Service Agreement (UK)
PSB	Public Service Bargain
PSBR	Public Sector Borrowing Requirement (UK)
PUMA	Public Management Service of the OECD
RIA	Regulatory Impact Analysis
SAI	Supreme Audit Institution (the generic title given themselves by national audit offices)
SEM	Sound and Efficient Management Initiative (EU Commission)
SES	Senior Executive Service
SOA	Special Operating Agency (Canada)
SRA	Strategic Results Area (New Zealand)
TQM	Total Quality Management
UNPAN	United Nations Public Administration Network
VBTB	Van Beleidsbegroting Tot Beleidsverantwoording (From policy budgeting to accountability budgeting) (Netherlands)
WGA	Whole-of-Government Accounting
WGI	Worldwide Governance Indicator
ZBB	Zero-Based Budgeting
ZBO	*Zelfstandige Bestuursorganen* (Dutch autonomous public bodies)

1 Comparative public management reform: an introduction to the key debates

We've got a government in a box, ready to roll in.

(General Stanley A. McChrystal, senior American commander in Afghanistan, speaking at the beginning of an offensive to retake territory from the Taliban in southern Afghanistan, February 2010—quoted in Filkins, 2010)

1.1 Purpose

We think General McChrystal was sadly mistaken. No government can be instantly rolled out from a box, not even in far less adverse circumstances than obtained in southern Afghanistan in 2010. In this book we are looking, not at Afghanistan, but at the relatively stable and prosperous democracies of Australasia, Europe, and North America—and yet we remain less optimistic about what can be achieved (and how it can be done) than the American commander. Understanding what is and is not possible in public management reform (which is, of course only one part of government reform) and seeing over what timescales changes of different types may be hoped for, should be valuable knowledge. We cannot offer a six-steps-to-success cookbook (and we rather doubt if anybody can), but we can draw out an international map of the debates and the events of the last generation. From this we may elicit some cautious conclusions about what has and has not been achieved under widely varying circumstances. Our aim is thus to provide a comparative analytic account of public management thinking and reform in twelve developed countries over a period of thirty years.

Lest our opening scepticism be interpreted as cynicism or 'negativity', we should also affirm that such a broad perspective actually provides plenty of evidence of beneficial change, and that we certainly think that good management can and does make a big difference to the impacts and legitimacy of governments. Examples of successful reforms will be cited as we go along. It is just that the imagery of conjuring good government out of a box finds no resonance at all in the massive corpus of evidence that we are about to review. For good reasons, that we will explain, it can never be that simple—or that quick.

1.2 **Scope**

We focus on public management reform, defined for our purposes as:

Deliberate changes to the structures and processes of public sector organizations with the objective of getting them (in some sense) to run better.

This is a deliberately open and wide definition which clearly leaves all sorts of important questions still to be answered. For example, 'structures or processes' could be the organizational structures of ministries and agencies, or the processes by which public servants are recruited, trained, promoted, and (if necessary) dismissed, or the legal and administrative relationships between the citizens using public services and the organizations providing them (as in a 'citizens' charter, for example). And 'getting them to run better' could mean getting these organizations to run more efficiently, or ensuring that they are more responsive to the citizens who used them, or focusing more strongly on achieving their official objectives (reducing poverty, promoting exports, etc.). It should be obvious that these different kinds of objective will sometimes trade off against each other, for example a more Spartan, efficient service that minimizes the taxpayers' money spent on each of its activities may not simultaneously be able to increase its responsiveness to citizens or effectiveness in achieving policy goals. So the phrase 'in some sense' may stand for some difficult choices and decisions about what the priorities really are. Reforms and 'modernization' almost always necessitate some awkward choices of this kind—decision-makers are obliged to decide what they think is most important—they can seldom hope to have everything at the same time.

The empirical area (locus) to which we apply this definition of reform is very broad, but yet it is still much less than the total field of public management. In brief, we have chosen to apply ourselves mainly to *central government in twelve specific countries, plus the management of the European Commission.* Thus, obviously, we do not deal with reforms in the hundreds of other countries, or with reforms at regional or local level, or with reforms in international organizations other than the European Union (EU), Commission. Central government, however, means much more than ministries and 'high politics'. It includes vital-but-unobtrusive services like registering births and deaths (central in some countries, local in others), or issuing driving licences. It includes both regulatory and executive agencies, which may be at arm's length from ministries and ministers, often with a degree of statutory independence. It involves major services such as national police forces, and public hospitals, schools and universities. In most countries these services employ far more staff and spend much more money than do the ministries themselves. However, the qualifying phrase 'in most countries' is important. The split of services between central governments (our focus) and subnational governments varies a lot between countries, and also somewhat over time. Thus, for example, central government is responsible for a much bigger share of services in New Zealand or the UK than in Germany, Finland, or the USA (OECD, 2009*a*, p. 57).

Yet this broad sweep still leaves a lot out. In all countries, governments seek to achieve many of their purposes through contracts or partnerships with non-governmental organizations (NGOs). In some countries (such as the USA) this zone of 'contracted out' yet still public activity is truly enormous, and some critics have begun to write of the 'hollow state' (e.g. Milward and Provan, 2000). It includes the work of charitable organizations and other 'non-profit' bodies that form part of civil society, as well as for-profit companies that inhabit the market sector. Some of these contractors and partners are quite small, local organizations, while others are large and multinational. In other countries, such as Germany or Belgium, religious and social foundations ('civil associations') continue to play an important role in providing key social, health care, and educational services. Thus this zone embraces both purely commercial contracting and sub-contracting, and more close and intimate 'public private partnerships' (PPPs—Bovaird and Tizzard, 2009), or long-standing charitable provision. We will not focus directly on most of this activity. We do note the shifts towards contracting out and partnerships, and we observe that this has been pursued to different degrees and in different ways in different countries, but we do not study these hybrid organizations per se. However, the growth of this penumbra to the core public sector is a key feature of 'governance' and 'network' approaches, and we will need to return to it at various points in the book.

Figure 1.1 should help clarify our focus. Our book is concerned with reform in the right-hand side of the inner circle—where it is marked as 'management'. Indeed, it is mainly concerned with only the upper quartile of that circle—the shaded part that relates to *central* government rather than sub-national governments.

Yet Figure 1.1 is itself far from perfect—like most diagrams it clarifies some issues while raising others. For example, it shows a 'borderzone' between the public and private sector (this is a zone that most scholars accept has grown over the past few decades). In this zone, for example, a private company may be contracted by government to provide a public service, or government may lay down regulations to govern safety in civil associations such as sports clubs or even churches. In a way the idea of a border*zone* may not be the most

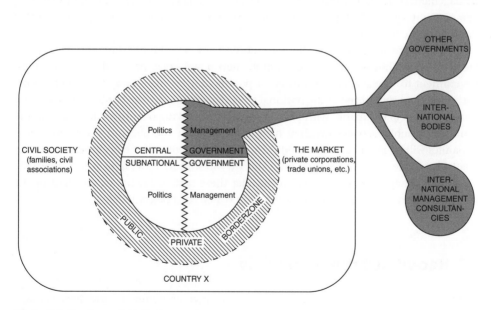

Figure 1.1 The focus of this book

realistic graphic representation. It is perhaps a bit too neat for what are in practice a myriad of complex, overlapping public 'tentacles' which reach out deep into both civil society and the business sector. Similarly the tentacles of the private sector reach into the heart of government. Government offices may be cleaned by private sector contractors. Government computers may be supplied and maintained by private sector companies, and so on. However, rather than attempt a potentially confusing figure that involved overlapping spiders' webs, we chose a simple and static representation—just to get started.

A second noteworthy feature of Figure 1.1 is the jagged line between 'politics' and 'management' that crosses the inner circle of the government system (both at national and subnational levels). The jaggedness is our rather feeble attempt to represent another set of relationships that are probably too complex to be entirely captured in a simple graphic. Suffice it to say here that the sensitive relationship between the political and the managerial has been a perennially debated issue within the academic field of public administration and management (see, e.g. Peters and Pierre, 2004). It will be touched on again in almost every chapter, but particularly in Chapter 6. Our focus is on management, but the insights of many previous scholars tell us that we cannot understand *public* management without also paying attention to political structures and processes.

A third feature of the figure is the channel connecting public management *within* the government system with 'other governments', 'international bodies', and 'international management consultancies', all of which lie *outside* the particular country which may be under consideration. Once more, this is a form of graphical shorthand. It is intended to depict the fact that—increasingly—reform ideas circulate round international networks, not just national ones. Governments copy other governments. Ministers and civil servants also swap ideas at meetings of the OECD, or the EU Council of Ministers, or the World Bank. Governments in many countries have also made increasing use of advice from management consultants, and the big management consultancies are multinational companies (Saint Martin, 2005). We will have a lot more to say about the emergence of this international community for reform later.

It is important to realize that the main borderlines between the different elements in Figure 1.1 may shift over time. For example, new powers may be devolved from central government to subnational authorities, or powers may be taken away from subnational authorities and centralized at the national level. The public–private borderzone—as mentioned above—may expand, with private corporations taking over more and more of the running of public services (as they have done in both the UK and the USA). These dynamics will be noted and discussed throughout the book, but we begin here with this relatively simple, static representation. Later we will shift to 'moving pictures', especially in the final chapter, where we will reconsider these basic elements in the light of the considerable amount of empirical information which the book will deliver.

1.3 Recent debates in the field

Of course, in one chapter we cannot cover *all* the different arguments and debates that a growing and increasingly international community of public management scholars have spawned over even the past ten years, let alone a longer period. We have had to be quite selective, so in the following sections we pick out what we consider to be the most important or interesting topics, and attempt to summarize the arguments. Those who wish to go deeper are urged to consult the references that we supply as a starting point for further study.

These are the issues we have chosen:

- Why has public management reform become a much more prominent issue than it was in the 1950s or 1960s? (Section 1.4)
- What has been the main direction of reform? (Section 1.5)
- Has there been a global convergence on one particular way of managing the public sector, or are there a variety of models? (Section 1.6)
- Internationally, how successful has the New Public Management (NPM) been? (Section 1.7)
- What other models—apart from the NPM—have been influential? (Section 1.8)
- What, in particular, are we to make of 'networks'? (Section 1.9)
- And what is the significance of the so-called shift from government to 'governance'? (Section 1.10)
- What are the implications for public management reform of the global economic crisis which began in the second half of 2008? (Section 1.11)

Finally, we also introduce some more epistemological or methodological issues:

- What kind of answers should we be looking for—models and menus? (Section 1.12)
- What kinds of methods are used in comparative research? (Section 1.13)
- Reflections and conclusions: management reforms caught between 'is' and 'ought'? (Section 1.14)

Most of these issues are closely interconnected, so one section leads into the next. All these issues will—as indicated earlier—reappear at various levels of detail as you move through the later chapters of the book.

1.4 Why has public management reform become a much more prominent issue than it was in the 1950s or 1960s?

Back in the 1950s, public management reform was different in two particular but fundamental ways. First, it was generally treated as a technical or legal, rather than a political or economic matter—it was usually a question of rather dull organizational and procedural changes. It was not normally something that party leaders or the mass media made much public fuss about. There was nothing like the stream of reform white papers and glossy brochures which we have become accustomed to more recently in many European countries and in North America. Second, it was an essentially national or even sectoral matter. Germans made their reforms in the light of German circumstances and history, as did the French, the British, the Americans, and so on. There was little *international* debate about such issues, and the usual assumption was that each country ploughed its own furrow. This attitude was reinforced—in many countries—by the important role constitutional and administrative law played in administrative reform. The relevant framework of law was very different in France from that in the UK, and in the USA it was different again—therefore the reforms themselves were likely to be different. International *fora* such as the OECD Public Management Committee or the United Nations Public Administration Network (UNPAN)—which subsequently became influential talking shops for public management reform—did not then exist. Neither did the multi-national management consultancies which, since the late 1980s, have come to play such an influential role in the reforms of many countries. The enormous subsequent growth of institutionalized, international management networks had not yet taken place (Sahlin-Andersson and Engwall, 2002; Saint-Martin, 2005). Similarly, in the academic world, we know of no group of scholars who at that time made *comparative* public administration (as it would then have been called) a consistent focus for debate, research, and publication. As far as the developed world was concerned, there were a few isolated works, frequently of a predominantly legal/constitutional nature, and that was all (Pollitt, 2011). There was, however, a considerable body of comparative 'development' administration pertaining mainly to the developing world, and frequently setting up Western models as the ideal towards which developing countries should aspire.

With the advantage of hindsight, we can see that this began to change in some countries in the late 1960s and early 1970s, and then began to affect many more from the late 1970s/early 1980s. The first wave—which was principally concerned with more rational strategic policymaking and evaluation—took place mainly in the USA, the UK, and France (Premchand, 1983; Pollitt, 1984; Wildavsky, 1979). It coincided with, and was part of, a period of 'high modernism' when rapid advances in science and technology, combined with a huge growth in the university-based study of the social sciences, seemed to hold out the promise of a more rational 'designed' set of public policies and institutions (see, e.g. Dror, 1971 or *The reorganization of central government*, Cmnd 4506, 1970).

The second wave seems to have been connected to the global economic disturbances of the 1970s, and the spreading belief that governments had become 'overloaded' and that Western welfare states had become unaffordable, ineffective, and overly constraining on employers and citizens alike (e.g. King, 1976; Held, 1984; O'Connor, 1973). One might say that the modernist optimism of the 1960s had been replaced as a spur to reform by the dismal prospect of fiscal crisis and governmental over-reach. At any event, there arose a fast-spreading desire to make government more businesslike—to save money, increase efficiency, and simultaneously oblige public bureaucracies to act more responsively towards their citizen-users (e.g. Boston et al., 1996; Pollitt, 1990). This time the trend was more widely felt so that, for example, among our selected countries, Australia, Canada, the Netherlands, New Zealand, Sweden, the UK, and the USA all launched major programmes of central government reform during the 1980s. It later became known as the New Public Management (NPM). It is a term which has (rather confusingly) come to be used to cover a very wide range of reforms in an equally broad spread of countries.

This second wave began during times of global economic downturn, but continued through the subsequent upturn. The drive for greater efficiency and improved service quality spread to more and more countries and lasted through the 1980s and well into the 1990s. (Its character is elaborated in the following section.) But, as the 1990s progressed, its 'personality' began to change. Reforms stayed high on many political agendas, but the talk turned to 'governance', 'partnerships', 'joined-up government'/'whole of government', and then to 'trust' and 'transparency'. In other words, the agenda seemed to shift. This was a complex process, proceeding faster and further in some countries than in others (as had the earlier reform waves). Efficiency and quality did not disappear from view—both remained as persistent concerns—but they tended to be overshadowed by these newer totems. Precisely *why* the agenda changed in this way is not yet entirely clear. To some extent there was a reaction against some of the unwanted or unpopular effects of the earlier, second wave of reform. The reforms of the 1980s and early 1990s had tended to fragment public sector organizations, producing fewer large, multi-purpose forms and more single- or few-purpose organizations, each pursuing more explicitly defined sets of goals and targets (Bouckaert et al., 2010). What is more, these new agencies were often deliberately positioned at arm's length from ministers, partly in order to give the managers greater freedom to manage (Pollitt et al., 2004). But as more and more such organizations came into existence governments began to realize that there were both coordination problems (getting many different public sector organizations cooperatively to pursue the same overall policy objective) and problems of political accountability (the arm's length agencies were harder for ministers to control, but in most cases, if they did unpopular things, it was still ministers who got the blame from the media and the public). For these reasons, therefore, 'strategy', 'joining up', and 'inter-service coordination' all rose up political agendas.

Another slogan that achieved very wide circulation was 'e-government'. There was no shortage of ideas about how the rapidly developing information technologies could revolutionize public sector productivity, provide citizens with faster, better information and access to services, and even usher in a new wave of participatory democracy. Governments in many countries made large investments in new computer systems and web-based communications systems. Sometimes these did indeed bring substantial benefits, but there were also many cases of spiralling costs and systems which under-performed or failed to work altogether (Committee of Public Accounts, 2000; Dunleavy et al., 2006*a*; OECD, 2005*a*). Whilst we will mention some of these projects as we go through the book, and while there is no question but that developments in Information and Communications Technologies (ICTs) have been very important for governments, the point to make here is that e-government is not a model in itself. Neither does it line up exclusively with any one of the models mentioned in this chapter (NPM, networks, governance etc). In effect, there are many versions of e-government: an e-government that reinforces traditional bureaucratic hierarchies, an e-government that facilitates the NPM, an e-government that is designed to promote networking and wider concepts of governance. A great deal depends on the particular context in which a given e-technology is introduced, with what purposes, and so on (Bekkers and Homburg, 2005).

It is hard to know whether this shifting agenda—governance, partnerships, e-government, and so on—constituted a 'third wave', or, if it did, quite how to characterize that wave. (Indeed, it should be emphasized that writing in terms of 'waves' is no more than a general heuristic—the detail of public sector reforms often turns out to be more like geological sedimentation, where new layers overlie but do not replace or completely wash away the previous layer.) Since the late 1990s, different commentators have favoured very different emphases—some have given pride of place to 'governance', some to 'networks and partnerships', some to 'transparency' and 'participation', some use the general term 'post NPM', and some just refer to 'globalization'. Here we will simply make a very brief note of some of these 'big ideas', continuing to a more detailed treatment of them later in the book.

In addition to strategy and 'joining up', the late 1990s and early 2000s brought a rising political awareness that governments appeared to be losing public trust. To some extent politicians themselves exacerbated this by exploiting the 'politics of fear'—playing on the fear of terrorism, but also the fear of the collapse of the pensions system or the health care system or some other key state system. The idea that this apparent loss of trust could be restored by offering the public more transparent and responsive services began to appear in speeches and official documents (although, as we shall see later, it is not clear at all that trust in the political system can be restored by such an approach—Van de Walle et al., 2008). Parallel to this—and related to it—this was also a time when many countries adopted new freedom of information legislation. In 1986 only eleven countries had freedom of information legislation, but by 2004 the number was fifty-nine (OECD, 2005b; Roberts, 2006).

Perhaps even more important, this was a period when 'globalization' became a subject for widespread political and media discussion. This seemed to have major implications for public administrations, for at least two reasons. First, governments needed to develop the capacity to represent themselves effectively in the ever-expanding international networks of international institutions (Held, 2004). The 'Little Englander' (or 'Little German' or 'Little Australian') option of just looking after one's own domestic business and ignoring international organizations and networks began to look more and more costly and unrealistic, even if some populist political fringe groups could still win attention by aspiring to withdraw from the EU or the United Nations or whatever. Second, on the economic front, governments, through their own efficiency or inefficiency, and through a variety of regulatory arrangements, helped sustain—or handicap—national economic competitiveness.

These different pressures each appeared to point towards reform in the basic machinery of the state. One might even say that, as national governments became less dominant, and less authoritative actors in their own territories (because of, inter alia, globalization, decentralization, the rise of an active citizenry, and a more aggressive mass media), so the spotlight fell even more harshly upon public management. Public management became one of the most politically popular answers to a range of these challenges—here, at least, was something ministers in national governments seemingly could fashion and control—their own organizations and staff. When, in 2008, the world was suddenly engulfed in a global financial and economic crisis, sure enough, public management was soon to the fore. Politicians and other commentators in various countries demanded new systems of national and international regulation for financial institutions. Ministers, who had radically unbalanced public finances by using huge sums of public money to prop up failing banks and commercial firms, were soon to be found promising that yet more reforms would ensure that the now-necessary public spending cuts would focus on 'waste' and would not lead to real quality reductions in basic services such as education and health care. Instead, even more 'productivity' would be squeezed out of services that, in some cases, had already officially been raising productivity for the past quarter century. After some months of this kind of rhetoric, however, it became increasingly clear that 'waste-bashing' and productivity improvement alone would not do the trick. These were important components, but the sheer scale of expenditure reductions that were needed meant that 'real' cuts in 'real' services were unavoidable (Pollitt, 2010a). By the autumn of 2010 there were large-scale demonstrations against public service cuts all over Europe.

Thus public management reform has come far from the dusty, technical, and legalistic days of the 1950s. It has become a key element in many party manifestos, in many countries. It has internationalized. It has acquired a body of doctrine, and a set of competing models and approaches. In short, it has 'arrived'.

1.5 **What has been the main direction of reform?**

As indicated above, the period from the mid 1960s to the late 1970s is frequently regarded as the golden age of planning. But our book begins its review from 1980, and by that time the planners were already well in retreat. Neither Mrs Thatcher, the then British Prime Minister 1979–89, nor Ronald Reagan, the US President 1980–8 were any friends of planning. They, and many of their advisers, favoured a more 'business-like' approach. Gradually, partly through doctrine and partly through trial and error, this general attitude crystallized into a more specific set of recipes for public sector reform. By the early 1990s, a number of influential commentators appeared to believe that there was one clear direction—at least in the anglophone world. This general direction was soon labelled as the New Public Management (NPM) or (in the USA) Re-inventing Government (a seminal article here was Hood, 1991). A pair of American management consultants, who wrote a best-seller entitled *Reinventing Government* and then became advisers to the US vice president on a major reform programme, were convinced that the changes they saw were part of a global trend. They claimed that 'entrepreneurial government' (as they called it) was both worldwide and 'inevitable' (Osborne and Gaebler, 1992, pp. 325–8). At about the same time the financial secretary of the UK Treasury (a junior minister) made a speech claiming that the UK was in the forefront of a global movement:

All around the world governments are recognising the opportunity to improve the quality and effectiveness of the public sector. Privatisation, market testing and private finance are being used in almost every developing country. Its not difficult to see why.   (Dorrell, 1993)

The increasingly influential Public Management Committee of the OECD came out with a series of publications that seemed to suggest that most of the developed world, at least, was travelling along roughly the same road. This direction involved developing performance management, introducing more competition to the public sector, offering quality and choice to citizens, and strengthening the strategic, as opposed to the operational role of the centre (see, e.g. OECD, 1995).

There have been many definitional disputes and ambiguities about exactly what the key elements of this general direction were supposed to be: 'There is now a substantial branch industry in defining how NPM should be conceptualized and how NPM has changed' (Dunleavy et al., 2006a, p. 96; see also Hood and Peters, 2004). For the purposes of this book we will assume that the NPM is a two-level phenomenon. At the higher level, it is a general theory or doctrine that the public sector can be improved by the importation of business concepts, techniques, and values. This was very clearly seen, for example, when the then US vice president personally endorsed a popular booklet entitled *Businesslike Government: Lessons Learned from America's Best Companies* (Gore, 1997). Then, at the more mundane level, NPM is a bundle of specific concepts and practices, including:

- greater emphasis on 'performance', especially through the measurement of outputs
- a preference for lean, flat, small, specialized (disaggregated) organizational forms over large, multi-functional forms
- a widespread substitution of contracts for hierarchical relations as the principal coordinating device
- a widespread injection of market-type mechanisms (MTMs) including competitive tendering, public sector league tables, and performance-related pay
- an emphasis on treating service users as 'customers' and on the application of generic quality improvement techniques such as Total Quality Management (TQM) (see Pollitt, 2003a, chapter 2)

Dunleavy et al. have usefully summarized this as 'disaggregation + competition + incentivization' (Dunleavy et al., 2006a). However, it would be wrong to assume that this formula was necessarily internally consistent. As a number of commentators have noted, there is some tension between the different intellectual streams that feed into the NPM, particularly between the economistic, principal-and-agent way of thinking, which is essentially low trust, and the more managerial way of thinking which is more concerned with leadership and innovation—and more trusting of the inherent creativity of staff, if only they are properly led and motivated (Pollitt, 2003a, pp. 31–2). The former stream emphasizes the construction of rational systems of incentives and penalties to 'make the managers manage'. The latter emphasizes the need to 'let the managers manage' by facilitating creative leadership, entrepreneurship, and cultural change. Other writers have drawn a distinction between 'hard' and 'soft' versions of NPM (Ferlie and Geraghty, 2005). The hard version emphasizes control through measurement, rewards, and punishment, while the soft prioritizes customer-orientation and quality, although nevertheless incorporating a shift of control away from service professionals and towards managers. This seems to map quite closely onto the low-trust/high-trust tensions mentioned above.

Consistent or not, the NPM was soon controversial. To begin with, it was perceived as having cultural, ethical, and political features which did not 'fit' certain countries (particularly France, Germany, and the Mediterranean states). In France and in the European Commission, for example, it was commonplace to hear NPM concepts disparagingly referred to as 'Anglo-Saxon ideas'. Furthermore, by the late 1990s it was coming under increasing attack, even in those countries where it had started earliest and gone furthest

Table 1.1 Three waves of reform thinking

Period	Characteristics of Dominant Discourse
Mid 1960s to late 1970s	Rational, hierarchical planning and cost-benefit analysis. Science and expertise will produce progress.
Late 1970s to late 1990s	New Public Management. Business techniques to improve efficiency. Rise of 'better management' as the solution to a wide range of problems.
Late 1990s–2010	No dominant model. Several key concepts, including governance, networks, partnerships, 'joining up', transparency, and trust

(i.e. Australia, New Zealand, the UK, and the USA). This did not mean that it suddenly 'stopped'—not at all. Indeed NPM-type reforms are still going forward in quite a few countries, even as this third edition is being written. But it did mean that other models—alternatives—were frequently being advocated and discussed, and that NPM reforms themselves were no longer seen as *the* solution to a wide range of public sector problems. As noted above, there was a 'third wave' of ideas, which embraced the concepts of globalization, governance, networks, partnerships, transparency, and trust.

The discussions of this section and the previous one are summarized in Table 1.1. It should be emphasized once more that these periods and categories are very broad-brush—the real detail of public management reform over the past three decades does not, unfortunately, separate into three neat waves. What is more, both the rhetoric and the practice around each wave was more dominantly present in some countries than in others (Australasia, the US, and the UK tended to be the most enthusiastic, and to try to 'export' these ideas to other countries).

Finally, it could be added that our reform waves were probably related to deeper currents, such as macro-economic changes, technological developments, ideological shifts, and so on. However, these inter-relationships were complex, and, fascinating though they are, are not our principal focus in this book.

1.6 Has there been a global convergence on one particular way of managing the public sector?

We must immediately begin to elaborate the over-simple picture portrayed by Table 1.1. We have already seen that some voices claimed that there was convergence, and that that convergence was towards the NPM model. Here are just two examples of that—the first a leading American professor and the second an equally influential Australian:

The movement has been so striking because of the number of nations that have taken up the reform agenda in such a short time and because of how similar their basic strategies have been.   (Kettl, 2005, p. 1)

There are various ideas of what is involved in public management reforms. However, as the process has continued there has been convergence as to what is involved in the reforms.   (Hughes, 2003, p. 51)

Yet this was far from a universal view. One group argued that NPM had not delivered what it promised, and they will be dealt with in the next subsection. More pertinently here, another group brought forward a more subtle argument—that the 'reach' and penetration of NPM ideas had been greatly exaggerated, especially by the early enthusiasts such as Osborne and Gaebler. This developed into quite an extensive scholarly argument about what was the real degree of 'convergence' in public management reforms, internationally. Were all countries heading in the same direction and, if not, was there some other sort of pattern? We (Pollitt and Bouckaert) cannot claim to be neutral bystanders in this debate because, both in previous editions of this book and in other works, we have argued that there *has* been an undue focus on NPM, and this has missed a lot of other reforms and combinations of reforms that have been launched. In the Mediterranean countries, for example, while there have been some NPM elements, a focus on them alone gives a very distorted picture of what has been going on over the last quarter century (see Ongaro, 2009). A plausible case can also be made for the idea that the countries with strong Napoleonic traditions were busy with other kinds of reform and attempted reform, and only followed the NPM in limited and selective ways (Kickert, 2007). In Germany, while some NPM-type reforms certainly took place in subnational governments, the federal government has never adopted NPM on a large scale (Bach et al., 2010; Jann et al., 2006; Wollmann, 2001). And even right next door to the UK, in Belgium, the NPM 'flavour' has been quite weak (Brans and Hondeghem, 2005; Broucker et al., 2010; Pollitt and Bouckaert, 2009). In short, national histories and characteristic national patterns of institutions have had a tremendous influence (Lynn, 2006). We will see much more of this variety later in the book.

Another important point—and another one that adds to the complexity of the picture—is that even where a particular new model is adopted, it is rather unlikely that it will simply replace all previous ideas and practices. In public management reform, new brooms hardly ever sweep entirely clean. Rather they shift some of the dust away but then deposit new dust on top of remaining traces of the old. Overall:

Defining periods in the evolution of any complex system, such as public management systems in advanced industrial countries, is a tricky task. New developments accrete and accumulate while older trends are still playing out and apparently flourishing.   (Dunleavy et al., 2006*b*, p. 468)

However, even if we accept that the true picture is far more varied than the convergence enthusiasts suggest, we are left with the question of how and why many leading academics and politicians came to believe that 'a similar process is underway throughout the developed world' (Osborne and Gaebler, 1992, p. 325). We suggest there are several reasons, and they are worth rehearsing here because they also function as general warnings about the generic difficulties of international comparisons.

First, there is a language issue. All the leading NPM countries are predominantly anglophone (Australia, New Zealand, the UK, and the USA). Much of the NPM literature has been anglophone. Many politicians and academics from these countries listen and read predominantly or exclusively anglophone sources. So it is easy to get an exaggerated impression of how prevalent these types of reform are elsewhere in the world. (One healthy development over the past decade or so is that the academic community discussing these issues has broadened so that we are hearing more and more from scholars in countries such as Brazil, China, Italy, Japan, Korea, Mexico, or Spain—who can speak English even if the mother-tongue anglophones can only occasionally speak their languages.)

Second, individuals from these same anglophone countries seem to have been able to colonize key positions in the main international agencies that 'spread the word' about what was going on—especially the OECD and the World Bank. The influence of these agencies was wide: it was not just the 'Anglo-Saxon' states where they got a favourable hearing, but, eventually, such initially resistant administrations as France (Bezes, 2010) and Norway (Christensen et al., 2007, pp. 28–30).

Third, there is a major issue about the types of evidence employed in the debate. As we will see in the next section (and throughout the book) there are many gaps, diversions, and outright failures that stand between the *announcement* of a reform policy and the success-ful *implementation* of that policy. In fact in the public management field it is very common for officially announced reforms only partly to reach their objectives, or to fade away altogether. Some scholars have even shown a pattern where essentially the same rational-istic, performance-oriented reform is introduced over and over again, despite the fact that it never seems to work remotely as originally hoped and declared (Brunsson, 2006; Sundström, 2006). However, if we quickly scan the web or the newspapers, most of the information we find is about reforms which are being debated or which have recently been adopted and announced. There is much less information in these sources to tell us exactly how the reforms have been implemented—how widely and with what degrees of measured success. (Chapter 5 deals at length with this whole problem of defining and assessing 'results'.) One of us has written about this (Pollitt, 2002), suggesting that the life of a reform can be divided into stages, and that at each stage the challenge of research is somewhat different. A simple division of stages recognizes four (Table 1.2):

Table 1.2 helps us to understand why the spread and impacts of NPM (or any other fashionable model) may sometimes be exaggerated. Basically, it is quicker and easier to research the headlines of talk and decision than to go out into the field and look in detail at operational practices and final outcomes. Thus, for example, a quick survey of official

Table 1.2 Researching public management reforms

Stage	Description	Research?
Talk	More and more people are talking and writing about a particular idea (e.g. contracting out)	Quick and cheap. Monitoring what people are talking and writing about is fairly straightforward
Decision	The authorities (governments, public boards, etc.) publicly decide to adopt a particular reform	Again, quick and cheap. The public decisions of the authorities can usually be located quite quickly (on the Net, often without leaving one's desk)
Practice	Public sector organizations incorporate the reform into their daily operational practices	Probably requires expensive and time-consuming fieldwork. This needs both funding and access
Results	The results (outcomes) of the activities of public agencies change as a result of the reform	Final outcomes are frequently difficult (and expensive) to measure. Even more frequently there is an attribution problem, i.e. one cannot be sure how much of the measured change in outcomes can be attributed to the reform itself, as opposed to other factors

Developed from Pollitt, 2002.

documentation shows that executive agencies in the UK, Sweden, Finland, and the Netherlands all have performance indicator systems. This could be seen as an example of convergence, with a strong NPM flavour (performance measurement and results-oriented management are central planks in the NPM model). What detailed fieldwork reveals, however, is that these indicators are used in very different ways and with different consequences in the four countries (Pollitt et al., 2004). Before leaving this point we should note that the Talk-Decision-Practice-Results framework has several implications for comparative analysis. Inter alia it suggests that we should try to compare like with like (decisions with decisions, or results with results). Comparing (say) talk and decisions in country A with practice in country B is potentially misleading (and unfair).

Fourth, there has almost certainly been a kind of 'multiplier' effect. That is, as attention has focused on business-derived NPM reforms, a community has grown up in whose interests it is to create new ideas and techniques, and therefore further reform. There is nothing necessarily sinister about this, even if it can often be construed as a form of self-interest. It is simply that more and more people take up public sector roles after some training in 'management', and more and more consultancies depend on winning and subsequently sustaining contracts to facilitate reform. For example, the UK public sector spent approximately £2.8 billion on consultants in 2005–6, a 33 per cent increase on what the level had been only two years previously—in fact central government spent more on consultants per employee than did comparator private sector firms! (National Audit Office, 2006, pp. 5 and 15).

Furthermore, individuals increasingly move between different management roles—as practising managers, as consultants, as academics, or as contributors to the now-extensive specialist media concerned with communicating management ideas (Sahlin-Andersson and Engwall, 2002, pp. 14–19). More and more governments have set up one or more specialist management reform units, such as the Prime Minister's Public Service Delivery Unit (UK), the Public Management Department of the Finnish Ministry of Finance, the French Directorate General for State Modernization, the Norwegian Ministry of Government Administration and Reform, and so on. Members of these organizations may themselves have consultancy experience or they may become consultants afterwards, trading on their experience gained near the heart of government reforms. More profoundly, these units and departments help to institutionalize 'modernization' and 'reform', continually putting forward programmes and targets, drawing attention to new management ideas and techniques and generally keeping the rest of central government 'on its toes' (for a vivid account of how intrusive this can become, see Barber, 2007). As we said at the beginning of this chapter, a real community has emerged, complete with its own terminology, doctrines, procedures, and networks. And, more often than not, these 'communities of discourse' have been heavily influenced by NPM ideas (again, see Barber, 2007, where the Head of the Prime Minister's Delivery Unit strongly criticizes the traditional public service professions, but praises inspirational, generic business-school texts such as John Kotter's *Leading Change* (Kotter, 1996)).

For all these reasons, therefore, there has been a tendency to over-concentrate on the NPM. This is not an attempt to argue that NPM is not important—clearly NPM ideas *have* achieved a very wide international spread, and *have* directly inspired many reforms in many countries. But they have not been universal—the idea of a global trend, at least in its strong form, is something of a mirage—and neither has the NPM been the only kind of reform that was going on (even in those countries that were NPM-intensive, like New Zealand and the UK, but especially in those countries that only borrowed from the NPM toolkit cautiously and selectively, like Finland, France, or Japan).

1.7 Internationally, how successful has the New Public Management (NPM) been?

Elements of the NPM have been widespread, but have they worked? There is no straight-forward 'yes' or 'no' answer to this, partly because many policymakers (and some scholars) start from a strong normative commitment either pro- or anti-NPM, and they are never likely to agree with each other. However, that is far from being the only reason. It is also the case that it is very difficult systematically to evaluate large-scale public management reforms (and in quite a few cases the governments concerned have not been all that interested in scientific evaluation anyway) (Pollitt, 1995; Wollmann, 2003; Pollitt, 2009). We will spend a little time briefly summarizing why this is so difficult, before moving on to look at what 'results' have nevertheless been observed.

To examine reforms and their results, we first need some kind of conceptual framework. Therefore we detour from our main story here in order to introduce a fairly orthodox framework within which to discuss 'performance'—see Figure 1.2.

In the figure, terms such as 'efficiency' and 'effectiveness' are given fairly specific mean-ings, whereas readers should be warned that in 'real-life' reform talk they are frequently used in loose, vague, and/or inconsistent ways. Thus, for us, efficiency is the ratio between inputs and outputs, whereas effectiveness is the degree to which the desired outcomes result from the outputs. For example, if lessons are delivered (outputs), do the students actually learn (outcomes)? Note that it is therefore perfectly possible for a given policy to increase efficiency while decreasing effectiveness, or vice versa. For example, a new approach to managing hospital operating theatres may increase the rate at which a partic-ular surgical procedure is carried out (greater efficiency) but in doing so lead to more mistakes being made by doctors and nurses, so that the effectiveness of the operations falls (the clinical outcomes deteriorate). Or, more commonly perhaps, there may be an improvement in efficiency (police check more alcohol licences per month), but no change in the outcomes (levels of teenage drunkenness remain the same). An example of increas-ing effectiveness whilst decreasing efficiency would be if a university replaced a retiring group of run-of-the-mill professors with highly paid top rank international 'stars'. Students might learn more, and research outcomes might improve (both measures of outcome) but the cost per student would go up (and therefore efficiency would go down) because of the higher salaries demanded by the new super-professors.

Some would object to this framework on the grounds that it is over-rationalistic. It assumes, for example, that socio-economic problems are addressed by distinct programmes which have discernible objectives (against which effectiveness can subse-quently be measured). But sometimes, such critics might point out, policies exist

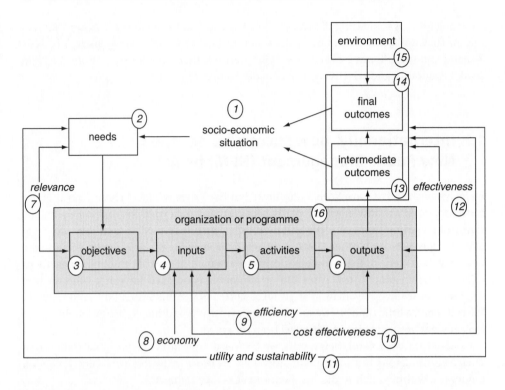

Figure 1.2 Performance: a conceptual framework

without clear objectives, or with contradictory objectives, or a particular problem is addressed by many different policies, which are not well coordinated and which carry with them conflicting approaches to, and conceptualizations of, the original problem that is to be solved. Others would say that the framework assumes a hierarchy of decision-makers, and that, increasingly, we live in societies where 'governance' is conducted in networks which do not behave like hierarchies. We accept that such criticisms have considerable force. Policymaking often *is* messy and inconsistent (and that is one reason why evaluating the results of reforms can be so difficult). Nevertheless, it is hard to discuss reform policymaking without assuming that that it is a purposive activity with some shape or pattern to it, and the framework used in Figure 1.1 has proved a powerful tool in the hands of some public administration scholars who have wanted to assess the results of particular policies (e.g. Boyne et al., 2003). It is also more or less the framework employed in many official documents, and therefore gives us a way of discussing reforms in the reformers' own terms. So we will use it, while acknowledging that reality often leaves us with something much less neat.

Even if we do use such a framework, however, there are a number of well-known reasons why systematic evidence of causal connections between reform programmes (not just NPM reforms but most types of reform) and improvements in outputs and outcomes may be very hard to come by:

- Changes in organizational structures are frequently a central feature of public management reforms, but usually such changes are connected to outputs and outcomes only by quite long causal chains. For example, a function is taken out of a department and made into an executive agency. A new top management is introduced. Performance targets are set up. Management appraisals are geared to the achievement of these targets. New working methods are introduced. Staff are reassigned. New training is conducted. Measured performance improves. But would that have happened anyway, even if the first and/or second steps in this process had been absent? What is it among all these changes which is actually producing the improved results—all these things or only one or two of them? Reforms themselves are thus typically multi-faceted, so that there is always a question of which elements are working and which are not.

- Different stakeholders may take very different views of both the justifications and meanings of the reforms, and even of their results (see, e.g. Hartley et al., 2008).

Even in an ideal world—where policymakers had a strong commitment to feedback and evaluation—the two aforesaid difficulties would apply. But in the real world such a commitment is quite rare, and there are therefore other issues which prevent the observer getting a clear picture of the precise results of particular reforms. For example:

- There may be no evaluations at all, because the new reform is politically sensitive and its promoters want to drive forward, minimizing the possibility of critical comment, and resulting doubts, distractions, and delays. When Mrs Thatcher's administration introduced an internal market to the National Health Service (NHS) from 1989, the government was initially opposed to any official evaluation of this huge reform (although some useful academic evaluations were mounted post hoc). Similarly, when President George W. Bush created the vast new Department of Homeland Security, no official evaluation was put in place. Indeed, the US Congress has a long record of launching reorganizations for symbolic reasons and then quickly losing interest in the operational consequences (Kettl, 2009).

- In both practical and political terms a reversal of a reorganization is just not feasible, so any idea that a negative summative evaluation will result in a change back to what was there before is unrealistic. The reorganization has already created a de facto new reality, which lessens the room for manoeuvre for the evaluators. The most they may be able to do is offer a formative-type evaluation which helps the existing management cope better.

- Evaluations are often put into place too late, so that they can have no clear view of the baseline performance, prior to the reform (as was the case with the academic evaluations of the UK National Health Service internal-market reform).

- An evaluation is set up, but before it can be completed, policy has moved on again—policymakers can't wait for the full set of results (Walker, 2001).

Finally, it is important to note that virtually all the constraints and barriers noted above apply not just to NPM-type reforms, but to large-scale reforms in general. We will see later that evidence for the success of 'network' and 'governance'-type reforms is just as hard—or harder—to interpret as that pertaining to the NPM.

This has been quite a lengthy—and gloomy—detour into the problems of evaluating management reform. Fortunately, despite these difficulties we do know something about the results of reform. There have been a number of reasonably rigorous studies which have identified attributable changes in outputs and outcomes. Most of these have concerned specific reforms rather than broad programmes of reform, and some of have identified clear improvements—for example, studies of US federal public procurement (Kelman, 2005) or human resource management (Thompson and Rainey, 2003) or British educational programmes for pre-school children from socially disadvantaged localities (BBK NESS site, 2009). Then there are a few studies which have tried to get a bigger picture, such as the series of studies by Boyne and his partners at Cardiff. In one of these, the conclusion was reached that the NPM reforms of the 1980s and 1990s in UK education, health care, and housing had a) raised efficiency, b) improved responsiveness to service users, but c) reduced equity (Boyne et al., 2003). Exactly *why* these impacts followed from the reforms was less clear—understandably there tends to be something of a trade-off between the breadth of evaluations (Boynes' was wide) and the degree to which the researcher is able to trace the precise processes and mechanisms that have produced the apparent outcomes. We will revisit some of these tricky issues in Chapter 5, which directly addresses the question of the results of reform.

The multiple difficulties in pinning down the effects of public management reforms do not seem to have deterred both practitioners and academics from trying to come up with indices of success. On the contrary—the period since the late 1990s has seen a veritable explosion of comparative, international indicators of 'good governance', 'bureaucratic quality', 'transparency', 'e-government', and other aspects of modernization (see, e.g. Accenture, 2008; Advisory Group on Reform of Australian Government Administration, 2009). This has begun to attract a good deal of academic attention—for example, in 2008 the *International Public Management Journal* ran a special theme issue on 'ranking and rating public services', and other publications have also begun to appear (Dixon et al., 2008; see also Pollitt, 2010*b*). For the moment we will simply note that these international league tables have in some instances become quite influential (governments are embarrassed when their government sinks down the table, and implement programmes to raise their scores), and that they provide useful examples of what is involved, conceptually, empirically and practically in trying to summarize the 'success' or 'failure' of whole governments. We will return to international league tables at various points in the book, but especially in Chapter 5 ('Results').

1.8 What other models—apart from the NPM—have been influential?

There has been no shortage of models. From governments we have heard of various national formulations—the 'New Zealand model' (Boston et al., 1996), the Canadian 'La Relève' (Bourgon, 1998), the Belgian 'Copernicus' model (Hondeghem and Depré, 2005), and the German 'slim state' (Sachverständigenrat 'Schlanker Staat', 1997). We need not—indeed cannot—go into all these here, but it is worth noting that governments seem to like to have their own variant, both internally, to show their domestic originality and

COMPARATIVE PUBLIC MANAGEMENT REFORM: THE KEY DEBATES **19**

uniqueness, and sometimes externally, as a 'product' to be marketed on the international marketplace for public management reforms.

Alongside governments, academics have also been fruitful in their invention of new models. We have publications which discuss the Napoleonic model (Ongaro, 2009), the Neo-Weberian State (NWS—Drechsler and Kattel, 2008; Lynn, 2008), the French model (Bartoli, 2008), and the Nordic model (Veggeland, 2007). The Nordic model, for example, is said to put 'heavy weight on government and public solutions and interventionist measures. Universal welfare and social security arrangements with high public expenses are basic welfare principles, and tariffs and a high degree of job security dominate labor market relations' (Veggeland, 2007, pp. 121–2). Most of these models have established themselves in the anglophone literature by first distinguishing themselves from what they take to be the 'Anglo-Saxon model', which is itself usually a version of the NPM. Veggeland, for instance, characterizes the Anglo-Saxon model (in contrast to his favoured Nordic one) as putting weight on market solutions, low public expenses, and limited government. More general models offered by academics searching for 'the next big thing' include Digital-Era Governance (DEG) (Dunleavy et al., 2006b) and the New Public Governance (NPG—Osborne, 2010). Our own suggestion, in the previous edition of this book, was of the Neo-Weberian state (NWS). In essence, this was an attempt to modernize traditional bureaucracy by making it more professional, efficient, and citizen-friendly. It was particularly characteristic of the stable, prosperous, Western European democracies which had sizeable welfare states—including Germany, France, and the Nordic group. It was therefore not a universal model, but one limited to particular kinds of state. It reflected a more optimistic and trusting attitude towards the state apparatus than the NPM. The NWS will be one of the three high-level models we refer to throughout the book, the other two being the NPM and the NPG. These three models are helpful in organizing large quantities of empirical material, and we will come back to them shortly (sections 1.9 and 1.10).

The attempt to establish reform models and trends has overlapped with scholarly efforts to identify administrative 'traditions', and to show how these have influenced reforms (and sometimes absorbed or defeated them). One recent work identified, inter alia, Anglo-American, Napoleonic, Germanic, and Scandinavian traditions (Painter and Peters, 2010). These traditions are, in a sense, another kind of big model—they are the models of the past, still built into institutional structures, procedures, and ways of thinking.

We do not have the space to go into each of these national or regional models, or traditions, here (although we will refer to some of their features when dealing with specific countries in later chapters). We do, however, need to take a closer look at some of the broader academic models which have been advanced—models which describe, not particular countries, but larger features of the organizational *ensemble* which constitutes the public sector. Two of these have been especially popular—networks and governance. The next two sections introduce them.

1.9 **Networks**

Since the early 1990s a huge literature on 'networks' has sprung up. It stretches far beyond our field of public management, but within that field has spawned many new publications and debates (for overviews, see Klijn, 2005 and Agranoff, 2007; for a much-cited application see Milward and Provan, 2000). A father figure in this is the social theorist Manuel Castells who in 1996 published a hugely influential book entitled *The Rise of the Network Society* (for an updated edition, see Castells, 2010).

Again, this is not the place to go into the (endless) details of the academic discourse on networks in public administration, but it is important to see how, in general terms, this upsurge of scholarship relates to the arguments over the NPM and convergence. Most commonly, network theorists present the network form as something which is growing, because it is flexible and fits well with the increased complexity (as they see it) of the modern world. Networks are said to have properties which make them superior to both hierarchies and markets (the other two major organizational forms). Therefore networks are an alternative to the NPM, which is itself a mixture of hierarchies (the political and managerial leaders declare strategies and set targets) and markets (units performing public sector tasks are supposed to compete with one another, and individual staff compete for performance pay bonuses). Indeed, in many network texts the replacement of hierarchies by networks is made to sound almost inevitable:

Problems cannot be solved by organizations on their own. Hence, hierarchy as an organizing principle has lost much of its meaning. The model of the 'lonely organization' that determines its policy in isolation is obsolete. (...) Equally obsolete is the image of government at the apex of societal pyramid. (...) Horizontal networks replace hierarchies.   (Koppenjan and Klijn 2004: p. 3)

It would be wrong, however, to leave any impression that the 'network model' is novel, clear, cut and dried. On the contrary, there are a range of definitions, some of them conflicting (Pollitt and Hupe, 2011). Some claim that networks have to be self-organizing, while others point out that, in reality, many networks are organized by one or two dominant members. Others say that networks are essentially voluntary, yet some others argue that membership of certain networks may be a practical necessity, if one's organization is going to survive. Many commentators suggest that networks are 'horizontal' and may therefore be contrasted with bureaucratic hierarchies, but specific case studies have found that there may be a strong 'pecking order' in some networks, with one player (often the government) de facto 'on top' and calling the shots. Those with a sense of history point out that networks, both formal and informal, are certainly not new (Pemberton, 2000). Governments have often operated through networks, and it is not entirely clear whether the growth of analysis of, and talk about, networks noted here represents a real underlying growth of the form, or just an increase in interest in something that has been there for a long time. The debate about networks is far from concluded.

1.10 **What is the significance of the so-called shift from government to 'governance'?**

Since the late 1990s 'governance' has become an immensely popular term, with both academics and practitioners. It appears in almost as many versions as there are authors writing about it. A standard governance text (Pierre, 2000) opens with two experts offering, respectively, five and seven different meanings of the term (see Hirst 2000 and Rhodes 2000). Other authors speak of 'hybrid governance' (Hupe and Meijs 2000), and 'operational governance' (Hill and Hupe 2009), and 'public sector governance' (Australian Public Service Commission, 2007), and 'New Public Governance' (Osborne, 2010). There are many other varieties, including one that stresses the significance of changes in relationships within government, and between governments and their citizens which are facilitated by contemporary ICTs—this one is termed 'Digital-Era Governance' by its inventors, Dunleavy et al. (2006*b*). It is therefore understandable that Bovaird and Löffler (2003: 316) describe the attempts to 'fix' the concept as like trying to 'nail a pudding on the wall'. To be charitable, there may be a rough common core residing in the notion that steering society or making policy increasingly requires the active participation of a range of actors in addition to government itself. This broad thought alone, however, is far from being entirely new, and does not adequately explain the recent attractiveness of the term.

The concept of governance draws strength from its claim to represent a wider, more inclusive concept than 'government' alone. Yet it is not an *alternative* to government, because government remains as one of its principal constituent elements. From a governance standpoint, one 'sees government as only one institution among many in a free market society' (Stivers 2009: 1095). The danger here is that the concept of governance is made to appear to transcend previous tensions and contradictions, such as public versus private, or bureaucracy versus market. Similarly, it may mask traditional social science concerns with conflicting interests and logics. In a good deal of the writing about governance these conflicts are largely assumed away.

Good governance is said to entail the steering of society through networks and partnerships between governments, business corporations, and civil society associations. Thus it is closely linked to the network model described in the previous section—indeed, one of the foremost network theorists has more recently taken to writing about 'governance networks' (Klijn, 2008). And the NPG model referred to in section 1.8 above is explicitly connected to network theory (Osborne, 2010, p. 9). Thus it would be wrong to think of 'governance' as a model which has superseded and displaced the network model—rather it is a wider model which as to some extent absorbed the earlier—and continuing—work on networks. A typical definition is the following:

Governance entails a move away from traditional hierarchical forms of organization and the adoption of network forms. It also entails a revision of the relationship between the state and civil society in a more participatory direction. Governance is finally said to be responsible for shifting the emphasis away from statute law to more flexible forms of regulation and implementation. The state is thus claimed to be superseded by a 'networked polity' where authority is devolved to task-specific institutions with unlimited jurisdictions and intersecting memberships operating at sub- and supra-national levels.   (Bellamy and Palumbo, 2010)

An obvious question for both governance and networks is 'Well, do they work?' Unfortunately the variations in the definitions of these models, as well as the problems of evaluation described in section 1.7 above mean that no clear answer can be given. Even less than for the NPM can we say 'yes, it (whatever 'it' is defined as!) works well under conditions x and y'. We do have quite a few good case studies of networks and attempts at governance in action, but what they tend to show is that these approaches work well sometimes and fail at other times. There are, of course, plenty of suggestions for what the 'success factors' might be, but nothing that can be convincingly formulated into an operationalizable general model. Contexts, it seems, are very important, and this is a message which will recur many times before the end of this book.

To conclude these sections on models, Table 1.3 provides a very crude summary of the core claims of each major model, and some suggestions on further reading.

As indicated above, we could have chosen any number of models upon which to focus, but have settled for three—NPM, NWS, and NPG. A larger number would quickly have become unwieldy. We would suggest that our selection usefully covers a wide range of

Table 1.3 Big models—big claims: the basics

Model	Core Claim	Most Common Co-ordination Mechanism	Some Key Sources
NPM	To make government more efficient and 'consumer-responsive' by injecting businesslike methods	Market-type mechanism (MTMs); performance indicators, targets, competitive contracts, quasi-markets	Hood, 1991; Lane, 2000, Osborne and Gaebler, 1992; Pollitt, 1990
NWS	To modernize the traditional state apparatus so that it becomes more professional, more efficient, and more responsive to citizens. Businesslike methods may have a subsidiary role in this, but the state remains a distinctive actor with its own rules, methods, and culture	Authority exercised through a disciplined hierarchy of impartial officials	Dreschler and Kattel, 2008; Lynn, 2008; Chapter 4 of this book
Networks	To make government better informed, more flexible and less exclusive by working through 'self-organizing' networks rather than hierarchies and/or market mechanisms	Networks of interdependent stakeholders	Agranoff, 2007; Castells; 2010, Klijn, 2005
Governance (of which NPG is one variant)	To make government more effective and legitimate by including a wider range of social actors in both policymaking and implementation. Some varieties of governance explicitly rest on a 'network approach', and most of them emphasize 'horizontality' over vertical controls	Networks of, and partnerships between. stakeholders	Pierre and Peters, 2000; Frederickson, 2005; Kaufmann et al., 2009; Bellamy and Palumbo, 2010; Osborne, 2010

reform paradigms. In the NPM we have the original reaction against traditional bureaucracy and 'big government'. The new model was to be business. Management was the key skill. Markets and incentives were the key mechanisms. In the NWS we have a different emphasis. Yes, the state apparatus requires modernization, but no, the world of business does not hold all the answers. Traditional bureaucracy has virtues which should be preserved (clear accountability, probity, predictability, continuity, close attention to the law). The key is to find ways to combine these with more efficient procedures and a more flexible and responsive stance towards the needs of an increasingly diverse citizenry. Subsequently, the NPG attempted to move beyond the old arguments between the state and business, and to show that complex modern societies could only be effectively governed through complex networks of actors, drawn from government itself, the market sector, and civil society. The emphasis was on networks, partnerships, and negotiated but ultimately voluntary cooperation, not on competition (like the NPM) or enlightened and professional hierarchies (like the NWS).

1.11 What kind of answers should we be looking for—models and menus?

Up to this point we have written as though the best way of describing and classifying what has been going on internationally in public management reform is in terms of big, general models—NPM, NWS, NPG, and so on. And it is true that many of the contributions to the literature proceed in this way—they focus on how far NPM has gone in Norway compared with New Zealand (Christensen and Lægried, 2001), or in Italy versus Flanders (Verschuere and Barbieri, 2009), or they examine the compatibility of NPM reforms with the basic assumptions and practices underying 'Napoleonic' types of regime (Ongaro, 2009). From a comparative perspective this approach has a number of advantages, but it also carries risks. One risk is that it may lead scholars to try to force the local details in country X into a pre-set frame (more or less NPM, more or fewer Public–Private Partnerships—PPPs), whereas perhaps the main significance of the changes in X is their relationship to something else, perhaps something that has gone on before in that country or sector, and which is unique to that country or sector. It may be that these big models are pitched at such a high level of generality that they miss much of the significant detail and difference. If so, deeper understanding of particular reforms may come from viewing them within a more specific, detailed story within a specific country or small group of countries. Better explanations may be generated by looking at particular contextual factors (the balance between political parties; the state of the budget; the nature of local cultural norms, and so on), than by positing big international models driven by equally generic global trends.

The problem with local detail, of course, is that, however illuminating by itself, it is just local detail. International comparison is not possible or meaningful unless *some* features can be identified which are sufficiently common to be compared across boundaries. There are various ways of doing this, but one way is to think in terms of specific management tools or instruments. For example, one could think of the set of tools which promote competitive behaviour in the public sector—such as contracting out, performance-related pay, and indicator systems that produce public 'league tables' of schools or hospitals or freedom of information legislation. (Notice that these are not real tools—you can't pick them up and bang them on the table—they are *ideas*, portable assemblies of concepts, formalized practices, and assumptions about how to do things. Nevertheless, they appear to be more specific and operationally definable than the big models of NPM, etc.) Or one could consider the set of tools which are supposed to enhance public service quality, such as TQM, the Common Assessment Framework (CAF), or minimum standard setting in health care or education (accident and emergency patients will all be seen within thirty minutes; each child in class will spend so many minutes per week reading aloud to the teacher, and so on). Looking at specific tools and techniques like this clearly leads to analysis at a 'lower' (more detailed and specific) level than focusing exclusively on the big models. Yet it can still be used in a comparative way—we can ask what percentage of public sector organizations in a given country or sector use a given technique, or group of techniques, and we can also go deeper and try to find out exactly how they are used. We might term this a 'menu' approach, in the sense that we are asking what the menu of reforms is in a particular country or jurisdiction or sector, and how and why menus differ in different times and places. In this vocabulary the particular tools are individual dishes/ *plats*, while the menu is an overall list of what is on the table. Notice that, like a menu in a restaurant, there are different reasons why a dish may delight, or fail to satisfy. It could be that the recipe itself is flawed. Or it could be that the chef is incompetent in putting together the ingredients. Or it could even be that the dish is perfect, but the customer comes from a different culinary culture, and just doesn't like 'that kind of thing' (as when the English throw up their hands at the idea of the French eating snails, or vegetarians recoil from a traditional working-class dish of pig's trotters). Furthermore, we may imagine that menus may be more or less *coherent*, in the sense that, for a given palate, some dishes go better with others and some clash. Thus, a particular management tool may fit well with others, or it may in some way contradict them or lessen their impact. Thus, for example, a coherent NPM menu might include disaggregation of large, multi-purpose organizations, competitive contracting out, performance measurement, performance-related pay, business-style accruals accounting, and so on. Introducing, say, statutory lifetime secure tenure for senior civil servants to this menu would create a tension because it belongs to a different kind of model.

An important qualification here would be to say that, although particular management tools do often belong to similar families (or coherent menus) it should not be assumed that each individual tool is *exclusively* associated with one model, and cannot be fitted into any other. The connection is often looser than that. Thus, for example, performance measurement may feature within an NPM approach, but it can also function—in a somewhat different way—within a modernizing, NWS approach (e.g. Pollitt, 2006a). Figure 1.3 shows a selection of tools/dishes, and indicates that many of them do not have a one-to-one relationship with one model/menu.

Thus Public–Private Partnerships (PPPs) feature in both the NPM and the NPG paradigms. And contracting out is a main dish on the NPM menu but can also be used as a side dish (dotted line) within both the NWS and the NPG models. Performance measurement

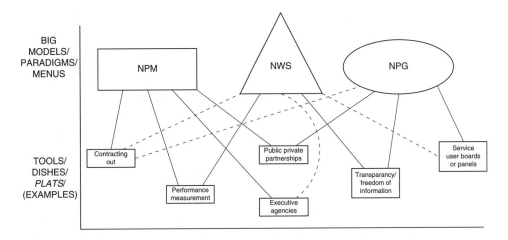

Figure 1.3 *Plats* and paradigms

is particularly associated with the NPM, but may also be used, in a less command-and-control way, within other approaches. In fact most individual dishes can feature on more than one menu, although their prominence may vary from one to another

1.12 What methods should we be using for the comparative analysis of public management reforms?

This question may not have been a headline in most of the numerous books and articles which have appeared during the past decade, but it is often lurking just below the surface. It is quite obvious that a wide variety of approaches are used, from econometric-style multiple regressions to political science classifications of different types of political systems, to excursive interpretations of the influences of different national cultures. In short, comparative public administration partakes of the deep epistemological, ontological, and associated methodological differences which characterize the whole sweep of the social and economic sciences (see Pollitt and Bouckaert, 2009, chapter 9).

An obvious first question is 'what should we compare with what?' Constitutions? Legal systems? Methods for recruiting and appointing civil servants? Levels of expenditure on particular types of programme? Dominant value systems among public officials? The list is endless and the choice difficult. One needs a focal question or questions to guide one's choice. For this particular book, our general orientation can be deduced from what has already been said above. We want to compare *deliberate changes to the structures and processes of public sector organizations with the objective of getting them (in some sense) to work better* (Section 1.2), focusing mainly on *central government*. To do this we will focus on two levels: first, what broad *models of reform* have been in play, and second, within that, what *menus of tools and techniques* have been selected by individual countries? So we will be comparing programmes of reform and tools of reform—the first in part an analysis of rhetoric (talk and decisions—see Table 1.2), the second an analysis of decisions and practices (again see Table 1.2). On both levels we will look for patterns (groupings of similarities or dissimilarities between countries). Can we see regional, or cultural, or ideological groupings? We will also trace how these patterns may have changed over the three decades which we study. (Cross sectional comparisons—snapshots at a single time— although common, have considerable limitations for the study of public policy and management, where big changes usually take years rather than weeks—Pollitt, 2008.) Are there international trends, cycles, pendulum swings? One interesting question under-lying this will be whether broad models, dominant in a particular country, *can* be changed? Are the differences between (say) France and the UK fundamentally the same as they were thirty years ago, or do we have cases where countries have been able to make deep, planned changes to their ways of managing their public sectors? To read all the books and articles on 'transformation', one might think that revolutions and break-throughs were commonplace. General McChrystal (see the quotation at the head of this chapter) may think that new systems of government can be rolled out in 'in a box', but examples of the successful implementation of such schemes appear to be exceedingly rare. The story we will tell shows things are usually rather more complicated than that.

However, this is not primarily a 'theory and methods' book: it is a book about what has happened and why. Our strategy, therefore, has been to push on with the story/ies of reform while occasionally bracketing issues of theory or method, so that readers can follow them up if they need to. Theories and methods thus feature as a kind of intermittent subtext (as has already been exemplified, for example, in the discussion of different views of convergence in Section 1.7). More substantively, if the reader wishes to consult a brief note on comparative methods as related to public management reform, s/he should look at the first section of the Appendix.

1.13 What is the significance for public management reform of the global economic crisis which began in the second half of 2008?

The global economic downturn has plunged most of our twelve countries and their governments into a new era—one of public-spending cutbacks and austerity. This con-trasts with what were for many (but not all) the boom years of 1995–2007. Yet at the same time the pressures for reform and improvement are no less than they were before—indeed, these pressures may become even more intense.

Historically, the connection between public management reforms and episodes of financial austerity has been a variable one. Over the past thirty years we can find several episodes of financial austerity and many waves of public management reform, but the two are not necessarily closely connected. Sometimes major reforms occur without any precipitating financial crisis (as with the US National Performance Review under President Clinton, or the reforms of the second term of the Blair administration in the UK). But sometimes they clearly originate in such crises (as did the famous New Zealand reforms of 1984–90). And sometimes financial crises are managed with straight 'cutback management', but no fundamental system reforms.

In fact, the implications of financial austerity for management reform are ambiguous. On the one hand, austerity makes reform more difficult, because reforms cannot be lubricated with new money, and objectors and recalcitrants cannot be 'bought off'. But on the other hand, a sense of crisis can make it easier to consider radical options and more fundamental changes than would otherwise get onto the agenda of feasibility.

Further, making *sustained, aggregate* savings in public spending is extremely hard to achieve. The UK, for example, has undergone many, many rounds of 'cuts', but a scholarly study indicated that only one—the so-called 'Geddes Axe' in the 1920s—seems to have actually resulted in a sustained reduction in the level of public spending. Mrs Thatcher was famous for the severity of her spending cuts, yet after six years in power her central government current spending was higher than it had been a decade previously (Dunsire and Hood, 1989). The current situation is one in which fiscal and political considerations are in serious tension. The fiscal logic is to make large cuts. The political logic is that cuts on this scale are both profoundly unpopular (vote losers) and possibly beyond the limits of political feasibility, especially for fragile regimes. At the time of writing we can see quite large-scale public resistance—including public demonstrations—against the cuts in public services which the international community is demanding from Greece as the price of a large financial loan. It remains to be seen, in each country, which logic will win out.

Making cuts can be approached in different ways. One distinction is between cheese-slicing approaches ('everyone must cut back by 5%') and more prioritized approaches ('we will reduce programmes X and Y because they are not very effective, but increase programme Z because it is effective and is a high political priority'). Both can lead to management reforms, but in different ways. With cheese slicing, operational managers and professional-service deliverers are obliged to find ways of reducing their budgets by the 3 per cent or 5 per cent, or whatever the decrement is determined to be. But these reform adoptions are somewhat decentralized, and the central authorities are not themselves choosing either which services are going to be winners and which losers, or exactly what types of reform are to be implemented.

Cheese-slicing approaches are common, but have been relatively little researched. One recent interesting piece of work suggests that—faced with a sudden percentage budget reduction—local managers can be rather adaptable in protecting core activities and top priorities through a variety of tactics (Meier and O'Toole, 2009). The authors stress, however, that their research only applies to the short run, and that some of the actions taken would become more damaging/less sustainable if (as seems to be the case now) the cuts continue over a number of years.

In between the two poles of cheese slicing and strategic prioritization come strategies that attempt to make efficiency savings. Each approach has its own advantages and disadvantages; see, for example, Table 1.4.

In practice it is often possible to fashion strategies which combine features of all three approaches. For example, ministers can decide that certain high-priority programmes will be protected, but that outside those sectors cheese slicing should be imposed. Or ministers may first decide to go for cheese slicing, then efficiency savings, and only later, when the first two have not yielded enough, move on to the more ambitious setting of

Table 1.4 Three approaches to cutbacks

Approach	Advantages	Disadvantages
Cheese slicing	Sounds egalitarian ('everyone must meet his share'). Ministers avoid directly choosing which programmes will be most hurt. Detailed decisions delegated to programme specialists who probably know what they are doing (and can be blamed if their decisions turn out to be unpopular or hurtful)	Programme specialists may make politically very unpopular choices. And/or they may make self-interested choices which hurt effectiveness whilst protecting service providers (themselves). May also incentivize budget holders to pad their budgets so that there will be 'fat' to be cut next time round.
Efficiency gains	Sounds less threatening/more technical—'doing more with less'. So it may be claimed that savings can be made without too much pain. Also sounds 'modern' and 'managerial' and may thus appeal across party or ideological lines.	Usually requires considerable innovation—organizational and technological changes which may not work, or may not work for some time. Probably will not yield enough by itself to correct the large fiscal imbalances
Centralized priority setting	Looks more strategic and leaves politicians directly in control. Enables the government to protect the most effective programmes (*if* they have reliable data on effectiveness)	Ministers become visibly and directly responsible for painful choices. And, unless they consult carefully, they may make choices with consequences they do not fully foresee, but they are unlikely to understand the internal complexities of the services which are being cut

For more detailed discussion, see Pollitt, 2010a.

central priorities. Some academics have suggested that this is a natural order of business (i.e. to move from the top to the bottom of Table 1.4, over time). Each stage requires a more sophisticated information base, and a more advanced management capacity. The historical record, however, suggests that the sequence is seldom as neat as this. What we can be reasonably sure about, however, is that:

Cutback management, like most pressing organizational concerns, brings forth an army of consultants who are ready to offer prescriptions to remedy the problems. (Pandey, 2010, p. 568)

One thing that can be said with certainty is that the public sector consequences of the 2008–11 economic downturn will still be unfolding when you read this book. As this is being written in late 2010, the UK government has just announced a programme of £81 billion of cuts over four years. It is estimated that half a million public service jobs will disappear, and another half million private sector posts that depend on public sector expenditure and contracts will also go. Furthermore, these consequences—in the UK and elsewhere—will not be confined to the expenditure cuts. They may also sometimes put pressure on the integrity of public servants; they may lead to increased corruption (simply because in many countries public procurement expanded as part of fiscal stimulus packages, and public procurement is an area of public management that we know historically is vulnerable to waste and corruption); they may strengthen the need for lobbying to be better regulated; they may intensify the pressures for 'joined-up', whole of government approaches (OECD, 2009a, pp. 20–30). They may well make it harder for the public sector to recruit and keep the kind of talent it needs.

1.14 **Reflections and conclusions: management reform caught between 'is' and 'ought'**

The debates referred to above have taken place in a mixed, increasingly multinational community, consisting of academics, public servants, management consultants, and politicians. It is therefore unsurprising that the reasons for becoming engaged with these arguments have differed. Some participants want to find the best way forward—reforms that will work to solve some real (or imagined) problems. Some want to justify a recent choice of a new direction—to defend a new policy against attacks from the political opposition or criticism from the media. Some wish to package and sell sets of ideas ('best practice', 'the reinvention model', 'World Governance Indicators' etc.). Management consultants, 'experts', and governments all do this (e.g. Federal Ministry of the Interior, 2006; Kaufmann et al., 2007; Osborne and Gaebler, 1992; Prime Minister and Minister for the Cabinet Office, 1999). Some hope to sound progressive and look good at an election. And some—mainly the academics—simply want accurately to describe and explain what is happening or has happened in the world of reform.

This mixture of motives means that the dividing line between descriptive and analytical ('is') statements and normative ('ought') statements is frequently hard to find. The desire to understand and explain is often tangled up with the desire to promote and support a particular kind of reform. Those reading the literature (which obviously includes those of you who are reading this book) need to be especially sensitive to the likely interests of the author(s), to unspoken assumptions, to the strength of evidence in relation to the size of the claims being made, and so on. This is what used to be called 'source criticism', and it is a vital technique for those who wish to investigate the literature on public management reform. For example, a student who researched public management reform solely by visiting government websites would be likely to come up with a picture of what was going on that was both over-simple and over-optimistic. Even texts produced by academics cannot be assumed to be 'neutral', partly because many public management academics also work in consultancy and advice roles, but also because the academic world is itself divided between competing theoretical and methodological camps (Pollitt and Bouckaert, 2009, chapter 9).

We can advocate source criticism and we can comment on the contested nature of the literature, but of course we cannot ourselves entirely escape from this ongoing contest. On the one hand we can assure readers that this book is not written to promote any particular reform or to satisfy any particular 'customer'. We have striven to be impartial, and to look for good quality evidence from wherever we can find it. (This has meant, inter alia, that in some places we have used evidence and ideas sourced from others in the academic world with whom we differ over a range of issues. Nevertheless, if they have interesting findings or insights, we gladly adopt them, even if there remain other theoretical or normative disagreements between us.) Our general stance is sceptical but (we hope) appreciative of the sheer complexity and difficulty which reformers themselves routinely face—and which academics who wish to understand what is going must also grapple with. Yet despite these good intentions and despite our academic independence, we cannot claim to sit atop Mt Olympus and offer a God's-eye view of what has been happening. To make any sense at all we have to employ some theories and conceptual frameworks and methods and, as soon as we do that, we necessarily import particular sorting devices that screen out some elements and screen in others. This process has already begun—as we warned, our conceptual framework for assessing results (Figure 1.1, above) would be regarded as unduly rationalistic by some.

Thus, both material interests and theoretical perspectives greatly influence the kinds of knowledge that are formed concerning public management reform. This is not a cause for despair: it is simply a sign that this branch of knowledge is heavily engaged with the real world, warts and all. After all, in most countries public management reform affects the daily lives of most of the population. In many ways it is more important than the ephemeral thrills and spills of 'high politics', because it may have direct impacts on the enduring basics—education, health, crime, safety—things whose effects last far longer than the transient personalities and slogans that so often occupy the headlines. In this spirit, we welcome you to our attempt to make sense of the last thirty years of reform.

2 Problems and responses: a model of public management reform

> Reform means change in a direction advocated by some groups or individuals. It does not necessarily mean improvement.
>
> (Rubin, 1992)

2.1 Why has there been so much reform?

Over the last three decades there appears to have been a huge amount of public management reform. It is difficult to be certain—there are no readily available, common, and commensurable units in which we can count and compare what has been happening. Yet the present authors share, with many other commentators (e.g. Kettl, 2000; Christensen and Lægreid, 2001; OECD, 2005*b*; Lynn, 2006), an impression of a wave of reforms across many countries. Of course, there was also reform in earlier periods (see, e.g. König, 1996, pp. 44–5; Pollitt, 1984; Savoie, 1994; Bouckaert, 1994). However, the changes since 1980 have—in many countries—been distinguished by an international character and a degree of political salience which mark them out from the more parochial or technical changes of the preceding quarter century. In some countries there have been deliberate attempts to remodel the state. In many countries reform has been accompanied by large claims from politicians to the effect that wholesale change, with sharp improvements in performance, was both desirable and achievable. As we explained in the first chapter, there has been more 'hype' about administrative change, in more countries, more or less simultaneously, than ever before.

If this impression is even approximately correct, then one question must be 'why?' What are the forces driving the reformers? Why is it that, on the one hand, many countries have participated in the stampede to remodel their public sectors while, on the other, some have been much more cautious? How can we explain both the similarities and the differences between what has happened in this country as compared with that? Chapter 1 offered a first, very brief, overview of these questions, but that was only to scratch the surface. The development of more systematic answers will occupy much of this book. A useful first step is to develop a general model of the process of management reform, and that is the task we address in this chapter.

It is important to note that this is a different kind of model from those we introduced in the previous chapter (NPM, NWS, NPG, etc.). *They* are usually presented either as normative models of desired states (objectives to be achieved) or as models of reform processes that are under way (thus, many commentators have claimed that actual reform paths are shifting from NPM to NPG). The model we are about to outline here is not of that type. It is a general model of how and why public management reform takes place. It is entirely agnostic as to what current trends are or where things should be going. It simply models the forces and influences affecting reformers, be they believers in NPM, NPG, or a flat Earth.

2.2 A model of public management reform

The model we will propose is intended as a first approximation. Its purpose is to provide a framework for subsequent discussion by depicting the broad forces which have been at work in both driving and restraining change. A model such as this is a conceptual map, a diagram of forces, and a heuristic device. From it and within it we can develop more detailed sets of typologies and more specific theories which will classify and explain specific patterns and trends, both within individual countries and across groups of countries. The model is therefore a way of learning—as anyone attempting to draw even a simple diagram of the influences on reform will quickly discover for themselves. It will also serve to structure a lot of the empirical material which we subsequently introduce (e.g. in the country cases in Appendix B).

Figure 2.1 shows our model. It represents an inductive synthesis of what we have learned about the process of reform in many countries. It is as simple as we could make it without doing injustice to the real complexity of the processes we are endeavouring to identify and assess. Even so, it is complex enough to require some explication.

2.3 The forces at work

Let us first consider the broad architecture of the model, since this embodies a number of our key assumptions and concepts. A first, and very important point is that the model takes the government of a single country as its framework. This is already something of an over-simplification, because, as we noted in Chapter 1, and will continue to discuss later in the book, international organizations and networks frequently play important parts in such reforms (see, e.g. Mahon and McBride, 2009). Nevertheless, the key reform decisions are usually formally taken by national governments, even if they proceed under the influence of wider networks or international organizations like the OECD or the World Bank. So that is where we begin.

At the centre of the figure lies the process of elite decision-making. That is no accident, since one of our theories is that most of the changes we are concerned with have been predominantly 'top-down', at least in the sense of having been conceived and executed by executive politicians and/or senior civil servants. Of course (as the diagram explicitly

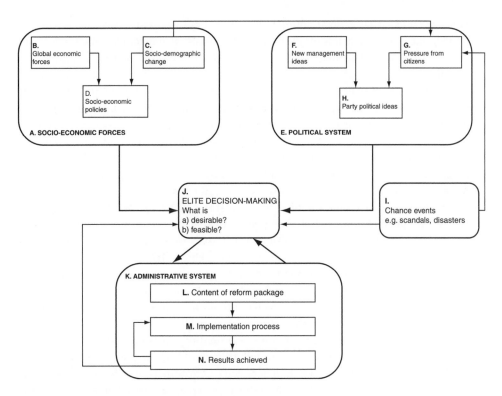

Figure 2.1 A model of public management reform

acknowledges), these elites may be heavily influenced by ideas and pressures from elsewhere (including the international influences just mentioned), and, furthermore, their plans may be blown off course. (In addition, over time, elites change their composition—they are themselves not a fixed entity.) Nevertheless, public management reform—certainly in central governments—is a process that tends to begin in the upper, rather than the lower reaches of governance, and which allows for a measure of choice as to the specific instruments and techniques which are chosen. Notice that, within box J, we distinguish between elite perceptions of what reforms are *desirable* and elite perceptions of what reforms are *feasible* (the elites are the same in both cases). This distinction reflects the commonplace of political life that, as Sir Michael Jagger once sang, 'You can't always get what you want' (even if you are a president or prime minister). There are obstacles—economic, ergonomic, and legal—and there are also conservative forces which resist change (and are not necessarily wrong to do so!). Reformers are frequently in the position of desiring something more than what they actually propose, but 'censoring' their own aspirations in the interests of framing a lesser package that stands a better chance of being accepted. Notice, also, that perceptions of what is desirable are not merely identifications of what is technically optimal. They are very much *cultural* as well as technical, as, equally, are perceptions of what is feasible (which will usually be calculated in terms of the norms and expectations of other key actors).

There are three other general points to be made about the centrality of elite decision-making in the model. First, it is the exception rather than the rule for reform schemes to be comprehensive, even in intent. Reformers try to improve this or that institution or programme, or sometimes a whole sector (health, education), but they seldom attempt to remodel the entire sweep of public sector institutions in one go. Goodin (1996, p. 28) expresses this point well: 'Typically, there is no single design or designer. There are just lots of localized attempts at partial design cutting across one another, and any sensible scheme for institutional design has to take account of that fact.' Even the reforms in New Zealand between 1984 and 1993, which were unusual for the extent to which they formed a coherent whole and were (initially at least) driven by one small group, evolved over time and were significantly affected by a host of practical considerations which blunted the purity of the theories which lay behind them (Boston et al., 1996, pp. 81–6).

The second general point is that it is easy to exaggerate the *degree of intentionality* in many reforms. The final results of reform efforts (box N in the diagram) may bear only a loose relationship to the intentions embodied in the elite's original manifesto for change (box L). Again, Goodin makes the point: 'Institutions are often the product of intentional activities gone wrong—unintended by-products, the products of various intentional actions cutting across one another, misdirected intentions or just plain mistakes' (Goodin, 1996, p. 28). Thus, although we locate elite decision-making at the centre of the process of reform, and although we would maintain that intentional acts of institutional redesign have been crucial to the story we have to tell, this should not be read as an elevation of organizational elites into God-like designers who are routinely able to realize bold and broad schemes of improvement. On the contrary, we envisage their schemes as frequently vulnerable to cognitive limitations, cross-cutting actions, politico-administrative road-blocks, and unforeseen developments of a wide variety of kinds (see March and Olsen, 1995, chapter 6, for an extended account of the pitfalls, both cognitive and motivational, and Hammond, 1996, for a brilliantly argued demonstration of why having more of one kind of desired result often inevitably means having more of another kind of problem as well). The most prominent of these complicating factors are discussed further later in this chapter, and subsequently.

The third general point is that—as this explication of the model will hopefully make clear—public management reform does *not* usually consist of a few elite persons coming along with a bright idea. Neither the persons nor the ideas appear out of a vacuum. The elite usually has quite distinctive channels of recruitment. The ideas nearly always come from *somewhere*—a management consultancy, an academic, a neighbouring government, the OECD, or whatever. The whole point of our model is to see the elite decision-making in the centre as a process that is powerfully shaped by a much wider context.

Surrounding the elite decision-making at the heart of Figure 2.1 there are, therefore, three large groups of elements. In the top left there is a group of economic and socio-demographic factors (A, including B, C, D). In the top right there is a group of political and intellectual factors (E, including F, G, H). In the bottom half of the figure there is a group of administrative factors (K, including L, M, N). It is from the interplay between these principal elements that management changes emerge.

We will now proceed to examine each of these influences in rather more detail, beginning with the socio-economic factors (box A). (Those wishing to see how these factors interact in specific cases should go to the individual country files in Appendix B, where developments in each country are set out using exactly these same categories.) Box A itself represents the general set of these factors, which is both broad and diverse. Some such factors can be thought of as *structural*, in the sense that they are deep-rooted and long-lasting. The population structure would be one example. We may not immediately think that population changes would have much effect on public management reform, but that would be a mistake. For example, two of the reform-prompting problems which many governments face at the moment are the increasing costs and complexity of the welfare state (which have a lot to do with the presence of a larger percentage of elderly people in our populations), and the difficulty of adequately staffing the public service, because the big cohorts that were born in the 1940s and 1950s, and which joined the public service in the 1960s and 1970s, are now retiring, all within a short space of time (e.g. Management Advisory Committee, 2003). Others may be more ephemeral, such as short-term economic cycles of upturn and downturn. Certain of these are likely to have a definite and discernible impact on state administrations, and it is these which are identified in boxes B, C, and D.

Box B represents the influence of global economic forces. Some commentators ascribe a large and dominating influence to these (for thoughtful critiques of such arguments see Held, 1998 and Scholte, 2000). It is often said that the globalization of capital markets and the growth of multinational corporations and international trade have weakened the control national governments are able to exert over 'their' economic policies. It is therefore no longer possible for a government to sustain for very long a level of public spending that global money markets deem to be imprudent. The intensification of international competition has also obliged governments to give greater attention than ever before to the competitiveness of 'their' firms. Firms are unlikely to compete effectively if they are weighed down by either high taxes (to finance high public spending) or by tedious and heavy bureaucracy. What is more, national and local governments are more restricted than they used to be in their ability to address costly and painful social problems such as unemployment.

As a consequence of increased capital mobility and tax competition, the power of all national governments to tax capital assets and capital incomes has been reduced. By the same token, national monetary policy can no longer reduce interest rates below the international level in order to stimulate productive investment, and higher rates of tax mean that running fiscal deficits to expand aggregate demand has become more expensive. National governments have thus largely lost their ability to avert rising unemployment through the strategies of macro-economic management that were still relatively effective in the 1960s and 1970s. Hence, the more social policy systems were implicitly premised on continuing full employment, the more they have come under stress (OECD, 1997c, p. 211). More recently, we have seen how problems in the finance sector can quickly spread from finance to the 'real economy', and from country to country, until they amount to a global economic crisis (GEC). Governments then felt obliged to 'rescue' banks by huge expenditures which, in turn, unbalanced public budgets so that severe cuts in public-spending programmes become inevitable. Reforms are then *de rigueur*, as governments try to 'do more with less' so as to preserve popular front-line public services even while budgets are being slashed.

Thus we have one set of reasons for widespread public sector reforms—to restrain public spending, lighten the bureaucratic burden, and reshape social policies that can no longer be afforded.

These are powerful arguments. They are widely rehearsed and believed. However, it is important not to exaggerate their explanatory power. Whilst it seems entirely probable that global economic forces have been a vital background factor in prompting consideration of administrative reform, they do not usually determine the precise form or timing or degree of that reform. Some of the detail necessary to support this contention will be presented later, but it can immediately be pointed out that the pattern of management change has differed considerably from country to country, suggesting that the effects of global markets are not uniform. Furthermore, the timing of particular reforms in particular countries frequently does not correlate at all to economic crises. Even when the 2008 GEC had made it obvious that large public-expenditure cuts were necessary in the UK, the political parties repeatedly postponed defining the precise targets and full extent of these (very unpopular) cuts while they struggled for electoral advantage.

Finally, it should be noted that economic pressures do not themselves translate directly into some particular *type* of management reform. Reformers need ideas—models or patterns or plans or visions of how the public sector could be better organized. Markets may provide the pressure to do something, but they do not supply the ideas of exactly what to do.

In practice, a further problem with those commentators who present 'globalization' as a dominant and determining influence on institutional changes is that the concept itself is frequently deployed in a vague or even contradictory manner. For a satisfactory analysis one would need, at a minimum, to distinguish the different mechanisms and modalities involved in the increasing interconnectedness of world financial markets, extensions to free trade, technological standardization and internationalization (e.g. the global spread of certain brands of computer software or hardware), and what one might term cultural globalization (McDonalds, certain films, fashions, sporting events, etc.). Too often these rather different processes are all lumped together in a single, utopian or dystopian fashion.

In short, *economic* forms of globalization *do* seem to have been a major influence on institutional change, but one which has acted through a number of other, intervening variables. These other variables have been crucial in determining the precise shape and timing of the reforms in particular countries.

Socio-demographic change (box C) is a second background pressure of considerable importance. By this we refer to the pressures arising from changes in the pattern of life for millions of citizens in each of our countries. They are too numerous to list in their entirety here, but include, most notably, increased life expectancy, changes in the patterns of family life (especially a higher incidence of single-parent and single-person households), and a considerable rise in the average level of unemployment as compared with the boom years of 1950–73. Some data on these trends is given in Appendix A. The basic effect of many of these social changes has been to increase the demand falling upon state-provided or state-financed services—particularly health care, social care, and social security. For example, in the early 1990s the average amount of health care resources consumed by the average British or American person over the age of 75 was calculated as being between six and ten times the amount consumed by a middle-aged person. Thus, to have an increasing proportion of elderly people in a population implies a considerable growth in welfare expenditure. In most modern states, social security (pensions, unemployment benefits, and other benefits in cash and kind) is the largest single item in the state budget, and health care is frequently the second largest. Broad changes in the levels of demand for these services therefore translate into significant public expenditure increases—just as global economic pressures are pushing in the other direction. In some countries commentators have painted frightening scenarios of state finances collapsing under unsupportable welfare burdens, with millions of citizens being deprived of their expected rights and benefits.

How does all this affect public management reform? Again, as with the globalization of capital and trade flows, the impacts are indirect. An increase in the number of pensioners or of the unemployed does not by itself produce a particular type of organizational change. But what it does do is provide powerful incentives for politicians and civil servants to look for ways of easing the strain on the system. These may include lowering the rates of increase in benefits (e.g. by de-indexing them from wages and salaries), narrowing the categories of eligibility (so as to concentrate on the 'most needy'), or increasing charges and co-payments by the beneficiaries. But they have also tended to include changes which have more obvious impacts on the ways in which such services are organized and managed. For example, streamlining may be implemented with a view to reducing administrative overheads; commercial and voluntary sector participation in the process of provision may be encouraged and/or there may be wholesale restructurings of the relevant departments and agencies in an attempt to build in stronger incentives to economy and efficiency (see, e.g. for the US, Petersen, 2000 or, for Sweden, Micheletti, 2000).

These background pressures therefore reflect themselves in foreground socio-economic policies which may oscillate quite rapidly over time (box D). For example, in pursuit of social-security savings, many European governments have raised the minimum age for entitlement to a state pension. Or, in the economic field in the mid and late 1990s, EU member states struggled to meet the Maastricht 'convergence criteria' which would qualify them to join the European single currency. This put downward pressure on public spending and public debt, and may well have somewhat increased the numbers of unemployed, at least in the short term. It was, therefore, a policy with considerable and diverse effects on the administrative apparatuses of those states concerned. It was of particular interest as a *supranational* initiative.

We can now move to the second cluster of influential factors—those concerned with the political system. To begin with we need to take into account the general, structural features of this system, which are represented in Figure 2.1 by box E. These features may make management reform more or less straightforward. For example, in Germany a strict constitutional law makes it difficult, if not impossible for major restructurings to take place at the federal level, whereas in the UK the process of changing the machinery of government has long been remarkably easy, usually involving only secondary legislation that can easily be passed through the legislature by the executive (Pollitt, 1984, 2007). Note here the important role that the law can play in facilitating, shaping, or sometimes restraining public management reform. Moving to another aspect of the political system, it may be observed that, in countries such as Finland or Belgium, which are characterized by consensual political systems and coalition governments, the process of management reform is likely to be less harsh and combative than in countries such as Australia or the UK, where the political systems are more adversarial. A final example would be the high degree of protection which the constitutions of Germany and the Nordic countries afford to regional/local/municipal government. This usually means that central governments in these countries find it relatively difficult to extend the reforming process to the local level—unless and until there is a reasonable coalition of political support for reform at that level itself. Contrast this with Mrs Thatcher's ability, in the UK during the 1980s, actually to *abolish* the Greater London Council and the six metropolitan county authorities when she found herself in disagreement with their politics and policies. These contrasting features of different political systems are to some extent *structural*—as in the electoral system and the corresponding pattern of political parties—and to some extent *cultural*—as with the heavy emphasis on relatively 'polite' collective discussion and agreement which characterizes systems such as those of the Netherlands and Sweden.

In contrast with the constraints and restraints which often flow from the deep structures of political systems, there are also, within those same systems, dynamic elements. One such that is of particular importance for our theme is the influx of new management ideas into the public sector (box F). Over the last two decades this has generated a rich flux of ideas about how to manage almost anything, from a corner shop to 'Great Britain, plc'. These ideas have echoed around business schools, corporate boardrooms, government seminars, and even airport bookstands (see Pollitt, 2003*a*, chapter 7). There has been considerable inter-country borrowing, facilitated by international bodies such as the Public Management Service of the OECD (PUMA) and the World Bank. There can be no doubt that the selling of management ideas was one of the growth industries of the 1980s and 1990s (Sahlin-Andersson and Engwall, 2002). Equally there can be little doubt that the writings of the gurus and the presentations of the management consultants have influenced political and civil service leaders in a number of the countries examined in this book. Perhaps the most celebrated case was the intellectual line of descent which ran from generic management writers such as Peter Drucker and Tom Peters through the authors of the American best-seller *Re-inventing Government* (Osborne and Gaebler, 1992) to the major US federal government report *Creating a Government that Works Better and Costs Less: Report of the National Performance Review* (Gore, 1993).

Of course, management ideas, however fashionable, very seldom get translated in a pure form directly into specific reforms. Rather they flow into a larger pool of ideas, drawn from a variety of sources, which are made use of by political and administrative elites (box J). Nevertheless, generic management ideas have been prominent on the face of public sector reforms, perhaps especially in Australasia, North America, and the UK, but also, more recently to some extent even in France (Bezes, 2007; Eymeri-Douzans, 2009). In these countries (and, to a lesser extent, others) generic approaches and techniques such as Management by Objectives (MbO), Total Quality Management (TQM), benchmarking, outsourcing, and Business Process Re-engineering (BPR) have been widely adopted within the public sector (Lane, 2000; Pollitt and Bouckaert, 1995; Thompson, 2000). These are the individual dishes or *plats* we referred to in Chapter 1, items which can be combined to make more or less coherent models/menus. Alongside these specific management techniques, and often interwoven with them, organizational design principles based on micro-economic theories have also been extensively used. In New Zealand, for example, public choice theory, agency theory, and transaction cost economics were all influential (Boston et al., 1996, chapter 2).

In Chapter 1 we stressed the growing internationalization of public management. Certainly this has become increasingly true for management ideas, both those generated by gurus and business schools and those which derive from micro-economic theory. Departments and units charged with administrative reform have their own international networks, both bilateral and multilateral. The Public Management Service of the OECD was an influential nodal point in these networks from the late 1980s onwards (see, e.g. OECD 1995, 2005; Halligan, 1996*a* and Premfors, 1998). Other networks have also emerged, such as the 'Reinventing Government' conferences that came from the Clinton/Gore reforms in the USA, but were then marketed internationally as 'Global Forums', or the World Bank's promotion of a specific set of ideas about what constitutes 'good governance' (Arndt, 2008).

Box G in Figure 2.1 represents pressure from citizens. It should immediately be acknowledged that management reform is not usually at the top of the citizenry's list of priorities. Neither is it a topic upon which most men and women in the street have very specific suggestions to offer. If we define reform as deliberate changes to governmental structures and functions, then we must immediately concede that most citizens know very little about these structures and functions, except at the top surface, or 'sharp end', of a government website or service counter or police cordon. It would be simply unrealistic to expect citizens to generate detailed proposals for reforming an inner machinery of which they know not much, and about which they have only very limited incentives to learn. However, although lay citizens are unlikely to be brimming with concrete proposals for better management, they can and, on occasion, do exert pressure for change. If, for example, citizens become used to very rapid and customer-friendly transactions in banks, building societies, and shops they may become progressively more and more discontented with post offices or benefits payment agencies which are slow, inflexible, and inhospitable. Such discontent with low standards of service in state institutions may then be expressed to political representatives, or the media, who then communicate them onwards to the elites (box J). More dramatically, if it is widely believed that civil servants are corrupt, or that a particular service is being delivered in a seriously inequitable way, then public opinion may mobilize to create pressure for reform. Thus, while the views of citizens seldom seem to be the driving or shaping force for particular reforms, there can be circumstances in which they constitute an important background influence. For example, the fatal explosion of a firework store in the Dutch city of Enschede in 2001 crystallized a major debate in that country concerning alleged laxity and 'cosiness' in regimes of public regulation.

Box H identifies party-political ideas as a further influence on public management change. Political parties acquire ideas about how they would like to govern, and these include issues of structure, style, and process. For example, a party may decide that it wishes to 'reduce bureaucracy' or to 'decentralize and put power closer to the people'. Or it may adopt more specific proposals such as creating a special ministry or agency for the environment, the regions, the family, gender mainstreaming, inland security, or any other topic which happens to be prominent or fashionable. Party-political ideas may be more or less ideologically charged. One doctrine that was influential in a number of countries during the 1980s and 1990s was that of privatization. When construed as a consistent preference for private over public provision, this doctrine had a very obvious and immediate impact on the public sector—it reduced its size. Australia, New Zealand, and the UK all pursued vigorous privatization programmes of this type, and the doctrine was also applied, albeit in a less unremitting way, in Canada, France, the Netherlands, Sweden, and the USA. More recently a number of political leaders have proclaimed the need for more 'joined-up' government, with greater integration between hitherto separate policies or services (see, e.g. Bogdanor, 2005; Kernaghan, 2009; OECD, 2002; Pollitt, 2003b).

Party-political ideas are sometimes internally generated and derived from a specifically political agenda that party activists are developing (box H). On other occasions the ideas may come from outside, from popular movements among the electorate (box G) or from the worlds of business or academia (box F). It is clear, for example, that in relation to public management issues, the ideas of the 1980s Conservative governments in the UK, and of the 1984–90 Labour governments in New Zealand, were extensively influenced by the theories of public choice-school economists (Boston et al., 1996; Pollitt, 1993). Equally, the Republican administration of President Reagan was heavily populated with business advisers, while its Democratic successors during the mid 1990s also made deliberate use of what it called 'Lessons learned from America's best companies' (Gore, 1997).

It should be noted, *en passant*, that all these flows of ideas can be greatly strengthened by amplification in the mass media. Political systems have become more and more closely attuned to, and bound in with, the mass media, and if a reform idea can achieve exposure on national TV or in the main newspapers it will be virtually guaranteed at least some serious political attention. While the detailed technicalities of reform (e.g. accruals accounting versus cash-based accounting) are unlikely to catch the attention of TV pundits or mass-circulation daily newspapers, more general ideas (that the railways are a mess and need re-organizing, or that too many people are defrauding the welfare system) do receive wide media exposure, and help to increase pressure for management reform. We have not devoted a specific box to the media in Figure 2.1, but one can perhaps think of the TV and the press as a general influence that can (sometimes quite suddenly) 'heat up' a particular part of the diagram, amplifying the volume and force of communications and discussions of particular issues.

Summing up the play of ideas, one scholar wrote:

Public sector reform is in fashion and no self-respecting government can afford to ignore it. How a fashion is established is one of the most intriguing questions of public policy. Part of the answer lies in *policy diffusion* brought about by the activities of international officials (whose zeal for administrative reform mysteriously stops short at the door of their own organizations), by meetings of public administrators, academics and the so-called policy entrepreneurs. (Wright, 1997, p. 8).

There is one influence which operates outside the main groupings of socio-economic forces, political system factors, and elements of the administrative system. Box I represents the effect of chance events such as scandals, natural or man-made disasters, accidents, and unpredictable tragedies such as shootings or epidemics. Whilst these can clearly partake of socio-economic or political factors (trains can collide because of lack of public investment in maintenance or signalling equipment; a crazed gunman may bear a grudge against the government), their most obvious features are their newsworthiness and their unpredictability. The effect of such events on reform programmes may not be obvious, but occasionally it is significant. For example, the Cave Creek disaster in New Zealand (when an observation platform collapsed in a public reservation) sharply focused media attention on the issue of public accountability in a newly decentralized system (Gregory, 1998). The explosion at Enschede, mentioned above, had a similar effect in the Netherlands. In the USA the disaster that destroyed the 'Challenger' space shuttle led to a major overhaul of the National Aeronautics and Space Administration (NASA), one of the largest federal agencies. Thus, physical accidents have a tendency to transmute into organizational or even institutional crises. At a more personal level, senior ministers are prone to a variety of 'accidents' (including ethical misdemeanours, sexual indiscretions, or simple illnesses), and occasionally individuals with strong reforming ideas may arrive or depart for reasons quite unconnected with their management priorities.

Accidents and disasters come in many different forms and sizes, and the examples given in the previous paragraph far from exhaust the catalogue. We also need to remember that disasters can be global in reach and that, except for a few unlistened-to prophets, the global economic collapse of 2008 came as a quite unexpected and sudden tidal wave. Its impacts on public administration were vast and various, and at the time of writing we are still seeing new ones crop up almost every week.

Taking a broad view, therefore, the upsurge of reforms in the last twenty years or so can be attributed to an intensification of a number of factors, but perhaps particularly global economic forces, socio-economic change, and the supply of new management ideas (B, C, and F). However, these pressures do not enjoy free play over a smooth surface. On the contrary, they soon wash up against countervailing forces—not only the recalcitrance of those groups with a vested interest in the status quo, but also less animated sources of resistance. Existing ways of doing things may be entrenched in laws or regulations or cultural norms which take time or political majorities (or both) to change. At the strong end, a particular kind of management change may require an adjustment to a country's constitution—or, in the case of EU institutions—to the founding treaties. Furthermore, even if the majority are agreed that the existing administrative structures or procedures are inadequate, it may be hard to agree on what to do instead (especially if, as is often the case, reform in one direction raises risks in another). Or it may simply be that to manage in a new and desired way may require a considerable investment in new information technology, new accounting systems, and/or new training programmes for the staff concerned, before it can be put into practice. All these factors represent the *costs of change* and they also help determine the *timescale* of change (Pollitt, 2008). Often reformers underestimate the extent of these until they get close to them (as they approach or get into implementation—box M).

Many of the costs of change can be thought of as being associated with the dismantling of existing political and administrative systems in order to 'make room' for the new. In every country, much history and many political bargains—and therefore some wisdom—is built into existing systems. Such systems are archaeological maps of past struggles and settlements (March and Olsenn, 1995, p. 205). Economists and political scientists increasingly employ notions of 'path dependency' to show how certain laws, rules, and institutions can create heavy disincentives for change, because so much is already invested in the existing ways of doing things (Pierson, 2000; Pollitt, 2008; Pollitt and Bouckaert, 2009). Consider the business of the UK driving on the right, while most of Europe drives on the left. At first sight it seems a pointless and occasionally irritating, or even dangerous anomaly—why not just pass a law that requires all countries to drive on the same side of the road? But then think of all the previous investments in the UK in favour of driving on the right—car plants which make right-hand-drive cars, road markings, road signs, driving tests, and many other things that would have be (expensively) changed. Then there would have to be a huge campaign to retrain every driver, and complex and possibly disruptive arrangements for the day when the changes would actually be made. All in all, the disincentives against change are considerable, even without allowing for the fuss about 'surrendering to the Brussels' bureaucracy' which the nationalist media would presumably make.

Similarly, with management reform, staff are obliged to relinquish old ways and learn new. Well-oiled networks of information and influence are disturbed and new, less certain ones put in their place. Politicians who were used to one configuration of authority within those state agencies that most interested them now have to get used to a new pattern, and possibly one which will be more difficult for them to influence or communicate through. And so on. We have already discussed the restraining effects of political structures (box E), and we will now move on to look at the corresponding structures of *administrative* systems. The two act jointly to temper the ardour of the reformers with the sober difficulties of shifting the status quo. Thus we depict them as enclosing and surrounding the more specific and dynamic pressures of the moment.

Administrative systems (box K) are often difficult to change in more-than-incremental ways. For example, the UK civil service is built around a core of generalists, whereas many continental civil services, including the French and German, consist mainly of staff trained in law. A cultural and disciplinary difference of this type cannot be eliminated overnight—it influences the way in which officials conceptualize and approach a wide variety of issues. Structural differences can also be significant: in Sweden and Finland central government for long consisted of a group of modest-sized ministries surrounded by a circle of relatively independent administrative agencies which had responsibility for most operational issues. This was a more decentralized system than that which obtained (until recently, at least) in France or the UK. Many of the issues for which local or municipal authorities in the UK would deal directly with a central ministry, would be taken care of by agencies in Finland or Sweden. For the Nordic countries, to change required new legislation and a reconsideration of the highly political issue of relations between central government and municipalities. It could be done (and to some extent has been), but not quickly or lightly. A third example would be personnel regulations. These are clearly necessary to ensure that public servants behave with propriety and consistency. Yet they tend to develop a momentum of their own. Over the years huge manuals are built up, with each unusual occurrence leading to more paragraphs or pages being added to the magnum opus. It can be very difficult fundamentally to reduce or revise this tangle of interlocking rules and regulations. When, in 1993, the American vice president launched the National Performance Review, the federal personnel manual was presented as a symbol of traditional, over-complex bureaucratic rule-making, and a copy was ceremonially burned on the lawn of the White House. The reality was less impressive than this publicity stunt—a huge civil service could not really throw away all its internal rules, and most agencies seem to have continued to apply most of the rules as before. As one American colleague put it to us, 'The copy that was burned cannot have been the only one'. Personnel regulations have become notable constraints on reform in a number of countries—perhaps especially Belgium, France, and Italy—and also for the European Commission.

At a more pedestrian level, administrative systems can still be hard to budge. Consider a straightforward benefits-claiming system. Claimants come to a social security office and fill in a form. The form is then checked by counter staff who, if the claim is in order, make the appropriate payment. Let us suppose that a decision is made to reform this system by introducing computerized technology. In theory the new procedures will be quicker and less staff-intensive. Large efficiency gains are predicted. In practice even this simple-sounding reform can involve extensive complications. Hundreds, if not thousands of staff will need training to use the new computer technology. The educational qualifications needed for counter staff may need to be increased. Public service unions are likely to be concerned about any such changes, and are even more likely to resist attempts to reap efficiency gains which take the form of staff reductions. The purchase of the necessary computer software may be less than straightforward (Bellamy and Taylor, 1998, pp. 41–51; Hudson, 1999; Margetts, 1998; Dunleavy et al., 2006*a*). Questions about linking the data held on the new system to other computerized government data banks and about the security of personal details held on file may also arise, and these are likely to have legal implications. And so on. To manage the change well will take considerable forethought, planning, and time. To announce the reform is the easy part; to carry it through requires patience and resolve. During the 1980s and 1990s the UK Department of Social Security struggled hard to implement a huge computerization project called the 'Operational Strategy', but in the end the results fell well short of what had been forecast (National Audit Office, 1999, p. 25).

Despite these potentially formidable obstacles to radical or rapid change, reform programmes *are* launched, and frequently *do* make an impact. In Figure 2.1 boxes L, M, and N represent this more dynamic aspect of the administrative system. These activities—announcing reform packages, implementing changes, and achieving results—are the main focus of the remainder of our book, and their treatment here will be correspondingly brief.

The *content* of reform packages (L) are the product of the interaction between the desirable and the feasible, mentioned above. When announced, such packages frequently display a considerable rhetorical dimension, playing harmonies on the styles and ideas of the moment. They attempt to establish, or reinforce, discourses which support the particular institutional changes under consideration. Here is an example from the USA:

If somebody had said in 1993 that within 10 years the federal government would be smaller, customer-driven, worker-friendly, and run like America's best companies, they would have drawn . . . jeers.

But that was the challenge that President Clinton handed down four years ago when he asked me to reinvent the federal government—to put the wheels back on. We agreed right then that we needed to bring a revolution to the federal government: we call it reinventing government.   (Vice President Gore, 1997, p. 1).

Or this, from the Minister of Finance in a new, right-wing Danish government in the autumn of 2002:

The public sector must learn to think, act and be managed on the same terms as the private sector. The old bureaucrats must be smoked out!   (Pederson, 2002, p. 2)

Reform announcements are therefore as much texts to be interpreted as they are blue-prints for administrative action. Some reform announcements come to rather little, so it is always advisable to check how far the initial promises have been realized in the medium term. In this they are no different from most other political manifestos. It is also important to recognize that *announcing* reforms and *making recommendations* may become activities with a value of their own, without any necessary follow-through. Politicians, consultants, and academics can make quite decent livings out of producing statements and reports, even if little else happens in the longer run. Many countries can show at least some examples of political and managerial rhetoric outrunning measured achievement (for a long-term Swedish example, see Sundström, 2006).

The process of *implementation* (M) is a particularly important stage of the reform process. The 'science' of administration is hardly exact. Much is learned during the attempt to put reform ideas into practice, and some of that learning frequently translates into departures from the original design. During the 1970s an Anglo-American academic literature focus-ing on this stage appeared, and much of it was fairly pessimistic about the chances of reform packages actually unfolding according to plan. One particularly influential work was subtitled 'How Great Expectations in Washington are Dashed in Oakland' (Pressman and Wildavsky, 1973). It explained how top-down reforms were implemented through long chains of decisions and many levels of administration, and the chances of success were no better than the strength of the weakest link. Although subsequent scholarship has suggested that this mainly linear model of the implementation process is too simple, the basic point about the complexity of the process running from ideas to actual accomplish-ments stands firm (Hill and Hupe, 2002).

Indeed, the complexity of implementation processes may well be on the increase. More and more programmes are delivered through networks of organizations rather than by a single implementor (Kickert et al., 1997; Osborne, 2000; Rosenau, 2000). These networks may include different levels of government, independent public corporations, public/private hybrid bodies, commercial firms, and voluntary, non-profit associations. The NPM doctrines referred to in Chapter 1 have amplified this kind of fragmentation (Bouck-aert et al., 2010). Furthermore, implementation networks increasingly need to be interna-tional—most obviously for policies in fields such as telecommunications, transport, the environment, or communicable diseases. The implications of all this for manage-mentreform are complex. If such reforms are to be effective it seems they will often have to take the whole of a network as their 'unit of analysis', rather than just a single organization. However, both the available theories and the available authority could easily be inadequate for such a task. Ideas about how to design or redesign networks of different types of organization are in short supply. And the authority to carry through integrated reform of a whole network may not exist—each member of the network being its own master in the matter of management change.

Another problem that can arise during implementation is that individual reforms, though they may make good sense in themselves, may contradict or detract from other reforms which are being carried through at the same time. For example, the Assistant Auditor General of Canada, commenting on the slow progress made by various public service quality improvement initiatives during the early 1990s, observed:

Our review of relevant documents and our discussions with service managers indicated that they had many reasons for not having made more progress toward the government's repeated commitments. The reasons included the public service strike of 1991, government reorganisation in 1992, the change of government in 1993 and the subsequent Program Review and associated cutbacks, as well as re-engineering exercises carried out by individual departments. (Auditor General of Canada, 1997, para 14.65)

Implementation is also a crucial stage in the sense that it can directly feed back to the elite decision-makers' ideas about what to do next—whether to continue along a given path or change tack. For example, in New Zealand, a particularly elaborate and sophisticated performance-management system was put in place from the mid 1980s onwards. By the mid 1990s, as this system matured, it was recognized that there were dangers in too tight a focus on measurable outputs. The ultimate objectives of programmes (to educate children, lower unemployment, etc.) could be displaced by an intense concentration on how well lessons were delivered, how many unemployment training courses had been held, and a host of other measures of process and output. With this concern in mind, the New Zealand Senior Public Managers Conference for 1997 had the title and theme 'Raising our game: from outputs to outcomes'.

Finally we come to the end of this long and complicated road—the achievements that eventually accrue from the process of reform (box N). These might, or might not, bear a close resemblance to the original aspirations of the politico-administrative elite. Whether they do or not, like the implementation phase, these 'results' are likely to feed back into earlier stages of the process—particularly to elite perceptions of what types of change are desirable and feasible (J). In practice—as we shall see in Chapter 5—the 'final results' of reform are frequently difficult to identify and/or attribute with any confidence (National Audit Office, 2010). Rhetoric and reality can be very hard to disentangle. Indeed, ultimately 'the final reality' *cannot* be wholly separated out, because it is so thoroughly impregnated with the competing discourses through which it is constituted. Furthermore, although new administrative structures and processes may unmistakably exist, it is often a problem to know just how far they can be attributed to some preceding reform (Pollitt, 1995; Pollitt and Bouckaert, 2001). In interviews, practitioners very often trace specific impacts back to a variety of influences, of which a particular reform is only one. In short, the process is usually messy rather than neat.

2.4 **Concluding remarks**

We have now presented our model of the 'why' and 'how' of public management reform. It depicts the process as multifaceted and liable to modification at a number of different stages. It embodies interactions between background socio-economic influences, political pressures, specific ideas that are in current circulation, and features of the administrative system itself. It identifies both pressures *for* change and sources of resistance *against* change. It reserves a role for the unintentional and the accidental. It already hints at, and allows for, considerable variation between countries, not least because they enter into the process of change from different starting points, in the sense that each country has its own distinctive political and administrative system (E and K). It incorporates several important feedback loops, as reformers learn from the process of implementation (and with the internationalization of the 'market' in management ideas, governments frequently look for lessons from the experiences of other countries, not just their own).

Yet the model is limited in various significant ways. Presented as it is in Figure 2.1 there is a danger that it will be interpreted or used in a static manner ('just fill in the boxes'). But the boxes each represent sets of processes, and further processes then ensue *between* the boxes. It is important to realize, therefore, that it is the interactions within and between the boxes that bring real reforms to life. These interactions may be very short term (an earthquake, an election result), or medium term (setting up a new agency), or long term (weeding out corruption, or adjusting the pension and health care systems to deal with a population containing a much higher percentage of elderly people). The temporal aspect of reform is often crucial (Pollitt, 2008), but is not apparent from Figure 2.1.

There is therefore still a lot to be 'filled in'. In particular, to breathe life into the model we need more detailed accounts of what goes on inside some of the key boxes—particularly typologies of different types of political (E) and administrative (K) regimes. Once we have those in place it should be possible further to develop the dynamic features of the model, by relating particular regime types to specific trends in reforms. At that point, the schematic and heuristic model that is Figure 2.1 can begin to accommodate specific explanatory theories. For the moment it is simply a starting point—a logical model, certainly not a unified theory. It can accommodate within its 'boxes' quite a wide variety of more specific theories—more, in fact, than we will have room to introduce within this book. We will, however, make a start. The socio-economic forces of box A, though important, will be treated primarily as background factors, and are analysed comparatively in Appendix A, and for individual states in the country files of Appendix B. In the next chapter we therefore focus on boxes E and K—the political system and the administrative system. Here, we will argue, one is able to see quite a strong set of explanatory connections between, on the one hand, the types of national structures and processes and, on the other, particular patterns of management reform.

3 | Many houses: types of politico-administrative regime

Every house has many builders, and is never finished.

(Paavo Haavikko, in Lomas, 1991)

3.1 The starting point for management reforms

The model of public management reform developed in the previous chapter laid considerable stress on the characteristics of the existing political and administrative systems as shaping influences over processes of management change (boxes E and K in Figure 2.1). These systems provide, as it were, the existing terrain—the topography over which reformers must travel. To continue the analogy, it is obvious that different countries display different topographical features, and therefore different challenges to those who wish to carry through reform. For example, a US president must get his/her reforms through an independent-minded and powerful Congress, whereas a British prime minister with a majority can much more easily push reforms through the British parliament. In this chapter we will offer relevant classifications for such differences, and will then use these to examine and locate the twelve countries which fall within our scope. We will also attempt to use the strategy on the other entity in our study—the European Commission—although its application in that unique case is less straightforward (Section 3.8).

Some accounts of public management reform say little or nothing of contextual differences of the kind to which the discussion of this chapter is devoted. They concentrate entirely on the characteristics of the reform tools themselves—strategic planning, performance budgeting, Total Quality Management or whatever —the 'dishes' in Figure 1.2. In our view such accounts are seriously incomplete. Their attention is, in effect, confined to the intervention alone, with minimal analysis of variations in the contexts in which the intervention takes place. Yet there is ample evidence from many studies of public administration that context can make a huge difference to the effects yielded by a particular model or tool of management change (e.g. Bouckaert et al., 2008; Lynn, 2006; Pollitt, Van Thiel, and Homburg, 2007; Savoie, 1994; Wilson, 1989). Conceptually identical, or at least similar, reforms develop differently in one national (or sectoral or local) context as compared with another.

On the other hand, it would be misleading to think of politico-administrative systems as some kind of unchanging bedrock, to which every reform must adapt itself or fail. In our model of the process of change (Figure 2.1) *every* element is subject to change, though at different speeds. Thus even the fundamentals of political systems (e.g. constitutions) and administrative systems (e.g. the educational and cultural characteristics of the higher civil service) can and do change over time. The UK is famous for its one-party governments and its 'first-past-the-post' majoritarian voting system. Yet at the time of writing it has a Conservative/Liberal Democrat coalition government and has recently carried out a referendum to consult the public on electoral reform. Some commentators are doubting whether it will ever return to simple majoritarian government, which would make a fascinating case study if anyone is revising this book in another ten years' time. Equally, both Belgium and the Netherlands have long been known for their stable, consensus-based systems, but that may now be changing. In both countries, over the past decade or so, the party system itself has evolved, throwing up new, populist parties which have been able to gain influence very fast. These newcomers have not by any means wanted to join in the old consensual game on the old consensual terms, so there has been a certain volatility that was not previously apparent. The phrase from Paavo Haaviko's poem which introduced this chapter sums up the situation well—the house is never entirely stable and complete. However, these kinds of systemic features usually tend to change only gradually—or at least infrequently—and may therefore be regarded as much more stable/less dynamic features of the reformer's environment than, say, the play of economic forces or the changing fashions in management ideas (Lijphart, 1999, p. 254; Pollitt, 2008, pp. 16–20).

Towards the end of the chapter (Section 3.9) we comment on another type of regime— the *ancien régime*, or 'traditional bureaucracy', which recent reforms are often said to be departures—or escapes—from. We raise some questions about the accuracy of this picture of the past, and about the value shifts which are both explicit and implicit in the contemporary debate over 'bureaucracy'.

3.2 Politico-administrative systems: the key features

From the very beginning, comparative approaches to the study of politics and public administration have been intimately concerned with the question of what features to select as the most sensible and illuminating basis for comparing one state, or subnational jurisdiction, with another. It makes sense here to concentrate on features which, prima facie, seem likely to affect the process of management reform. In the relevant academic literature, there is no shortage of suggestions as to what these might be. We have borrowed heavily from this corpus of comparative work. Typically, the key features identified by leading authors include *structural*, *cultural*, and *functional* elements (see De Jong et al., 2002, for a useful overview). Those we have chosen are as follows:

1. The state structure (including the constitution)—this is clearly a structural feature.

2. The nature of executive government at the central level—this is a mixture of structural and functional elements. This includes the nature of the political system —in

particular whether it operates according to majoritarian or a consensus-oriented principles (Lijphart, 1984, 1999).

3. The way relationships work between political executives (ministers) and top civil servants ('mandarins')—a functional element, but heavily conditioned by cultural values and assumptions. One way to think of this is to regard it as a bargain between the two elites (Hood and Lodge, 2006). For example, top civil servants may be treated as an independent group of 'trustees' (or 'magistrates' or 'technocrats'), or they may be regarded as 'agents' for the politicians—'battle troops for political masters to command and redeploy' (Hood, 2002, p. 319). As trustees, top officials receive a generous share of discretionary authority and a high social status. As agents of the politicians they may receive operational autonomy and the pleasures of being trusted confidants, closely protected by the politicians, but only for as long as the latter are in power. The German (Hegelian) idea of a civil service probably comes closer to the former (trustee) model, while most top American officials are more of the 'battle troops'. The career paths of the two elites may be largely separate (as in the UK) or extensively intertwined, as in France, where, for example, the Prime Ministers Jospin and Juppé and the Presidents Mitterand and Chirac had all attended the famous training school for top civil servants, the *Ecole Nationale d'Administration* (ENA).

4. The dominant administrative culture. We here take administrative culture to refer to the expectations the staff of an organization have about what is 'normal' and 'acceptable' in that organization—'the way we do things around here'. It therefore provides the context for ethical relations within the public sector. Such beliefs and attitudes manifest themselves in numerous different ways, including the symbols and rituals of the organization, and its stories, jokes, and myths (Geertz, 1973; Handy, 1993; Hofstede, 2001). Cultures will vary from country to country and, indeed, from one organization to another (Demmke and Moilanen, 2010; Lalenis et al., 2002, pp. 18–41; Schedler and Proeller, 2007). Yet at the same time there are factors encouraging some elements of international cultural convergence—not least the Internet and global media, but also including specific organizations within the field of public management such as the World Bank or the OECD.

5. The degree of diversity among the main channels through which the ideas come that fuel public management reform—this reflects both cultural and functional elements. Thus in some countries advice on management reform may come mainly from a small and relatively homogenous elite while in others it may come from several competing sources.

These five key features are depicted in tabular form in Table 3.1. In the following sections we discuss each feature in turn.

3.3 The basic structure of the state

Here there are two basic dimensions. The first refers to the degree of *vertical* dispersion of authority—that is, how far authority is shared between different levels of government.

Table 3.1 Types of politico-administrative regimes: five key features of public administration systems

	State Structure	Executive Government	Minister/ Mandarin Relations	Administrative Culture	Diversity of Policy Advice
AUSTRALIA	Federal Coordinated	Majoritarian	Separate Mildly politicized	Public interest	Mainly civil service until 1980s
BELGIUM	Federal	Consensual (though becoming more polarized)	Politicized	*Rechtsstaat*	Mainly consultants and universities
CANADA	Federal	Majoritarian	Separate	Public interest	Mainly civil service but more political advisers since c.2000
FINLAND	Unitary Decentralized Fairly fragmented	Consensual	Separate Fairly politicized	Used to be Rechtsstaat, but now more plural	Mainly civil service
FRANCE	Unitary Formerly centralized Coordinated	Intermediate	Integrated Fairly politicized	Predominantly *Rechtsstaat*	Mainly civil service Some consultants since 2000
GERMANY	Federal Coordinated	Intermediate	Separate Fairly politicized	*Rechtsstaat*	Mainly civil service (plus a few academics)
ITALY	Unitary Increasingly decentralized	Coalition	Politicized	*Rechtsstaat*	A broad mixture
NETHERLANDS	Unitary; Fairly fragmented	Consensual	Separate Fairly politicized	Originally very legalistic, but has changed to pluralistic/ consensual	A broad mixture: Civil servants, academics, consultants, other experts
NEW ZEALAND	Unitary Centralized Mildly fragmented	Majoritarian (until 1996)	Separate Not politicized	Public interest	Mainly civil service
SWEDEN	Unitary Decentralized	Intermediate	Separate Increasingly politicized	Originally legalistic, but has changed to corporatist	A broad mixture. Corporatist processes bring in academic experts, business people, and trade unions
UK	Unitary Centralized Coordinated	Majoritarian	Separate Not politicized	Public interest	Mainly civil service until 1980s Recently think tanks, consultants, political advisers
USA	Federal; Fragmented	Intermediate	Separate Very politicized	Public interest	Very diverse: political appointees, corporations, think tanks, consultants

Some states are highly centralized, with all significant decisions concentrated at the top level, some much more decentralized. The second dimension concerns the degree of *horizontal* coordination at central government level—that is, how far central executives are able to 'get their acts together' by ensuring that all ministries pull together in the same direction. This dimension ranges from the pole of 'highly coordinated' to 'highly fragmented'. As we stressed in the previous section, these basic features can change (for example, a number of countries have recently declared that they are pursuing better horizontal coordination—see 6, 2004; Bogdanor, 2005; Bouckaert et al., 2010; Christensen and Lægreid, 2007*b*; Kernaghan, 2009*b*), but on the whole such change is quite slow.

In terms of the first dimension, the vertical dispersion of authority tends to be greatest within federal constitutions and least within the constitutions of unitary and centralized states. In a unitary state there is no *constitutionally entrenched* division of state power. Central government retains ultimate sovereignty, even if particular authority is delegated to subnational tiers of government. In a federal state, the constitution itself prescribes some division of sovereignty between different bodies—for example in the USA between the federal government and the state governments or, in Germany, between the federal government and the *Länder*. Of the countries included in this study, Australia, Belgium, Canada, Germany, and the USA are federal states.

However, we wish to distinguish further within the category of 'unitary' states. Some of these may be highly centralized (e.g. France, at least until the 1980s' decentralization reforms; New Zealand; the UK), whilst others are extensively decentralized (e.g. the Nordic states, where many powers have been delegated from ministries to agencies, and where local governments (counties, municipalities, etc.) have statutorily well-protected independence from central government). In such circumstances the degree of *de facto* decentralization in a unified state can equal, or even exceed, the decentralization of a federal state (incidentally, the concept of decentralization is notoriously complex and we are only skating over the surface here—see Pollitt, 2005). In Sweden, for example, the reforms of the 1980s and 1990s further decentralized an already decentralized state, expanding the 'local state' at the expense of an increasingly anorexic group of central ministries (Micheletti, 2000; Molander, Nilsson, and Schick, 2002).

What are the consequences of these distinctions for public management reform? All other things being equal, reforms in highly decentralized states (whether they be unitary or federal) are likely to be less broad in scope and less uniform in practice than in centralized states. In decentralized states, different entities are likely to want, and to be able, to go in different directions, or at least not all in the same direction at the same time. The federal governments in Washington DC or Brussels or Canberra simply *cannot* order the subnational governments to reform themselves in particular ways. In Germany, the *Länder* have tended to grow in strength (even aspiring to separate representation at European Community level), and different *Länder* have adopted varying stances towards administrative reform (Schröter and Wollmann, 1997). Indeed, it is often argued that federal states have the advantage that they form 'natural laboratories', where one approach can be tried in one state or at one level, while another is tried elsewhere. Even if external pressures are similar, states within a federation may adopt quite widely varying trajectories for management reform (see Halligan and Power, 1992, for Australia; see Vancoppenolle and Legrain, 2003, for Belgium). By contrast, one may refer to the actions of Mrs Thatcher's administration in the unitary UK when, in 1986, irritated with certain local authorities for a mixture of doctrinal and administrative reasons, central government simply abolished the Greater London Council and the six largest metropolitan county councils.

Another possible contrast between a highly centralized state and a highly decentralized state concerns the *focus* of management reforms. Central governments in centralized states tend to be more heavily involved in the business of service delivery (education, health care, etc.) than do the central governments of decentralized states (where these functions tend to be taken care of by lower tiers of government). It has been suggested that this may lead reformers in such centralized states towards a narrower focus on service-specific outputs and results (as in New Zealand during the late 1980s and early 1990s), rather than towards a more strategic concern with policy impacts and overall outcomes (as in Australia during the same period—see Holmes and Shand, 1995). Behind this concern one may often detect budgetary preoccupations—if central government is responsible for running major welfare state services such as social security, health care, or education, these are likely to dominate its overall spending profile. When pressures to restrain public spending mount it is to these services that ministries of finance are obliged to turn their attention, as we are currently witnessing in the aftermath of the 2008 global economic crisis. Of course, even where local governments provide such services, central government may to a considerable extent be paying for them. In such circumstances, central government may seek to offload cuts onto local authorities, sometimes icing the cake by promising local authorities greater freedom to shift spending within a block budget—but making the total size of the block smaller than previously. Something like this happened, for example, in the Netherlands in the 1980s, in Finland during the mid 1990s, and in the UK in the aftermath of the 2008 GEC.

Among our unitary states, Finland and Sweden have been rather decentralized throughout the period under consideration. New Zealand and the UK have remained highly centralized throughout the same period (although in the UK case one must qualify this to the extent that powers have been devolved to Scotland, Wales, and Northern Ireland). New Zealand and the UK are also the countries which have carried through the most vigorous, broad-scope management reforms among the twelve states under consideration (which therefore fits with our analysis). France is an interesting case because, having been famously highly centralized until the early 1980s, it then embarked upon a series of structural decentralizations, the full effects of which have been profound. The impacts of these changes appear to have included a modest decline in central government's share of both total public expenditure and total taxation.

Table 3.2 shows two indicators of centralization—and reveals truly impressive differences among our twelve countries. Clearly some countries are much more 'centre-heavy' than others. The expenditure column shows New Zealand with an astonishingly high central government presence (almost 90 per cent of general government spending) followed by the UK at 71.6 per cent and the USA at 56.3 per cent. Meanwhile Belgium, Canada, Finland, and the Netherlands each record less than 30 per cent, with Germany claiming the lowest share of all—19.1 per cent. The employment column shows that both Italy and the UK have more than 50 per cent of their public service labour force in central government (the figures for New Zealand were not available, but would probably

Table 3.2 Distribution of general government expenditure and employment by level of government

Country	% of General Government Spending by Central Government (2006)	% of General Government Employment by Central Government (2005)
Australia	N.A.	11.4
Belgium	23.2	18.4
Canada	29.6	13.6
Finland	29.9	22.0
France	35.0	46.8
Germany	19.1	16.5
Italy	33.5	57.4
Netherlands	29.5	27.5
New Zealand	89.3	N.A.
Sweden	43.9	14.7
UK	71.6	50.7
USA	56.3	13.0

Sources: OECD 2009a, pp. 57 and 69. The data in the first column for NZ and the UK is for 2005. In the second column the employment data for Belgium and France is from 2004, and for Finland it is a mixture of 2004 and 2005.

have shown an even bigger share). Germany, however, employs fewer than 20 per cent of its public servants at the centre, and Australia is almost down to 10 per cent. Taking the two columns together we can see that expenditure and employment do not necessarily go together. Sometimes they do—heavily decentralized countries such as Belgium and Germany are low on both. But in other case there is an apparent disconnect—most notably in the case of the USA, where the federal government spends 56 per cent of the money but employs only 13 per cent of the staff. The main explanation here is that subnational governments actually run many of the national (federal) programmes, so they have the staff, while the federal government pays but does not actually operate. The UK also shows quite a substantial difference of a similar kind—central government has half the staff but spends over 70 per cent of the money. These are therefore countries where the power of the purse is quite centralized, even if the actual activities are relatively decentralized.

We now turn to the second dimension of structure—the degree of horizontal coordination within central government. How far are one or two central ministries able to ensure that all the others take the same approach to matters of particular interest? This is a difficult variable to estimate, because it tends to be more a matter of convention and less clearly written down in constitutional or statutory provision than are questions of the distribution of powers between different levels of government. One is obliged to rely more on the impressions of knowledgeable observers and participants. Allowing for this, there do appear to be some significant differences between countries.

In some countries there is a tradition that one, or sometimes two, ministries 'call the shots' as far as administrative reform is concerned. Other ministries have to fall in line. In New Zealand, for example, the Ministry of Finance and the State Services Commission were able to drive through the huge changes of the ten-year period after 1984 (Boston et al., 1996). In the UK, the Treasury is usually able to get its way, especially when it is in agreement with the Cabinet Office. In several states, one effect of the GEC has been, at least temporarily, to strengthen the role of ministries of finance. Other countries, however, are more fragmented in this regard. In the Netherlands, no ministry enjoys the degree of pre-eminence held by the New Zealand Ministry of Finance or the UK Treasury. In the USA, the picture is complicated by the unusual strength of the legislature. The strong direct links between, on the one hand, the Senate and the House of Representatives and, on the other, the individual departments and agencies, and Congress's ability to 'micro-manage' federal organizations, sometimes cut across the intentions of the President and the executive leadership (see Appendix B: USA, country file, and Peters, 1995). In France, although the *grands corps* form a strong 'glue' at the top of the system, the state as a whole has for some time been regarded as a 'fragmented machine' and 'Ministerial structures are always in turmoil' (Rouban, 1995, pp. 42, 45). Nevertheless, we must again enter the caveat that changes do sometimes occur. In 2005 the creation of a Directorate General for State Modernization (within the Ministry of Finance) marked a lessening of the fragmentation in public management reform (Bezes, 2007). Germany is more fragmented still: 'Instead of having one single powerful actor or agency, possibly at the national level, that would take the lead, and have the say in public sector reform issues, the German politico-administrative system has a multitude of such arenas and actors' (Schröter and Wollmann, 1997, p. 187; see also Bach and Jann, 2010).

3.4 The nature of executive government

Whatever the *scope* of central government might be, what goes on within that scope will be shaped by the working habits and conventions of that particular executive. Comparativist political scientists have developed a useful typology of these conventions, the basic features of which are as follows:

Single-party or minimal-winning or bare majority: where one party holds more than 50 per cent of the seats in the legislature;

Minimal-winning coalitions: where two or more parties hold more than 50 per cent of the legislative seats;

Minority cabinets: where the party or parties composing the executive hold less than 50 per cent of the legislative seats;

Oversized executives or grand coalitions: where additional parties are included in the executive beyond the number required for a minimal winning coalition (Lijphart, 1984; see also a slightly changed but fundamentally equivalent classification in the later Lijphart, 1999, pp. 90–1).

The importance of these types is that each tends to generate a different set of governing conventions. Of course, following elections, the executive of a given country *can* change from one of these types to another, but in practice such shifts are comparatively rare (such as the 2010 change in the UK from a single-party system to a minimal-winning coalition—at least for the time being). In most countries the electoral system produces fairly stable results and thus executives tend to build up entrenched habits of government. In general terms these habits tend to become more consultative and consensus-oriented/less adversarial the further one moves down the above list (i.e. single-party majorities tend to go along with majoritarian styles of governance, while minority cabinets and grand coalitions tend to behave in a more consensual fashion). The implication of this for public management reform is that the sweeping changes—which are highly likely to be those which will disturb the widest range of interests—are less and less feasible the further one moves away from the first category of executive government—single-party or minimal-winning or bare-majority governments. We do not wish to suggest that the pattern of reform can simply be 'read off' from the type of executive—but it is a significant background influence which shapes the boundaries of what is politically feasible (in terms of Figure 2.1 this is the political system—box E—influencing elite perceptions of what is feasible—box J).

The 'track records' of our twelve countries would appear to lend general support to this line of reasoning. If we examine the clearly majoritarian governments (Australia, Canada, New Zealand until 1996, and the UK) and compare them with the clearly consensual regimes (Finland, Italy, and the Netherlands), there can be little doubt that the scope and intensity of management reforms were greater in the former group than in the latter. However, there is also an intermediate category where the application of this 'rule of thumb' does not work out so clearly.

These first two features—the state structure and the nature of executive government—combine to exercise a very significant influence on the speed and scope of public management reform. In Table 3.3 we show the two factors together, and the groupings it reveals seem to fit rather well with much of the recent history of management reforms that we will be unfolding in the next chapter and in Appendix B. *Very crudely* (and we will want to refine this proposition as we go along) *the speed and severity of management reform have*

Table 3.3 State structure and the nature of executive government

NATURE OF EXECUTIVE GOVERNMENT

Majoritarian ←——— Intermediate ———→ Consensual

STATE STRUCTURE	Majoritarian	Intermediate	Consensual
Centralized (unitary)	New Zealand UK	France	Italy Netherlands
Intermediate	Sweden		Finland
Decentralized (federal)	Australia Canada USA	Belgium Germany	

Source: Loosely adapted from Lijphart, 1984, p. 219 and 1999, pp. 110–11 and 248.

declined as one moves from the left to right, and the scope of reform (the amount of the public sector any one reform programme affects) has declined as one moves from top to bottom.

This kind of analysis rests on a whole set of definitions and approximations, and it is important to examine these carefully. That having been said, such a scheme leads to two important propositions. First, deep and rapid structural reforms to the administrative apparatus tend to be less difficult in majoritarian regimes than in consensual ones. The general reason for this is that such changes usually create 'winners' and 'losers', and the more consensual the regime, the more likely it is that the losing interests will be directly represented in the executive, and will seek to prevent, delay, or dilute the envisaged changes. Thus, consensual regimes are less inclined to, and, in terms of political feasibility, less capable of dramatic, radical reforms than are strongly majoritarian executives. The latter can force through their own schemes even against opposition from a range of other interests. In case this sounds like a 'plug' for majoritarian regimes, let it also be said that these same qualities mean that majoritarian governments may be more prone to disruptive policy reversals. In the UK, for example, during the period of 'New Labour' government from 1997 to 2010, many commentators noted that the rapidity of departmental and other reorganizations was leading to confusion, cynicism, and some short-term loss of performance (Pollitt, 2007; White and Dunleavy, 2010). A long-term comparison with Belgium showed a much more modest rate of structural change in the more consensual, federal state (Pollitt and Bouckaert, 2009). (We should note, however, that towards the end of our period Belgium was becoming less and less consensual, as the struggle between Flanders and Wallonia intensified).

As a footnote to this section of the argument, we should note that Yesilkagit and De Vries (2004) challenged the notion that consensus democracies are unable to match majoritarian regimes in the radicalness of their reforms. They argued that reforms in the (consensual) Netherlands were as far reaching as those in (majoritarian) New Zealand. We find their argument unconvincing, for several reasons. First, the idea that the Netherlands has ever carried through reforms as radical as those in New Zealand between 1984 and 1993 strikes us as a misreading of the record (compare the country files in Appendix B). Second, they argue that studies have not looked closely enough at the implementation phase, where consensus democracies may have some advantages. We think this is wrong on both counts. First, there *have* been studies of implementation (e.g. Pollitt et al., 2004; Pollitt and Bouckaert, 2009) which *do* show a 'softer' approach in consensual regimes. Second, our argument has never been that consensus democracies are poorer at implementation. On the contrary, we acknowledge that a consensually conceived reform may even have a better chance of surviving the implementation phase (and less chance of being thrown aside when a government changes—Pollitt 2007). 'Softer' is by no means necessarily 'weaker'. Finally, Yesilkagit and De Vries suggest that the institutions of majoritarianism will not by themselves explain reform outcomes. But that has never been our argument: as Figure 2.1 and the sequence of this chapter make clear, our argument is that having a majoritarian regime and culture is *one* (important, but not all powerful) factor that seems, looking at twelve countries over thirty years, to be an important part of the explanation for the patterns and partial patterns which we see.

The second proposition is that more centralized countries find it less difficult to carry out sweeping, synoptic reforms than more decentralized ones. This is one reason why, for example, we will find that management reforms in New Zealand and the UK have been deeper and wider than in Canada and the USA (both federal, decentralized states), despite the fact that all four of these countries are usually majoritarian rather than consensual democracies.

The form of the political executive can thus affect change at several stages in the process of reform. First, it influences the degree of leverage that can be created to launch a programme of reform. Second, it may affect the stability of reforms, once carried through (consensually based innovations are hypothesized to have a higher life expectancy than single-party-based innovations, which are more likely to be overturned when a rival party gets back into power). Third, there may also be an impact on the sense of 'ownership' of reform measures. Insofar as these are seen to have emerged from a broadly based consensus of political opinion, they may assume a legitimacy among the public servants who have to carry them out. If, however, specific reforms are perceived as the doctrinaire instruments of a single party or group, then public servants may resist taking any 'ownership', regarding them with resentment, as alien impositions which may be delayed or diluted as much as possible. This kind of resistance may be even more likely where senior civil servants are independent, high-status 'trustees' rather than politically patronized 'agents' (Hood and Lodge, 2006). In terms of Figure 2.1 the nature of executive government (E) may thus affect not only perceptions of desirability and feasibility (J) but also the contents of reform packages (L), the implementation process (M), and the extent of reform eventually achieved (N).

We have looked at the clearest-cut cases—the extremes of majoritarianism and consensualism. Now let us examine some more 'mixed' examples. France is in an intermediate position—it has a multi-party system, but possesses a very strong executive figure in the shape of the president. When the president is of a party which is also a major party in the government, France has quite a majoritarian 'tinge'. During these periods (e.g. 1982–4, 1988–92, and 2002–), extensive public management reforms have been carried out (see entry for France in Appendix B). However, at other times, the president has had to work with a prime minister who is not of the same party (*cohabitation*) and during these interludes policymaking is likely to be more cautious. Overall, France may be said to have an intermediate regime, and to be a 'middling' player in terms of the extent and intensiveness of its management reforms. Thus the hypothesized connection still stands.

Italy is a second 'mixed' case. During the 1990s it experienced deep political crisis, and moved from a proportional/coalition system towards a more majoritarian system, and from a highly centralized system towards a system with strong regions, provinces, and municipalities. The executive continues to be a coalition, but usually now with a dominant party. These shifts have been accompanied by a wave of administrative reforms (Ongaro, 2009). From the perspective of our model, it would be convenient to claim that the upsurge in administrative reform was linked to the move towards a more majoritarian system. In truth, however, what we have witnessed during the past fifteen years has been a confusion of initiatives, heading in several different directions. The grip of the centralized bureaucracy certainly seems to have weakened, and the concept of 'consumer service' has gained some ground, but the smoke has not yet cleared from the various political and administrative battles, and Italy is hard to classify with much confidence. This is partly because some of the factors which are most stable in other countries—such as the party system or the balance between national and subnational levels of govern-ment—have been in prolonged flux in Italy (Ongaro, 2009). It is also because the 'imple-mentation gap'—the chasm between official reform pronouncements and achieved organizational change 'on the ground'—may well be larger in Italy than in countries such as Canada, Finland, Sweden, or the UK (Ongaro and Valotti, 2008).

A third case would be Finland, again an intermediate case, but further towards the consen-sual end of the spectrum than France or Italy. Here the state structure is unitary, and oversized coalitions are common. The political culture is one of consensual caution and mutual accom-modation. Inter-party disputes certainly occur, but their tone is seldom as fierce as is common in France or Italy or the UK. In the Finnish case we find a history of substantial but non-doctrinaire reforms which have been implemented calmly and continuously over a period of two decades and which have traversed the periods of office of a number of coalition govern-ments of varying mixtures of parties (see Appendix B and Pollitt et al., 1997).

Before concluding this section it is worth examining two further cases, Germany and the USA. In the German case the *structure* of the state is federal and extensively decentralized (the 'subsidiarity principle'), while the form of executive government has usually, but not always, been that of a minimal-winning coalition (for 71 per cent of the time between 1945 and 1996—Lijphart, 1999, p. 110). The effects of the state structure have been profound:

Lacking a single, possibly centrally-located powerful protagonist and trend-setter in public sector reform matters and, instead, disposing of a multitude of such arenas and actors each interacting in its own right, it almost follows from the 'logic' of the German federal system that public sector reform activities are bound to proceed in a disjointed and incrementalist rather than a comprehen-sive and 'wholesale' manner.   (Schröter and Wollmann, 1997, p. 188)

The effect of the nature of the executive government has been less clear. In theory the minimum-winning coalition provides a strong Chancellor with good possibilities for carrying through reforms. In the specific case of public administration, however, this possibility tends to be outweighed by the structural factors referred to above. Most public servants are not employed by, and most public programmes are not administered at, the central (federal) level. Also, the federal government's freedom of manoeuvre is restricted by the Federal Civil Service Framework Law. Considerable change has, however, taken place at the level of the *Länder*, and in particular cities.

Finally, the USA is a fascinating example of an executive with mixed characteristics. On the one hand, in relation to the nature of executive government it is quite strongly majoritarian (one-party cabinets for 89 per cent of the period 1945–96). This would lead one to hypothesize the possibility of vigorous, broad-scope management reforms—at least during those periods when the president is of the same party as holds the majority in Congress (at other times there may be an American parallel with the French *cohabita-tion*, although one in which the legislature is relatively much more powerful than it is in France). However, state structure pushes in quite a different direction. The USA is a decentralized, federal state, with a somewhat rigid constitution. One further element needs to be taken into account. The US legislature (House of Representatives plus Senate) is unusually strong relative to the executive, and, furthermore, the executive does not wield the same control over same-party members in the legislature as is enjoyed by, say, the British Cabinet. These factors further qualify the picture of majoritarian strength, and change the hypothesis in the direction of a more cautious assessment of the executive's reform capacity. When one comes to examine the track record of reform, it is a mixture. From time to time presidents have loudly proclaimed their intentions fundamentally to reform the management of federal departments and agencies, but actual achievements have lagged far behind (Ingraham, 1997; Pollitt, 1993; Mihm, 2001; Radin, 1998, 2000; Schick, 2001; GAO, 2001). White and Dunleavy (2010, p. 23) describe the situation as follows:

All US departmental reorganizations have to be approved by Congress, and changes are generally opposed because of their inevitably disruptive effects on the existing structure of congressional committees and sub-committees, many of whose powerful incumbents often stand to lose out from any reorganization.

This 'more mouth than muscle' picture closely corresponds with the two dimensions depicted in Table 3.3.

Of course, although state structure and the nature of executive government do seem to be important determinants of change, they usually act in combination with other factors. They permit, but do not, of themselves, 'drive'. That requires the intervention of some dynamic agency, such as a flow of new ideas allied to determined leadership. Rhodes (1997, p. 44) reviewed the UK experience and came to this answer:

[W]hy was the pace of change in Britain greater than elsewhere in Western Europe? Three factors were of overriding importance. First, Margaret Thatcher pushed through reform of the civil service. The phrase *political will* is commonly used to explain the government's determination. *Strong, directive and above all persistent, executive leadership* is longer but more accurate.

Second, there are few constitutional constraints on that leadership, especially when the government has a majority in Parliament . . . Central administrative reform in Britain does not require a statute, only the exercise of Crown Prerogative, or executive powers.

Finally, the government evolved a clear ideological strategy to justify and sell its various reform packages. It attacked big government and waste, used markets to create more individual choice and campaigned for the consumer.

3.5 Mandarin/minister relations

In all countries, major public management reforms usually involve both executive politicians and senior public servants. Together they usually constitute the main part of the elite which makes the crucial decisions about reform (box J in Figure 2.1).

However, the relationships between these two elite groups vary considerably from one country to another, and over time. This is the question of what kind of 'bargain' or deal exists between top politicians and top civil servants (Hood and Lodge, 2006). What do they expect from each other? For example, are political careers separate from, or integrated with, the careers of 'mandarins'? (Pierre, 1995). Are senior civil service positions themselves politicized, in the sense that most of their occupants are known to have (and have been chosen partly because they have) specific party political sympathies? Mandarins can still be politicized in this sense even if their careers are separate from those of politicians (as often happens in Germany). Or again, how secure are senior civil service jobs? Do mandarins enjoy strong tenure, remaining in post as different governments come and go? Security of tenure actually seems to have been declining in a number of our selected countries, including Australia, Canada, France, Italy, and New Zealand—see also Demmke and Moilanen, 2010, pp. 96–103. Or are their fortunes tied to party political patronage, so that they face some form of exile—of 'being put out to grass' if the party in power changes? Or are they employed on performance-related contracts, so that they can survive changes of government, but not a repeated failure to reach their performance targets?

Unfortunately, scholars have as yet failed to agree on a single, robust way of classifying these important differences. The Hood and Lodge scheme (2006—we will come back to it in the next chapter) is a good start, but its originators themselves recognize that its categories are neither mutually exclusive nor jointly exhaustive. We are therefore left with a slightly messy situation, in which we are reasonably convinced that the type of bargain *is* likely to affect the direction and speed of public management reform, but where we can as yet describe that connection only in a fairly ad hoc, descriptive way.

The effects of different 'bargains' on management reforms may be quite subtle. They concern, in particular, 'ownership' of reforms at different levels within the administrative system. Thus, where ministerial and mandarin careers are integrated, one might imagine that the ownership of reforms at the highest levels would be more easily achieved than in systems where the two career paths are entirely distinct. So in a system such as that of the *grands corps* in France, where many ministers would share closely intertwined careers with the senior civil servants, the shaping of reform packages can rely upon shared perspectives and a common professional socialization to an extent that would not usually be the case in, say, Canada or the UK. However, in a French-type system of integrated careers the problem of ownership may reappear lower down the hierarchy, where rank-and-file public officials feel little kinship or identification with the politicized high-flyers of the *grands corps*. In terms of Figure 2.1 the French problem may be with the implementation process (box M) more than with the original shaping of the 'package' (box L)—as does indeed sometimes seem to have been the case.

Another one of the variables mentioned above—that of the politicization of top posts—adds its influence in roughly the same direction. It creates a bigger gap between the mandarins and the rank and file than would otherwise exist, and may lower the legitimacy of the former in the eyes of the latter. However, in its extreme form—where the occupancy of top civil service positions changes on a large scale following the election of a new political executive—the effect may be one of creating instability in the reform process. This would particularly dog administrative reform because reshaping organizations and standard operating procedures tends to take several years to carry through (Pollitt, 2008). We can illustrate this with several examples. Germany (Götz, 1997) and Finland (Tiihonen, 1996) offer cases of moderate politicization where the party political affiliations of senior officials have been important but where a change of government did not result in the wholesale 'slaughter' and replacement of the mandarinate. In the Finnish case, the governments were coalitions and the style was consensual, and these factors enabled considerable continuity and stability to be achieved in public management reform. In the German case, the effects were masked by the long tenure of the Kohl-led conservative–liberal coalition, and, in any case, when German governments change there are opportunities for mandarins who are unsympathetic towards the new regime to take study leave or be moved to a variety of less politically sensitive roles (Götz, 1997). The American example is more extreme. The 'spoils system' results in an incoming president rapidly replacing a large number of senior officials in Washington, producing an odd situation which one American academic has memorably described as a 'government of strangers' (Heclo, 1977). The number of political appointees grew from 451 in 1960 to 2,393 in 1992 (Kettl et al.,1996, p. 82) and has grown further since. Change on this scale certainly disturbs continuity. As we will see later, the reform programme of the National Performance Review, which had been given great prominence by Democratic President Clinton and Vice President Gore during the mid and late 1990s, almost instantly disappeared when Republican George W. Bush came to power in 2000. One group of American scholars describe the general problem as follows:

It is one thing to rely on political appointees to set basic agency policy. It is quite another to appoint so many political appointees that they extend deeply into an agency's middle management. These extra layers increase the distance from the government's top to its bottom and can frustrate the ability of top leaders to give voice to their policies. The layers complicate the flow of information in both directions. They hinder the always difficult job of translating broad goals into specific goals and manageable objectives. They create an artificially low ceiling on the career paths for the bureaucracy's long term officials and, therefore, impose additional frustrations on the federal government's career work force.   (Kettl et al., 1996, p. 83)

This state of affairs may be contrasted with what passes for normalcy in Canada, New Zealand, or the UK. In these countries few overtly party-political appointments are made to the upper reaches of the public service, and 'mandarins' can normally expect to serve out all or most of their working lives within the upper reaches of the state machine. This brings, in equal measure, the benefits of continuity and accumulated knowledge, and the drawbacks of conservatism ('seen it all before') and limited breadth of experience. In these countries the career patterns of ministers and mandarins are largely separate. Even here, however, an important qualification must be entered. In most of these countries the category of 'political advisers'—individuals who are neither politicians nor career civil servants, but who are doctrinally sympathetic to the party in power—has grown in numbers and influence since the mid 1990s (Aucoin and Savoie, 2009; Peters and Pierre, 2004)

3.6 The philosophy and culture of governance

Having considered the 'normal habits' or 'traditions' of government (consensualism, majoritarianism, and their variants) and the relations between ministers and mandarins, we can now begin to examine the 'normal beliefs' of administration. Can distinctive administrative cultures be identified, each with its own characteristic pattern of values and assumptions and, if so, how do these affect the process of administrative reform?

A number of writers have argued for the existence of two particularly strong models: 'Most public administrative systems seem to be guided either by the *Rechtsstaat* model or by the Anglo Saxon notion of the "public interest"; very few systems fall between these two models, which appear to be inherently inconsistent and irreconcilable' (Pierre, 1995, p. 8). In this connection, the 'Napoleonic' states (including France and Italy) constitute an important sub-family within the *Rechtsstaat* model (Ongaro, 2009, pp. 252–63).

From the *Rechtsstaat* perspective, the state is a central integrating force within society, and its focal concerns are with the preparation, promulgation, and enforcement of laws. It follows from this that most senior civil servants will be trained in the law and, indeed, that a large and separate body of specifically *administrative* law will have been created. In such a culture, the instinctive bureaucratic stance will tend to be one of rule-following and precedent, and the actions of both individual public servant and individual citizen will be set in this context of correctness and legal control. The oversight of such a system will require a hierarchy of administrative courts, such as the *Conseil d'Etat* in France and Belgium or the *Bundesverwaltungsgericht* in Germany. The typical values of this approach will include respect for the authority of the law as a socially necessary and integrating force, attention to precedent, and a concern with equity, at least in the sense of equality before the law. All in all:

[I]t has become sufficiently clear now that, in countries like France and Germany, the issue of New Public Management in the civil service meets with cultural premises that differ from those in Anglo-Saxon countries.   (König, 1997, p. 222; see also Bouckaert, 2007 and Ongaro, 2009, p. 223)

By contrast, the 'public interest' model accords the state a less extensive or dominant role within society (indeed, use of the phrase 'the state' is rare within originally 'Anglo-Saxon' states such as Australia, New Zealand, and the UK). 'Government' (rather than 'the state') is regarded as something of a necessary evil, whose powers are to be no more than are absolutely necessary, and whose ministers and officials must constantly be held to public account by elected parliaments and through other means. Of course, the law is an essential component of governance, but its particular perspectives and procedures are not as dominant as within the *Rechtsstaat* model. All citizens are under the law, but law is usually in the background rather than the foreground, and many senior civil servants have no special training in its mysteries (as in the UK case, where the majority of senior officials are 'generalists'). Civil servants are regarded as simply citizens who work for government organizations, not some kind of special caste or cadre with a higher mission to represent 'the state'. The process of government is seen as one of seeking to obtain the public's consent for (or, at least, acquiescence in) measures devised in the public (general, national) interest. It is recognized that different social interest groups compete with one another, sometimes in fiercely adversarial ways. In this context, government's job is to play the part of a fair and trusted referee, and not to get drawn in on one side or another. Fairness and independence of the play of sectional interests are therefore key values, with pragmatism and flexibility as qualities which may be prized above technical expertise (or even above strict legality).

What are the implications of each of these approaches for public management reform? In general terms we might expect that *Rechtsstaat* systems would be 'stickier' and slower to reform than public interest regimes. This is because management change would always require changes in the law and, culturally, because senior civil servants who are highly trained in administrative law may find it more difficult than generalists to shift to a 'managerial' or 'performance-oriented' perspective. There is at least some circumstantial evidence to support this interpretation. For example, French and German civil servants often found it surprising that the UK executive agency programme could, within a decade, have transferred more than two-thirds of non-industrial civil servants out of ministerial departments and into a new form of organization without much new legislation being required (see Appendix B: UK country file). By contrast, the small amount of restructuring that has taken place in the federal German government has sometimes been explained as partly a result of the constraining nature of the basic framework laws in that country (Schröter and Wollmann, 1997).

However, Pierre's categorization into two distinct camps is now fifteen years old, and is beginning to look a bit dated. More recent work argues that the polar classification of *Rechtsstaat* versus public interest is too crude, and that nowadays not a few, but most, civil-service systems are mixtures (Demmke and Moilanen, 2010, p. 9; Hood and Lodge, 2006). In a number of the countries under consideration there has been a considerable shift away from a highly legalistic state form, but towards something other than a straightforward public interest model. The Netherlands, Finland, and Sweden all fall into this mixed category. The Netherlands went through a period of 'dejuridification' after the Second World War, and its administrative culture now appears as a complex mixture, with a rather open attitude that brings a range of experts and representative groups into the policy-making process. There are also remnants of the old 'pillarization' mind-set, insofar as it can still be considered important to ensure that the administrative decision-making process balances representation from each of the major social groups. It is an essentially consensual approach, very different from the more closed and juridical purity of a full *Rechtsstaat* philosophy. In both Finland and Sweden a training in law has in the past been normal for higher public officials, but, as with the Netherlands, this juristic dominance has been considerably diluted over the past forty or fifty years. In both countries, civil servants now come from a wide variety of disciplinary backgrounds, and the culture of upper civil service could be said to have as much to do with satisfying the demands for 'coordination', 'partnership', 'responsiveness', and 'leadership' as with a strict application of law. In both countries, also, there is a sense of the weight, centrality, and continuity of the state—senior public servants are not quite the anxious, harassed breed one often finds in Washington, DC or sometimes in Whitehall.

There is therefore much more to administrative culture than just a bipolar scale running from *Rechtsstaat* to public interest—as the expansion of writing about organizational cultures and traditions over the past two decades testifies (see, e.g. Hood, 1998, Painter and Peters, 2010; Schedler and Proeller, 2007). To summarize all that literature is beyond us, but it may be worth selecting one particular approach, so as to illustrate the additional insights that a cultural perspective can afford. Hofstede's *Culture's Consequences* (2001) examines variations in values and organizational norms across fifty countries. It is based on a quarter century of research and a wide range of studies and surveys—but is not specifically focused on the public sector. It is relatively unusual in that it actually attempts to quantify certain dimensions of culture. It produces measures for what Hofstede argues are five critical cultural elements:

- Power distance: the difference between the extent to which a boss can determine the behaviour of a subordinate, and the extent to which the subordinate can determine the behaviour of the boss. This is closely connected with the norms which exist in a given culture about equality and inequality. A high power distance implies a high tolerance for the existence and manifestation of inequality. For example, Hofstede tells a story of seeing a Dutch prime minister holidaying at an ordinary Portugese camp site, and suggests that, while this was not unusual in the Dutch culture (power distance index 38), it would be much less likely to be the choice of a French prime minister (power distance index 65).

- Uncertainty avoidance: the extent to which the members of a culture feel threatened by uncertain or unknown situations. Here one might compare, say, Belgium (index 94) with Sweden (index 29).

- Individualism versus collectivism: 'individualism stands for a society in which the ties between individuals are loose: everyone is expected to look after him/herself and his/her immediate family only. Collectivism stands for a society in which people from birth onwards are integrated into strong, cohesive in-groups, which throughout people's lifetime continue to protect them in exchange for unquestioning loyalty' (Hofstede, 2001, p. 225) The USA, a famously individualistic society, scores 91 on the individualism/collectivism index, while Finland scores only 63.

- Masculinity versus femininity: 'Masculinity stands for a society in which gender roles are clearly distinct: men are supposed to be tough, assertive, and focused on material success; women are supposed to be more modest, tender, and concerned with the quality of life. Femininity stands for a society in which social gender roles overlap: both men and women are supposed to be modest, tender, and concerned with the quality of life' (Hofstede, 2001, p. 297). On this dimension the scores of Germany (66) and Italy (70) can be contrasted with the lower masculinity/higher femininity scores of Sweden (5) and the Netherlands (14).

- Long-term versus short-term orientation: 'Long term orientation stands for the fostering of virtues oriented towards future rewards, in particular, perseverance and thrift. Its opposite pole, short term orientation, stands for the fostering of virtues related to the past and present, in particular, respect for tradition, preservation of "face" and fulfilling social obligations' (Hofstede, 2001, p. 359). Here the variation between 'our' countries does not appear to be so great, but there is nevertheless a significant difference between, on the one hand, Canada (23) and the USA (29) and the more long-term orientation of Finland (41) and the Netherlands (44).

Table 3.4 sets out Hofstede's findings for the twelve countries covered in our book.

What, the reader may well ask, does all this have to do with public management reform? Quite a lot, we would suggest. Although Hofstede's measures are usually taken from general surveys, and are not focused specifically on civil servants or politicians, they presumably reflect the broad cultural climates in which management reforms will have to be announced, interpreted, promoted, and resisted in each particular country (Bouckaert, 2007). As a major recent comparative study of the civil services in twenty-seven EU states puts it: 'we agree that there is a connection between the culture of a nation or region, the

Table 3.4 Indicators of different cultural aspects in different countries

	Power Distance		Uncertainty Avoidance		Individualism/ Collectivism		Masculinity/ Femininity		Long- /Short-Term Orientation	
	Index	Rank	Index	Rank	Index	Rank	Index	Rank	Index	Rank
Australia	36	41	51	37	90	2	61	16	31	22–4
Belgium	65	20	94	5–6	75	8	54	22	38	18
Canada	39	39	48	41–2	80	4–5	52	24	23	30
Finland	33	46	59	31–2	63	17	26	47	41	14
France	68	15–16	86	10–15	71	10–11	43	35–6	39	17
Germany	35	42–4	65	29	67	15	66	9–10	31	22–4
Italy	50	34	75	23	76	7	70	4–5	34	19
Netherlands	38	40	53	35	80	4–5	14	51	44	11–12
New Zealand	22	50	49	39–40	79	6	58	17	30	25–6
Sweden	31	47–8	29	49–50	71	10–11	5	53	33	20
UK	35	42–4	35	47–8	89	3	66	9–10	25	28–9
US	40	38	46	43	91	1	62	15	29	27

Rank 1= highest rank
Source: G. Hofstede, *Culture's Consequences* (2001), Thousand Oaks, Sage Publications, p. 500.

way management in civil services is structured, how reform pressures are perceived and how reform priorities are adopted' (Demmke and Moilanen, 2010, p. 3). Hofstede's dimensions help us understand why what appears to be exactly the same reform may be very differently received in different cultures. We would expect, for example, equal opportunities regulations to have an easier passage in Sweden than Italy (and we would expect the percentages of senior civil servants who were female to be higher, on average, in the Nordic countries than in the Mediterranean countries). We would expect quality improvement techniques that rely upon egalitarian discussion circles as their main mechanism to work less well in France than the Netherlands—at least if staff of different ranks were involved in the same discussion group. We would expect people in high uncertainty avoidance cultures to be more alienated from, and suspicious of, their governments, and therefore, on average, less 'believing' in their responses to reform (Hofstede, 2001, p. 171). We would also expect staff in high uncertainty avoidance cultures to be more concerned with rule-following and more reluctant to risk changing jobs—both factors of some importance for those reformers who want to deregulate bureaucracies and encourage more rapid job change in the public service. As we will see in Chapters 4 and 5, the introduction of flexible employment contracts in civil service jobs does indeed appear to have gone much further in New Zealand and the UK (UAI scores of 49 and 35) than in Belgium or France (UAI scores 94 and 86).

At the very least, this kind of analysis may challenge, or at least refine, the kind of crude parading of national stereotypes to which discussions of different countries' bureaucracies and political systems an easily descend. At best it may offer an insight into the specific ways in which particular reforms are extensively 'translated' as they move from one country to another (Czarniawska and Sevón, 1996; Smullen, 2010).

3.7 Sources of policy advice

The final aspect of the administrative system which we wish to suggest is of significance is the diversity of the key sources of advice to ministers on reform issues. (We are here referring exclusively to advice on management reform issues. Advice on other types of policy innovation, such as defence policy or economic policy, may be taken from different networks.) In principle, political executives could take management advice from a wide range of sources—from their own political parties, from their mandarins, from management consultants, from academic specialists, from business corporations, or from political or policy think tanks. Since about 1990 international bodies have also played a growing role in advice-giving. For our twelve countries the OECD has been particularly active and influential (see, e.g. OECD, 1995, 2005, 2009*a*). In Eastern Europe and the developing world, the World Bank and the European Commission have been important (see, e.g. Demmke and Moilanen, 2010; Kaufmann et al., 2007). The basic proposition here is that the wider the range of customary sources of advice, the more likely it is that new ideas— especially those from outside the public sector—will reach ministers' ears in persuasive and influential forms. Thus, for example, new management ideas (box F in Figure 2.1) will have an earlier and better chance of getting a sympathetic hearing from executive politicians.

One particular trend which has affected many (but not all) of our twelve countries has been the increasing politicization of advice to ministers. The specific form which this has taken has varied from one country to another, but over the past two or three decades the prominence of 'political advisers' or politically flavoured senior civil service appointments has grown in Australia, Belgium, Canada, Germany, the UK, and the USA (see, e.g. Aucoin and Savoie, 2009; Peters and Pierre, 2004). Alongside, and sometimes overlapping with this trend has been another one—that of the increasing role played by management consultants, even at the highest levels (National Audit Office, 2006; Sahlin-Andersson and Engwall, 2002; Saint Martin, 2005). Both these trends represent a broadening of the stream of advice on management reforms, and both are also controversial. It is not self-evident that corporate management consultants or party political 'fixers' are necessarily better placed to give advice on how to reshape ministries and major public services than the civil and public services themselves.

Beyond this, the source of a particular reform idea may influence its perceived legitimacy and 'ownership' (a point already made in the section on minister/mandarin relations). Rank-and-file civil servants may be more suspicious of innovations that are believed to come from one particular political party or from 'whizz kids' in a fashionable think tank. Achieving 'ownership' of reform right down the hierarchy may be less difficult if it is perceived as having a significant 'home-grown' element, that is, if the innovation is seen to be based on accumulated experience within the civil service itself, rather than being a forced 'import'. Of course, these reactions will themselves be influenced by the administrative culture. Ideas from big business may be accorded greater face legitimacy in a pro-business, anti-government culture such as prevails in the USA, than in a strong, proud state-centred culture such as has existed for some time in France.

Contrasts are not hard to find. Consider the differences between France and the UK during the 1980s. In France, reform policies emerged from within the 'usual networks' of members of the *grands corps*—mandarins and politicians with shared ENA backgrounds and intertwined careers. In the UK, Mrs Thatcher was well known for her suspicions of the civil service and went out to right-wing think tanks for many of her reform ideas. Or again, we may note a similar contrast between Germany and the USA. In Germany most reform projects have been hatched within the public service itself, sometimes helped by advice from specialist academics (Schröter and Wollmann, 1997). In the USA, President Reagan called in teams of businessmen to propose changes in the federal administration, most infamously the Grace Commission and its 2,000 businessmen (Pollitt, 1993, pp. 91–5). In 1984 Grace delivered 2,478 recommendations for improving efficiency and cutting 'waste', but the implementation of many of these ideas seems to have been lost track of within a fragmented, sceptical, and probably resentful federal bureaucracy. In Canada, too, Prime Minister Mulroney exhibited considerable suspicions of the career bureaucrats, and made a virtue of seeking business advice (Savoie, 1994).

Finland, the Netherlands, and Sweden are each different again. The major Finnish public management reforms of the early 1990s owed most to the thinking of senior public servants. External participation from business people or consultants was the exception rather than the rule (though one or two of the civil servants themselves had some business experience). By contrast, Dutch reforms emerged from a procession of committees and enquiries which featured not only civil servants but also academics, auditors, and individuals from the business world—there was a fairly open market place of advice and ideas. Sweden probably fell some way between Finland and the Netherlands—there was some 'external' debate and participation, but senior public servants kept a firm grip on the helm, and were never in the position of US or British or Canadian civil servants in being obliged to implement a reform agenda that had been substantially set by business advisers to the government, external think tanks, or management consultants.

3.8 The European Commission: a special case

The European Commission is obviously a special case, because it is not a sovereign nation state. Furthermore, as a supranational authority, much of its business is conducted *with* nation states, and thus cannot be considered in the same breath as relations between a national government and its own subnational tiers of government. We agree with the many commentators who have warned against simple comparisons between EU institutions and national governments. However, despite these *sui generis* aspects, much of the analysis which we have applied above to the twelve countries in our set can also be applied to the Commission. We would argue that the third, fourth, and fifth features of our general analysis see Sections 3.5, 3.6, and 3.7 above) can be related to the Commission without too much difficulty, and that the main differences arise with the first and second—state structure and the style of executive government. So we will tackle these two more problematic features first.

In terms of the vertical dispersion of authority we cannot neatly label the Commission as either federal or unitary. Certainly it is not federal in the sense of having inferior tiers of authority below it, sharing powers in a way that is defined by a single constitution. Yet there are some resemblances: the Commission very much operates within the framework of treaties (Rome, Maastricht, Nice, Lisbon, etc.) and these define the relationships which are supposed to obtain between the Commission, other EU institutions, and member states themselves. In this sense one might speak of the Commission working within a quasi-federal, treaty-framed environment, although one in which the other 'levels' are not at all 'inferior'. One obvious difference, for example, has been that, whereas the national level in most federal states retains responsibility for foreign and defence policies, within the EU, member states have fiercely guarded their independence in these respects, and moves towards developing common approaches in these areas, though significant, remain limited and fragile.

On the other hand, the definition of 'unified' does not seem to fit very well either, because, although the Commission is itself a unified body, so much of its work depends on arriving at cooperative agreements with member states, each of which is an independent sovereign power in its own right. In this sense, therefore, only the most extreme Europhobes would liken the Commission to a powerful unitary state on the model of France or the UK.

Furthermore in the last fifteen years or so we have seen a growth in the number of agencies which have been spun off from the Commission to perform a variety of tasks. This growing complexity has been enough to prompt the EU institutions to launch a large-scale evaluation of their agency systems (Rambøll/Euréval/Matrix, 2009).

Moving onto the question of horizontal coordination, we may immediately observe that the Commission has strong vertical divisions and is often difficult to coordinate (Middlemass, 1995; Page, 1997). Each Directorate General (DG) is to a significant extent a law unto itself. The most powerful horizontal controls have traditionally emanated from the budget and personnel DGs (although current reforms are lessening these in certain respects—see Appendix B). In short, however, the Commission is vertically a quite fragmented body.

Given these structural characteristics, what might one deduce about management reform? Perhaps simply that broad-scope, radical reform of the kind carried through in unified, centralized states such as New Zealand and the UK would be difficult. The historical record would seem to bear this out. There has been a tortuous history of partial, incremental reforms (and failed reforms—Spierenberg, 1979). Until the mid 1990s there was no general restructuring or reorientation towards modern styles of management— indeed, 'management' itself was not seen as particularly important by most senior Eurocrats (Stevens and Stevens, 2001, p. 148). The Commission was, for the most part, an old-fashioned bureaucracy. In the late 1990s and early 2000s there was a major management upheaval, centred around what became known as the 'Kinnock reforms' (see EU Commission file in Appendix B), but since then the pace of change appears to have slowed once more. Recently the EU machinery has been focused on larger problems of public legitimacy (the initially failed attempt to introduce a new 'constitution'), enlargement, and the economic/currency crisis.

The second 'key feature' in our analysis is the nature of executive government—the habits or style of governance. In the Commission's case this is much more consensual than majoritarian, although political parties play only a very subdued role. The Commission itself (i.e. the body of Commissioners) is an expressly collegial body, where it is vital for proposers of reform to gain common assent (sometimes through complicated trade-offs between apparently unrelated issues), or at least to secure reluctant acquiescence. It is composed of people with executive political experience (typically ex-ministers from the member states), but they must deal with what is, in effect, a rival, and in some ways more powerful political executive in the shape of the Council of Ministers. The Commission is also accountable to the European Parliament. The latter used not to be a particularly strong political force, but since the late 1990s it has acquired new powers and has begun to flex its muscles.

Moving on to what in Table 3.1 is termed 'minister/mandarin relations' we may say that the Commission is unique, and uniquely complex. To begin with, it has what in terms of most nation states would be regarded as an 'extra' political layer. The 'mandarins' are the Directors General, the permanent heads of the Commission's services. Above them floats the first political layer—the Commissioners, who, although appointed, are generally politicians by background (see previous paragraph). However, beyond the Commissioners lies another powerful body of executive politicians, the Council of Ministers from the member states. Just to make matters more complicated still, each Commisioner has a *cabinet* of personally appointed officials, who offer policy advice and (not infrequently) clash with the Directors General. Finally, we may note that, while *cabinet* positions are temporary (they do not last beyond the tenure of the individual Commissioner) both they and the career Directors General, and the two grades immediately below them ('A2s' and 'A3s'), are politically influenced appointments (Page, 1997). The upshot of all this is a very complex set of relations between senior career officials and 'their' Commissioners. Their careers are not usually intertwined after the French fashion, but the mandarin ranks are certainly politicized, and there is a large group of politicized temporary officials in the *cabinets*. Yet for most of the permanent officials the 'bargain' seems to be more of 'trustees' or 'technocrats' than 'agents' for a particular political regime (the terms are again borrowed from Hood and Lodge, 2006). They enjoy extremely strong tenure and have only recently begun to be subject to any organized form of individual appraisal (Levy, 2004). Many of them serve most of their careers in Brussels, where they enjoy high salaries and a variety of privileges.

As for the administrative culture of the Commission, it still bears distinct traces of the predominant French influence during its formative years. Many French practices and titles continue, including the existence of strong separate hierarchies (in the DGs) and the predominantly regulatory and legalistic cast of mind. Although there is considerable internal variation (as one might expect in an organization whose staffing policies deliberately mixed officials from such a diverse range of national backgrounds), the predominant impression is of a hierarchy that would score quite highly on both Hofstede's power-distance index and his index of uncertainty avoidance (see Section 3.6, above). 'Playing it safe', not challenging one's superiors, addressing problems by making and then following very detailed procedural rules—these are familiar cultural 'norms' within the Commission to this day. The Commission is thus more *Rechtsstaat* than public interest, and can seem a strange place for new arrivals from countries such as Sweden or the UK, which have somewhat different traditions. Cultural change is, however, an almost inevitable consequence of the successive enlargements of EU membership. New *fonctionnaires* from the Central and Eastern European states, combined with the influx from the 1995 enlargement, are gradually making their impact on the Commission's atmosphere and style (Ban, 2010*b*).

With respect to policy advice, that which reaches Commissioners may be said to be fairly diverse. In addition to advice from the DGs, Commissioners take the views of their own *cabinets*, and, not unusually, may tap sources within the administration of their own member state. They are also bombarded with evidence and demands from the multiplicity of pressure groups which have set up in Brussels. Whilst this is an exceedingly complex system it is not a closed one; indeed the channels are almost certainly more diverse than in some member states.

In sum, therefore, one could say that, within the Commission, the feasibility threshold over which management reforms must pass is rather high. The Commission is a collegial, consensual body, and its operative Directorates General are vertically strongly divided from each other. No single source of power and authority is therefore strong enough to drive through across-the-board changes against significant resistance. The pressure of public opinion is weak and indirect: this is because of the intervening 'layer' of member states, because of the relative feebleness of the European Parliament (whose own legitimacy, as indicated by electoral turn-outs, is not high) and because the Commission anyway does not itself provide the kinds of public services which would bring it into direct contact with the public. Other 'difficult to change' factors should also be mentioned. The Commission mandarins have separate and secure careers—they do not need constantly to 'show results' in order to keep their jobs (Page, 1997, p. 87). The top three grades in the hierarchy are fairly politicized, but in a way which tends to focus the occupants on sexy political topics and on what can be achieved within the four-year term of a Commission, rather than on longer-term structural change. The administrative culture carries significant elements of *Rechtsstaat*, and the resort to legal rules and standard procedures is, if anything, intensified by the difficulties of running such a multi-lingual, multicultural organization. All these features combine to make the life of the would-be management reformer difficult.

Yet, despite all this, broader political pressures and external currents of management ideas have at least placed large-scale administrative modernization on the Commission's agenda. When a new Commission took office in 1995 it launched a Sound and Efficient Management Initiative (SEM 2000). This was quickly followed by MAP 2000 (Modernizing Administrative and Personnel Policy) which focused on internal reforms to the Commission's own machinery. However, this (Santer) Commission collapsed in disgrace and an unprecedented mass resignation in 1999. The circumstances of the fall of M. Santer and his fellow commissioners guaranteed that reform would be high on the agenda of the new leadership (the Prodi Commission), and, under the leadership of Vice-President Kinnock significant reforms in audit, financial management, and human resource management were proclaimed (European Commission, 2001). It appears that real changes have been made, but that progress is quite slow, and that the main emphasis of the reforms has become—in path dependent fashion—centralizing and regulatory (Levy, 2003; Stevens and Stevens, 2001—see Appendix B for further details). In some particular respects, however, more radical changes have occurred—perhaps most noticeably in recruitment procedures (Ban, 2010*a*).

3.9 Traditional bureaucracy: the *ancien régime?*

A good deal of the rhetoric associated with public management reform vividly contrasts the new (= good) with the old (= bad). The name given to the old—that against which the modern, reformed public sector organization stands out as superior—is usually something like 'traditional bureaucracy' (e.g. Hughes, 1998, chapter 2). The big models first introduced in Chapter 1—NPM, NWS, and NPG—are all, in different ways, reactions to this grand old model from the past. Politicians, in particular, never seem to tire of 'bashing bureaucracy' and portraying it as both restrictive and wasteful (although as soon as something goes wrong the same politicians often demand new oversight bodies and new regulations). The global economic crisis provoked a new round of rhetoric as leading politicians in several countries claimed (however improbably) that huge savings could be achieved by cutting out 'bureaucratic waste', while leaving front-line public services unharmed.

Before concluding this review of regime types it is therefore necessary to explore a little further this *ancien régime*—to understand what was supposed to be wrong with it and to clarify its relationships with the various dimensions of the politico-administrative world which have been discussed in sections 3.2 to 3.8 above.

Osborne and Gaebler (1992, pp. 11–12) are fairly typical of at least the Anglo-American-Australasian critique of traditional bureaucracy:

Our thesis is simple. The kind of governments that developed during the industrial era, with their sluggish, centralised bureaucracies, their preoccupation with rules and regulations, and their hierarchical chains of command, no longer work very well. They accomplished great things in their time, but somewhere along the line they got away from us. They became bloated, wasteful, ineffective. And when the world began to change, they failed to change with it. Hierarchical, centralised bureaucracies designed in the 1930s or 1940s simply do not function well in the rapidly-changing, information-rich, knowledge-intensive society and economy of the 1990s.

This traditional model is commonly linked with the ideal-type rational/legal bureaucracy proposed and analysed in the writings of Max Weber (Weber, 1947). This type of organization was characterized by:

- fixed spheres of competence;
- a defined hierarchy of offices;
- a clear distinction between the public and private roles (and property) of the officials;
- specialization and expertise as the basis for action;
- full-time, career appointments for officials;

- management by the application of a developing set of rules, knowledge of which was the special technical competence of the officials concerned.

This, then, is the type of regime which is said to be in need of replacement by more flexible, fast-moving, performance-oriented forms of modern organization. Of the various types of administrative culture which have been discussed earlier in this chapter, it is fairly clear which one is closest to the traditional model—it is the *Rechtsstaat*. The culture is one of high power-distance and high uncertainty avoidance—indeed, the reduction of uncertainty and the increase in predictability are claimed to be among its chief virtues. The critique favoured by Osborne and Gaebler, Hughes (and many others) therefore leads towards the conclusion that countries like Germany are 'behind' and need to take up 'reinvention' or the 'New Public Management' more vigorously—to follow the 'leaders' such as New Zealand, the UK, or the USA.

Unfortunately, however, what one might term the 'NPM story' is misleadingly neat and over-simple. There are many detailed criticisms which could be made of it—see Pollitt, 2003a, chapter 2—but here we will confine ourselves to just three general points. First, it is dazzlingly clear that there has not been just one type of administrative regime in existence, but several (Demmke and Moilanen, 2010; Lynn, 2006; Ongaro, 2009). So to reduce the past to a single system is to do a considerable injustice to the variety of history. Second (by way of extension to the first point), even if some parts of some public sectors 'fitted' the image of the traditional bureaucracy, others definitely did not. Thus in the UK (as in most other Western European states), the most expensive and labour intensive sectors of state administration—health care and education—were never legalistic bureaucracies. On the contrary, they were heavily professionalized organizations in which individual professions were able to exercise a great deal of discretion, sometimes in a rather collegial, rather than hierarchical manner. Clarke and Newman (1997) call this 'bureau-professionalism', to distinguish it from pure bureaucracy. Third, the accounts of traditional bureaucracy given by the NPM 'school' tend to be rather one-sided. They emphasize the negatives ('rigidity', 'centralization', etc.) but ignore or underplay the positives, such as continuity, honesty, and a high commitment to equity in dealing with the citizen/public. In his seminal article on the NPM, Hood terms these 'theta-type core values', and comments that, even if NPM reforms do increase frugality and efficiency, these gains could be 'bought at the expense of guarantees of honesty and fair dealing and of security and resilience' (Hood, 1991, p. 16—see also, for a sophisticated defence of bureaucratic characteristics, Du Gay, 2000).

Our conclusion is *not* that the negative features of the 'traditional model' are fantasies, with no basis in reality. Every reader can probably vouchsafe some personal experience testifying to the capacity of public (and private) bureaucracies to work in infuriatingly slow and inefficient ways. However, it is a long—and unjustified—leap from there to the idea that the governments of the industrialized world previously operated their public sectors as Weberian-style traditional bureaucracies, and are now able to move, without significant loss, to a new, modern type of organization which avoids all the problems of the past. As this book will continue to demonstrate, public sectors have not all come from the same place and are not all headed in the same direction. Modernization often involves losses as well as gains (Chapter 7 is particularly concerned with this theme).

Each country is different (though there are some groups and patterns), and within each public domain, individual sectors have distinctive organizational cultures of their own. The idea of 'bureaucracy' as a single, and now totally obsolete, *ancien régime* is as implausible as the suggestion that there is now a global recipe which will reliably deliver 'reinvented' governments.

3.10 **Concluding remarks**

The main points of this chapter can be straightforwardly summarized. Features of the existing politico-administrative regime are likely to exert a significant influence over both the *choice* of reforms to be adopted and the *feasibility of implementing* certain types of reform. State structures, the nature of central executive government, relationships between ministers and mandarins, the prevailing administrative culture, and the diversity of channels of advice all have effects on which ideas get taken up, and how vigorously and widely these are subsequently implemented. Thus, certain regimes look as though they are much more open to the 'performance-driven', market-favouring ideas of the NPM than others: particularly the 'Anglo-Saxon' countries, Australia, Canada, New Zealand, the UK, and the USA. Other countries—especially the continental European states of Belgium, France, Finland, Germany, and Italy—have been structurally and culturally less hospitable to such ideas, but have responded to pressures by developing a different reform mix of their own, sometimes selecting from and transforming NPM tools as they do so. However, whatever type of reform may be desired, not every country has an equal capacity to *implement* new arrangements in a coherent, broad-scope way. For structural reasons, executive power is less centralized and focused in, say, Belgium, or the USA, than in New Zealand or the UK.

Continental Europe is significantly different. It is dominated by Germany and France, each with its own strong administrative tradition. Of the two, France finds it less difficult to make broad changes, to the extent that it remains fairly centralized and is governed by a president with strong powers. In federal Germany some of the constraints on change are entrenched in constitutional law, so one might expect change to be difficult at the federal level, though more in evidence at the lower levels of *Länder* and municipalities. Belgium is federal, and therefore structurally closer to Germany, but carries an inheritance of administrative arrangements which is predominantly in the French style. Unsurprisingly with this background, compounded by the linguistic and political divide between the Flemings and the Walloons, change has hitherto been slow (see, e.g. Pollitt and Bouckaert, 2009). Italy is in transition, but has clearly launched some major reforms, even if implementation has been highly uneven. Finally, there are the three north-western European states—Finland, the Netherlands, and Sweden. These differ among themselves in a variety of ways, but share a general disposition towards consensual, often meso-corporatist styles of governance. This tends to blunt the sharper corners of the NPM, leading to less outright criticism of the state bureaucracy, a cautious rather than a wildly enthusiastic approach to MTMs and to privatization, and a less rapid (some would say less ruthless) style of implementation than prevailed in New Zealand and the UK.

The above remarks are a brief foretaste of what is to come. In the next chapter, and in Appendix B, there will be more detailed accounts of the reform trajectories in each of the twelve countries, and of the EU Commission. These will therefore provide a test for the predictive powers of the politico-administrative variables here identified and discussed.

4 Trajectories of modernization and reform

4.1 From regimes to trajectories

In the previous chapters we examined the relatively enduring—yet nevertheless evolving—politico-administrative regimes of twelve countries, plus the European Commission. Now we shift focus to more rapid and short-term forms of change: the reforms themselves. How far can it be said that everyone has been following more or less the same route, albeit from different starting points in terms of their politico-administrative regimes? Are there clear patterns, and if so, of what kind, or is the story really one of ad hockery dressed up as strategy?

Our first step was to use the model of change advanced in Chapter 2 to organize the elements of what seemed to be the 'basics' of each country's experience into some sensible categories. The results of that exercise may be seen in tabular form in Appendix B, where there is a summary for each country, and chronological tables of key events. Appendix B should be used as an adjunct to the whole book, but especially to this chapter. Here in Chapter 4 we adopt a broad comparative perspective, looking for patterns of similarity and difference. We do this by employing the concept of *trajectories* to help us sort out the data.

4.2 Trajectories and scenarios: a conceptual preliminary

A trajectory, as defined here, is more than a trend. A trend is simply some pattern in the data (e.g. if the rainfall goes up every year for ten years, that is a trend). A trajectory, by contrast, is an *intentional* pattern—a route that someone is trying to take. It leads from a starting point (an alpha) to some desired place or state of affairs in the future (an omega). Thus a *scenario* consists of three basic elements: an initial state, a trajectory, and a future state (see Figure 4.1).

Scenarios may exist at various levels of specificity. They may amount to little more than a set of vague ideas and orientations. Or they may be developed into a strategic plan, with specified actions, timescales, and objectives. Scenarios are not always complete, in the sense that one or more of the three basic elements may be missing. For example, if there is only an omega—a vision of the desired future—but no clear specification of alpha or of trajectory, one might speak of a *utopia* or perhaps a *paradigm*. Thus one could consider the

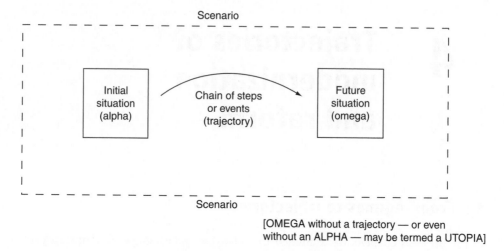

Figure 4.1 The concept of a trajectory

big models from Chapter 1—say the New Public Management (NPM), Neo-Weberian State (NWS), and New Public Governance (NPG)—as omegas, destinations, or ideal worlds that certain groups wanted to get to. Alternatively, there may exist a critique of the status quo (alpha) and a desire to move in a certain direction (trajectory), but no well-developed picture of the final state that is aimed for. This could be thought of as a kind of drifting with the tide, and there is certainly evidence of a good deal of that in the world of management reform ('everyone seems to be doing this so we had better try it too').

To anticipate, we are of the view that fully worked out scenarios, with each of the three main elements clearly analysed and described, are the exception rather than the rule in public management reform. The real world is usually more untidy, with poorly specified visions of the future, inadequate analyses of the status quo, and partial and sometimes conflicting or oscillating trajectories for different aspects of the administrative apparatus. This untidiness is understandable—it can occur for reasons of limited capacity for reform policymaking, or because ambiguity and vagueness may suit the political leadership (leaving their options open and holding together varied coalitions of opinion), or because of genuine uncertainty about what the best course of action may be (organizational change is not something political leaders are necessarily either trained for or even especially interested in). At this stage we may note—to anticipate Chapter 5—that if the trajectories and/or the omegas are vague then the question of how one assesses *results* immediately becomes problematic. 'Did we do it?' becomes 'We did this and that, but was this what we originally intended?'

4.3 The main components of reform

Table 4.1 sets out some of the main components of reform trajectories, and these headings will be used as a template for the following sections and subsections.

We have selected five main components for the substance (or 'what') of reform, plus three for the process (or 'how'). The first four divisions are conventional: finance (4.4), personnel (4.5), organization (4.6), and performance measurement (4.7). The fifth and final 'what' component is rather different: it is transparency and open government (4.8). Then we have a section on implementation (4.9) which looks at three 'how' processes: top down/bottom up, legal dimensions, and organizational processes. These topics are reviewed in the following subsections, before a final overview analysis is developed in Sections 4.10 to 4.12.

4.4 **Trajectories in financial management reform**

Budget reforms have been widespread, and have been driven by two particular external pressures. The first has been to restrain the growth of public expenditure for macro-economic reasons. The second has been to increase efficiency and effectiveness. These reasons have, of course, redoubled since the advent of the global economic crisis in 2008.

These circumstances appear to have strengthened the hand of central budget agencies within most governments, just as they did during the earlier fiscal crises of the 1980s (Wanna et al., 2003, p. 253).

Clearly, therefore, the need to restrain expenditure goes up and down with the (increasingly international) economic cycle and also according to the strength or weakness of the particular economy. The Norwegians, for example, with a small population and a huge revenue from offshore oil and gas, have experienced less budgetary pressure than any of the twelve countries covered by this book. Currently Brazil and China (for example) are not at all facing the extreme pressures on public spending that feed daily headlines in Germany and the UK. The second pressure has been that for performance improvement within the public sector—for types of budgeting and financial management

Table 4.1 Aspects of trajectories: context (what) and process (how)

Starting Position: Alpha	What Trajectory: scope and components	End Position: Omega
	— Finance: Budget, Accounts, Audits	
	— Personnel: Recruitment, Posting, Remuneration, Security of Employment, etc.	
	— Organization: Specialization, Coordination, Scale, (De)centralization	
	— Performance Measurement Systems: Content, Organization, Use	
	How Trajectory: Process of Implementation	
	— Top-down vs Bottom-up	
	— Legal Dimensions	
	— Task allocation: (New) Organizations	

which will stimulate greater efficiency or effectiveness, or higher quality, or some mixture of the three.

Taken together, these pressures have led to what in effect has been an expansion in the scope or purpose of budgeting. Instead of the former situation, in which budgets were mainly a process by which annual financial allocations were incrementally adjusted, legalized, and made accountable to legislatures, budgeting has become more intimately linked with other processes—planning, operational management, and performance measurement. Greater integration of these different systems has been a stated objective in many countries (OECD, 2009a, pp. 92–4). Long ago Caiden (1988) described this broadening and complexifying of the budget agenda as the emergence of 'super budgeting'. More recently, the OECD observed that 'Since the early 1990s almost all OECD member countries have been working to improve the quality of their public expenditure by implementing a focus on results to their management and budgeting systems' (OECD, 2002b, p. 2). In parallel, financial management, which often used to be the preserve of financial management specialists, has now become an element in the training and professional socialization of many, if not most, middle managers and professionals (see Zifcak, 1994 on early initiatives in Australia and the UK). All of this can be seen as a shift towards an NPM model, where the emphasis is on results and efficiency, and budgeting becomes the business of many managers, not just specialist finance officers.

The reforms which have served the *savings* objective have not always fitted well with the reforms that would be required to encourage *performance improvement*. For example, the first reaction of some governments to expenditure pressures was to 'cheese slice', that is, to strengthen the hand of central finance ministries to cut back programmes from the top down.

The depth and incidence of the cuts depended on the political opportunities (some targets are politically 'harder' than others—e.g. it may be easier to cut new weapons systems than to cut pensions) and on the severity of the macro-economic position (e.g. New Zealand in 1984 and Finland in 1992 were in more severe circumstances than either country was in 1998). In general, however, this kind of approach sits uneasily with performance improvement. This is because opportunistic cheese-slicing generates a highly unpredictable and negative environment for operational managers, in which they may suddenly find they have lost part of their budget for no good performance-related reason. Managers may come to see themselves as the victims of particularistic interventions from seemingly all-powerful central finance departments. On the other hand across the board percentage cuts (e.g. everyone loses 3%) can be delegated to managers to make final decisions, thus 'distancing' the actual selection of cuts from executive politicians and leaving them in the hands of those people who presumably know more about the actual practical details of the programmes than anyone else (Pollitt, 2010a). In the 1980s and 1990s, for example, UK health authorities were subject to annual 'efficiency savings' of a fixed percentage, but were left to themselves to decide how these should be achieved.

A second route to savings is perhaps more compatible with performance improvement (though no programme manager enjoys budget reductions, however they are executed). It is to adopt or increase the use of frame- or block-budgeting, as was done by a number of countries, including Finland, Sweden, the USA, Belgium, and Italy, as part of its *decentramento* (decentralization) reforms. Here the central ministry sets and polices broad ceilings (frames), but within those delegates responsibility for allocation to particular services, programmes, or projects to local politicians and/or managers. In Finland, for example, the introduction of frame-budgeting in 1994 meant a change from a system in which central agencies had been heavily involved in regulating and controlling individual local services to a new relationship in which central government fixed a formula-determined total for each municipality and left local politicians to decide how to distribute that total between the various activities (see Appendix B: Finland country file). This approach does permit the local determination of priorities. However, as many commentators have pointed out, it also neatly delegates the unpopular business of making painful choices between competing priorities—in Italy, for example, the process of decentralization has been accompanied by vocal concerns from the provinces and regions that they are being delegated new tasks from the centre without adequate resources to carry them out ('unfunded mandates' has long also been a regular complaint from the states in the US federal system, where subnational governments are responsible for delivering many of the federal government's programmes). Frame-budgeting also required some redesign of budgetary procedures, in that there needed to be clear and separate phases to the budgetary discussion—first, the determination of aggregate financial frames (and therefore a debate about what the most appropriate formulae should be) and then, second, a detailed local discussion of what allocations there should be to specific programmes (and how the performance of those programmes should be measured). In a study of budgetary behaviour in Australia, Canada, Germany, Japan, Mexico, and the UK, the US General Accounting Office concluded that: '[A]ll six governments departed from previous budgeting approaches and imposed "top down" overall limits on government spending…Despite… variation, each represented a multi-year approach that sought to reduce overall real spending' (General Accounting Office, 1994, p. 6). A later study of Australia, Canada, Denmark, the Netherlands, New Zealand, Sweden, the UK, and the USA concluded that central budget agencies 'have essentially attempted to force the various policy actors to operate within control frameworks with longer horizons, rather than the more immediate, one-off deals and bilateral arrangements of past eras of public budgeting' (Wanna et al., 2003, p. 259).

A third approach is to make cuts strategically—for executive politicians to say, in effect, 'Programmes A and B are our top priorities, so cuts must fall on C and D'. There are not many examples of this being successfully accomplished (Pollitt, 2010a) but the Canadian Program Review of 1994 is often advanced as one good case (see Canada country file, Appendix B). At the time of writing, the Cameron administration in the UK is undertaking a programme of deep cuts in public spending, but has claimed it will ring-fence (protect) the National Health Service (very popular with voters) and the defence budget (the armed services are currently fighting in Afghanistan and are in receipt of enormous public sympathy for the desperate job they are being asked to do). This is clearly a sort of strategic prioritization, although in practice it is very difficult fully to protect the 'front line', and governments frequently lack the precision control tools to enable them to do so effectively.

Turning to those aspects of financial management reform which are more related to *performance* than to savings, one finds a number of partial trajectories. A first step is sometimes simply to publish some performance information alongside the annual budget documents (though it may be difficult or impossible to relate specific 'performances' to specific financial allocations). A second step is to begin to change the format and contents of the budget itself, typically by moving away from line item budgeting towards some more performance-sensitive type of categorization, or by trying to link up budgeting with new processes of strategic planning. A third, and more ambitious step is to change the procedure of budgeting itself, for example, by altering the incentives to key budget actors or by fundamentally changing the structure or timing of the budget discussion, or even by attempting to alter the role of the legislature in the budget process (Pollitt, 2001).

Figure 4.2 diagrams the OECD's view of how far each state has got in developing performance budgeting.

It shows a considerable range, from extensive use in Finland and Australia to much more limited use in Belgium and Germany. (We might add that, in 2007, the European Commission did not have what could be termed a performance budgeting system, although the reforms of 2000–4 had introduced a rather elaborate 'Activity-Based Budgeting' system – see Appendix B.) To some extent this reinforces the overall picture that is already beginning to emerge—that some countries (e.g. Australia, the Netherlands, the UK, and the US) have pushed faster and further with modernization than others (Belgium, Germany, Italy). The former group includes (but is not confined to) the strongly pro-NPM states, and the latter group includes some of the more NWS-oriented states.

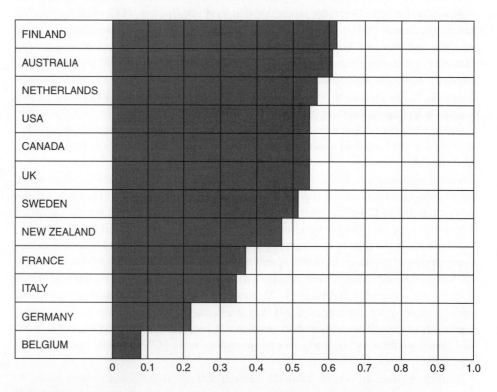

Figure 4.2 Extent of use of performance budgeting by central governments, 2007

Source: Adapted from OECD, 2009a, Table 20.1, p. 93.

Yet some of the details do not quite fit this rather-too-simple 'big picture'. New Zealand, for example, appears halfway down the chart, despite being a trail-blazer in financial management reform between 1984 and 1993. And some NWS-oriented states appear much higher up than others—if there is a pattern it is a ragged one, with much variation. But before we over-interpret this chart we should note that the OECD itself provides a cautionary footnote: 'This index examines the degree to which the OECD countries have put a performance budgeting system in place. However, it does not measure how successfully these systems operate in practice' (OECD, 2009a, p. 93). As we noted in Chapter 1 (section 1.6, especially Table 1.2) there can be a big gap between a formal decision to 'have' a particular reform (benchmarking, performance budgeting) and the day-to-day practice of government agencies. Furthermore, as the OECD explains, the index of use shown here was put together on the basis of a survey of central budget officials (where 0 = no use of performance budgeting and 1.0 = the existence of a comprehensive performance budgeting system). We should note, however, that central budget officials are hardly a neutral audience for these questions. They are by the very nature of their jobs heavily involved in budget reform, and may well have opinions as to what the 'right answer' to questions put to them should be. Even if they answer in a totally impartial, clinical way they may simply not know what actually goes on inside all the line departments and agencies when they compose their budget bids (it is not in the least unusual—or surprising—to find senior officials in the core executive who are not fully aware of actual practices in the ministries and agencies). We are perhaps rather labouring all these qualifications, but for a good reason. Similar caveats will apply to much, if not most, of the data exhibited in this chapter (and equally to some of the results data introduced in the following chapter). The plain fact is that doing good international comparisons is complex and difficult work (Pollitt, 2011). Public management scholars always need to be cautious when confronting apparently clear and decisive tables showing that country X 'scores' 0.7 and country Y only 0.4.

Canada provides a good illustration of the aforesaid difficulty of 'reading' budget reforms. In the early 1980s the federal government introduced a range of budget-modernizing measures—a Policy and Expenditure Management System (PEMS), a Multi-Year Operational Plan (MYOP) and an Operational Framework Plan (OFP). On paper this system sounded highly rational. In practice, however, under the Mulroney administrations from 1983, the PEMS system singularly failed to persuade or enable ministers to achieve their expenditure targets. It was partially replaced in 1989 and then in 1995 completely superseded by a new Expenditure Management System (EMS). EMS managed to deliver the first balanced budget for more than a decade, but even then the relationship between budget allocations and performance was debatable. Indeed, this is far from being just a technical issue. A decade later, after a series of scandals, the Canadians adopted a Federal Accountability Act (2006—see Canada country file). This established a parliamentary budget office, extended the authority of the Auditor General, and introduced a four-year cycle of departmental spending reviews, accompanied by systematic evaluation.

During almost half a century many countries have experienced considerable and persistent difficulties in trying to establish close links between the performance of programmes and their budget allocations (General Accounting Office, 1997; Pollitt, 2001).

There is no particular reason to believe that the latest generation of budget reforms will enjoy more than marginally greater success than previous efforts.

This leads directly to a more general point. Budgeting is an intensely political process, and actual behaviours can be very difficult to change—even when formal procedures are modified. Even when budgetary reform is implemented successfully, it may take years for all the various organizations concerned to become comfortable with and fully practice the new procedures. Finally, the process of budget reform is continuous, so it is inevitable that by the time this book is in print, further initiatives, not recorded here, will have been launched.

Bearing these caveats in mind, one can discern a broad pattern in budget reform. Since 1980 major changes to enhance the performance focus of budgeting have been implemented in the majority of our twelve countries (see, e.g. Wanna et al., 2003), and some modest moves in that direction have taken place even in the more reluctant countries, such as Belgium and Germany. Thus, for example, the Dutch and US governments have taken steps to change the format of budget documents, and to display much more performance information (either in the basic budget document or alongside it) than would have been usual twenty, or even ten, years ago. In 2001 the French government made a major shift to programme budgeting, which one book described as *'une véritable réforme de l'Etat'* (see *Loi Organique relative aux Lois de Finances* (LOLF), in the France country file in Appendix B). However, this still left the French some way short of the intensity of performance-linkage which had been achieved in New Zealand nearly a decade earlier (Trosa, 2002—the quotation comes from the back cover). One way to categorize the modernization of budgeting is to break it down into a number of steps (whereas the OECD index of performance budgeting aggregates these different steps into a single index). One begins with a traditional budget—line item and cash-based. The first step is simply to add on some performance information to this budget, without changing the basics. All our countries have done this— to some degree at least. The second step is to change the format of the budget, for example by aggregating line items into programmes, or by formally attaching performance information to most or all the line items. This can tell you how much it costs to maintain a military presence in Afghanistan, rather than just knowing from a line item budget how much was spent on boots, ammunition, fuel, etc. The third step is to alter the timing and sequence of the budget procedures, so as to try to ensure that the new information in the budget gets properly considered (e.g. by introducing a preliminary, more 'strategic' or 'whole of government' stage to the discussion before the debate moves on to which department or programme gets what). A fourth step is to alter the very basis of the budget by shifting from a cash base to accruals accounting (as discussed in more detail in the next section). We can say that a number of our countries have now reached that fourth stage— Australia, Canada, Finland, the Netherlands, New Zealand, Sweden, and the UK. Thus the fit with our models—NPM and NWS—is not at all a neat one. It should be remembered that budgetary reform can appear within both an NPM- and a NWS-inspired approach. For NPM enthusiasts, it is about performance, results, and efficiency. For NWS advocates it is more about modernizing financial control systems so as to be able to express broad political and strategic priorities more clearly in resource allocation.

Also, just *making* a budget is not the same as implementing it. Thus, alongside the reforms in budget preparation, many countries have witnessed parallel attempts by central budget agencies to increase both the frequency and the precision of monitoring. Wanna et al (2003, pp. 261–2) found that in Australia, New Zealand, the Netherlands, Sweden, and the UK 'ministries and agencies have become obliged to report and explain any deviation from their appropriated funds continually to the [central budget agency]'. Performance budgeting is one way of trying to achieve more active monitoring. National frameworks which attempt to sort budget items into a simpler, more policy- or programme-related order have multiplied. The Dutch VBTB reduced 800 line items to about 150 policy categories, asking 'What do we want to achieve?', 'What steps shall we take to achieve it?', and 'What will it cost?' (Van Nispen and Posseth, 2006). Canada developed a Management Accountability Framework (MAF). Australia had an Outcome Framework (Hawke, 2007; Blöndal et al., 2008). Sweden introduced a common activities structure with forty-eight policy categories (Küchen and Nordman, 2008). The UK has a system called FABRIC, a performance information architecture which is linked to the Public Service Agreements.

The broader debate about transparency (see section 4.8, below) has left its mark on budgets. Making budgets more transparent implies that budgeting becomes less exclusively a technical operation within the executive government and more a communication with the legislature and civil society. Some of the performance-budgeting reforms mentioned above were supposed to make the purposes of expenditure much clearer, although the reactions of parliamentarians to these reforms has by no means always been enthusiastic. An international survey suggested that some of the countries we have studied are among those with the most 'open' budgets—France, New Zealand, the UK, and the USA (Carlitz et al., 2009).

If we now move from budgetary reform per se to the (closely related) modernization of accounting systems, we find a roughly similar pattern of country trajectories (Table 4.2).

Table 4.2 Accounting trajectories

	Full Cash Basis	Combination of Cash and Accrual Basis	Full Accrual Basis (*)
Australia			X
Belgium	X		
Canada			X
Finland		X	
France			X
Germany	X		
Netherlands	X		
New Zealand			X
Sweden		X	
United Kingdom			X
United States			X

Source: Selected from Khan and Mayes, 2009, p. 2. Note that this data was originally drawn from the OECD/World Bank Budget Practices and Procedures Database, and that data for Italy is apparently missing.
(*) Full accrual basis means financial statements are prepared on the basis of accrual-based national or international accounting standards, also sometimes referred to as generally accepted accounting principles (GAAP)

Again, Australia, New Zealand, and the UK are among the countries which appear to have made the most far-reaching changes, with Finland, Sweden, and the USA having moved, but not quite so far, the least change being visible in Belgium, Germany, Italy, and the EU Commission. This is the pattern which seems to appear if one defines three broad positions, beginning with a traditional, cash-based accounting system, then a shift to double-entry bookkeeping, possibly with elements of cost analysis, modified cash or modified accrual and, finally, the development of full accrual accounts with a focus on providing performance-related information. Internationally, budget and management reforms have increasingly converged within a variety of shared performance architectures.

This is not a place for a full exposition of the different bases for keeping public accounts. There is space only to point to the very basics of our threefold classification. In pure cash accounting, a public sector entity is given a budget, calculated in cash terms, and proceeds to spend the money, keeping records of each cash disbursement (and incoming payment) so as to ensure neither an overspend (which may actually be illegal) or an underspend (which is likely to act as an invitation to the political level to arrive at the conclusion that not so much money is needed, and that the budget can therefore be cut in the following year). In the EU Commission, for example, an elaborate cash system used to operate until recently in which each piece of expenditure had to be approved by three separate officials, as, first, legal, then, second, in accordance with the programme, then, third, as affordable (there is sufficient cash to pay it). A problem with this type of system is that, by itself, it gives few incentives for efficiency, or even economy. The name of the game easily becomes that of simply spending the money allocated, within the financial year. EU officials, for example, seemed to worry about 'absorption' (i.e. their ability to spend all the money allocated) at least as much as they did about efficiency and effectiveness of expenditure. Even after the reforms of 2001–2, the EU budgetary system contains few incentives to 'save'. The money in the budget is there, it cannot be saved or switched for use elsewhere, and therefore it has to be spent.

The shift to double-entry bookkeeping marks a significant change from this position. It brings public accounts closer to the private sector model. Every transaction is entered on the accounts twice—once as a credit and once as a debit. If wages are paid, for example, the sum involved can be shown as a *credit* to the organization's central cash account and, simultaneously, a *debit* to the wages account. This approach is founded on the perspective that the organization is a separate business, in which its total assets must, by definition, remain equal to its capital plus its liabilities. It can be used to raise consciousness of a wider range of management issues than is usually provoked by cash-based accounting. In particular, if double-entry bookkeeping includes capital assets (land, buildings) it can stimulate managers to make more efficient use of these resources, rather than treating them as a 'free good', as often occurs in cash-based systems. On the other hand, much depends on the *organizational level* at which the books are balanced, and on the extent to which links to performance are made explicit. If double-entry systems are confined to a high level, and accounting itself is performed as a very centralized function, far from 'street level' management, then the impact on most managers may be limited.

Our third stage, accruals accounting, brings the public sector on to as near as possible a comparative basis to the private sector (lowering 'grid' in anthropological terms—Hood, 1998). It means that government organizations report commitments when they are incurred (rather than when the cash is actually disbursed), allow for the valuation and depreciation of all capital assets, and present annual 'balance sheet-type' financial statements (Likierman, 1998; Khan and Mayes, 2009). When coupled with a system of decentralized financial management it can form the basis for a close link between resource allocation and performance management at the level of individual agencies and programmes. At the time of writing, full accruals accounts for public sector entities were being produced by Australia, Canada, France, New Zealand, the UK, and the USA.

The significance of these shifts in accounting practices for management is considerable. So long as a cash-based system prevails, without double-entry bookkeeping or accruals accounting, it is hard to make either global or specific links between expenditure and cost, and between cost and performance. Managers are not faced with the full costs of their use of assets, and performance measurement, if it exists, tends to be a separate system from financial management. On the other hand, the application of accruals systems is not equally straightforward for all different types of service and circumstance, and reform can create perverse incentives as well as advantages (Pollitt, 2000b; Straw, 1998; Newberry and Pallot, 2006). It can also be less immediately understandable than cash accounts for lay persons—including citizens and members of parliament. In both New Zealand and Sweden there was some evidence that expenditure figures on the new accruals accounting basis caused misunderstandings among parliamentarians.

When reform takes place it has frequently been a step-by-step process, moving from pilot projects to larger scale roll-outs, or from one part of the public sector to others (which means that distortions can arise during the sometimes long transitional periods, when one part of the public sector is operating according to one set of accounting principles and another is following a different set). For example, in the UK, accruals accounting was introduced in the National Health Service before it was adopted for central government, and in the Netherlands double-entry bookkeeping was required for some agencies but not for their parent ministries. Furthermore, our three broad 'stages' of accountancy are inevitably a somewhat over-neat classification of detailed practice. In the real world, governments blur these categories considerably, by adding performance elements to basically cash-based systems or by introducing partial accruals accounting with lots of exceptions and special features (see HM Treasury, 1998, pp. 132–54).

The most recent major trend in public sector accounting has been the interest in Whole-of-Government Accounting (WGA—see Grossi and Newberry, 2009). This parallels the interest in 'joined-up government'/'integrated public governance' that we will deal with in Section 4.6 on organizational changes. Like joined-up government, it seeks to see the big picture, to bring all the various public sector actors within one framework. It has an obvious logic—to hold a government to account one needs to see the whole of what is going on—not just departmental expenditures but also agency expenditures as well as previously 'off books' expenditures and liabilities such as those located in Public–Private Partnerships (PPPs). All these should be brought together in a single account. It is a logic which has come to seem all the more forceful in those countries where public services have been fragmented into many organizations, and where much has been contracted out or 'partnerized' (again, see Section 4.6). One can see in it some trace of NPG ideas—that we need to see the big picture, including all the different actors, both public and private, that may contribute to the delivery of a policy. The new OECD database, Government at a Glance, explicitly refers to the need for a broader concept of governance (OECD, 2009a) Yet there are also echoes of NPM—perhaps a kind of Mark 2 NPM where the fragmentation of Mark 1 is overcome by fitting all agencies into one set of accounts, so that the government can have one *financial* picture, even if there continue to be autonomous management and specialization in operational matters. WGA could even be said to be compatible with NWS ideas, in that NWS reasserts the unity of the state, and the need for modern methods of coordinating public actions.

There is often ambiguity about how far the WGA envelope is supposed to spread (is it all central government, or central *and* local, or *all* bodies that spend public money and own public assets?). The wider, more ambitious definitions of WGA imply a challenging degree of centralization in accounting practice, and do not seem to have been fully implemented anywhere. Furthermore it does not seem to be clear what the balance is between objectives of macro-economic steering and micro-economic management (Grossi and Newberry, 2009). Finally, neither is it clear who is demanding WGA—who will really use it, and for what? Despite these questions, WGA projects are going forward in several countries, albeit often with delays and setbacks. It is noticeable, however, that the biggest efforts seem to be being made by the core NPM states—Australia, New Zealand, and the UK. Developments in continental Europe are far more limited and cautious, and are less firmly wedded to business models.

Completing the financial circle, we now turn briefly to reforms in public sector *auditing*. Again, we distinguish three stages (and again, these should be regarded as no more than rough approximations to the complexities of detailed practice within each country and sector). The first stage is that of *traditional financial and compliance auditing*. Here the basic concern of the auditor is with legality and procedural correctness. Has the money been spent on duly approved objects, through the correct procedures? Is there evidence of unauthorized expenditure or corruption? The second stage is to add *investigations of some performance issues* but still staying close to financial issues. For example, auditors may be empowered to search for waste—items which have been purchased at unnecessary expense, or items which have been perfectly legally purchased but which are not being used very much (the school purchases a computer but no teacher can use it, so it sits in the storeroom). Another extension of traditional audit is to extend it into a deeper questioning of data quality ('validation'). The figures presented to Parliament or Audit Office may add up, but how reliable are they? Have all transactions been recorded, and recorded accurately? This is, in effect, an audit of the performance of the organization's internal auditing system. The third stage is the development of *full-blown performance auditing* as a distinct activity, often with a separate unit or section of the national audit office to develop performance auditing expertise. Full-blown performance auditing may still be concerned with financial issues (economy and efficiency) but it may also move on to look at non-financial performance, for example are visitors satisfied with the national museums, does the national weather bureau forecast the weather accurately? The development of performance auditing over the last quarter century has been considerable, but it has been taken much further in some countries than others (National Audit Office, 2005; Pollitt et al., 1999).

Performance auditing now exists in most of our twelve countries, but it is carried out on a larger scale and in a more ambitious way in some than in others (OECD, 2005, p. 95). Australia, Canada, Finland, the Netherlands, New Zealand, Sweden, the UK, and the USA are the countries where it is furthest developed. In some of these—especially Sweden, the UK, and the US—the Supreme Audit Institutions (SAIs) have examined the scope for borrowing techniques and concepts from evaluation, but have not created separate units to carry out evaluations per se. Elsewhere, however, the place of performance audit is not so developed or clear cut. In France there is no doubt that the magistrates of the *Cour des Comptes* can, and often do, analyse performance aspects, but the performance audit function has been separated from more traditional, compliance-oriented forms of audit only slowly and partly, and the general culture is still highly legalistic. In Germany the main emphasis of the *Bundesrechnung-shof* has been on compliance and financial auditing, though some performance elements are also covered. The European Court of Auditors has a definite capacity for performance audit but, in practice, seems to find most of its staff resources drawn into the identification of fraud and the provision, since 1994, of an annual statement of assurance (DAS) to the European Parliament (National Audit Office, 2005; Pollitt et al., 1999).

Thus far the discussion of audit has been exclusively in terms of external audit by independent audit offices. In practice, the work of external audit organizations is made either much easier or much more time-consuming and difficult according to the state of sophistication of *internal* audit within public sector organizations. In short, reform of auditing usually entails more than just remandating, retraining, and reskilling the national audit offices. It also requires matching changes in internal audit services. We are not aware of substantial comparative research in this area, but in general, internal audit and control practices seem to have developed considerably since the mid 1990s (OECD, 2005, pp. 90–3). For example, the crisis that led to the fall of the Santer Commission in 1999 helped to ensure that the introduction of an internal audit service would be a high priority for the next leaders of the Commission (European Commission, 2000). Similarly, in Belgium, the Copernicus reform announced in 2000 that henceforth each federal ministry would have an internal audit service. Probably internal audit has become one of the boom professions within the public sector (Put and Bouckaert, 2010).

4.5 Trajectories in personnel management/HRM

[T]he often prevailing perception that civil services are reform resistant is clearly wrong (Demmke and Moilanen, 2010, p. 4)

4.5.1 The volume and direction of reform

As Chapter 3 made clear, different countries entered the 1980s with contrasting legal and cultural assumptions about the nature of public service (even the words are treacherous here—'public service' already suggests an Anglo-American-Australasian perspective, by contrast to continental countries in the *Rechtsstaat* tradition, which might rather regard civil servants as 'state officials', or some such term). Yet despite differences of 'starting line' most countries suffered similar pressures, and were obliged to find some response. Certainly there has been no shortage of activity (the following list is selective, not comprehensive):

- Australia: 1983 Amendment of the Public Service Act; 1987, 1993, 1995 Guidelines on Official Conduct of Commonwealth Public Servants; 1990 Guidelines on Appraisal of Performance of Senior Executive Service; 1999 Public Service Act.

- Belgium: 1994 new civil service statute; 1997 introduction of a personnel appraisal system; 2000 Copernicus reform plan, including many aspects of personnel management.

- Canada: 1989 new Personnel Management Manual; Public Service 2000 initiative; Public Service white paper; 1992 Public Service Reform Act.

- European Commission: 1997 Modernization of Administrative and Personnel 2000 programme; 2003 creation of European Personnel Selection Office, and major reform of recruitment system.

- Finland: 1994 State Civil Servants Act; 2005 pensions for state employees brought closer to system for private sector pensions.

- France: 1989 Prime Ministerial circular on public service renewal included some personnel reforms. In the mid 1990s proposed personnel reforms helped provoke extensive public sector strikes. In 2007 the new President, Sarkozy, launched a series of reforms designed to ensure, inter alia, that only 50 per cent of those civil servants who were retiring would be replaced.

- Germany: 1989 law amending working provisions for civil servants; 1994 Public Service Reform Act; 1996 amendments to the law relating to federal civil servants.

- Italy: reforms of public employment law in 1993 and 1997; 1998 decree allows political bodies to make top official appointments; 2009 tightening of rules to enforce annual performance rankings.

- Netherlands: 1993 delegation of detailed negotiations on labour conditions from Ministry of Home Affairs to eight sectors (state, judiciary, municipalities, etc.); 1998 extension of Senior Public Service terms to all 1,500 top management positions.

- New Zealand: 1988 State Sector Act; 1991 Employment Contracts Act. By 2005 93 per cent of staff were on open-term contracts (OECD, 2005, p. 172).

- Sweden: 1990 modification of Public Employment Act. Lifelong employment has been replaced by employment on permanent contract for more than 75 per cent of government staff (OECD, 2005, p. 172); 1991 public sector pensions made more like private sector pensions.

- UK: 1992 Civil Service (Management Functions) Act; 1993 Civil Service Management Code; White Papers *The Civil Service: Continuity and Change* (1994) and *The Civil Service: Taking Forward Continuity and Change* (1995).

- USA: 1978 Civil Service Reform Act (including creation of a Senior Executive Service); 1994 Federal Personnel Manual abandoned (with ceremonial burning of a copy on the White House lawn, as part of National Performance Review (NPR)); 1994 Federal Workforce Restructuring Act. After 2001 President G. W. Bush introduced new, more private sector forms of employment for staff in the Departments of Homeland Security and Defense.

The Global Economic Crisis of 2008 ushered in hard times for many civil servants in many states. Salaries were frozen or cut in most of our twelve countries, numbers were drastically reduced in several, and pension rights were reduced in various ways (higher retiring age, less generous pensions for those who were not yet near retirement). Most of these measures were characterized by the same broad orientation (Farnham et al., 1996; Balk, 1996; Horton et al., 2002; Hondeghem and Nelen, 2002). Politicians wanted civil services which were more flexible and responsive, more focused on getting results, more skilful and, if possible, less numerous (and therefore less expensive in total). After the GEC the downward pressure on numbers became acute. Civil servants, meanwhile, while not averse to some of these demands, also sought to retain existing privileges and protections. They obviously did not want drastic downsizings with compulsory redundancies, and neither did they want salary freezes or other arrangements which would further erode their material rewards in comparison with the private sector. In some places (France, the EU Commission) they had strongly entrenched unions and fought long and hard to stave off erosions of their basic conditions of service (Howard, 1998). Nevertheless in the crisis atmosphere of 2008–10 many protections and privileges were scaled back—even in the European Commission. Occasionally, constitutional protections were so formidable that it was almost impossible for governments to effect radical change (as for German federal civil servants). In other cases, resistance was either less well organized or less embedded in legal rights, and fundamental changes were driven through. For example, security of tenure was significantly reduced in Australia, New Zealand, and the UK. Substantial downsizings were carried through in Australia, France, Finland, New Zealand, the UK, and the USA (though one has to be careful in interpreting the statistics because in some cases staff were transferred to other parts of the public sector).

Personnel changes seldom came first on the reform agenda. It was much more common for them to follow—sometimes at a considerable distance—innovations in financial management, organizational structures, and management techniques. In this respect Australia was not unusual (at least not for the Anglo-Saxon countries):

Financial management dominated the reform programme of the 1980s. In the latter half of the decade, the limitations of this emphasis were increasingly acknowledged and pressures to broaden the directions being taken and to reduce the subservience of management processes to financial questions. Other forms of management were increasingly being advocated, human resource management assuming a prominence from the end of the 1980s.   (Halligan, 1996*b*, pp. 102–3)

However, this positioning of Human Resource Management (HRM) reform as 'last in the line' certainly changed with the GEC, when HRM reform itself became a way of achieving desperately needed economies.

As far as the member states of the European Union are concerned, a recent comparative analysis suggested that there had been a number of fairly widespread trajectories (Demmke and Moilanen, 2010, pp. 3–4):

- a transition from centralized to decentralized determination of employment conditions
- a shift from statutory to contractual or managerial governance
- a development from career systems to post-bureaucratic (position systems)
- a delegation of responsibilities to managers
- an alignment of pay levels with private sector practices
- a change to special retirement schemes.

In this respect, therefore, there does seem to be a degree of convergence. It should not, however, be exaggerated. As we know from Chapter 3, different countries started from very different positions. As with budgetary reforms, some have moved further and faster than others, and the gap between the formal system and the way operational decisions are made in practice may in some cases be rather large. Demmke and Moilanen themselves, having identified these widespread and important trends, nevertheless arrive at the conclusion that 'the emergence of a new European-wide organizational model in the national civil services cannot be identified' (2010, p. 95).

It is perhaps easiest to understand these trajectories of change in respect of a 'base case'. This base case is very general, and applies to both the *Rechtsstaat* and the public interest countries (Chapter 3, Section 6). In it, a typical civil servant is assumed to be:

- a tenured, career appointment—not dependent on the whims of transient politicians or on one's civil service superior (although dismissable, with difficulty, in cases of extreme dereliction of duty or of criminal actions);
- promoted principally in relation to qualifications and seniority;
- part of a unified civil service, within a distinct and particular national framework of terms and conditions (including national pay scales).

These are all features which made being a civil servant different from most private sector jobs (and increasingly different during the 1970s and 1980s, as the nature of private sector employment itself became more precarious). They are also features which, at least in the core NPM countries, came to be seen as inhibiting the greater responsiveness and efficiency which it had become fashionable for politicians and public alike to demand. In Australia the Public Service Commissioner, explaining the main thrust of the 1999 Public Service Act, said:

As public servants we need to walk the same fields and gaze the same blue skies that inspire innovation in the private sector. Central to that is the need to bring our employment arrangements more into line with the wider Australian community. Does anyone really believe that, protected by a monopoly status and inadequate scrutiny, we can defend an approach to management that we now know is at least twice as expensive as best practice?   (Shergold, 1997, p. 33)

Note the elements in this quotation—the setting up of the private sector as the standard to be attained, the emphasis on cost saving, and the suggestion that the public service is over-protected and 'feather-bedded'. One should beware of accepting all this at face value. For example, it is easy to exaggerate the prevalence and influence of the three distinctive features mentioned (e.g. many categories of civil servant in the UK never had particularly strong tenure, low pay was common, and there had long been many non-career and part-time appointments, especially in the clerical grades). Studies which do show high average pay in some parts of the public sector often overlook the fact that those staff are, on average, significantly more highly qualified than the private sector comparison group. Nevertheless, the popular stereotype of a tea-drinking, probably not very efficient, yet secure and well-pensioned civil servant was never far from media reporting and political characterization, especially by neo-conservatives. In the UK and the USA this trend has been amplified by the GEC, to the point where it seems as if the hunt is on for any public servant paid more than a modest amount. Even in France, a country with a proud tradition of a powerful and talented civil service, there was a period when '[F]rom a model of social success, the civil servant became an awful figure, the pure representation of waste and incompetence' (Rouban, 1997, p. 150). In the Netherlands, generally a more consensual and incremental politico-administrative system than Australia or New Zealand, the early 1990s saw steps being taken to 'normalize' the status of government employees, and in 1992 it was agreed that the general pension fund for public employees would be privatized. In Italy a 1993 reform contractualized the basis of most civil servants' employment, and as a result these staff were subsequently governed mainly by private labour laws (Demmke and Moilanen, 2010, p. 74). Even in Belgium, steps were taken to lessen the differences between public sector and private sector employment (Brans and Hondeghem, 1999; Hondeghem, 2000; Hondeghem and Vermeulen, 2000). In the European Commission the reforms at the beginning of the twenty-first century saw the introduction of regular individual appraisals, and of large-scale management training. Furthermore the Commission's recruitment system was fundamentally overhauled, and replaced with one that includes assessment centres and competency tests for the most promising candidates (Ban, 2010a).

The three indicated characteristics therefore became easy foci for reform. We will now look at each of the three features in turn.

4.5.2 **A tenured career**

The directions of change here were to make careers less secure, and to encourage larger inflows and outflows of staff so that a smaller and smaller proportion of civil servants were 'lifers' and a larger and larger proportion had experience of other ways of doing things. A typical development in NPM countries was the appointment of top officials (especially agency chief executives, but also, in some cases, the heads of ministries) on two-, or three-, or five-year performance-related contracts. The most extreme case is again New Zealand. There, all members of the Senior Executive Service (see 4.5.3) have to reapply for their own jobs after five years, except for the heads of ministries (called Chief Executives), who enjoy a provision which permits their contracts to be extended (Boston et al., 1996, pp. 117–20).

Elsewhere, there has been less change. In Belgium, Canada, Finland, France, Germany, and Sweden most top civil servants are career 'mandarins' with long experience and well-established personal networks (see, e.g. Bourgault and Carroll, 1997). France is perhaps rather different from the other countries in this group, to the extent that the members of the *grands corps* frequently move in and out of jobs in the business world, and therefore could not be accused of being monkishly bureaucratic. Indeed, one problem is that, with falling civil service prestige, increasing numbers of these mandarins have been leaving for the better-paid positions in the private sector (Rouban, 1997, p. 147). In the European Commission the permanent A-grades continue to enjoy great security of tenure, although since the Kinnock reforms their performance has now come under more systematic formal appraisal than in the past (see European Commission file, Appendix B). The USA is different again: here members of the Senior Executive Service have tended to be narrowly specialist and, in any case, are obliged to work within a system where so many of their colleagues are short-term political appointees (Kettl et al., 1996, p. 56; on the 'spoils system' see Appendix B: USA, country file).

4.5.3 Promotion by seniority and qualifications

Here the shift was to link promotion more to results and responsiveness, often by embodying the required results in an annual agreement or quasi-contract, containing specified individual targets and priorities. Usually the change was only partial—seniority and qualifications were still elements in the overall calculation—but the intention of making civil servants more sharply focused on specific and usually short-term objectives was quite clear. This new emphasis was frequently reinforced by linking pay as well as promotion to 'track record' in achieving results (see 4.5.4).

A further important development in a number of countries was the creation of some form of Senior Executive Service (SES) (Australia, Canada, New Zealand, the UK, and the USA—see Ban and Ingraham, 1984; Boston et al., 1996, pp. 117–20; Halligan, 1996b, pp. 86–7). This kind of grouping was supposed to bring a variety of benefits ('supposed' because in every case there were significant difficulties in achieving the originally proclaimed goals). Basically an SES was intended (with slightly different emphases in each country) to create a more mobile, flexible, responsive, and managerially competent group at the top of the public service. An SES would be more mobile because provisions would allow the easier recruitment of competent executives from outside the normal career ladder of the civil service, and because the terms and conditions would explicitly include horizontal movement within the politico-administrative machine ('horses for courses'). It would be more responsive partly because the right (wo)man could be moved into the right place at the right time, but also because promotion was intended to be for the 'can do' individuals with track records of achievement, rather than by seniority and precedence. As the UK Conservative government put it:

Entry to the Senior Civil Service from within a department or agency would be marked for the individual concerned by leaving negotiated group pay arrangements and moving to individually-determined pay, and by acceptance of a written contract of service.   (Prime Minister et al., 1994, p. 37)

This type of system was usually backed up by some form of Performance-Related Pay (PRP) (in both Australia and the USA this was also intended to be a way of circumventing general civil service pay restrictions so as to be able to retain 'high flyers'). Experiments with performance pay have been implemented in most of our twelve countries, and elsewhere, but often with mixed or downright disappointing results (Gaertner and Gaertner, 1985; OECD, 1993b; Perry and Pearce, 1985; Perry et al., 2009). Again, the pattern is of the widest use coming in the core NPM countries (and, on this score, the USA), with more cautious and limited projects in the Nordic countries and France. It is perhaps typical of the more sceptical approach of the continental European countries that, in Finland and Sweden, while PRP is legally possible, many public departments and agencies decline to avail themselves of it, arguing that it would be divisive and unhelpful. Additionally, managerial competence can be increased by bringing in outsiders with managerial backgrounds as well as by the provision of intensive high-level management training programmes (Op de Beeck and Pollitt, 2010). The advantages of this trajectory are thus obvious, but it has potential disadvantages too. Concerns about the dangers of increasing the number of short-term fixers and 'yes-men' (and 'yes-women'), and endangering the promotability and security of those who give 'frank and fearless' advice, have been expressed in several countries, including Australia, Belgium, Canada, and the UK.

4.5.4 **Part of a unified national service**

In this case the thrust in quite a few countries was towards decentralization of personnel authority, initially for the day-to-day management of individuals, but increasingly also in terms of a widening range of terms and conditions, so that, ultimately, line managers could hire and fire on terms they set according to local conditions, and the concept of a unified public service was for all practical purposes abandoned. This direction of change had many ramifications. Pay, hours of work, required qualifications, disciplinary and dismissal procedures—all these and more might cease to be matters of national negotiation by management and union leaders and be decentralized by organization, region, or occupational group. The new philosophy was succinctly enunciated in a UK White Paper in 1994:

No two civil service organisations are identical, any more than two organisations elsewhere in the public or private sectors. It is right that pay and grading systems, like other management arrangements, should be attuned to individual circumstances and relevant labour markets. (Prime Minister et al., 1994, p. 26)

In Australia, as in the UK, the outline shell of a unified public service was retained but, with the 1999 Public Service Act:

It is departmental secretaries and agency heads who will determine the remuneration, conditions and terms of employment. No longer will the legislation distinguish between public servants on the basis of whether they are permanent or fixed-term. It is secretaries who will decide how they will employ public servants and on what conditions of engagement. It is they who will assign duties and delegate responsibility. (Shergold, 1997, p. 34)

In New Zealand the government moved away altogether from the concept of a single, unified service. The 1988 State Services Act established departments, under their Chief Executives, as the employers of their own staff. The Annual General Adjustment (of pay) and public service-wide negotiation of non-pay conditions of service were abolished (Boston et al., 1996, chapter 10). The public sector came under the provisions of the Labour Relations Act, which had previously been meant for the private sector. By the early 2000s, however, the New Zealand government was seeing the need to find other ways to re-emphasize the unity of the senior civil service (see New Zealand country file, Appendix B).

This kind of 'normalizing' trajectory, where the civil service is 'deprivileged' and increasingly treated on the same fragmented and locally varying terms as private sector employment, has certainly not been followed by all countries. France, Germany, and the European Commission are notable and weighty exceptions. In Italy the terms of civil service employment have been brought somewhat closer to those prevailing in the private sector, but there are still significant differences, especially for more senior grades. The MAP 2000 initiative by the European Commission was proclaimed as a major decentralization in personnel management, and this tendency was taken further by the Kinnock reforms (see European Commission file in Appendix B). Nevertheless, by comparison with what had already been implemented by the core NPM countries, it was quite timid and conventional (European Commission, 1997*b*, 2000). In Belgium, Germany, and France, the state servant remains a very distinct category—legally, culturally, and politically. As we saw to be the case with financial management reforms, the northern European states have followed a path somewhere between the NPM enthusiasts, and the more conservative *Rechtsstaat* regimes. Finland and Sweden have made provisions for performance-related pay, and for more decentralized and results-oriented styles of personnel management. Yet these countries have not more than marginally dismantled the essential unity of the civil service. The same could be said of the Canadian federal civil service (Bourgault and Carroll, 1997, but for more recent concerns see Aucoin and Savoie, 2009). In the Netherlands, career management of top civil servants was actually *centralized* during the mid 1990s (Mazel, 1998).

The USA is once more a unique case. In theory a scrupulously fair and impersonal merit system provides a national framework for recruitment and job classification:

However, the federal government's uniform merit system today is neither uniform, merit-based, nor a system. It now covers barely more than half—56%—of the federal government's workers. Only 15% of the federal government's new career employees enter through the system's standard testing-and-placement process. (Kettl et al., 1996, p. 1)

Despite much debate during the 1980s and 1990s, no comprehensive reform was agreed or implemented (so in this respect the USA was unlike Australia and New Zealand). The problem, in the complex and fragmented US political system, is that:

Civil service reform is on everyone's list of jobs that must be done—but it is high on virtually no one's list. It has too little sex appeal to excite political interest; and though everyone agrees on the need for change, the consequences of *not* reforming the civil service never seem great enough to force it onto the policy agenda. (Kettl et al., 1996, p. 2)

Instead of head-on reform, what has tended to happen in recent years is that the executive has, so to speak, worked around the edges of the merit system, circumnavigating it rather than conquering it. Thus President G. W. Bush, for example, was able to introduce new, more private-sector-like HRM procedures in the new Department of Home Security and in the Department of Defense. And the process of contracting out federal work to the private and non-profit sectors (see USA country file, Appendix B) also tends to diminish the importance of the rump of the traditional civil service. In short, the USA, while far from the European *Rechtsstaat* model in political temperament and rhetoric, was nevertheless home to an often rigid and unreformed (or perhaps one should say partially and incoherently reformed) core civil service.

4.5.5 Interpreting the big picture on HRM

Here it may be useful to return to the idea of 'public service bargains' which was introduced in the previous chapter (Section 3.5). Figure 4.3 shows the basic schema developed by Hood and Lodge (2006). We should remember that these bargain categories are usually applied to *senior* civil servants—those who actually interact with political leaders—whereas much of the legislation and reform previously referred to covers the majority of public servants, at all levels.

In general, we can say that there are strong (but not universal) trends towards 'de-privilegization' and away from trusteeship. In a number of countries, bargains of types B1a and/or B1b are becoming less usual, and bargains of type B2a are becoming more common. Furthermore, the growth in the numbers and influence of political advisers in countries like Belgium, Canada, the UK, and the USA mean that in those states the category of B2b bargains has gained prominence—especially subtype B2b2. Yet there are also cases where the bargain between politicians and mandarins remains one in which senior civil servants are treated as an independent group of technocrats or magistrates (B1b). The French *grands corps* still fall in this category, as do most senior German civil servants. And we must remember that in almost every system there are particular groups which are exempted from the more general trends—such as the exemption of Italian judges, prosecutors, prefects, and diplomats from the 1993 reform which contractualized most other civil service appointments (for a general treatment of these many differences and details, see Demmke and Moilanen, 2010). So there is more than one omega, and more than one trajectory, but the dominant direction of travel is that of reducing the distinctiveness of the rules governing many public service jobs, from the top to the bottom of the hierarchy.

Finally, we can ask how all this relates to the three big models—NPM, NWS, and NPG. Clearly, many of the developments we have cited in this section possess an NPM-ish flavour, especially moving towards private sector types of employment contract and the introduction of performance-related pay. Yet at the same time we have noted the reluctance of some states—Germany, for example, and to a lesser extent France and the Nordic states—to go very far down this road. In those cases the vision has seemed to be more NWS-ish: that it is important to keep the public service somewhat distinct from private sector employment, and to continue to endow at least some parts of it with special status and protections. In this particular context the significance of NPG thinking is hard to assess. Presumably its advocates would urge that civil servants be trained to network and collaborate with a range of other stakeholders. If so, there is some evidence that these ideas are indeed beginning to infiltrate training programmes for top civil servants (Op de Beeck and Pollitt, 2010). But what the implications might be for civil service recruitment, pay, and conditions are not clear.

4.6 Organizational trajectories

The restructuring of organizations is a ubiquitous feature of public sector management reforms (for details on the twelve countries, see Appendix B). Of the many different

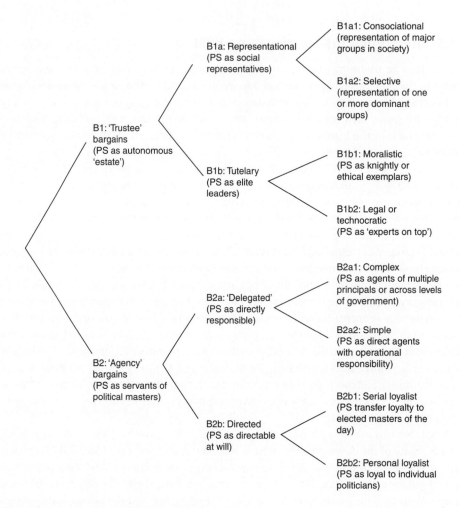

Figure 4.3 Some types of public service bargain

Source: Hood and Lodge, 2006, p. 21, Figure 2.1.

possible ways of classifying these restructurings we have chosen a fourfold scheme which is fairly 'mainstream' in terms of classical organization theory, namely:

- specialization (should institutions be single-purpose or multi-purpose?)
- coordination (by what means should coordination across different functions, levels and sectors be achieved?)
- centralization/decentralization (what functions should be centralized/decentralized, and to what degree?)
- scale (what is the optimal size for organizations?).

A brief overview may first be useful. As a broad generalization it can be said that the main thrust of the early Australian/New Zealand/UK reforms from 1980 until the mid 1990s was towards organizations which were more specialized; towards coordination by means of market mechanisms and contractual and quasi-contractual relationships, instead of through hierarchies of authority; towards decentralization of authority from the centre towards the periphery (in both hierarchical and geographical terms); and towards decreasing the size of public organizations by breaking up and downsizing large bureaucratic organizations (Boston et al., 1996; O'Toole and Jordan, 1995; Peters and Savoie, 1998). Trends towards specialization and fragmentation have also been discernible in Canada, France, and the Netherlands (though to a lesser degree than in the core NPM countries), but are much less marked in Belgium, Finland, Germany, and Sweden, each of which has retained its central ministerial or directorate structure with only limited fragmentation, downsizing, or 'hiving off'. The EU Commission has also acquired a growing penumbra of agencies (Rambøll/Euréval/Matrix, 2009). Of course some of these systems—the German and the Swedish for example—were already highly decentralized, so it can be argued that they had less 'need' of reforms of this type. The USA sported a fairly fragmented and specialized administrative system from the start (see Appendix B: USA country file) and has been concerned to try to develop overall systems which will permit greater coherence (e.g. common accounting procedures, common reporting procedures through the Government Performance and Review Act). As for decentralization, almost everyone seems to believe in it, though, as we shall see, it takes on a different personality in different contexts (Pollitt, 2005).

During the twenty-first century, however, a new trend has appeared. Especially in those countries which had undergone the most radical fragmentation (Netherlands, New Zealand, UK) the tide turned towards better coordination. This has taken a variety of forms (although nowhere has it become the reconstruction of traditional, large, multi-functional departments) but it has been a discernible trend nonetheless. Strengthened coordination—both vertically and horizontally—is also much facilitated by the intelligent application of modern information and communications technologies. One promising interpretation is that the earlier, specializing and fragmenting reforms unintentionally produced difficulties for policymakers, who could no longer control all the autonomous 'bits' as they wished, and so started to look for devices that would enable them to be more coordinated, 'joined-up', or strategic (Bogdanor, 2005; Bouckaert et al., 2010). A further development of this is the idea that the reaction against fragmentation merged with pressure to use new ICTs so that a model of 'Digital-Era Governance' has now emerged (Dunleavy et al., 2006*b*). Two of the key themes of this new model are said to be 'reintegration' (putting back together what NPM had put apart) and 'needs-based holism' (simplifying the entire relationship between the citizen and the state, so that the former only has to go to one website or place to get all his/her requirements dealt with).

The signs of attempts at improved coordination are clear to see. One popular initiative has been to develop some form of strategic planning. This has been tried (in different ways) by Australia, Canada, Finland, New Zealand, and the UK. The New Zealand system of Strategic Results Areas (SRAs) and Key Results Areas (KRAs) is probably the best known (Boston et al., 1996, pp. 282–3; Matheson, Scanlan, and Tanner, 1997). In Canada, the 1994 Program Review exercise was intended to put an end to the fragmented and volatile policymaking which was seen as a characteristic of the preceding Mulroney administrations (Aucoin and Savoie, 1998). In Finland, a 'Strategy Portfolio' was developed and the government tried to take a strategic overview of government organization (*High Quality Services, Good Governance and a Responsible Civic Society*, 1998*a*, especially pp. 19–22, and the later consultancy report, Bouckaert, Ormond, and Peters, 2000). In the UK, following a period of distaste for central planning and coordination under Mrs Thatcher, the Blair Labour government committed itself to better 'joined-up', horizontally coordinated policymaking. It set up cross-departmental reviews in areas such as criminal justice and services for young children, and conducted a comprehensive review of all government spending (Chancellor of the Exchequer, 1998, especially pp. 33–41; Pollitt, 2003*b*). The four dimensions will now be examined in more detail, in sequence.

Specialization. Alternation between a preference for broad-scope, multi-purpose organizations and, by contrast, a predelection for tight-focus, specialized organizations has been one of the salient features of the history of administrative thought. The idea that specialization is the basis of good administration can trace its supporters back through Adam Smith and Jeremy Bentham. The opposite doctrine—that consolidation is good—has been advanced by, inter alia, Sir Edwin Chadwick and Karl Marx (Hood and Jackson, 1991, pp. 114–16). The pendulum may swing twice within a single generation, witness the shift in UK central government from a preference for large, omnibus central ministries (favoured by both Labour and Conservatives in the late 1960s and early 1970s) to the 1990s' model of downsized and relatively focused ministries surrounded by shoals of specialized executive agencies (Pollitt, 1984; O'Toole and Jordan, 1995) and then back to ideas of 'joined-up government' (Bogdanor, 2005; Office of Public Services Reform, 2002; Prime Minister and Minister for the Cabinet Office, 1999).

During the 1980s the international swing was towards more specialization, most clearly in those countries which were the most influenced by the application of micro-economic reasoning to questions of institutional design. This took place at all levels—micro, meso, and macro. Thus in New Zealand 'the preference for single-purpose organisations and the separation of potentially conflicting functions has led in some cases to a plethora of functionally distinct, but nonetheless quite interdependent, organisations' (Boston et al., 1996, p. 88). But by the late 1990s there was much discussion in New Zealand government circles of the drawbacks of having such a large number of ministries to deal with such a small population. In 2001 a Review of the Centre initiative was launched aimed at strengthening strategic capacity and encouraging a 'whole of government' approach (Bouckaert et al., 2010, pp. 108–13; Gregory, 2006).

New Zealand is probably the clearest, but is not the only case. In the UK the Next Steps programme, launched in 1988, led within ten years to the creation of more than 140 specialized executive agencies (Chancellor of the Duchy of Lancaster, 1997). In France more than 200 *centres de responsabilité* (CDRs) were set up after 1989. In the Netherlands many *Zelfstandige Bestuursorganen* (ZBOs) were created during the 1980s, and since 1991 more than twenty specialized agencies have also appeared (Ministerie van Financiën, 1998)). The Canadians moved more cautiously, but there, too, some 'Special Operating Agencies' (SOAs) were carved out of the federal ministries (the first five appeared in 1989—see Appendix B: Canada country file). In Italy legislative decree number 3,000 of 1999 led to the setting up of a number of *agenzie*, some with their own legal personalities and some as units within ministries. Germany, however, is generally an exception to the trend. There, the main 'receiving positions' for the flow of decentralized functions has been not specialist

agencies (though a few of these have been set up) but rather multi-functional local authorities (Wollmann, 2001). Indeed, the number of federal agencies, which had increased since
the 1960s, actually began to decline during the 1990s (Bach and Jann, 2010).

In sum, one might say that the use of specialized administrative and managerial bodies
appears to have grown in at least ten of our twelve countries—at least up to the early 2000s. It
has also taken place in the EU Commission, although there the main growth perhaps came a
little later (Rambøll/Euréval/Matrix, 2009). The creation of agencies was particularly popular
(Pollitt et al., 2004; Pollitt and Talbot, 2004; Peters and Bouckaert, 2003).

Coordination. In a traditional hierarchy, coordination is ensured by the exercise of
authority from the top. Coherent and consistent orders are passed down the line. Central
staff units, supporting the top administrators, check lower-level proposals to ensure that
they all fit the strategy, that precedents are observed, and that division X does not set out
along a line that contradicts what is being done at division Y. Regulations are issued from
the centre which all must observe. When new situations occur, new regulations are
formulated to deal with them, and these are fitted into the existing body of law and
procedure which guides every part of the organization. Such exercise of hierarchical
authority is, however, not the only way of achieving coordination (Thompson et al.,
1991). Coordination can also be achieved less formally, by voluntary cooperation within
a network. This form of 'solidarity' tends to be more easily achieved where objectives are
widely shared among all network members, communications are easy and full, and the
scale of operations is modest (Pollitt, 2003*a*, chapter 3). A third mode of coordination is
the market mechanism. The miracle of the market is that a price mechanism enables the
activities of many producers/sellers and consumers/buyers to be coordinated without any
central authority ordering it so. The 'hidden hand' of supply and demand does the work,
and with the assistance of modern communications and information technologies, that
work can be accomplished with great speed (think of e-Bay). As we saw in Chapter 1, each
of these three different primary modes of coordination tends to 'lead' one of our three big
models of reform—market mechanisms for the NPM, hierarchy for the NWS, and networks for the NPG (Table 1.3). Note, however, the significant complication that the
purposes of coordination are not necessarily the same in all instances. A market mechanism
may be a brilliant way to coordinate the buyers and sellers of a defined product, but less
good at coordinating, say, food inspectors and food retailers, or sick people and
health care.

Although it is conceded that under certain conditions—most influentially specified in
theoretical terms by Williamson, 1975—hierarchies may be preferable to markets, the
main weight of NPM arguments has been that there are many hitherto unseen opportunities to 'marketize' relationships within the public sector. Indeed, just as certain words
such as 'decentralization' and 'empowerment' have become unassailably positive in their
connotations, 'hierarchy' and 'hierarchical' have become invariably negative—within the
NPM discourse, but also among those who advocate more network-type coordination
(NPG). Even where an indisputably hierarchical relationship remains, there may be an
attempt to package it into a quasi-contract, where the 'agent' ('subordinate', in old-
fashioned hierarchical terms) agrees to supply the 'principal' (superior, boss) with a
defined set of outputs within a fixed time period and at a predetermined cost. In the
countries which were most enthusiastic about NPM there was therefore a wide-scale

substitution of market and quasi-market coordination and contractualization for hierarchical coordination (Lane, 2000, elaborates the theoretical underpinning for this tendency). In New Zealand, for example, the chief executives who run ministries agreed an annual quasi-contract with their minister, promising to deliver specified outputs which were then supposed to lead to the outcomes at which the minister and his/her government were aiming. In most countries contractualization did not infiltrate so high up the chain of minister/mandarin command. Slightly lower down, however, contractualization and marketization have spread widely in Australia, New Zealand, the UK, and the USA, and to a lesser extent in Canada, the Netherlands, and Sweden. It has gone hand-in-hand with many of the measures of specialization referred to in the previous subsection. Thus, for example, where a pre-1991 District Health Authority in the UK might have given an instruction to a local hospital, in the post-1991 'provider market' it contracted for defined services with a legally independent corporation—the NHS trust which the previously 'directly managed' hospital had become. The two parts of the previously hierarchical National Health Service had specialized into a purchaser and a provider, joined by contract. The example of the Canadian Special Operating Agencies provides a further illustration of the general logic:

The SOA is based on the same theoretical models as organisational forms being adopted by other governments and large corporations. The models are more contractual than hierarchical; provide greater autonomy to individual units of the whole; and rely more on market mechanisms then central decisions to allocate resources.   (Auditor General of Canada, 1994, p. 2)

This spread of contractual and quasi-contractual relationships provoked a certain amount of academic concern, both by legal theorists worried about the inadequacies of the relevant areas of administrative law (Harden, 1992; Bouckaert, 2002a) and by public administrationists who pointed to the difficulties of writing 'complete' contracts in conditions where the providers of services have much more information than the purchasers and/or users (Le Grand and Bartlett, 1993).

Not all countries have been as enthusiastic about the potential of market-type mechanisms (MTMs) and contractualism as New Zealand, the UK, and the US. Such devices have been used more sparingly in Germany, France, and even the Nordic countries (see, e.g. Wollmann, 2001). Here limited local experiments have been more characteristic than sweeping marketizations of entire sectors.

Merging departments has for long been one way of improving coordination. Of course, this route rather contradicts the trend to specialization, noted above, but it is a device that has been used by some countries. While New Zealand was allowing the number of its ministries to proliferate, its neighbour, Australia, was reducing its population of departments from twenty-eight to eighteen (1987—see Appendix B). In 1993 Canada followed suit, reducing the number of federal departments from thirty-two to twenty-four (see Appendix B). These initiatives were reminiscent of much earlier (1960s' and early 1970s') attempts by UK governments to rationalize the pattern of ministries by creating large, 'strategic' departments (Pollitt, 1984). In Italy in 2000 a population of more than twenty ministries were merged and slimmed to just a dozen. In the UK the 2000s brought a number of departmental mergers (e.g. the tax department with the customs and excise department) but the overall number of ministries did not change much (White and

Dunleavy, 2010). There was not much change of this kind in the US (where it is anyway more difficult to do), except for the 2002 creation of a huge Department of Homeland Security (see US country file, Appendix B). In France, 2008 witnessed quite large-scale mergers, with the Ministry of Finance merging with the Ministry of Employment and Public Servants to produce a Ministry of the Budget, Public Accounts, and Civil Administration (see France country file, Appendix B).

Another feature in a number of central governments has been an attempt by politicians themselves to exert greater control over the bureaucracy (Peters and Pierre, 2004). This phenomenon will be discussed in more detail in Chapter 6, but it should be noted here as, in effect, another species of coordination effort. It has been particularly noticeable in Australia, New Zealand, the UK, and the USA, but softer echoes have also been heard in Belgium, Finland, the Netherlands, and Sweden. In all these countries the numbers of temporary appointments and political advisers has grown—although the absolute number varies enormously from just a handful to large numbers. Australia offers perhaps the clearest case. As Halligan puts it (1996*b*, p. 82): 'Reform programs [during the Labor governments of 1983–93] were driven by a foremost concern of Labor—political control—which had come to be regarded both as an end in itself and a means to implementing party policy. To achieve this required a redistribution of power between the bureaucracy and the politicians.' To achieve this, the capacity of the Prime Minister's office and cabinet were enhanced, the pattern of ministries was radically altered (1987), ministers made more active use than hitherto of their right to influence senior bureaucratic appointments, and much greater use was made of specially recruited ministerial advisers. This trend was further amplified during the later Howard administration (1996–2007).

To conclude this review of coordination, it should be remarked that, even where traditional hierarchies remained in place, the instruments of hierarchical coordination tended to change. In particular there was a shift from control and coordination by rationing inputs and regulating procedures to a greater emphasis on coordination by targets and output standards. The majority of the twelve countries became active in developing indicator sets for the performance of almost every imaginable public service (for Australia see Department of Finance, 1996; Department of Finance and Administration, 1998*a* and *b*; Development Team, 1998; for Canada, see Mayne, 1996; Treasury Board of Canada, 1996; for the Netherlands, see Leeuw, 1995; Mol, 1995; for the UK, see Carter et al., 1992; Chancellor of the Duchy of Lancaster, 1997; Likierman, 1995; Pollitt, 1986, 1990; for the USA, see Radin, 1998). Some, however, are still at a fairly undeveloped stage. In Germany there has been much more reform at local and provincial (*Länder*) level than in the federal government. Large parts of the Belgian and Italian public sectors appear to have little in the way of output or outcome targets. Equally, the key Kinnock reform documents from the European Commission (2000, 2001) stop well short of providing a set of quantitative criteria by which the success of individual reforms and programmes might later be judged.

Decentralization. Decentralization, ministers and mandarins have said, makes possible more responsive and speedy public services, better attuned to local and/or individual needs. It facilitates 'downsizing' by leading to the elimination of unnecessary layers of middle management. It even produces more contented and stimulated staff, whose jobs have been 'enriched' by taking on devolved responsibilities for financial and personnel management, and by escaping from the overburden of centralized regulation. Given all these benefits it is little wonder that almost every country (and the European Commission) seems to be officially in favour of decentralization (Pollitt, 2005). Like virtue, however, decentralization is differently construed by different parties, and is far easier to preach and praise than to practise. If we are to describe the actual trajectories in a way that carries some real meaning then we have to distinguish between different aspects of decentralization— different alphas—as well as between rhetoric and reality.

One way of deconstructing the concept of decentralization is to recognize that it is a process which contains at least three strategic choices. These are depicted in Table 4.3.

The first choice is therefore between *political* decentralization, where the decentralized authority is transferred to elected political representatives (e.g. when central government decentralizes a power to local government) and *administrative* decentralization, where authority is passed to an appointed body such as a UK Urban Development Corporation or a Swedish agency. The second choice is between transferring authority to another body which is selected by *competitive* means (e.g. through competitive tendering for a local authority refuse collection service), and transferring authority by *non-competitive* means (e.g. where a UK Health Authority transferred some of its authority to an NHS provider trust). A third choice is between *internal* decentralization (where the act of transfer takes place 'within the walls' of an existing organization) and *external* decentralization, where the authority is transferred to a separate, external body (which might be an existing one or a new, specially created one). When authority to spend up to $X without seeking permission is delegated from the Principal Finance Officer to senior line managers, that is internal decentralization. When authority was transferred from a UK local education authority to a grant-maintained school under Mr Major's Conservative government, that was external delegation (Pollitt, Birchall, and Putman, 1998).

The balance between these different forms of decentralization has been rather different in different countries. Once more, different countries have *started* from very different positions. Thus, for example, central governments in France, Sweden, Finland, and the UK, have each praised the virtues of decentralization, but in the early 1980s, France and the UK were relatively centralized countries, while the two Nordic states were both already extensively decentralized (see Chapter 3 and Appendix B). Germany had been very decentralized since the Second World War, at least by Franco-British standards (Schröter and Wollmann, 1997; Wollmann, 2001). Taking this into account, we can say that administrative decentralization has been the preferred form in New Zealand, while political decentralization has been the dominant type in Belgium, Finland, Germany, France, and Sweden. Few new powers have been given to local governments in New Zealand and the UK. In each case decentralization has transferred authority to a range of specialized administrative bodies. However, the UK did experience a very significant act of political decentralization when the Blair administration created elected assemblies for Scotland and Wales (see UK country file, Appendix B). In France probably the most significant single reform of the last three decades was the decentralization to local and regional *elected* authorities carried out by the Mitterand Presidency and the socialist government from 1982 (see Appendix B, France, and de Montricher, 1996), though various forms of administrative decentralization have continued to be announced ever since. In Germany, it is local governments which have probably gained

Table 4.3 Strategic choices in decentralization

Either	Or
Political decentralization	Administrative decentralization
Competitive decentralization	Non-competitive decentralization
Internal decentralization	External decentralization (devolution)

most from the delegation of functions by higher levels in the three-tier system. In Finland and Sweden there has been both political and administrative decentralization, but the transfer of responsibilities to the municipalities and counties has been a central plank of their respective reform programmes. In Italy, one of the consequences of the political crisis of the early 1990s was a marked swing towards decentralization (*decentramento*), both of a political and of an administrative kind. Meanwhile, in Belgium, the political tensions between the Flemish and Walloon communities has led to an increasing delegation of federal powers to the sub-federal level (see Belgium country file, Appendix B).

Turning to the distinction between competitive and non-competitive decentralization, we see a roughly similar pattern. The competitive approach was prominent in Australia, New Zealand, and the UK, but much less so in the central or northern European countries. The USA has certainly been enthusiastic about contracting out (but in a sense had less to commercialize, at least at the federal level). Perhaps the extreme case was the much criticized contracting out of many military and security activities during the Iraq war (Scahill, 2007). Canada (again at the federal level) was generally somewhat more cautious. This, of course, follows from the pattern of enthusiasm and caution over the use of MTMs, as discussed above.

As for the internal/external distinction, it is safe to say that all countries practised both types to some extent, but that the NPM countries have probably undertaken more *external* decentralization, because they have been the ones who have been keenest to create new, autonomous, and specialized bodies, and then devolve powers to them. France has also been fertile in setting up new subnational authorities, in line with the government's wider strategy of political and administrative decentralization, and has also continued, over the years, to create many more or less autonomous *établissements publiques*. The picture in the Netherlands is complicated. The creation of ZBOs and departmental agencies can be taken as evidence of external decentralization by central departments. On the other hand, during the 1980s and 1990s, '[S]pending departments often held out resolutely (and with success) against the transfer of powers to provinces and municipalities' (Derksen and Korsten, 1995, p. 83). At a detailed level one can trace how the concept of a decentralized executive agency, imported from the UK, was in Dutch central government successively 'translated' into something less radical and more narrowly focused on financial flexibility (Smullen, 2003). Other countries (e.g. the Nordics) have also practised devolution, but have tended to rely more on existing local governments as the recipients of new responsibilities (Micheletti, 2000). There has been some divergence between Finland and Sweden, however, with respect to central agencies. Whereas, during the mid 1990s, the Finns downsized the numbers and functions of their central agencies, the Swedish agencies remain extremely powerful and, in many cases, have received even greater devolved power from their ministries than hitherto (OECD, 1998; Molander, Nilson, and Schick 2002).

It would, however, be quite misleading to suggest that there was a global rush towards decentralization, with the only differences between countries being which types of decentralization they prefer and how far they have gone. Centralization is also part of the picture: as some authority has been decentralized, simultaneously there have been significant instances of a tightening of central control and oversight. One fairly prominent case has been the way in which pressures on public spending have strengthened the hands of treasuries and central finance ministries in a number of countries. For example, there is a general perception among officials that economic constraints have reinforced the dominance over other ministries of the Finnish Ministry of Finance and the New Zealand and UK Treasuries. Certainly since the advent of the 2008 GEC, finance ministries have gained influence in many countries. Furthermore, centralization has not been exclusively a matter of finance. There are countless instances, especially perhaps in the NPM countries, of central authorities using performance indicator systems or standard setting, to reassert control over lower tiers or local units. In the UK, central government forced national 'league tables' on every school and hospital, and from 1988 for the first time imposed an (increasingly detailed) national educational curriculum on all state schools. Under Mr Blair's New Labour administration the intensity of central target-setting and monitoring actually increased (Barber, 2007). In the EU there have been examples where the 'harmonization' of some product or rule or procedure across Europe has resulted in a *de facto* centralization on the Commission in Brussels. Furthermore the administrative reforms of the Prodi Commission in some ways decentralized 'horizontal' functions to the Directorates General, only to re-articulate them in a particularly centralized and bureaucratic fashion within each individual DG. Thus the idea that everything is travelling in the direction of decentralization (still more 'freedom') is, to say the least, over-simple.

Scale. Obviously, scale is intimately connected with some of the other dimensions of organization discussed above. In addition to the general pressure for 'downsizing' which arrives from the savings objective, the trends towards specialization and decentralization also indicate reductions in the average size of many public sector organizations. The ideal public sector agency, as envisaged by the enthusiasts and visionaries of the NPM and reinventing government movements, will be 'flat', flexible, specialized ('focused'), and decentralized, and therefore very probably quite *small*. These approaches to reform include a deep doctrinal suspicion of large central bureaucracies. Such organizations represent (as we will see in subsequent chapters) the 'old world' from which many NPM reformers were determined to escape. The US Vice President put it like this:

Big headquarters and big rule books never have kept the government from making big mistakes. In fact, they often kept front-line workers from doing things right. So we asked agencies to cut layers of supervisors, headquarters staff, and other management control jobs by 50%. (Gore, 1996, p. 16)

However, the 'small-is-beautiful' vision is evidently not universally shared—indeed the recent trend of re-asserting coordination (noted at the beginning of Section 4.6, above) has led to a number of mergers and re-absorbtions of arms-length bodies into central departments. For example, while central ministries have been considerably reduced in size in New Zealand and the UK (Boston et al., 1996; HM Treasury, 1994), in Finland the reforms of the 1990s actually led to slight growth in the size of central ministries, as they absorbed some of the functions previously performed by central agencies (Ministry of Finance, 1997). In 2001 the Blair administration merged elements of social security, and employment advice and placements, and work benefits into a giant new Department of Work and Pensions (White and Dunleavy, 2010, pp. 53–9). Faced with the 9/11 terrorist onslaught President G. W. Bush merged twenty-two different organizations into one Department of Homeland Security. In France President Sarkozy also launched ministry mergers.

In general the continental European countries have been less enthusiastic about 'down-sizing' as an overall goal. The EU Commission itself has grown considerably. Between 1977 and 1997 the number of Commission staff grew by 104 per cent, with an increase of 150 per cent in the policymaking 'A' grades. However, it should be noted that the EU budget grew by 206 per cent in real terms over the same period, and, since it is widely acknowledged that the tasks of the Commission expanded rapidly during the 1980s, it can be argued that the extra staff were needed to cope with new responsibilities. Nevertheless, the organizational development of the Commission has certainly not followed the NPM trend: it has specialized only to a limited extent, created only weak forms of horizontal coordination, did not begin to decentralize in any significant way until right at the end of the 1990s, and has grown in size.

Some of these trends in organizational structures can easily be related to one or more of our three models of reform, but others are more ambiguous in this respect. As indicated above, much of the downsizing and administrative decentralization (and fragmentation) of the 1980s and 1990s was associated with reformers of an NPM persuasion. However, as a knock-on effect, some of the re-centralization and mergers of the 2000s—in those same core NPM countries—have clearly also been in reaction to unwanted consequences from the earlier fragmentation. Overall, therefore, NPM thinking has had a big effect on organizational structures in many countries. NWS thinking probably also had effects, but they were less obvious, at least for Anglophone audiences. This was partly because they lay more in defending existing structures rather than proposing new ones, and also because such activities of preservation and cautious modernization seemed to require less trumpeting than did the self-conscious paradigm-breakers of the core NPM states. Thus NWS states such as Germany or Sweden already enjoyed quite decentralized systems, and were more hesitant and selective about putting basic public services at arms length from democratic local government through either managerial autonomizations or contracting out. Further decentralization certainly occurred, especially in Sweden, but it was mainly within the framework of regional/county/local authorities and not by ejection to new autonomous agencies or to private sector contractors—or certainly not to the same extent as in the UK or the USA. Finally, we may ask whether NPG thinking appears to have influenced trends in organizational restructuring. This is hard to say. To begin with, NPG thinking has only been popular for a decade or so, so we cannot expect to find evidence of its effects in the 1980s or early 1990s. Then there is the point that the precise structural implications of NPG are not terribly clear. That we should expect more net-working and partnerships, and more bodies to ensure consultation and participation—all that is obvious. But what specific changes should we expect in the machinery of central government? The NPG theorists seem to have had little to say about this as yet. One observation would be that the recent moves to amalgamate central ministries and agencies which we have seen, in different ways, in France, New Zealand, the UK, and the USA, probably would not be seen as very NPG-ish. On the contrary, it seems to signal a return to hierarchical control by ministers and their top officials. Some of the moves towards joined-up government also have this top-down quality, but others are more bottom-up and might command more enthusiasm from NPG advocates (6, 2004; Christensen and Lægried, 2007b). To be a little harsh, one might say that no clear trend towards NPG structures is yet widely observable, not least because, theoretically speaking, it is not yet obvious what such structures would actually look like. The NPG 'movement', thus far, has had more to say about what the *external* relations of government should look like than its *internal* structures.

4.7 **The measurement of performance**

It is clear from the previous subsections that increased measurement of performance has been a central feature of public management reform in many countries. These accounts of financial and personnel management, and organizational restructuring, have already partly dealt with performance measurement, so this section can be correspondingly brief. There are, however, some generic measurement issues which it makes sense to address here.

Performance measurement certainly is not new. Indeed, it is as old as public administration itself. In the latter part of the nineteenth century there were already schemes in place in the UK and the USA for measuring the performance of teachers in state schools. Woodrow Wilson was writing about the need to design an administrative system that would perform well against efficiency criteria, and F. W. Taylor was advocating a generic approach towards measuring the efficiency of workers (Dunsire, 1973). Acknowledging all this, however, does not prevent one from recognizing that interest in measuring public sector activities has blossomed over the last quarter century (Bouckaert and Halligan, 2008; Boyne et al., 2006; Kettl and Kelman, 2007; Moynihan, 2008; Pollitt et al., 2010; Talbot, 2010; Van Dooren et al., 2010). 'Performance remains the mainstream focus of international public management' (Bouckaert and Halligan, 2008, p. 196), and the GEC is likely to make this even more true in the near future. The performance 'movement' has developed along several dimensions:

Measurement is becoming more *extensive*. More levels . . . and more fields . . . are included. Performance measurement is becoming more *intensive* because more management functions are included (not just monitoring but also decision-making, controlling and even providing accountability). Finally, performance measurement becomes more *external*. Its use is not just internal, but also for the members of legislative bodies, and even for the public. (Bouckaert, 1996, p. 234)

It may be useful to look at each of these dimensions in turn. The growing *extent* of performance measurement was best exemplified in the NPM countries, although significant measurement initiatives were also to be found in Canada, France, the Netherlands, the Nordic states, and the USA. We therefore turn to the UK for an assessment of the full extent of the trajectory:

No public sector employee has escaped the ever-extending reach of performance evaluation schemes. The pressure to meet targets or performance standards, whether hospital waiting lists, school exam results, crime clear-up rates or university research ratings—has introduced profound changes in public organisations. As PIs [performance indicators] have become increasingly linked to resource allocation and individual financial rewards, so organisational cultures and individual behaviours have been transformed.   (Carter, 1998, p. 177. This wave of measurement went on to reach even greater heights under the Blair and Brown administrations of 1997–2010—see, e.g. Barber, 2007)

Examples of the spread of performance measurement to new fields can be found in many countries. Often they have been tied in with developments in information technology (e.g. Bellamy and Taylor, 1998, pp. 68–70). In the USA the 1993 Government Performance and Results Act effectively mandated PIs for every federal agency (Radin, 1998). Subsequently, performance measurement seemed to expand in every direction, generating debates in which some American experts saw performance management as *the* wave of the future (Kettl and Kelman, 2007), and others found it critically flawed and liable to lead to perversions (Radin, 2006). In Australia performance measures were widely introduced during the 1980s and the systems were tightened and toughened by the neo-conservative Howard government after 1996 (Department of Finance and Administration, 1998*a*, *b*). In New Zealand the system of Strategic Results Areas and Key Results Areas (mentioned above) required wide-scope PI systems. In the Netherlands during the 1990s a strategy of progressively integrating performance measurement with the budget process has been pursued (Sorber, 1996), and this took a further twist with the introduction of the VBTB budgeting system from 1999. In several countries, initiatives to raise the quality of public services have led directly to a wider scope for performance measurement (e.g. the UK Citizen's Charter from 1991; the French Public Service Charter from 1993; the 1994 Declaration of Service Quality and 1995 Quality of Service Initiative in Canada).

One might suppose that the extension of PI systems would proceed in a rational fashion, with relatively straightforward, tangible services (e.g. refuse collection, the mail) being measured first, and then more individually variable, less concrete services such as health care and education, and finally, perhaps, non-tangible, non-routine services with a high subjective content such as the provision of policy advice or the coordination of different agencies in the pursuit of some general policy goal (Bouckaert and Ulens, 1998). In practice, however, any such logic is hard to find. In the UK, for example, one of the earliest national PI schemes (from 1983) was for the National Health Service (Pollitt, 1986). What is perhaps a clearer pattern is that the powerful have been better able to postpone or deflect the tide of measurement than other groups. Thus, within health services, the activities of nurses and receptionists have been measured far more intensively and openly than the quality of clinical decision-making by doctors, although in a few countries, gradually, the medical citadel is crumbling (Pollitt et al., 2010). In the core NPM countries, at least, the public can read plenty of reports containing measures of the performance of teachers, police, social workers, social security clerks, and specialist agencies, but few, if any, measuring the performance of MPs or ministers (the USA may offer a rare exception to this generalization, at least in respect of the voting and attendance habits of members of Congress and Senate).

Extending PI systems is not only a matter of finding hitherto unmeasured sectors or organizations and subjecting them to 'the treatment'. It is also a question of broadening the scope of measurement in a more analytical sense—of beginning to measure efficiency and effectiveness, not just inputs, processes, and compliance (see Figure 1.2 for a diagrammatic representation of these distinctions). The desire to measure outcomes as well as outputs has been a common theme of debates since the late 1990s, at least in the core NPM countries (Bouckaert and Halligan, 2008). As noted elsewhere, many national audit offices have extended their work beyond questions of regularity and legality, beyond even the hunting-down of waste, to embrace more sophisticated concepts of efficiency, effectiveness, and service quality (Pollitt et al., 1999). This shift of measurement systems beyond the relatively mundane issues of input and process, towards the more politically sensitive and methodologically challenging problems of assessing effectiveness has proved both difficult and controversial. For example, consider the words of a New Zealand minister, reflecting upon the way in which, with what was then one of the world's most sophisticated performance measurement systems, New Zealand public servants nevertheless tended to over-concentrate on outputs (e.g. cases completed) at the expense of the final *outcomes* (e.g. satisfied clients):

One [danger is that] risky, unattractive, but nevertheless important functions might start to fall between the cracks, or that absurd demarcation disputes might arise, of the kind that used to be endemic in the cloth-cap trade unions of old. If 'output fixation' distracts departments from outcomes, and 'contract fixation' encourages them to ignore everything that isn't actually specified, aren't these things very likely to happen?   (East, 1997)

These more ambitious uses of PIs—to assess impacts, guide programmes, or help decide the fate of policies—are perhaps less difficult for the public service cultures of the 'public interest' administrative systems to absorb than for the *Rechtsstaat* systems. The latter are more used to trying to guide administrative behaviour by the formulation of precise laws and regulations, than by giving more discretion and then measuring results (Bouckaert, 1996, pp. 228–9). In general, performance management, although definitely present, has gone less far in countries like France and Germany than it has in Australia, New Zealand, the UK, and the US (Bouckaert and Halligan, 2008).

Thus the NPM countries have been at the forefront of the more *intensive* use of PIs. Over the last twenty years one may discern a trajectory which runs from the use of PIs principally as supplementary or background information towards their use for a variety of management purposes—to inform specific decisions, to compare different organizations or functions (benchmarking), to determine budget allocations, and even as a major input to decisions concerning motivation, career development, and promotion of individuals. An example would be the research quality ratings given to UK university departments on the basis of their published output, research grants, and honours won, PhDs awarded, and other factors. This elaborate national exercise, which has been conducted roughly every four years since the 1980s, now directly and formulaically produces each department's allocation of baseline research funding. Planning to achieve a 'high score' in this assessment has become a core component of the management of most university departments. Similarly, the use of PIs in the UK National Health Service has evolved from unsystemic internal use by health authorities to published national league tables which have serious immediate consequences for low-scoring organizations (Pollitt et al., 2010). In short, the use of PIs, having once been an 'extra' or novelty, has been progressively integrated with other aspects of management. This can significantly sharpen the management of public services and the orientation of those services to their users. On the other hand it can also lead to various pathologies where the activity of measurement itself distorts the administrative process in undesirable ways (Bevan and Hood, 2006; Bouckaert, 1995*b*; de Bruijn, 2002; Pollitt, 2003*a*, chapter 2).

Finally, we turn to the *external* use of performance measurement—not exclusively for internal management purposes, but to inform legislatures, taxpayers, service users, and a variety of other stakeholders. For those who know where to look (and, more importantly, for those who are interested in looking) the official publications of the 2000s contain far more performance information than was available in 1980. Gradually these data sets are being refined so as to reduce the weaknesses and poor presentation of some of their early versions. In the case of the NHS, for example, the first national sets of PIs were unwieldy and unwelcoming, and overwhelmingly concerned process issues such as average lengths of hospital stay. Over the years, however, the presentation and explanation of this information has improved enormously, and, though there are still many possible improvements that can be discussed, at least a number of indicators or proxies for clinical outcomes are now included in the package. In some cases, performance information is given considerable publicity by the mass media (the 'league tables' of English state schools, for example), although in others the 'take-up' of such data by politicians has been disappointing (Bouckaert and Halligan, 2008, p. 201; Johnson and Talbot, 2007; Pollitt, 2006*b*). Some governments and parliaments have begun to take special steps to improve the relevance and accessibility of PI data for politicians (e.g. in the Canadian case, Duhamel, 1996). Finally, it should be noted that during the past decade *international* performance league tables have become a major growth industry, and several of these attract significant publicity in the mass media (e.g. Arndt, 2008; Dixon et al., 2008; Grek, 2008). Examples of this new trend will be discussed in the next chapter.

In the terms of Chapter 1, performance measurement is a tool or dish, not a big model. In fact it connects to more than one of our three main models (see Figure 1.4). It has been a central plank of NPM reforms. But it is also associated with NWS-style modernization efforts. Certainly there are no shortage of PIs in countries like the Netherlands and Sweden (Pollitt, 2006*a*) or France and Italy (Bezes, 2007; Ongaro, 2009). (However, they may not be used in quite the same 'command and control' ways that became prevalent in the UK during the late 1990s and early 2000s—Pollitt, 2006*a*.) A modern professional manager in the NWS mould would expect to use PIs, inter alia, to check that the services the state was delivering were timely and efficient, and that they were generating good levels of satisfaction among the citizens who used them. The role of performance measurement within NPG is less clear. Whilst it is certainly not ruled out, some of the main texts within this stream of thinking scarcely mention it (Klijn and Koppenjan, 1997; Teisman et al., 2009; Osborne, 2010). One sometimes has the impression that the advocates of NPG are reluctant to discuss performance measurement, for at least two reasons. First, they associate it with the enemy—NPM. Second, they do not yet appear to have a strong answer to the difficult question of 'how are we to measure the performance of a network?'

4.8 Transparency and open government

One widespread and noticeable tendency has been the embrace by many countries of concepts of 'transparency' and 'open government'. In 1980 only a few states had Freedom of Information (FoI) legislation—most notably Sweden (since the eighteenth century) and the USA (since 1966). But by 2005, fifty-nine countries had adopted laws of this kind (Roberts, 2006, pp. 14–15). Among them were Australia (1982), Canada (1982), Germany (2005), New Zealand (1982), and the UK (2002). The underlying idea seems to have been that citizens were entitled to see both what their governments had decided and how they were deciding it—that transparency was a fundamental feature of a democracy. This line of reasoning constituted a development of an older, more limited, debate about *accountability* (Pollitt and Hupe, 2011).

Although the rhetoric around transparency and openness may seem to have been principally concerned with rendering *politicians* more visible and accountable, it also held considerable implications for *public managers*. Traditional bureaucracies have long been associated with secrecy, and with the idea that the possession of information is a form of power. Therefore to expect bureaucrats suddenly to become 'transparent' and 'open' was quite a leap. Further, 'An attempt to remove restrictions on access to information is [...] a challenge to social hierarchy within public agencies' (Roberts, 2006, p. 49). Additionally, the development of ICTs meant that public access to documents took on a more immediate and comprehensive form. Were citizens to be allowed to peer into the internal email traffic of a ministry? How fast was this access supposed to be—could Joe Public read today's submissions to the Minister and, if not, why not (Roberts, 2006, pp. 199–230)?

Unsurprisingly, in practice, governments drew new defensive lines to protect their most sensitive forms of decision-making (Roberts, 2006). Certain categories were excluded from most freedom of information provisions (e.g. defence and security). Privacy considerations also pointed to the need for some restrictions (it would be wrong, for example, for the opening up of public records to lead to the personal details of citizens' health or financial circumstances becoming publicly available). Procedures for applying for documents were made more or less elaborate, and this itself prevented instant access. Fees were applied to discourage frivolous requests. Politicians and their officials found new ways (or rediscovered old ways) of having discussions off the official record—without leaving a documentary trail. Privatized and contracted-out services were often deemed to be beyond the reach of FoI legislation. And so on. Furthermore, the pro-transparency effects of more sophisticated ICT systems seem, in some instances at least, to have been offset by a slackening of the traditional bureaucratic punctiliousness in record-keeping—especially in the more fragmented, high NPM regimes (Pollitt, 2009*a*; Weller, 2002). The new Public–Private Partnerships sometimes found themselves working more to the confidentiality norms of their private, corporate partners than to the higher standards of public accountability. Yet despite all these qualifications, the 'transparency movement' has made a real change to the daily lives of many public officials. Even the 'Eurocrats' have to reckon with the fact that, sooner or later, what they write or say at meetings may well become 'public' (Regulation, 2001). We may also note that the most intensive use of FoI provisions nearly always comes not from individual citizens, heroically holding their public authorities to account, but from corporate interests (looking for technical or commercial information), or from lobby groups and journalists, looking for a story. Humble citizens, on the whole, made little use of FoI, so its proponents' claims it would increase citizen participation and trust have thus far found little evidence to support them (Worthy, 2010).

Interestingly, transparency is *not* something which seems to fit neatly into some of the groupings which we have found are important for other aspects of reform. Thus we cannot say, for example, that the core NPM states were way ahead (or behind) in the transparency stakes. In fact the leading countries come from rather different categories—Sweden and the USA. The UK FoI legislation was rather late in coming and turned out to be quite restricted in practice, whereas the consensual Dutch, for example, were more open. It could be argued that transparency should be something especially associated with the NPG. After all, the ideal from an NPG perspective might be a horizontal network of mutually interdependent actors, freely exchanging information, open to new members, and informing and consulting each other on all important moves. It sounds much more open than a traditional, secretive, bureaucratic hierarchy. Yet it is evident that there are often considerable practical difficulties standing in the way of any such vision being realized. One is that partnerships with private sector companies often mean that different actors in networks operate to different standards of transparency—the private companies claim large areas as 'commercial-in-confidence'. Even non-profit organizations from the civil society sector may not relish being asked to meet the same standards of disclosure as a government ministry or public agency.

4.9 Modes of implementation

In this subsection we move from the 'what' of reform to the 'how'. This poses an immediate problem. It is usually harder for academics to obtain systematic information about *how* reforms are being put into practice than about what the reforms are. Governments are frequently keen to announce what they are going to do but are understandably less energetic in offering a blow-by-blow account of how things are going. Some aspects of implementation are particularly hard to research and write about: it is only rarely that we get scientific accounts of the strengths and weaknesses of individual leaders and managers, of the resentments and conflicts which reforms so easily stimulate, of the compromises and threats by which these are often settled, and so on (though journalistic treatments are more common). There is plenty of circumstantial evidence to indicate that such factors can be influential in determining the success or failure of some innovations, but these things can rarely be subject to rigorous testing (although see Kelman, 2005).

What can be seen from the outside is the broad direction and energy of implementation that seems to be characteristic of a particular government during a particular period. Even this is partly impressionistic, but, pending more systematic comparative evidence, is worth recording nonetheless. Here we will quickly review three aspects:

- the extent to which reform has been a *top-down or bottom-up* exercise
- the extent to which *new organizations and structures* have been created specifically to advance reform (the alternative being the pursuit of reform through existing structures)
- the *intensity* of reform, that is, have governments barged ahead, trampling opposition underfoot, or have they tiptoed delicately, consulting and cooperating with the other stakeholders (such as public service unions) as they go?

The distinction between top-down and bottom-up reforms has itself to be used with some caution. These are not two separate categories but poles on a spectrum which passes through 'top-down-guided bottom-up' and even 'middle outwards'. So there are more intermediate cases than pure polar examples. Furthermore, since our focus is principally on central governments, it must be acknowledged that what constitutes the 'bottom' of central government (let alone the EU Commission) may still be far from the street.

Bearing these caveats in mind, we can go straight to a major generalization about implementation. It is that *all three aspects have in practice gone hand in hand*, that is, those countries which have employed more top-down strategies also tend to have created more new institutions *and* to have pushed on with reform at a more intense pace. Furthermore *the core NPM countries again stand out as a separate group*—it is they, more than Germany and France, more than the consensual Dutch and the Nordics, more even than the voluble Americans or the somewhat quieter Canadians, who have driven reforms from the top, with relentless speed, throwing up all manner of new organizations—and new *types* of organization—as they have rushed onward. The range of implementation styles therefore matches very well the characteristics of politico-administrative regimes which were identified in the previous chapter.

There is space here only to offer brief illustrations of these generalizations, although evidence for them continues to accumulate throughout the remainder of the book. One way of doing this would be to compare the reform process in, say, Finland, Germany, and the UK (i.e. an active modernizer of a roughly NWS-ish character, a country that has been fairly conservative with respect to management reform, and an 'NPM-enthusiast')

In Finland, considerable reforms have been implemented, and the numbers of civil servants has been markedly reduced, but this has been done in a low-key way and at a relatively leisurely pace. Furthermore, high levels of continuity have been maintained despite the existence of five different coalition governments over the relevant period. The reform programme that was launched in 1987/8 was still being 'rolled out' twelve years later (although by then there were naturally new items on the agenda as well). It was conceived and coordinated mainly by the Ministry of Finance and, in that sense, was fairly 'top down'. It was of broad scope, affecting all or most of the central government, but could not directly apply to the municipalities, which enjoyed the constitutional autonomy which allowed them to decide on their own reforms. A good example of a central government reform would be results-oriented budgeting, one key element of the broader programme. It began with a small number of voluntary pilot projects from 1988, and then developed into a government decision to extend the system to all ministries and their agencies. The target was to have the system fully in place by the beginning of 1995—seven years after the launch. On the organizational dimension, new forms of state-owned company were a significant innovation, and the system of central agencies was extensively remodelled during the mid 1990s, but the ministries themselves remained largely undisturbed. Personnel reforms were placed on the statute book, but came into use only slowly and on a limited scale. The Finns paid close attention to reforms throughout the OECD world, and were active members of PUMA and other international bodies, but they imported reform ideas cautiously and selectively, adapting them to fit the Finnish politico-administrative system. Privatization and quasi-market mechanisms were elements of the NPM package that the Finns treated with considerable reserve. There was no 'rush to the market', and no large political constituency for the idea that the market was automatically superior to the 'nanny state' (Ministry of Finance, 1997; Pollitt et al., 1997). The shift from a Social Democrat-led coalition (1995–2003) to a Centre Party-led coalition (2003 onwards) did not mean any great change in modes of implementation.

The federal German government was more conservative than its Finnish counterpart. There was no broad programme of management reform at the federal level (though there was considerable activity in a number of municipalities—see Appendix B). The main laws governing the civil service were not changed. No flocks of new organizations were created. There was no drastic downsizing. German activity at PUMA and in other international *fora* was modest in terms of active participation in the global debate about management reform. Many of the leading German academics appeared to be lukewarm or actively hostile to NPM thinking (König, 1996; Derlien, 1998). When faced with the huge administrative challenge of reunification, the government decided not to innovate, but to transplant virtually the whole of the existing system in West Germany to the former East Germany—to create what was, in effect, a new Weberian state out of a defunct Communist one. Overall there was plenty of modernization in Germany, but it took place mainly at local and provincial levels, and it proceeded in an incremental fashion, with many local variations (König and Siedentopf, 2001; Wollmann, 2001). Implementation at federal level tends to proceed by way of pilots or programmes within one or two ministries, rather than by 'fanfare' changes right across the federal government (Bach and Jann, 2010).

The implementation process in the UK was more hectic, harsh, and sweeping than in either Finland or Germany (and it began in 1979, almost a decade earlier than in Finland). Wave after wave of broad-scope reform followed each other, often to the accompaniment of assertively doctrinaire statements by ministers. Most change was decidedly top-down. In central government Rayner Scrutinies (1979) were followed by the Financial Management Initiative (1982), the Next Steps Programme (1988), the Citizen's Charter (1991), the Private Finance Initiative, the downsizing of a number of ministries (1994–7), the introduction of accruals accounting right across central government, and various other new systems. Extensive personnel reforms led to wider application of individual contracts for senior public officials, extensive use of performance-related pay and the decentralization of most personnel authorities to individual ministries and agencies. Central government also drove radical reforms in subnational and local government, often in a directive manner that would have been impossible in either Finland or Germany. MTMs were imposed on the National Health Service, education, and community care. Many new types of organization were created, including urban development corporations, city technology colleges, grant-maintained schools, an Audit Commission, NHS trusts, various types of public housing agency, and so on. Nor did the advent, after eighteen years in opposition, of a Labour government (1997) lead to any slackening of the pace of change. On the contrary, if anything the catalogue of restructurings, realignments, and re-badgings intensified (Office of Public Services Reform, 2002; Pollitt, 2007; Prime Minister and Minister for the Cabinet Office, 1999). Furthermore, the mood of this was often combative. A good flavour of the Blair reform process can be had from the book *Instruction to Deliver*, an account by the head of the Prime Minister's Delivery Unit (Barber, 2007). He refers to 'the danger of underestimating the extraordinary deadweight force of institutional inertia' (p. 72), to the fact that 'the plans that were returned to us from the departments... varied from the barely adequate to the absolutely dreadful' (p. 85), and asserts that 'Bold, sustained leadership is a prerequisite for transformation; professions, left to themselves rarely advocate more than incremental change' (p. 144). Barber makes it clear that his favourite reading consisted of upbeat generic management texts by American business school professors.

This sense of urgency and top-down pressure was not confined to the New Labour government of 1997–2010. It characterized a wide range of sectoral reform polices over a long period. Thus, for example, a recent comparative study of policymaking in the police and hospital sectors, in England and Belgium, 1965–2005, found a consistent difference in terms of the speed and scope of management reforms (Pollitt and Bouckaert, 2009). Throughout these four decades there had been more change, and more radical change in England. An American scholar summed matters up well when he wrote 'the kind of changes brought about by Mrs Thatcher and Mr Blair... are unthinkable in the United States. They are, as well, unthinkable on the Continent' (Lynn, 2006, p. 120).

At first sight our three big models—NPM, NWS, and NPG—may appear to be about content/substance rather than modes of implementation. However, a little further thought shows that they have, at the very least, some implications for implementation. That is because each (Table 1.3) adopts a particular dominant (though not exclusive) mode of coordination. Logically, therefore, one might suppose that these modes of coordination would also be the prime ways in which supporters of these models would try to get their distinctive types of reform put into action. In which case we could expect to see NPM reforms implemented through market-type mechanisms, NWS reforms implemented through hierarchies, and NPG reforms being negotiated through networks. Unfortunately, the historical record suggests that there has been no such neat correspondence. Some of the biggest NPM reforms (such as the introduction of a quasi market within the UK National Health Service from 1989) were implemented by a fierce use of hierarchical authority, beating down opposition and criticism. Hierarchical authority has also often been used to make NPG partnerships or NPM contracting out mandatory. Major reforms such as the French LOLF or the US NPR or the radical New Zealand changes of the 1980s have all been founded on statutory authority, with new laws being pushed through parliaments by executive governments. Indeed, it seems that few of the most significant reforms covered by this book have been implemented without at least a dose of hierarchical authority to speed them on their way. (One is reminded of Adam Smith here—it is sometimes forgotten that he saw quite clearly that competitive markets required active maintenance by government authority if they were to survive and not degenerate into cartels.) So, although we may profitably discuss alternative coordinating mechanisms for the day-to-day management of public services, we should also remember that our chosen field—structural and procedural changes in central government—lies close to political and legislative power. This means that it is frequently conflictual and that, in consequence, the implementation of reforms very often requires a measure of power and authority to get them off the ground. Insofar as any of the three models fails to allow for that, they will remain inadequate or incomplete guides to the actual business of reform.

4.10 Summary: multiple omegas, multiple trajectories, and unforeseen developments?

In Chapter 1 the questions was first posed as to whether all twelve states were following one, basically similar route (first mapped out by the Anglo-American countries), or whether, at the other extreme, there was no discernible pattern to the multiplicity of reforms—just a national and international game of reform ad hockery? On the basis of the evidence developed above—and set out at greater length in Appendix B—what can now be said in response to this question?

A first, perhaps rather obvious, observation is that the story as told here lies somewhere between the two extremes. There is more than one route but, on the other hand, the picture is not chaotic. Some trends and partial patterns seem to stand out rather clearly. The points of departure (alphas) were, as the previous chapter made clear, very different from each other (Lynn, 2006).

A second point is that trajectories would be much more likely to converge if every government in every country shared the same omega—the same vision of the desired future arrangements that the reforms were intended to propel that jurisdiction towards. However, it does not seem that there *is* such a universally shared vision. Some seem to have had the relatively modest ambition of 'lightening' the existing bureaucracy, through deregulation and streamlining, and simultaneously saving money by tightening up on budgets and financial management. For most of the 1980s Germany fell into this category—at the federal level, though not locally. So did Italy, as well as the European Commission. One might think of this as an essentially conservative strategy of maintaining as much as possible of the status quo by taking steps to make current structures and practices work better—tightening up rather than fundamentally restructuring.

Other states (or the same states at different periods) have been somewhat more adventurous. They have acknowledged the need for fairly fundamental changes in the way the administrative system was organized. Such changes typically included budget reforms which move towards some form of results or performance budgeting, some loosening of personnel rigidities (but not necessarily the abandonment of the concept of a distinctive career public service), extensive decentralization and devolution of authority from central ministries and agencies, and a strengthened commitment to improving the quality and responsiveness of public services to citizens. Within this group of modernizers there are different emphases as between managerial modernization (concentrating on management systems, tools, and techniques) and participatory modernization (giving greater salience to devolution of authority to subnational governments, and to developing user-responsive, high-quality services, and forms of public participation). We might term the two emphases *Modernizing (managerial)* and *Modernizing (participatory)*. Both fall within the broad model of NWS, first outlined in Chapter 1 (and about which we will be saying more in a moment). The two strands are not directly opposed, or mutually wholly exclusive, but in practice each country in each period seems to be stressing the one side rather than the other. Broadly (and this is *very* broad) one might see something of a north–south difference in continental Europe, with the participatory modernizers tending to be more in the north (Finland, Netherlands, Sweden) and the managerial modernizers being a bit further south (France and, later on, Belgium and Italy).

Further, one might link these shades of difference with deeper cultural orientations—the northerners being more open and egalitarian, the central and southern Europeans more hierarchical and technocratic (Bouckaert, 2007). Within both sub-groups of modernizers, moves to privatize state-owned commercial organizations have been selective and gradual, with intermediate forms such as state-owned enterprises or companies being extensively resorted to before, or instead of, outright privatization. In a way Germany belongs to this group also—as is clear from the many subnational reforms which took place from the mid 1980s onwards. In Germany, however, there was also a striking increase in participation (again at the subnational levels), mainly through the introduction of locally binding referenda, from the early 1990s onwards (Wollmann, 2001). However, our main focus here is on central governments and, at that level, a serious move towards modernization came very late (at the end of Chancellor Kohl's third term) and even then did not make much headway. Thus, for example, the basic official document describing the federal public service in 2009 remained heavily concerned with legal categories and rules, and said remarkably little about specific reforms, other than in the relatively innocuous area of e-government (Federal Ministry of the Interior, 2009).

A third group also wanted to make substantial—sometimes fundamental—reforms, but held a particular view of what the most successful kind of change was likely to be, namely, the introduction of more competition and MTMs and business-like methods *within* the public sector. They were the core NPM states. These countries favoured quasi-markets, large-scale contracting out and market-testing, contractual appointments and performance pay for civil servants, more people brought in from outside the traditional career pattern and a general reduction of the distinctiveness of the public sector vis-à-vis the private. They were also the most enthusiastic about importing private sector techniques such as accruals accounting, Business Process Re-engineering (BPR), benchmarking, and franchising into the public sector. Australia, New Zealand, and the UK all fit this category, at least for considerable parts of the period under scrutiny. Occasionally the Netherlands,

Finland, and Sweden (the 'northern Europeans') have ventured into this territory, but only selectively, remaining more usually among the modernizers of the previous group.

Finally there is also the omega or possibility of a *minimal state*, where everything that could possibly be privatized is privatized, leaving only a 'nightwatchman' administrative apparatus, performing core functions that the private sector is quite unable or unwilling to perform. Massive privatization and wholesale downsizing of public sector organizations would be key features of this approach. None of our twelve countries has consistently adopted this minimizing position, which has existed in full-blown form only in the tracts of right-wing politicians and theorists. Rhetorical empathy for such minimalism had been found on the lips of President Reagan, but there the gap between practice and vision was particularly wide. More generally, the USA remains difficult to classify: there have been strong elements of modernization, but also a considerable thrust towards marketization. It is certainly not Weberian, but at the same time it is, in part, highly legalistic and sometimes very bureaucratic.

Canada is also rather an 'awkward customer' from the point of view of our typologies, since during the 1980s and early 1990s it shared much of the marketizing rhetoric of Thatcher and Reagan, but did not in fact go far in implementing those ideas. Whilst the culture is not of a strong central state like France, it has clung to the tradition of a fairly stable and neutral senior civil service, unlike the American 'spoils' system. One might say that it was in the NPM camp as far as its openness to Anglophone marketizing ideas was concerned, but that its federal divisions, and the continuing anchor of a non-partisan central civil service have helped to moderate the scope and pace of change, and to preserve considerable elements of modernization.

Thus there *is*, in our view, a pattern. We might say that there are two obvious groupings, and then a few 'hybrid' or 'hard-to-classify' cases (although these are important exceptions). The first, and best-known grouping is that of the NPM marketizers—Australia, New Zealand, the UK and, in words if not always in deeds, the USA (though in that case we should repeat that more radical examples of NPM can easily be found at the subnational level rather than the federal level). We call this the *core NPM group*—they all see a large role for private sector forms and techniques in the process of restructuring the public sector. The second grouping are the continental European modernizers—Finland, France, the Netherlands, Italy, and Sweden (and Belgium and Germany, if one goes below the federal level). They continue to place greater emphasis on the state as *the* irreplaceable integrative force in society, with a legal personality and operative value system that cannot be reduced to the private sector discourse of efficiency, competitiveness, and consumer satisfaction. They thus continue, in modern form, their nineteenth- and twentieth-century traditions of strong statehood and a high status for the top, career civil servants. Of course, the pace and precise mixture of change has differed between members of this modernizing group. Reform has come later and more gradually to the 'central Europeans'—Belgium and Germany—than to the 'northern Europeans'—Finland, the Netherlands and Sweden. France has matched the pace of the northern group, but for long was more resistant to marketizing ideas, and to much of the Anglophone rhetoric around NPM. Since 2000, however, and particularly since Sarkozy took on the Presidency in 2007, it looks as though NPM-type ideas are gaining a somewhat firmer foothold at the heart of the French administration (see France country file, Appendix B). Italy has been quite volatile on the surface—especially in the mid 1990s—but simultaneously exhibits some deeper cultural and organizational continuities.

A further distinction is that the 'northerners' have given their modernization efforts a stronger citizen-oriented, participatory flavour than the central Europeans. Nevertheless, when compared with the core NPM group, we can say that the continental Europeans as a group—north and south—have shared a more positive attitude towards the future role of the state and a less sweepingly enthusiastic attitude towards the potential contribution of the private sector within the public realm (Lynn, 2006; Ongaro, 2009; Pollitt et al., 2007).

4.11 Back to the models: the Neo-Weberian State (NWS)

The NPM group of states are well known in the Anglophone literature, and there is a huge literature discussing the NPM model (e.g. Boston et al., 1996; Christensen and Lægreid, 2001; Hood, 1996; Kettl, 2000; Lane, 2000; Pollitt, 1995, 2003a). The second group—the continental modernizers—are much less well advertised, and are sometimes portrayed simply as laggards or faint-hearts, who have been slow to climb aboard the NPM train. There is something of this to Gualmini's interesting account of reforms in Europe and the USA (we would take issue with some of her distinctions and explanations, but her basic 'ranking' is not dissimilar to our own—Gualmini, 2008). Our interpretation, however, is much more positive. We believe that what we see in the continental European states is a distinctive reform model, one which we decided to call the *Neo-Weberian State (NWS)*. This was briefly introduced in Chapter 1, but now we have looked at some of the trajectories and examples, it may be time to spell out this model in rather more detail. Compared with its much better-known cousin, the NPM, we see the NWS as bearing the following emphases:

'WEBERIAN' ELEMENTS

- Reaffirmation of the role of the state as the main facilitator of solutions to the new problems of globalization, technological change, shifting demographics, and environmental threat
- Reaffirmation of the role of representative democracy (central, regional, and local) as the legitimating element within the state apparatus
- Reaffirmation of the role of administrative law—suitably modernized—in preserving the basic principles pertaining to the citizen–state relationship, including equality before the law, privacy, legal security, and the availability of specialized legal scrutiny of state actions
- Preservation of the idea of a public service with a distinctive status, culture, and—to some extent, though perhaps not as much as in the past—terms and conditions

'NEO' ELEMENTS

- Shift from an internal orientation towards bureaucratic rule-following towards an external orientation towards meeting citizens' needs and wishes. The primary route to achieving this is not the employment of market mechanisms (although they may occasionally come in handy) but the creation of a professional culture of quality and service

- Supplementation (not replacement) of the role of representative democracy by a range of devices for consultation with, and the direct representation of, citizens' views (this aspect being more visible in the northern European states and Germany at the local level than in Belgium, France, or Italy)

- In the management of resources within government, a modernization of the relevant laws to encourage a greater orientation on the achievement of results, rather than merely the correct following of procedure. This is expressed partly in a shift in the balance from ex-ante to ex-post controls, but not a complete abandonment of the former. It may also take the form of a degree of performance management (see Section 4.4, above)

- A professionalization of the public service, so that the 'bureaucrat' becomes not simply an expert in the law relevant to his or her sphere of activity, but also a professional manager, oriented to meeting the needs of his/her citizen/users.

When we introduced this NWS model in the previous edition of this book, it created a small academic stir. All sorts of extensions and interpretations of the concept began to be aired (see, e.g. the special issue of *The NISPAcee Journal of Public Administration and Policy*, 2008). For example, Eastern European scholars began to debate how far the NWS could serve as a model for the reconstruction of their post-Communist administrations. Regrettably, we cannot pursue all these interesting directions here. What we can do, however, is to try to clarify what we mean and what we don't mean in our deployment of the NWS model. It arose as a way of trying to identify some rather general common denominators that we thought we saw in the reform records of the six continental European states covered by this book, as compared with the core NPM states of Australia, New Zealand, the UK, and the USA. So it was originally intended primarily as a summary description, not a theory, and not a normative vision or goal either. However, some other commentators have subsequently used it as a normative vision, and so in this third edition we too have allowed it something of that quality. In this mode, like NPM and NPG, NWS serves as an omega. It is a vision of a modernized, efficient, citizen-friendly state apparatus. Further, it is *not* correct to identify NWS (as one or two commentators have done) as 'Weber plus NPM'. Careful reading of the 'neo' elements will show that they do not add up to the familiar NPM recipe of disaggregation plus competition plus incentivization (Dunleavy et al., 2006*a*, pp. 97–102).

Subsequently Lynn (2008), among others, has pointed out that, before it can do much more explanatory work, the NWS classification needs to be connected with some kind of theoretical framework. Were its elements (as spelled out above) dependent or independent variables? If NWS was an approximately accurate portrayal of differences between certain continental European states and the core NPM states, then why did these differences arise? These are excellent points, but, again, we cannot go far with them here. We hope it will suffice if we offer a general indication of the line of our response. It would be that the NWS—insofar as it captures a set of real differences—represents a particular instance of path dependency. In this case the path is one where the image of a strong state that is well placed to help its citizens can still be used to generate positive political returns (legitimacy). One could say, therefore, that the general idea of an NWS had been constructed as part of a political strategy responding to globalization and party political de-alignment. In this sense it could be seen as a defensive strategy by previously corporatist regimes (Germany, France, the Netherlands, Sweden) to try to protect the 'European social model' and the 'European administrative space' from the depradations of globalized neo-liberalism. 'Trust us, we can modernize and become both efficient and citizen-friendly' might be the message.

We are also aware that the label itself, 'Neo-Weberian State', may surprise some continental experts. Among German scholars, for example, the modernizers have sometimes characterized themselves as *anti*-Weberian or, at least, as moving away from the *Welt von Max Weber*. We would not disagree with their contention that many of their reforms could be seen as diluting or adding new features to the original Weberian ideal type. Nor would we deny that the conservatives who opposed these modernizers could be seen as wanting to hang on to the old systems and the old values—as defenders of the Weberian heritage. Yet, looked at from the *outside*, what is striking—in comparison with the core NPM states— is how far the underlying assumptions of a positive state, a distinctive public service, and a particular legal order survived as the foundations beneath the various national packages of modernizing reforms. What was going on, it seems, was the modernization of the Weberian tradition, not its outright rejection: a process of addition, not demolition (even if some of the additions fitted on the foundations rather awkwardly). Consider the following summary of French reforms:

In France, the importance of administrative law, the successful experience of nationalized, monopoly, public service providers in the post war period, and the idea of a 'general interest', represented at local level by the prefect, explain many of the distinctive features of the hybrid modernization reforms.   (Guyomarch, 1999, p. 171)

Finally, the radical marketizers and anti-state minimizers, who were quite common in the UK, New Zealand, and the USA, never commanded the same degree of political voice in either the central European states or even the northern group. Their omegas (Figure 4.1) were different. The prophets of the core NPM states envisaged an entrepreneurial, market-oriented society, with a light icing of government on top. The northern variant of the NWS foresaw a citizens' state, with extensive participation facilitated by a modernized system of public law that would guarantee rights and duties. Proponents of the central European variant of the NWS favoured a professional state—modern, efficient and flexible, yet still uniquely identified with the 'higher purposes' of the general interest.

However, the precision of the NWS model—or the NPM or the NPG for that matter— must not be exaggerated. As we said at the beginning of the chapter, omegas are frequently vague, or incomplete, or both. So the pattern is very rough and approximate, for both political and organizational reasons. Politically, governments change and may hold different visions of the future, so that, following elections, certain types of reform are de-emphasized and other types given greater salience. Thus, in the US, the arrival in power of the Clinton Democrats resulted in an end to the neglect and sometimes scorn which the federal civil service had suffered between 1980 and 1992. At least in rhetorical terms, it shifted reform away from a mixture of minimalism (especially under Reagan) and marketization and towards modernization as the dominant *motif*. The election of President George W. Bush inaugurated a swing back to marketizing and contracting out, although 9/11 meant that in some areas (the new Department of Homeland Security) state provision and intervention actually increased.

A second set of political reasons for 'untidiness' is to be found among the pressures represented by external socio-economic forces (Figure 2.1, box A) and by political demands (box E). These can blow chosen trajectories off course. Consider, for example, the balance between three basic types of reform objective. First there is the objective of reducing public expenditure, or, at least, restraining its rate of growth. Second, there is the laudable desire to design better-performing public services—higher quality, greater efficiency, and so on. Third, there is the aim of sharpening accountability and transparency, and thereby—hopefully—enhancing the legitimacy of the administration in the eyes of the public. These three objectives—all of them widely held and proclaimed among our twelve countries—exist in some tension with each other. Trouble for governments may blow up on any of these three fronts at quite short notice. An economic crisis (the GEC of 2008) heightens the need for economies and cuts. Revelations of low standards in, say, nursing homes or public transport, may lead to strident and popular calls for something to be done. The discovery of cases of corruption or gross waste or concealment of important decisions may fuel calls for greater transparency and stricter accountability procedures (as happened with the European Commission crisis in 1999). When one or more such events occur political leaders and their senior officials have, temporarily at least, to alter the balance of their efforts. 'Firefighting' may lead to some neglect of longer-term visions. Progress along a particular trajectory, or towards a particular omega, wobbles or halts. In particular, the GEC has clearly led to major reform 'detours' in a number of countries: 'Cutback management . . . brings to the fore the trade-off between short-term goals and long-term goals' (Pandey, 2010, p. 568).

Organizational factors may also intrude to spoil the possibility of any truly neat pattern. There are frequently implementation difficulties, and these can persuade governments to change instruments, or to 'soft pedal' on types of reform about which they were previously very enthusiastic. Mr Major's UK Conservative government soon retreated from the rhetoric of vigorous competition with respect to the NHS provider market, and took steps to see that it was closely managed, in an effort to avoid volatility (Pollitt, Birchall, and Putman, 1998). Following criticism, the Dutch government of the mid 1990s became more cautious about creating highly autonomous ZBOs and tended to favour more controllable departmental agencies instead. In the 1990s M. Jospin's government in France retreated from some of its public service reform proposals when faced with large-scale strikes by resistant trade unions.

More fundamentally, different governments have different *capacities for reform*, according to regime type (as explained in Chapter 3). During the 1980s, for example, the gap between rhetoric and actual implementation was perhaps particularly wide in Canada and the USA. Between 1998 and 2006, a number of reforms were announced in Germany. but in 2008 the view of at least one German scholar was that 'So far, most of the reform programmes consist of rhetoric' (Reichard, 2008, p. 47). During the 1990s one may question the extent of actual reform achievements within the European Commission, despite the impressive-sounding rhetoric of SEM 2000 and MAP 2000 (The Evaluation Partnership, 1999; see also the European Commission file in Appendix B).

4.12 Back to the models: the New Public Governance (NPG)

A final, but important qualification concerning the 'big picture' we are attempting to paint in this chapter is that we do *not* see the history as simply a clash between NPM and NWS. That is both far too simple and much too static. To begin with, there have been many routine reforms in most of our countries that do not particularly fit into *any* of the three big models introduced in Chapter 1—improving emergency answering services, for example, or putting tax forms or birth certificates online. Cumulatively such 'routine' and unremarkable reforms can be very significant, but one of the drawbacks of taking an approach which is structured by big models or theories is that these sorts of changes too easily fall out of the picture.

Additionally, as we remarked in Chapter 1, there are plenty of other suggested models in circulation, any of which can be used as a lens through which to categorize the reforms of the last three decades. More particularly, there is a widespread and somewhat chaotic theoretical debate about what (if anything) has 'succeeded' NPM as a dominant model for the immediate future. We mentioned this in Chapter 1 (Sections 1.8 to 1.10) and we now turn to the idea that could probably be described as the 'leading candidate' to succeed NPM, namely *governance*. In this book we have followed the NPG (Osborne, 2010) as one of our three big models, but it is far from being the only version of governance (Pollitt and Hupe, 2011). So in the remainder of this section we will explore rather further both NPG and another governance model, 'Digital Era Governance' (Dunleavy et al., 2006*b*).

The NPG is presented as 'the shadow of the future'—the next stage after, first, traditional public administration and, then, NPM (Osborne, 2010, p. 6). The NPG paradigm (*sic*) is said to be rooted within network theory. It is worth quoting at length how one of its most vocal advocates defines it:

It posits both a *plural state*, where multiple interdependent actors contribute to the delivery of public services, and a *pluralist state*, where multiple processes inform the policymaking system. Drawing upon open natural systems theory, it is concerned with the institutional and external environmental pressures that enable and constrain public policy implementation and the delivery of public services within such a plural and pluralist system.   (Osborne, 2010, p. 9 – original italics)

For its part, Digital-Era Governance (DEG) is said to be 'now the most general, pervasive, and structurally distinctive influence on how governance arrangements are changing in advanced industrial states' (Dunleavy et al., 2006*b*, p. 479). Whilst any technological determinism is denied, its proponents nevertheless envisage a 'strong, underlying, upward momentum' (p. 490). The key features of DEG are:

- Reintegration: digital technologies facilitate the joining-up of fragmented government (left behind by NPM) and siloed government (left behind by traditional bureaucracies)

- Needs-based holism: radically to simplify the relationship between agencies and their clients, using digital technologies and re-engineering processes to strip out unnecessary steps, repetitions, and duplications

- Digitization: electronic channels replace traditional ones. The agency *becomes* its website.

(Dunleavy et al., 2006*b*, p. 481)

How far can these two governance models be related to the kinds of evidence we have introduced in this chapter, and to the interpretations of it we have presented? Our assessment is: only to a very limited extent, for reasons we will now explain. First, neither NPG nor DEG has been set up as a model to use in *comparative* analysis. On the contrary, as was earlier the case with the NPM (but is not the case for the NWS), they are both basically presented as 'global waves'. There is nevertheless a difference between the two models on this score. Whereas Osborne's book on NPG makes very little reference to the possibility of systematic differences between countries, Dunleavy et al.'s treatment of DEG most certainly does. They see the actual incidence of DEG as being mediated by 'a wide range of cognitive, behavioural, organizational, political, and cultural changes' (2006*b*, p. 468). Thus, although the literature has yet to develop this aspect, the door is open to an examination of how different political systems, institutional structures, cultures, etc., amend, adapt, or delay the DEG trajectory. Perhaps in a few years it will be possible to write a book like this one, examining how far the DEG model has got in different countries and why it has gone further in some than in others. Certainly Dunleavy et al. already envisage a range of possible trajectories, not just one highroad. Furthermore their own analysis of e-government schemes in seven countries already draws out some interesting hypotheses. Among these is the idea that a high NPM orientation towards organizational fragmentation and contracting out, combined with weak government handling of powerful international IT corporations, produces the worst results (as, for example, in the UK), whereas a much more cautious approach to NPM, plus retention of a strong government in-house capacity to deal with IT companies leads to far better outcomes (as in the Netherlands—see Dunleavy et al., 2006*a*). However, at this point in time it is not possible comparatively to apply the DEG model across the broader horizon of public management reform as a whole—it is just too early, and the necessary data has not been assembled. Dunleavy et al. themselves acknowledge that 'Like any other "over the horizon" projection, our predictions may partly misfire' (p. 489).

The NPG shares with DEG the use of the term 'governance', to denote the inclusion within the governing process of other social actors apart from governments themselves. But for our purposes it is different in almost every other way. To begin with, as you can see from the definition given above, NPG is an extremely broad and abstract model. Although it specifies certain features (e.g. resource allocation is to be made through 'networks and relational contracts'), it is largely descriptive and lacking any theoretical 'motor'. It can be hard to decide what is *not* NPG. Indeed, its status as a model is itself ambiguous: 'it is being presented both as a conceptual tool with the potential to assist our understanding of the complexity [of twenty-first-century policy implementation and service delivery] and as a reflection of the reality of the working lives of public managers today' (Osborne, 2010, p. 6). Yet within a page it is also being claimed that 'from being an element within the PA and NPM regimes ... public governance has become a distinctive regime in its own right' (p. 7). Many conceptual schemes are offered, but not much empirical evidence. NPG is therefore still a long way from being an adequate theoretical vehicle for a comparative, empirical analysis such as this one. It is too broad and too general, and gives little clue on why, how, and when specific things are likely to happen. For the moment, at least, it does not add much to the conceptual weaponry we already have in the shape of the analysis of different types of national 'house' in Chapter 3. (Thus, if we wish, we can already discuss better coordination, 'joining-up', contracting, and so on (see 4.6 above) without needing to posit a whole new 'regime' or paradigm.) Nevertheless, there is a great deal of debate around governance at the moment, so we will continue to make references to the NPG as one of our three 'red threads' running through the remaining chapters of the book. Whilst the NPG model may at present appear to be rather vague and idealistic, it is nevertheless focused on some core contemporary features of politics and society (governments sharing power with other social actors in a range of informal ways). It may yet be developed into something more theoretically precise and operational.

4.13 In conclusion

Overall, therefore, our interpretation is that, whilst there has undoubtedly been great diversity, and while many trajectories turn out to be partial or interrupted, there is a rough but discernible longer-term pattern beneath the welter of detail. Whilst this pattern certainly does not mean that each individual reform instrument (performance budgets, contracting out, etc.) can be ascribed exclusively to one single trajectory (still less to one group of countries and not to others) it *does* suggest that there are some usually continuing broad differences between different groups of countries. The trajectories and rhetorics of reform were significantly different as between, first, the Anglo-Australasian-American core NPM enthusiasts; second, the early and participatory modernizers in northern Europe (NWS—modernizing/participatory) and, third, the somewhat later, more managerially oriented modernizers in central Europe and the EU Commission (NWS—modernizers/managerial). It also seems likely that these differences are indeed related to the types of politico-administrative regimes which were analysed in the previous chapter. In terms of trajectories or strategies, not every country has played the NPM game, and certainly not many are doing so now. There is a kind of path dependency, but there is more than one path, and the specific mechanisms that reinforce certain actions and punish others (i.e. the mechanisms which reinforce the path) differ somewhat between majoritarian states and consensual states, between centralized systems and decentralized systems, and between different cultures (Pollitt, 2008, pp. 40–51). The mechanisms are procedural, structural, and cultural—would-be reformers can be rewarded or frustrated by procedural rules, institutional structures, or cultural norms (Pollitt and Bouckaert, 2009, pp. 153–8). They can tackle these with greater or lesser skill, and greater or lesser willpower, but they cannot wish them away. That is why the actual content of the reform (the specifically proposed actions and techniques) is never more than half the story.

There is, of course, another, uncomfortably sharp question, which has been waiting in the wings throughout this chapter. It is whether any or all of these trajectories actually *work*? Can any of these many reformers in many countries realistically claim that their omega has been reached? That is, what have been the *results* of the many efforts at reform? The next chapter wrestles with this by no means straightforward issue.

5 Results: through a glass darkly

You have to have a long-term strategy but unless it delivers short-term results no one will believe you.

(Michael Barber, former Head of Prime Minister Blair's Delivery Unit, 2007)

The performance of public organizations cannot be reduced to a single dimension, and is inescapably contestable.

(Boyne et al., 2006)

5.1 Results: a slippery concept

The question of what has *resulted* from all the many reforms is obviously an absolutely fundamental one. Yet it is not at all simple. The label 'result' can be applied to many different aspects, and may incorporate a variety of concepts. Talk and decisions and even cultural shifts, as well as actual actions, may be considered as important types of 'result' (Brunsson, 1989). Changes in citizen attitudes are another possible result. But if, in opinion surveys, citizens are shown to 'feel' that some service has got better, or worse, is that the final word on the matter, or dare we risk being branded as 'anti-democratic' by suggesting that citizens can sometimes be mistaken? Perhaps instead of popular opinion, we should place our faith in expert evaluations. Yet much seems to depend on who is evaluating what, for whom, and why. The top experts may be able to discriminate between the scientifically first-rate professional evaluation and the only upper-second division evaluation, but most citizens and politicians would be struggling to be sure of the difference. Even if you simply ask the top officials in an organization what they think about a reform they have just been through, these knowledgeable 'insiders' frequently express widely varying opinions of whether it was a success or not (for the case of the Kinnock reforms in the EU Commission, see Ellinas and Suleiman, 2008). A full discussion of 'results', therefore, embraces the wider questions of 'results for whom, defined by whom, against what criteria, and in pursuit of which objectives?' It would be all so much easier if the popular question of 'And what were the actual results?' could just be given a straightforward, concrete answer, but in public management reform, frustratingly perhaps, such straightforwardness is the exception rather than the rule.

It should also be noted that 'results' are closely tied to the concept of 'performance', and performance became one of the core concerns of those advocating the NPM. Performance also outgrew and outlived the NPM, and today remains a central concern for many theorists and practitioners, whether they be sympathetic to, or opposed to, NPM ideas (see, e.g.

Bouckaert and Halligan, 2008; Boyne et al., 2006; Kelman and Kettl, 2007; Moynihan, 2008; Talbot, 2010; Van Dooren and Van de Walle, 2008). Advocates of NWS and NPG trajectories also believe that their models will bring, in some sense, better-performing governance.

The remainder of the chapter is divided into seven main sections, each with a number of subsections:

5.2 The big picture: comparing the performance of governments internationally
5.3 Types of result and challenges to assessing them
5.4 Saving money—economies
5.5 Improving efficiency
5.6 Increasing effectiveness
5.7 Enhancing citizen satisfaction and trust
5.8 Beyond the production model for performance: systems, capacities, orientations, visions
5.9 Conclusions and reflections

We begin with two sections that engage with some of the conceptual and practical problems of assessing results. Thus in Section 5.2 we plunge straight into a particularly striking kind of result—the internationally comparative indicators of 'good governance' which have multiplied in number and increased in prominence over the past decade or so. We look at these both because of their intrinsic interest and because of the ways in which they prompt methodological questions over measurement and interpretation. That leads us straight into a section (5.3) where we enumerate some of the key challenges in defining, measuring, and assessing results. Inter alia this involves distinguishing between a number of different levels at which results can be defined and assessed, and between a number of different dimensions or aspects of performance.

In the following four sections we look at evidence concerning some typical categories of results—saving money (5.4), improving efficiency (5.5), increasing effectiveness (5.6), and enhancing citizen satisfaction and trust (5.7). These are related to the performance framework which was introduced in Chapter 1 (Figure 1.2). After this (5.8) we look at some other conceptions of improvement, which are less related to the idea of government as a producer of goods and services. Finally (5.9) we reflect on what is known and what is not about the results of public management reform.

This is thus a long chapter. We think this is justified because of the centrality of the 'results' issue for most public managers and their governments. One might say that the more educated, sophisticated, and aware citizens become, the less they are likely to be satisfied with their governors offering stirring visions and vague promises of a better tomorrow, and the more likely they are to ask the question, 'Yes, but where are the results?'

5.2 The big picture: comparing the performance of governments internationally

Each year since the late 1990s the World Bank has published a collection of 'Worldwide Governance Indicators' (WGIs), which apparently measure each country's achievements in governing themselves. The WGIs are organized into six main indicators/scores:

- Government effectiveness
- Voice and accountability
- Political stability and the absence of violence
- Regulatory quality
- Rule of law

Obviously these dimensions cover both politics and management (see Figure 1.1), so we will choose here to look more closely at one which seems to have a high management element—government effectiveness. The government effectiveness scores of our twelve countries in the 2009 'edition' of the WGIs are shown in Table 5.1, below.

It is worth interjecting at this point that the WGIs were among a large and growing number of such international indices—more than 400 comparative indices existed by 2007 (Inter-American Development Bank, 2007). We have selected the WGIs here because a) they are among the best known and b) their construction has been extensively discussed, and therefore they provide a useful basis for looking at some of the problems of 'results'. At first sight the WGIs certainly appear formidable: in their 2008 form they included 441 individual variables taken from 35 different sources produced by 33 different organizations (Kaufmann et al., 2009, p. 7).

What do we see in Table 5.1? At first it appears that the majority of scores have declined between 1996 and 2008—that government effectiveness is actually declining. Then there is the obvious 'odd man out'—Italy, which has dramatically lower scores than all the other countries. At the other end of the scale Sweden, by a narrow margin from Finland, takes

Table 5.1 Government effectiveness scores (World Bank Governance Indicators)

Country	1996	2002	2008
Australia	1.66	1.82	1.90
Belgium	2.01	1.99	1.36
Canada	1.93	2.09	1.93
Finland	2.11	2.21	1.95
France	1.79	1.81	1.54
Germany	1.85	1.81	1.85
Italy	0.88	0.93	0.39
Netherlands	2.29	2.09	1.86
New Zealand	2.16	1.81	1.76
Sweden	2.19	2.07	1.99
UK	2.04	1.93	1.74
USA	2.22	1.82	1.65

Source: Kaufmann et al., 2009, pp. 86–8.
Note: Scores range between a theoretical maximum of 2.5 and minimum of −2.5. Thus, for example, in 2008 Somalia scored −2.5.

the prize as the most effectively governed state among our dozen. Exactly where a country ranks in tables like this tends to make the headlines—newspapers and the media like to portray such 'results' as 'rising' or 'falling', and to blame or praise the governments concerned. For example, an analysis of media coverage of the Programme for International Student Assessment (PISA) (another international table, this one concerned with educational performance) concluded that 'most of the [British] media focused on where the UK education system ranked internationally and tended to concentrate on the negative results using populist and catchy sporting equivalences—being "beaten", "slump in the world league", and "failed"' (Grek, 2008, p. 1).

One message from this chapter is that 'results' are very seldom as simple as this. Aggregate indices such as the WGIs in Table 5.1 conceal a multitude of methodological decisions and uncertainties, and are actually rather difficult to interpret. And the media's favoured language of winners and losers is usually unhelpful, and not infrequently actively misleading.

In support of these cautionary words, consider the following issues in relation to the World Bank's government effectiveness scores (Arndt, 2008; Pollitt, 2010b):

1. The measures are not linked to any underlying *theory* of effectiveness. 'A framework is needed before we measure government effectiveness or propose specific models of what government should look like. Given the evidence of multiple states of development, the idea of a one-best way model actually seems very problematic' (Andrews, 2008, p. 379).

2. The World Bank's operational *definition* of 'government effectiveness' (and even more of 'good governance') is woolly and very general. They say it is 'capturing perceptions of the quality of public services and the degree of its independence from political pressures, the quality of policy formulation and implementation, and the credibility of the government's commitment to such policies' (Kaufmann et al., 2009, p. 6). This definition raises as many questions as it answers, for example whose perceptions? What do they mean by quality (a notoriously slippery term)? How can they measure the average 'credibility', when some believe passionately in what a government is trying to do and others are highly sceptical or cynical? In fact the World Bank does not measure these perceptions themselves at all—they take a whole series of measures from a number of other organizations and aggregate them together to form the index.

3. The *actual measures* which go to make the aggregate score are a tremendous mixture with no obvious coherence or logic. They include 'the quality of bureaucracy', 'the quality of public schools', 'the quality of personnel', time spent by senior business managers dealing with government officials, public satisfaction with roads and highways, and a number of other items.

4. The *aggregation procedure* for scaling and weighting all these very different measures so that a single number comes out at the end is complex and debatable.

5. *Changes over time* are not at all easy to interpret. The sources used to compose the aggregate indicators vary somewhat from year to year. A change between, say, 2002 and 2008 may mean that there has been an actual change in effectiveness, but it could also mean a) that there has been a change in perceptions by the people monitored, but that this is a false indicator because there has been no underlying real change or b) that

the ratings of other countries have changed (WGIs are designed so that the global average and standard deviation remain the same, so a change in one country's ratings usually changes all the other countries' ratings) or c) that there has been a change in the number and/or composition of the sources from which the World Bank draws its data. This is one reason why we cannot assume, from Table 5.1, that actual effectiveness has declined in most of the countries shown. Even the World Bank itself recognizes these difficulties (World Bank, 2008, p. 3).

There are other problems. Even if one accepts the government effectiveness indicators at face value, it turns out that the most effective governments exhibit very different patterns of institutions, processes, and practices. When Andrews (2010) examined the high-scoring countries of Australia, Belgium, Canada, Germany, Denmark, Hong Kong, the Netherlands, Singapore, Sweden, the UK, and the USA, he found that 'good governments can look very different' (p. 11) and that, in the area of public financial management at least, several of the key 'best practices' were no more likely to be adopted by governments scoring highly on effectiveness than by governments scoring much further down.

However, even if all these criticisms of the WGIs are accepted as having force, that should not be read as a general rejection of all international performance comparisons. The WGIs are unusual in several respects. First, they are extremely ambitious, aiming to sum up the whole universe of 'good governance' in just six aggregate scores. Second, they are similarly ambitious in the breadth of their coverage—212 countries, including the richest and the poorest, liberal democracies and corrupt dictatorships. Third, they are based on an aggregation of many different data sources, not on data gathered by the World Bank itself for this specific purpose. Many of the other international comparisons are less grandiose/more focused in their aims and methods. One example at the other end of the spectrum might be the OECD's PISA project, an attempt to measure educational proficiency at age 15 across sixty-five countries (OECD, 2007). Here the exercise is confined to a somewhat smaller group (sixty-five) of (mainly) developed countries, and the measures are derived from specially constructed tests, administered in a similar way in each country. The result is a series of performance measures which are highly respected by many (though not all) educational professionals, and which have certainly had effects on educational policy-making in several countries, including Finland and Germany (see Hautamäki et al., 2008). Table 5.2 gives some idea of what these 'results' look like.

Yet even these carefully collected numbers from carefully administered tests have their limitations (see, e.g. Goldstein, 2004). For example, they are frequently treated as though they are a comparative test of the effectiveness of national educational systems. But they are not really well fitted to do that job. First, they are cross-sectional rather than longitudinal and so do not offer an analysis of development over time. Thus a country that started with a very low performance but made huge strides forward would still appear lower down than a country that had initially had an excellent education system but which was gently declining. Furthermore, PISA involves testing students against a test, not against what might happen to be the educational objectives of that particular school system.

Table 5.2 PISA reading scores, 2006

Country	Reading Score	Standard Error
Australia	513	(2.1)
Belgium	501	(3.0)
Canada	527	(2.4)
Finland	547	(2.1)
France	488	(4.1)
Germany	495	(4.4)
Italy	469	(2.4)
Netherlands	507	(2.9)
New Zealand	521	(3.0)
Sweden	507	(3.4)
UK	495	(2.3)
USA	Not shown	
Kyrgystan	285	(3.5)

Source: Extracted from Table 4, OECD, 2007, p. 47.

5.3 Types of result and challenges to assessing them

The examples of the World Bank's WGIs and of PISA lead us into a wider discussion of the difficulties of finding, measuring, and interpreting 'results'. To begin with, one needs to decide what one means by a result. It may be useful to distinguish between four broad levels of results, as follows:

First, *operational results*. This is perhaps the simplest and most concrete sense of 'result'. In principle, operational results are discrete and quantifiable. More outputs are obtained for the same inputs. Without additional expenditure a programme succeeds in reaching a higher percentage of its target population. The police crack down on car theft, and succeed in halving the number of vehicles which are broken into (and so on). Operational results may be found at the micro, meso, and macro scales. Examples might be a local office which provides the same service with one fewer staff (micro), or a government which manages to reduce the overall rate of growth of public expenditure (macro).

Second, there could be improved *processes* of management or decision-making. Related matters (such as health care and social care) are better coordinated. 'One-stop shops'/ 'single window' arrangements are examples of this—the particular decisions taken and the information given are not necessarily any different, but they are all conveniently available in one place. Processes are streamlined (e.g. planning applications are now processed in only 70 per cent of the average time which they used to take). In the language of economics, transaction costs are reduced. Much 're-engineering' is about this kind of improvement. The assumption is normally that process improvements of this type will lead directly to improvements in operational results—that is, to better or more outputs and outcomes. Of course, in practice it is necessary to check that this assumption actually holds—public sector re-engineering projects, for example, do not always produce identifiable effects on final outcomes, or even on outputs.

Changes in process are frequently intended to signal a shift in administrative cultures—indeed they are often made with a definite consciousness of their symbolic impact. A status report on the US National Performance Review (NPR) lists ten pieces of evidence that government is starting to work better:

- Over 90 per cent of National Performance Review recommendations are under way.
- The President has signed twenty-two directives, as well as performance agreements with seven agency heads.
- Over 100 agencies are publishing customer service standards.
- Nine agencies have started major streamlining initiatives.
- Agencies are forming labor-management partnerships with their unions.
- Agencies are slashing red tape.
- The government is buying fewer 'designer' products and doing more common-sense commercial buying.
- Throughout the federal government 135 're-invention laboratories' are fostering innovation.
- The government is shifting billions of dollars in benefits to electronic payments.
- The federal government is changing the way it interacts with state and local governments (National Performance Review, 1994, p. 5).

It is noticeable that these were all process improvements.

Third, a 'result' may take the form of some broad change in the overall *capacity* of the political or administrative system. The pattern of institutions may be redesigned so as to be more flexible, with the intention that this will make the system more resilient in dealing with pressures which are expected to arise in the future. For example, it may be decided that all senior civil service appointments will be competitive and open to any applicant, rather than being confined to those already in the civil service and at the relevant level in the hierarchy. In a way, capacity changes are process improvement writ large. They mean that government organizations are now able to do more things within a given period of time, or can do things better—in a more evidence-based or flexible way.

Fourth, and finally, 'results' may be assessed relative to the degree to which the system has shifted towards some *desired or ideal state*—in the language of Chapter 4, an omega. This is perhaps the most strategic sense of result. It is also the most obviously doctrinal or ideological. If the ideal is very small, 'light' state apparatus, with most activities undertaken within the private, market-oriented sector (as seems implicitly to be the case with some international measures—Van de Walle, 2006), then public management reforms may be judged in terms of how far they have moved the system in the direction of this vision.

It is immediately apparent that the first and second levels are more precise and concrete and—potentially at least—quantifiable, than the third and fourth. The third and fourth are both 'systems-level' kinds of results, and both involve somewhat abstract and intangible changes, including value shifts and cultural transformations. The claim that 'we issued more licenses last year with 10 per cent fewer staff' is a claim about an operational result, and can probably be checked fairly closely. The claim that 'we are working more closely together this year and have the skills and ability to handle bigger crises' (a claim of enhanced capacity) is far more difficult to test.

A moment's thought will also indicate that results—at any level—lead to further results. On level four the 'result' of a determined drive towards minimizing the state/maximizing the market may, for example, be a backlash of voters who wish to safeguard the welfare state and who succeed in electing a different government which then slows or reverses the original strategic direction. On level one a 20 per cent improvement in the productivity of a particular tax collection office in region X may lead top management in the taxation service to launch an investigation as to why the other collection agencies (in regions Y, Z, etc.) are not making similar efficiency gains.

There is one last matter to be attended to before we come to the results themselves. We need to revisit our usage of familiar performance terms such as 'efficiency' and 'effectiveness'. Despite (or perhaps because of) the frequency of their usage, one should not assume that such terms always have the same meaning. Terms such as the famous 'three Es' (economy, efficiency, and effectiveness) are drawn from a generic input/process/output/outcome framework that was introduced in Chapter 1 (Figure 1.2,) and which is very

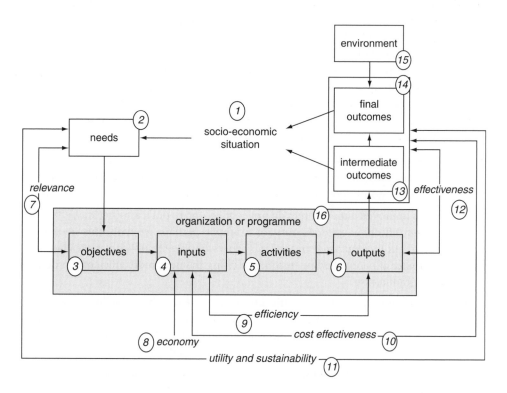

Figure 5.1 Performance: a conceptual framework

widely used in both the study and practice of public management. For convenience, we reproduce it here as Figure 5.1.

This model mainly concerns the first two levels of result discussed above—operational results and process results. The model can itself be applied on various different scales. For example, it can be deployed at the macro scale, taking the entire apparatus of public administration as the unit of analysis—the 'thing' that produces the output. More commonly, however, the input/output model is applied at a meso scale—to programmes (e.g. health care, job creation, road construction) or to individual institutions or organizations (a tax collection agency, a police force). In each of the sections which follow we will try to look at 'results' first at the level of whole countries, then at the level of reform programmes, and finally at the level of individual organizations.

The model assumes that institutions and/or programmes are set up to address some specific socio-economic need(s). They establish *objectives* concerned with these needs, and acquire *inputs* (staff, buildings, resources) with which to conduct activities in pursuit of those objectives. *Processes* are then those activities which take place inside institutions, in order to generate outputs. Processes would thus include, for example, teaching in a school, or recording and labelling within a warehouse. The *outputs* are the products of these processes—what the institution 'delivers' to the outside world (academic qualifications, school reports or, in the warehouse case, issued stock). The outputs then interact with the environment (especially with those individuals and groups at whom they are specifically aimed) leading to intermediate and then final outcomes (e.g. students getting jobs and achieving competence within them, or stock items being used by their purchasers). Ultimately the *value* of both the processes and the outputs rest on the outcomes. Finally, the production model of performance can also be used on a micro scale. Parts or all of it can be applied to the work of individuals, teams, or small groups. In this book, however, we will operate mainly at the macro and meso scales.

Having thus clarified the conceptual vocabulary of results and performance we can quickly point to some very common challenges in identifying results and the reasons for results. These include the following:

1. Policy objectives are expressed in very vague or even contradictory terms, meaning that it is hard to know when outputs and/or outcomes match the intentions. This has been a standard observation in policy studies for forty years or more.

2. Efficiency is improved but outcomes do not change—or, to put it another way, efficiency improves but effectiveness does not. For example, perhaps we write this book more quickly than our previous one, and the publishers are able to publish it more cheaply— yet the number of people buying, reading or citing the new, more efficiently produced book does not increase.

3. A particular performance target is hit, but at the cost of other (usually unmeasured) activities being quietly downgraded and/or neglected (Bevan and Hood, 2006). It is often said that what is measured gets attention, but the supply or organizational attention is limited, so choosing *what* to measure becomes a critical task.

4. Outcomes improve (or deteriorate) but it is not clear that this change is the result of the organization or programme. This is known as the 'attribution problem', meaning that

changes in outcomes may be attributed to the programme/organization, whereas in fact they are caused by something else. A classic case is when the public employment service is blamed because it fills fewer jobs than it did last year. But the fall may be due to worsening macro-economic conditions, over which the public employment service has no control (and for which it has no responsibility). Or there may even be a misunderstanding about the direction of the 'arrow of causation'. Some Swedish studies seemed to show that, whereas some had claimed that certain reforms had led to expenditure savings, it actually seemed more probable that forced expenditure reductions had led to reform (Murray, 1998).

5. There are changes in the way the programme is organized or the results are measured (or both) which means that it becomes impossible precisely to compare the outputs and/or outcomes *before* the programme started with those *after* the programme has had time to take effect. For example, a study of twelve UK schools, hospitals, and public housing organizations which had been given greater decentralized management autonomy was unable to say whether this had produced better results because 'there is little systematic before and after data' (Pollitt et al., 1998, p. 164).

In conclusion, it may be worth emphasizing the point that these multiple difficulties in assessing 'results' mean *both* that failures or weak performances may be missed *and* that successes or significant improvements may go unsung. We should not assume that what we cannot see clearly must be either all bad or all good.

5.4 Saving money—economies

One apparently easily understood result is economy (see Figure 5.1 above)—the saving of inputs (which could be actual cash, or materials used, or staff needed—all of which can be translated into monetary terms). We say 'apparently' because 'savings' is itself a term which is used in a variety of ways. As any experienced budget official knows, a 'saving' may mean any one or more of the following:

1. a reduction of the financial inputs compared with the previous year using the current price basis in each year (i.e. not allowing for inflation);

2. a reduction of the financial inputs compared with the previous year, using the same price base for both years (so that, for example, if the nominal/current cash spend in the previous year was 100 and the nominal/current cash spend this year is 105, but general inflation has been 10 per cent, then this will be counted as a saving, despite the fact that the nominal spend is higher);

3. a reduction in the financial input for year X compared with the previous *forecast* input for year X (such reductions may still leave the inputs higher than they were in the previous year);

4. a reduction in inputs with no reduction of the services provided/activities conducted (i.e. an efficiency gain in terms of Figure 5.1);

5. a reduction in inputs which leads to a reduction in the services provided/activities conducted (which may even mean an efficiency *loss*, depending what the relative proportions of the reductions in inputs and outputs turn out to be);

6. a reduction in unit costs (e.g. the cost per application processed). If activity volumes increase then perfectly genuine savings in unit costs may nevertheless be accompanied by an increase in the budget (because the latter is determined by unit cost × quantity, so the increase in quantity may outweigh the reduction in unit costs);

7. the transfer of an activity from one part of the state to another (e.g. from central government to local government) so that one jurisdiction can show what appears to be a 'saving', though the system as a whole has made no saving;

8. the transfer of an activity out of the state sector altogether (privatization). In this case the government 'saves' money (at least in terms of gross public spending) and also wins a one-off receipt in the form of the sale price. The citizen may or may not benefit. Taxes may go down, or not; the citizen may now have to buy the same service from the private sector at the same or even a higher price; or may benefit from lower prices and higher efficiency—these outcomes all depend on situationally specific factors of markets, regulatory regimes, management skills, and other variables;

9. a purely hypothetical future event (as in 'if we make these changes to our working patterns now then in two years' time we should be able to reduce our overheads by 15 per cent').

Claims that savings have been made should therefore always be subject to further questioning and scrutiny, in order to determine precisely what is meant and what the implications may be for outputs and outcomes. With that caveat in mind we will now look at some of the broad evidence concerning 'savings'.

Despite (or perhaps because of) all the alternative versions of what it means, saving money has certainly been a salient objective for many countries, and a major influence on public management reform—especially since the global economic crisis of 2008, but also long before that. One might remember, for example, the EU's Maastricht 'convergence criteria', which included the standard that public sector deficits must be held below 3 per cent of GDP. These were a major spur to reform in Italy and several other EU member states—and something of a spur to 'creative accountancy' also.

In this and subsequent sections we will begin at the country level, then go to the level of reform programmes, and finally address examples at the level of individual organizations or units.

Table 5.3 shows changes in the ratio of government spending to GDP in the twelve countries between 1980 and 2006. It is immediately apparent that, although the shares go up and down somewhat, the rank order between countries has remained fairly stable over the quarter century covered. There remains, for example, a huge difference between the 'small state' US (consistently below 40 per cent of GDP) and the 'big state' Sweden (usually above 60 per cent, though recently down to 54 per cent). Similarly there is a consistent contrast between 'small state' Australia and 'big state' France.

Table 5.3 General government expenditures as a percentage of GDP (all figures percentages)

Country	1980	1985	1990	1995	2006*
Australia	33.8	38.7	34.8	37.4	34.9
Belgium	59.0	62.5	55.2	52.1	48.4
Canada	40.5	47.1	46.9	48.5	39.3
Finland	36.6	41.6	41.2	61.6	48.9
France	46.1	52.2	49.9	54.4	52.7
Germany	48.5	47.6	46.0	54.8	45.3
Italy	41.7	50.9	53.0	52.5	49.9
Netherlands	57.5	59.7	55.6	56.4	45.6
New Zealand	n.a.	n.a.	n.a.	41.4	39.9
Sweden	61.6	64.7	61.4	65.1	54.3
UK	44.8	46.2	42.1	43.9	44.2
USA	33.7	36.7	36.1	37.0	36.4

Note: The figures for 1980, 1985, and 1990 come from OECD (1992), *OECD Economic Outlook: Historical Statistics, 1960–1990,* Paris, OECD, but the figures for 1995 and 2006 are on a somewhat different basis and come from OECD (2009), *Government at a Glance 2009,* p. 53.

However, here we are looking for evidence of economies. During the most recent period (1995 to 2006) the GDP share has fallen in eleven of our twelve countries—paradoxically rising only in the intensively and repetitively reformed UK! Particularly large falls are visible in Canada, Finland, Germany, the Netherlands, and Sweden. Before jumping to the conclusion that this means public management reforms have been successful in producing savings, however, several qualifications must be made.

First, the pattern between countries does not always fit what one might expect from a crude reading of the record of management reform. For example, Finland and the Netherlands—both consensual, cautiously reforming regimes—achieved large reductions while the UK—a self-styled 'world leader' in reform—was the only country whose public share went up. So there may well be something else behind these aggregates.

Second, the figures tell us little about what kind of 'savings' may have been involved here. In particular they give no clue as to whether reductions in the share of GDP taken by public spending have been achieved with no losses in efficiency, effectiveness, and quality, small losses, or severe deterioration in the overall standards and scope of public services. Neither do they tell us to what extent the 'results' have been gained by transferring large sets of activities to the private sector. In fact there are no good international, comparative data sets to show what in these senses has been the 'price that has been paid' for 'savings'. Indeed, the methodological problems in constructing such a data set are enormous.

A third qualification is that much depends on the state of the economy at the time the measurement is taken. If the economy is depressed, various kinds of social protection expenditures rise and tax revenues fall. The public sector tends to loom large while the private sector contracts or ceases to grow so rapidly—as has happened in 2008–10, after the OECD measurements in Table 5.3 were taken—hence the big deficits with which so

Table 5.4 Employment in general government as a percentage of the labour force (all figures percentages)

Country	1985	1990	1995	2005
Australia	26.9	23.0	13.9	13.6
Belgium	20.4	19.3	16.9	17.1
Canada	20.2	20.3	17.9	17.1
Finland	25.3	23.2	21.0	21.3
France	20.5	20.4	21.6	21.9
Germany	15.5	15.1	12.2	10.4
Italy	15.2	15.6	14.2	14.2
Netherlands	15.1	12.9	13.1	12.8
New Zealand	27.0		20.0	
Sweden	32.7	31.6	29.8	28.3
UK	21.6	19.5	12.9	14.6
USA	14.8	14.9	14.6	14.1

Note: The figures for 1985 and 1990 come from OECD (1992), *OECD Economic Outlook: Historical Statistics, 1960–1990*, Paris, OECD, but the figures for 1995 and 2006 are on a somewhat different basis and come from OECD (2009), *Government at a Glance 2009*, p. 53.

many governments are currently struggling. For this reason the public spending:GDP ratio can change quite rapidly because of general economic conditions, without this implying anything about the underlying state of management reform.

Another common measure of the size of the state has long been the number of staff employed. For comparative purposes this can be expressed as a percentage of the total labour force. Table 5.4 gives this information for the period 1985 to 2005.

Here we see a more mixed pattern than in Table 5.2. As we might expect, the rank order shows Sweden, Finland, and France as large-scale employers throughout the period, and the US as a much smaller-scale employer throughout the period. The dynamics, however, are interesting. Australia, Germany, New Zealand, and the UK all show very substantial reductions in the percentages of their labour forces which were public servants. Of these all but Germany have carried through large-scale programmes of privatization and contracting out during the period in question. This does look like a real shrinkage of the state, although to the extent that public services have been contracted out, the governments are still *paying* for them, even if they are no longer *staffing* those activities. Obviously, like government expenditure as a percentage of GDP these figures are ratios, so much depends on how private sector employment has grown, or decreased. But at least we can say that, as an overall trend, the share in total employment is down (five countries substantially down, six modestly down, and only one slightly up).

Now let us turn to the welfare state. Much popular comment, and a good deal of academic literature, has subscribed to the proposition that the welfare state is in retreat. However, if we look at the OECD figures for 'social expenditure' (which includes pensions) they seem to tell a different story—see Table 5.5.

In fact, since 1985 the share of the economy represented by social expenditure has risen in eleven of our twelve countries. Only in the Netherlands has it decreased. One

Table 5.5 Social expenditure as a percentage of GDP

Country	1980	1985	1990	1995	2000	2005
Australia	10.6	12.5	13.6	18.3	19.7	18.2
Belgium	23.6	26.1	24.9	26.3	25.3	26.4
Canada	13.7	17.0	18.1	18.9	16.5	16.5
Finland	18.0	22.5	24.2	30.9	24.3	26.1
France	20.8	26.0	25.3	28.8	28.1	29.5
Germany	24.6	24.7	23.9	28.0	27.5	27.9
Italy	18.8	21.7	23.4	23.6	25.0	26.5
Netherlands	25.2	25.7	26.0	24.5	20.6	21.6
New Zealand	17.2	17.9	21.8	18.9	19.3	18.5
Sweden	27.1	29.4	30.2	32.5	29.1	29.8
UK	16.9	20.0	17.3	20.8	19.9	22.1
USA	13.5	13.5	13.9	15.8	14.9	16.3

Source: OECD National Accounts at a Glance Database, accessed 3 September 2010.

possible conclusion here would be that, since Table 5.3 showed most countries reducing the share of general government expenditure, therefore other areas of spending (not social expenditure) must have carried the brunt of any reductions. This fits with a detailed recent analysis by Castles (2007) who concluded that 'in the vast majority of these countries [the OECD countries], it was not the welfare state, but the core expenditure state, that was being cut back [during the 1980s and 1990s]' (Castles, 2007, p. 21). However, these core cuts were usually insufficient to match the continuing growth of social expenditure, so another feature of these years was increasing debt—the average level of gross liabilities in eighteen OECD countries rose from 40.9 per cent of GDP in 1980, 63.7 per cent in 1990 and 70.0 per cent in 2001 (Castles, 2007, p. 28). Within this general trend, however, there was a large variation between countries, with Greece, Belgium, and Italy standing out as having unusually high levels of debt over the whole period since 1980—a situation which led to Greece triggering a crisis in the Eurozone in 2010 (Wagschal, 2007—see also Appendix A).

To conclude this first examination of aggregate country-level statistics, it must reluctantly be admitted that it is hazardous to draw any strong conclusions at all about public management reform solely from macro-economic statistics of government spending and staffing. The connections are too indirect and uncertain, and the spending figures are affected by too many other factors, which cannot be attributed to management reform. What is more, the figures themselves often contain inconsistencies and variations which make them only very cautiously and approximately useful for inter-country comparisons (see United Nations, 2001, Part 2 for a succinct account of some of these technical difficulties). Once again, therefore, hard 'results' are difficult to find.

If we now move down from the level of whole countries to specific reform programmes, or, below that, specific organizations, we can locate rather more definite information about economies. Oliver (2003) tried to make a detailed study of the UK 'Next Steps' reform, a process whereby a series of executive agencies were created to take over work previously done by ministries or other central government bodies. The first three agencies were set up in 1988, and by 2001, 126 agencies existed, employing 57 per cent of all civil servants. This was therefore a large-scale reform. The broad idea of the policy was that agencies would be focused on performance targets set for them by ministers, that they would be professionally managed, and that they would achieve greater economy whilst also increasing efficiency and effectiveness. On the economy front, however, James found that in the ten years following the reforms, expenditure in real terms rose by 19 per cent, which was actually more than the 13 per cent rise which had characterized the ten years before the reform (James, 2003, p. 110).

At the level of individual organizations, very clear examples of economizing can frequently be found. For example, re-organizing an organization's purchasing so as to buy in bulk and 'off-the-shelf' can often lead to large savings. On many occasions, re-engineering administrative processes so as to cut out redundant steps has saved money (and time). Reducing staff sick leave by reducing stress and providing early warning and better support has on a number of occasions led to overall economies because temporary staff are needed less often, and so on. These items are not 'high policy' or flagship reforms, but they are the stuff of everyday good management.

5.5 Improving efficiency

An efficiency increase (or productivity gain) is usually defined as an improvement in the ratio of outputs to inputs (see Figure 5.1). As such it may come about via a variety of quite different circumstances:

- where resources (inputs) decrease and outputs increase;
- where resources remain the same and outputs increase;
- where resources *increase* but outputs increase by an even larger amount;
- where outputs remains static but resources decrease;
- where outputs *decrease* but inputs decrease by an even larger amount.

It is important to know which of these situations one is dealing with. For example, in the 1970s and 1980s both British Steel and British Coal considerably increased their average productivity. This sounds fine until one realizes that both corporations were contracting fast—closing down plants and throwing many people out of work. Productivity rose as fewer and fewer steel plants/coal mines—the most modern and productive ones—were left.

Improving efficiency has attracted an enormous amount of management attention in every public sector covered by this book. Yet the available evidence of efficiency gains is patchy and incomplete. There are a number of comparative international tables of government efficiency, but most of them are poor measures of input/output ratios as we defined them in Figure 5.1 (Van de Walle, 2006 offers a good critical overview). Take, for example, a 2008 Working Paper of the International Monetary Fund, bearing the promising title *Determinants of Government Efficiency* (Hauner and Kyobe, 2008). It comes to the 'resounding conclusion' that 'higher government expenditure relative to GDP tends to be associated with lower efficiency' (p. 1). But when one examines the calculations closely, a tremendous conceptual mess emerges. Not all its problems can be enumerated here, but, for example, primary and secondary school enrolment rates (an *input*) are used as an educational *output* indicator, and the physician to population ratio is defined as a health *output*. They also make huge and improbable leaps of faith in order to complete their calculations, such as assuming that the results of expenditure occur immediately, without any lag (p. 5). Finally, it is interesting to note that countries with high spending relative to GDP, far from coming low down the WGIs we looked at earlier, tend to cluster round the top of that particular league table—the high-spending Nordic countries usually feature heavily in the top ten of most international comparisons of good government.

But perhaps it is worth looking at a somewhat weightier and more widely publicized efficiency league table, the one published in the World Competitiveness Yearbook. It rates our chosen countries as shown in Table 5.6.

This shows a wide spread, with Australia and the US coming at the top of the efficiency league and Italy coming way below all the others, But what, exactly, does it tell us? Van de Walle (2006, pp. 441–2) explains that most of the indicators relate to how easy or difficult governments make it for investors to invest in their countries, and that 'many relevant aspects of the organization of an administration are neglected'. The bias is towards efficiency defined as free trade and limited government intervention.

One generalization would therefore be that, at the level of whole governments or public sectors, there is remarkably little that meaningfully compares efficiency as we have defined it (and our definition is a fairly standard one in public administration). Thus, for example, the OECD 2009 publication *Government at a Glance 2009*, which at

Table 5.6 Government efficiency 2003 according to the IMD's world competitiveness yearbook

Country	2003 Score	2003 Rank (out of 29)
Australia	89.91	1
Belgium	43.74	19
Canada	76.83	5
Finland	77.62	3
France	44.80	18
Germany	50.22	17
Italy	25.41	27
Netherlands	59.09	14
New Zealand	69.63	8
Sweden	64.12	11
UK	53.06	10
USA	78.02	2

Source: Extracted from Table 1 in Van de Walle, 2006, p. 439.

the time of writing is probably the most comprehensive and careful comparative attempt to measure government activities, contains virtually no measures directly comparing inputs and outputs.

As we move from the country level to the programme level, and even more to the level of individual organizations or activities, the picture improves. Sweden, for example, was a pioneer in developing productivity studies. In a series of studies their Ministry of Finance concluded that there had been:

a huge plunge in productivity starting in 1960 and continuing up to 1980, [then...] a continued productivity decrease 1980–90 in the public sector as a whole but at a much more modest rate—0.3 percent per year. In the central government sector there was in fact an increase in productivity of 0.6 per cent per year.   (Budget Department, 1997, p. 7)

Within these general trends, however, the investigations found big differences between particular agencies and services. For example, over the period 1980/1 to 1991/2, the Companies Department of the Patent and Registration Office increased its productivity by 84 per cent, but the productivity of the main Patent Department in the same organization fell by 29 per cent (p. 63). This report should alert us to the fact that, even where robust aggregate efficiency measures can be found for a country, they are likely to conceal big variations between individual organizations, and that those who wish to reproduce successful reforms would be well advised closely to investigate the reasons for those variations.

Turning to the micro level, let us now, for illustrative purposes, examine one of the relatively rare high-quality, independent scholarly studies of a measured improvement in efficiency. Kelman and Friedman (2009) focused on the attempt within the UK National Health Service to reduce waiting times in hospital accident and emergency (A&E) departments. They were especially concerned to see whether the apparent improvements brought about by a vigorous targeting regime had also led to dysfunctional 'side' effects. The specific target they investigated (one among many—see Pollitt et al., 2010) was that in A&E departments 98 per cent of all patients would be treated within four hours of arrival. Surveying 155 hospital trusts they found that the percentage achieving this target was 1.24 per cent in the third quarter of 2002 but had risen to 59.4 per cent by the third quarter of 2007. This very marked improvement was attributed to the government campaign, commencing at the beginning of 2003, which featured the target as part of an overall system for publicly rating hospitals as having three, two, one, or zero 'stars', and which later offered hospitals cash incentives for meeting the target. No evidence of any dysfunctional effects were found.

This was a particularly sophisticated, detailed, and careful study. It demonstrated, beyond reasonable doubt, that waiting times were dramatically reduced, and that certain kinds of possible dysfunctions did not appear to take place. Yet even here, there is room for controversy—the contestability referred to in the second of the quotations which opened this chapter has not entirely vanished. To begin with—as Kelman and Friedman themselves footnote—'both budgets and staffing for the NHS, including A&E departments, increased significantly during this period...and we do not claim that all the overall improvement reflected in performance was due to attention to the target' (p. 929). So perhaps this was not wholly or even mainly an efficiency improvement, because better outputs were partly or wholly explained by more inputs. More seriously though, close to the time that the Kelman and Friedman article was published, so was the report of an inquiry into events at Mid Staffordshire NHS Foundation Trust (Healthcare Commission, 2009). This trust hospital had come into the news because of extraordinarily high mortality rates, and evidence of widespread dissatisfaction among patients. The Healthcare Commission concluded, inter alia, that 'there were deficiencies at virtually every stage of the pathway of emergency care', and that 'Doctors were moved from treating seriously ill patients to deal with those with more minor ailments in order to avoid breaching the four-hour target' (Healthcare Commission, 2009, p. 129). Over a three-year period Mid Staffordshire had suffered between 400 and 1,200 more patient deaths than would have normally been expected. So we seem to have two studies, each thorough, pointing in different directions. On the one hand, an academic statistical analysis of 155 hospital trusts finds 'no evidence for any of the dysfunctional effects that have been hypothesized in connection with this target' (Kelman and Friedman, 2009, p. 917), while on the other hand, a detailed official review, based on extended investigation 'on the ground' (300 interviews and 1,000 documents) finds plenty of evidence of just such distortions and dysfunctions. Of course, one could say that Mid Staffordshire was only one hospital trust out of 155, and was quite exceptional. One could also point out that the big improvement in national average waiting times in A&E had presumably saved an unquantified number of lives. On the other hand, 400–1,200 excess deaths is rather a large exception and, at the very least, points to the limitations of a purely statistical approach to organizational analysis. A later detailed inquiry into Mid Staffordshire concluded that 'there can no longer be any excuse for denying the enormity of what has occurred', and that 'a high priority was placed on the achievement of targets, and in particular the A&E waiting time target. The pressure to meet this generated a fear, whether justified or not, that failure to meet targets could lead to the sack' (Francis, 2010, pp. 3 and 16). Mid Staffordshire seems to have been an unusually tragic example of—in our terms—true effectiveness being abandoned in the pursuit of a particular kind of measured efficiency.

Other examples of efficiency gains are less complicated—and much less consequential. So, for example, the UK Social Security Child Support Agency reduced its cost per cleared application by 37 per cent between 1993/4 and 1994/5. Over the same period the UK Employment Service reduced its cost per placed unemployed person by 7.2 per cent (see Chancellor of the Duchy of Lancaster, 1997, respectively pp. 128 and 65). Under the impact of the Kinnock reforms, the European Commission reduced the average number of days it took to make payments from 54 in 1999 to 42.9 in 2003 (Ellinas and Suleiman, 2008, p. 713). And so on. These are the kind of unsung but cumulatively significant efficiency gains which public management reforms are delivering all the time.

5.6 Increasing effectiveness

If good aggregate measures of efficiency are rare at the level of a whole country (section 5.5, above) then measures of country effectiveness are an endangered species. New

Zealand is a case in point. Certain outcomes—both positive and negative—were observable in the period of the great management reforms of 1986–92 (see Appendix B: New Zealand, country file). Unemployment reached new heights and then, in the early 1990s, dropped. Inflation also rose and fell. Crime and youth suicides rose. And so on. But were these the results of *management* reforms, or policy changes, or changes in external circumstances (the continuing dynamic of the global economy), or some mixture of all three? As it happens, New Zealand was a country that built up an unusually sophisticated system of performance measures for its public services. Yet most of these measures were of outputs, not outcomes.

Attribution problems of this kind are present in almost every country. In Australia, for example, the 1992 evaluation of management reforms concluded that 'the new framework has strong support and is seen, overall, to have increased the cost effectiveness of the APS (Australian Public Service) including outcomes for clients' (Task Force on Management Improvement, 1992, p. 52). However, closer inspection shows that the causal link suggested here was far from proven, and, in another part of the very same report, a rather different emphasis is given:

since the reforms took place at a time of rapid social and economic change, there is no definitive way of separating the impact on cost, agency performance and clients (among other things) of these broader changes and the government changes which accompanied them.   (Task Force on Management Improvement, 1992, p. 8)

Real and substantial gains in effectiveness are often associated with innovations in management approach. Donahue (2008) reports on a successful reform in the Maine office of the US Occupational Safety and Health Administration (OSHA). The State of Maine had rather a poor safety record, and 'continued downward pressure on its budget and workforce' meant that by the mid 1990s 'OSHA and its state affiliates had fewer than 2,000 inspectors to enforce job safety and health regulations at more than 6 million workplaces' (Donahue, 2008, p. 96). At this point the Maine office devised a new strategy, which offered companies a choice. Either companies remained subject to a conventional inspection, as before, with violations commonly being found and fines being levied, or they chose a new regime. In the new regime companies were to develop their own comprehensive safety plans—in consultation with OSHA and with their own workers. Out of 200 Maine companies, 184 chose this new option. Spending by the companies to reduce hazards went up (including in areas where OSHA would not have had jurisdiction to require changes), and most participating companies experienced reduced rates of workplace injury and illness.

5.7 Enhancing citizen satisfaction and trust

Another way of conceiving 'results' or impacts is to use citizens as final arbiters, and to ask them to say how good or bad particular services are. Many public services now routinely sample their users' views of the services they have received. One particularly interesting exercise has taken place in Canada, where in 1998 a mail survey of 2,900 Canadian

Table 5.7 Citizens' assessments of public and private services (Canada)

Service	Mean service quality score (0-100)	
	1998	2005
Visiting public library	77	84
Private mail and couriers (private)	68	74
Supermarkets (private)	74	71
Banks/credit unions (private)	51	71
Canada Post	57	70
Receiving care in a public hospital	51	70
Using municipal public transport	58	68
Sending one's child to public school	54	66
Taxis (private)	57	64
Internet service providers (private)	-	64
Get/renew passport	66	65
Department stores (private)	-	64
Canada Revenue (tax collection)	55	62
Insurance agencies (private)	55	60
Telephone companies (private)	63	59
Average rating across all public services	60	70
Average rating across all private services	62	66

Source: Adapted from Exhibit 2.5, Erin Research Inc. (2005), p. 15.
Note: The 1998 figures come from the Erin Research Inc. (1998). The 1998 sample sizes were 2,546–794, while the 2005 figures come from *Citizens First 4* (sample sizes 1,319–6,731).

citizens was commissioned, seeking comparative judgements as between selected public and private sector services. This survey (Erin Research Inc., 1998) was repeated several times, with similar questions being asked of the same services. If we compare the 1998 survey with the 2005 survey we get the scores summarized in Table 5.7.

Contrary to some popular beliefs, these surveys show that the public have quite selective views of the quality of services from public and private sectors—some public services scoring high and others low, with the private sector services similarly scattered. They also show an average improvement for both public and private services over the seven years between the surveys, although the degree of improvement is larger for the public services.

In principle, such surveys could be undertaken before and after major reforms (this was not the design of the Canadian survey) and would provide one way of registering any shift in public satisfaction levels. In practice, such before-and-after studies are not terribly common, although there are a few (e.g. concerning passenger satisfaction with rail journeys before and after improvements, where changes have definitely translated into higher scores). What *Citizens First* does do, however, is to dispel any government-bashing idea that (in Canada at least) public services are all bad, or that public services *in toto* are getting worse. *Citizens First* is not methodologically perfect (in particular the response rates are low—see Bruning, 2010)) but it has the great advantage of being longitudinal as well as cross-sectional and, overall, is one of the best sources we are aware of for citizens' assessments of public services.

Elsewhere we have suggested that the relevant variables for service user satisfaction are quite complex (Pollitt and Bouckaert, 1995). Much depends on the expectations of the various parties concerned, and satisfaction levels may go up and down as much because *expectations* vary as because the underlying 'producer quality' of the service changes. Indeed, one strategy for a cynical government that is determined to raise satisfaction scores might be to attempt to lower public expectations (which may almost have been the case with some governments in certain instances—for state pensions for example). Thus the measurement of perceived quality in public services is by no means just a technical issue. It has political and psychological elements, and these make 'satisfaction' a moving target, something which may jump to a new position as soon as, or even before, it is achieved.

Over the past few years, academic and practitioner interest in citizens' views have expanded from a (relatively) straightforward concern with how *satisfied* they were with this or that service, to a more complex concern with issues of *trust*. 'Trust' has become a focus for debate and rhetoric. It is widely assumed (and often explicitly claimed) that citizen trust in government has been falling, and that something should be done about it. Trust is thus treated like a result that needs to be improved, and reforming public services is frequently said to be one important way of achieving this. If only there was more citizen choice and participation, and more responsiveness and flexibility on the part of the service providers (the argument runs) then citizens would be more inclined to trust the authorities and believe that their taxes were being well spent. And if these better results were measured and published, even those citizens who did not use a particular service would be reassured that their taxes were not going to waste and that the public sector could be relied upon.

Scholarly analysis casts several doubts on this version of events. Thomas (2009) offers a deft summary of why 'trust' has become such a slippery term. One can distinguish between 'local trust' (e.g. interpersonal trust) and 'global trust'(e.g. trust in government). One can distinguish between trust and confidence (although some researchers and survey questions assume they are the same). Trust can be broken down into different components—emotional/affective, cognitive (calculative), intentional, and behavioural. The *Harvard Business Review* defines three types—strategic, personal, and organizational (Galford and Drapeau, 2003). Trust fluctuates over time—it is not fixed. Some scholars think that 'real trust' always takes time to build up, whereas others think it can be created quite quickly. Psychologists suggest that different individuals with different backgrounds have different capacities for trusting. Some studies list more than fifty factors which are believed to promote trust (Thomas, 2009, p. 223).

It is also worth mentioning that the popular assumption that trust levels have been falling dramatically throughout the Western world may simply not be true. Such evidence as is available does not seem to support such an assertion (Van de Walle et al., 2008). If we look at Tables 5.8 and 5.9 we can see data from the World Values Survey and the Eurobarometer.

Table 5.8 Confidence in the civil service (World Values Survey)

Country	1981	1990	1995–7	1999–2000
Australia	47	–	38	–
Belgium	46	42	–	45
Canada	51	50	–	50
Finland	53	33	34	41
France	52	49	–	46
Germany	32	38	48	39
Great Britain	47	46	–	46
Italy	27	25	–	33
Netherlands	44	46	–	37
New Zealand	–	–	29	
Sweden	46	44	45	49
USA	58	60	51	55

All figures are percentages of those expressing 'a great deal' or 'quite a lot' of
confidence in their national civil service.
Source: Adapted from Van de Walle et al., 2008, p. 58, Table 1.

Table 5.9 Trust in the civil service (Eurobarometer surveys)

Country	Autumn 1997	Spring 1999	Spring 2001	Spring 2002
Belgium	29	37	46	51
Finland	38	43	46	43
France	47	44	49	45
Germany	37	43	48	45
Italy	24	27	27	29
Netherlands	58	57	52	55
Sweden	50	45	51	60
UK	46	44	45	48

All figures (except dates) are percentages of respondents saying that they tended
to trust their national civil service.
Source: Adapted from Van de Walle et al., 2008, p. 59, Table 2.

The World Values Surveys (Table 5.8) do not show a clear pattern. Ten of our countries
have scores for both 1981 and 1999/2000. Of these, three are significantly down, three are
marginally down, and three are up—hardly an international collapse of confidence. In a
number of countries, confidence appears to be fairly stable over time. The Eurobarometer
surveys (Table 5.9) give even less support to any assumption of generally declining trust.
Among our eight European countries, between 1997 and 2002, trust in the civil service is
up significantly in four cases, up marginally in two, and down a little in two. Belgium is

interesting as a country that has risen enormously, but the first, 1997, measure was taken during the national trauma over the failure of the police and judicial services to deal with the paedophile, Marc Dutroux.

However, to return to our previous point, one political claim has been that it will be possible to increase trust *by displaying good performance (results)*—irrespective of whether trust was previously static, falling, or even increasing. Why is this claim doubtful? Consider, for a moment, the conditions that would have to be fulfilled before this could be the case. These conditions include the following:

1. The performance information would have to reach the citizen.
2. The performance information would have to be paid attention to by the citizen.
3. The performance information in question would need to show a good performance, not a weak one. (Or, to be more precise, it would have to show a performance equal to, or higher than, the public's expectations—a highly variable and subjective standard.)
4. The performance information would have to be understood by the citizen.
5. The performance information would have to be trusted by the citizen.

Taken together, this is a very demanding set of conditions. The information we have about how the public use performance information is very patchy, but that which there is does not suggest that any of these stages is likely to be particularly easy. More positively, we can say that actual, concrete experiences are often influential, whereas the wider idea that, in the absence of personal experience, many citizens will read and believe published official data (such as the Canadian *Citizens First* reports referred to earlier in this section) is highly suspect. *Citizens First 5* claimed that 'service impact' (citizens' actual experiences of public services) had a strong impact on 'confidence in the public service', and that, both directly and indirectly, it also influenced 'confidence in government' (Erin Research, 2008, pp. 5–12). However, the authors of that report also acknowledged the complexity of the subject (and note that they are here talking about *confidence*, rather than trust):

confidence is based on experiences that accumulate in individuals over years and decades. In general, confidence measures change rather slowly. It is probably more difficult to build confidence than to lose it—a single critical event can do considerable damage.   (*Citizens First 5*, 2008, p. 9)

5.8 Beyond the production framework for performance: systems, capacities, orientations, visions

As we indicated earlier, the performance framework encapsulated in Figure 5.1 is certainly not the only way to think about results. Figure 5.1 envisages results as produced on a kind of assembly line, but one can also see improvements in public management in broader, possibly less mechanical, and sometimes more explicitly normative terms. The aim becomes not higher measured efficiency or satisfaction but the creation of a particular type of relationship between state and society—a small state, for example, or an administrative machine which is open and flexible instead of bureaucratic, or a public administration whose culture is consistently to focus on the individual citizen's needs.

Sometimes management reforms are ad hoc and functional. Sometimes they are emergency measures, designed to stave off a crisis, real or anticipated. But there are also occasions when management reforms are carried through with the aim of realizing some larger vision of how things should be in some imagined future world. (And certainly there are occasions when reforms, although they may also be driven by functional pressures, are *announced* and clothed in terms of one of these 'big ideas'—'good governance' or ' the big society', or whatever.) These imagined futures may be framed in very general terms, or in more specific ways, but they serve a useful function as rallying points and guidance for the faithful and as siren calls to the as-yet agnostic. In terms of the trajectories discussed in Chapter 4 they are highly normative omegas, which may or may not be accompanied by plans for how to get from here to there. They are a desired result, but in a much larger and more diffuse sense than the outputs and outcomes we have mainly been discussing up until now.

There was certainly something of this visionary element to Mrs Thatcher's reforms, encapsulated in the phrase from her 1979 election manifesto, 'Rolling back the state'. There was a similarly vivid (and almost certainly more coherent) vision informing the New Zealand reforms of 1984–94 (Boston et al., 1996, pp. 3–6). No one could accuse Vice President Gore of being without a vision for the NPR—many publications elaborate on the theme of reinventing government so that it 'works better and costs less'.

In other countries the vision was perhaps less strongly enunciated, less combative towards the status quo ante, but there were nonetheless elements of idealism and futuristic imagery. The Finnish government recommitted itself to a combination of democracy and egalitarianism (*High Quality Services, Good Governance and a Responsible Civic Society*, 1998a). The new 1994 'purple coalition' in the Netherlands committed itself to the 'primacy of politics', and the reining-in of unaccountable quangos (Roberts, 1997). In Germany one might say that there was at first a conscious rejection of 'fashions and fads' in favour of the virtues of the existing system (Derlien, 1998), and then, at the end of the long Chancellorship of Helmut Kohl, a brief flirtation with the vision of a 'lean state' (though in practical terms it did not come to much). In Belgium, the new 'purple–green' coalition from 2000 launched a modernization process, called 'Copernicus', referring to a fundamental change based on a vision.

Of course, academics adore ideal models and utopian visions. They (we) take an intense interest at the merest whiff of a new 'paradigm', and tend to react by polishing, systematizing, and elaborating the fragmentary visions proclaimed by political leaders, so as to be able to analyse them—and subsequently often to damn or praise them. Politicians, on the other hand, usually have the street-wisdom to cast their references to the desired future in rather more vague, malleable, and ambiguous terms. The purposes and skills of the two groups are different. Since we are academics rather than politicians it will come as no surprise when we say that the 'teasing out' of visions can be a useful and illuminating exercise. This is not the place to do justice to all the various schemata which have been offered (though we have already introduced the NPM and the NWS) but it may be helpful to pause long enough to look at one example.

Peters (1996b) suggests that four main visions may be identified within the national and international rhetorics of public management reform:

- *The market model*, which holds out the prospect of extensive privatization and therefore of a much smaller public sector—and one that will itself be infused with market-type mechanisms. Citizens become consumers and taxpayers, the machinery of government shrinks to a policymaking, lightly regulatory, and contract-letting core. This corresponds to the 'NPM group'—those countries which we identified as having a marketizing trajectory in the concluding section of Chapter 4.

- *The participatory state*, which lays great emphasis on the empowerment and participation of citizens in the running of 'their' administration. Like the market model, it envisages radical decentralization and a sharp move away from bureaucratic hierarchies. Unlike the market model, it is suspicious of the divisive and inegalitarian features of competitive markets and confident of citizens' ability and willingness to play a more creative part in their own governance. We would see this model as corresponding with the 'northern Europeans'—the NWS modernizers of Finland, Sweden, and the Netherlands.

- *Flexible government*, which is opposed to the rigidities and conservatism attributed to permanent organizational structures and individuals with permanent, highly secure careers. The remedy is a 'temporary state', with shifting squadrons of adaptable and re-adaptable organizations, each purpose-built to address the most salient issues in the current, but rapidly changing environment. Advanced information technology is frequently seen as a major force in this new state of affairs, which can be represented as less 'doctrinaire' or 'ideological' than either the market model or the vision of participatory government (Bellamy and Taylor, 1998; Hudson, 1998). The temporary state is likely to be an extensively contract-based phenomenon. There is no one group of countries which we would suggest as exemplars of this particular vision. Rather it appears as a subsidiary element in many reform programmes, but probably more so in the NPM group of countries than the NWS group (and least so among the 'central Europeans'—Belgium, France, and Germany).

- *Deregulated government*. This vision is built on the assumption that the public service and its organizations are full of creative ideas, relevant experience, and well-motivated people—if only they can be released from the heavy constraints of bureaucratic regulations. This vision is perhaps the least widespread of the four, being mainly confined to those—such as public service unions and professional groups—who share its optimism about the character and motivation of civil servants. It is essentially a version of the modernized state, but rather different from the participatory state described above. Again, it is seldom the sole or dominant element in reform programmes, but can play an important subsidiary role, perhaps especially in the more heavily bureaucratized countries of continental Europe.

As Peters makes clear, each of these visions has aspects of silence or even incoherence, lying quietly alongside its 'headline' messages. That none of the four has been implemented in a pure way will come as no surprise, given the constraints on radical change identified in Chapters 2 and 3. Nevertheless, in certain countries the 'flavour' of one dominant model can be tasted in the key speeches and documents of reform. Thus the New Zealand reforms clearly owed much to micro-economic thinking that favoured a market model (see Appendix B: New Zealand, country file). The Finnish reform documents lean more towards the participatory model: 'earlier administrative reforms have been experienced to have increased the bureaucracy of administration. The government wants to ensure the democratic development of the policy of governance' (*High Quality Services, Good Governance and a Responsible Civic Society*, 1998a, p. 8). The Belgian Copernicus programme placed great emphasis on modernizing personnel management and releasing civil servants from the shackles of outdated bureaucratic procedures (Appendix B, Belgium country file).

Let us take a moment to look more closely at two examples of these popular visions—first, the idea of a new, more participatory, citizen-friendly administration and, second, the idea of 'joined-up government'. First, then, the notion of putting clients, customers, users, patients, passengers (or whatever) first has been given tremendous rhetorical emphasis in many jurisdictions and in many countries. The NPR in the USA, the *Citizen's Charter* in the UK, the 1994 French programme *Année de l'accueil dans les services publiques*, the Belgian, Italian, Portuguese, and Finnish service charters, and more—all claim to increase client orientation. Furthermore, modern quality-improvement techniques such as TQM are founded on the centrality of customer requirements, and have been introduced in parts of the Australian, Belgian, Canadian, Dutch, Finnish, French, New Zealand, Swedish, UK, and US public sectors, as well as being promoted by some parts of the European Commission.

However, achieving a client orientation is not straightforward. While the UK *Citizen's Charter*, which was strongly driven from the centre of government, made some impact, its Italian equivalent quickly faded out (Schiavo, 2000). Or consider the case of the reforms to the Australian Public Service (APS). A 1992 survey of Australian citizens indicated that 73 per cent of those who had had prior contact with a given agency thought its quality of service had remained the same, and 26 per cent thought it had changed (about three-quarters of whom thought it had changed for the better). At the same time members of the Australian Senior Executive Service (SES) were asked whether *they* thought that the reforms had led to an increased client focus, and 77 per cent said they thought it had. Only 51 per cent of lower grade staff were of the same view. This—and other evidence within the same report—shows a complicated picture in which perceptions of client emphasis and of quality improvements depend to some extent on where the respondent sits. The senior staff appear to be more optimistic than more junior staff, while only a minority of citizens notice much difference.

Much depends on the expectations of the various parties concerned, and satisfaction levels may go up and down as much because *expectations* vary as because the underlying 'producer quality' of the service changes. Thus the measurement of perceived quality in public services is by no means just a technical issue. It has political and psychological elements, and these make 'satisfaction' a moving target, something which may jump to a new position as soon as, or even before, it is achieved.

Our second 'vision' is that of joined-up government, or 'integrated public governance' (6, 2004; Bogdanor, 2005; Kernaghan, 2009*b*). The basic idea here sounds quite simple, but its practical manifestations can easily become rather complicated. The vision is that in an 'integrated' or 'joined-up' system, on the 'demand' side citizens will be able to go to one place to access a wide range of public services, and on the 'supply side' different agencies of government—at all levels—will work together so that policies and programmes do not contradict or duplicate each other. Gaps between different programmes (e.g. between hospital care for episodes of acute illness and the subsequent social care provided to discharged but still frail patients at their homes) will be managed away. In its most ambitious form joined-up governance also includes non-profit and commercial organiza-tions that are involved in delivering public services, so that the whole ensemble moves sweetly and smoothly together, without 'turf wars' between different department—or between central and local government—and without citizens having to give the same information to different parts of government more than once, or needing to go to more than one website or office. Furthermore, the whole process can be facilitated and speeded up by the wonders of modern ICTs. They enable managers to practise 'disintermedia-tion'—the stripping out or radical simplification of the sometimes long chains of inter-mediaries involved in delivering public services (Dunleavy, 2010).

Who could possibly be against such a sensible and convenient-sounding approach? It is no surprise that echoes of the integration vision have been heard in many of our countries—particularly Australia, Canada, Finland, New Zealand, and the UK, but also in France, the Netherlands, and Sweden. Many specific changes have been made to try to realize this vision (the Centrelink agency in Australia and Service Canada are two prominent examples—see respective country files in Appendix B). Yet not all has been plain sailing. As Bouckaert et al. (2010, pp. 25–32) note, the vision of integrating/joining-up is but the latest manifestation of an age-old issue in public administration—coordina-tion. And there are a number of common reasons why attempts at coordination may not work:

1. Simple lack of interest by the agencies concerned—they continue to 'plough their own furrows' and have no incentive to spend extra energy on joining-up.

2. Partisan politics, as when one agency is under the authority of a politician of one party and the other is under the authority of another, e.g. Labour local authorities in the UK which, during the 1980s did their best to slow down or undermine policies coming down from Mrs Thatcher's government in London.

3. Genuine differences of view between different professions and their agencies as to what is the best way of tackling specific types of problem, e.g. teachers do not always agree with social workers as to what is best for problem pupils.

4. Conflicting time scales or routines, so that agencies which are supposed to be making joint commitments to cooperate find they have different budgeting or planning cycles, or elections at different times, or other time-related procedures which make it hard to enter into commitments at the same moment.

5. Different procedures and even different concepts of accountability. Some of those involved may see their primary accountability as being direct to elected

representatives, while others are accountable to management boards, and others still to professional associations and standards. The question of who is accountable when a joined-up service involving several different agencies goes wrong can be both complex and contentious.

Ultimately, therefore, there are a number of major difficulties in assessing visions and systems improvements. First, there is a need to separate out the substance from the rhetoric, a distinction which is often far from straightforward. Many government documents and speeches, in several countries, have claimed a 'system transformation' of one kind or another, only for closer empirical study to show that there has actually been high continuity between the old and the new (e.g. Ingraham, 1997 on the US NPR; Pollitt, Birchall, and Putman, 1998 on the British Conservative government's decentralization reforms of the late 1980s and early 1990s; more generally see Pollitt, 2002).

Thus, for example, the empirical basis for conclusions about cultural change at the systems level is usually slender. The number of studies where researchers have been able to measure broad shifts in attitudes and beliefs over time (essential to a full identification of cultural shifts) is small indeed. Most of the limited number of works that do exist measure at a single point in time and then hypothesize what the results imply for cultural change (Rouban, 1995; Talbot, 1994). Nevertheless, such fragments as we have help to cast some light on the claims that management reform has produced cultural change. A survey of French civil servants, carried out in 1989, drew an interesting distinction between professional values and broader social values. It then concluded that:

Professional values depend closely on the nature of the job and the strategic position within ministerial circles. They can therefore evolve and can be improved with training. However, the transformation of these values cannot be so great as to modify the global conception that civil servants have of the relationship between public administration and political spheres, or the ranking of social values which determine their professional success. One cannot change civil servants' social values through administrative reform. Such a change requires extra-professional resources. (Rouban, 1995, p. 51)

This line of interpretation may help to explain why, in a number of jurisdictions, it has seemed possible to change—for example—civil servants' attitudes towards the 'customer', but much less so other attitudes, such as a distrust of politicians or a scepticism towards the benefits of MTMs within the public service. Rouban went on to argue that the perceived legitimacy of administrative reforms varied up and down the hierarchy, usually being highest with senior civil servants, but only so long as they could continue to control the process of change itself. This finding of a variable adhesion to reforms, correlated with rank and position, has been replicated in other countries also. A large survey of staff carried out in conjunction with an Australian 1992 evaluation of the management reforms of the previous decade found evidence that public servants at different levels exhibited significantly different degrees of belief in the usefulness and impact of the reforms (Task Force on Management Improvement, 1992). US federal staff exhibited significant levels of scepticism towards the NPR and Government Performance and Result Act (GPRA) reforms of the 1990s (General Accounting Office, 2001).

There is an even more stubborn difficulty in assessing the claim that a system has acquired greater flexibility, capacity, integration, and so on. How are these claims to be tested?

Presumably the counterfactual is the way that the old (previous) system would have tackled the new circumstances and pressures. But that is a very difficult criterion to apply: who can say exactly how the old system would have performed? Nor does it help that the most prominent voices saying that the new system is better/worse are frequently insiders with strong and obvious interests in conveying a picture of either progress or decline.

One of the most sophisticated attempts to improve capacity was the series of departmental Capability Reviews launched by the UK Cabinet Office from 2005. Within eighteen months all seventeen major departments were reviewed using an advanced model of capability that had ten elements, including several each in the areas of leadership, delivery, and strategy. The direct costs to the Cabinet Office of conducting this major exercise were £5.5M. Intensive follow-up procedures tracked departmental responses to aspects of their work which had been found wanting, and significant improvements were recorded. Undoubtedly, many beneficial changes resulted from this programme. Yet, when the National Audit Office came to review it, they found that 'Departments cannot yet show any clear impact on outcomes' (p. 8); that departments found it difficult to separate the influences of the Capability Reviews from all the other changes going on at the same time; and that there was a divergence between measured capability and departmental performances as measured by the (separate) system of Public Service Agreements (National Audit Office, 2009)

All in all, the category of transformatory vision and systems improvements, while appealing in theory, is very hard to pin down in empirical practice. The dangers of hindsight are considerable, and the risks of perceptions being distorted by a few salient incidents or episodes are high. There is also a temptation to see change in an over-coherent way—to presume that all the changes one sees were intentional, rather than forced or accidental, and, further, to assume that they were related to each other within some overall 'systems approach' (this common bias is challenged at length in the intriguing book, *The Reforming Organization*, Brunsson and March, 1993). It is also misleading to assume that there are singular entities called 'the public service culture', or 'public opinion about reform'. As indicated above, such research as has been carried out conveys a more fragmented and variegated picture. Organizational cultures seem to depend to some significant extent on role and rank, and they shift more quickly along some dimensions than others, with some basic elements of social values which may be beyond the power of reformers to change. As Hofstede (2001) indicates, the basic patterns of national cultures probably change only very slowly – over generations rather than between elections. Public opinion is also a complex issue, with no easy or straightforward link between the success of reforms and the perceived legitimacy of the politico-administrative system. As for perceptions of better integration/joining-up, there seems to be little if any empirical work at the level of whole systems. Some local studies indicate measurable improvements, but the big picture remains obscure.

The most, perhaps, that one can say is that the politico-administrative system in some countries appears to have undergone deeper change than in others. As is clear from Chapters 3 and 4, high-change countries (in management terms) would include New Zealand and the UK, and low-change countries would include Belgium and Germany (although both underwent considerable change at subnational levels). The other countries considered in this book are stretched out somewhere in between. Whether the many innovations in the high-change countries are all to be considered as *improvements*, however, is another question altogether. Some commentators, for example, clearly believe that sticking with a strong existing system is better than playing around with flawed and ephemeral fashions in management reform (Derlien, 1998; Pollitt, 2007).

To conclude this section, it might be said that, while visions play an important role in shaping the rhetorical dimension of reform, it is hard to use them as a means of assessing the results of the reform process. For the zealots, the ever-closer approximation of reality to the vision is the abiding concern, but the zealots are usually few in number. Even the most powerful spokespersons for a particular view are obliged to compromise and exercise patience. Mrs Thatcher left the level of UK public spending only marginally different from that which she had found in 1979. President Reagan bequeathed a huge public sector deficit and a federal civil service little altered in size by his eight years at the helm. President G. W. Bush, also an advocate of fiscal prudence and small government, presided over the transformation of a federal surplus into a big deficit, and left an enlarged federal workforce. The enthusiastic privatizers in the new Dutch government of 1982 and the new Swedish government of 1991 found that they could not transfer to private ownership anything like as much of their respective public sectors as they had at first envisaged. For the reasons developed in chapter 3 (and to be elaborated in chapter 7) purity of vision must almost always be tempered with an understanding of political, economic, and functional constraints and trade-offs. Therefore, even those who are advocates of a particular vision, and who wish to assess 'results' in terms of that vision, must make allowances for the strength of the forces of tradition, inertia, and recalcitrance—for path dependency. Sometimes the new vision looks surprisingly like some previous vision, but with a new label. In such cases a longer historical view makes reforms look more like waves or cycles around certain persisting ideas rather than new directions (Pollitt, 2008, pp. 59–74). Talk, decisions, and actions frequently diverge. Our argument has been that the strength of these forces depends to a considerable extent on the nature of the politico-administrative regime in question, and the extent to which the new vision which is proposed cuts across, or goes along with its grain.

5.9 Conclusions and reflections

5.9.1 Initial overview

This has been a long chapter but the conclusions may be briefly stated. First (Sections 5.1 to 5.3) 'results' may be looked for in different ways, in different places, and on different levels and scales. Overall, one might say that at the time of writing the 'results' wineglass is half empty—and half full. It is half empty because so often, following a reform, we still lack details about confidently attributable outcomes, or about efficiency, or even just about outputs. In some countries the 'results and performance' mindset is still little developed in practice (e.g. Belgium or Italy) but in others it has reached high levels of intensity and sophistication (e.g. Australia or the UK). Fifteen years ago one of us pointed out how patchy the evaluation of NPM reforms then were internationally (Pollitt, 1995), and in 2010 it remains the case that many major reforms—even in the 'performance-minded' countries—are launched with little or no attention to evaluation (e.g. White and Dunleavy, 2010).

On the other hand the glass could be seen as half full. Certainly there is much more performance data around than fifteen or twenty years ago, and more of it is in the public domain. Whilst much of this is case-specific there is also rapidly increasing attention to international comparisons. Some of these may be conceptually or methodologically weak (see our earlier discussion of the World Bank's WGIs) but others are more sophisticated (e.g. the PISA educational scores—see Hautamäki et al., 2008) or just more cautious and detailed (e.g. the OECD's *Government at a Glance 2009*).

For some commentators the most significant evidence lies in the 'changed climate', the existence of new 'talk', and the promulgation of visions of privatization, marketization, participation, deregulation, and flexibility. In short, the crucial evidence is the growth of a new community of discourse, with its main production centres usually located in the 'Anglo-Saxon' countries and certain international organizations such as the OECD, the IMF, the Commonwealth Secretariat, and the World Bank. For others the focus is the record of decisions—the publication of White Papers and national review documents, the enunciation of programmes such as citizens' charters or Public Service 2000, and the passing of laws decreeing administrative reform. Others, however, look for 'hard' evidence in the form of actions and impacts. Most—though not all—of this chapter has been devoted to that kind of search. It is itself a large domain, within which one may look for macro-level effects or local impacts, for concrete outputs or longer-term outcomes, and so on. One's judgements on the achievements of reform are likely to vary considerably according to which of these various types of result—and corresponding species of evidence is given the greatest weight (Pollitt, 2002).

Where one looks is, in turn, influenced by where one sits. The three most obvious sitting positions tend to generate rather different 'vibrations' about management reform. The state apparatus itself, and particularly the political heads of department, tend to report steady progress—everything is in hand and remaining issues are being vigorously addressed (e.g. Chancellor of the Duchy of Lancaster, 1997; Commonwealth Secretariat, 1993; Gore, 1996; Cabinet Office, 2008). Management consultants tend to focus more on the future, on the potential of new techniques and systems to solve the perceived problems of today. They do issue warnings, but these are usually about the constraints which may inhibit progress rather than about the nature of that progress itself. This may be considered understandable for a group the existence of which depends partly on the membership being able to sell innovatory concepts and techniques. Academics are undoubtedly the least optimistic of the three groups, worrying about what may be lost as well as what is gained, expressing caution about long-term effects, and generally hedging achievement claims with qualifications and critique (e.g. Boyne et al., 2003; Derlien, 1998; Dunleavy and Hood, 1994; Ingraham, 1997; Pollitt and Bouckaert, 2003; Radin, 1998, 2000).

There are also differences *within* each group. The differences among members of the state elite itself are perhaps the most interesting, since this is the group that one might suppose would be most likely to speak with one voice. One obvious divide is between legislatures and executives. Another is between executives and independent audit offices (with the latter, as is their role, being more critical). A third is within the executive itself, between central finance departments (on the one hand) and operational departments (on the other). One brief example may illustrate these differences of perspective.

In 1996 the President of the Canadian Treasury Board made an annual report to the legislature, entitled *Getting Government Right: Improving Results Measurement and Accountability* (Treasury Board of Canada, 1996). The minister claimed that:

We have already achieved tangible results in this area. For example, modernizing the financial management system, better reporting to Parliament, improving how we use information technologies, and adopting alternative ways of delivering government services.   (Foreword)

However, when the Auditor General's Office reviewed these documents they made a number of strong criticisms, including:

[...] The President's report does not distinguish evaluation from other forms of review [...] The President's report presents an overly optimistic picture of progress for an activity which is undergoing major change and dealing with many important challenges [...] The Treasury Board should ensure that its report to Parliament credibly represents the performance of review and includes specific measures on evaluation.   (Auditor General of Canada, 1997, sections 3.80, 3.83, 3.85, and 3.86)

At the same time a Parliamentary Working Group was considering the same documentation. In their own report they also expressed critical views:

One of the perceived shortcomings of these documents, as expressed by MPs, was the lack of objectivity in the reporting. Many respondents suggested that it was inappropriate for departments to be reporting on their own performance—the perceived result of which was 'feel good' documents that said little about the true performance of the department.   (Duhamel, 1996, p. 14)

To complete the circle, we might add that parliaments themselves—including the Canadian one—have been less than exemplary in making use of performance data, even when this has been supplied to them (Johnson and Talbot, 2007; Pollitt, 2006*a*). There has perhaps been a tendency to succumb to the temptation of grabbing a few headlines by highlighting unusual or extreme statistics, but not to work through, or try to understand, the broad picture which is presented to them.

As for internal differences of perspective within executives, the European Commission offers many examples of tensions between different Directorates General, some of which involve management issues (e.g. Middlemas, 1995, pp. 247–55). The SEM 2000 and MAP 2000 initiatives, for example, were seen as coming mainly from the 'horizontal' parts of the Commission—DGIX (personnel), DGXIX (budgets), DGXX (internal control), and the Secretariat General. As such, aspects of the reforms were regarded with suspicion and were slow-pedalled by certain 'operational' ('vertical') DGs, which regarded them as belonging to someone else's agenda, and potentially burdensome. Evidently, views of the Kinnock reforms of 2002–6 also vary considerably among the Eurocrats (Ellinas and Suleiman, 2008).

Finally, we come to the academic community which is, of course, famous for its ability to argue over how many angels may dance on the head of a pin. Views of reforms are no exception. As indicated above, many academics are both critical and sceptical, perhaps especially of NPM-type reforms. But others, more supportive of particular reforms, attack these critics and accuse them of various crimes, such as lacking theoretical rigour, using 'primitive' methods, or even displaying 'cranky skepticism' (e.g. Kelman, 2007, 2008).

5.9.2 Data, criteria, attribution

The foregoing sections have been peppered with references to the incomplete, ambiguous, or downright inadequate state of the available data. It is also clear that data availability varies sharply according to how one defines 'results'. To return to the distinctions we made in Chapter 1 (see Table 1.2) the records of results *talk* are voluminous, and the analyst's problems are mainly to do with information overload. The records of *decisions* concerning results (target-setting, the creation of performance management procedures) are also very extensive. The situation with the *practice* of results-based management is more complex. The available information on inputs, savings, process improvements, and outputs is vast. There can be little doubt that, in many public sector organizations in many countries, the work process has intensified: more measured outputs are being generated per pound spent or per member of staff employed. Not all of this information may be entirely reliable, but it would take a giant dose of cynicism to arrive at the conclusion that nothing had changed, and that the productivity of specific organizations had remained static.

Where the information begins to get thin is at the two next stages. First, what have been the costs of the many measured improvements in productivity, in terms of other activities foregone, stress, and reduced loyalty or commitment among the public sector workforce, loss (or gain) of trust by the public, and so on? In most cases there are few answers here: these hidden costs could be very high or very low, and there could also be hidden benefits, which the bald statistics of productivity fail to capture.

More importantly, however, information about what may be regarded as the final stage—the ultimate outcomes of all the reform talk, decision-making, and action on society at large—is both sparse and ambiguous. As we said earlier, results lead to more results, and it is the search for the final, end results in this chain—the 'final outcomes' as they are sometimes referred to in the literature—that is most difficult. This is partly because most governments do not seem to have looked very vigorously for this type of information, but partly also because such information is difficult and expensive to collect, and then hard to interpret.

There is therefore something of a paradox at the heart of the international movement in favour of performance-oriented management reform. The reformers insist that public sector organizations must reorient and reorganize themselves in order to focus more vigorously on their results. They must count costs, measure outputs, assess outcomes, and use all this information in a systematic process of feedback and continuous improvement. Yet this philosophy has clearly not been applied to many of the reforms themselves, which thus far have been evaluated only occasionally, and usually in ways that have some serious methodological limitations (Pollitt, 1995; Pollitt and Bouckaert, 2003).

Finally, it may be observed that information itself means little until it is combined with some *criterion*. An increase of 5 per cent may be good if the criterion for success is an average increase elsewhere of 2 per cent, but poor if the average elsewhere is 8 per cent. Contracting out refuse collection may be deemed a success if the criterion to be applied is cost per bag collected but thought to be a problem if the criterion is promoting equal opportunity of employment. The main point here is that there is often room for debate about which criteria are the most appropriate and, in any case, there seem to be fashions for particular criteria or measures, which come and go. Indeed, there is quite a persuasive theory that suggests that this kind of change over time is necessary, to prevent particular performance indicators getting 'worn out' and becoming the target for excessive gaming and manipulation (Meyer and Gupta, 1994):

a number of factors, especially the tendency of performance measures to run down or to lose the capacity to discriminate good from bad performance, trigger ongoing creation of new performance measures different from and therefore weakly correlated with existing measures. (Meyer and Gupta, 1994, p. 309; see also de Bruijn, 2002)

5.9.3 Who needs results?

One mildly controversial conclusion can be drawn from the foregoing. It is that, if 'results' are defined in a narrow way as scientifically tested data describing the final outcomes of changes, then *the international management reform movement has not needed results to fuel its onward march*. This will come as no surprise to analysts who stress the symbolic and rhetorical dimensions of politics and institutional life (Brunsson, 1989; Brunsson and Olsen, 1993; Hood, 1998, 2005; March and Olsen, 1995; Power, 1997). Nevertheless it does represent what might politely be termed a discontinuity within some of the paradigms used by the proponents of reform themselves—particularly the hard-edged, performance-driven visions of core NPM enthusiasts and, more recently, the 'doing more with less' rhetoric of politicians and officials faced with implementing large, recession-induced public-spending cuts.

Equally, 'results' of another kind *are* needed to maintain the momentum of reform. A continuing high level of production of talk and decision-making is probably essential. Until now, the flow of White Papers, charters, and 'new initiatives' has been unceasing since the early 1980s. Every country has to have a reform programme of some sort, or at least to be seen to be discussing one. One may ask whether this procession of talk and decision is now a permanent feature of governance, or whether it is conceivable that the flood tide may begin to ebb? If public management reform *did* fall from fashion that would not imply that institutions would cease to change. It would simply mean that reforms were no longer so newsworthy—they would resume the status of technical adjustments, which is what they were mainly seen as during some periods in the past.

5.9.4 Regimes, trajectories, and results

Finally, we should ask what are the connections between the politico-administrative regimes described in Chapter 3, the reform trajectories chosen by different jurisdictions and commented upon in Chapter 4, and the picture of 'results' put together here in Chapter 5?

In an ideal world the regime types would influence the reform trajectories, and evidence would show that given trajectories led to specified but different mixtures of results. The connecting mechanisms or processes (what works and what doesn't) would also be clear, and the would-be reformer could thus inspect the local regime and then choose a reform trajectory which would generate the mix of benefits and costs which s/he most desired.

Unfortunately neither we nor anyone else can 'fill in' all the spaces in this ideal model. Chapter 4 did show that some broad connections could be established between types of politico-administrative regime and the choice of reform trajectories. Even those links were subject to exceptions and deviations, temporary or otherwise. However, there is then a considerable 'disconnect' between trajectories and results. The record does not permit confident and specific statements to be made concerning the different mixtures of results that will be harvested from each main trajectory. On the contrary, there are conflicting claims, with advocates advancing the respective merits of different models and approaches (Derlien, 1998). These arguments are only occasionally backed up by results data, and, when they are, the attribution of effects is usually disputable.

On the other hand, it would be wholly mistaken to draw the conclusion that public management reform was a meaningless charade, played only by the cynical or the stupid. On the contrary, it is absolutely clear that many of the changes made have carried definite 'payoffs' for particular groups and individuals, even if longer-term outcomes remain comparatively obscure. To explore these issues further requires, first, a disaggregation of the 'players', and, in particular, a further examination of the role of management reform at the interface between politics and management. This will be undertaken in the next chapter. It also requires the development of a closer analysis of some of the trade-offs and paradoxes which have come to light in Chapters 4 and 5. They will be the subject of Chapter 7. Finally, in Chapter 8, it will be possible to return to the overarching question of the likely connections between different reform strategies and their consequences for relations between politicians, public servants, and the rest of society.

6 Politics and management

The dividing line between the political and the apolitical has been shifting in the
direction of the political, and more positions that once would have been off limits
for political tampering are now clearly subject to political pressures and appointments.
We may well debate the desirability and efficacy of this change, but it does appear to
have become a reality of modern government.

(Peters and Pierre, 2004)

6.1 Forwards to the past?

At this point we shift gear. In Chapters 2, 3, 4, and 5 we have been engaged in building a
model of the process of management reform, classifying key contextual features which
differentiate one country's regime from another, identifying alternative trajectories for
change and examining the evidence as to the results of this change. Each of these chapters
has therefore been intended to help build up a general picture of what has been happening—in word and in deed—in the world of public management reform. In the remainder
of the book, however, we stand back from this picture in order to reflect upon and interpret
some of its broader features. We shift mood from construction towards deconstruction,
from creating an accurate and convincing depiction towards exploring its contradictions
and acknowledging its limitations.

From the outset we have argued that public management cannot be adequately com-
prehended without reference to the crucial relationships which exist between administration and politics, and between administrators and politicians. In making this point we are
just one more member of a large chorus (e.g. Flynn and Strehl, 1996; Götz, 1997, p. 753;
Lynn, Heinrich, and Hill, 2001; Hood and Lodge, 2006; Peters and Pierre, 2004). However,
while there is wide agreement that this frontier is an important one, there appear to be
varying opinions as to what is taking place along the borderlines. Some have seen 'management' (in the sense of modernized public administration plus privatization) invading
politics and taking over slices of political territory (e.g. Clarke and Newman, 1997; Pollitt,
1993, chapter 1; Stewart, 1994). Others, in apparent contrast, suggest that management
reform has been a vehicle by which executive politicians have gained a tighter grip of their
officials (Halligan, 1997; Peters and Pierre, 2004).

At this point it may be useful to examine more closely the concept of a 'frontier' between
management and politics. This frontier is related to, but by no means necessarily identical
with, the boundary between civil servants and politicians. According to most contemporary definitions, 'politics' is not limited to certain persons (elected politicians) or
to specialized arenas in which an action takes place (Parliament, ministerial offices,

'smoke-filled rooms', etc.). More commonly, politics is defined by the *processes* involved. In particular, political activity is that which involves the exercise of power, especially the mobilization of various kinds of resources in order to achieve a chosen set of ends in a situation where the interests of the various parties concerned potentially or actually conflict (Leftwich, 1984). Thus, even public servants in Westminster-type systems, though they may remain 'neutral' and scrupulously avoid 'party politics', nevertheless frequently engage in 'political' processes, in the sense that they bargain and negotiate and deploy resources of money, information, and presentational skills in order to improve the chances of success for policies and programmes with which they are associated. For example, a senior civil servant charged with implementing his or her minister's policy of privatizing a public utility, will negotiate with the various parties involved and attempt, on the minister's behalf, to make the policy work. Similarly, the chief executive of a hospital may negotiate with the local trade unions over redundancies or terms and conditions and the head of a government regional office will bargain with other powerful local figures (local government officers, local business leaders, and so on) to try to promote regional development. In these senses, then, many public servants are involved in 'politics', even if they stay scrupulously clear of 'party politics'. Indeed, the more 'networking' and 'partnering' a government attempts (i.e. the more the New Public Governance or similar models become reality), the more likely it is that officials will be involved in bargaining and persuading roles. To the popular definition of politics as the process which determines 'who gets what, when, and how' we would therefore add the thought that, albeit within legal frameworks and (possibly) under explicit guidance from elected politicians, the person making such determinations will often be an appointed official.

From such a perspective some interesting interpretive possibilities open up. The apparently contrasting views referred to above (between those who believe that the domain of management is increasing and those who argue that political scrutiny is increasing) become more understandable and—to a degree, if not entirely—mutually reconcilable. For example, it could be simultaneously true that politicians are intervening more in public administration *and* that the sphere of public management has begun to encompass more and more issues which used to be mainly the preserve of politicians. These are, then, crucial, boundary issues for public management, and they deserve more detailed consideration here. We will focus on four key questions:

1. Has public management reform shifted the borderline between politics and administration, and, if so, in what way?

2. What are the main implications of the new trajectories and models of public management for elected politicians (in both executive and legislative roles)?

3. How far does the notion of 'public service bargains' enable us to understand changes to the borderlines?

4. What is the relationship between public management reform and public attitudes towards politicians and civil servants?

Our answers to all four of these questions—perhaps particularly to the final one—are tentative. As usual, the available evidence is less than complete, and different directions are visible in different places and periods. We may also note that one feature of the rhetoric surrounding a good deal of management reform (perhaps especially in the core NPM group of countries) has been that it has drawn attention *away* from these overtly political issues—the emphasis has tended to be placed on saving money or improving the public services received by citizens rather than on the effects of all this upon basic political and constitutional relationships. The implication has seemed to be that management can be a professional and technical exercise, relatively free of 'politics'. Typical of this dominant emphasis was Vice President Gore's characterization of the US National Performance Review exercise as one aiming at a government which 'works better and costs less'. Typical also was Mrs Thatcher's bold assertion that moving 70 per cent of the civil service out of conventional departments and into a new type of executive agency had no constitutional significance:

The government does not envisage that setting up executive agencies within departments will result in changes to existing constitutional relationships.   (Prime Minister, 1988, p. 9)

However, after two decades of intensive change across many countries, we are far from alone in suggesting that the 'three Es' and improved 'customer service' are only one dimension of the picture: the relations between politics and administration have changed too.

Having addressed the four questions listed above, the chapter concludes with some synthesizing comments on the extent to which 'politics' may represent a structural limit to the effectiveness and reach of management reform.

6.2 Has public management reform shifted the borderline between politics and administration?

There have, in any case, been significant changes in the nature of politics in many OECD countries, quite apart from the impacts of management reforms. Specifically, there has been an erosion of the perceived legitimacy of government and an increase in the volatility (decrease in the party loyalty) of most electorates. More sectors of politics—including management reform—have developed through international rather than purely national networks (Halligan, 1996a; Held et al., 1998; Kettl, 2000; Manning, 2001). Finally, economic pressures have meant that in most OECD countries, the era where ministers made their reputations by introducing big new programmes has long passed. We have moved into an era of largely 'technical politics' rather than the welfare state construction of 1945–75. Executive politicians are now usually engaged in stream-lining, repackaging, marginally modifying, or actually downsizing ('decrementing') ex-isting programmes, rather than any heroic new efforts. Publics tend to be vigilant against reductions in popular and basic welfare state services (health care, education, pensions), yet more sceptical and more demanding (in terms of service standards) than in the past *and*, at the same time, more resistant to tax increases. Furthermore, in most countries the mass media have become more aggressive and sceptical, no longer accepting the 'official line' or deferring to the minister's authority or access to expertise. To put it bluntly, it is even more difficult being a minister than it used to be, partly because the kinds of things a minister gets to do today are inherently less popular than those that were being done during the boom years of the 1950s and 1960s, and partly because the public audience out there are more sceptical, less deferential and less trusting. One should add that it is also more difficult being a 'mandarin'. Rouban (1997, p. 148) is referring specifically to developments in France, but his words apply to most of our other countries as well:

The time is over when civil servants, representing an all-mighty State, could steer most actors of the social life and could impose their choice without too much difficulty. Moreover, the classic political game has been changed. Controversies are no longer built along the lines of ideological frontiers but involve technical arguments that often cross the political parties boundaries.

Within this context, management reform ministers have been caught in the dilemma captured by the Peters and Pierre quotation at the beginning of this chapter: on the one hand they have sought greater control over the bureaucracy and its programmes, but on the other they have seen advantages in decentralizing responsibility and trying to sit 'above' the dangerous cauldron of day-to-day operational failures and achievements. Generally speaking, it might be said that NPM in the Anglo-Australasian style contains contradictory ideas (or, at least, ideas which exist in some tension with each other). NPM doctrine holds that decentralization is good, and letting/making managers manage is good, but also that political control and accountability need to be strengthened *and* that consumer power should be strengthened. This conundrum—which will be explored further in the next chapter—looks rather like an 'eternal triangle'. The grass in the other two corners is always greener. Nor have continental European states—which, as we have seen, have not embraced NPM to anything like the same extent—been able to avoid problems. In France:

Many civil servants have perceived modernisation as a means to put them in charge of political choice that had not been decided upstream, as a tricky game whose winners are always the politicians who can get rid of embarrassing responsibilities in a time of budget cuts and, simultaneously, of high defensive corporatism.   (Rouban, 1997, p. 155)

Decentralizing devices such as frame budgeting (Sweden, Finland) or delegation to provincial or regional tiers of government (Belgium, Canada, Italy, USA) have clearly been used partly in order to transfer the political pain of sharp prioritizations and downsizings from the national to subnational levels of government (from one set of elected politicians to another—although within each jurisdictional level there may also be some passing on of 'hot potatoes' to officials). However, at least in these cases the arguments have taken place *within* the political sphere, between different strata of elected representatives.

The precise ways in which these tensions play themselves out are therefore shaped by the type of regime in which they occur (see Chapter 3). In the 'Anglo-Saxon' regimes (Australasia, UK, USA) where politics and government in general tend to be held in lower esteem, it has been less difficult for politicians to retreat from responsibility for the management of public services (indeed, easier for them to pursue outright privatization). Thus, many developments have seemed to signal a shift of the borderline in favour of management, so that its empire (both private and public) has grown, while the empire of politics appears to have shrunk. This has been done in the name of efficiency and consumer responsiveness. Yet executive politicians have also been cunning. They have, in effect, reasserted the distinction between politics and administration (though now calling the latter 'management'), making managers responsible for achieving targets, but at the same time they have frequently retained powers of intervention so that, if things go badly wrong in the public eye, then the politicians can appear to ride to the rescue with inquiries, inspection teams, restructurings, and all the other paraphernalia of crisis management. This generalization would apply, for example, to UK executive agencies, grant-maintained schools and NHS trust hospitals, and to the Belgian Commission on the Dutroux (child abuse) scandal and the Dutch inquiry into the firework explosion at Enschede.

Beneath the surface, the process of letting—or making—public sector managers manage has not been so simple. There have been countervailing currents and considerable centralization, partly through the establishment of ever more sophisticated performance indicator and target regimes, underpinned by rapidly advancing information technologies. In the UK, a general shrinkage of the public sector has been accompanied by an extraordinary growth of central auditing, inspecting, and monitoring bodies (Hood et al., 1999; Power, 1997). As we have seen, executive politicians have transferred their focus for control from inputs to outputs, via processes. This may account for the somewhat ambiguous responses from public service managers themselves—they have experienced greater freedom to deploy their inputs (e.g. switching money from staff to equipment, or vice versa) but at the same time they have felt themselves under closer scrutiny than ever before as far as their results are concerned. Even where an activity has been fully privatized—as with the UK public utilities such as gas, water, electricity, and telecommunications—politicians have gradually been obliged to give more attention to arrangements for the public regulation of the resultant private corporations (Foster, 1992).

What is clear is that, in the UK, but also in other Westminster-influenced systems, the additional pressures which NPM reforms have put on traditional concepts of public accountability have not been met with any clear and coherent new doctrine to cope with the new circumstances. The problems are increasingly widely recognized, but most politicians have shrunk from the task of articulating a 'new model' (Barberis, 1998; Behn, 2001; Pollitt, 2003a, chapter 4; Stone, 1995).

In an interesting analysis of reforms in two strong NPM countries (Australia, New Zealand) and two modernizers from the 'northern European' group (Norway, Sweden), a pair of Norwegian scholars paid particular attention to the effects of the implementation of NPM practices on politicians. Their conclusions are worth citing.

The distance between political leaders, on the one hand, and the actors, institutions and levels to be controlled, on the other, is increasing, and autonomy from political leaders is more evident. The new administrative and institutional actors are less loyal than in the traditional system, more instrumental and individually oriented, and less preoccupied with collective interests, public accountability and ethos.   (Christensen and Lægreid, 2001, p. 304)

Note the emphasis here on a changing culture among the new administrative elites. Christensen and Lægreid go on to note the additional complexity these changes bring for accountability systems before finally delivering a sober verdict:

Our conclusion is that these changes may in fact undermine political control. Managerialism may allow executives to exercise greater control over state agencies, but it is greater control over less... The changes also create ambiguity concerning the role of managers, because they are caught in cross-pressure between politicians and customers. (Christensen and Lægreid, 2001, p. 309)

In the more consensualist and decentralized regimes (the northern European group identified in Chapter 4) the 'anti-government' theme has not been as strong as in the core NPM group. Instead, the rhetoric has stressed modernization, with the political elites largely holding to their usual role of directing a substantial state apparatus, and the mandarins continuing to play a strategic role with relatively little challenge to their status and competence. Considerable decentralization has taken place (Sweden, Finland) but this has been more political decentralization (to subnational elected authorities) rather than managerial decentralization on the New Zealand/UK model. One should remember, however, that these countries were already administratively more decentralized than the UK, with both Sweden and Finland having strong traditions of national boards and agencies and Sweden, in particular, possessing only quite small central ministries (see Sweden country file, Appendix B). In general change in the Nordic countries, although often flavoured with NPM ideas, was more incremental and cautious than in Australia or New Zealand (Christensen and Lægreid, 2001). In the Netherlands the trajectory was slightly different, with a significant growth in appointed quangos (ZBOs) during the 1980s. However, this trend soon attracted political criticism (including some accusations that the ZBOs were being used to create well-paid jobs for sympathizers of the ruling Christian Democrat party), and in 1994 an incoming left-right 'purple coalition' made restoring 'the primacy of politics' one of its leading slogans. Departmental agencies with more sharply defined accountability became the preferred vehicle for decentralization of central government tasks, rather than ZBOs, and the national audit office made a series of well-publicized reports aimed at improving the public accountability of autonomous bodies (e.g. Algemene Rekenkamer, 1995, 2002)

In sum, neither in the Nordic states nor in the Netherlands has the borderline between management and politics moved much, one way or the other. On the other hand, these regimes have shared in the shift to systems of output rather than input controls, even if this move has not been as vigorously reinforced by personnel reforms (performance appraisals, annual results targets for individual public servants) as in the most pro-NPM countries.

In Germany and France the politics/administration frontier has not shifted very much either. Neither has significantly dismantled central civil service controls; neither has created flocks of powerful new quangos to take over functions formerly under direct political oversight (Germany already possessed a large and significant set of para-statal, corporatist organizations with responsibilities for carrying out public functions). France has implemented a significant privatization programme, but cautiously, and nowhere near as sweepingly as the UK or NZ. Germany was already extensively decentralized and France has carried through a major decentralization programme since 1985 but, as in the case of the Nordics, these have been primarily acts of political decentralization (to local and regional *elected* bodies) not pure managerial decentralization. Administrative decentralization has certainly taken place, but not on the same scale as in the UK or

New Zealand (Guyomarch, 1999; Trosa, 1995; cf. Pollitt et al., 1998). In short, political and civil service elites (which, significantly, in both countries are intermingled rather than separate—especially in France) have retained their grip. The politically led state, even if leaking legitimacy, is still seen as a major, socially integrating force to be reckoned with. There have been significant attempts to begin to shift large, rule-following bureaucracies towards a more performance-oriented approach, but this has been both patchy and a largely internal matter. It has not been accompanied (as in Australia/NZ/ UK/USA) by general rhetoric about how 'political influences' have to be removed/minimized and professional management/business-like approaches substituted. On the contrary, while the first edition of this book was being written a prominent German scholar expressed himself thus:

Not only would it be undesirable to once again in German history have senior civil servants conceal their functionally politicized role, it is also hardly imaginable how to turn them into a-political managers. Possibly, the formal neutrality of civil servants in the UK and the absence of the safety valve of temporary retirement could be reasons for the easy adoption [in the UK] of a managerialist role understanding.   (Derlien, 1998, pp. 23–4)

Nor have the German or French publics been copiously supplied with 'league tables' of 'results' as has been the fashion in the UK and, to a lesser extent, the USA and New Zealand. The Anglo-American-Canadian rhetoric of citizen 'empowerment' has been far more muted in *Rechtsstaat* regimes, where the dominant legal perspective and the distinctiveness of the state sphere make such concepts more difficult to conceive or fill with any sensible meaning. Citizen justice and citizen rights, *Conseil d'Etat* style is very different from consumer choice in the style of John Major's *Citizen's Charter*, as the 1992 *Chartes des Services Publics* illustrated.

   Among the central European group of states, Belgium and Italy remain to be commented upon. Both have witnessed extensive political decentralization (see country files in Appendix B), but it is not clear that this has much altered the borderline between politics and administration or, at least, not in any lasting way. In Belgium the federal civil service has, if anything, probably lost some status, alongside politicians, amid the public anger at the Dutroux affair and other administrative and political scandals of the 1990s. On the other hand the politicians have responded by considerably expanding their political patronage—the number of discretionary contract appointments has grown (OECD, 2007) and proposals to reduce the size of the (politicized) ministerial *cabinets* were the first casualty of the Copernicus reform (see Belgium country file, Appendix B). In Italy, confidence in the political system fell to very low levels in the late 1980s and early 1990s, and there were even two 'non-political', technocratic governments in the mid 1990s. However, there too, there is little evidence that the civil service has been the beneficiary of the loss of confidence in politicians. Rather it, too, has a low status in the eyes of the public. Table 5.9 showed 2002 levels of 29 per cent for Italian trust in the civil service, as against 51 per cent for Belgium, 45 per cent for France, 48 per cent for the UK, 43 per cent for Finland and 60 per cent for Sweden. Italy was the only country below the 40 per cent level. So, although both countries have begun real reforms, it is hard to see that these have yet led to any restoration of the status and authority of national civil servants. Neither does the available evidence show any sustained reversal of the fall in the standing of politicians. Direct evidence of a shifting borderline between political and managerial power is not plentiful—either in Belgium or in Italy—but we can at least say that there is little to indicate a major accretion of authority to either ministers or mandarins (even though the Belgian 'purple-green' coalition made the 'primacy of politics' a key programme issue).

6.3 What are the main implications of the new trajectories and models of public management for elected politicians?

Here we face the same problem that arose in Chapters 1 and 4—how many of the various models which have been put forward should we select for attention? Our choice is to follow the main lines discussed towards the end of Chapter 4: that is, to look at the NPM, then the Neo-Weberian State (NWS), and finally 'New Public Governance' (NPG).

Looked at by and large, these three models have rather different versions of the roles of politicians and officials. Most of the early NPM writings said very little about politicians—the debate was all about how to give more authority to managers, although within a performance framework that ensured that their performance would be measured and would be aligned with the strategic goals that were handed down from the politicians. The correct framework of incentives would ensure that these managers performed in the public interest. Politicians were left with a strategic role—setting broad goals but keeping their hands off the day-to-day business of running the machine, which should be delegated to professional managers. They were to act as chief executives, or even chairmen of the board, not 'fixers'.

The NWS, by contrast, was closer to the traditional pattern. Officials were there to implement communally decided and politically defined policies, and they were to do this professionally and using high technical skills, but without any presumption that they required large increments of extra autonomy or discretion in order to work effectively. They were still very much servants/representatives of the *state*, and as such were not conceived of as autonomous managers, and certainly not as 'entrepreneurs' (cf. Osborne and Gaebler, 1992). Politicians were very much part of the picture, and were not assumed to be confined to a strategic role—if they chose to intervene in detail, then civil servants had to accommodate themselves to that—politicians could legitimately be interested in the *minutiae* as well as the strategy.

The NPG complicates the whole picture by taking a 'network' approach, and positioning both politicians *and* public servants as no more than rather special players in a larger game. In this game all sorts of other 'stakeholders' also carry both legitimacy and influence—companies, non-profits, and civil society associations of many kinds. Instead of being final and authoritative decision-makers, politicians, in this scenario, become joiners-up, deal-makers, people who seek to build and maintain the networks from which agreed policies will emerge, as well as the networks of organizations (partnerships, collaborations) that will implement those policies. Civil servants are also drawn into this ever-shifting web of agreements and deals, for it is they who will have to do much of the 'footwork' with local/national/international stakeholder groups in order to prepare the ground for their political masters to confirm and legitimize the outcomes of on-going, multi-lateral negotiations and consultations. In this model, civil servants certainly have to have management skills, but these are far more than merely technocratic—they must also include the ability to sound out diverse interests, suggest possible compromises, build partnerships, guide networks, and generally *negotiate*. It was significant that, in an excellent recent overview of the 'metagovernance' of networks, the authors repeatedly referred to 'politicians and public managers', without making any distinction between their roles (Sørensen and Torfing, 2009). They acknowledge the need to recruit or train new types of public manager because some of the existing ones 'will be unable or unwilling to change their role from rule-observing bureaucrats to strategic developers and from case and programme managers to network managers' (ibid., p. 254).

One interesting implication here is that the enormous growth of 'leadership' training for senior civil servants—a trend which has been seen in some continental European states as well as in the core NPM states—may mean different things in different countries (Pollitt, and Op de Beeck 2010). In fact there may be separate 'brands' of the 'new public leadership' according to whether the NPM, NWS, or NPG model is preferred (Bouckaert, 2010). Table 6.1 expresses these contrasting models in simple form.

The first thing to say about the correspondence between the empirical evidence on the one hand and the NPM, NWS, and NPG models on the other is that it is not a close or comfortable fit for *any* of the three. Politicians, it seems are often reluctant to accept or confine themselves to the roles these models assign to them—or, at least enough of them are reluctant, enough of the time. And civil servants have difficulties too. Some of these are indicated in Table 6.2.

It should also be pointed out that, while all these models probably fit some situations quite well, they certainly do not fit all the vast range of roles which public servants are called upon to perform. Thus in one situation—say looking for partners to redevelop a run-down city centre, a public servant may be expected to act entrepreneurially, but in another, such as administering a pension fund or conducting a public inquiry, s/he is not. So part of the problem with each of these ideal-type models is that they are each models of only a subset of the situations which politicians and their officials have to deal with (Pollitt, 2003, pp. 161–8). We will now explore the problems of each model in more detail.

Table 6.1 Roles for politicians and civil servants: three ideal-type models

Model	Role for Politicians	Role for Civil Servants
NPM	Strategic goal setting	Autonomous managers, sometimes entrepreneurs, held to account through performance frameworks plus incentives. Mainly working in arms length agencies
NWS	Traditional—takers of authoritative decisions, both big and small	Professional implementers of a) laws and b) politicians' decisions. Technically expert. High quality service to clients. Public service ethical code
NPG	Forgers and guarantors of compromise deals between multiple stakeholders	Network managers; partnership leaders; negotiators; searchers for leverage, synergies

Table 6.2 Weaknesses in the three ideal-type models

Model	Role for Politicians	Role for Civil Servants
NPM	Strategic goal setting: *but politicians often do not wish to be confined to this role. They want to get involved in the detail*	Autonomous managers, sometimes entrepreneurs, held to account through performance frameworks plus incentives. Mainly working in 'arms length' agencies: *loss of sense of a unified public service and increasing distance from ministers reduces responsiveness*
NWS	Traditional—takers of authoritative decisions, both big and small: *less of a problem than NPM or NPG, but there are an increasing number of situations in which it is very hard for politicians to take decisions and make them stick*	Professional implementers of a) laws and b) politicians' decisions. Technically expert. High quality service to clients. Public service ethical code. *Civil servants may experience a tension between their role serving politicians and their role of being responsive to citizens and clients*
NPG	Forgers and guarantors of compromise deals between multiple stakeholders: *some politicians may be good at this, but there are other pressures on them, and in any case the lowest common denominator of what can be agreed between stakeholders is not necessarily the best solution in the public interest*	Network managers; partnership leaders; negotiators; searchers for leverage, synergies: *hard to maintain clarity of accountability for civil servants. May even be hard to maintain a dividing line between what civil servants do and what politicians do*

Weaknesses indicated in italics.

The NPM model seems to have the poorest fit with the evidence, although that may be partly because a) it requires the biggest shift away from traditional political and administrative roles and, b) it has been tried out more extensively than either of the other two, so its flaws are better known. According to the NPM model, the new role held out for ministers is as strategists and opinion-leaders. They will clarify and communicate visions and values, choose appropriate strategies and identify, allocate, and commit resources at the macro-level. The managing/operations will then be done by professional managers, whose performance will subsequently be appraised against clear objectives and targets.

There seems little evidence that this is a credible vision of any likely reality. Most senior politicians, in most countries, have not been trained for such a role, and the pressures on them are not likely to encourage them to adopt it. They may learn the rhetoric—particularly if it enables them to shed responsibility for policy failures—but not much more. The story of the politically dismissed Director of the UK prison service vividly illustrates the dangers: a minister who, faced with an embarrassing series of incidents, tried to save his political reputation by blaming his official, even though the latter had achieved all the performance targets set out in his contract (Lewis, 1997). There were similar events with the responsible CEOs for railways in the Netherlands and Belgium. Politically, the incentives are still short term: to make popular announcements of new initiatives, to intervene dramatically when things appear to be going wrong, to follow popular opinion rather than try to educate it, to take up single issues (mirroring the media) rather than to develop integrated strategies, and so on. (As is often wrily observed in government 'all failures are operational'.) And there is evidence that this is exactly what happens (Talbot, 1996 for the UK; Zifcak, 1994, chapter 5, for Australia; Molander et al., 2002 for the steering of Swedish agencies; Radin, 1998 for the Government Performance and Results Act in the USA). 'While the intellectual exercise involved in defining goals and measures of success has its own rigor, it does not fit comfortably into the fragmented decision-making process in both the White House and the Congress' (Radin, 1998, p. 313).

In consensualist political systems the attraction of the NPM vision of ministers as strategists seems even less than in the majoritarian systems of Australia, Canada, New Zealand, and the UK. In Belgium, the Nordic states, and the Netherlands ministers are not far-sighted strategists—their political success and survival depends upon their skills and creativity in putting together coalitions of support to steer through particular pro-grammes. This is even more true for EU institutions. In these environments clear state-ments of strategies and priorities may actually prove counter-productive: the ability to be all things to all (wo)men is much more useful. Lists of objectives will typically be either a) very long and inclusive or b) shorter but so general and capaciously phrased as to exclude very little. In neither case will the list of objectives be very useful operationally but, more importantly to the politicians, in neither case will potential allies be needlessly alienated. Nothing in the NPM can change this political dynamic, which has been recognized by numerous public administration scholars over more than half a century.

Again, as far as the substantive content of management reform is concerned, nothing has happened to alter the diagnosis made by many previous writers on public sector organizational reform, namely that such reforms have little interest for most ministers, as they are not 'vote-catchers', and because they yield results only over long periods of time, if at all. *Announcing* reforms may be mildly rewarding (e.g. Gore, Thatcher, Lange, Howard, Blair), but following them through and checking to see if they worked are not high-priority tasks for most politicians. As the OECD—a leading influence in NPM-type reforms for a decade or more—put it in 2002: 'There are political advantages in launching reform initiatives, and political disadvantages in carrying them through. Hence the prevalence of reform initiatives abandoned before the critical mass-point of cultural change' (OECD, 2002, p. 8; Pollitt, 2009). Of course, when organizational boundaries are changed, politicians take an interest, either to protect their 'patch' or to try to gain 'territory', but this is hardly the perspective of the strategic figure implied in much of the NPM literature.

The analysis in the previous paragraph is even more true for the second group of politicians—those in the legislatures. Their careers are hardly ever shaped by organiza-tional reforms, their constituents are seldom interested in them or knowledgeable about them, and there is little incentive to get involved in such matters, except in the most superficial ways, or as constituency advocates in particular cases when things go wrong ('crippled widow denied disability benefit', etc.). Legislatures have been very slow to make constructive use of the increase in performance information available to them (Johnson and Talbot, 2007; Pollitt, 2006). Most MPs simply don't have the time or inclination to get involved in the details of management. Describing the US Congress' reaction to the National Performance Review Kettl (1994, p. 49) vividly crystallized the problem:

Congress, by practice and the Constitution, attacks problems by passing laws. The NPR seeks to solve problems by improving performance. Congress as an institution works on the input side. The NPR focuses on the output side. Congress has little incentive to worry about results and, in fact, has long indulged itself in a separation-of-powers fantasy that absolves it from any complicity in the executive branch's performance problems.

Turning to the NWS, we should first acknowledge that, of the three, this model represents the smallest movement away from a traditional system, and therefore it might be expected to cause fewer 'waves'. Nevertheless, it is not problem-free. While politicians are not assumed to have to change their behaviour very much, new aspects have been stitched on to the role of civil servants. They are supposed to have become more professional managers, and they are supposed to have learned to behave more responsively to the individual clients of public services. Whilst these are both laudable objectives, there is always the possibility that one or both of them may come into tension with what the directing politicians want. Thus, for example, civil servants as professional managers work out a rational, justifiable scheme for decentralizing and relocating government offices to areas where they will be cheaper and will bring maximum benefit to the local economies, but the politicians have other ideas. They want some of the relocations to be directed to areas which are politically marginal constituencies, or which are loyal to the party in power. Or again, civil servants, attempting to respond to citizens' wishes, carry out opinion surveys and organize focus groups to determine how hospital services should be reorganized within a particular region, but ministers are persuaded by the representatives of the medical profession and the big construction firms that what should actually go ahead is a big new hospital that will involve the closure or run-down of many existing local services. Civil servants are then left looking manipulative or untrustworthy to the local residents who put energy into developing a plan of their own. In the English expression, they are 'hung out to dry' by their political bosses.

The 'professionalism' of the NWS manager is therefore a particularly circumscribed kind of professionalism. It is a professionalism that can only rarely assert the necessity of following its own standard and procedures. Quite often these procedures must bend or even break before the superior force of a political imperative. The best hope for the NWS manager may be in a system such as the Danish or Finnish or Swedish, where there is deep mutual trust and long-established stability, so that politicians are prepared to allow their managers considerable discretion to act 'professionally', and the managers, in their turn, are unquestioningly obedient once a political imperative is declared to them (see, e.g. Kettl et al., 2004). The problem for reformers, of course, is that these Nordic states achieved this condition, not through some particular reform package, but historically, over decades or even centuries of evolution.

It is hard to assess the NPG model because it is often formulated in such a vague and general way (Osborne, 2010). However, it is reasonably clear that it would involve civil servants in extensive 'networking' activities, dealing with a range of groups from the market sector and civil society. In these instances the public officials would not be simply 'messengers', handing down what their ministers had told them they wanted. On the contrary, they would have constructive and creative roles, looking for synergies between different stakeholders, encouraging innovatory solutions, and so on. Rather like the 'entrepreneurial' public officials in the NPM model, this can leave civil servants rather out on a limb. Furthermore, this model tends to assume that, if one gets all the stake-holders around the table with one or more skilled 'network facilitators', then an agreed compromise solution will be found. Unfortunately, this does not always happen, either in practice or even in theory.

The NPG model is still evolving, and has the support of many academics who see it as the answer to problems of governability in complex, cosmopolitan societies. However, it is also widely acknowledged that it has weaknesses and 'silences'. One of these is how one measures the effectiveness of networks, since the somewhat hierarchical 'production model of performance' (see Figure 5.1) is held not to apply to NPG (Sørensen and Torfing, 2009, pp. 239–43). A second is the role of politicians. Network theorists see the need for a new interpretation of 'political primacy':

This primacy is not so much based on the right to define the substance of government policy based on an *ex ante* interpretation of the general interest, but on the capacity to initiate and guide societal discourses aimed at the exploration of interests, the creation of solutions, and thus the *gradual discovery* of the common interest.   (Klijn and Koppenjan, 2000, p. 385—original italics)

This leaves open the question of whether politicians themselves are, on the whole, likely to want to give up their previous form of 'primacy' for this new version. It seems from quite a few case studies of networks that many politicians (understandably) wish to reserve to themselves the right at any point to back out and claim a unique and higher legitimacy as elected representatives. In the case studies analysed by Klijn and Koppenjan, the politicians emerge (to use their words) as 'spoilsports' as often as they do 'playmakers' (ibid., see also Pollitt, 2003, pp. 57–67).

A third problem, which also directly concerns us here, is the issue of democratic accountability. One advantage of traditional hierarchies is that accountability leads up from one level to the next in a nice straight line. It may not always work like that in practice, but in principle it is understandable and clear. By contrast, in the myriad, plastic networks of NPG, how can we see who is responsible for what? Although supporters of network governance, Sørensen and Torfing put the issue with admirable candour:

on the basis of the liberal norms of representative democracy, governance networks appear to be rather undemocratic. There is no equal participation of citizens within a given territory, since only the relevant and affected groups have access to a particular governance network. There is no free and open competition among different political elites to represent the relevant and affected citizens, as the participating stakeholder organizations often possess a monopoly in representing particular function-ally defined groups of people. Finally, democratic control and accountability is weak due to the fact that network participants are not elected, but rather (self) appointed.   (2009, p. 243)

Thus *both* politicians and public managers may be able to use networks to edge away from the usual constraints and transparencies on their activities. The answer to this problem proffered by Sørensen and Torfing is quite a complex and demanding list of principles and tools for 'network metagovernance' (p. 248). Perhaps the proposal which is most relevant to our frontier between politicians and public managers is the following:

The relevant political authorities and public agencies must assign responsibility for strategic gover-nance of particular networks to the politicians and public managers who are directly or indirectly involved in the networked governance processes and, therefore, have the required knowledge of the organizational and political landscape to act as metagovernors.   (p. 254)

It has to be said that this is not an entirely convincing proposal—in several respects. First, it seems to assume that 'the relevant political authorities' *can* just arrange the meta-governance of networks (although much of the network literature stresses how networks cannot be ruled or directed). Second, it further assumes that the 'relevant political autho-rities' will act in a long-sighted, strategic, and principled manner—but it is precisely the fact that they *don't* always do this that causes the problem in the first place! Third, we again have here an instance of NPG writing in which no distinction is made between the roles of politicians and managers. They are all in it together, not only collaborating and negotiat-ing and developing new relationships, but also, now, acting as 'metagovernors'. One must ask whether public managers are either trained or suited to such a role—and, indeed, what politicians (or the citizenry) would think if their officials began to behave in that way? Neither is it only academics who proclaim such bold but problematic futures for 'gover-nance'. Consider the following extract from a particularly gushing recent UK Treasury report about taking a 'whole area' (spatially integrated) approach to public services, an approach which the report refers to as 'Total Place':

The challenges identified by Total Place will require all public leaders to take a broader view of the leadership task in public services. Future leaders will not only be people who can work across organizations on behalf of their places, but people who engage effectively with peers, communities, the third sector and with local democratic representatives. They might be political leaders, chief executives, and chief constables; equally they might be programme managers, frontline staff or members of the public.   (HM Treasury, 2010, p. 59)

To conclude this section, we may remark that any model which assigns a new role to politicians is at risk of being embarrassed by their lack of cooperation. It is as well to remember an observation which was originally applied to attempts to establish profes-sional, career public services, independent of political influence, but which could also, perhaps be applied to all three ideal models—NPM, NWS, and NPG:

in government, politics is still trumps and if political leaders have the desire to impose their will over the public sector it is very likely that they will win; they may win by covert strategies, but they will win.   (Peters and Pierre, 2004, pp. 288–9)

6.4 How far does the notion of public service bargains help us to understand changes at the borderline between politicians and civil servants?

The three ideal types we examined in the previous section (NPM, NWS, NPG) are all broad-scope models of how the whole of the public sector can be run. Whilst they do—as we have just seen—have considerable implications for the borderline(s) between politicians and officials, it may be that the concept of public service bargains (PSBs) may help even more. After all, the PSB concept is specifically built for, and focused on, the frontier between politics and administration.

The main types of PSB were set out in Figure 4.3. The discussion of trajectories in Chapter 4, Section 5, suggested that, although there were significant exceptions, a general tendency could be discerned in which civil services moved away from trustee type bargains and towards agency type bargains. This, though, is no more than a useful summary description. It does not yet tell us what the reason or reasons for such a change may have been. That, perhaps, is most cogently summarized in the title of Peters and Pierre's 2004 book, *Politicization of the Civil Service in Comparative Perspective: The Quest for Control*. The hypothesis is that, faced with more complex, rapidly changing societies, with faster-moving, more aggressive media, and with dwindling popular loyalty to specific political parties, executive politicians have reached for any tools that appear likely to offer them more protection. One such device is to surround themselves with cohorts of politically loyal, media-savvy and, if possible, substantively expert 'advisers'. An empirical review of the New Zealand experience with advisers put the matter very clearly:

there is a sense among our respondents that policy-making is simply more difficult these days than it once was. Intractable policy problems, a more intrusive media that operates in real time . . . exponential increases in the amount of information policy-makers must absorb and master, and a more demanding and discerning public are among the characteristics of a contemporary policy environment which places ministers under increasing pressure.   (Eichbaum and Shaw, 2007, p. 465)

In PSB terms, such advisers are agents, not trustees. Most of them will be brought in on term contracts, although a few may be career civil servants who turn out to have the requisite sympathies and skills. We have seen a growth in the numbers of this sort of operative in Australia, Belgium, Canada, France, the Netherlands, New Zealand, the UK, and the US—although starting from very different previous levels, and appointed in a variety of ways. Some may be agents subject to short-term direction (B2b in terms of Figure 4.3), while some may be given delegated authority and allowed to go off and do their master's work at a distance (B2a). Some may have only one master (B2b2), while others may have several (B2a1).

This is an important development 'on the borderline'. It could be said that it means that the 'border' itself has been getting wider—the importance of this zone in between pure politician and pure career trustee has been growing. However, it has clearly not been a particularly simple or uniform process. Indeed, the original book by Hood and Lodge acknowledges that PSBs are usually informal rather than formal, and that they do not come in a single form but vary over time and place—Hood and Lodge, 2006, p. 24. The book also describes an almost endless series of ways in which one PSB can morph into another—and back again. So the taxonomy itself becomes rather complex.

Empirical work is only just beginning to come in, and thus far it suggests that we are not witnessing a simple transition from one type of PSB to another. Thus the PSB for Danish permanent secretaries has not become particularly managerial, despite some reforms which might seem to point in that direction. The PSB for top Dutch officials has acquired a slightly more managerial flavour, but still has consociational/trustee elements and might be best described as a hybrid. In Belgium, what was previously a B1a1 trustee/consociationalist type of bargain with agency/serial loyalist overtones (B2b1) has moved towards a complex delegated agency type (B2a1). As Eichenbaum and Shaw (2007) make clear, the effects of a growth of political advisers may be positive or negative for both politicians and career bureaucrats. Expert advisers may screen out certain proposals from the career civil service as politically too sensitive—thus restricting the range of options open to ministers. Alternatively, they may raise the quality of policy proposals coming from the civil service by constructively challenging them at an early stage, and making them more politically manageable. They may be doctrinaire and short term, or they may work in partnership with top civil servants to encourage innovatory but rigorous thinking. The games played in the borderlands between politicians, political advisers, and 'trustee' civil servants are not necessarily zero-sum, but they are by no means necessarily 'win-win' either.

Taken together, these findings confirm a very general direction of change in most countries, but not much more. We would also have to acknowledge that there have been some moves back towards re-emphasizing a unified, career public service—especially in those countries where the NPM-style fragmentation had gone furthest—Australia, New Zealand, and the UK (Advisory Group on Reform of Australian Government Administration, 2010; Whitcombe and Gregory, 2008). Overall, therefore, the PSB framework is helpful but itself quite slippery. It tends to confirm the trajectories we have already described in Chapter 4, and to reinforce the perception that there have been significant differences between core NPM countries and NWS countries.

6.5 What is the relationship between public management reform and public attitudes towards politicians and civil servants?

On the face of it the question 'What do the citizens think about public management reform?' may seem both fundamental and straightforward. Surely, in a liberal democracy, this is the ultimate test of any government action or programme? Such assumptions are further supported by both political rhetoric around the issue of rebuilding citizens' trust in government and by a widespread debate concerning the apparent loss of legitimacy by governments throughout the Western (and Australasian) world. The academic fascination with this began a long time ago, and has embraced academics of very different theoretical persuasions (see, e.g. Habermas, 1976; Nevitte, 1996; Nye et al., 1997). Some write of a loss of legitimacy, others of a decline in deference, others still of a loss of trust, or of confidence. There are interesting differences between these concepts (legitimacy/deference/trust/confidence), but from the point of view of management reform they all point towards a more critical and possibly recalcitrant audience for attempts to remodel at least those public sector organizations which deal directly with the citizenry.

Unfortunately, the question itself is packed with doubtful assumptions. For example, do most citizens know anything about the many reforms which have been proclaimed and implemented by OECD governments? They are seldom the stuff of TV news or newspaper headlines. Even if they may have encountered some references to reforms, are most citizens sufficiently interested to pay any attention? If we take one of the most extensively (and expensively) promoted reforms, the UK *Citizen's Charter*, one survey indicated that 71 per cent of citizens had heard of it (ICM, 1993), but other research indicated that very few people possessed any accurate knowledge of what was in it (Beale and Pollitt, 1994). This ignorance of actual mechanisms and substance survived despite a government campaign that had mailed a glossy leaflet to every household in the land. Six years later, a Labour government printed 100,000 copies of its annual performance report and made them available at £2.99 in the supermarkets. Only 12,000 were purchased, and under the terms of the contract many thousands had to be bought back by the government (BBC News, 1999, 2000). In Italy, the proud launch of their own citizen's charter escaped the attention of most Italians (Schiavo, 2000). In Belgium the citizen's charter was professionally published in the State Monitor, as royal and ministerial decrees, and therefore remained at the administrative level (Bouckaert et al., 2003). One imagines that more technical reforms—such as the 'reinvention labs' in the US NPR, or results-oriented budgeting in Finland and Sweden—would remain completely unknown to the vast majority of the populations of the countries in question.

Yet lack of knowledge may not be the most serious barrier. Equally distorting can be the possession of *false* information or serious conceptual misconceptions. Take, for example, the average American's view of the efficiency of federal programmes. Surveys show that most Americans believe that more than 50 per cent of the expenditure in social security programmes goes in overheads. The true figure is less than 2 per cent (Bok, 1997, p. 56). Surveys in the UK in the 1960s were said simultaneously to reveal majorities against 'nationalization' but in favour of 'public ownership'.

However, let us set the (major) problems of citizen ignorance and indifference on one side for a moment, and concentrate on those issues where citizens do, it seems, hold definite opinions. After all, surveys in a number of countries have been carried out with questions such as 'How do you rate the overall performance of government?' or 'Do you have no confidence/some confidence/a great deal of confidence in politicians/civil servants/bank managers/doctors?' and there has been no difficulty in obtaining responses and adding them up to percentage 'answers'. It is on the basis of time series of surveys of this genre that some political scientists have identified a problem of declining legitimacy and trust in many liberal democracies (for summaries, see Nye et al., 1997; the Pew Research Centre, 1998). This is certainly interesting data, but the problems of interpretation are considerable. For example, two important questions are what are respondents thinking of when they declare their opinions on the overall performance of government, or their level of trust? What they read in the newspaper last week? A recent TV appearance by the Prime Minister? The government's decision not to increase the state pension by the full rate of inflation? The poor service the respondent received in the post office that morning? Furthermore there is the question of the rationale behind the opinion. *Why* does the respondent think that state pension decisions/macro-economic policy/counter service at the post office is good or bad? What expectations did s/he bring to the question, and how were those expectations formed? Unfortunately, only a few surveys can offer any help with these sorts of questions—we may know *what* the average citizen thinks, but seldom *why* they think it.

Quite apart from what may lie behind the percentages in the survey reports, it seems that the gloomy picture of falling confidence may itself result from a narrow reading of too few sources. In a careful examination of international figures on trust in government, Van de Walle et al. (2008) arrive at the conclusion that

The findings contradict the political and the popular discourse. Empirically, there is little evidence of an overall long-term decline in trust in government, although there are institutions that have suffered from a loss in trust. (p. 61)

This ushers us into a more complicated landscape. First, opinions as to overall governmental performance, or levels of trust, do not necessarily correlate closely with opinions on much more concrete and specific issues (e.g. how adequate is the postal service?). It seems quite possible for citizens to maintain a generalized cynicism or mistrust of 'government' whilst simultaneously being reasonably satisfied with many of the specific public services they actually make use of (Canadian Centre for Management Development, 1998a and b). The level of this generalized dissatisfaction with government is 'strongly connected to how people feel about the overall state of the nation' (Pew Research Centre, 1998, p. 1). Meanwhile, as we saw in Chapter 5, citizen opinions of specific public services may go up (Table 5.7 showed a general improvement in mean service quality scores for specified Canadian public services—and a bigger average increase for public services than for private). In the UK too, the 1993 ICM survey found that the public's perceptions of improvements in services by no means put private sector services consistently above those provided by the public sector—for example, NHS doctors and state postal services were placed somewhat above building societies and far above banks (ICM, 1993, p. 16).

Certainly, there is no firm ground for the assertion that the public would like the welfare state to be 'rolled back' and replaced by private modes of provision. For example, a 1993 attitudinal survey of New Zealanders showed

strong endorsement for the notion of a universalist rather than a residualist welfare state, including support for more taxes (although not necessarily a willingness to pay more tax personally), as well as an underlying conviction that politicians are out of touch and unworthy of the government's trust. (Vowles et al., 1995, p. 97)

Similarly, more recently, the 2002 Swedish election results could be interpreted as a vote for public services rather than tax reductions. Even in the USA, supposedly the stronghold of anti-government, pro-private sector sentiments, it has been shown that: 'Fully 72% of Americans believe that government should see to it that no one is without food, shelter or clothing... as many as felt that way in the 1960s' (Pew Research Centre, 1998, p. 7).

Respondents are frequently able to distinguish between different groups of actors in the process of governance. Most commonly they extend a tolerable degree of trust towards civil servants, but a considerably lower (and falling) degree towards political leaders. For example:

surveys suggest that the public's frustration is directed more at politicians who lead government than at civil servants who administer it. By a margin of 67% to 16% the public has more trust in federal workers than in their elected officials to do the right thing. In that vein 69% now say that they have a favorable opinion of government workers—an improvement from the 55% that held that view in a 1981 *Los Angeles Times* national opinion survey. (Pew Research Centre, 1998, p. 2)

Thus, if President Reagan was right in saying that the federal government was part of the problem rather than part of the solution, it was the politicians rather than the bureaucrats he should have been aiming to reform! Furthermore—for the USA at least—it is not so much failures in the *efficiency* of elected politicians that provokes public distrust, as the perception that such leaders are failing to uphold high moral standards (Pew Research Centre, 1998). This is extremely interesting material, as it carries the implication that public management reform is unlikely to contribute much to enhancing the legitimacy of a particular, current government, for two solid reasons. First, the public *do* distinguish between political leaders and civil servants, and the bulk of their distrust is directed at the former. Second, the deepest roots of discontent with the political leadership do not grow out of perceptions of their incapacity to manage affairs, but rather from their (perceived) untrustworthiness or low moral standards. Finally—just to complicate matters further— the public may well also draw distinctions between different *types* of politician. They may trust local politicians more than national politicians. Or they may respond more favour- ably to a question about how far they trust 'parliament' than to one about how far they trust 'government'. All in all, it looks as though publics may be quite discriminating and sophisticated in their judgements, and as though sweeping generalizations about a loss of public confidence in (by implication) *all* government in *all* countries are inaccurate and misleading.

Third, citizen responses can be highly context-specific, and need to be interpreted in the light of that. For example:

> it appears that fire services are always rated highly by citizens while municipal planning services are rated much lower. This may reflect the nature of the services: one is an essential service; while the other is a regulatory function that may impact on some citizens negatively, in order to ensure fairness in protecting other citizens, such as in zoning regulations. *Thus a rating of 7.0 would be a poor score for a fire service, but an excellent score for a planning service.* (Canadian Centre for Management Development, 1998b, p. 6, italics as in the original)

Thus, ideally, analysis of citizen opinion needs to be topic specific (some services are inherently more popular than others) and person specific (politicians are distrusted more than civil servants). One also needs to know something about the citizens' own experiences (are responses coming from those who have little knowledge and no experi- ence to be counted as equally valid as those from other citizens who are regular, indeed, 'expert' users of the particular service in question?). The question of 'trust in government' turns out to be as complex as government itself.

Indeed, the concept of legitimacy itself is far from simple. To say that one accepts the current government, or the current system of public administration, as legitimate is a statement which may conceal a range of states of knowledge and a variety of attitudes. Attitudes may range from reluctant acquiescence ('I suppose there isn't any alternative') through lukewarm acceptance to enthusiastic approbation.

In sum, we may conclude that the public's attitude to management reform in particular, and to public administration in general, is both complex and as yet only lightly re- searched. Most of the public probably know little about most specific reforms. Most of them are also capable of simultaneously maintaining a spectrum of attitudes towards the state apparatus, distinguishing between different groups of actors, different services, and questions of greater generality or specificity. Some of their attitudes may be deeply founded and hard to shift (for example, the widespread apparent support, in many countries, for the continuance of the basic fabric of the welfare state), while other opinions may be quite volatile, easily altered by new information or experiences. Thus bold assertions that the public have lost confidence in public services, or that they 'want' less bureaucracy, or that they are demanding higher quality, frequently turn out to be fragile—and therefore inadequate as platforms upon which to erect specific programmes of reform.

6.6 Politics and management: an overview

The relationship between politics, public management, and public opinion is a contentious area, and one in which systematic data is at best patchy. Having made these caveats, we will attempt to draw out a few broad propositions from the arguments and evidence advanced above.

First, public management reforms *have* altered the relationships between elected and appointed officials, in a number of countries and a number of ways. In this sense, at least, they are not 'neutral'. It seems likely that these changes have been greatest in the core NPM countries, somewhat less in the northern group of European countries, and smallest in the central European group. Second, there is an absence of convincing evidence concerning the willingness or ability of executive politicians to fulfil the mandates they are given within each of our three ideal models—but particularly the parts they are given to play within the NPM and NPG frameworks. The kindest thing that could be said about reform models which cast politicians in such roles would be that they are unproven and seem to fly in the face of known incentives to behave in a more traditional 'political' fashion. Third, managers do appear to have gained extra authority in a number of ways, but at the same time political control has been vigorously reasserted in many of the twelve countries. There is no *necessary* contradiction between these two developments—the public sector is large and diverse enough for both to be happening at the same time. In specific cases, however, there may be a quite definite tension. In some of these cases, this has taken the form of difficulties between career civil servants and the enlarged ring of political advisers who surround and attempt to protect ministers. In others, civil service managers, granted greater autonomy, have behaved *too* entrepreneurially, and have taken risks or made decisions which have brought embarrassment to their political bosses. Fourth, any suggestion that public management can be radically depoliticized (in the sense of 'political' outlined above) is either a misunderstanding or is contradicted by evidence from many countries. The allocation of, say, health care resources or decisions about educational standards or major public infrastructure projects are all inherently 'political' decisions, whether they are taken by powerful politicians or tough public managers (or, indeed, medical doctors or teachers). The public will often see the political authority as ultimately responsible—or, at least, sharing responsibility—however much ministers may protest that these are technical or professional decisions which have been taken by the appropriate officials. Fifth, there is a certain ambiguity in much of the rhetoric around strengthening accountability and increasing transparency, insofar as some executive politicians have used the new politics/administration split to redefine policy weaknesses as managerial ('operational') failures. This enables political leaders to shuffle off direct responsibilities for things going wrong—or, at least, to try to. Furthermore, it appears that legislatures have been slow to take up and use the increased flow of performance data which greater transparency and the contemporary emphasis on outputs and outcomes affords. With Chapter 5 in mind, one might say that even when a 'real result' manages to climb over the conceptual, methodological, and political barriers, and escape into the wider public world, it is often left wandering around looking for an audience. Sixth, any simple picture of public opinion as being 'for' or 'against' 'big government' is misleading. Such evidence as is available shows that, however limited the public's knowledge may be of the specifics of reform, popular attitudes towards government are multi-faceted and, in some respects, quite sophisticated.

One further conclusion that might be drawn is that there is a strong need for a more realistic model of the role politicians can and should play in the running of the state apparatus. Neither the representative democracy/public-interest model of the Anglo-Saxon countries nor the continental *Rechtsstaat* model seems sufficient to cope with the new forms and practices which have emerged. It is not so much that these traditional models are wrong, more that they are, by themselves, inadequate to present-day circumstances. More controversially, one might suggest that any rethinking of these matters ought to focus at least as much on the induction and training of politicians, and on the framework of incentives and penalties surrounding them, as on reforming the public service or yet again reshuffling its organizations. Why is it usually assumed that it is the civil servants who are in need of reform, but not ministers or the other politicians who may hope to become ministers in due course? This is *not* to advocate some modern version of Platonic guardians and neither, certainly, is it a plea for MPs to be forced to take MBAs. However, it *is* to suggest that the preparation of politicians for high office has, in many countries, been a 'no-go' area for reformers for too long. If it is in fact the *politicians themselves* who are most widely and deeply distrusted, then perhaps there are sound democratic reasons for bringing their readiness for the tasks they are confronted with to the fore as an item on the agenda for public debate.

7 Trade-offs, balances, limits, dilemmas, contradictions, and paradoxes

> [T]he major paradoxes, with their unpalatable medium term and long term implications, appear to be general and permanent in character and seem to be rooted in misunderstanding, in the policy contradictions which characterise the reforms and in the naivete of the reformers themselves.
>
> (Wright, 1997, 12)

7.1 Reform optimism/memory loss

A prominent, but frequently unremarked feature of the public sector reforms of the last twenty years has been a large optimism about the *potential of management itself* (Pollitt, 1993, pp. 1–5). Few boundaries seem to be envisaged for the exercise of this set of dynamic and purportedly generic skills. At the beginning of the most intensive period of reform a British cabinet minister expressed himself thus: 'Efficient management is the key to the [national] revival . . . and the management ethos must run right through our national life—private and public companies, civil service, nationalized industries, local government, the National Health Service' (Heseltine, 1980). Such optimism stands in contrast to an older tradition of speaking and writing about the running of public sector organizations, one that sees these activities as subject to a number of widespread, 'built-in', and possibly inevitable limitations and trades-off. In traditional, permanent bureaucracies, cautionary wisdom about such administrative constraints was built up, case by case and over time, and used by seasoned career officials to warn politicians of the likely limitations of their proposed innovations (which, in administrative form, were seldom as novel as the politicians may have supposed). Since the 1970s, however, in the most radically reforming countries, this kind of cautious mandarin has gone out of cultural fashion in favour of the 'can-do' chief executive (see Pollitt, 2003*a*, chapter 7 for an analysis of management gurus and the representation of managers as heroes and visionaries, and Peters and Pierre, 2004 for an account of the politicization of the higher civil service). Furthermore, in these same countries, a combination of downsizing, the spread of term contracts for senior officials and higher rates of turnover of various categories of staff has operated to shorten institutional memories, so that fewer and fewer in the organization are likely to know of the precedents of ten or twenty years ago, or to wish to bring these inconveniences to the attention of their political masters (Pollitt, 2000, 2008).

The grip of the 'lessons of history' has been further weakened by the popularity of the notion that, catalysed by rapid economic and technological change, the business of management is constantly confronting *new* challenges, and therefore, by implication at least, rapidly leaving *old* concerns far behind. Best-selling texts with titles such as *Thriving on Chaos: A Handbook for a Management Revolution* (Peters, 1987) or *Re-engineering the Corporation* (Hammer and Champy, 1995) have encouraged the belief that the past is irrelevant. Consider the following advice from the founding fathers of re-engineering:

Re-engineering is about beginning again with a clean sheet of paper. It is about rejecting the conventional wisdom and received assumptions of the past. Re-engineering is about inventing new approaches to process structures that bear little or no resemblance to those of previous eras.   (Hammer and Champy, 1995, p. 49)

It might be objected that the cited sources are concerned with the private sector. In fact the management 'gurus' in question insist that their insights apply to *all* organizations (see, e.g. Hammer and Champy, 1995, pp. 218–19), and their work has certainly been taken up and noticed by governments in a number of countries. Furthermore, there is a parallel stream of rhetoric specifically focused on government. Probably the most read and talked-about English language text on government reform of the last decade is replete with declarations such as the following:

the bureaucratic model developed in very different conditions from those we experience today... Today all that has been swept away. We live in an era of breathtaking change... Today's environment demands institutions that are extremely flexible and adaptable... It demands institutions that *empower* citizens rather than simply *serving* them.   (Osborne and Gaebler, 1992, *Reinventing Government*, p. 15)

Without wishing to deny the evident truth of changing conditions for government, we do wish to register some scepticism concerning what one might term the 'history is dead, everything is new' school of management thought. On the contrary, as governments have geared up to tackle the problems of the late twentieth century, the record (as we read it) shows many examples of old constraints and trades-off reappearing in new clothes.

In this chapter, therefore, we wish to take seriously the concept of there being intrinsic constraints and limits to administrative reform. This is hardly revolutionary. It has been espoused, in different ways, by a number of the most distinguished academic writers on public administration and management. For example, just after the Second World War, Herbert Simon famously noted that the 'principles' of public administration were more like proverbs and, like proverbs, tended to come in contradictory pairs (Simon, 1946). Charles Perrow envisaged bureaucratic processes as being inherently beset with dilemmas, in which to organize in one way was inevitably to pay a serious price in another (Perrow, 1972). Christopher Hood developed an extended typology of 'limits' to administration, in which administrative dilemmas and non-linearities commonly conspired to distort the process of implementation in the direction of inefficiency, corruption, or even counter-intentional effects (Hood, 1976). Hood and Jackson, following in the footsteps of

Herbert Simon, later drew attention to the way in which administrative arguments often come in matching pairs, with advantages and disadvantages trading off as one moves from one polar principle to its opposite (Hood and Jackson, 1991). More recently, Hood has articulated an even more elaborate scheme of constraints, using grid/group cultural theory in an attempt to demonstrate that each administrative philosophy carries not only intrinsic limitations but, beyond that, the seeds of its own decay (Hood, 1998; see also 6, 2004). One of us has traced the way in which administrative fashions have swung between centralization and decentralization (Pollitt, 2005). Many other writers have noted a tendency for organizations' reforms to move in cycles or waves (e.g. Davis et al., 1999; Light, 1995; Talbot and Johnstone, 2007). Recently one group of scholars produced a whole book about the 'paradoxes of modernization', subtitled *Unintended Consequences of Public Policy reform* (Margetts et al., 2010).

Whilst we do not follow any of these authors exactly, we do believe that their shared perception that the administration of public programmes commonly exhibits deep-seated and recurring types of dilemmas and contradictions—and therefore limits and cycles—is accurate. The substitution in Anglophone environments of the magical word 'management' for the unfashionable 'administration' does little to change the types of limits with which these analysts were concerned (though it may lead to an increase in the proportion of certain types of problem in relation to other types). Obtaining reliable information about tax-evasion behaviours or coordinating a variety of agencies which are all delivering services to the unemployed are activities which pose fundamentally similar organizational problems whether the public officials concerned deem themselves to be rule-following bureaucrats or performance-chasing managers. Neither do the wonders of information technology dissolve the need to balance, choose, and recognize limits. Vastly improved capacities for data processing and rapid communication certainly make possible styles of governance, coordination, and (not least) supervision which were difficult or unachievable previously. However, ICTs cannot resolve logical contradictions, bruised motivations, ergonomic constraints, or problems of competing and divergent values (Hudson, 1998). They may, however, help decision-makers to muster a clearer or more detailed picture of the options before them—whether this clarity is welcome or not.

To further investigate these limits and contradictions we will take three steps. First (7.2), we will attempt to define the various kinds of problem concept a little more precisely. Second (7.3), we will list some contemporary candidates for trade-offs, limits, etc. Third (7.4–7.11), we will examine each of these candidates in more detail, relating them to the empirical material offered elsewhere in this book, and also to the three main models of reform that we introduced in Chapter 1. We end with a short, reflective summary.

7.2 The vocabulary of balance and contradiction

Thus far we have referred to 'constraints', 'limits', 'trades-off', and 'problems'. In an attempt to be slightly more precise we will henceforth distinguish between:

Trade-offs: where having more of one desideratum, or lessening one problem, inevitably diminishes some other wished-for quality or increases a different problem. This is therefore a situation where decision-makers are obliged to *balance* between different things which they want, but cannot feasibly have more of all at the same time—indeed, where to have more of one entails having less of another. An example that Hood (1976) gives is that of appointing long-serving local officials, which is likely to increase local knowledge and continuity but simultaneously to increase the number of instances where the local officials 'go native' or succumb to the temptations of corruption. On the other hand one can send in mobile officials whose allegiances are to the centre and who know they will soon be posted on elsewhere. Choosing this second route reduces corruption and the dangers of the official developing excessive sympathy for the perceived difficulties faced by the administered local population, but it also reduces the local knowledge available to the administering organization, and thereby increases the chances that the local population are managing to evade or pervert the intended system of controls. Trade-offs can easily lead to cycling, as going one way eventually produces drawbacks (corruption among long-serving locals) so that the alternative begins to look more attractive, until, that is, the drawbacks of the other course also become manifest—in the above case the lack of local knowledge on the part of the loyal, but short-term incumbents posted from the centre. Then the return swing begins.

Limits: we will use the dictionary definition of a limit as 'a point, degree or amount beyond which something does not or may not pass' (Harrap's *Chambers Encyclopedic English Dictionary*, 1994, p. 741). Can there be limits of this kind to reforms? Yes: for example, more efficient management of hospital in-patients can reduce the average length of stay for certain surgical procedures by 20 per cent, or 30 per cent, or even more. This frees up bedspace for a higher patient throughput, shorter waiting times, and so on. However, the length of stay for, say, an artificial hip replacement cannot be reduced to zero. At any given state of medical knowledge and technology there will be limits of this kind. Similarly, the cost of identifying and fining a speeding motorist can be greatly reduced by the installation of automatic cameras and computerized billing of fines, but some cost will remain. One danger for management is to believe that a particular process of reform that yielded X per cent savings or a Y per cent speed-up last year can be made to do the same thing this year and next year. Another type of limit which frequently occurs in public administration is the error rate. Errors occur in classifying things and people, in making payments, in recording observations and measurements, and so on. Good management may well be able to reduce these rates from, say, 10 per cent to 2 per cent, but they often cannot reduce them from 2 per cent to zero, and to try to do so can result in a great deal of wasted effort.

Dilemmas: situations in which the manager is faced with a choice of two or more unsatisfactory alternatives, that is, in which the available decisions about a given problem cannot be made in such a way as to *solve* the problem, but only to substitute one set of undesirable features for another. A dilemma is thus the limiting case of a trade-off, in that it is a trade-off in which the situation remains negative whichever option is chosen. Sometimes rooting out public service corruption and/or incompetence may take on the characteristics of a dilemma. To publicize the problem lowers the standing of that part of the public service, undermines public trust, and may even encourage increased citizen recalcitrance ('why should I pay my taxes if they are putting them in their own pockets?'). On the other hand, not to publicize the problem may allow it to continue and can prevent the formation of a sufficient coalition of support to ensure that real action is taken.

Another concept to which we will resort is the paradox. Paradoxes are seeming contradictions: statements which appear self-contradictory and false, and yet may contain a particular kind of truth. The dictionary example is often 'More haste, less speed'. Some commentators have found a whole string of paradoxes entwined in the rhetoric and practice of contemporary administrative reform (Wright, 1997). Some of these are pitched at the level of whole countries or systems, others at the level of specific institutions or practices. Wright begins his account with a striking example of a macro-paradox:

The first major policy paradox is that the most radical reform programmes appear to have been introduced in countries with the most efficient administrations, in other words, in those countries with the least need!   (Wright, 1997, pp. 9–10)

Earlier chapters in this book have contained some possible reasons for this curious state of affairs. Perhaps (chapter 3) it has been the countries which are constitutionally and politically most *able* to make big changes to their administrative arrangements that have done so. Yet these are also probably the countries *which had already made significant modernizations of their public sector organizations in the past* (for the same reason). However, our account here will mainly address more specific propositions within the portfolio of current reform ideas. One might argue, for example, that the statements which have been made in a number of countries to the effect that public management reforms will make public servants more accountable to political leaders *and simultaneously more accountable to the citizens who use public services*, though appealing, are paradoxical. How can public officials serve two masters, masters who are quite unlikely to have identical needs or preferences? Further examples occur when policymakers say that they intend to empower middle managers in the public service whilst at the same time radically downsizing the numbers of that group who will continue in public employment. *Perhaps* these apparent dissonances can be harmoniously reconciled, but it is not immediately obvious how.

It must be allowed that sometimes, at least, what sounds to be an incompatibility *is* an incompatibility, and cannot be reconciled. In such cases we may speak of straightforward *contradictions*. Guy B. Peters is one comparativist who has suggested that, while the contemporary nostrums of public management reform appear to contain a number of contradictions, some at least of these can be resolved into a question of finding an appropriate *balance* rather than a question of choosing between wholly incompatible alternatives (Peters, 1998a). In effect he is saying that some contradictions are really trade-offs rather than absolute contradictions. Thus one may think of a contradiction as a case of a very steep-sided trade-off—that is, as a situation in which having more of one benefit immediately and sharply reduces another benefit. Now we turn to more specific cases.

7.3 Public management reform: some candidate contradictions and trade-offs

As noted in Section 7.1, many writers have noticed apparent contradictions or tensions within the body of contemporary management prescriptions. We will draw on these to compile our own shortlist of 'candidate contradictions'—sets of prescriptions which at first sight appear incompatible, or at least unstable, and which therefore merit further discussion and investigation. The shortlist does not pretend to be exhaustive. It is no more than a selection of issues where there is some empirical evidence that problems have indeed occurred—illustrative but not comprehensive.

Our list includes some (seemingly) incompatible paired statements and some more complicated/less obvious combinations. Each will be explained in the sections that follow. The shortlist is set out below:

1. Increase political control of the bureaucracy/free managers to manage/empower service consumers.

2. Give priority to making savings/improve public service quality.

3. Promote flexibility and innovation/increase citizen trust and therefore governmental legitimacy.

4. Motivate staff and promote cultural change/weaken tenure and downsize.

5. Reduce burden of internal scrutiny and associated paperwork/sharpen managerial accountability.

6. Develop more partnerships and contracting out/improve horizontal coordination ('joined-up government'; 'integrated service provision').

7. Increase effectiveness/sharpen managerial accountability.

8. Promote open government and transparency/protect privacy.

7.4 Increase political control of the bureaucracy/free managers to manage/empower service consumers

Each of these three prescriptions features regularly in the rhetoric of public management reform. There is no doubt that reform leaders such as (among others) Thatcher, Reagan, and Mulroney wished to reassert (as they saw it) political control over the bureaucratic machine (Savoie, 1994). It was part of the NPM formula. It was also an intention among the French political leadership (Rouban, 1997), at least some elements among Swedish politicians (Pierre, 1995), and the Australian Labor governments of the 1980s (Halligan, 1997). Equally, there is no doubt that increasing the freedom managers have to manage has been a recurrent theme in countless texts and speeches—though more so for those favouring an NPM approach than those who prefer NWS or NPG. For example, a key line in the report which led to the UK's creation of 130 plus executive agencies, employing more than two-thirds of the non-industrial civil service, was: 'At present the freedom of an individual manager to manage effectively and responsibly in the civil service is extremely circumscribed' (Efficiency Unit, 1988, p. 5).

Finally, the empowerment of customers is a theme which has been repeatedly on the lips of politicians bent on reform, especially in the Anglo-Saxon countries. One US National Performance Review document puts it like this: 'Once President Clinton signed the Government Performance and Results Act in August 1993, strategic planning and listening to the "voice of the customer" was no longer just a good idea—it was the law' (National Performance Review, 1997*b*, p. 6). However, this theme is by no means confined to those of an NPM-ish tendency. Both NWS and NPG have their own versions of customer empowerment. Within the NWS it is a question of improving official consultation with citizens before new policies and projects go ahead. The modernized bureaucracy is to be a 'listening organization': the state is to be a friend and partner, not a stern schoolmaster. For NPG it is a matter of government working through networks that include representative groups of citizens, be they residents (for planning issues), patients and carers (for health care issues) or drivers and passengers (for public transport issues). Optimal polices will emerge (or be 'co-produced') from horizontal networks of participating stakeholders. Thus the empowerment/participation theme appears in all three of our models, and has many different aspects and angles (Pollitt, 2003*a*, pp. 83–111).

The problem with these superficially attractive formulations can be encompassed in the question 'How is it possible to give managers greater freedom and yet at the same time place them more under the control of ministers *and* oblige them to be more responsive to newly empowered consumers?' Is it conceivable that all three corners of this triangle can be strengthened simultaneously (minister power, manager power, consumer power), or is this simply a contradiction? As Hood (1998, p. 208) puts it: 'Since not everyone can be "empowered" at the same time, who exactly is to be empowered against whom, and how, is a key test of cultural bias in visions of modernization.'

If it is assumed that the appropriate concept of power and authority in this case is zero-sum (i.e. power is a fixed quantum, so that a gain here must be balanced by a loss somewhere else), then this particular NPM 'recipe' is a three-way contradiction. However, it is possible, on the basis of a different assumption, to interpret these claims in a more sympathetic (or at least paradoxical) light. Such a sympathetic reading might run along the following lines:

1. Managers can have greater freedom over the marshalling of their resources (combining inputs and processes in different and perhaps innovative ways) while at the same time ministers are offered a clearer picture of what is achieved—the outputs and outcomes of all the newly unencumbered management activity. So both politicians and managers can increase their control—though of somewhat different things. The clearest expression of this philosophy has been the New Zealand system in which ministers are deemed responsible for objectives and outcomes, and they then contract with the heads of departments (chief executives) for packages of measured outputs that are calculated to produce the desired outcomes (Boston et al., 1996; Halligan, 1997).

2. Similarly, empowered consumers (or citizens) may have access to better information about the performance of a service, and may enjoy improved means of complaint/ more efficient redress if things are not to their liking, and may participate in planning and prioritizing the service through a variety of mechanisms (these empowerments manifesting themselves in the shape of charters, better complaints systems, user panels, etc.—though whether the majority of citizens actually want to spend more time doing these things is an open question). At the same time, managers can gain

new freedoms to arrange their resources in ways that are calculated to maximize consumer satisfaction. There is no *necessary* contradiction between these two separate but complementary spheres of autonomy.

3. Thus, all three groups—politicians, public service managers, and public service users—*can* gain greater control, each in their own corner. Power is not zero-sum but rather variable: everyone can be a winner.

Is this a convincing defence against the charge of contradiction? Perhaps, but only if some rather demanding conditions are met. Three deserve particular mention. First, politicians must refrain from interfering in the management sphere (the allocation, manipulation, and combination of different kinds of resource; the motivation of staff; the establishment and maintenance of suitable organizational structures, systems, and processes) and confine themselves to setting strategies, scrutinizing 'results', and taking action if the results are short of target. Second, the priorities and targets handed out by the political leaders must be both clear and reasonably congruent with the demands and expectations of consumers (otherwise managers will be being asked to dance simultaneously to two discordant tunes). Third, where there are different organizations and levels involved in service delivery (as there very frequently will be), all must work within the same, shared set of objectives, targets, values, and—to some extent at least—procedures. Otherwise there is the likelihood that managers will receive conflicting messages from above and consumers will encounter different priorities, standards, and attitudes in different parts of the 'shop'. If one or more of these conditions is transgressed, the likelihood of the triangle being squared (so to speak) will be reduced.

The question of how often the above conditions actually *are* met (and how often they are not) is an empirical one, and the rate may vary with regime type, organizational culture, political ideology, and so on. Insofar as governments attempt to pursue the different visions of NPM, NWS, and NPG, one might expect different rates of different types of failure. Under NPM, in practice, politicians seem to want more control rather than less—which threatens managerial autonomy rather than enhancing it. Certainly, in a number of our countries, doctors, headteachers, social work managers, and many civil servants would see themselves as *more* closely measured and monitored than, say, thirty years ago. And the NPM doctrine that big multi-purpose bureaucracies should be broken up into smaller, more nimble, single-purpose agencies is likely to make joined-up service delivery more, rather than less difficult to achieve. Within an NWS perspective achieving overall coherence across services and sectors may be a slightly less formidable challenge, but the problems of reconciling popular citizen demands received through participative channels with political directives coming down from ministers are just as tricky as within an NPM model. As for giving managers more autonomy, that has (rhetorically at least) been less of a priority within continental European states than in the core NPM states. Insofar as managers become more professional, it may be possible for them to have more autonomy from direct political control, but only as long as they operate within clear professional guidelines and standards. Coming to NPG, its more disaggregated and fluid vision of governance makes the achievement of common standards and joined-up delivery even more problematic than under NPM. There is also an implication that managerial autonomy will not be a high priority—instead managers will be expected to perform 'boundary-spanning' roles, liaising between different stakeholder groups in an endless search for (shifting) consensus and network legitimacy. More importantly, perhaps, in a network model the elected politicians lose some of their specialness—they are no longer the unique bearers and arbiters of the general interest, so, far from reasserting control, they are supposed to be sharing it (Pollitt, 2003, p. 65).

Empirically, it is clear that there have been many occasions in many countries when the vision of mutual, three-cornered empowerment has been announced but not achieved. Some have been recounted earlier in this book. Particularly in welfare state services such as health care, education, personal social services, and social security the figure of the empowered service user has in practice been hard to find (e.g. Clarke and Newman, 1997, chapter 6; Evers et al., 1997; Flösser and Otto, 1998; Harrison and Pollitt, 1994, pp. 125–34). 'Shop front' public service staff may have had customer service training and been enjoined to deal more flexibly with individual service users, but meanwhile managers seem often to have extended their domain without conceding any substantial space for 'consumer power'. In other cases, managers have been pulled in different directions by irreconcilable demands from political bosses and service users (see Pollitt, 2003a, chapter 4 for an extended analysis of these issues).

Nor is the evidence on the second side of the triangle especially encouraging. As we saw in the previous chapter, politicians have not been spectacularly willing to relinquish their former habits of detailed intervention. In some research, managers have recorded more political 'interference', not less (Halligan, 2002; Talbot, 1994). In a number of countries, ministers have appointed extra political advisers and taken other steps to tighten, not loosen, their grip on what their officials are saying and doing (Peters and Pierre, 2004; Chapter 4, Sec. 4.6, above). Nor have ministers necessarily been prepared to spell out their values in a sufficiently precise manner to give managers a clear set of priorities to work to (and therefore, by derivation, a clear set of targets to aim at).

As for the achievement of coordination between different levels and types of organization (the third condition), there can be no doubt that 'partnership' and 'networking' have become extremely fashionable in most of our ten countries and with the EU Commission (e.g. Chancellor of the Exchequer, 1998; Osborne, 2000, 2010; Rosenau, 2000). Being in fashion and being well understood are, however, not at all the same thing. A now substantial literature demonstrates that most governments are still on the steep part of the learning curve as far as these pluriform approaches to service delivery are concerned (e.g. Davies, 2009; Christensen and Lægreid, 2007b; Lowndes and Skelcher, 1998; Peters, 1998b). The available 'technologies' for ensuring 'seamless' service are therefore still experimental and uncertain, so it would be reasonable to conclude that the third condition cannot be satisfied regularly and with certainty.

To sum up: first, the reformers' claims to empower consumers, free managers, and strengthen political control are not always and not necessarily contradictory. Unfortunately, however, the conditions for their simultaneous achievement are difficult to cultivate, so that, in practice, these three aims often do collide or, perhaps less dramatically, one or more of them is simply sidelined or forgotten. In a perfect world the three objectives might be compatible. In the real world public managers usually find themselves facing trade-offs or even downright contradictions. In the post GEC circumstances of severely reduced expenditure (in some countries) the perfect world may be further away than ever.

7.5 Give priority to making savings/improving public sector quality

At the time of writing this is a particularly prominent issue. In many countries politicians, faced with the need to cut public expenditure in the aftermath of the GEC, are claiming that cuts can be made—or most of them can be made—without reducing the quality of basic public services. Indeed, some of them are claiming that the quality of services can continue to improve while major financial savings are nevertheless harvested. Such claims have evoked widespread scepticism among expert commentators as well as among public servants themselves.

Yet to suppose that expenditure reduction and improvement were *always* diametric opposites—irreducible contradictions—would be highly simplistic. Tighter control of public expenditure has figured as one of the most frequent and most powerful motives for public management reform—in almost every country we have surveyed. Some of these reforms have been widely beneficial, and some have undoubtedly achieved the twin desiderata of 'working better and costing less'. New technologies and new organizational processes have both played their parts in such successes. For example, sharing buildings and computer systems between different agencies can simultaneously reduce costs and make access simpler for citizens (HM Treasury, 2010).

We should also note that it is sometimes possible to sidestep the apparent contradiction— at least on the level of concepts and rhetoric. In the field of social security in the UK, for example, much effort has been concentrated on improving the *process* of claiming—training counter staff to be more friendly, smartening up premises, speeding up processing activities, and so on. Not unreasonably, this is often referred to as 'quality improvement'. Meanwhile, however, the actual benefit levels have been tightly controlled, and, in the cases of a number of benefits, eligibility categories have been narrowed. Thus is the paradox 'resolved'—expenditure (substance) is reined in, but 'quality' (process) is improved. The benefit claimant loses some purchasing power, but the process of getting the money becomes quicker and more civilized.

A further step is to see that the apparent contradiction between cuts and quality actually has a paradox folded within it. This 'nested' paradox is that the apparent contradiction is more likely to become a real one in those jurisdictions *which are already most efficient in service delivery*. This is because the ability to make savings and at the same time improve service seems to be closely connected with the amount of spare capacity in the system (Murray, 1998), and the most efficient jurisdictions are those which are carrying the least spare capacity. In jurisdictions which are already super-efficient there is no 'fat' left to cut, and enforced economies are bound to carve into the bone of real services. For politicians, 'waste' is a wonderful thing—so long as one can claim to find more of it, one can also promise to cut relatively painlessly. And since 'waste' is a concept that is hard to define and operationalize, there is always room to argue that there is more waste 'in there' to be found. Popular anti-bureaucratic rhetoric encourages the belief that waste is widespread and can be readily identified and punished. However, a more sophisticated view, proposed by a long line of organization theorists and public administration scholars, would be that a certain amount of 'redundancy' or 'slack' in an organization is essential to facilitate innovation, flexibility, and positive workforce attitudes (Berg, 2010).

Yet another step is to acknowledge that technological advance will sometimes be able to 'solve' the apparent contradiction. A technological leap forward may enable managers of a public service simultaneously to save money and to push up quality and productivity (see, e.g. some of the examples in National Audit Office, 1999). There is an empirical question as to how often such technological breakthroughs occur, and there is a further empirical question about how well new technologies are implemented (Margetts et al., 2010; Hudson, 1998; Dunleavy et al., 2006a). Nevertheless, new ICTs will sometimes be able to resolve the contradiction, which is no doubt one reason why they are such a universal favourite as an ingredient of the rhetoric of public management reform.

We are left, then, with a context-dependent view of the apparent contradiction between improved performance and expenditure savings. In contexts where a system is already fairly efficient, and where there is no technological breakthrough to hand, the contradiction may be real—cuts will diminish quality. The argument in favour of 'slack' or 'redundancy' is an argument for a modest margin, not for a large slice (which would then become genuine 'waste'). Therefore in much less efficient systems, the contradiction can be circumnavigated by removing excess spare capacity/waste. In systems where technological change is rapid, the contradiction may sometimes be solved by technological innovation, assuming it is competently implemented. There is a final, important point. Size matters. Preserving or enhancing quality is likely to be much less difficult if the size of the cut is 3–5 per cent rather than 20–30 per cent. One of the reasons why much of the independent commentary on the UK Labour and Conservative governments in 2009 and 2010 was so sceptical was that they were promising that the 'front line' of public services would be preserved despite the fact that very *large* cuts were clearly coming down the pipeline.

Do these conclusions apply equally to all our three main models? In the broadest sense, probably yes. However, the types of contexts most frequently faced are likely to differ as between the three visions, and in that sense one could say that NPM, NWS, and NPG refract the cuts and quality problem in different ways. From within an NPM perspective, cuts versus quality resolves itself into a question of efficiency and management. If waste can be reduced— often by the application of market-type mechanisms—then quality can be preserved while economies are secured. Quality standards are written into formal contracts (with external providers) or quasi-contracts (with government agencies) to ensure that the achievement of budgetary targets is not at the expense of service quality. If the provider substantially fails to achieve either the budgetary or the quality targets, then another, more efficient provider can be brought in. Quality is, in effect, packaged up into an annually re-defined set of indicators.

The cuts and quality problem is seen somewhat differently from within an NWS perspective. Here quality is more a matter of publically motivated professionalism—of constantly supporting and re-inforcing a sense of bureaucratic pride and commitment to continuous improvement. If cuts have to be made, then they will need to be carefully prioritized in terms of overall government policy, and subsequently every step must be taken to support public organizations to make the necessary economies with the minimum damage to motivation, trust, and longer-term organizational capability. These values and capacities are seen as the underpinnings of real, professionally led quality, a quality that does not have to be beaten into service organizations by targets and penalties, because it is already deeply embedded in the public service culture. The public will trust these organizations (it is hoped) because they represent continuity and reliability, not something which is contracted out and 'performed' in order to fulfil a temporary contract. Greater efficiency is, of course, very important, and modern professionals will possess the management skills to seek it out. But they will do this not so much because it is a target in their annual appraisal as because to improve efficiency is part of a larger, internalized, self-image and organizational culture of modernized, citizen-oriented service provision.

The NWS and NPM visions are both too narrow for advocates of the NPG. In this model cuts and quality are not matters for the government alone or even (as in NPM) for government and its contractors. Both budgets and quality standards are things which will have to be negotiated through networks of stakeholders. No central authority can 'impose' them on everyone else. Solutions may be diverse: in one sector, stakeholders may be prepared to tolerate some lowering of standards in order to save money, whilst in another sector citizen groups or civil society associations may decide to pay more (fees or taxes) in order to prop up the standards of some particularly valued service.

The problems with each of these 'solutions' are fairly obvious. What if the NPM managers cannot find the necessary efficiencies? Or what if contractors talk of efficiencies but actually implement hidden quality reductions in complex services (such as health care or education) where quality is hard to pin down and define in a contract? What if the faith the NWS advocates place in right-thinking public service professionals proves misplaced, and these individuals prove to be self-interested first and citizen-oriented only second? Or what if the public service managers are simply not very good managers, and, too cosy in their secure jobs, are low on innovation and unimaginative in hunting down new ways of improving efficiency? What if the networks of NPG just fail to agree on a way of dealing with a painful budget situation, with different stakeholders 'passing the buck' to others? Or what if different parts of different networks agree to different kinds of solution, generating a patchwork of measures that are neither equitable nor egalitarian from the overall perspective of citizens? All of these risks are real, and any of them may result in unfair, inequitable cuts or unfair, inequitable losses of quality.

7.6 Promote flexibility and innovation/promote citizen trust and increase legitimacy

The possible contradiction between these two appealing propositions is not necessarily obvious. The tension arises in those situations where continuity, trust, and predictability are likely to be the qualities most sought after by the majority of service users. In such circumstances the excitements of constant change and innovation become counter-productive. Confusion and mistrust may grow. Take, for example, the issue of local post offices, which have been a focus for debate in a number of our countries, including Finland and the UK. Many small, (often rural) post offices are uneconomic to maintain. Therefore efficiency-promoting innovations are proposed (remote electronic means of conducting the same transactions; the relocation of the postal services in local shops rather than separate premises, closures). However, the public reacts against these 'improvements'. At least one section of the public values the cultural and social aspects of the local post office—they want stability and continuity. In Finland it seems that some persons trust a post office with their personal business but do not wish to reveal details of the same to their local shopkeeper (an interesting example of the public servant being perceived as more trustworthy than the business person). In the UK, the post office is sometimes claimed to be the last social centre or meeting place in small rural settlements (Business and Enterprise Committee, 2009).

Part of the problem with innovation is that it frequently requires users as well as service providers to learn new tricks. This tends to be far more difficult for some sections of society than for others, and innovations thus, unintentionally, acquire inegalitarian aspects. One could see this in the post office example mentioned above: citizens in rural areas lose their post offices and may have to learn to use remote systems; citizens in big cities get to keep them. More generally one can consider the extensive academic debate around the 'digital divide'—the ever-widening chasm between those citizens who can and do use computers and those who can't or won't (Castells, 2001; Fountain, 2001; Norris, 2001). As more and more public services go on-line the social and political handicap of not being able to use electronic channels becomes more profound. Optimists believe this divide is becoming less important as the older, non-computerized generation dies out, and in a number of countries governments have attacked the problem (with some success) by subsidizing the extension of broadband Internet connections. Even if this is true, however, the digital divide is only one of a series of divides that will constantly appear in a highly technological society subject to rapid change. If it is not Internet access then it will be mobile phones or access to advanced medical technologies or an inability to use some other new and sophisticated device.

A case which affects many millions of citizens in a number of countries is that of pensions. Governments have, in several instances, come to realize that their previous planning of pensions has been inadequate, and that they are unlikely to be able to afford all the demands that will fall on them in the future, as the elderly increase as a proportion of the total population. Legislation is therefore introduced to change national pension systems—sometimes restricting eligibility (usually by increasing the retirement age), sometimes changing terms, sometimes incentivizing citizens to take up private occupational or personal pension schemes rather than rely on the state pension. Many innovations in pension provision are attempted: some with very good intentions, some to save money. The outcomes are mixed. One outcome has been that stability and predictability has been lost in an area where stability and predictability over long time periods are of the essence. Citizens have lost trust in the ability of the state to provide for their old age—there has been considerable anxiety, and some commercial pension companies have taken advantage of the confusion to advertise their wares (Marmor et al., 1990). In some cases, commercial schemes have been perfectly satisfactory. In other cases there have been well-publicized examples of schemes being very poor value for money, or of companies failing, or of schemes being sold to citizens who did not really need them, thus adding to public disquiet. Thus attempts to innovate—at least some of them well intentioned—have ended up damaging citizen trust and amplifying confusion and anxiety.

Our overall analysis would be that *there is no fundamental or universal contradiction* between innovation on the one hand and stability and continuity on the other. Indeed, there are occasions when innovation is required *in order* to maintain continuity—such as when back-of-office automation allows the same service to be delivered to a larger number of users without unacceptable increases in cost. This having been said, however, there are also specific contexts in which public managers do face at least a trade-off between innovation and one or more of the values of stability, continuity, predictability, trust, and (as we saw in some of the above examples) egalitarianism. Such contexts confront public service managers with difficult problems of balancing divergent desiderata, and possibly disadvantaging certain sections of the community, even if an improved service is supplied to other sections of a community. Given the pervasive cost pressures and the prominence given to innovation within current reform ideology, it is likely that trade-off problems of this kind occur quite often. It is not our impression that the literature on management reform—either academic or professional—fully reflects this. Furthermore we should be cautious in equating citizen trust of a particular service with citizen perceptions of the legitimacy of governments or politicians (Chapter 5, Sec. 5.7, above; Van de Walle et al., 2008). There are good reasons to doubt whether the two would usually be closely connected, so even if successful innovations rapidly attract citizen support and trust, this may well not translate into improved legitimation scores for the government.

Our three models could be said to give different emphases to the two sides of this equation. Whilst, in the abstract, everyone is in favour of flexibility and innovation, and everyone is also in favour of increasing trust and legitimacy, NPM, NWS, and NPM tend to focus most intensely on different aspects. NPM has an efficiency focus, and innovation is seen as a major way of cutting costs and increasing productivity. Trust and legitimacy have been much less prominent concepts within the NPM discourse. Trust and legitimacy are, however, more to the fore in the NWS model, where the credibility of representative democratic politics, coupled with the professionalism and trustworthiness of the bureaucracy are prime foci. Flexibility and innovation do have a place within NWS, but mainly as adjuncts to the central idea of a modernized, professional public service. Meanwhile NPG sees the involvement of a wider range of stakeholders as the key to both more innovation and greater citizen trust. A network approach is said to be much more flexible than a traditional bureaucratic hierarchy (though, in practice, networks can often turn out to be clumsy and slow-moving). It is also claimed that wider participation will bring greater trust in its train.

7.7 Motivate staff and promote cultural change/weaken tenure and downsize

A whole chapter of the US National Performance Review booklet *Businesslike Government* was given over to 'Creative License: Unleashing the Creative Power of Government Employees' (Gore, 1997, p. 25). In many countries—particularly those where the civil service was most harshly criticized during the 1980s—the mid and late 1990s saw attempts to 're-vision' and 're-motivate' public servants. 'The Public Service of Canada requires a transformation in its people, its culture and its leadership', and 'The Public Service of Canada needs champions and leaders' (Bourgon, 1998, pp. 21, 23). 'We must restore faith in the public service ethos, and convey the message that we can only deliver better government if we harness and use the talents of the civil service and other public servants' (Clark—the minister with civil service responsibilities in the new Blair government in the UK—1997, p. 3). And so on. The contradiction here is with the threat to public service jobs, security, and pay posed by expenditure cutbacks and management reforms. To tell public servants that they are highly valued at the same time that many of them are being 'let go' may strike many public servants as ironic, or worse. Even the most sympathetic official statements often contain a sting in the tail: 'Absolute job security is not something that any employee... can expect in the competitive modern world. But we do want to look at ways of reducing insecurity, so as to minimize distractions from policy goals' (Clark, 1997, p. 20).

Can this apparent contradiction be resolved? We find it hard to see how it could be. Indeed, there have been obvious instances where the contradiction has been seen only too clearly by the staff concerned (e.g. in New Zealand—Boston et al., 1996, pp. 211–24; in the USA with respect to the NPR's downsizing targets—Kettl, 1994, pp. 13–21; or during the public service strikes in France in the mid 1990s). Phrases such as 'expecting the turkeys to vote for Christmas' (UK) and 'from rowing to steering to abandoning ship' (USA) came our way from public servants as we researched this topic.

That said, the contradiction may be lived with—even softened somewhat. Certain factors promise to assist in this. To begin with, there is the brutal fact that the public servants who matter most will be the ones who survive downsizing. It is possible to envisage—NPM style—a smaller, less bureaucratic, more highly skilled, perhaps even better-remunerated public service, within which morale could be restored and a new performance-oriented culture solidly entrenched. Those who lose their jobs frequently also lose their voices—they are now 'outsiders', at best an embarrassment to the survivors. Note, however, that this vision depends on the perception that a new phase of relative stability has been attained. Continuing, repeated downsizings (like those which have taken place in Europe and the USA in industries such as coalmining or shipbuilding) destroy any basis for confidence and commitment. They replace the proposition of 'pain today, jam tomorrow' with the unattractive 'pain today, more tomorrow'. They also undermine institutional memory, reduce the chances of survival for any 'public service ethic', and lead to a 'hollowed out' and ultimately less competent form of government (Perry and Hondeghem, 2008; Pollitt, 2008). In the aftermath of the 2008 GEC, the danger is precisely that downsizings will be so deep and so prolonged that the confidence even of the survivors will be badly shaken. In such cases the basic contradiction is left naked for all to see, and employing institutions must expect many of their remaining staff to become cautious and defensive, and perhaps to lose some of their public service motivation.

How do our three models accommodate this potential contradiction? In a nutshell one might say that NPM prioritizes downsizing over motivation (to achieve efficiency), NWS prioritizes motivation over downsizing (to preserve a high quality public service), and NPG does not seem to have much distinctive to say about this particular issue, unless it is that downsizing is something that needs to be negotiated with all the key stakeholders (which sounds nice but does not do much to change the underlying reality). None seems to offer a way of resolving what is often a harsh and painful choice.

7.8 Reduce burden of internal scrutiny and associated paperwork/sharpen managerial accountability

The evidence seems to indicate that this particular tension is more a question of balance than of outright contradiction—although in practice it is easy for the balance to be lost. The tension between the two arises because to sharpen managerial accountability so often involves operational managers having to make new returns to the top of the organization, to provide data for new performance indicators systems, quality improvement schemes, or performance audit scrutinies. Although what is being asked of operational managers is (in principle at least) a different *kind* of information—output and outcome oriented rather than input data—it can still become an onerous burden, perhaps even exceeding in volume and complexity what was required under the status quo ante. It has sometimes been referred to as a kind of 're-bureaucratization'.

Radin (1998) shows how easy it is for a series of individually well-intentioned reform measures to produce a heavy weight of requirements upon public managers. In the USA, the Paperwork Reduction Act of 1995 was aimed at eliminating unnecessary paperwork and reducing the burden on form-filling for citizens and firms. Introducing the bill, President Clinton spoke of the need to 'conquer the mountain of paperwork'. This in itself appeared an unexceptional objective, although, as Radin points out, it also placed limits on the collection of the kind of performance data that would be required to fulfil the aspirations of the 1993 Government Performance and Results Act. Meanwhile, however, federal managers groaned under a series of new measures, including:

- The Federal Managers' Financial Integrity Act, 1982—which requires annual assurance of the adequacy of controls.

- The Chief Financial Officers' Act, 1990—which requires annual accountability reports.

- The Government Management Reform Act, 1994—which requires annual financial statements to the Office of Management and Budget.

- The Information Technology Management Reform Act, 1996—which also requires annual reports, this time showing how information technology is being used to help programmes achieve their objectives.

- The Federal Financial Management Improvement Act, 1996—which requires reports on financial systems compliance by agency heads, inspectors general, and the head of the Office of Management and Budget (OMB).

- REGO 111 of the National Performance Review, 1996—which requires annual reports from agencies on how they are responding to the principles of the NPR.

The above is by no means a complete listing of all the *new* information demands, let alone the ongoing ones.

This is not just a tale of some particularly American exuberance or excess. Parallels can be found in a number of other countries where reform has been given a high profile. After documenting an 'audit explosion' closely linked to new styles of management, Power (1997, p. 142) comments that: 'it is clear that in the UK and elsewhere during the 1980s and the early 1990s auditing acquired an institutional momentum which insulated it from systemic enquiry'. New processes of audit or quasi-audit were devised and applied in almost every main branch of the UK public sector (Hood et al., 1999). By 2008, the UK Cabinet Office was issuing reform documents which clearly acknowledged that central government had overloaded public service delivery organizations with targets and measures and controls (Cabinet Office, 2008; see also Barber, 2007).

We said at the beginning of this section that we considered the tension between reduced paperwork and increased performance monitoring to be a question of balance, rather than of inherent contradiction. The above examples indicate that balance is not automatically guaranteed—it is a trade-off which has to be consciously constructed and then actively maintained. The paperwork/electronic form-filling burden on middle management *can* be reduced, if the performance monitoring regime is carefully designed, focused and regularly reviewed so as to prune 'excess growth'. This is the optimistic view. A less sanguine perspective would be to see the whole process as a cyclic one in which monitoring and auditing systems possessed in-built tendencies to 'put on weight', but these were, from time to time, corrected by bursts of 'dieting' (reforms). This would perhaps explain why, in several countries, clear-outs of regulations and paperwork requirements seem to be hardy perennials rather than 'one-off' reforms. It would also allow for the fact that there is some evidence of performance indicator systems cycling between a smaller number of key indicators and a larger number of detailed indicators (Pollitt, 1990; Pollitt et al, 2010c; Bouckaert and Hallingan 2008, see Chapter 8). What one is seeing here is therefore a trade-off rather than a contradiction: the trade is between, on the one hand, simple, light monitoring controls which permit subtleties and complexities and 'gaming' to squeeze round or through them and, on the other, detailed, heavy systems which capture more of the complexities and ploys, but which are burdensome and expensive to operate (de Bruijn, 2001). Over time the grass on the other side of the trade-off often looks greener, hence the cycle.

In principle this particular trade-off could appear within any of our three main models. However, in practice, it is most closely associated with the NPM. It is in the core NPM states where the phenomenon has been most clearly visible. One might add, though, that a sort of parallel may be emerging within NPG. In this case, however, what happens is that governments make increasing use of partnerships and networks to try to get their business done, but then attempt to steer these relationships by developing more and more elaborate procedural rules for them (Huxham and Vangen, 2000). As for NWS, this model is hardly immune from such problems, not least because it is the one of the three which has moved the least distance from the traditional, rule-bound bureaucracy.

7.9 Develop more partnerships and contracting out/improve horizontal coordination (joined-up government; integrated service provision)

The difficulty with this pair of proposals is that, *ceteris paribus*, partnerships and contracting out *increases* the difficulty of coordination (Bouckaert et al., 2010; Huxham and Vangen, 2000). This is because relationships become multiple and horizontal instead of two dimensional and vertical, and because coordination can no longer be ordered (as in a hierarchy), but must be negotiated. Agentification can have some of the same effects—as Rhodes (1997, p. 53) puts it of the Next Steps reforms in Whitehall: 'the most obvious result of the new system is institutional fragmentation'. There is some evidence that 'agentification' has exacerbated coordination problems in at least New Zealand (Boston et al., 1996, p. 88) and the UK (Office of Public Services Reform, 2002).

None of this is to say that partnerships and contractual relationships cannot also carry benefits. They may stimulate innovation and policy learning; they may introduce new expertise; they may increase flexibility. Such benefits are, of course, not automatic: there is always the danger that poor management will fail to grasp the opportunities that are presented to them. But the existence of benefits is not the point here: the point is that there is a tension between the harvesting of these benefits and the simultaneous arrival of certain penalties in the form of loss of coordination at a higher level (Bovaird and Tizzard, 2009). To be even-handed between both sides of the equation, it must also be acknowledged that the *potential* for coordination that exists under more centralized systems is by no means always taken advantage of. What we suspect, therefore, is that there probably *is* a trade-off (not a contradiction) here, and that in practise significantly increased resort to partnerships and/or contracting out are frequently purchased by some loss of policy or programme coordination (Löffler, 1999). It is for politicians and public to say whether any given trade-off is acceptable, but so long as the rhetoritcians of reform insist that nothing is lost, the trade-off issue cannot be properly investigated, weighed, and debated.

Partnerships are, of course, a key element in the NPG model, and are also widely used in NPM approaches. Contracting out has been a mainstay of NPM, and is also used, perhaps rather less vigorously, within NPG (and, selectively, within NWS). This is therefore a trade-off that may be faced within all our three models, but which is likely to be more frequently occurring in NPM and NPG. A study of the UK civil service reform programme from 1999 to 2005 noted that:

[T]he emphasis on 'internal markets' and the separation of 'purchaser and provider' were, by 2002, being seen as potentially damaging to the delivery of corporate and cross-cutting priorities and to the achievement of key governance principles such as transparency, stakeholder engagement, diversity and fair and honest behaviour.   (Bovaird and Russell, 2007, p. 326)

7.10 Increase effectiveness/sharpen management accountability

It may not be immediately apparent why there should be any tension between these two objectives. Are they not both perfectly sensible and compatible? If we consider the observations of the Canadian Auditor General, reporting on performance management reforms, we can see that this is not necessarily so:

Outputs are results that managers can control, while the outcomes managers are trying to accomplish are influenced by factors outside their programs.   (Auditor General of Canada, 1997, pp. 5–8)

A glance back at Figure 5.1 will show that effectiveness is a question of securing the intended *outcomes*, while efficiency is a matter of optimizing the input/*output* ratio. A good deal of evidence, spread over many years and from a number of countries, indicates two, alternating difficulties:

1. When managers are enjoined to concentrate on concrete outputs (licences issued, grants given, training courses completed) they tend to lose sight of outcomes and, therefore, to stress efficiency rather than effectiveness.

2. When, alternatively, managers are asked to concentrate on outcomes and effectiveness, it is hard to hold them responsible and accountable, for several reasons. This is because the attribution of outcomes to the actions of individual units or organizations is frequently obscure or doubtful, and also because, for many public programmes, measurable outcomes manifest themselves over such extended time periods that they cannot provide a sensible basis for annual accountability exercises anyway (Pollitt, 1995; Pollitt and Bouckaert, 2003). A teacher may be held responsible for his/her students' test scores but can s/he also be held to account for the jobs they subsequently get, and how well they perform them?

There appears to be a dilemma, or at least a trade-off, here. Go for outputs and you are likely to lose sight of effectiveness; go for effectiveness (outcomes) and you lose the chance of clear accountability for individual managers and their units. The easy answer is to say 'go for both simultaneously' (de Bruijn, 2001, p. 17). Unfortunately that is more easily said than done. Accountability systems are likely to slide towards outputs, as more quickly measurable, more easily attributable, and much less costly to monitor. At a 1997 conference for senior New Zealand public managers the then minister for the civil service made 'output fixation' and the neglect of outcomes one of his chief themes (East, 1997). This theme was also echoed in parts of the UK government's 1999 White Paper *Modernising Government* (Prime Minister and Minister for the Cabinet Office, 1999).

There is an even more controversial aspect to the effectiveness/accountability relationship. This is pungently expressed by Wright (1997, p. 11):

A great deal of public policy is about rationing, about the distribution of scarce resources, about zero-sum games and opportunity costs. For rationing to work over any length of time it must either be ignored, obfuscated or it must be legitimised. It is an intrinsically difficult exercise to undertake by a democratic society in peacetime and in periods of stagnation or depression . . .

However, some of the current reforms, driven by good intentions, seem designed to undermine those three essential props: ignorance is being replaced by defined rights and obfuscation by transparency. Even more significant is the *delegitimation* of the process: decisions about rationing are being removed from politicians and self-regulating professions like teachers and doctors and they are being transferred to *managers* and to entrepreneurs, who quite simply lack the essential legitimacy to spread the essential misery [original emphasis].

In the light of these considerations, what can be said about the relationship between the drive for greater effectiveness and the drive for sharper management accountability? First, we are definitely *not* arguing that this is a sharp contradiction, with a steep-sided collapse of an effectiveness-orientation the moment the authorities begin to try to build management accountability, or vice versa. Second, there does, however, seem to be a tension between a focus on outputs and a focus on outcomes, with most of the cards (measurability, timeliness, attributability, cost) being stacked in favour of outputs. This is not so much a trade-off as a balance which is difficult to hold against the slide towards 'output fixation'. Third, Wright opens up a deeper and more obviously political dilemma: that, for services which are rationed, the process of clarifying accountability and shifting it more to managers and away from public service professionals, may result in a loss of legitimacy and an increase in litigation and dispute.

How does this balance relate to our three models? Rather obviously, it cuts across them all. Both outputs and outcomes are, in principle, important in all three. The kind of slide towards outputs we have mentioned here could occur within a state aspiring to NPM, NWS, or NPG. If any distinction can be drawn between the three models (which is doubtful) it might be that NPM (with its intense focus on managerial efficiency) could be more likely to overconcentrate on outputs, while NWS (with a longer-term perspective and an orientation towards social solidarity and improvement) might lean more towards outcomes. On the other hand, NWS-type reforms may easily become more process-oriented (meet standards, follow guidelines), and in this case outcomes may drift away over the horizon. NPG advocates seem to be slightly uncomfortable with both elements. Network theorists have for some time worried about how outcomes might be evaluated and what accountability in networks might mean (e.g. Klijn, 2005, pp. 272–7). We must admit, however, that the whole of our discussion in this paragraph is quite speculative, and we know of little direct evidence that would resolve these musings one way or another.

7.11 Promote open government and transparency/protect privacy

In this case the tension is fairly obvious. Governments deal daily with millions of individual citizens. So if the call for open government means that governments should tell their citizens exactly what they are doing, and should open all their communications for public scrutiny, then an enormous amount of personal data is going to be open to those who are curious, unscrupulous, or commercially exploitative (or all of these things). Making all these documents anonymous may be technically possible, but may also be prohibitively time-consuming and expensive. (There is also the issue of when and how far political decision-makers themselves should be entitled to privacy, or secrecy. Some of the most sensitive political deals—the Northern Ireland peace process, the Oslo agreement between Israel and the Palestinians—can only be achieved in private. This is a large and complex subject which cannot be dealt with here—but see Roberts, 2006).

By way of illustration, let us quickly look at two cases. Over the past two decades DNA analysis has developed as (among other things) one of the most useful diagnostic tools available to the police. Most Western countries now have national DNA databases of one sort or another. There is no doubt that they help in the solution of many crimes. However, they also throw up a range of issues about privacy. First of all, under what circumstances are the police allowed to 'invade your privacy' and demand that you submit to a DNA swab? (This varies from country to country, in some cases according to the seriousness of the crime.) Second, how and how long should that record be stored? Third, who should have access to it—just the police, or also your defence lawyers, or other government agencies, such as social service departments or tax inspectors or the secret service? Fourth, how far should the organization operating the DNA database be allowed to exchange information with similar databases in other countries (countries which may have different privacy laws or different standards of implementation of such laws)? At each stage there is clearly a balance to be struck between effectiveness in fighting crime and the protection of personal data. Different balances are chosen by different countries, so that, for example, the UK and neighbouring Belgium have very different databases. The British one is very large and includes (at the time of writing) all sort of records, even for individuals who have never been charged with a crime. The Belgian one is quite small, and basically one has to be convicted of a very serious crime before one's record is kept.

A second example would be the 2001 EU regulation that says that any EU citizen can demand copies of emails or memoranda exchanged between EU officials on a particular topic, and must be supplied with them within fifteen working days (Regulation, 2001). Transparency in action one might say—a good thing. But now consider some of the practical consequences. Environmental pressure groups, or companies worried about a possible new regulation, ask the EU Commission for all the emails exchanged on topic X between 21 April and 14 May 2010 (the evidence is that, in most countries where freedom of information is legislated, the main users are journalists, companies, and pressure groups, not individual citizens). To begin with, this is a huge task. Officials will have to go through hundreds or thousands of emails before handing them over. This will be time taken away from actually getting on with their policy work. Major discussions may be required when something sensitive appears in this flow. It will also show up in detail the exact positions taken by individual, named officials and politicians in internal negotiations. It will reveal any colourful phrase or expression of frustration by any party to these communications. So what will be the likely result? Most obviously, an elaborate internal machine for vetting information releases (Roberts, 2006, pp. 86–106). Next, a reluctance on the part of policy-makers to record their most critical and sensitive thoughts on paper or email, so that the official record becomes more bland and informal, unminuted discussions in the corridor or the office become more frequent and important. Third, governments may find themselves working under a self-imposed handicap when dealing with private sector corporations, which now enjoy far greater scope for concealing their thoughts and actions than do the governments themselves (Roberts, 2006, pp. 150–70).

The implication of this brief discussion is that there often *is* a trade-off between openness/transparency on the one hand and privacy on the other. Roberts (2006, p. 226) puts it succinctly:

Indeed, it would be ironic if transparency laws that are justified in the name of human rights had the effect, in practice, of compromising civil liberties. And it is far from clear that a radically heightened capacity for monitoring *governmental* activity is necessarily in the public interest.

There is, of course, a huge variation from one sector to another. In some, the trade-off may be gentle or uncontroversial. But in others—crime, health, and finance for example—strong arguments may arise as to where the balance should be struck.

These problems affect all three of our main models. Whether the regime is NPM, NWS, or NPG, a balance must be found. The NPG model perhaps poses the issue in a particularly challenging and complex way because of its stress on the participation of a variety of stakeholders in policymaking and management/delivery. Are all these stakeholders going to be equally open and accountable, or is it acceptable for, say, private companies to be able to operate with greater confidentiality than the governments for whom they are working and by whom they are paid?

7.12 Reflections: balances, limits, dilemmas, and paradoxes

Looking across the various 'candidate contradictions' reviewed above, one can allow that not all are insurmountable. Some can be avoided—they are implementation dangers rather than fundamental logical contradictions. Others are more apparent than real (paradoxes), and in other cases still, there may be a deep-lying tension, but the edge can be taken off it by skilled leadership and implementation. A considerable residue, however, remains. The various components of what has become the vision of a modernized public sector do not add up to an integrated and harmonious whole:

Tensions such as the conflict between 'career service' and 'spot hiring' approaches to organising top public servants, legalist and managerial visions of organisational process, competition-centred and oversight-centred approaches to control over public services, are not likely to disappear through some ultimate 'modern' resolution.   (Hood, 1998, p. 221)

The scope of our investigation has in some ways been narrower than Hood's—he seems to be attempting to establish a set of timeless and universal trade-offs, pictured in a group/grid matrix of administrative cultures in which both his four 'pure' administrative philosophies and attempts at hybrid combinations are fundamentally unstable. We have focused more specifically upon selected elements (dishes/*plats* in the language of Chapter 1) that are important within out three main models—NPM, NWS, and NPG. We are more interested in the extent to which these elements can be reconciled in logic and also confirmed as mutually compatible by empirical observations. Our focus is therefore less on an exploration of the explanatory value of any one overarching taxonomy. Thus, while we entirely concur with Hood's proposition that certain tensions cannot be 'disappeared' by contemporary models of management reform, we also want to discriminate between the more and the less 'do-able'. In the preceding sections we have therefore reached towards a set of conclusions concerning our eight 'candidate contradictions'. We conclude the chapter by briefly recapitulating these tentative 'findings'.

1. *Increase political control of the bureaucracy/free managers to manage/empower service consumers*: in a perfect world these could just about be compatible. In the real world there

is frequently a trade-off between one or more of the three corners of this triangle. In some contexts the trade-off becomes so sharp as to merit the title of a contradiction.

2. *Give priority to making savings/give priority to improving public service quality*: there is no general contradiction: much depends on the specific circumstances, especially whether the organization(s) in question has/have spare capacity ('slack'), and/or whether technological advances offer the possibility of productivity gains. With complex services, the picture may be complicated because quality may have many aspects and/or be difficult directly to observe. This opens up the danger that service providers will conceal reductions of quality, or will emphasize quality gains on one aspect while obscuring reductions on other, less visible dimensions.

3. *Promote flexibility and innovation/increase citizen trust and therefore governmental legitimacy*: there is no fundamental contradiction here. However, there are specific contexts in which politicians and/or managers are obliged to trade off between, on the one hand, innovation and, on the other, values such as stability, predictability, continuity, and trust. Not infrequently management innovations can relatively disadvantage certain sections of the community. Also the equation of citizen trust in a particular public service with the same citizens' attitudes towards the government as a whole is often misleading. Citizens are fully capable of forming one judgement about a particular service and quite another about the overall legitimacy of the political leadership.

4. *Motivate staff and promote cultural change/weaken tenure and downsize*: this appears to be the most obvious and inescapable contradiction. It can be softened by sensitive management and, of course, it can be rhetorically papered over. But it is not clear why many public service staff should be reassured. There is therefore a price to pay for the contradiction in terms of loss of morale, loyalty, the attractiveness of a public service career, and possibly, therefore, effectiveness.

5. *Reduce burden of internal scrutiny and associated paperwork/sharpen managerial accountability*: this seems to be principally a question of balance. However, while it may not be a contradiction, intelligent and determined implementation is required if the balance is to be first constructed and then, subsequently, maintained. Some core NPM countries have suffered 'audit explosions', 'initiativitis', and 'target overload'.

7. *Develop more partnerships and contracting out/improve policy and programme coordination*: we suggest that there is an underlying trade-off here. The slope may be sharp or gentle, depending on context. Sometimes the benefits will clearly outweigh the losses, but sometimes they will not. The literature on partnerships is now huge, and some scholars have begun the task of identifying the general conditions which are likely to influence this trade-off (see, e.g. Bovaird and Tizzard, 2009).

8. *Increase effectiveness/sharpen managerial accountability*: whilst this does not appear to be a direct contradiction, there does seem to be some tension between these two objectives, and there is evidence that the balance is hard to hold in practice. There may also be an underlying dilemma—for rationed services—between transparency and legitimacy.

9. *Promote open government/transparency/protect privacy*: there are real trade-offs here and, at the poles, contradictions. Many states have needed to adjust their privacy

legislation in relation to new technological developments such as mobile phones, DNA analysis, and electronic banking. This will no doubt continue. Most of these new laws and regulations are clearly balancing between openness and privacy, and the balance has been struck somewhat differently in different countries. There is also an underlying question about the impact of very high levels of transparency on the ability of officials and politicians to arrive at compromises and do deals.

All our three big models have problems with these trade-offs and contradictions. Some dilemmas and trade-offs may show up more obviously within one model than another (as suggested above), but others cut across all the models. Indeed, some may even be relatively timeless, in the sense that, historically, they pop up time and time again, in different contexts and slightly varying forms, constituting true limits (or at least hard choices) in public administration (Hood, 1976).

8 Reflections

The art of government is in procrastination and in silence and in delay;
  blazing bonfires left to burn will soon consume themselves away.
Of evils choose the least: great foes will tumble down in time, or wither, one by one.
He that rules must hear and see what's openly or darkly done.
All that is not enough: there comes a moment when to rule is to be swift and bold;
  know at last the time to strike—it may be when the iron is cold!

Sir Robert Cecil to Queen Elizabeth I from Benjamin Britten's opera Gloriana.
Libretto by William Plomer

8.1 Introduction

This is where we return to the beginning—to the key debates which were introduced in Chapter 1. Between there and here we have introduced a small mountain of evidence, referred to hundreds of research studies, and summarized dozens of theoretical approaches or conceptual frameworks. So where does that leave us with respect to the questions we started out with? And what seem to be the implications for future research in public management—research that we hope many of the readers of this book will be engaged with, in one way or another?

Amalgamating some of the bullet points on the question list we originally introduced in Section 1.3 (p. 5) we arrive at a set of four fundamental questions about what has been happening—and what is likely to happen in future. These are:

- What have been the main trajectories of reform, 1980–2010?

- What have been the results of these reforms?

- What are the implications of this experience for the future?

And last, but not least:

- What kind of answers are we looking for, and what kind of answers can we reasonably expect to get?

Sharp-eyed readers will notice that this list does not contain any 'why?' questions—the questions are all of the 'what?' variety. This may trouble those who argue that it is 'why?' questions—questions where a theory is used to explain why something has or has not happened—which are the high ground of academic life. So let us say quickly that in no way do we seek to demote explanatory issues. Indeed, we see a whole host of 'why?' questions standing immediately behind our 'what?' questions. In fact we have been discussing those throughout most of the book (for example, the model of the reform process in Chapter 3 and the 'many houses' discussion in Chapter 4 were very much concerned with reasons why this reform or that reform took place, or that particular approach was *not* adopted in a given country). Nevertheless here we give the headline to the 'what?' questions, for several reasons.

First, good descriptions are important because we believe that a good part of the international discussion of reform trends is seriously oversimplified and resorts to stereotypes, and that it is therefore important to try to establish just exactly what *has* happened, before launching into conclusions and prescriptions. Although this book gives a more detailed account than most, we are still conscious that it contains a number of lacunae and quite a lot of 'thin ice'. Even so, it is considerably more nuanced and detailed than many official reports, consultancy publications, and even academic analyses. One can understand why—the simple model and the memorable sound bite ('banish bureaucracy!', 'steering not rowing!', 'the network society!') are attention-grabbers. They increase the chances of getting your story onto crowded political or academic agendas. Second, theory-building and theory-testing—which we fully accept is central to the social science project—are themselves in part dependent on the availability of good descriptions. In the empirical social sciences it is not much use having a beautiful abstract theory with only partial and unreliable data to feed into it. In fact the sheer number and variety of public management models (which we noted back in Chapter 1) may to some degree reflect an unsatisfactory database on reforms. If we had better, more systematic and comparable descriptions of what has been happening in different countries, some of these models would probably fall, because they would be seen to be seriously incomplete, or to explain what happened in jurisdiction X but not at all what happened in jurisdiction Y. Third, this book is as it is because we have found, both among our own students and among those of a number of our colleagues at other universities, a real demand for just knowing what has happened. Intelligent students know that they cannot always trust government White Papers to tell the whole story. They also know that confining themselves to documents operating only at very high levels of aggregation (such as are found in the World Bank's World Governance Indicators (Chapter 5) or even many OECD publications) is not enough. They can find numerous case studies, many of them excellent, but it is more difficult to find reform stories from many countries brought together in one place and in an explicitly comparative format. Hence the satisfaction of this need is one of our objectives in writing this third edition.

8.2 What have been the main trajectories of reform, 1980–2010?

There is no doubt that NPM reforms were a major international trend during the 1980s and 1990s. Beginning in the mid 1980s in New Zealand and the UK they spread rapidly to many other countries and, by the early 1990s had become the 'new norm' in the many publications and discussions of the influential PUMA group at the OECD (e.g. OECD, 1995). Even countries which were culturally resistant to the NPM package as a whole (such as France or the Nordic countries) tended nonetheless to adopt or experiment with specific tools such as results budgeting or contracting out. In the language of Chapter 1, they selected certain dishes from the menu, even if they did not want the whole NPM cuisine. Finally, we beg leave to differ from those who have pronounced that the NPM is now 'dead' (e.g. Dunleavy et al., 2006b). At the time of writing, individual NPM- type reforms continue in a number of countries. The global economic crisis has in some ways even revived those parts of the NPM menu that claim to yield short-term savings—such as large-scale contracting out. Indeed, a detailed reading of Dunleavy et al. shows that they themselves do not really mean 'dead', because they freely acknowledge that some elements continue to spread. Terms such as 'decline' or 'decay' might carry a more accurate connotation than 'dead'.

Yet (as we argued in Chapter 1) it would be a dangerous oversimplification to claim that public management reform during the 1980–2000 period consisted of a global (or even an OECD) convergence on the NPM model. Many important reforms were not at all part of NPM packages—such as the French decentralization reforms of the early 1980s, or the amalgamation of Australian ministries in the mid 1980s, or the agency reforms in Finland in the early 1990s, or the somewhat chaotic Italian changes following the political crisis in 1994. They were responses to perceived domestic problems, principally addressed to those problems and not—or not much—derived from the international NPM agenda. There was a generalized cautiousness towards NPM from a number of continental European states, and the development of an alternative trajectory which, in Chapter 4, we characterized as the NWS.

Now we can return to the question raised in Chapter 1: the question of how best to characterize what has been happening since the NPM tide began to stall or recede—since, say, 2000 in most of our twelve countries. Throughout this book, and especially in Chapters 4, 5, and 6 we have periodically referred to three ideal type models—NPM itself, NWS, and NPG. As we said at the outset, these are far from the only models we could have explored, but, on the other hand, they are all models which have been, and still are being, extensively discussed within the academic community that studies public management. They express different principles of coordination—NPM favours market mechanisms designed and guided to yield outcomes which are in the public interest; NWS displays a professionalized and consultative form of hierarchy; NPG is based on a network approach, yielding an inclusive view of the wide range of organizations that needs to be involved in the governance of complex, pluralistic societies (Bouckaert et al., 2010). Furthermore, they have penetrated—at least to some extent—the vocabulary of reformers themselves. Practitioners in a number of countries have referred to specific themes which are clearly related to these academic models, such as the need for a more businesslike approach (NPM), the importance of preserving the

'European social model' and modernizing the state (NWS), or the desirability of more partnership working and networking (NPG). Collectively the three models represent, in a sense, the first and second generations of reform: first, NPM, as a clean break with traditional, hierarchical bureaucracy, and then NWS as an emerging alternative to NPM, and NPG as a broader approach which many academics have argued has succeeded—or is succeeding— NPM, and which is, to some extent, a conscious reaction to NPM's limitations.

So the three models are useful in a variety of ways. They express different principles of organization and different views of the preferable relationship between the state, the market sector, and civil society. As such they can serve as guiding heuristics or, beyond that, as visions. They can stimulate debates and provide frameworks for the analysis of specific reforms. What it is evident they do *not* do, however, is to provide a neat empirical map of where our twelve countries have come from, are now, or appear to be going to. The empirical map, in fact, is a pretty messy one, and shows every sign of remaining so. One cannot point to a single country and say, 'There we can see an example of NPM/NWS/NPG in full working order.' Even the famous NPM reforms in New Zealand between 1984 and 1993—radical though they undoubtedly were—were not 'pure'. There were many departures from the model and the doctrine (Boston et al., 1996), and within a decade elements of the reform were being dismantled or significantly modified (Duncan and Chapman, 2010). Equally, the numerous reforms in most European countries that have been proclaimed as promoting networking, partnership, and public participation have invariably co-existed with areas in which governments have still exercised the right to act decisively and hierarchically. When we examine a specific reform in a particular subset of organizations, we may sometimes find (to use the language of Chapter 1) coherent menus, with a series of mutually supporting tools being deployed in an attempt to realize a particular trajectory and vision. But when we look across the whole of any given public sector, the menu is always mixed—different tools are being used for different purposes in different parts of the operation.

As we have tried out the three models on our empirical evidence, another limitation has gradually become apparent. It is that each model attends to some aspects of public administration—the aspects it wants to give importance to—but tends to ignore or omit others. Thus the NPM, for example, says little directly about politics and seems, implicitly at least, to use an overrational and rather unrealistic set of assumptions about what politicians can, and want, to do (Chapter 6). It also tends to focus on the inner workings of individual organizations, and pay less attention to the 'big picture'—the shape of the network, the history of a given sector, the particular provisions of a specific constitution, and so on. The NWS vision, by contrast, has its strength in reminding us what states *can* do and how important democratic politics is as a guiding and monitoring force. It accepts that there are particular contexts where the state must coerce its citizens, where public order must be sustained, even at some price in terms of individual liberties. It places the public service ethic closer to the centre of attention and avoids the simplistic assumption that everyone is a self-interested utility maximizer. On the other hand, the NWS perspective is much less clear about how the state should deal with some of the other powerful players in the policy process—big corporations, intergovernmental organizations, and international non-governmental organizations. Furthermore, it tends to assume that public officials *will*, either always or usually, prove pliable to sensible, modernizing reforms. It perhaps needs to pay more attention to what is to be done when reformers encounter extreme inertia or recalcitrance among the affected staff—as does sometimes occur. The NPG approach is probably better at dealing with the 'external' parts of the picture than either the NPM or the NWS, because it is essentially outward-looking. But it remains largely silent about how, internally, the core of the state should be organized and what issues, if any, the state needs to reserve to itself. It also struggles to explain how traditional values of democratic accountability and transparency will be maintained in complex networks of partnerships and collaborations. '[I]n some ways the growth of partnerships has tended to add to institutional complexity in the public sector rather than necessarily to simplify it . . . The "organic" nature of different partnerships, and their variability from one area to another, also add to difficulties in attributing policies and understanding how they might be changed, not only for citizens, but also for public sector decision-makers themselves' (Dunleavy, 2010, p. 14).

The big models, then are less than comprehensive. And, meanwhile, the empirical map is composed of many partial trajectories, and some reversals or shifts in course. In the UK, as in New Zealand, the 2000s witnessed a partial (but only partial) retreat from the market-type mechanisms which had been introduced at the height of the NPM era. Actual reform packages have frequently included elements drawn from more than one of our models—for example the Blair government (1997–2008) praised partnerships and networking, yet simultaneously imposed one of the most detailed, top-down systems of performance measurement the world has yet seen. One may also notice a certain tendency towards alternations or cycles in reform (Pollitt, 2008, pp. 51–9). As remarked in Chapter 7, it has long been observed in public administration that there is a tendency for policy prescriptions to be packaged up in contradictory or opposing principles—now decentralization is the answer, now centralization (Pollitt, 2005), or now specialize tasks, now consolidate them (Hood and Jackson, 1991; see also Simon, 1946). Each prescription at first seems to make sense in itself, but after it has been applied for a while its disadvantages become more apparent, and eventually there is a movement to go the other way because it is perceived that now we have *too much* of what was formerly thought to be a good thing (too much autonomy, too much audit, too many performance indicators, and so on). We have perhaps seen this most clearly in the rapidly reforming countries—thus British governments swung from organizational disaggregation and then back to aggregation between 1988 and 2005 (Talbot and Johnston, 2007). More widely, Davis et al. found some tendency towards cycling between aggregation and disaggregation in Australia, Canada, and the UK over the longer period of 1950–97 (Davis et al., 1999) and Light found 'tides of reform', ebbing and flowing, in the USA between 1945 and 1995 (Light, 1997). The existence of such cycles does not rule out trajectories: one can have a trajectory that lasts for a decade or more and then the fashion changes—the previous trajectory is seen to have gone too far, and a new trajectory begins, not returning to the point of origin, but at least somewhat abandoning elements in the previous direction of travel. But to see these patterns one usually needs to look at developments over quite a substantial period of time—probably decades. Short-term examinations of the latest reform will not pick up the larger, longer-term patterns (Pollitt, 2008; Pollitt and Bouckaert, 2009). In the language of geological and evolutionary time 'arrows' (trajectories) can co-exist with 'cycles'—indeed, in order to make sense of evolution we need to understand the interaction between the two (Gould, 1988).

Now let us return to our models. Even if a particular government *were* able to craft and implement a somehow 'model pure' reform, that would not mean that that public sector then became an equally pure example of NPM or NWS or NPG. That is because no reform could conceivably simultaneously touch every nook and corner, every aspect of the

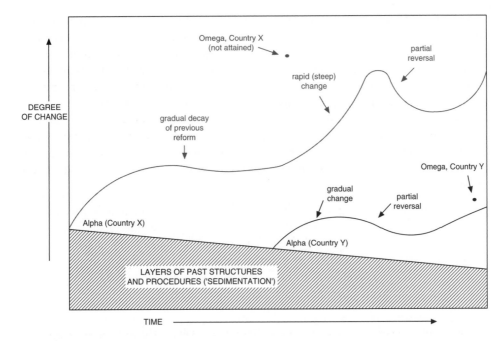

Figure 8.1 Some patterns of reform

modern state. There are always exceptions—sectors or organizations where, for special reasons or just from oversight or neglect, the previous system and culture survive (e.g. Pollitt and Op de Beeck, 2010). When in Chapter 2 we used the metaphor of reform as part of a process of geological sedimentation—new layers being deposited upon old—we were simply echoing an observation that has been made time and time again by observers of reform. Thus the old merit system survives in a substantial part of the US federal service, the influence of the graduates of ENA remains high within the French system despite some weakening reforms, the consensual culture continues to be a significant factor in the Dutch system, despite recent changes in the party system that could be construed as more polarization—and so on and so forth.

Figure 8.1 gives a visual impression of some of this complexity. It shows reform trajectories in two countries, X and Y. Country X begins first (with an alpha at the left-hand margin). It aims high (omega high up the figure, just over halfway across). It does not achieve this, but it does achieve substantial change. The change process, however, is not smooth.

It begins with a reasonably rapid period of change, but that then slackens off, and there is even some gentle slipping back. A second wave of reform is more radical (steeply rising slope of change), but, after a while, there is a crisis of some sort and a partial (but far from total) reversal. At the right hand-margin rapid change is resumed, and the finishing point shows very substantial change since the beginning (alpha). Even so, this change has been built over a continuing substratum of older structures and procedures, which are only gradually fading away (striped area at the bottom of the figure). Country Y begins later, and sets its sights lower (the omega is much lower = less change, than for Country X). Its rate of change is also lower (slopes less steep). Like country X, it has a period of partial reversal, but ends up quite near its (more modest) omega. Country Y has achieved less change than Country X, but has come closer to its goals. One might think of Country X as a radical NPM reformer and Country Y as a more cautious NWS reformer, although they do not have to be this—they are no more than abstract, illustrative examples of the kind of complexity which our historical approach has revealed, over and over again.

Nevertheless, despite this 'messiness', and all these necessary qualifications, the story we have told has not been one of chaos or randomness, without shape or direction. Just as the period 1980–2000 *was* characterized by a widespread interest in NPM, so certain themes have grown in prominence internationally since the turn of the century. These include:

- The development of integrated services/joined-up government/'whole of government' approaches. These apply both to the 'production' of policies (developing integrated analyses of cross-sectoral or 'wicked' problems) and to the delivery of services (one-stop shops, single portals for all government services, etc.). Attempts to integrate at the service(operational) level seem to have been almost universal, but efforts to develop whole-of-government strategies have been confined to a more limited subset of countries.

- The promotion of e-government as a solution to many problems, and as a major facilitator of the integration sought in the first bullet point, above. Again, virtually every country has had some sort of programme here.

- More networking and partnership with other social partners/stakeholders. Almost all our governments have adopted this, at least on the level of rhetoric.

- Improved transparency and more open government. Transparency has become an international buzzword (and like all such, means many different things in different contexts). But no one can be against transparency.

- Strengthening the political support and protection for ministers (by more political advisers, more professional media offices/'spin doctors', more opportunity for political executives to remove and replace their top civil servants if they are found to be unsympathetic to the government's specific policies). There has been *something* of this in all our twelve countries, but the amount of it varies enormously, from the addition of a handful of political advisers to a spoils system that embraces the whole of the upper reaches of the administration.

Do these elements, taken together, constitute a new model, to which we can give a name? Our interpretation would be no, or, at least, not quite—only in an indirect and partial way. Certainly it could be said that a number of these themes are consonant with the NPG model (integration/holism, e-government, networking, and partnerships). Yet not all of them are. Strengthening the control of executive politicians could even be said to be a move *against* the tide of governance, and back towards a more hierarchical, representative politics. However, there is a deeper point. It is that a number of these themes can be formulated and reformulated to fit in with different management paradigms. In terms of the 'menus and dishes' discussion in chapter 1 (See Figure 1.3, pp. 25), these are dishes which can be presented within different menus, some more and some less coherent.

Consider the first two—integrated services and e-government. Each of these can be approached from within more than one of our three main models (NPM, NWS, and NPG). Thus integrated services can comfortably feature on either an NWS or an NPG trajectory. Within the former, one might expect the emphasis to be on better bureaucratic coordination—health care and social care authorities are reorganized so as to work more closely together, or local authority services are coordinated more closely with central government services (multi-level government). Within NPG, however, the same theme takes on a somewhat different hue. A holistic approach becomes a more ambitious affair, with the focus being on the coordination of government and non-government actors through networks and partnerships. Similarly with e-government—Dunleavy et al. (2006a) have shown that different governments have approached this in very different ways. In some, almost everything has been contracted out, NPM style, to private companies—even the business of designing the contracts themselves. Government has retained little capacity or expertise of its own. In others, however, government has preserved a strong central capacity and has used this to ensure that, where private companies have been involved, there has been real competition and a stronger, more informed assessment of their proposals—one might think of this as a more NWS approach to e-government (although Dunleavy et al. do not themselves refer to that model). Within an NPG approach, one might expect that the emphasis would be different again—perhaps accentuating the joint design, commissioning, and use of computer systems between public authorities and their partners in the market sector and civil society. In a four-country comparative study of ICT policies, Homburg comes to the conclusion that these policies tend to follow pre-existing institutional patterns and cultural attitudes, and that, in consequence, they are significantly different in the Denmark, the Netherlands, the UK, and the US (Homburg, 2008).

Therefore, although we can see a pattern of sorts in reforms since 2000—certain themes and tools that are internationally echoed and reproduced—these do not amount to a single new model or menu. Rather, as suggested in Chapter 1, we have a menu of dishes (tools), and different customers are selecting different combinations, and flavouring the same dish with different paradigmatic sauces. In an interesting recent study of public financial management in Australia, Belgium, Canada, Germany, the Netherlands, Sweden, the UK, and the US, Andrews arrived at the following conclusion:

> Conceptualising governance constructs as menu items, to be chosen, rather than essential elements of a one-best-way model, is, I believe, an important step to better understanding why good government looks different in different settings.   (Andrews, 2010, p. 30)

Within all this there are certainly elements of path dependency—the differences between the different 'houses' which we set out in Chapter 3 have not vanished. There is still a spectrum running from stronger state solutions to stronger market solutions, and there is still a difference between heavily centralized and majoritarian polities like New Zealand and the UK, and strongly decentralized and more consensual polities like Germany and Sweden. The internationalization of public management thinking may well have reduced the strength of these national differences, but it has by no means eliminated them. Furthermore, according to our reading of the evidence, these differences become more marked the further one moves down the sequence from talk to decision to practice and finally to results (Table 1.2, p. 13). To put it another way, the impression that 'everyone is doing NPM' (or governance, or transparency) is strongest if one confines oneself to reading policy statements and plans. As one moves through to practice (not to speak of results) one finds that, for instance, Belgium 'does' transparency very differently from the UK (Pollitt and Bouckaert, 2009), and Canada and the Netherlands 'do' e-government very differently from Australia and the UK (Dunleavy et al., 2006a, pp. 83–134). The structural and cultural substrata of public administration are often more durable than the latest reform.

8.3 What have been the results of these reforms?

Results are often the 'elephant in the room' for management reforms. As Chapter 5 showed, they can be remarkably difficult to pin down, even (perhaps *especially*) for the biggest, most loudly trumpeted reforms. Of course there may be masses of 'evidence', but on closer inspection (in the language of the performance framework from Chapter 5), most of it turns out to be about changes in activities and procedures rather than about actual outcomes. To an extent, therefore, public management reform has been more a matter of faith than science (Pollitt, 1995). We can think of public management as 'a social and perhaps a quasi-religious movement, arguably part of a broader "managerial" movement' (Hood, 2005, p. 13). Many reforms have been launched on the basis of a vision, an omega, rather than on the basis of anything that could be regarded as hard scientific evidence. Afterwards—sometimes many years afterwards—it is usually hard to collect the evidence of what worked and what didn't, and why. Supporters of the particular reform attribute anything good that happened to the reform, and critics similarly attribute almost anything bad that happened to the same reform, but both sides have difficulty in proving their attributions.

Yet it would be wrong to exaggerate this problem. It *is* a big problem at the level of whole reform programmes—the NPR in the USA or the 1980s Hawke administration reforms in Australia or the 'joined-up government' reforms of the Blair administration in the UK—but it is less difficult at a more local and specific level. Thus we may not know whether the NPR or Mrs Thatcher's 'Next Steps' programme 'worked', but it is easier to see whether changes to emergency call handling in the Sussex Police Force have improved public opinion ratings of the service, or whether reforms to the New Zealand health care system have reduced waiting lists for the hospital treatment of specified conditions. In Chapter 5, for example, we referred to clear evidence that a determined performance management reform by the UK government had radically reduced average waiting times in hospital accident and emergency departments (Kelman and Friedman, 2009). We also know that new data-matching procedures by the UK Department of Work and Pensions helped to halve benefit fraud in the years following 2000/1 (Chief Secretary to the Treasury, 2009, p. 29). We are told that by pooling budgets across several different government agencies a programme called Wraparound Milwaukee has reduced the need for residential treatment for seriously disturbed children in that city, and has halved the cost per child of that treatment (Chief Secretary to the Treasury, 2009, p. 39). During the Clinton/Gore National Performance Review, a new, simpler way for employees to make small purchases by using

Visa cards was extended across the federal government resulting in claimed savings of more than $12 billion (Gore, 1997, p. 49). There are many, many such examples and, while some of them may be oversimplified or exaggerated or ephemeral, it is hard to doubt that positive results are frequently achieved, and that sometimes they are successfully embedded, and last over the longer term.

The overall conclusions, therefore, are threefold. First, it is very difficult to be sure what is the net spectrum of results from large, complex programmes of public management reform. To some extent these big reforms are undertaken as matters of faith rather than proven 'science', and this is a feature that has not changed noticeably over the whole period of our study (cf. Pollitt, 1984 with White and Dunleavy, 2010). Second, this difficulty is frequently compounded and amplified by the fact that government themselves do not put credible evaluation procedures in place—or certainly not early enough. It is hard to avoid the conclusion that the politicians launching management innovations do not always see the careful, independent assessment of their long-term costs and benefits as a particularly important aspect of the reform process. Third, the methodological challenges of accurately assessing results are somewhat less (although still tough enough) if the focus is on a single, specific reform in a single, specific location or organization, or limited set of locations and/or organizations. Thus, some of our most convincing and 'hard' evidence comes from these more focused and disaggregated studies, where one can trace the complex actions and reactions as the reform unfolds (for a positive example, see Kelman, 2005; for a less encouraging case, see Sundström, 2006).

8.4 What are the implications of this experience for the future?

The story as we have told it seems to have a number of implications for those conducting research—or even simply studying—public management reform.

First, and most positively, international comparison can be seen to be a powerfully enlightening and informative exercise. It may be difficult to do well, but it frequently brings forth contrasts and alternatives which are so strong that they seem robust—that is to say that it is hard to believe that they could be merely artefacts of the way the data has been collected or some other bias. For example, reform has been consistently wider, deeper, faster, and more rigorously implemented in the UK than in Belgium (Pollitt and Bouckaert, 2009). It has been accomplished with less overt party political warfare and accusatory stereotyping in the Nordic countries than in Australia or New Zealand. It has resulted in far deeper changes to the procedures and culture of the top civil service in Australia, New Zealand, and the UK than in Germany or France. It has 'hollowed out' the French or Swedish (or even Canadian) public services much less than the American federal service. All this, taken over a thirty-year period, tells us that the strength of the big models of reform is less than overwhelming. Certainly there are international currents, and certainly particular models and, at a more detailed level, specific tools (dishes) become fashionable and attract a lot of interest. But they have never been strong enough, compelling enough, to push all our twelve states down the same road. There is, to put it positively, a good deal of room for choice and interpretation. There is room for strategies and political preferences and different balances between the state sector, the market sector, and civil society. Even now, post GEC, governments may 'have to' save money, but there is almost always more than one way of doing it. Governments may 'have to' address changing demographics, or climate change, or the digital revolution, or any number of other challenges, but for each there is more than one way of organizing and managing the government's response. In short, there is something worth arguing about.

Furthermore—to extend this first point—comparison opens up a treasure chest of examples of adaptation. As we have seen, it is not only that different countries have inclined more to one model than another, it is also that they have taken specific tools (performance-related pay, benchmarking, public–private partnerships) and used them in contrasting ways. It seems that management tools are made of bendy plastic, not rigid metal, and it seems they are used by different craftspeople for somewhat different jobs. Again, there is plenty of space for discussion and choice, for creating new menus by combining particular dishes in new ways. And there are also some warnings—negative, perhaps, but still very useful to have. These tend to be about the use of particular tools in particular contexts. Thus, for example, the aggressive implementation of individualistic performance-related pay in team- or consensus-based organizational cultures is likely to create rather high counter-waves. Or the attempt to use precisely specified ('complete') contracts in situations where it is hard to define the precise level and quality of outputs one wants—or perhaps will want in the future—may lead to the organization letting the contract finding itself locked in to a set of increasingly inappropriate incentives. Or the wholesale contracting out of complex technological functions runs the risk that public authorities may not be able to retain sufficient in-house expertise to monitor and evaluate the contractors who are providing the actual service.

Second, an overview of the evidence thus far encourages a certain scepticism concerning reformers' incessant claims to be on the verge of 'transforming' this or that, or becoming (to use a phrase that was popular in the late Blair and Brown administrations in the UK) 'world class' at almost any aspect of public service provision you care to name. The deep, sedimented structures of most of our twelve public sectors are hard to shift in such fundamental ways. At the end of 2009 the UK public expenditure minister issued a White Paper in which he said:

[R]eform must accelerate through making full use of the new strengths we now have: more empowered citizens, the knowledge and commitment of our public servants, especially those at the frontline, and our vibrant communities. It will require a premium on transparency, innovation and flexibility.   (Chief Secretary to the Treasury, 2009, pp. 15–16)

This picture was unrealistic to the point of romanticism. It was a White Paper issued by a deeply unpopular government which knew it had to make huge cuts in public spending, but was putting off discussing them in any detail until after the imminent election (which it lost). Would most citizens, if surveyed, have declared themselves 'empowered'? Unlikely. Would most frontline public servants, ground down by reform after reform, and burdened by unprecedented levels of central control, have recognized this buoyant picture? Probably not. Were these 'vibrant communities' the same as those being described at exactly the same time as 'the broken society' by the Leader of the Opposition?

Unfortunately, this is far from being the only example of hyperbole in official publications. Something else which has changed in the thirty years since 1980 has been the vocabulary and style of public administration reform documents. In many of our countries (Australia, France, the Netherlands, New Zealand, the UK, and the USA), the sober reports of the 1970s have given way to 'designer' documents replete with sound-bite phrases, up-beat photos and diagrams, and managerial buzz words. They claim that the machinery of government is on the verge of 'transformation', 'smarter' government, citizen empowerment—that the authorities are about to achieve all manner of radical change. Yet within a short time these texts are largely forgotten. How many people now remember the official documents of the late 1980s and 1990s which, in some cases were promising things which sound suspiciously similar to what is still being held out as just round the corner today? These included: citizen-focused government (e.g. Prime Minister, 1991), a government that 'works so much better and costs so much less' (Gore, 1997, p. 2), benchmarking (Department of Finance, 1996), quality through market competition (HM Treasury, 1991), and more joining up and integration of services (Prime Minister and Minister for the Cabinet Office, 1999).

More importantly, we can see that many of our (admittedly imperfect) indicators show the rank order of different countries to be remarkably similar to what it was many years ago. The 'high trust' countries (especially the Nordic group) remain relatively high trust and the low trust countries (e.g. Italy) remain low. The big spenders (Sweden) remain big spenders, the middling big spenders (France, Germany) remain middling big spenders, and the lean states (USA) remain lean. The law-oriented culture may have diminished, but relatively speaking it remains much more prominent in Belgium, Germany, and France than in the UK. Of course all these countries have moved—they have carried out real reforms and made real changes. But they seldom if ever turn out to be as transformational as the rhetoric, and the relativities between countries do not change at anything like the same speed as the announcements of new reforms.

This leads to a third observation. It is that the timescale for effective management reform is often far longer than a) the timescale of media attention and b) the timescale of strong political interest. The application of many of the tools mentioned in this book takes twelve to thirty-six months before the reform is fully bedded-in and one can see the whole range of effects—positive and negative, expected and unexpected. Serious efforts to get close to a new model or paradigm (e.g. NPG or the 'Digital state') take much longer, probably a minimum of five years and sometimes double that. Thus stability of purpose and continuity of practice are important ingredients in successful reform (Pollitt, 2008). Yet stability and continuity are increasingly hard to come by in today's high-speed world. However, some systems seem better able to support complex, longer-term reforms than others. If we return to the 'many houses' of Chapter 3 we can see that the relative ease or difficulty with which management reforms can be carried through may well have some bearing here. At one extreme we have some rather slow-moving systems where reform has difficulty in achieving the kind of momentum which it needs in order to build its identity and attract sufficient support. The German federal government seems to be one such environment. Belgium, for somewhat different reasons, is also a candidate, at least in the sense that an increasingly fragmented and fractious political system currently has difficulty in agreeing on any fundamental machinery reforms. At the other extreme it can be so easy to promulgate reform—the checks and balances are so flimsy—that governments may be tempted to pile one political initiative on top of another, creating a merry-go-round of reforms which soon induce reform fatigue among the officials concerned—and possibly cynicism among the on-looking citizens. At times the UK seems to have belonged in this category (Pollitt, 2007). It is the countries in between—where reforms require hard work over time to construct the necessary political consensus, but which then have a good chance of long-term survival in a less adversarial system—that may have the best hope of sticking to agreed trajectories and eventually firmly embedding reforms. Finland, Sweden, and, to a lesser extent the Netherlands, typify this kind of system.

Finally, fourth, we might suggest that our thirty-year view lends some support to the idea that a proportion (not all) of the most fundamental choices in public management involve trades-off or balancing acts between different underlying values or principles (as discussed in Chapter 7). Do we want continuity and stability or ever-increasing choice and innovation? Efficiency or equity? Effectiveness or efficiency? Expertise or diversity? As already mentioned, over the past fifty years a number of notable academics have characterized public administration knowledge as often having a proverbial or contradictory character (Hood and Jackson, 1991; Simon, 1946). Of course we want all these things, but the pursuit of one value (efficiency, say) is gradually realized to have a deleterious effect on another (equity, say). At which point the currents of reform rhetoric may swing round and stress the other value or values. But if they are vigorously pursued for a while, it will be eventually realized that things are quietly becoming less efficient, and the tide will turn once more. This is not to argue that the story of reform is one of an unending swing between fixed poles (the values). Rather what seems to happen is that the *level* to which we realize each value (or, at least, aspire to realize it) shifts upwards. Furthermore the value itself may be redefined to fit new circumstances (du Gay, 2005). Thus the efficiency with which we issue driving licences or pay pensions has climbed over the years, and our notions of equity may have become more inclusive, but still the reform ball bounces between them, and balance can be lost, even if it is a balance set at a higher or more ambitious level. Thus (for example) in many countries we have attained levels of transparency and accountability undreamed of thirty years ago, and yet we still demand more of these attributes. We have more choice than ever before, but we read in countless reform documents that we need yet more. In some countries efficiency drives have been a fairly constant presence for a quarter of a century, and yet we are told we must make more efficiency gains.

8.5 What kind of answers are we looking for, and what kind of answers can we reasonably expect to get?

This is rather a fundamental question and one which, logically, it could be argued should have come at the beginning of the book rather than the end. Our priority, however, was to get to the facts (and alleged facts) about reforms first—to 'get our hands dirty'—so we have left the more metaphysical question until now. So, what kind of answers might we expect from a study of management reforms? There is a spectrum that runs something like this:

1. Clear identification of certain models or forms or techniques that work well in most places, times, and circumstances. These could be big models/paradigms like NWS or NPG, or they could be individual tools such as single-purpose, contractually framed executive agencies, or contracting out or performance-related pay. These would therefore function as generic solutions, based on law-like generalizations—serving within a classic nomothetic approach to knowledge (Kay, 2006).

2. More limited and conditional generalizations, usually of the form 'this usually works in this way under these conditions and in these circumstances'. Thus, for example, we might say 'performance-related pay works best when tasks are simple and easily measurable, and when staff can control the circumstances of their own productivity, and where the general culture is fairly individualistic'. These are thus conditional and probabilistic hypotheses (and may thus be rather complex/less than elegant). They are explicitly contextualized. Nevertheless, they may be generalizable across quite broad territories—for example, our proposition that centralized executives within majoritarian systems have the capacity to make more radical management reforms and formulate and decide them more quickly than decentralized executives within consensual systems. (Notice that this does *not* mean that centralized, majoritarian regimes necessarily or automatically *will* carry through radical reforms. It means they *can*, but this potential will only be realized if there are competent—and sometimes lucky—leaders who have ideas and actually want to use up political capital in trying to put these ideas into effect.)

3. No big, generic laws or generalizations—not even those hedged about with probabilities and conditions—but a shopping basket full of assorted insights and rules of thumb that seem to have some transferability from one place to another. Thus we may observe that the tighter performance measures are linked to explicit penalties and incentives, the more impact they will have on behaviour *and* the more gaming and cheating is likely to arise, or that crises often offer a window of opportunity for would-be reformers. Such insights may encourage us to build bits of explanatory theory (it is not too difficult to see why strong penalties and incentives may tempt more people to indulge in gaming), but they do not 'add up' to any general theory that categorizes (still less explains) patterns of public management reform. Although they can stimulate theory-building they are more usually a type of 'craft knowledge' or practitioner's wisdom, rather than formal academic theory. In this sense category 3 type answers are different from category 2 type answers, but there is also a degree of overlap between the two categories—the boundary between them is not sharp.

4. No workable generalizations. Every situation is unique. The world is too complex and uncertain for us to predict anything with much confidence. All we can do is to describe, with hindsight and in narrative form, what seems to have worked and what seems to have failed in a series of distinctive and highly chance-influenced circumstances. This is the polar, pure type of the idiographic approach to knowledge

(Kay, 2006). And in the hands of some writers it is pushed even further because of their insistence that there is no one version of the story which is better than the others, but only a range of alternative stories. The conclusion is then arrived at that a range of 'decentered narratives' are about as much as we can hope for (Bevir and Rhodes, 2006).

We are not the only interpreters of the material we have selected and shaped for inclusion in this book. Any reader has the opportunity to draw their own conclusions. But, for what it is worth, our own view is that answers at the two extremes (1 and 4 above) are either unlikely (type 1) or unambitious (type 4). Readers are invited to search for type 1 generic 'laws'—we find it hard to think of any that, under inspection, do not quickly dissolve into qualifications and conditions and exceptions. Thus, for example, a detailed study of Lijphart's (1999, p. 301) general proposition that consensus democracies outperform majoritarian democracies with regard to the kindness and gentleness of their public policy orientations finds that it does not seem to apply very well to Belgium and the UK (Pollitt and Bouckaert, 2009, pp. 158–67). Similarly, the generic hypothesis in Osborne and Gaebler's best selling *Re-inventing Government* (1992) that all governments would soon be obliged to follow the road of the 'entrepreneurial spirit' has been shown by repeated studies not to apply in all sorts of places (e.g. Bouckaert et al., 2008; Ongaro, 2009; Pollitt et al., 2007). As far as the other pole is concerned—type 4—we acknowledge both that highly idiographic studies can be quite fascinating and convincing, and that there may be certain topics or issues where we cannot get any further than type 4. But to claim that type 4 answers are the *only* robust ones available seems a considerable exaggeration. There are many type 2 and type 3 generalizations that work pretty well most of the time, and which, at the very least, give researchers and reformers an illuminating way into particular situations, even if these generalizations may require a certain amount of refinement and qualification as one goes along. If evidence of this is needed, the reader need go no further than Sections 8.2 and 8.3 above, both of which include a number of type 2 and 3 general-izations which we believe are robust and which approximately conform with the volumi-nous evidence we have reviewed elsewhere in this book.

The implications of this analysis for further research are fairly clear. In a nutshell, most public management researchers should be aiming at generating knowledge of types 2 and 3, rather than 1 or 4. They should be looking at the way specific tools behave (and are adapted) in specific contexts rather than trying to build models of global governance or—at the other pole—lovingly recording, blow-by-blow, the evolution of the multiple view-points of different stakeholders concerning the organization of the municipal refuse collection service in Pudsea. They should also be tracing and analysing the way specific ideas and concepts are spread and sold and move from one arena to another. It is therefore in categories 2 and 3 that the modest hopes for some sort of cumulative knowledge about public management reform mainly lie. The big models are stimulating, and will surely keep on coming (it is actually quite easy to invent a new one, or, at least a new variation on an existing one). Yet they do not take one very far, either in analysing actual reforms or in prescribing what might be done in future. Worse, they can grievously mislead their users into thinking that they *really* know what is happening in country X or Y, or that it is *just* an example of NPM or NPG, or whatever.

Public management reform, we have suggested, is not a science, not a piece of managerial technology, and certainly not a predetermined and inevitable outcome of 'globalization' (or some other supposed universal imperative). It is a partly political, partly organizational, partly economic, and partly technological process with quite uncertain outcomes. It is informed by an assorted, untidy accumulation of knowledge which is sometimes sufficient, but not infrequently incomplete, faulty or misapplied. Yet reform is inevitable—one only has to try to imagine a world in which there would be no public management reform to see how extremely improbable such a state of affairs must be. We give the last word to Machiavelli:

[N]o government should ever imagine that it can adopt a safe course; rather it should regard all possible courses of action as risky. This is the way things are: whenever one tries to escape one danger one runs into another. Prudence consists in being able to assess the nature of the particular threat and accepting the lesser evil.   (Machiavelli, 2003, p. 73 [original, *c*.1516]).

■ APPENDIX A

The Socio-Economic Context

A.1 The scope and purpose of Appendices A and B

Chapter 2 introduced the model of public management reform which we have referred to throughout the rest of the book (see Figure 2.1). In that model, socio-economic forces (box A in Figure 2.1) are given an important, though not finally determinative role, in setting the climate for management reform. Here in Appendix A we offer a brief descriptive summary of what that climate has been like during the past twenty-five years. Then, in Appendix B we move on to the specifics in each country, and offer a brief 'file' summarizing the history of reform in that state.

The two appendices together provide some basic facts about the twelve countries covered in the main text. Unlike many other multi-country studies, this book is *not* organized into single-country chapters. It is deliberately and, we hope, advantageously, organized by model and theme—thus permitting a more integrated, less sequential form of inter-country comparison. However, one price that is paid for this type of integration is that the reader is not offered neat little summaries of each country's recent history and arrangements. Left thus, readers who were not already familiar with the relevant aspects of a particular country's constitution, policies, and so on, would be at a considerable disadvantage. To offset this possible handicap, Appendices A and B offer this type of information in a conveniently packaged form. The contents of the package are closely patterned on the model of public management reform introduced in Chapter 2. The sequence is therefore as follows:

APPENDIX A

- some information on major economic indicators for each country (i.e. data which helps to 'fill in' the larger box 'A' in Figure 2.1);
- some information on key sociodemographic indicators for each country (i.e. data which helps fill in box 'C' in Figure 2.1).

APPENDIX B

- a set of 'country files' which give snapshots of each country, organized in exactly the same categories as Chapter 2 and including, inter alia, details of the major management reforms since 1980. Each 'file' concludes with a table summarizing key events.

A.2 Major economic indicators

As the model in Chapter 2 proposes, macro-economic features influence public management reforms. Writing at a time when the GEC is directly causing cutbacks, public service wage freezes, and urgent reforms to try to maintain quality in the face of reduced inputs, it should not be difficult to persuade readers of this connection. However, it is not only in the aftermath of crises that the economic situation exerts an influence. Rather it is a constant presence. When the economy is doing well, tax revenues rise and social expenditure falls (because there are fewer unemployed). When a government bears a heavy load of debt a considerable slice of its expenditure must be devoted to paying interest, and/or repaying the principal, and is therefore not available for spending on public services. And so on.

In the following pages we look at some significant macro-economic indicators. Most of the statistics have been extracted from the OECD's admirable *Factbook 2010*. We look at GDP growth, and, as a rough proxy for the exposure of governments to international economic cycles, we examine the share that international trade represents of GDP.

Then we go to government spending and government debt.

Three major limitations to this data should, however, be acknowledged at the outset. First, it is seldom, if ever, possible to read off conclusions about a country's economic health from a single indicator. Second, some of these indicators are 'snapshots'—indicators of the state of a variable at a particular point in time or, at best, over a

Table A.1 Real GDP growth

Country	1995	2000	2005	2008
Australia	4.1	1.9	3.0	2.3
Belgium	2.4	3.7	1.8	1.0
Canada	2.8	5.2	3.0	0.4
Finland	3.9	5.1	2.8	1.0
France	2.1	3.9	1.9	0.4
Germany	1.9	3.2	0.8	1.3
Italy	2.8	3.7	0.7	−1.0
Netherlands	3.1	3.9	2.0	2.0
New Zealand	4.2	2.4	3.0	−1.1
Sweden	4.0	4.4	3.3	−0.2
UK	3.1	3.9	2.2	0.6
USA	2.5	4.2	3.1	0.4

Source: OECD Factbook, 2010.

three- or five-year average. Third, as we pointed out in Chapter 2, economic pressures may often provide the context in which governments think they are obliged to launch public management reforms, but they do not determine what those reforms will be. One cannot read off either individual models or individual measures (instruments) from economic trends.

Most countries showed quite strong growth from 1997 onwards, peaking in 2000/1. Then there was a dip before a renewed growth surge took place from 2003. This collapsed with the 2008 GEC, the first effects of which are clearly visible in the much lower growth figures for most of our countries in 2008 (actually negative for three countries—and negative for most OECD countries in the following year). At the time of writing reliable figures for 2009 were still coming in, but already it can be seen that some of our countries suffered badly (see Table A.2)

The falls shown in Table A.2 are steeper and deeper than the falls experienced during the two previous major global economic downturns (1981–2 and 1992–3).

It should not be forgotten that, by global standards, all twelve countries studied in this volume are rich. However, there are considerable differences within this rich countries' club. All other things being equal (which is a big assumption), a super-rich country such as the USA or Germany will have more room for manoeuvre, in both public and private spheres, than a significantly less

Table A.2 Changes in real GDP between the first quarter of 2008 and the third quarter of 2009

Country	% Change in GDP
Canada	−3.1
France	−3.2
Germany	−6.3
Italy	−6.5
UK	−5.9
USA	−3.5

Table A.3 International trade in goods and services as a percentage of GDP

Country	1995	2000	2005	2008
Australia	19.4	22.5	21.0	24.6
Belgium	63.5	76.8	78.2	85.3
Canada	35.7	42.7	35.9	34.3
Finland	32.6	38.7	39.6	45.0
France	22.2	28.1	26.5	27.7
Germany	23.7	33.2	38.5	44.1
Italy	23.8	26.6	26.0	29.1
Netherlands	56.5	67.3	65.4	72.6
New Zealand	28.6	34.7	28.9	32.8
Sweden	36.4	43.4	44.9	50.5
UK	28.3	28.6	28.1	30.4
USA	11.6	13.0	13.2	15.2

Source: OECD Factbook 2010.

Table A.4 General government expenditures as a percentage of GDP

Country	1995	2000	2005	2008
Australia	38.2	35.2	34.8	34.3
Belgium	52.1	49.2	52.2	50.1
Canada	48.5	41.1	39.3	39.7
Finland	61.4	48.3	50.3	49.0
France	54.4	51.6	53.4	52.7
Germany	54.8	45.1	46.9	43.8
Italy	52.5	46.1	48.1	48.7
Netherlands	56.4	44.2	44.8	45.9
New Zealand	42.2	39.2	39.1	41.1
Sweden	65.3	57.0	54.0	51.8
UK	44.1	36.6	44.1	47.5
USA	37.1	33.9	36.2	38.8

Source: OECD Factbook 2010.

rich country such as New Zealand or the UK. Obviously size isn't everything: Belgium is quite small (population 10 million) but the deep tensions between the Wallonian and Flemish communities have certainly made it a difficult country—at the federal level—to govern.

Next, Table A.3 shows international trade as a percentage of GDP. Clearly there are huge differences here. For the Netherlands and Belgium, international trade is a large component of their national economies—73 per cent and 85 per cent respectively. For Australia (24%), France (28%) and, most of all, the USA (15%) it is much less significant. What is most noticeable, however, is that for all countries (except, marginally, Canada) the importance of international trade has grown over the

Table A.5 General government gross financial liabilities (as a per-centage of GDP)

Country	1995	2000	2005	2008
Australia	42.5	25.4	16.9	14.3
Belgium	135.4	113.8	95.9	93.5
Canada	101.6	82.1	71.6	69.7
Finland	65.2	52.3	48.5	40.7
France	62.7	65.6	75.7	75.7
Germany	55.7	60.4	71.1	68.8
Italy	122.5	121.0	119.9	114.4
Netherlands	89.6	63.9	61.1	65.8
New Zealand	51.3	37.4	27.4	25.3
Sweden	81.0	64.7	60.7	47.1
UK	51.6	45.1	46.1	56.8
USA	70.6	54.4	61.3	70.0

Source: OECD Factbook 2010.

period as a whole. This suggests that the global economy is indeed becoming more interconnected with respect to trade, and that means it is more likely that where some countries go up or down, so do the others. Obviously, however, trade is not the only factor in global economic interconnectedness. Equally, if not more important, has been the globalization of capital and investment markets. This can also have effects on public management reform. One has only to consider, for example, the catastrophic effects of international investments on the British or Irish banks during the 2008 GEC, and the knock-on impacts on public spending in those countries.

The figures for general government expenditure (Table A.4) confirm the broad comparative picture developed earlier in the book. There are relatively generous Nordic countries (usually over 50%) and relatively parsimonious Anglo-Saxon countries (Australia and the USA below 40%, New Zealand and the UK usually just above). The continental governments emerge as 'big state' countries, with Belgium and France usually over 50 per cent and Italy and the Netherlands usually high in the 40s. However, the general trend is downwards during the period of growth between 1995 and 2005, although this is, of course, a drop in *proportion*, and says nothing about absolute levels of spending (if the absolute level remains the same and the

economy grows quickly, then the proportion will obviously fall).

Now we move on to government debt (Table A.5). Here there are interesting differences. In the period 1990–5 (not shown on the table) debt as a percentage of GDP had risen in all our twelve countries except New Zealand. After 1995, however, a majority of these countries took the opportunity of a long boom to reduce this ratio. Others did not do this, so that we see major reductions in Australia, Belgium, Canada, Finland, the Netherlands, and New Zealand and Sweden, but a growing proportion of debt in France and Germany. Even more striking is the variation in national debt levels. Belgium, Italy, and Canada began in 1995 with debts of more than their annual GDP. At the same time Australia recorded only 42.5 per cent and New Zealand 51.3 per cent. Belgium and Italy remained highly indebted throughout the whole period (though each eased the proportion down a bit), while Canada radically reduced its ratio. Of course it has to be said that Table A.5 ends on the brink of an abyss. The figures for 2008 do not yet more than marginally reflect the impacts of the GEC which, in many countries, led to a ballooning of debt as governments spent to prop up financial and industrial institutions, and to pay benefits to rapidly increasing numbers of unemployed persons.

A.3 Key sociodemographic indicators

The need to restrain public expenditure (and thereby hold down rates of taxation) has featured frequently throughout the book. Most of the largest elements of expenditure within the twelve public sectors under examination are strongly influenced by sociodemographic factors. Typically pensions, health care, and education are the largest spending programmes. Unemployment benefits tend to be much smaller in volume, but have attracted a great deal of public attention, especially as the nature of both employment and unemployment has been changing since 1980, as compared with the 1950s and 1960s. Part-time employment has grown almost everywhere (although at different rates in different countries), and there has been a shift in employment away from younger people and from older men.

Among our twelve countries welfare states vary hugely, not simply in terms of the shares of expenditure they absorb, but also in terms of their basic structures and procedures. However, all, to a significant degree, have both fiscal and social problems to face. Expert studies sometimes classify welfare states into a Scandinavian model, an American model, and a continental European model. The Scandinavian model is relatively generous, and places emphasis on the provision of social services as well as on cash payments. The American model is relatively parsimonious, leaving a wider range of service provision to the private sector than is the case in its Scandinavian counterpart. There is also a political willingness to tolerate more extreme inequalities in income distribution and therefore, in both the US and the UK cases, the continuing existence of substantial pockets of deep poverty. The continental model is more 'generous' than the American, but less service-oriented (and therefore less employment-intensive) than the Scandinavian model. The emphasis is on cash transfers. If you look back to Chapter 5, Table 5.5 gives an aggregate picture of social expenditure in our twelve countries. Notice that, in every country except the Netherlands, it has grown in importance in the quarter century after 1980. In 2005 the proportion was highest in Sweden (29.8%), France (29.5%) and Italy (26.5%). It was lowest in The USA (16.3%), Canada (16.5%) and Australia (18.2%). Differences of 10 per cent or more of GDP between the biggest social spenders and the smallest are huge differences which, all things being equal, would get even bigger as the population ages and unemployment rises.

The different models are also financed in different ways. All use some combination of general taxes, payroll taxes, and mandatory insurance, the exact balance between these different forms varying a good deal. As a basis for welfare expenditure, payroll taxes are particularly vulnerable in a globalized economy because they add directly to the cost of labour and, when employment falls, revenue shrinks more rapidly than it would from, say, a tax on consumption or even a general tax on incomes. An OECD study summed up as follows:

[T]he implication seems clear enough: in order to increase their sustainability, each of these three types of welfare state must primarily attend to its specific problems. The Scandinavian model must reduce its dependence on very high levels of taxation; the American model must find ways of alleviating the distress of the working poor; and the continental model must find ways to increase levels of employment without running into the problems of the other two models. (OECD, 1997c, p. 218)

Returning to the sociodemographic particulars, pensions are obviously affected by the age structure of the population. *Ceteris paribus*, the higher the proportion of the population which is retired, the higher will have to be public pension expenditure, and the smaller will be the proportion of the population which is in work and therefore capable of making some contribution to this expenditure through current taxation. In practice matters are rather more complicated than this, for a variety of reasons. For example, in different countries different proportions of the retired population are covered by private pension schemes, and the adequacy of these schemes also varies. Also, many older people may still be active participants in the labour market, and variations in the extent to which this takes place can also influence the 'need' for state pensions. Further, it is the case that pensionable age varies from country to country (and since the mid 1980s there has been a trend towards shifting the age of entitlement *upwards*, so as to moderate demands on public expenditure, and this has accelerated recently leading, *inter alia*, to large strikes of public sector workers in France in 2010). All these variations are important, but underneath them net changes in the elderly population remain a significant 'driver'. In all twelve countries the percentage of elderly persons in the population as a whole has been increasing, but at different rates and over slightly different time periods. Table A.6 gives some information about this.

Table A.6 Population aged 65 and over as a percentage of the total population

Country	2000	2005	2010	2020	2050
Australia	12.4	12.9	14.3	18.3	25.7
Belgium	16.8	17.2	17.6	20.7	27.7
Canada	12.6	13.1	14.1	18.2	26.3
Finland	14.9	15.9	17.3	22.8	27.6
France	16.1	16.4	16.7	20.3	26.2
Germany	16.4	18.9	20.4	22.7	31.5
Italy	18.3	19.6	20.5	23.3	33.6
Netherlands	13.6	14.2	15.5	19.8	23.5
New Zealand	11.8	12.0	13.3	17.1	26.2
Sweden	17.3	17.3	18.5	21.2	23.6
UK	15.8	16.0	16.5	19.0	24.1
USA	12.4	12.4	13.0	16.1	20.2

Source: OECD Factbook 2010.

From Table A.6 it can be seen, for example, that in 2010 Germany and Sweden have the highest percentages of over-65s. For all twelve countries, the share of 'dependent elderly' has already been increasing and will increase even more in the period up to 2050. The next decade will be a time of particularly rapid expansion of the elderly population as the post-Second World War 'baby boom' retires. This will put very considerable pressures on the welfare state, and we can expect to see many more reforms in this sector. However, the size of the longer-term forecast increases (up to 2050) vary a good deal from country to country. Belgium, Finland, Germany, and Italy will end up with a very high proportion of over 65s—as much as a third of the total population in the case of Italy. In the Netherlands, Sweden, and the USA, by contrast, this group are predicted to form between 20 and 23 per cent of the total population.

The relative size of the elderly population is very important for health care spending. For example, in the UK it was calculated that, in 1990, the average gross per capita expenditure for hospital and community health services for 16–44 year olds was £115. The equivalent annual expenditure per 85 plus capita was £1,875. Between 1971 and 1990 the population of people aged 85 and over had risen from 485,000 to 866,000 (Harrison and Pollitt, 1994, pp. 19–21).

Of course, there is no assumption that each country is equally generous in its social expenditures, or that there is some uniform balance between expenditures on different social groups. Some countries seem to emphasize the needs of the elderly, others the needs of, say, the young, or the unemployed (OECD, 1997c, pp. 63–80).

Another aspect of ageing populations—and one of particular relevance for this book—is the effect on the staffing of the public service. In 2010 we are in the middle of a wave of retirement that will leave some public agencies with only a very thin layer of experience at the top. As the OECD says:

Maintaining the government's capacity to deliver the same level and quality of services remains a complex issue. Significant staff departures create an opportunity to bring staff with new skills into government, downsize the workforce where needed, decrease staff costs...and re-allocate human resources across sectors. However, this can lead to loss of capacity and the need to postpone the retirement of some key staff. In addition, given the large share of government employment in many OECD member countries, these high replacement needs could risk pre-empting the private sector's access to new labour market entrants. (OECD, 2009a, p. 72)

To illustrate the scale of the problem we can note that in 2005 Canada, Finland, France, Sweden, and the USA each had more than 30 per cent of their central government staff over the age of 50.

Table A.7 Income inequality mid 2000s

Country	P90/P10	P50/P10
Australia	3.95	2.09
Belgium	3.43	1.97
Canada	4.12	2.14
Finland	3.21	1.86
France	3.39	1.82
Germany	3.98	2.08
Italy	4.31	2.11
Netherlands	4.27	2.06
New Zealand	2.83	1.77
Sweden	2.79	1.72
UK	4.21	1.99
USA	5.91	2.69

Source: OECD Factbook 2010.
Notes: The table shows two measures. The P90/P10 ratio is the ratio between the upper bound value of the ninth richest decile of the population to the upper bound value of the poorest 10% (first decile). The P50/P10 is the ratio of the median income to the upper bound value of the poorest 10%.

Table A.8 Foreign-born populations as a percentage of total populations

Country	1995	2000	2006	2007
Australia	–	7.4	7.7	–
Belgium	9.0	8.4	8.8	9.1
Canada	–	5.3	6.0	–
Finland	1.3	1.8	2.3	2.5
France	–	–	5.6 (2005)	–
Germany	8.8	8.9	8.2	8.2
Italy	1.7	2.4	5.0	5.8
Netherlands	4.7	4.2	4.2	4.2
New Zealand	–	–	–	–
Sweden	6.0	5.4	5.4	5.7
UK	3.4	4.0	5.8	6.5
USA	6.0	6.6	7.4	–

Source: OECD Factbook 2010.

For Australia, Germany, the Netherlands, and the UK this figure was between 20 and 30 per cent (data was not available for Belgium, Italy, or New Zealand—OECD, 2009a, pp. 72–3).

There is a range of other social developments which can affect social and economic policies, apart from changes in the proportion of elderly persons. One of them is the level of income inequality, which seems to be connected to a wide range of social problems. High levels of inequality seem to be associated with greater problems of, *inter alia*, violent crime, drug use, imprisonment, mental health, obesity, teenage births, and educational performance (Wilkinson and Pickett, 2010). Even in otherwise wealthy societies, pockets of poverty also tend to become pockets of crime and health problems and low educational attainment—and each of these obviously has significant implications for the public services. Table A.7 shows levels of income inequalities in our twelve countries.

Clearly there are significant differences here. The USA is by far the most unequal country on these measures. Canada, Italy, the Netherlands, and the UK are also fairly unequal. At the other end of the spectrum come Sweden and New Zealand. Since the mid 1980s inequality has risen in all our countries except France (*OECD Factbook 2010*, p. 235). Interestingly, the proportionate rise has been highest in countries which were previously rather egalitarian, particularly New Zealand and Finland. However the USA and Germany have also seen quite substantial increases. It seems unlikely that the effects of the GEC (not yet registered in these figures) will do much to lessen inequalities, and possibly quite the contrary. A final, but important point is that all this data refers to *income* inequalities, not inequalities of wealth. The latter, in most cases are even greater than the inequalities of income.

Finally, we live in a period of considerable international migration, for economic, political, and other reasons (one of the authors of this book is currently an immigrant). This movement of persons brings a range of individual and collective benefits, but can also lead to political, economic, and cultural tensions. The presence of a substantial body of immigrants in a country faces the government of that state with various challenges—first of all, what citizen rights to extend to them, and then a whole range of questions concerning how to 'tune' public services to deal with a multilingual, multicultural community. Table A.8 shows that some of our twelve countries (Australia, Canada, New Zealand) contain large percentages of foreign-born residents, while others have only proportionately small groups (especially Finland). (*En passant*, it should be noted that *foreign-born* residents may not be *foreigners*, because they may have taken the nationality of their new country of residence. How quickly and easily they can do that depends on the local laws and procedures, which vary considerably among our twelve countries.) In all the eleven cases where the OECD has data there appears to have been a substantial increase in the foreign-born population over the period covered. In one case there is no longitudinal information. Collecting information about foreign-born residents can be a sensitive political and legal issue, and some governments do not do

Table A.9 Estimated total populations 2010

Country	Estimated population, 2010
Australia	21.5M
Belgium	10.8M
Canada	33.6M
Finland	5.3M
France	62.5M
Germany	82.8M
Italy	59.0M
Netherlands	16.4M
New Zealand	4.4M
Sweden	9.3M
UK	62.3M
USA	308.9M

Source: OECD Factbook 2010.

it, or only do it very occasionally. The general trend, aided by economic liberalization, has been for greater international movement.

Finally, it may be worthwhile to remind ourselves that sheer size matters, and that we are dealing with very differently sized countries in respect of population. These range from quite small and fairly socially homogenous countries like Finland and New Zealand, to large countries with very substantial foreign-born populations, such as the USA and Germany. Table A.9 shows estimated total populations in 2010.

Country Files and Tables of Events

AUSTRALIA

A. Socio-economic forces: general

Australia is a very large country, with a relatively modest population of 21.5 Million (2010). For key economic and socio-demographic data see Appendix A.

B. Global economic forces

Like New Zealand, Australia relinquished most of its protectionist policies of the 1950–75 period as no longer viable. Unsurprisingly, therefore, competitiveness has become a major issue for governments of all political colours. International trade represents a somewhat more modest proportion of the Australian economy than for the majority of our twelve countries (see Table A.3).

C. Sociodemographic change

Two features of the 1970s and 1980s which tended to dilute the previous assumptions of Australia as an overwhelmingly white, post-colonial society were, first, an influx of Asian immigrants and, second, an increasingly strong demand for political (including territorial) rights by the aboriginal peoples. By the early twenty-first century immigration was a major political issue with the Howard government attempting to make political capital out of its tough stance with respect to asylum seekers and refugees. However, the pressures of an ageing society have thus far been somewhat less than those experienced by most Western European states (4th lowest proportion out of twelve countries in 2010—see Table A.6). Nevertheless, the passing into retirement of the 'baby-boomer' generation is currently imposing considerable strain on the Australian Public Service (see Australian Public Service Commission, 2004).

D. National socio-economic policies

Australia and New Zealand were both obliged, during the 1980s, to move away from previous protectionist policies which had involved a high degree of state regulation and intervention in the economy. 'Increasingly both countries turned to the private sector and the use of market principles within the public sector, which have been linked to broader programmes of economic reform' (Halligan, 1997, p. 17). Also like New Zealand, one component in the shift of economic strategy was a recognition that a higher proportion of both imports and exports were now coming from Asia, rather than from Europe (Castles et al., 1996, pp. 24–6).

The Hawke Labor government increased public spending as a percentage of GDP. However, the terms of trade deteriorated sharply in 1985/6 and the second half of the 1980s witnessed an intensified effort at expenditure reduction. This, in turn, focused efforts to increase public sector efficiency and streamline government. By the mid 1990s the Australian economy was performing better, and has generally recorded an above-OECD average record for a number of years.

It might be said that the transition to new macro-economic and micro-economic policies was both sharper and more painful in New Zealand than Australia. During the 1985–92 period Australia enjoyed much better economic growth and employment growth than New Zealand (Castles et al., 1996). Micro-economic reforms were mediated through corporatist negotiations with the Australian trade unions, whereas the New Zealand reforms had a more 'imposed' quality.

The effects of the 2008 GEC were somewhat muted by a healthy surplus and the continuing

Chinese demand for resources. Nevertheless, the government had to act to contain an emerging deficit. It tried to stimulate the economy through infrastructural funding, but much of this was poorly implemented. Overall, Australia probably escaped from the GEC with less economic damage than most of our other eleven countries.

E. The political system

Australia is a federal state, in which the state level is strong and, indeed, served as a 'laboratory' for some of the public management reforms which were subsequently introduced at the federal (Commonwealth) level (Halligan and Power, 1992).

At the Commonwealth (central) level, Australia has a bicameral legislature, with the upper house being directly elected, with control by non-government parties, and quite well endowed with legislative powers. The Senate has a strong committee system and capacity (often mediated through minority party senators) to block legislation. The electoral system is majoritarian, being based on an alternative vote procedure where voters are asked to indicate their first, second, third (etc.) preferences among candidates, and the preferences of those who voted for the candidate with the lowest number of first preferences are redistributed until one candidate emerges with an absolute majority of first preferences. Governments are usually dominated by a single party, either the Australian Labor Party (ALP), as between 1983 and 1992, or Liberal-National coalitions (as for the whole of the period from 1950 to 1972, and again from 1996–2007). The dominant style of politics is adversarial (Australia is mildly famous for the boisterousness of its political exchanges).

F. New management ideas

Australia was exposed to the same tide of 'Ricardian' or rational choice micro-economic thinking as other Western states, but does not seem to have been as directly and powerfully influenced by this as was New Zealand (Castles et al., 1996)—or, at least, not until the Howard-led National government of the mid 1990s. Australia was also within the global reach of the parallel wave of generic managerialist ideas such as TQM, benchmarking, re-engineering, and so on. In this case, the concept of a distinctive *public* service seems to have been strong enough to dilute the impact of such generic concepts and their associated techniques

somewhat more than in either New Zealand or the UK. Nevertheless, both rational choice and generic managerialism certainly exerted an influence, during the 1980s—as in the UK and the USA right-wing think tanks began to play prominent roles in debates about government and public affairs (Zifcak, 1994, p. 19). However, their ultimate impacts on the central government machine were less than sweeping (Halligan and Power, 1992, chapter 5). By the late 1990s, however, the Howard government was strongly advocating a familiar mix of downsizing and outsourcing in order to concentrate on 'core activities', more flexible and decentralized labour relations within the public service, stronger and more entrepreneurial public service leadership, and continuous benchmarking for performance improvement. 'Public–private partnerships' became a leading idea, and outsourcing was accompanied by a restructuring of the Australian framework of regulatory institutions (Steane, 2008). The Labor government which came to power in 2007 continued to favour partnership, but gave greater emphasis to a) technologically facilitated integration of services, across the federal government but also with other levels of government and b) a strengthened central capability for leading and managing the Australian Public Service (APS) 'ensuring greater consistency for a united APS' (Advisory Group on Reform of Australian Government Administration, 2010, p. x).

G. Pressure from citizens

As with most other countries, there is no evidence of popular opinion demanding some specific and particular programme of management reform. Like elsewhere, however, some effect was probably felt from the public's unwillingness to continue putting up with poor service or bureaucratic obstructions. The Howard government (1996–2007) sometimes played on negative images of the public service to support its neo-conservative policies. A report of 2009 claimed that a better educated and informed citizenry was a major source of pressure for high quality and individually responsive public services (Advisory Group on Reform of Australian Government Administration, 2009, pp. 6–7).

H. Party political ideas

By the time Labor came to power in 1983 there was a growing consensus that the public service elite had become too much of a 'law unto themselves', and there was an appetite for a reassertion of political direction. This generalized sense that the public service required reform was clearly illustrated in the incoming government's White Paper on the public service (Commonwealth, 1983) and the 1984 Public Service Reform Act.

When, after a narrow victory in 1993, Labor's run of office finally came to an end in 1996, their National Party successors brought with them an at least equal suspicion of self-interested behaviour by the public service, combined with a stronger enthusiasm for privatization and the institution of market-type mechanisms within the public sector. As a departmental secretary in the Howard administration put it in 1997: 'It is important that the APS [Australian Public Service] takes what practices and experiences it usefully can from the private sector. We have often lagged behind private sector efficiencies, largely because we have lacked the edge of competition and the reality of meaningful performance targets' (Hawke, 1997, pp. 40–1). The 2007 victory of the Labor party brought back a less anti-civil service attitude, but also continued the later Howard period's tendency to want to increase ministerial (central) control of policy implementation.

I. Chance events

None of great significance for public management reform. However, the 'children overboard' incident during the 2001 general election became very controversial, and led to a number of subsequent inquiries and commentaries, most of which suggested that decision-making and record-keeping practices at high levels had become both highly informal and rather slack (e.g. Weller, 2002, p. 89).

J. Elite decision-making

From 1983 onwards there was a consistent desire by the Labor governments (1983–96) and their National successors to assert full political control over the Australian public service (Halligan, 2001). During the 1980s 'Managerialism offered both a new approach for directing the public service and a rationalization for exerting greater political control' (Halligan, 1996b, p. 77). On the other hand, while the Labor politicians knew the direction in which they wanted to travel, they were not devotees of one particular model of reform: 'Australia has followed a more pragmatic mixture of principles and practice

in contrast to the theory-driven reform in New Zealand' (Halligan, 1996b, p. 79). The long period in office after 1983 meant that Labor politicians were able to build up confidence and knowledge in their reform efforts. Thus, for example, important new reforms were launched in 1987, after ministers had had some opportunity to observe what worked and what didn't in Canberra.

The Howard government, from 1996, was perhaps more 'pure' in its doctrines, and vigorously espoused the neo-conservative ideas of downsizing, contracting out, and privatizing. However, it claimed to stick to the principle of an apolitical public service, albeit one with much less of a monopoly of policy advice than formerly (Halligan, 2001). Despite this, controversies arose about senior appointments and the removal of a number of senior officials from their positions. From 2008 the Rudd government said that it would avoid this kind of behaviour, and would seek to embrace evidence-based policymaking (Rudd, 2008).

K. The administrative system

At the beginning of our period (1980) the Australian Public Service remained in the classic 'Westminster' mode—separate political and mandarin careers, a strictly party-politically neutral, permanent career service, a near monopoly of policy advice to ministers, and strongly hierarchical, high levels of unionization. This 'Westminster model' was extensively changed during the two following decades. Tenure was now less secure; the presence of partisan advisers within the system was much more extensive; levels of unionization—and the role of the unions—was reduced; user-charging, quasi or actual contracts, and outsourcing extensively replaced administrative hierarchies. The size of the APS declined through most of the last twenty years, falling especially steeply between 1994 and 1999 (from more than 160,000 to fewer than 120,000—Advisory Group on Reform of Australian Government Administration, 2009, p. 2). It grew after 2005, fairly much regaining its absolute 1994 level by 2008. However, because the Australian labour force as a whole had grown during this period the 2008 APS represented only 1.5 per cent of the total workforce, as compared with 1.8 per cent in 1994.

Furthermore, the Howard government pushed through a good deal of privatization and contracting out of services. Public–private partnerships were favoured for what had been mainly purely public tasks. For the civil service this meant a greater emphasis on skills connected with contracting, quality monitoring, and general regulation—that is, arm's-length rather than hands-on activities.

L. Contents of the reform package

In 1983 the first priority of the new Labor government was 'to re-establish ministerial control and greater responsiveness to government policies and priorities' (Halligan, 1997, p. 31). This meant reform of the Australian public service so as to shift the balance of power between bureaucrats and politicians more in favour of the latter. Actions included a number of components which were designed to reduce the permanency of public servants, diversify sources of policy advice to ministers, and increase both managerial competence and the responsiveness of public servants to the government's political priorities. A central vehicle for this was the creation of a Senior Executive Service (SES) as part of the 1984 Public Service Reform Act. The effects of this were not particularly radical to begin with, but when combined with the 1987 restructuring (see below) led to much more mobility and diversity in the upper reaches of the service.

The key developments during the long Labor term of office from 1983 to 1996 included the following:

- 1983: Launch of the Financial Management Improvement Program (FMIP), including strong elements of corporate management and programme budgeting, plus mandatory evaluation to 'close the loop' for a new system of results-oriented management (see Zifcak, 1994).
- 1984: Public Service Reform Act—creation of a Senior Executive Service. One aim was to make recruitment to senior public service appointments more open and competitive.
- 1987: Major restructuring of central departments. Twenty-eight portfolio ministries were merged to produce sixteen large departments. In particular, 'mega' departments emerged with responsibility for Foreign Affairs and Trade, Education, Employment and Training, and Transport and Communications. These changes forced a considerable reshuffling of senior posts. A Department of Administrative Services (DAS) was formed, which subsequently became associated with a strong drive to increase competition. Greater emphasis was also placed on

creating a tighter regime for the Government Business Enterprises (GBEs)—the growing number of public sector units and activities which had been 'corporatized'. (Subsequently many of these were privatized—see below.)
- Late 1980s: Beginnings of a sequence of significant sales of public sector assets, for example, Defence Service Homes Corporation (1988–90), Qantas airline (1992–5), and Commonwealth Bank (1994) (for more detail, see Halligan, 1996b, p. 34).
- 1993: Publication of the Hilmer Report, *National Competition Policy*, recommendations from which were subsequently embodied in an intergovernmental agreement to seek competitive neutrality (a 'level playing field') as between public and private sectors.

The Howard administration from 1996 continued and intensified the processes of privatization and contracting out. Other key developments included the 1999 Public Service Act, which significantly 'deprivileged' the senior public service, although it did include a statutory list of APS 'values'. It also included a full devolution of personnel management powers to agency heads, leading some commentators to argue that the unity of the APS was under threat. Certainly the Australian Public Service Commissioner did not seem to be left with many executive powers (Australian Public Service Commission, 2004) The Howard government also carried through further contracting out, and there was a shift to accruals accounting, and an intensification of the existing performance measurement regime. Changes initiated in 1999/2000 introduced a system of accruals-based output and outcome measurement. It was part of a 'long term, iterative process' (Hawke, 2007, p. 13). Whilst many observers believe that this has involved considerable sharpening of the performance focus, and also improved transparency, there have also been recurring disappointments concerning the quality of performance information and the limited use that is made of it for budgetary decision-making (Hawke, 2007, p. 14). There was also a major drive to restrain government regulation—a 'meta-regulatory regime'—carried out under the Competition Principles Agreement (see Morgan, 1999).

In 2004 the Management Advisory Committee published *Connecting Government: Whole of Government Responses to Australia's Priority Challenges*. This signalled a recognition that agencification, strict performance targets by agency, contracting out, and other aspects of recent policy were producing unwanted effects of fragmentation and loss of coordination. Reintegration through whole-of-government approaches was called for (see also Bouckaert and Halligan, 2008, appendix V).

A further important document was the 2007 Australian Public Service Commission *Building Better Governance*. It declared the principles of good governance to be:

1. Accountability
2. Transparency/openness
3. Integrity
4. Stewardship
5. Efficiency
6. Leadership

The Rudd administration (from 2007) declared that it had no in-built preference for public or private sector provision, but would base decisions 'on the available evidence on how to deliver services efficiently and effectively' (Rudd, 2008, p. 5). It said it would reinvigorate the tradition of an independent public service, build the capacity for strategic policymaking, strengthen integrity and accountability, increase participation, and develop evidence-based decision-making.

One of the first major structural changes was the December 2009 announcement that Human Services agencies (including Centrelink and Medicare) would be increasingly co-located and the Chief Executive Officers of these agencies would be drawn back into the Ministry. The aim was better coordination across services and closer integration of policymaking and implementation (Bowden, 2009). A later report (*Ahead of the Game*, Advisory Group on Reform of Australian Government Administration, 2010) reinforced this commitment to 'joined-up' government, both across the federal government and vertically, with states and local authorities. It also emphasized the need for a more integrated and strategic approach to the management of the APS, recommending the creation of a new Australian Public Service Commission, with enhanced powers. It was accepted by the new Prime Minister, Rudd. The main recommendations of the report were:

1. More integrated, citizen-centred services
2. More open government
3. Enhanced policy capability
4. Reinvigorated strategic leadership
5. A new Australian Public Service Commission

6. Align employment conditions across the APS, and strengthen workforce planning
7. Regular reviews of agency effectiveness and efficiency

M. The implementation process

Compared with countries such as the Netherlands or even the United States, the implementation of public management reforms in Australia looks to have been a fairly centralized process. Prime Ministers and the former Department of Administrative Services (later Finance and Administration, and then Finance and Deregulation) have generally been able to get their way—although all such observations need to be taken in a context where the focus is principally on the Commonwealth government and not on the (independent) State level. Sometimes the style of implementation has been gradual and incremental (as with much of Finacial Management Improvement Programe (FMIP), sometimes rapid and sweeping (as with the 1987 restructuring of departments). During the Howard/National government of 1996–2007 the implementation process sometimes appeared sudden and harsh. This, in turn, generated unusually virulent opposition.

N. Reforms actually achieved

As indicated above, Australian governments not only carried through a series of significant public management reforms, they also committed themselves to a more extensive application of evaluation than did most of the other countries covered in this book. Thus, for example, the FMIP was subject to a series of evaluations, both internal and independent (Halligan, 1996*b*; Zifcak, 1994, pp. 96–9), and in 1992 the whole sweep of reforms was reviewed in an expensive and large-scale study (Task Force on Management Improvement, 1992).

The picture revealed by these and other studies is a mixed one. Real change has undoubtedly been achieved: the 'culture' of the public service has shifted; substantial state assets have been privatized; certain techniques such as user-charging, outsourcing, and benchmarking have been widely applied; and cost-consciousness and financial management skills have been considerably sharpened. The total size of the public service fell from 180,893 in 1986 (the peak year) to 143,305 in 1996, (Halligan, 1997, p. 39). By 2001 the number was down to 118,644 after which it began to rise again, reaching 155,482 by 2008 (Halligan, 2008, p. 14).

On the other hand, implementation has often been significantly slower than had been envisaged, and the costs of change have been high. For example, central finance divisions within departments were often reluctant to permit the degree of internal delegation of financial authority implied by the spirit of the FMIP, or 'corporate planning floundered as a technique designed to enhance political and departmental strategy' (Zifcak, 1994, p. 110). The big 1992 evaluation by the Task Force on Management Improvement found that enthusiasm for many aspects of the reforms was much more pronounced at senior levels in the hierarchy than lower down, where considerable scepticism appears to have existed. By the late 1990s the downsizings and perceived anti-public service attitudes of the Howard government seemed to be generating disruption and severe morale problems. However, by 2001 this drive was somewhat moderated, partly because it was realized that imposition from the top could be counter-productive (e.g. problems with ICT outsourcing).

The 2007 reforms (following Prime Minister Rudd's acceptance of the *Ahead of the Game* report (Advisory Group on Reform of Australian Government Administration, 2010) were vigorously promoted by both the Secretary to the Prime Minister and Cabinet Department, Moran, and the Public Service Commissioner, Sedgewick. Both toured the country explaining and recommending the reform to public-service and general audiences.

Key Events—Australia

Period	General	Organization	Personnel	Finance
1980–5	1981–3 Fraser (Liberal) as Prime Minister 1983–91 Hawke (Labor) as Prime Minister	The Hawke administration carried through many management reforms 1983 Report: *Reforming the Australian Public Service*	1985 Creation of Merit Protection and Review Agency (MPRA)	1984 Financial Management Improvement Programme (FMIP—see Zifcak, 1994)
1986–90		1987 Major departmental re-structuring—28 departments reduced to 18. Also, creation of Efficiency Scrutiny Unit	1987 Replacement of Public Service Board by Public Service Commission. 1989 Introduction of Senior Executive Service, together with performance appraisal for its members	1988 Programme Management and Budgeting
1991–5	1991–6 Keating (Labor) as Prime Minister	1995 Privatization of national airline (Qantas) and Aerospace Technologies. 1995 Further reshuffling of government departments	1992 New framework for Human Resources Management, and a strategic plan for equal employment opportunities 1995 Amended Public Service Act—allows for tenure or fixed term appointments	1992 Announcement of intention to introduce accruals accounting 1994 Audit Act strengthens public sector auditing
1996–2000	1996–2007 Howard (Liberal) as Prime Minister	1999 Reform of competitive and contracting out rules—the government wants to facilitate more of these activities. 1999–2002 Launch of several measures to promote e-government	1999 Public Service Act	1996–2000 Further steps towards the introduction of accruals accounting
2001–5		2002 Senate report on the 'children overboard' incident: highly critical of the Howard government's decision-making and record-keeping 2003 Uhrig report: criticized lack of consistency in the design of governance systems for agencies 2004 Creation of Department of Human Services 2004 Management Advisory Committee publishes *Connecting Government: A Whole of Government Response to Australia's Priority Challenges*		
2006–10	2007 General election: Rudd (Labor) replaces Howard (Liberal). 2010 Rudd stands down as leader of the Labor Party. Gillard takes over. General Election follows: Labor forms a minority government under Gillard	2007 Australian Public Service Commission publishes *Building Better Governance.* 2009 *Ahead of the Game:* blueprint for the future of the Australian government administration (Advisory Group on Reform, 2009). Accepted by the Prime Minister. 2009 New programme *Works for You* (Bowen, 2009) Includes further integration of service delivery between Centrelink, Medicare, etc. 2009 Australian Public Service Commission publishes *Challenges of Evidence-Based Policymaking*	2008 New Prime Minister sets out his aims for the Australian Public Service (Rudd, 2008)	

BELGIUM

A. Socio-economic forces: general

Belgium is a rather small country (32.500 km^2), with a relatively modest population (10.8 million in 2010). For specific key economic and socio-demographic data we refer to section A2 and A3 in Appendix A, including Tables A.1 to A.5.

B. Global economic forces

Belgium is a particularly open economy with imports and exports representing the highest percentage of GDP of the countries studied in this book (85%) (see Table A.3). Facing the convergence criteria for accessing the EMU in 1992, Belgium was confronted with the problem of its consolidated gross public debt which rose to 135.4 per cent of GDP in 1995. Due to the restriction policy pursued by the government, public debt could be reduced to 93.5 per cent of GDP in 2008, but mounted again to 100 per cent in 2010.

C. Sociodemographic change

Belgium is situated at the junction between the Latin and Germanic languages (Dutch, French, and German) and cultures. For many years these different cultures have been trying to find a fragile balance, leading to the creation of a federal state in 1993, after significant steps at the end of the 1980s and the beginning of the 1990s (a process that is still continuing and is explained more broadly in section E below).

Since the late 1970s and the early 1980s the classical welfare state, together with the social security system, have been subject to great pressure from the economic climate (increasing unemployment) and the ageing society. The social welfare system is advanced, though not as elaborate as that in Sweden.

D. National socio-economic policies

Faced with the problems of public debt and the increasing public sector expenditures, central government launched a strong programme of budgetary reform and restraint under the Dehaene government (1992). Thanks to this policy, Belgium was able to fulfil the Maastricht 'convergence criteria' for the EU monetary union (though only partially). The focus was one of downsizing the public sector and coping with the economic crisis by working more efficiently and effectively. The governments of the late 1990s enjoyed an easier position on public spending than their predecessors. The financial and economic crisis, the need to support and even save several banks, and the demographic evolutions are currently pushing the political elite to take measures, which are, however, being postponed because of the political impasse at the federal level.

E. The political system

Belgium is a federal state. In recent years, the country has evolved rapidly, via five stages of constitutional reforms (in 1970 ('cultural communities' and three regions), 1980 ('communities'), 1988–9 (Brussels Capital Region, and further strengthening of regions and communities), 1993 (constitutional recognition of a federal state), and 2001 (Lambermont Agreements including fiscal power and further devolution). The decision-making power in Belgium is no longer exclusively in the hands of the federal government and the federal parliament, but falls to communities on the one hand and regions on the other, which exercise their competences independently in different fields.

The redistribution followed two broad lines. The first concerns linguistics and, more broadly, everything relating to culture. It gave rise to the communities. Belgium has three communities, based on language: the Flemish, the French, and the German. The second main line of the state reform is historically inspired by economic concerns, expressed by regions who wanted to have more autonomous power. This gave rise to the founding of three regions: the Flemish, the Brussels Capital, and the Walloon. To some extent Belgian regions are similar to the American States or the German '*Länder*', except that legislation decreed by regions and communities are at the same level as federal legislation.

All these communities and regions have separate governments and parliaments. The federal state retains important areas of competence including foreign affairs, defence, justice, finances, social security, important sectors of public health and domestic affairs, etc. The country is further divided into 10 provinces and 589 communes. On the federal level, as well as on the community and the regional level, there is a multiparty political system and governments are composed by coalitions. The cabinets act collegially, with the prime ministers taking the role of *primus inter pares*.

Between the parliaments there are some differences. On the federal level, the legislature is bicameral (tending to an unicameral system in the future), with on the one hand, the House of Representatives and on the other hand, the Senate, which are elected every four years. On the community and regional level legislatures are unicameral and elected every five years.

For a long time the government was composed of Christian Democrats and Liberals or the Socialist Party. In the 1999 federal election the composition changed and the Christian Democrats lost their place in government. The Liberals made up a coalition together with the Socialist Party and the Green Party (the 'purple-green coalition' of Verhofstadt). The 2010 elections demonstrated two separated democracies with the Flemish Nationalist (NVA) as the largest party in Flanders, and the Francophone Socialists (PS) as the major party in Wallonia (the Liberal MR being the biggest in Brussels).

The Belgian system is slowly moving from a consensual to a polarized political system, with two increasingly divergent economies, political systems, and administrations, and with Brussels as a third, *sui generic,* politico-administrative system. After the elections of 2010 a caretaker government was responsible for the federal level, and a series of negotiators and mediators were in charge of the negotiations concerning the sixth stage of the constitutional reform. This resulted in a political impasse which at the time of writing risks a complete paralysis of central government. At the central level, since 2008, economic and political crises pushed state reform to the front of the agenda. One symptom of the impasse was the significant turnover in political leadership (Leterme I (March 2008 – December 2008), Van Rompuy (December 2008 – November 2009), Leterme II (November 2009 – April 2010—caretaker government during the European presidency).

Figure B.1 shows the implications of the five stages of the reform ('available today'), and the possible 'programme' for the sixth stage of reform.

F. New management ideas

The position on the junction of two main cultures (see section C above) has also an impact on the introduction of new management ideas. Since the process of federalization, especially at the end of

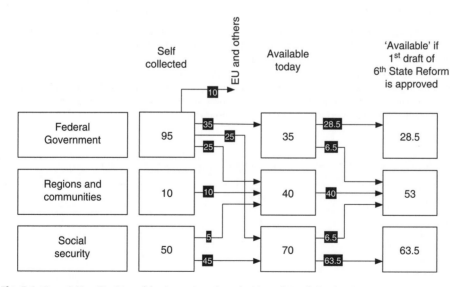

Fig. B.1 Financial Implications of further state reform for the Belgian federal system
Source: De Standaard, 18 August 2010, p. 6.
Note: All figures are billions of euros.

the 1980s and at the beginning of the 1990s, different rhetorics on public management have been displayed. The Ministry for the Flemish Community and Region was influenced by the NPM principles from the Anglo-Saxon world and organized and modernized itself according to these ideas (Bouckaert and Auwers, 1999). The Ministries of the French Community and the Walloon Region, as in France, were more reluctant, and applied their own strategy. They launched modernization plans. Although the aim of making public service more efficient, effective, and responsive was similar, the trajectory in the separate parts in Belgium was different in approach, scope, and speed (Vancoppenolle and Legrain, 2002).

The evolution on the national level (1999–2003) followed the same trajectory as the modernization of the Flemish Ministry. A lot of ideas used earlier in the Flemish Ministry were projected on the national level in the Copernicus programme, led by Minister Van den Bossche. After his term, there was a high turnover of responsible ministers and there was a political fragmentation of political portfolios, resulting in a loss of consolidation and new initiatives.

Cultural differences are significant in the Belgian context since its administration is multicultural. These differences affect a shared public sector reform programme.

G. Pressure from citizens

It is indeed hard to find out if there was any pressure from citizens, what this pressure was and whether pressure from citizens instigated governments to launch reform initiatives. In the beginning of the 1990s, with the elections of 1991, trust in the national government was a very low 31 per cent (*la Libre Belgique*, December 1991). The

government launched initiatives to reduce the gap with its citizens.

In 2000, with the proclamation of the Copernicusinitiative, there was a large-scale survey. On the one hand, this questionnaire was meant to be an information and communication strategy, but on the other hand, the low response to the survey was seen as a failure of the initiative (Bouckaert et al., 2001). The June 2010 elections demonstrated clear political victories for the Flemish Nationalists (NVA) on the Flemish side, and for the Francophone Socialists (PS) on the Walloon side of the country. The Flemish population gave a clear signal that it supported a significant state reform to improve the functioning of its public services and policies.

H. Party political ideas

As in the Netherlands, single parties are likely to be less significant and powerful than in countries with one-party-government and majoritarian systems such as New Zealand or (until 2010) the UK. Belgium has a proportional system, compulsory voting, and coalition governments. At the central level, increasingly, the diverging dynamics are along the line of the two major communities, and not according to cross border party political ideas.

In the 1980s and the early 1990s party political ideas (the Christian Democrats and the Socialist Party or the Christian Democrats and the Liberal Party) were focused on the reduction of the public debt and rebalancing the budget deficit, aiming to cope with the Maastricht convergence criteria. Because of this the public sector was subject to a downsizing operation. The question in Belgium was not one of the role of the state, and the privatization debate was never as prominent as in the Netherlands.

Table B.1 Cultural differences between the two linguistic communities in Belgium

	Flanders	Wallonia	Belgium
Power distance	61	67	65
Uncertainty avoidance	97	93	94
Individualism/collectivism	78	72	75
Masculinity/femininity	43	60	54
Long/short term	–	–	38

Source: Hofstede, 2001, p. 501.

After the elections of 1991 (and also in 1995) and the rise of the extreme right party, government policy was focused on the relation with the citizens, and the amount of (dis)trust in politics and the public sector. Therefore policies aimed at closing these gaps and making the public sector more responsive to the needs of citizens/users (e.g. Charter of the User of Public Services, 1992).

From 1999 till 2003 the purple-green government launched a broad scope and big objectives reform initiative for the federal public service (the Copernicus initiative). This programme was initiated by the federal (Flemish socialist) minister of public services, Van den Bossche, based on his experiences in the 1990s in the Flemish administration. The new (Francophone socialist) minister Arena (2003–4) announced after one month in office that the Copernicus project had ended (Hondeghem and Depré, 2005: 425–6). As a consequence, reforms lost their coherent framework and hence their momentum. Low profile, and incremental initiatives took over. In the period 2004–7 Minister Dupont (Francophone socialist) shared responsibilities with a state secretary for administrative reforms and a state secretary for IT. The subsequent turnover (Vervotte, 2007–8; Vanackere, 2008–9; Vervotte, 2009–), combined with the economic problems and the political mounting impasse, with its significant periods of caretaker governments, resulted in a limited and internal set of measures such as refinement of training, IT, tendering, internal mandates and contracts, and career pattern development. Even the much needed reforms in the judicial branch (which has been under pressure for at least a decade) were not realized to any significant degree (Hondeghem et al., 2010).

I. Elite perceptions of what management reforms were desirable and feasible

Most elite attention was focused on the federal process and on budgetary problems during the 1980s and the 1990s (Section D above). Management reforms therefore emphasized the economy—and input side of the public service.

Next to the budgetary focus, the gap between the government and the citizen was seen as a reason for the launch of initiatives to make the public service more accountable and responsive, following the elections of 1991.

In the late 1990s, when the budgetary restraints were fewer, government found an opportunity to

launch a major reform initiative (see Section L below). The Copernicus reform programme (1999–2003) remained, with a small elite around the responsible minister. Its ownership could not be broadened to the civil servants or the trade unions, partly because it was very consultant driven. Between 2004 and 2008 there was an absence of elite decisions in the field of public sector reform, and since 2008 the political elite has been absorbed by the debates about a sixth stage of state reform, to the detriment of solving the economic and financial crisis.

J. Chance events

In the 1991 national elections, the rise of an extreme right party was marked. Politicians and social scientists saw this as a sign of the low legitimacy of the political culture and the widening of the gap between citizens and politicians (Maesschalck et al., 2002).

In 1996 Belgium was startled by a paedophilia scandal (the Dutroux affair). The judicial system and the police forces were intensely criticized (Pollitt and Bouckaert, 2009). The authorities were shaken by 'The White March'—250,000 to 300,000 demonstrators in Brussels. Again this was a decline in trust in the institutions and politics in general.

In 1999 the dioxin food crisis had an impact on the elections and pushed the reform agenda and the creation of the Federal Food Agency. The 2009 Fortisgate, in which top magistrates were said to have violated confidential information on the Fortis bank, and the way the 2010 operations concerning the paedophilia cases in the Catholic church were conducted still did not produce significant reforms in the judicial branch.

It is debatable whether the effects of the 2008 GEC can be termed 'chance events', but certainly, for Belgium, a banking crisis, requiring strong government actions, was part of this period.

K. The administrative system

The original administrative structure of the Belgian state as established by the 1831 Constitution was quite simple. It was made up of three government levels: the central level and two subnational levels, provinces, and municipalities. This structure remained intact until 1970. Four revisions of the constitution made Belgium a federal state from 1993 (see Section E above). The federal civil

Table B.2 The development of public sector employment in Belgium

	1953	1964	1970	1980	1989	1995	2001
Ministries(*)					77,232	62,535	65,598
– national					(10%)	(7%)	(7%)
– regional	83,797	99,198	108,074	88,062	7,848	26,804	28,313
	(21%)	(19%)	(17%)	(10%)	(1%)	(3%)	(3%)
– total					85,080	89,339	93,911
					(11%)	(10%)	(10%)
Public instit.							
– national					166,098	149,575	127,814
					(21%)	(17%)	(14%)
– regional					13,634	47,888	55,169
					(2%)	(5%)	(6%)
– total	131,341	126,292	115,969	198,402	179,732	197,463	182,983
	(33%)	(24%)	(19%)	(23%)	(22%)	(22%)	(20%)
Particular	85,830	199,806	272,684	392,336	352,965	358,780	357,311
bodies (**)	(21.5%)	(38%)	(44%)	(45%)	(44%)	(40%)	(39%)
	(***)						
Local	97,200	98,010	120,299	184,643	188,556	244,729	285,843
government	(24.5%)	(19%)	(19%)	(21%)	(23%)	(27%)	(31%)
							(****)
Legislature		1,000	969	1,232	1,773	2,282	2,860
		(0.2%)	(0.1%)	(0.1%)	(0.2%)	(0.2%)	(0.3%)
TOTAL	398,168	524,306	617,995	864,675	808,106	892,593	922,908
	(100%)	(100%)	(100%)	(100%)	(100%)	(100%)	(100%)

(*) inclusive personnel of scientific institutions

(**) army, police force, justice, teachers

(***) exclusive teachers of private schools (approximately 80,000)

(****) figures of 2000

Table B.3 Employment in the core administrations at federal, state, and local levels in Belgium, 2007

	2007
Federal government	**83,871**
– federal public services	61,613
– scientific institutions	3,303
– public institutions	18,955
State government (regions and communities)	**68,517**
– Flemish government	39,310
– Walloon region	15,384
– French community	5,035
– German community	233
– Brussels capital region	6,911
– Community commissions in Brussels	1,644
Local government	**340,621**

Source: Hondeghem, 2010.

service has been severely reduced as a result of the different state reforms (see Tables B.2 and B.3, below). In terms of public employment the national level now represents only 17 per cent of the personnel in the public sector. In addition, many functions have been transferred to autonomous public institutions (Brans and Hondeghem, 1999, pp. 122–4).

The Belgian civil service is facing two main challenges. The first is associated with the legitimacy crisis of political institutions as a whole (see Sections I and J above). The second is related to the budgetary pressures and the ascendancy of the new managerial paradigm in the public sector. Civil Service reform has arrived on the agenda, albeit somewhat behind many other nations. There are, however, strong internal constraints on which reforms are likely to be implemented. These constraints are linked to the strong position of the civil service unions and the preoccupation of political actors with maintaining a balance of party-political power within the administrative system (Brans and Hondeghem, 1999, p. 121; Hondeghem and Depré, 2005).

The federal civil service is a modest administration, playing only a marginal role in the policy-making process. With the loss of important functions and powers to the new state levels, the federal level is now a laggard. Even major initiatives such as the Copernicus reforms have not fundamentally changed that pattern (see Section L below). The drivers for change are external: Europe, economic and financial crises, and the reform of the state.

L. Contents of reform package

Since the 1980s several different initiatives have taken place. In the 1980s most of these initiatives occurred against the background of stringent cutbacks of public expenditures and the diminution of the general public debt (see Sections D and G above). In the first half of the 1980s, under the fifth and sixth cabinet of Prime Minister Martens, the modernization of the civil service was inspired by these cutbacks (Bouckaert and François, 1999, p. 12). This modernization of the civil service never led to a rethinking of the role and the scale of the state. In many other OECD countries the privatization debate was more prominent at that time than it was in Belgium.

Between 1981 and 1989 several initiatives were launched to modernize the civil service:

- 1985: Appointment of a state secretary for modernizing the public service, attached to the prime minister
- 1987: Creation of modernization cells in the different ministries
- 1987: Creation of a secretariat of modernization
- 1989 Creation of the College of Secretaries-General (the highest civil servants of the ministries), and the enlargement of the power of this college in 1993

After 1991 the focus of the modernization process shifted. Macro-economic policy was still a priority. Instead of integrating the personnel management in this macro-economic policy, the focus moved to the rewarding and motivation of civil servants. Reforms at the Ministry of the Flemish Community triggered initiatives at the central level:

- 1991: First edition of the General Principles Royal Decree (KBAP) stated the overall principles for civil servants (and replaced the old statute Camu that went back to 1937). The KBAP was finally approved in 1994
- 1993: The creation of the Office for Modernization and Organization (ABC)
- 1995: The creation of a ministry of the civil service

The modernization of the civil service was more than just an attempt to improve efficiency and effectiveness. It was also used to try to close the gap between the citizen and the government (see Sections G and H above). Thus, after 1991, many citizen-related initiatives were started (Bouckaert and François, 1999, p. 30):

- 1991: Law on the motivation on administrative actions
- 1993: Charter of the User of Public Services
- 1994: Law on access to information
- 1995: Appointment of the federal ombudsmen

Most of the initiatives were launched on an ad hoc basis and lacked an overall strategy. Therefore there was little coherence between the different initiatives. However, with the establishment of the Cabinet in 1999 a major reform initiative was launched. The Copernicus reform (1999–2003), initiated and sponsored by the minister of reform, was a modernization plan covering many fields of the federal civil service. The initiative was built on four main trajectories:

- A modern HRM: In each new ministry HR experts were appointed and HR cells were created. The top managers were selected by assessment centres and interviews, and they received mandates for six years. For all civil servants the evaluation system changed and the renumeration—and career-planning systems were to be reformed. Education and training were a priority.
- A restructuring of the ministries: The former ministries were to be restructured and reformed. There were ten vertical, four horizontal ministries, and several programmatorial ministries (working on social themes crossing the entire policy field). The new internal structure of the ministries aimed to equip them to fulfil an important role in policy design, implementation, and evaluation.
- A new budget and control system: The new ministries were to have a large degree of autonomy in developing a policy strategy and in spending the budget. For this reason each ministry was to have its own internal audit, to monitor its economy and efficiency.
- improved communication, including both internal communication among civil servants and, on the other hand, externally with citizens.

Between 2004 and 2008, there was a continuation of process redesign, mandate systems, and internal contracts (with social security agencies). Also, there were some initiatives to install internal audits. After 2008, the degrees of freedom to launch a major public sector reform initiative were restricted by economic and political crises.

M. The implementation process

Past initiatives were not always coherent and often lacked an overall strategy. In 1989 a minister of the civil service was appointed (before that a secretary of state was attached to the prime minister). For a long time reform initiatives were a matter for the prime minister. In 1995 a separate ministry of the civil service was created and many reforms have been launched and sponsored by this ministry.

In the past initiatives were ad hoc and fragmented. Many separate ministries launched their own programmes and took individual initiatives. The modernization pressure came from the lower levels of government (communities and regions), especially the Flemish community.

The reforms started in 1999, under the leadership of Minister Luc Van den Bossche, were often perceived as fundamental and drastic. These reforms were coherent and inspired by an overall strategy, but initiated in a top-down way, which evoked some resistance during its implementation, especially from trade unions. The post-Copernicus period could be described as low profile, internal, and incremental.

N. Reforms actually achieved

In Belgium, policy and programme evaluations are not widespread. It is only since 1998 that the role of the National Court of Audit (*Rekenhof*) has changed and moved to performance auditing as well as traditional financial and compliance audits.

The only broad-scope evaluations of management reforms have been academic rather than internal (Hondeghem and Depré, 2005; Hondeghem et al., 2010; Bouckaer et al., 2010, see Chapter 10). Management reforms were introduced on an ad hoc basis and many individual initiatives have taken place in the separate ministries. Overall initiatives launched in the early and mid 1990s are still effective tools (access to information law, motivation law). Other initiatives have slowly faded out (e.g. the users' charter).

The most important goal for the Copernicus reform was to install a different culture within the civil service. Between 1999 and 2003 many initiatives took place such as the restructuring of the ministries, the appointment of the new top managers and leading officials, implementation of Business Process Re-engineering, and development of an HRM policy. The basic structure of the public sector still remains, as well as the major principles of its functioning (mandates, internal contracts, some audit functions). However, after 2004 no further major steps forward could be taken.

Key Events—Belgium

Period	General	Organization	Personnel	Finance
1980–5	1981 Martens PM (Christian Democrat) 1980–2: 2nd State Reform 1985 Martens PM	1980 Territorial: Transfer of national services and ministries to Regions and Communities	1982 Transfer of Direction of General Affairs and General Direction for Selection and Formation to Ministry of Interiors	1985 Programme Budgeting
1986–90	1987, 1988 Martens PM 1988 3rd State Reform 1989 Minister of Civil Service 1990 Crossroad Bank for Social Security	1985–8 State Secretary for modernization and information 1986 Report on the modernization of the civil service and creation of a secretariat 1988 Creation of the Brussels Region 1989 College of Secretaries-General 1989 Privatization initiatives (Brussels Airport Terminal Cy)	1987 School for Finance and Tax Law 1990 Policy for equality for men and women 1990 Corps of Civil Service Advisers	1989 Finance Law (as part of the 3rd State Reform) 1990–5 Zero Based Budgeting
1991–5	1991 Martens PM 1991 Law on the motivation of Administrative Action 1992 Dehaene PM (Christian Democrat) 1992–3 4th State Reform: Belgium is a federal country 1993 Charter of the Customer of the Public Service 1994 Law on the access of information 1995 Dehaene PM	1990–4 Merger of ministries (Public Works, Post and Communication) into Communication and Infrastructure, Agriculture and Small Commerces). 1991 Law on the reform of state companies 1991 Law on the reform of Public Credit Institutions: creation of two semi-public holdings 1991–3 Radioscopy: audit of federal ministries 1991 Establishment of State Companies 1992 1st wave of asset sales of State Companies and Credit Holdings 1994 2nd wave of Credit Institutions. 1994–5 State Companies become Public Ltd (Belgacom, Railways) 1995 Federal Participation Company as intermediate step to privatization of Credit institutions 1995 Federal Ombudsmen	1991 Reform of the Office for Selection and Recruitment 1993 Outplacement Service. Tobback Plan 1994 Royal Decree on the General Principles of the Civil Service 1995 Ministry of Civil Service 1995 Office for Organization and Management (ABC)	1991 Law on State Accountability 1992 Savings to get closer to the Maastricht convergence criteria
1996–2000	1999 Verhofstadt PM (Cons/Soc/Green) 1999 Minister for Administrative Reform	1996 Ministry for Social Affairs, Public Health, and Environment 1998 Agency of Simplification	1996 Reform of the Institute for Education and Training 1997 Flahaut Plan 1998 Evaluation System	1998 Court of Audit has competence for economy, efficiency, and effectiveness

continued

Continued

Period	General	Organization	Personnel	Finance
	2000 Copernicus reform plan of Minister Van den Bossche	1999 Action Plan for administrative simplification; government commissioner 1997 Royal Decree on social security agencies. 2000 Federal Agency for Food Protection	2000 Royal Decree on the General Principles of the Civil Service. 2000 Reform of Selor (recruitment) 2000 Mandate system for top civil servants	1998 Commission on the normalization of accounting 1998 Changing role of the Finance Inspectorate 1998 Public Debt Office 2000 New budget and control cycle 2000 Internal audit services (not implemented)
2001–5	2003 Verhofstadt PM 2003 5th reform of the state: Reform of electoral system: creation of provincial constituencies	2001–2 FEDICT: Ministry of ICT 2001–3 Reduction and abolition of ministerial cabinets (not implemented) 2001 Ministries: management boards and direction boards 2002 Operational autonomy and new personnel status for 10 social security agencies 2001–3 BPR 2002 Bankruptcy of SABENA (national airline)	2001 Ministry of Personnel and Organization 2000–3 Assessment of top managers 2002 Copernicus reforms in social security agencies 2004 Transfer of personnel to regions (5th State Reform)	2001 Royal Decree on the budget, accounting and audit of social security agencies 2002 Royal Decree on internal audit
2006–10	2007 Verhofstadt 2008 Leterme 1 (March–November) 2008 Leterme 2 (November–December) 2008 Van Rompuy 2009 Leterme (November–) 2010 elections in June with Leterme as caretaker government			2006 Redefined role for the Financial Inspectorate 2007 Royal Decrees on internal control, internal audit, and the Audit Committee 2009 Government Commissioner for Internal Audit (till 2010)

CANADA

A. Socio-economic forces: general

Canada is a very large country, but relatively thinly populated (33.6 million population in 2010). Like the USA, it is an ethnically diverse community, having been built up from successive waves of immigration from Europe and elsewhere.

B. Global economic forces

Again, see Appendix A. In 2008 Canada ranked 6th out of our twelve states in terms of the percentage of GDP represented by international trade.

C. Socio-demographic issues

For the general picture, see Appendix A. Canada has become a multi-ethnic and multicultural society—partly through immigration. By 2009 the number of Canadians whose first language was neither French nor English reached more than 6 million (out of a population of 33.5 million). More than 1 million had Chinese as their mother-tongue, and 455,00 had Italian; 626,000 defined themselves as belonging to one of the three recognized aboriginal groups (in addition to the official languages of English and French there are half a dozen 'recognized languages' spoken by the aboriginal groups). Canada, like other advanced industrial economies, is also getting older. Between 1961 and 1991 the number of citizens aged 65 and over increased 128 per cent, to 3.2 million (see Table A.6). Canada also has a relatively high divorce rate (2.8 per 1,000 population in 1992) and 60 per cent of female-headed single-parent families fell below the official low income cut-off (Statistics Canada, 1995).

D. National socio-economic policies

Relative to OECD averages, Canada suffered a disappointing economic performance during the 1980s. Control of public spending was a particular weakness. During the Mulroney administration (1984–93) public spending targets were repeatedly set and then missed. Between 1984 and 1993 the net public debt increased from $C168 billion to $C508 billion (Harder and Lindquist, 1997, pp. 80–1). However, the Chrétien administration (1993–2003) largely met its expenditure reduction targets, and in 1997/8 achieved the first balanced budget for thirty years. Growth in the first eight years of the twenty-first century was respectable.

E. The political system

Canada, like Australia, is a federal state with a 'Westminster' system (i.e. a first past the post electoral system, disciplined parties, and (usually) strong, majoritarian governments). However, a simple picture of single-minded centralism would be inaccurate:

In a country consisting of two 'founding' linguistic groups, four or five distinct regions, and the usual cleavages between classes and other divisions characteristic of all modern societies, a governing party must try to accommodate a representation of as many interests as possible. Aboriginals, historically marginalised in the political process, are also becoming contenders in the system. (Mallory, 1997, p. 16)

During the nineteenth and early twentieth century, central government appeared to dominate most of the significant governmental functions, but the growth of the welfare state shifted the balance in favour of provincial and local governments. Agreements between federal and provincial governments became more and more essential for policy progress on many items.

Although in many ways a more 'state-centred' and even 'state-trusting' society than its US neighbour, there is also a widespread popular suspicion of the Ottawa political elite. The underpinnings of federal authority have been eroded from several directions:

the whole system of government in Canada is beset by a number of forces which tend to undermine it. These include a pervasive anti-elitism and populism which undermines the authority of government and thus its will to deal with issues, a pervasive and exaggerated fear of mounting public debt and public bankruptcy, and a threat to the survival of the system by the danger of Quebec separation accompanied by serious regional discontent which could of itself lead to the dissolution of the union. All these threats to survival have occurred in the past, and have been successfully surmounted. This time they seem to have all come together. But one should not underestimate the enormous inertia of the system, as well as its flexibility, which may well ensure its survival and its capacity to adjust. (Mallory, 1997, p. 23)

In the twenty-first century, popular opinion has been further depressed by the 'sponsorship scandal' and other events (see Key Events at end of this country case). While it would probably be an exaggeration to say that the Canadian system was facing a crisis of trust, it was a moment for reflection and for attempts to rebuild lost confidence (for a subtle Canadian analysis of the difficult concept of trust, see Thomas, 2009; for an analysis of the 'critical moment', see Lindquist, 2006).

F. New management ideas

It is clear that Canadian ministers and senior officials were well aware of the currents of new management thinking which were flowing through the Anglophone world from the late 1970s onwards. Mulroney's administration (1984–93) made extensive use of business people and also 'borrowed'—at least in part—a number of public management reform ideas from the USA and the UK. Mulroney's own rhetoric mirrored the anti-bureaucratic, pro-private sector tone of Thatcher and Reagan (Savoie, 1994).

Just two examples will have to suffice. First, the Nielsen task force set up in 1984 took about half its members from the business community, and Nielsen himself was conscious of borrowing from Raynerism (UK) and the Grace Commission (USA) (Savoie, 1994, pp. 127–30). Second, the creation of politically sympathetic chiefs of staff in each department drew something from the US 'spoils system', and more specifically from President Reagan's expansion of that system during the early 1980s. The basic idea was to give ministers greater assistance in the task of getting the permanent bureaucracy to do their bidding.

Under the Liberal administration from 1993 the public service regained some of its self-confidence, and by 1998 the clerk to the Privy Council (the most senior civil servant) felt able to proclaim a 'Canadian model' of public management reform. This included a rejection of the proposal that minimizing government was always a good thing and an embracing of experiment and diversity in organizational forms (Bourgon, 1998; Gow, 2004).

As the 1990s unfolded—and even more after the turn of the century—issues of coordinated service delivery came more and more to the fore. Canada established something of an international reputation as a leader in forms of 'integrated public governance' (see Kernaghan, 2009a, b). Another growing concern was with Human Resource Management, and the need to address the loss of organizational memory and talent that could ensue as a very large percentage of senior civil servants (the 'baby boomers') retired within a short space of time. After the sponsorship scandal broke in 2004, specifically public sector notions of accountability and transparency featured heavily in political discussion (and informed the 2006 Federal Accountability Act).

G. Pressure from citizens

As elsewhere, citizens in Canada did not rush forward with specific proposals for management reform. However, a perceived dissatisfaction with government, and alleged citizen demands for greater accountability, were certainly a factor mentioned by executive politicians and senior officials as one reason for public management reform (e.g. Foreword to President of the Treasury Board, 1997).

It is important to disentangle the various strands and dimensions of citizen opinion, for example, by distinguishing the satisfaction levels of service users with a particular service from more general citizen views of the competence or trustworthiness of government at large (Canadian Centre for Management Development, 1998a). Much of the expressed distrust of government in general appears to have been focused on politicians and on government in general, with public servants being regarded with greater confidence. Furthermore, when due allowance for differences was made, user satisfaction levels with many public services were not systematically worse than with private sector services (Canadian Centre for Management Development, 1998b; Erin Research Inc., 2005, p. 15).

H. Party political ideas

The decisive shift towards public management reform came (as in the UK and the USA) when a right-wing government was elected in place of a somewhat 'worn out' centre-left government (in the Canadian case, Trudeau's Liberal government). Mulroney's Progressive Conservative administration was imbued with anti-bureaucratic rhetoric and carried with it a general suspicion of the established bureaucracy and its seemingly close previous relationships with long-standing Liberal governments. However, although the incoming administration had plenty of generalized prejudices against bureaucracy and in favour of private sector dynamism, there is no evidence that it had any well-worked-out scheme for public management reform, or any coherent set of operationalized ideas on which to base such a plan.

The popularity of private sector management concepts faded somewhat during the long life of the Mulroney government, and were certainly less to the fore during the succeeding, more 'state-friendly' Liberal government. It is not clear that Chrétien's regime had any distinct plan of conception for management reform per se, but it was determined to bring expenditure under control and to try to link that to a more positive agenda of modernization and developing alternative modes of public service delivery. Most of the specific ideas, however, seem to have come from the senior bureaucrats themselves.

From 1993 to 2006 there was a long period of Liberal rule. This began in an atmosphere that was more 'public service friendly' than had obtained under Mulroney, but that did not prevent the Chrétien government from making deep cuts in public expenditure. The Harper administration after 2006 was again rather cool towards 'public sector solutions'.

I. Chance events

Several chance events appear to have had some influence over the trajectory of management reform. One was the dropping of Erik Nielsen from the Mulroney cabinet in mid 1986—for reasons unconnected with his leadership of the programme review task force. This cannot have helped the implementation of the still-new report, which afterwards largely faded away. A second coincidence, of rather larger impact, was the Mexican currency crisis of late 1994, which by all accounts helped significantly strengthen the determination of the Chrétien cabinet to push ahead with the downsizings and programme adjustments of the Program Review exercise, in case Canada became the next state to suffer currency 'meltdown' (Aucoin and Savoie, 1998).

Although it would be possible to argue that the 2004–6 sponsorship scandal—which certainly had many consequences—was a chance event, such an interpretation is not favoured here. The corruption was planned, widespread, and long-lasting, and even

if the emergence of some of the evidence may have been accidental or unintended, the scandal as a whole cannot really be classified as a 'chance event'.

J. Elite decision-making

See Section G, above. The Mulroney administration developed a series of specific initiatives on the basis of some generalized attitudes and prejudices, but there does not seem to have been any coherent overall plan. Even the specific initiatives that were launched frequently encountered implementation difficulties (see Sections L and M below).

After the fall of the Progressive Conservative administration in 1993 there was a shift in ministerial preferences. More emphasis was now placed on finding creative forms of 'Alternative Service Delivery', on partnership operations with the provinces, on shrewd use of advanced information technology and on more transparent accounting to Parliament for results (Aucoin and Savoie, 1998; President of the Treasury Board, 1997).

Throughout, Canadian ministers and officials had to temper their enthusiasm for particular directions of reform with a recognition of the complex, multilevel, sectorialized nature of the political and administrative systems. They did not enjoy the powers of (say) New Zealand or UK prime ministers to drive through major reforms even against significant opposition. The picture of the 'Canadian model' drawn by the Secretary to the Privy Council (Bourgon, 1998) is essentially incremental and anti-doctrinal. It speaks of reform being carried out 'calmly, competently, without much fanfare' (ibid., p. 1). Considerable stress is laid on sharing and cooperation with the provinces.

Ten years later, Bourgon's model does not look to be such an accurate portrayal. Government decision-making has become more politicized and more centralized on the prime minister (Aucoin and Savoie, 2009). Furthermore, certain management reforms—especially the 2006 Federal Accountability Act, but also the Management Accountability Framework (MAF)—have been given considerable fanfares.

K. The administrative system

In February 2008 there were twenty-five departments, more than thirty crown corporations and roughly fifty other service organizations responsible to federal ministers. A strong form of ministerial responsibility prevails (ministers responsible for all the actions of their 'portfolio' of departments, crown corporations, service agencies, tribunals, etc., no 'accounting officers' along UK lines). A number of commentators have observed a movement towards centralization of power around the prime minister and his political advisers since the late 1990s (Aucoin and Savoie, 2009). On the other hand, it must be remembered that the proportion of public employment in central, as opposed to sub-central government in Canada is one of the lowest in the OECD (OECD, 2009a, p. 69).

The central agencies have remained relatively prominent—indeed they have probably increased their influence. The main ones are the Privy Council Office (approximately 300 staff), the Treasury Board Secretariat (800), the Department of Finance (700), the Prime Minister's Office (80), and the Public Service Commission (2,000) (Savoie, 1997). Management reforms tend to be led by the Privy Council Office and the Treasury Board Secretariat.

The public service itself is non-partisan, and deputy ministers (the chief officials in the departments) usually remain in place when the government changes. Nearly all deputy ministers are career civil servants. There is quite a strong 'mandarin culture', with considerable horizontal communication between senior civil servants in different departments (Bourgault and Carroll, 1997, p. 97). However, in the past decade or so the influence of political appointees and consultants has grown. Furthermore the 'churn' rates of deputy ministers and ministers has increased, so that the opportunities to form longer-term trusting relationships have probably diminished: 'There is increasing evidence to suggest that senior public servants have become more responsive to the political wishes of the prime minister's court' (Aucoin and Savoie, 2009, p. 110).

For those who want more detail, Dunn (2002) offers a comprehensive analysis of the Canadian system. Lindquist (2006) gives a detailed review of the HRM aspects.

L. Contents of reform

From a bird's-eye view, some of the history of management reforms in the Canadian federal administration appears as a bewildering series of overlapping and only loosely coordinated initiatives, many of which seem to fade away or lose momentum after a relatively short time. Several commentators confirm that—certainly under the Mulroney administrations of 1984–93—the political leadership lacked any 'grand design' and gave management issues only intermittent attention (documented in Savoie, 1994).

Mulroney came to power following a campaign which had been sharply critical of 'big government' in Ottawa, and which had promised greater 'frugality' and radical changes in the bureaucracy. He was re-elected in 1988 and finally lost office in 1993. During his period in power he launched a number of initiatives, including:

- A 1984 review, under Deputy Prime Minister Erik Nielsen, of existing government programmes, to make them 'simple, more understandable and more accessible to their clientele', as well as to decentralize them and cut out programmes for which there was not a demonstrable need.
- The creation, in each ministry, of a politically appointed chief-of-staff position at assistant deputy minister level (i.e. the second highest civil service grade).
- A target of a 15,000 downsizing of the civil service within six years.
- The 1985 Increased Ministerial Authority and Accountability initiative (IMAA). This was designed to give individual ministers and departmental managers greater flexibility in allocating and reallocating resources within their departments.
- From 1986, a 'make or buy' policy to encourage competitive tendering for public services.
- Also from 1986, the establishment of a privatization office.
- The 1988 establishment of the Canadian Centre for Management Development (CCMD), to strengthen management training for the Canadian public service.
- It was decided that deputy ministers (the most senior civil servants) could henceforth be called before parliamentary committees for questioning (Bourgault and Carroll, 1997, p. 3).
- The effective scrapping of the previous Policy and Expenditure Management System (PEMS) and its replacement, from 1989, with a new system of cabinet committees, centred upon an Expenditure Review Committee (ERC).
- A high-profile, broad-scope exercise entitled Public Service 2000 (PS 2000), which was to empower civil servants, cut red tape and improve service to the public. PS 2000 was

announced in December 1989. In 1990 a White Paper *The Renewal of the Public Service in Canada* was published.

- The creation of a new type of decentralized agency, the Special Operating Agency (SOA), which was to enjoy greater managerial flexibility, whilst remaining within the framework of ministerial departments. The first five SOAs were announced in December 1989. Others followed, and from the late 1990s major efforts were made to provide integrated (or 'joined up') services through SOAs such as Service Canada (Kernaghan, 2008, 2009*a*, *b*).

- Further reforms followed the fall of the Progressive Conservative administration in March 1993. Some of the more significant were:

  ○ 1993: Service Standards Initiative, to encourage departments and agencies to develop and publish service standards. By 1995 two-thirds of departments were said to be well advanced in this exercise.

  ○ June 1993: A radical restructuring of the machinery of central government by Mulroney's Progressive Conservative successor, Kim Campbell. The size of the Cabinet was reduced from thirty-five to twenty-three and a number of departments were merged or eliminated.

  ○ Campbell's government was short-lived. In October 1993 the Liberals, under Jean Chrétien, returned to power.

  ○ February 1994: A process of Program Review was launched. Unlike some previous expenditure reduction exercises this one was able to mobilize considerable collective support within Cabinet, and was carried through to implementation in the 1995 and subsequent budgets. It went beyond simple cost-cutting and entailed a broad reconsideration and prioritization of the role of the federal government in Canadian society (Aucoin and Savoie, 1998).

  ○ February 1995: A new Expenditure Management System (EMS) was introduced which considerably tightened the previous approach to the use of budgetary reserves. Under EMS it is assumed that all new programmes and programme increases will have to be financed by reallocations within departments' budgetary envelopes. The government also committed itself to the introduction of full accruals accounting.

○ June 1995: A Quality Services Initiative approved by Cabinet. Aimed at increasing measured client satisfaction.

○ 1996: Introduction of Improved Reporting to Parliament system (IRPP) with the aim of enhancing the accountability of ministers and departments to Parliament.

○ 1996: Secretary to the Privy Council launched an initiative named *La Relève* designed to tackle what was said to be a 'quiet crisis' in the Canadian public service: 'This was the result of years of downsizing and pay freezes, criticism, insufficient recruitment, and the premature departure of experienced public servants' (Bourgon, 1998, p. 18). Initiatives were invited from departments to revitalize the public service.

○ 1997: Publication of *Accounting for Results* (President of the Treasury Board, 1997) which for the first time brought together results statements for all departments.

○ 2000: Introduction of Results-based Management and Accountability Frameworks (RMAFs) to support the regular evaluation of transfer payments programmes.

○ 2001: Launch of the Public Service Modernization initiative, focusing on HRM and aiming to reduce detailed central control and introduce more flexibility.

○ 2003: Full implementation of accruals accounting in the federal government. (The original decision to introduce it had been taken in 1995—see Baker and Rennie, 2006.)

○ 2003: Treasury Board Secretariat introduced the Management Accountability Framework, which is used for appraising the performance of top civil servants.

○ 2004: Auditor General's report on what became known as the 'sponsorship scandal' initiated an intense political crisis, lasting for more than a year and signficantly contributing to the loss of popularity of the Liberal government of Prime Minister Martin, and its eventual electoral defeat in 2006 (Auditor General, 2004). A 1996–2004 federal sponsorship programme in the province of Quebec turned out to have been riddled with corruption. The programme was intended to raise awareness within Quebec of the federal government's contributions to the Quebec economy. The Auditor General's report revealed, inter alia, that up to $C 100 million of the $C 250 million programme had been paid to

Liberal Party-friendly advertising firms and crown corporations who had performed little or no work. Eventually the scandal tarnished both political and civil service reputations, and lowered public trust. Guité, the official in charge of the programme, was tried and convicted on five counts of fraud.

○ 2004–5: The Liberal government (now in a minority), defending itself against sponsorship scandal criticisms, introduced a whole series of reforms, including the creation of a Comptrollership General of Canada (Thomas, 2009, p. 241).

○ 2005: Launch of Service Canada, a hybrid agency offering a single window for the delivery of a wide range of public services (including employment insurance and pensions) for thirteen departments and agencies. Operates through a) Internet, b) telephone, c) conventional mail, and d) a network of local offices: 22,000 employees. Citizen-centred business model (Kernaghan, 2008). Reports to Minister for Human Resources and Skills Development.

○ 2006: General election. The Conservative party defeats the Liberals (after thirteen years in power). Harper becomes PM.

○ 2006: Federal Accountability Act made deputy ministers accountable to parliamentary committees, established a parliamentary budgetary office, extended the power of the Auditor General, and introduced a systematic evaluation of the government's grant and contributions programmes (McCormack, 2007).

○ 2006: New government website introduced Tools and Resources for Parliamentarians: (www.tbs-sct.gc.ca/tbs-sct/audience-auditoire/parliamentarian-parlementaire-eng.asp, accessed 15 April 2010). Intended to provide MPs with a simplified way of finding many government reports and plans.

○ 2008: General election. Harper Conservative government retains power, but as a minority.

M. The implementation process

During the 1980s the implementation process in Canada appears to have been a somewhat uncertain one, at least in the sense that a number of the initiatives petered out after a relatively short period. Examples of such disappointments include:

- 'Notwithstanding its early support, the Mulroney government did not follow through on the great majority of the Nielsen recommendations. ..Indeed, the great majority of programs reviewed are still in place and virtually intact' (Savoie, 1994, p. 130).

- The 'make-or-buy' policy of 1986 did not make much progress beyond the pilot project phase, and was abandoned in 1990.

- Despite the early development of a privatization plan, substantive progress on this policy had dwindled by 1987. The Department of Finance insisted that revenues from privatization sales should go into the Consolidated Revenue Fund, and departmental ministers became increasingly resistant to 'losing' 'their' crown corporations or subsidiaries.

- The success of IMAA was limited. Six years after its introduction only about one third of departments had agreed to sign an MOU with the Treasury Board, and those that did sometimes complained of a mass of paperwork for only limited real autonomy.

- 'Even its most ardent supporter admits that PS 2000 is not living up to expectations' (Savoie, 1994, p. 241). The expectation that central agencies would be cut back was not fulfilled. There was a widespread perception that PS 2000 remained a top-down exercise which produced more reports than action.

- Mulroney's programme for downsizing the civil service produced a reduction of only 15,000 and about half these positions were actually transferred to provincial governments or other parts of the public sector (Savoie, 1994, pp. 266–7).

- 'Although the experiences with SOAs have been positive, it is not clear whether they are sufficiently different from traditional departments to support flexible and innovative service delivery' (OECD, 1997, p. 44).

- During the 1980s 'governments became increasingly pre-occupied with the deficit and the debt, but were unable to come to grips with it. The period was characterized by unachievable deficit reduction targets and regular across-the-board cuts, primarily targeted at operations' (Harder and Lindquist, 1997, p. 80). Net public debt increased from $C168 billion in 1984 to $C508 billion in 1993.

After 1994, conditions for implementation eased. The Canadian economy began to improve, and a very experienced prime minister (Chrétien) was able to establish a relatively disciplined Cabinet. The 1994 Program Review exercise and the 1995 budget were generally regarded as successful exercises. However, there remained a doubt about the connections between the higher levels of the federal government—especially the central agencies—and 'middle management' in the operational agencies and the departments. Reforms might have achieved agreement at the top, but to what extent was implementation 'owned' by those outside Ottawa?

This tension continued into the twenty-first century, as the federal government became increasingly centralized, but at the same time the complexity of implementing 'integrated public governance' in cooperation with the provinces increased.

N. Reforms actually achieved

There has been no systematic evaluation of public management reform in Canada during this period, although there have been a number of specific reviews or assessments of particular initiatives. Notable among these have been the sometimes sharply critical reports of the Auditor General (e.g. Auditor General of Canada, 1993, 1997, 2004).

As indicated above (M), it appears that Canada suffers (or, at least, suffered) from a significant 'implementation gap', with many initiatives failing to meet anything like their full expectations. The 1994 Program Review exercise, thanks to a favourable set of political circumstances surrounding its launch, appears to be an important exception to this, but it would have been optimistic to expect such circumstances to continue indefinitely (Aucoin and Savoie, 1998). There are signs, for example, that implementation of elements of the 2006 Federal Accountability Act has been weak (e.g. some retreat on access to government information; an underfunded and tightly controlled parliamentary budget officer) (See also Bouckaert and Halligan, 2008, appendix V).

Some particular studies shed light on aspects of the reforms. For example, Bilodou et al. (2007) examined the productivity of five federal Special Operating Agencies before and after corporatization (there were twenty SOAs in all at the time they undertook their research). They found statistically significant increases in outputs for a majority of their cases, but other measures (cost efficiency) were less clear, and in any case there was great variation between individual agencies, with some indicating performance declines. Neither did this study include measurement of service quality or user satisfaction, so, overall, it cannot be interpreted as more than a mild endorsement of the idea that autonomization can sometimes increase technical efficiency.

At the time of writing we are awaiting the five year post-implementation review of the Public Service Modernization programme.

Key Events—Canada

Period	General	Organization	Personnel	Finance
1980–5	1981–4 Trudeau (Liberal) Prime Minister 1984 (June–September) Turner (Liberal) Prime Minister 1984–93 Mulroney (Progressive Conservatives) Prime Minister	Trudeau's was a rather tired administration (it was his 5th term as PM). Mulroney launched many reforms but few were effectively implemented (Savoie, 1994) 1984 Nielsen Task Force on Improving Government Efficiency (very 'NPM-ish', half composed of businessmen)		1981 Policy and Expenditure Management System (PEMS). This was a multi-year expenditure plan
1986–90		1990 First Special Operating Agencies (SOAs), e.g. Passport Office (see review in Auditor General of Canada, 2001)	1988 Creation of Canadian Centre for Management development (a kind of civil service college). Later became the Canadian School of Government 1989 Launch of Public Service 2000	
1991–5	1993 (March–October) Campbell (progressive Conservative) Prime Minister 1993–2003 Chrétien (Liberal) Prime Minister	1993 Number of departments reduced from 32 to 24. 1994 Declaration of Service Quality 1995 Quality Service Initiative, including a commitment regularly to measure citizen satisfaction (see Erin Research Inc., 1998, 2005, 2008)	1992 Public Service Reform Act	1994 Program Review exercise effectively restrained public spending and moved towards a balanced budget (Aucoin and Savoie, 1998) Expenditure Management System (EMS) Commitment to introduce accruals accounting
1996–2000	1996 Improved Reporting to Parliament (IRPP) project launched	1997 Creation of Citizen-Centred Service Network (later the Public Sector Service Delivery Council—Kernaghan, 2009) 1999 Creation of Government-on-Line (GOL), aimed at using IT to improve the quality of public services to citizens 2000 Service Improvement Intitiative (SII)—aimed at continuous improvement and standard-setting SII and GOL both concluded operations in 2006 2000 Creation of Canada Customs and Revenue Agency 2000 Publication of *Results for Canadians: A Management Framework for the Government of Canada*	1997 La Relève: report by the Cabinet Secretary on the state of the Canadian public service	2000 Results-based Management and Accountability Frameworks (RMAFs) to support the evaluation of transfer payment programmes

| 2001–5 | 2003–6 Martin (Liberal) Prime Minister | 2004 Auditor General's report on what became known as the 'sponsorship scandal'. This initiated an intense political crisis lasting for more than a year, and contributing to the fall of the Liberal government (Auditor General, 2004)

2005 Launch of Service Canada, a hybrid agency offering a single window for the delivery of a wide range of services on behalf of 13 departments and agencies (Kernaghan, 2008) | 2003 Full implementation of accruals accounting in the federal government (Baker and Rennie, 2006) |
| 2006–10 | 2006–8 Harper (Progressive Conservatives) Prime Minister

2008–? Harper (Progressive Conservatives) again Prime Minister, but now with a minority government | 2006 New government website—Tools and Resources for Parliamentarians (www.tbs-sct.gc.ca/tbs-sct/audience-auditoire/parliamentarian-parlementaire-eng.asp) | 2006 Federal Accountability Act—flagship legislation for the new Conservative administration. Created a Parliamentary Budget Office and extended the powers of the Auditor General. Introduced a systematic evaluation of grant and contribution programmes (McCormack, 2007). Deputy Ministers (the top civil servants) were made directly answerable to parliamentary committees (Franks, 2009) |

THE EUROPEAN COMMISSION

Preface

The European Commission is an 'odd one out' in this book, in the sense that it is *not* a national government, and, indeed, to think of it as though it were would be highly misleading. The Commission is one important component—the main 'executive' component—in the unique and tremendously complex formation of institutions that make up the European Union (see Peterson and Shackleton, 2002, for a clear treatment). A Commission reform document describes the Commission's original role as follows:

It was established to act impartially in the interests of the European Community as a whole and to act as guardian of the founding Treaties, notably by exercising its right of legislative initiative; controlling Member States' respect of community law; negotiating commercial agreements on behalf of the Community, implementing the common policies and ensuring that competition in the Community was not distorted. (European Commission, 2000, p. 1)

Over the years, however, the Commission took on a wide range of new tasks. Not only did it help to devise new policies and legislative initiatives (as originally intended), and not only did it carry out ever-more extensive regulatory functions (for example in relation to competition within the Single European Market), it also acquired a substantial burden of administrative tasks. By 2000 almost half the Commission's officials were engaged in the management of programmes and projects of various kinds. Thus it performs a significant set of *management* tasks, and forms a fit subject for treatment in this book.

A. Socio-economic forces: general

For details of the socio-economic forces affecting the member states, see the country files for Belgium, Finland, France, Germany, Italy, Sweden, and the UK, elsewhere in this Appendix.

The 'gross value added' for the fifteen member states' economies fell slightly in 1994 but then rose strongly for the rest of the period to 2000. The second half of the 1990s—unlike both the early 1990s and the early 1980s—was thus a period in which the EU as a whole was generally free from acute economic pressures (Eurostat, 2002, pp. 158–61). Growth then slowed significantly from 2001, but picked up again after 2003 until the GEC in 2008.

B. Global economic forces

See Appendix A and the country files for EU member states. By 1999 the EU was the world's largest single trading block in services, and was only slightly behind the USA in its share of total world transactions in goods. By 2008 the combined GDP of the twenty-seven member states (US $ 15.3 billion) exceeded the GDP of the USA (US $ 14.4 billion) and was far ahead of China (US $ 7.9 billion), though with a much lower growth rate (*OECD Factbook, 2010*). Like the USA, however, the EU has been pressured by the rapid growth and competitiveness of (especially) China, India, and Brazil. A continuing point of pressure has been the Common Agricultural Policy (CAP) which, although quite strongly reformed (and due to be reformed again), continues to provide a considerable measure of protection for EU farmers against agricultural products from elsewhere. The CAP is currently responsible for about 40 per cent of the EU budget, although this percentage has been declining for quite some time.

C. Sociodemographic change

The total population of the twenty-seven EU member states rose steadily from 693M in 1980 to 729M in 2005, (Eurostat, 2010, p. 154). Within this total, the proportions aged over 65 and over 80 also rose. Despite this absolute growth, however, the proportion of the world population living in the EU twenty-seven countries fell over the same period (1980–2005) from 15.6 per cent to 11.2 per cent.

Net migration has been the largest component of total population change in the EU since 1989. Since the second half of the 1990s most or all EU countries have experienced positive net migration (i.e. immigration exceeded emigration).

D. Socio-economic policies

It is only a slight exaggeration to say that, during the past two decades, the Commission has presided over a revolution in EU economic policy. After a period of stagnation in the late 1970s and early 1980s, the pace of policy development picked up. A landmark was the Commission's 1985 White Paper on the Single European Market. This was followed, the following year, by the Single European Act, which committed member states to completing a single market by 1993. This programme brought with it an enhanced role for the Commission, not only 'internally' as the regulator of the market, but also externally, as the central actor managing the interface between the single market and the wider world trade system. In 1988 the Council asked the Commission to develop a plan for achieving economic and monetary union (EMU). The eventual upshot of this was the launch, on 1 January 2002, of a single currency (the euro), watched over by a single, independent European Central Bank (ECB).

The Commission's presence in the social policy field is not nearly as soundly based in the European treaties as is its economic activity. Most of its resources are directed elsewhere. Nevertheless, by a variety of stratagems, the Commission has edged into social policy, especially in the areas of employment law, equal opportunities, and health and safety issues. Increasingly, also, the largest EU budget line—the Common Agricultural Policy (CAP)—is being converted into a vehicle for a kind of social policy for rural regeneration, environmental protection, and diversification.

E. The political system

The political system within which the Commission operates has evolved quite rapidly over the past twenty-five years. In institutional terms the system comprises the Commission itself (headed by the College of Commissioners—political appointments proposed by the member states), the Council of Ministers (ministers from the member states), and the European Parliament (members directly elected from the member states).

During this period the EU enlarged its membership four times. In 1981 Greece joined; in 1986 Portugal and Spain; in 1995 Austria, Finland, and Sweden. The most dramatic enlargement came in 2006 when Poland, the Czech Republic, Hungary, Slovakia, Lithuania, Latvia, Estonia, Cyprus, and Malta became members. This was followed, in 2007, by the addition of Bulgaria and Romania (creating the current EU of twenty-seven). The countries involved in the 2004 and 2007 enlargements

formed a much less economically developed group than the earlier members, and one which included states which had only emerged from Communist rule/membership of the Soviet Block since 1990. Clearly, each successive enlargement increased the size and complexity of the Council of Ministers. Since each member state has traditionally had at least one commissioner, it also changed the shape of the upper reaches of the EU Commission. Enlargements have also helped to generate an ongoing evolution of voting procedures, with more and more issues being assigned to qualified majority voting (where the number of votes allocated to each state is proportionate to its size) so as to avoid the potential deadlocks of a requirement of unanimity.

The political system has also changed in other ways. The European Parliament has developed its role considerably (Peterson and Shackleton, 2002, chapter 5). The first direct elections to this body took place in 1979. In 1980 the *Isoglucose* judgement of the European Court of Justice made it clear that the Council of Ministers could not adopt Community legislation without consulting the Parliament. In 1987 the Parliament gained further influence through a new cooperation procedure, which meant that, for certain categories of legislation, the Council of Ministers could only overrule the Parliament if it acted unanimously. The Maastricht Treaty of 1992 further extended Parliament's role. Finally the dramatic 1999 resignation of the entire College of Commissioners—the fall of the Santer Commission—was triggered to a significant extent by fear of an imminent vote of censure in the Parliament. This provided an indelible mark of the growing significance of the Parliament for the work of the Commission. Subsequently the Parliament carved itself a role in holding hearings and approving the candidates selected for the College of Commissioners.

Despite these many and significant changes, one original feature of the Commission's political position remains. As Christiansen (2001, p. 100) puts it, 'there is an inherent contradiction in the Commission providing both political leadership and an impartial civil service to the EU system'.

F. New management ideas

In general, it could be said that the Commission has not been particularly receptive to management ideas coming from outside—or, at least, not as far as the reform of its own structures and procedures have been concerned. It is self-consciously 'different'—unique—and has never been as open to private sector management ideas as, say, the governments of USA or the UK. The reforms since the mid 1990s (for details see below) have been very much 'home grown' and not directly modelled on those of any guru or school of thought such as NPM (Levy, 2004), even if they have shared some of the rhetoric ('decentralization', 'performance'). Since the 1999 collapse of the Santer Commission (see below), ideas of *strategy* and *transparency* have gained significant footholds within the Commission, and both these are obviously drawn from the wider international stream of public management ideas.

The Commission has also acted to facilitate the spread of certain management ideas among the member states. It has helped to promote TQM, and has supported the development of a simplified version of the European Foundation for Quality Management model of excellence, known as the Common Assessment Framework (CAF). For the main part, however, these activities have constituted the promotion of certain techniques *for use elsewhere* (in member states or in EU programmes which are administered on a decentralized basis) rather than within the core of the Commission itself.

G. Pressure from citizens

It is hard for citizens to exert any direct pressure on the Commission. On the whole it has few direct contacts with citizens—most EU programmes are administered by member states, with the Commission acting at a distance to formulate the objectives and rules, to supply some or all of the finance, and to regulate or monitor the activities 'on the ground'. The Commission does not itself provide extensive public services, as do national and local authorities.

Nevertheless, in a more general way the Commission—together with the Council and the Parliament—is certainly concerned at the general problem of falling trust in EU institutions and declining voter turnout at European elections (Peterson and Shackleton, 2002, pp. 8–9). This concern may well have been one motive behind the theme of 'transparency' which was embraced in the 2000 White Paper, *Reforming the Commission* (European Commission, 2000).

H. Party political ideas

The reform of the Commission does not seem to have been much affected by party political ideas.

The Commission is not 'run' by one or two parties, like most national governments. There is no direct channel by which the ideas of a particular political party could come to dominate the reform discussion within the Commission. This is not to say, of course, that politics do not have any influence. Changes in the upper reaches of the Commission are usually a focus for intensive 'bureau-politics', but that is a different kind of politics, not usually conducted along party lines.

I. Chance events

One may debate whether it was 'chance' or 'an accident waiting to happen', but the series of scandals and inefficiencies which gradually engulfed the Santer Commission (1995–9) certainly left their mark on the ongoing process of reform. The eventual resignation of that Commission made a fresh reform effort virtually inevitable. Arguably, however, it also biased attention towards an agenda of control (tightening procedures and audit) and away from the agenda of efficiency and performance (see, e.g. Committee of Independent Experts, 1999). The ensuing reforms embraced both themes, but some evidence suggests that the former, rather than the latter, has been more vigorously implemented.

J. Elite decision-making

Whilst there is certainly an 'elite' within the Commission, it is quite a diverse one. As far as reform is concerned the key actors are probably the commissioners themselves plus the directors-general (heads of the main vertical divisions within the Commission). These two groups come from all the member states, and therefore from a wide range of political and administrative cultures (Ban, 2010b). Even when they can agree that a particular reform may be desirable, they face a number of powerful constraints. In practice, major reforms would have to be acceptable to the Council of Ministers, and 'saleable' to the European Parliament. Last, but by no means least, the Commission is home to strong trade unions ('syndicates'), which have long practice in defending their members' strong tenure and not inconsiderable privileges.

The elite is advised by personal *cabinets* of officials (often quite young) and by ad hoc teams and task forces. The selection of members of these influential teams and *cabinets* is commonly quite personalized—this is not a transparent process based on qualifications and merit, but rather a commissioner picking (from those who are willing and available) individuals s/he thinks will be effective and loyal helpers in the process of forming and negotiating a set of feasible reform proposals.

Two of the stronger internal rules within the Commission are that the commissioners decide on proposals collegially, not individually, and that proposals which come up from within the Commission must be cleared and agreed horizontally with all the directorates who have a legitimate interest in the issue at hand. Both these rules help to ensure that the proposals of a single individual, or doctrinally committed group, are unlikely to be acceptable unless considerable compromises are made.

K. The administrative system

A popular image in the British mass media is that of a 'bloated Brussels bureaucracy'. In reality, while the Commission certainly possesses many of the classic characteristics of a bureaucracy (strict hierarchy, lots of 'red tape'), it is not at all large, relative to the long list of responsibilities attributed to it. The total number of Commission staff in 2007 was about 23,000 plus 9,000 'external' staff (detached, or temporary). These numbers included more than 2,000 translators and interpreters (to handle the need to translate the many documents and speeches into all the Community languages). The number of A-grade staff (the policy and management group) was just over 6,000.

At the top sits the College of Commissioners itself. These twenty-seven (one for each member state) are mainly ex-politicians, and are supposed to work on a collegial basis, not as individual ministers, each with their own unique sphere of authority (Christiansen, 2001).

The work is divided into more than twenty Directorates General (DGs) and a number of other services (most importantly, the Legal Service and the Secretariat General). The DGs (whose exact number varies over time, with mergers and new creations) are functionally defined (e.g. Agriculture, Budget, Energy, and Transport, etc.—see Peterson and Shackleton, 2002, p. 145). Most are sectoral ('vertical'—e.g. energy), but a few are horizontal, cutting across the sectors (e.g. budget). Traditionally DGs are fairly hierarchical, and the divisions between them are quite deep. In other words, the directors-general are powerfully placed

at the top of strong vertical ladders of authority, and horizontal coordination between these twenty-plus 'commands' is weak. For long the administrative culture of the Commission represented a blend of the hierarchical and legalistically-oriented French and German traditions. The 'Kinnock reforms' of 2000–4 aimed to improve strategic coordination but it is debatable how successful they were (see below).

The most senior official in the Commission is the Secretary General. All permanent staff enjoy high security of tenure. The nationalities of the A-grades in any particular part of the organization are deliberately mixed up so as to try to prevent the formation of 'national groups' which could influence a given programme or project (i.e. if you are an A-grade German, you are unlikely to have another German as your boss). There is an unofficial national quota system for the top three grades (A1 to A3). (Details of how all this works are spelled out in Page, 1997, but it should be noted that the Kinnock reforms since 2000 have had as one of their aims the reduction of the 'flags on posts', or quota system for top positions.)

The DGs report to the commissioner responsible for their particular function. The precise definition of functions, and the exact portfolios of individual commissioners change constantly over time, in roughly the same way as frequent re-allocations or definitions of function take place in many national governments. Commissioners are supposed to assume full political responsibility for the Commission's actions, with DGs being responsible for sound implementation. In practice the line between policy and implementation in the EU is probably even harder to draw than in national governments.

L. Content of the reform package

Between 1980 and the mid 1990s there were few attempts to reform the management of the Commission. During this period its tasks and size grew considerably, and in particular it took on more executive functions—running projects and programmes. The famous French President of the Commission between 1985 and 1995, Jacques Delors, was keen to expand the range of Commission activities, but seems to have been little interested in issues of efficiency or performance management. Expert observers refer to 'the inefficiencies and *immobilisme* that plagued the services' (Peterson and Shackleton, 2002, p. 156).

In 1995 the Santer Commission launched a programme entitled *Sound and Effective Management 2000* (SEM 2000), quickly followed, in 1997, by a further development called *Modernization of Administration and Personnel Policy* (MAP 2000). SEM 2000 was aimed at updating financial management practices and creating a system whereby EU programmes would be subject to regular, independent evaluation (European Commission, 1997a, 1998). MAP 2000 was aimed at decentralizing and simplifying the Byzantine system of personnel and administrative procedures (European Commission, 1997b). The Santer Commission also launched an exercise called DECODE (1997–9), which aimed at inventorizing staff and their functions. It was perhaps significant that such an elaborate and time-consuming exercise was needed simply so that the Commission could accurately see what its own staff were spending their time doing. SEM 2000, MAP 2000, and DECODE each got quite a long way before the end of the Santer Commission (1999), although none were entirely complete. A brief assessment of them is given in Section N below.

After the fall of the Santer Commission, the incoming Prodi Commission was obliged to make major reforms. It built upon these previous attempts at reform, and gave their own effort a high profile. It quickly published a White Paper on *Reforming the Commission* (European Commission, 2000). The major changes envisaged were:

- Strategic priority setting and resource allocation (particularly a system of Activity-Based Management, or ABM, plus a policy of 'externalizing' operational tasks and activities so as to be able to re-focus on policy priorities—see European Commission, 2000 and 2001a).
- Human resource management (decentralizing responsibility for staff management, and simplifying and clarifying procedures; introducing better training and career planning).
- Financial management (setting up a proper internal audit service and better 'fraud-proofing' of legislation; decentralizing financial controls to individual DGs).

Although there has been nothing since the Kinnock reforms which has matched them for comprehensiveness or public attention, there have been various moves to modernize different aspects of the Commission's working. Transparency has become a major issue (see, e.g. Regulation (EC) no.1049/2001). The theme of simplifying and reducing the regulatory burden has been a hardy perennial. One important innovation here has been the use of Regulatory Impact Assessment (RIA) to test the economic, social, and environmental impacts of new EU regulations—on this and most other reforms, see the Europa website (<http://ec.europa.eu>) for details. Last, but by no means least, the prospect of having to hire 4,600 new staff as the 2004 enlargement approached galvanized a big change in recruitment procedures (Ban, 2010a). A European Personnel Selection Office was set up in 2002 and has introduced a much more modern-looking system, including assessment centres and competency testing.

M. Implementation process

Implementation of the SEM 2000 and MAP 2000 reforms conspicuously lacked a central focus and leadership, and were eventually overtaken by the collapse of the Santer Commission.

The Kinnock White Paper had a clearer Action Plan (European Commission, 2000, Part 2), with many of the important actions falling to the Secretary General, a man who had previously been chief adviser (*chef de cabinet*) to Mr Prodi, the new president. Nevertheless, a quick persual of this document should suffice to convince the reader of the complexity of the implementation process for a reform of this type. It was also noticeable how, during implementation, the human resource management elements came to take up a larger and larger share of effort (Mr Kinnock himself felt obliged to attend many dozens of meetings with the syndicates) and the performance-oriented elements of the reforms seemed to take second place. Furthermore the rhetorical flourishes concerning decentralization seem to have lost out to a strong bureaucratic logic of further centralization in the name of tighter control (Levy, 2004).

The ongoing reform of recruitment procedures appeared to be accomplished with surprising ease, but a detailed analysis indicates that the implementation of these changes hold a number of potential pitfalls, and that their final impact is likely to be less than revolutionary (Ban, 2010a).

N. Results achieved

This is hard to say, not least because many elements within the recent reforms have been expressed in very general terms and/or are hard to measure. The reform package announced by Vice

President Kinnock in March 2000 included an action plan and, in 2003, the Commission published a progress review, in which it was claimed that real advances had been made with eighty-seven of the ninety-four recommended actions (European Commission, 2003). Further analysis indicates a somewhat less rosy picture, in that the majority of the 'actions' were preliminary or intermediate rather than final, and even some of the 'successes'—such as Activity-Based Management—may have fallen far short of what might be supposed from the management textbooks (Levy, 2004). There have certainly been important changes in procedure, such as the introduction of Activity-Based Management and the creation of an internal audit service. Financial procedures have changed—though whether they have become more efficient or effective in some more fundamental sense can be debated. The new emphasis on the individual responsibility of DGs, coupled with new promotion and grading procedures and annual activity plans *could* begin to shift the management culture, but at the time of writing there is little hard evidence that this has been achieved. As for the new commitment to strategy, there has been no shortage of annual and five-year strategy documents (see Europe website) but, again, it is not clear how far these go beyond paper exercises to paint a post hoc coherence over what remains underneath a fairly opportunistic collection of policies and programmes. Specific indicators or measures are rare (Ellinas and Suleiman, 2008, p. 713).

Turning to the growth of EU agencies, a recent evaluation suggested that there is plenty still to do if they are going to be firmly steered and effectively evaluated by the Commission (Rambøll/Euréval/Matrix, 2009). Finally, it should be mentioned that the Regulatory Impact Assessment process was recently given a fairly clean bill of health by the European Court of Auditors, a body that has often been quite critical of the Commission in the past (European Court of Auditors, 2010).

Whether there has been any basic shift in the bureaucratic and hierarchical culture of the Commission therefore remains doubtful. There is a sense in which the reforms have themselves been bureaucratized during implementation, so that the original rhetorical emphasis on a more performance-oriented approach has somewhat evaporated under the welter of new rules about financial procedure, internal audit, and personnel management (Ellinas and Suleiman, 2008). However, longer-term changes in the Commission's culture may come more from the influx of 'new blood' with different backgrounds, coming from the more recent member states, than from specific reform instruments (Ban, 2010*b*).

There was a formal evaluation of the earlier (1995–9) SEM 2000 reform programme. The evaluators found that some significant progress had been made in setting up financial units within each DG, and in embedding evaluation as a regular practice. However, they were of the opinion that the effectiveness of the implementation of SEM 2000 is being undermined by some basic problems which inhibit effective change (The Evaluation Partnership, 1999, p. 4). These problems included a lack of ownership and leadership, and a certain incoherence to the reform programme itself. It might also be said that in their original conception SEM 2000 and MAP 2000 were quite cautious and modest, if measured against the standards of major public management reforms in, say, New Zealand and the UK, or even France, Sweden, or the USA. This may not, however, be a fair yardstick. As this case file makes clear, the Commission is in several crucial respects quite *unlike* a national government.

It remains the case that the Commission is an exceptionally complex organization, and one in which it is extraordinarily difficult to formulate and execute fundamental reform. It does not provide many services direct to citizens, being mainly concerned with transferring funds to other bodies, and with regulation and legislative initiatives. Much of its work is carried on within tight legislative frameworks, which permit little discretion to individual managers. The basic rules for setting six-year budget totals through the Council of Ministers (the 'Financial Perspective') create a situation in which incentives for 'savings' and 'efficiency' have much less force than in some national systems (the European Parliament has frequently criticized the Commission for failing to spend up to the hilt). Its multiculturalism and collegiate principles further militate against implementation of the kind of fast, single-track reforms which have been possible in some of the NPM countries.

Key Events—European Commission

Period	General	Organization	Personnel	Finance
1980–5	1981–5 Thorn Commission 1981 Greece becomes a member state 1985–95 Delors Commissions			
1986–90	1986 Portugal and Spain become member states	Under Delors, the Commission acquires many new programmes and functions		
1991–5	1995–9 Santer Commission	1995 Sound and Effective Management programme (SEM 2000)		
1996–2000	1999 Fall of the Santer Commission following allegations of fraud and mismanagement (Committee of Independent Experts, 1999) Prodi Commission, 1999–2004 2000 White Paper *European Governance* (European Commission, 2000)	1996 Commission decision to create an evaluation unit in each directorate 1997 Modernization of Administration and Personnel policy (MAP 2000) 2000 Policy of externalizing operational tasks (e.g. by creating agencies)		
2001–5	2000–4 the 'Kinnock Reforms' 2004 EU enlargement from 16 to 25 member states 2004–9 First Barroso Commission	The Kinnock Reforms established a regime of annual strategic planning, with targets cascaded down to directorates 2005 Strategy for the simplification of the regulatory environment: introduction and growth of Regulatory Impact Assessment (RIA)	Introduction of annual appraisal interviews (with points for promotion) for all A grade staff 2003 Creation of European Personnel Selection Office 2004 Major influx of staff from the new member states	Introduction of Activity-Based Management (ABM) Introduction of an internal audit service 2005 New methodology for assessing the costs of regulation
2006–10	2007 Further enlargement—Bulgaria and Romania 2009–14 Second Barroso Commission	2006 Green Paper *European Transparency Initiative* 2007 Action programme for reducing administrative burdens	2007 Further influx of new staff from Bulgaria and Romania	2008 DG Budget publishes multi-annual overview of evaluations

FINLAND

A. Socio-economic forces: general

See Appendix A. Finland is a small country with a relatively homogenous population and a fairly egalitarian culture. It has created an innovative, successful economy, but its size and position (the extreme north-eastern corner of Europe, with a long common border with Russia) make it highly vulnerable to major downturns among its trading partners.

B. Global economic forces

See Table A.1 and discussion in Appendix A (above). Although Finland entered the GEC in a relatively strong position, it nevertheless suffered a sharp contraction in the economy, and public debt rose from 40.6 per cent of GDP in 2008 to 52.4 per cent in 2010.

C. Sociodemographic issues

See Appendix A. Finland faces the problems of an ageing population which are present in the rest of Western Europe, but to a more than average degree. Between 2010 and 2050 the working-age population is forecast to decline by 260,000 at the same time as the population over 65 will grow by more than 700,000. The government estimates that the multiplication of the elderly will translate into a need for 4,000 extra staff annually in municipal health and social care services (OECD, 2010, p. 7). Generally speaking Finnish society is relatively homogenous and peaceful. There is a different ethnic group (the *Saami* people) in the far north (Lapland) but their numbers are small, and their significance for a study of the reform of central government limited. In the last decade inward immigration from Russia has increased, and organized crime seems to have begun to seep in.

D. National socio-economic policies

Finland enjoyed a good growth rate and relatively low unemployment through most of the 1980s. From 1991, however, the sudden collapse of trade with its neighbour, the then Soviet Union, together with the more general recession in the West, sparked a severe economic crisis. Trade fell, banks

got into great difficulties, unemployment soared to unprecedented heights (18.4 per cent in 1994). Between 1990 and 1993 GDP volume fell by 12 per cent. Faced with these problems, central government launched a strong programme of budgetary reform and restraint. By 1997 growth had returned, budgetary discipline was maintained, and Finland was able fully to satisfy the Maastricht 'convergence criteria' for EU monetary union. By the late 1990s economic growth was once again healthy, although there was some concern at the high reliance of the economy on one firm—the mobile phone giant, Nokia. The GEC hit Finland quite hard, but previous prudence had put the government in a position where it 'will have relatively more room for discretionary fiscal stimulus in response to the pressures of the economic and financial crisis compared to most OECD countries' (OECD, 2010, p. 6).

E. The political system

Finland is a unitary state, though with a strong tradition of relatively autonomous municipal government, protected by the constitution (like Sweden). The basic pieces of legislation are the Constitution Act (1919) and the Parliament Act (1928). There is a multiparty political system and governments are usually quite stable coalitions. The Cabinet acts collegially, with the prime minister having less personal prominence than in the 'Westminster' systems of the UK and New Zealand. Formally the power of execution lies with a Council of State, consisting of government ministers and the Chancellor of Justice. There is a president, who is elected every six years, retains some responsibility for foreign policy and is commander-in-chief of the armed forces. In general it might be said that the Finnish president, while considerably more active and politically powerful than his/her German counterpart, is also nothing like as dominant as the French president. During the last fifteen years or so it is the Prime Minister's Office that has tended to gain new responsibilities and powers, while the President's Office has not (see Bouckaert, Ormond, and Peters, 2000).

The legislature (*Eduskunta*) is unicameral, with 200 seats. Eighty per cent of MPs tend also to be municipal politicians—so the interests of the municipalities are strongly represented at the centre. The three big parties in recent years have been the Social Democrats, the National Coalition (conservatives), and the Centre Party (originally an agrarian party). The reforming coalitions since the late 1980s have been led by the National Coalition (Holkeri, 1987–91), the Centre Party (Aho, 1991–5), and the Social Democrats (Lipponen's 'Rainbow Coalition', 1995–2003). From 2003 to 2010 (and continuing) the Centre Party led the governing coalitions. The Communist Party was a significant political force during the 1960s and 1970s, but has since lost most of its strength.

F. New management ideas

Finland has been an active member of many international organizations, both governmental and academic (e.g. PUMA, European Group for Public Administration). In that sense it has been open to, and acquainted with, the full range of contemporary management concepts and techniques as applied to the public sector (indeed, it prides itself on this—see Ministry of Finance, 2010, p. 7). However, it has not slavishly followed fashions, but rather carefully selected and piloted those ideas considered suitable for Finnish needs. To take two examples, TQM and ISO 9000 approaches to service quality improvement were widely adopted in Finnish local government and, in central government, accruals accounting practices in other countries were closely studied but then only partly adopted. Finnish central government has not made intensive use of management consultants to implement reform (in the way that occurred in, say, the UK). Consultants have been used to gather information, and a number of foreign academics have been used as advisers, but actual implementation has remained, for the most part, firmly in the hands of career civil servants.

G. Pressure from citizens

We are not aware of any evidence pointing to sustained pressure for specific reforms from the Finnish public—or, indeed, for reversal of any of the changes which have been implemented. During the 1980s and 1990s public attitudes towards the state appear to have been mixed. On the one hand, 'Finns are a people very loyal to the state, who see change as a governmental process rather than a grass root level reform of the society'

(Centre for Finnish Business and Policy Studies, 1996, p. 2). The radically anti-state attitudes which are common in the USA are rare in the Nordic countries. On the other hand, there have been a limited number of instances where popular discontent has been manifested over specific aspects of the changes—for example, over the closure of some small rural post offices and the substitution of postal counters in local shops. Senior officials are aware of the dangers of loss of legitimacy (Holkeri and Nurmi, 2002), and some of them believe that administrative modernization, including improvements in the quality of services, openness to greater citizen participation, and visible efficiency will help contribute to sustaining political stability and trust (see, e.g. *High Quality Services, Good Governance and a Responsible Civic Society*).

H. Party political ideas

Party political ideas per se have not had a big influence on public management reform in Finland. On the contrary, reforms have been mainly the work of a fairly small elite of senior civil servants and a few politicians. Media interest in the reforms has not been particularly strong either (Ministry of Finance, 1997, pp. 73 and 81). Finland did not experience strongly ideological governments with strong views about changing the role of the state in the way that the USA did under President Reagan or the UK under Prime Minister Thatcher.

I. Chance events

The collapse of the Soviet Union at the beginning of the 1990s had a significant, if indirect influence on public management reform. By triggering economic crisis it strengthened the hand of reformers, particularly with respect to budgetary reform (e.g. the rapid implementation of frame budgeting was seen as a vital part of regaining control of public spending). But most of the reforms (e.g. results-oriented budgeting) were already firmly on the agenda, before the economic downturn. The effects of GEC of 2008 could well be similar—to accelerate the implementation of ideas already in currency.

J. Elite decision-making

The process by which the first major Finnish reforms came into being from the late 1980s was quite long drawn-out and cautious. It was not a matter of a few individuals passionately advocating specific 'solutions' (which would be unusual anyway within the Finnish politico-administrative culture), but rather the gradual, consensual formation of a set of proposals for streamlining the state apparatus and, after 1991, for restraining expenditures in response to the sudden economic downturn. Within this process some central themes were the lightening of the bureaucratic 'weight' of central government (especially by reforming the national-level agencies), a shift from input budgeting to a stronger focus on results, a parallel shift to frame (block) budgeting for central transfers to municipalities, and a commitment to service quality improvement and some measure of decentralization.

From the late 1990s there was discussion among senior civil servants about the possibility of a second wave of reform. This would involve a fairly comprehensive restructuring of central government into different relational categories (e.g. organizations where the government was principally exercising the interests of an owner, organizations where the government's interest was as a direct service provider, and so on). This then became coupled to a wider agenda, embracing improved steering by ministries, e-governance, and strengthened citizen participation. Under the second Lipponen administration (1999–2003) ministers again became more directly and actively interested in management reform, especially the strengthening of the Prime Minister's Office and the improvement of horizontal coordination between ministries. This theme of horizontal coordination and the development of a stronger strategic ('whole-of-government') capability continued under the Centre Party governments of 2003–10.

K. The administrative system

For many years Finland, like Sweden, had an administrative system consisting of ministries, national-level boards (agencies) with considerable powers of rule-making and detailed intervention, and a municipal level. However, in the mid 1990s the agency level was subject to reform, shrinking its size and numbers and reorienting its role away from detailed regulation (Ministry of Finance, 1995, pp. 1–2—see also Section L below). It should be noted that, although this account is focused principally on the central state, local (municipal) government employs roughly three-quarters of the public sector workforce.

The population of central ministries has been fairly stable over the past two decades. In the 1990s there were twelve ministries and the Prime Minister's Office, which itself has the status of a ministry (Prime Minister's Office and Ministries, 1995). In 2008 the Ministries of Trade and Industry and Labour were merged to create a Ministry of Employment and the Economy (MEE). The Ministries of Finance and the Interior are the two with the most important responsibilities for administrative reform. In 2008 sections of the Ministry of the Interior with responsibility for regional and local administration and municipal IT were transferred to the Ministry of Finance. The latter has a budget side and a governance side.

Traditionally, each ministry has independent responsibility for implementation and control of laws and policies within their own sphere so, although the Ministry of Finance may be, in some general sense, the most powerful ministry, it usually cannot impose its own programmes on other ministries to the degree that has occasionally been possible in more centralized systems such as that in France, New Zealand, or the UK. However, by the beginning of the new century concern about this relative lack of coordination was growing, and a major report drew attention to the need for better integration across government (Bouckaert, Ormond, and Peters, 2000). A strengthening of the Prime Minister's Office, especially but not exclusively with respect to EU coordination, was one consequence of this debate. The theme of a need for greater 'horizontality' continued through to the time of writing, although the 2010 OECD report on Finland indicated that the ministerial 'silos' were still strong.

There is a career civil service, and political and 'mandarin' careers are usually separate. However, some of the top three levels of civil service appointment used to go to known sympathizers with particular political parties, according to a kind of informal 'quota' system (Tiihonen, 1996, p. 40). Since 2005 there have also been a number of 'political state secretaries' who were appointed only for the same duration as the minister, and who helped him or her in policy preparation. The permanent secretaries, however, remained the administrative heads of the ministries. Not all ministers had political state secretaries (9 out of 18 in 2005).

In the past, senior Finnish civil servants were mainly lawyers, but this balance has shifted over the past generation, with more people with a training in economics or the social sciences being recruited into senior posts. Public management reform has been mainly an 'insider' process, with senior civil servants playing a crucial role. External consultants, although used for certain purposes, have not been as influential as in, say, the UK or the USA (Ministry of Finance, 1997, p. 74).

L. The contents of the reform package

There was much internal discussion of reform during the early and mid 1980s, but the first major initiatives came with the arrival in office of the Holkeri government in 1987. The subsequent decade was then a busy one, with several main lines of reform unfolding simultaneously or in sequence. The three changes of government (1991, 1995, and 1999) did not appear to make any dramatic difference to the general thrust of the reforms, although possibly it could be said that the level of political interest in management reform (never overwhelmingly high among the majority of politicians) declined somewhat after 1994, but then revived from the beginning of the second Lipponen administration in 1999.

The main lines of the first wave of reform were as follows (See the pamphlet *Government Decision in Principle on Reforms in Central and Regional Government*, 1993):

- Results-oriented budgeting was piloted from 1987 and rolled out to the whole government from 1994. This required a number of potentially important changes, including the definition of results indicators for agencies (to enable their performance to be assessed more explicitly by their 'parent' ministries) and the creation of unified running costs budgets for ministries and agencies. The pilot projects appeared to show that significant running cost savings could be achieved, but that some ministries were slow to take up the challenge of using indicators as an active form of performance management (Summa, 1995).
- An Administrative Development Agency (later retitled the Finnish Institute of Public Management) was set up in 1987 to provide training and consultancy to support reform. The Agency/ Institute has been obliged to operate along increasingly commercial/self-financing lines. An attempt to sell it off during the late 1990s/early 2000s failed, and at the time of writing it continues as a state-owned company.

- The transformation of a number of agencies with commercial functions into, first, State Enterprises (twelve were created 1989–97) and then, subsequently and in some cases, State-Owned Companies. The law enabling the creation of State Enterprises was passed in 1988. The further transformation to state-owned joint stock companies included Post and Telecommunications and Railways.
- The introduction from 1993 of a framework budgeting system to control central government aid to municipalities. This was partly a decentralization measure, aimed at reducing the amount of detailed central intervention in municipal decision-making, but it was also a way of gaining firm control of the *totals* of municipal spending at a time of great budgetary pressure, and of delegating painful decisions about spending priorities down to municipal leaders. The total aid going to a given municipality was henceforth calculated as a lump sum based on the values taken by certain indicators, such as the number and age structure of the population. Later, framework management was developed into 'a central procedure steering the preparation of the State budget by the government' (*High Quality Services, Good Governance and a Responsible Civic Society*, 1998a, p. 10).
- A restructuring of the central agencies. This was also a decentralization measure. The agencies with commercial functions were turned into State Enterprises (see above). Others were merged or downsized, and their role was changed from that of regulation to one of providing research and development and evaluation to the ministries. Their internal governance structures were also changed—usually away from collegial forms towards more managerial and/or monocratic arrangements.
- Government data collection was streamlined and barriers to data transfer between different parts of the state were reduced.
- Regional state administration unified and lightened. The offices of different ministries at regional level were combined.
- Human Resource Management reforms, including provision for performance-related pay and for more decentralized management of staff. The main decisions and announcements here were made during the Aho administration (1991–5) but subsequent implementation was very slow.
- In 1998 it was announced that 'The quality as well as the citizen- and customer-orientation of

the services will be developed by means of a new type of Service Charters to be given to the customers' [sic] (*High Quality Services, Good Governance and a Responsible Civic Society*, 1998a, p. 15).

Thus the balance of the reforms leant towards decentralization, simplification, and tighter control of spending (Ministry of Finance, 1993; Puoskari, 1996). There was no great enthusiasm for widespread privatization, although the Finnish governments were quite prepared to privatize selectively, when it seemed to make sense on its own terms (e.g. the government printing company).

In the late 1990s a second wave of reform began. Considerable emphasis was placed on improving the quality of public services, and on encouraging citizen participation (Holkeri and Nurmi, 2002). To support this and other goals, a sophisticated national electronic portal on the public sector was developed and opened in 2002 (Romakkaniemi, 2001). There was also an attempt to tidy up some of the 'unfinished business' from the first wave of reforms, particularly the slowness of ministries to engage in active, performance-oriented steering of their agencies (Joustie, 2001). This had become a hardy perennial—some ministries gave little priority to performance measures, and there seemed to be no incentives for many managers to take them seriously. For example, in 2003 an audit indicated that only 9 per cent of agencies had approved productivity targets (Ministry of Finance, 2006, p. 22). A budget decree in 2004 emphasized the requirement of target setting and performance accounting, but it is not clear how fundamental the changes flowing from this were. In 2010 the OECD review still found a significant disconnect between budgeting and strategy, as did the Finnish National Audit Office (OECD, 2010; Pöysti, 2010). A new variant of this old problem has gained prominence because of the need to set targets for 'horizontal', joined-up programmes (see next paragraph).

A strongly emerging theme from the early 2000s was the need for better horizontal coordination, and for a 'whole-of-government approach'. The strategy-forming machinery in the Prime Minister's department was reinforced, and a number of studies of future challenges (population change, new technologies etc.) were carried out. (Finland began producing an annual Government Foresight Report for parliament as early as 1993.) Yet all this forecasting and planning and reporting evidently did not translate easily into action. In 2010 the OECD review concluded that: 'The government's whole-of-government vision is not being realized at the operational level' (OECD, 2010, p. 15). The Auditor General put it more bluntly: 'The Government's Strategy Document is not a genuine strategy' (Pöysti, 2010, p. 3).

M. The implementation process

Overall, the implementation process has been gradual and deliberate, with pilot projects and extensive training programmes to ensure the smoothest possible implementation. One does not get the sense of the hectic pace and urgency which prevailed during, say, 1986–92 in New Zealand or 1987–92 in the UK. Consider, for example, the introduction of performance-related pay. Legislation made this possible from the mid 1990s, but by 2004 only a minority of civil servants were in a PRP system (Ministry of Finance, 2006, p. 106). By 2010 PRP was theoretically in place for 100 per cent of government agencies, but there seems to be little information about its effects in practice. Unless there is slack in the budget (less and less likely since the GEC) it is hard to offer significant bonuses. And, in any case, the PRP has been introduced by separate collective bargaining at each agency, so the details of the schemes vary from one organization to the next.

At the highest level, the coordination of the reform programme was ensured by the creation of a ministerial committee on which all the main political parties in government were represented (Ministry of Finance, 1997, p. 69). Stability was also enhanced by the long-term participation of a small number of senior civil servants from the Ministry of Finance and the Ministry of the Interior. One Finnish commentator went so far as to term the Finnish approach 'technocratic' (Puoskari, 1996, p. 105).

The shift from a Social Democratic-led coalition (1995–2003) to a Centre Party–led coalition (2003–present) did not fundamentally alter the way in which public management reforms were shaped and implemented. The process remained, by, say, UK or French standards, a collective and relatively gentle one.

N. Reforms actually achieved

The reforms mentioned above (Section L) were all 'achieved', in the sense that relevant legislation was passed and new procedures were put in place. What is harder to determine is how vigorously the originally announced aims of the reforms were pursued, and how far they were eventually realized. In some cases (e.g. corporatization of former agencies into enterprises and then state-owned companies), change was undeniable and quite rapid. In others (e.g. the introduction of a new personnel regime into the public service), legislation has been passed, but the implementation seems to have been fairly slow. For example, a new system of job classification and payment by results was first introduced in the mid 1980s, but by 1997 covered only about 5 per cent of state employees (Ministry of Finance, 1997, p. 78). It is also clear that persuading ministries and agencies to adopt the spirit as well as the letter of results-oriented steering has been a fairly long drawn-out business and that, more recently, whole-of-government strategy-making has not penetrated far down the line into operational matters.

The number of personnel financed directly through the state budget fell by about 40 per cent (from 213,000 to 130,000) between 1989 and 1995 (thanks partly to the creation of off-budget state enterprises and companies, which accounted for about 54,000 of the reductions). Since 1995 it has continued at the lower level, and plans for the future are to replace only one in every two civil servants who retire.

At an early stage, the Finnish government supported a programme of evaluations of its reforms (Holkeri and Summa, 1996). It is not clear that these evaluations (for an example, see Pollitt et al., 1997 and Ministry of Finance, 1997) have had any clear and direct effect on subsequent decisions, but the evaluation function has now been firmly established in Finland as an ongoing component of modern public management (see, e.g. Ministry of Finance, 2006, pp. 115–29).

An interesting reflection on the major reforms of the 1987–97 period appeared in the 1998 Government Resolution *High Quality Services, Good Governance and a Responsible Civic Society* (1998a):

earlier administrative reforms have been experienced to have increased the bureaucracy of administration. The Government wants to ensure the democratic development of the policy of governance . . . On all administrative levels, the real possibilities of the citizen to influence matters as well as openness and transparency of administration will be increased. (p. 8)

In subsequent years this theme was intensified, and became one of the main dimensions of reform (Holkeri and Nurmi, 2002; Romakkaniemi, 2001).

Finally, we should mention the major OECD assessment of Finland's system of governance, published in 2010 (OECD, 2010). This acknowledged that Finland was basically a very well-governed country—one which frequently came at or near the top of international league tables for education, health care, e-government, and so on. At the same time, however, the OECD concluded that there were rigidities in the system that could hamper Finland in tackling the future challenges of demographic change, globalization, etc. In particular, the OECD was of the view that:

While the government has put much effort into strategic planning, its ability for collective commitment to a shared vision is hampered by a lack of horizontal collaboration in the development and translation of strategic priorities. (OECD, 2010, p.15)

Key Events—Finland

Period	General	Organization	Personnel	Finance
1980–5	Prime Minister Sorsa (Centre) 1983–7			
1986–90	Prime Minister Holkeri (Conservative) 1987–91 1988 First general reform programme	1987 Ministry of the Environment created 1987 Administrative Development Agency created From 1990: some agencies turned into public enterprises, including the railways and posts and telecommunications	1990 Faced with economic crisis government decides to leave 10% of government posts unfilled	1990 Frame budgeting announced
1991–5	Prime Minister Aho (Centre) 1991–5 Prime Minister Lipponen (Social Democrat) 1995–2003 1995 Finland becomes a member of the EU	A number of public enterprises are converted into joint stock companies. By 1995 there were 12 public enterprises and 15 public companies 1995 Administrative Development Agency becomes Finnish Institute of Public Management	1994 State Civil Servants Act. Brings terms closer to private sector conditions, although still under public law. Introduces possibility of performance-related pay	1991 12 agencies in pilot for results-oriented budgeting 1993 move to block grant financing of municipalities 1995 All agencies supposed to move to performance budgeting
1996–2000	1997 Governance project	11 provinces reduced to 5 1996 110 'one stop shops' 1998 quality strategy for public services, including public service charters (see *High Quality Services*, 1998) 2000 First national quality conference. More state activities are put into the form of joint stock companies	Slow spread of performance-related pay schemes 2000 Personnel 'barometer' introduced, and an annual reporting system on human resources	1997 Further reform of the state grant system 1998 statutory annual reports for ministries 1998 accruals accounting introduced for agencies
2001–5	Prime Minister Jäätteenmäki (Centre)—resigned after a few months because of scandal Prime Minister Vanhanen (Centre) 2003–10		2005 Pensions reform—similar pensions to the private sector 2005 Role of political state secretaries defined in law	2004 Government decision to strengthen performance management and management accounting
2006–10	2010 OECD public governance review of Finland (OECD, 2010)	2007 ALKU—programme for clarifying the role of regional level state administrations 2008 Merger of ministries of Trade and Industry and Employment, which became the Ministry	2009 Aftermath of GEC leads to freezing of civil service salaries and appointments. 2010 State universities become independent legal persons, employing their own staff	Continuing efforts to bring strategy and budgeting closer together, although the OECD review of

(continued)

Continued

Period	General	Organization	Personnel	Finance
	Prime Minister Kiviniemi (Centre) 2010–11	of Employment and the Economy (MEE) 2009 merger of agencies to produce the National Supervisory Authority Welfare and Health (Valvira) 2009 SADe programme for providing integrated services to citizens and businesses 2010 Six transport agencies were merged into two—the Transport Agency and the Transport Safety Agency		2010 suggested this had not yet succeeded

FRANCE

A. Socio-economic forces: general

For general background, see Appendix A. France is a large country (population 62.8 million in 2010) in a central position in the most economically advanced part of Europe.

B. Global economic forces

Again, see Appendix A for background.

Economic globalization brought increasing pressure upon the previous system of state-directed 'sectoral corporatism' (Jobert and Muller, 1987). In consequence there has been 'a more general loss of centrality of the state in social mediation and public policy' (Clark, 1998, p. 101). However, even if a number of major state companies have been privatized, the French state keeps significant minority shareholdings in Renault, SNECMA, Air France-KLM, EADS, and France Telecom. It also exercises substantial continuing state control in EDF (Electricité de France) and GDF (Gaz de France). Successive governments have been seen to have had very limited success in solving the problem of high unemployment (well over 10% for most of the 1990s, and back to that figure in 2010).

C. Sociodemographic change

See Appendix A.

D. National socio-economic policies

Traditionally France has sought a somewhat greater degree of state control over its economy than either Germany or the UK. This stance has come under increasing strain as the forces of economic globalization appear to have favoured more open, competitive economies, and as the EU has promulgated common fiscal rules for members of the eurozone (Jobert and Mueller, 1987). The continued failure to 'solve' France's fiscal deficit was an important factor behind the most important management reform of the 2000s—LOLF (see below).

E. The political system

The French political system is distinctive, belonging fully neither to the 'majoritarian' camp with the UK and Australasia nor to the consensual systems which prevail in the Netherlands and the Nordic countries (see Chapter 3). Elections are according to plurality and cabinets are usually one-party or a minimal coalition, but these majoritarian features are offset by the existence of a multi-party system and a strong, directly elected presidency.

During the period since 1980 there has been a fairly frequent alternation of the parties in office, with these sometimes matching the party identification of the president but sometimes not (the periods of *cohabitation*, as with the Chirac government under President Mitterand, 1986–8, the Baladur government, also under Mitterand, 1993–5 and the Jospin government under President Chirac, 1997–2002). Obviously, all things being equal, a President is stronger when his own party also forms the government (e.g. under President Chirac, 2002–7). Under Sarkozy (2007–), the presidentiality of the French political system seems to have become even stronger.

F. New management ideas

France has often been regarded as a country that has been quite resistant to the NPM ideas which emerged from the UK, the USA, and Australasia from the early 1980s. France has continued its own, distinctive thinking and rhetoric about administrative reform, centred on the themes of modernization and decentralization. However, during the 1980s there was a shift towards neoliberal ideas within the elite at the Ministry of Finance, albeit in the form of favouring the modernization of the public sector through private sector methods, rather than maximum privatization or the 'hollowing out' of the state (Clark, 1998, p. 103). The contractualization of public services, stressed as a key component of Prime Minister Juppé's 1995 circular *Reforme de l'Etat et des services publics*, was a reflection of this tendency. From the beginning of the twenty-first century 'managerialist' flavours strengthened further, first as Chirac escaped from *cohabitation* in 2002, and later even more, when the self-proclaimed 'modernizer', Sarkozy, became president in 2007. Meanwhile, quietly and incrementally, NPM-type ideas had gained ground within the Ministry of Finance and some other departments (Bezes,

2010). Two significant indicators demonstrate a shift towards new sources of ideas—first, that the position and the numbers of the elite 'corps' have decreased, and, second that the visibility of consultancy firms has increased.

G. Pressure from citizens

Most political scientists have regarded France as traditionally a state-centred system, where the intensity and variety of pressure-group activity has tended to be moderate in comparison with, say, the USA or the UK. The system has tended to sectoral corporatism rather than active pluralism, that is, governments have done deals with a smaller number of peak associations (big employers, big unions), rather than being particularly permeable to a wider range of interest or issue groups. Such deals have been facilitated by the frequency with which members of the *grands corps* move between government and business positions (*pantouflage*). Certainly, in respect of public management reform, the pressures from the citizenry in general appear to have been limited. Nevertheless, there has been a general decline in public confidence in the French system, and some popular critiques of the rigidity of some public services and of the corruption and remoteness of some of the state elite.

Societal tensions on, for example, safety, urban development, and migration resulted in a significant protest vote for a far-right candidate during the first round of the presidential elections in 2002. The 2010 pension reform (which shifted the actual pension age from 60 to 62 and the legal one from 65 to 67) is only the most recent reform attempt that has been resisted by large-scale demonstrations and strikes.

H. Party political ideas

In France neo-liberalism has been embraced by the right (especially when Chirac was prime minister, 1986–8) but has been interpreted in a managerial rather than a doctrinaire, anti-state fashion. This has meant that the 'modernization' theme was also acceptable (with some changes in the 'filling') by governments of the left. The public service 'renewal' programme of 1989–93 was negotiated with, and broadly supported by, the public service unions. However, left and right parted company over the desirability of reforms to social security

and central personnel regulation, where the right's attempts to push through changes sparked major public service strikes during 1995 (Howard, 1998). Also education reform was high on the agenda, causing major strikes in 2002. In the later stages of Chirac's presidency (2002–7) and under Sarkozy (2007–) market-favouring ideas steadily gained ground. However, once the global economic crisis broke in 2008, Sarkozy's rhetoric shifted to reaffirm the importance of the state, and the dangers of allowing markets to be deregulated.

I. Change events

On one view, the emergence of various cases of corruption could be viewed as chance events which have contributed to a crisis of confidence in 'an elite that had discredited itself' (Howard, 1998, p. 201). From another perspective, however, these cases are not so much one-off, chance events as 'business as usual' within a system in which certain forms of corruption and 'croneyism' had become endemic.

J. Elite decision-making

This general loss of perceived legitimacy has been a factor in encouraging the elite to launch such initiatives as the public service charter (Ministère de la Function Publique et des Réformes Administratives, 1992) and the *L'année de l'accueil dans les service publics* (Ministère de la Fonction Publique, 1994). During the French presidency of the EU (2000) there was an explicit focus on 'the public service: the social dialogue as a contribution to improvement'.

The limited move towards neo-liberal ideas as a basis for modernization has been mentioned above. There has been a widely shared desire to rehabilitate the reputation of the state apparatus, but differences as to how this might best be done. One line of tension is between the central politico-administrative elite (*Inspections des Finances, Cour des Comptes, Conseil d'Etat*) and the growing autonomy of the field services of ministries and the regional and local authorities.

The division of opinion here is perhaps between those who still believe that technocratic reforms, imposed by the centre, can ultimately succeed, and those who argue for a new and more inclusive form of political action. One view is that:

The strikes of 1995 made clear what should have been evident: France cannot be reformed by decree. Technocratic solutions, however well conceived, are not possible in modern, individualist democracies. (Howard, 1998, p. 216)

What has been noticeable, however, is not only that 'Anglo-Saxon' NPM ideas have been extensively remodelled and relabelled for use in France, but that the power struggles and debates over these 'new' ideas have played out very much within the usual elite networks (Bezes, 2007; Eymeri-Douzans, 2009). After 2002, however, private sector consultants begin to form an increasing presence in reform debates and reform planning. It is not yet clear whether, in the longer term, they will become a major player in state reform.

K. Administrative system

France has possessed a strong administrative tradition since at least Napoleonic times. Five main features of the system as it existed in the late 1970s may be noted (Clark, 1998, pp. 98–100):

- A tradition of state direction of the economy and society (*dirigisme*). As indicated above, this has weakened, but is still more salient than in, say, Germany or the UK.
- Centralized direction of the state apparatus by two sets of *grands corps*. The first set are administrative and comprise the *Inspection des Finances* (a kind of financial inspectorate), the *Conseil d'Etat* (the Council of State—a supreme administrative court) and the *Cour des Comptes* (the national audit office). This group recruit their members (*Enarques*) from the prestigious *Ecole Nationale d'Administration* (ENA). The second set are technical (e.g. *Ponts et Chaussées*) and recruit from the *Ecole Polytechnique* via various *Grandes Ecoles*. Members of the *grands corps* enjoy highly mobile careers and frequently take up top executive positions in the private sector or, indeed, in politics. For example, up to 1993, eight of the previous eleven prime ministers had been civil servants. And between 1997 and 2002 the president, the prime minister, and the ministers for finance and economic growth, foreign affairs, defence and the interior, justice, social affairs and employment, and the civil service were all *Enarques*! This elite group has long had 'low permeability' to 'outsiders' (Bezes, 2010).
- A strong central presence subnationally through the presence of a *préfet* (prefect) and many local

units of central ministries (deconcentrated State services) in each *département* and region. The prefect coordinates the deconcentrated State services and also has, since 1982, a steering authority. He/she is the representative of central government and used to hold a direct supervisory authority (*tutelle*) on the budgets of the local authorities. In 1982, prefects lost the direct supervisory authority over local administrative decisions. Since then regional and local authorities have gained a good deal of independence, although prefects have also moved to try to make the deconcentrated services they control technically indispensable to local authorities. The authority and determining position of the Regional Prefectures over the Departmental Prefectures was confirmed by a decree in February 2010. Since the regional prefects are (according to the LOLF) also regional budget holders, potentially they become strongholds for the reform of the territorial state.

- Division of the civil service into a large number of *corps* (1,800 at the end of the 1980s) each with its own educational entry requirements and its own set of hierarchically arranged posts, defined by a general civil service law, and its own professional *esprit*. This feature of the French administrative system has proved a source of considerable rigidity and resistance in the context of management reform. By 2010, however, the political and administrative position of the 'corps' seems to be in decline.
- The importance of a special body of administrative law in regulating administrative procedures and appointments. The French system 'is a "legal model" in the sense that it is regulated by legal rules which conceive the state administration as inhabiting an autonomous domain apart from civil society' (Clark, 1998, p. 100). The 'weight of legal entrenchment' (Bezes, 2010, p. 160) has usually acted as a break on management reform.

Each of these five features has come under strain during the last twenty years, but the modernization process thus far has probably made greater impact on the first and third than the other three.

L. Contents of the reform package

Initially, there was no one, single package that lasted for very long, but rather a series of separate initiatives by different governments which could, at best, be said to be grouped around certain broad themes. The two most prominent were, first, decentralization and deconcentration and, second, modernization. The strategic shift towards decentralization came in the mid 1980s, when the socialist government under President Mitterand removed the prefects' *tutelle* and created local collectivities as autonomous authorities. Direct elections were established for regional councils, and legislation during 1982 gave local collectivities significant new taxing and budget-making powers. The ripples spreading out from this deep change have continued through to the present (de Montricher, 1996), and have been amplified by the effects of EU regional policies: 'Decentralization seems to be a never-ending story in the French context' (Bezes, 2010, p. 166). The 'deconcentration charter' of 1992 marked a further step in shifting authority from the centre to the periphery. In the French context:

decentralisation means transfer of authority from the central state to regional and local governments. Deconcentration means devolution of competence and managerial authority to the local administrative units of central government . . . as well as the agencies. (OECD, 1997, p. 67)

Autonomy in personnel management, in budget management, and for administrative decisions has been transferred to the deconcentrated states services and the prefects. The main purpose was the promotion of a better policy coordination at the deconcentrated level (Albertini, 1998, pp. 145–56). Initiatives have been taken and new policy instruments have been introduced for a better *interministérialité*: extension of the coordination's mission of the prefects (1999), creation of a college of the *chefs de service* (directors of a deconcentrated state service), creation of discussion platforms between deconcentrated state services (*pôles de compétences*), introduction of a strategic approach at the regional level (1999), etc. In 1997, management autonomy was given to several national management support services by the creation of a new kind of internal agency: the Services of National Scope.

The second theme—modernization—came to prominence under Prime Minister Rocard in 1989, although earlier discussions and initiatives had occurred throughout the 1980s. In February 1989 Rocard issued an important circular entitled *Renouveau du service public* which contained a series of initiatives: the creation of responsibility centres (*Centres de responsabilité*—CDRs) within ministries,

personnel reforms, greater emphasis on decentralized management of field services and responsiveness to public service users, and the institutionalization of policy evaluation across many sectors of government. Renewal—or modernization—continued under the succeeding Cresson and Bérégovoy governments. In 1995 Prime Minister Juppé issued a circular, *Réforme de l'Etat et des services publics*, which proposed the reorganization of certain field services and an experiment in contractualizing the relationship between central ministries and their field services. The Jospin government set up several objectives on the second step of the *Réforme de l'Etat* (1997–2002): permanent evaluation of public policy, modernization of the deconcentrated level, modernization of the prefect's tasks, introduction of the strategic management, better transparency in public administration, better responsiveness to citizens' wishes and demands, and e-government. Thus 'the successive phases of "administrative modernization" have been characterized by a broad continuity of policy, rather than by partisan differences between governments of the Left and the Right' (Clark, 1998, pp. 106–7; Cole and Jones, 2005).

A third theme—one characterized by much greater divergence between the parties which held power—was that of privatization. During the period of the socialist government of 1981–6 extensive nationalizations were carried though (exactly the opposite of the trend which was beginning to develop in the UK). However, the neo-liberal government of Chirac (1986–8) reversed this, listing sixty-five companies that were to be sold off. During a relatively short period in office nearly 300,000 industrial workers and 100,000 bank staff were 'privatized' (Wright, 1989, p. 105). This flurry came to an end with the return of left governments in 1988, but when the right regained power in 1993, significant privatization resumed (e.g. steel in 1995). Despite, the left-wing label, the Jospin government sold assets of public companies (e.g. *Crédit Lyonnais* and *France Telecom*) to the private sector. However, the critics inside the socialist party after the presidential election in 2002 showed that a majority of the left political world remained opposed to further privatizations. In 2005 Electricité de France, said to be the world's largest utility company, was partially floated on the stock exchange. However, the state retained more than 80 per cent of the shares. Overall, the period since 1980 has seen a significant fall in the public sector's share of the French labour force.

In 2001 the *Loi Organique relative aux Lois de Finances* (LOLF) introduced programme budgeting and a connected system of performance indicators (the whole package was supposed to be implemented by 2006). Initially the budget was divided into 34 missions and 168 programmes. LOLF was a framework law or constitutional by-law, the passage of which required extensive agreement between legislature, executive, and presidency during a period of *cohabitation*, and was widely regarded as something of a miracle (Corbett, 2010). It 'triggered a process of managerialization' (Ongaro, 2009, p. 204). It also represented a systematization or 'roll out' of various reform tendencies that had been emerging since the early 1990s (Bezes, 2007). LOLF was initially focused on improving the executive's budgetary accountability to the legislature, but in practice it also became a vehicle for internal changes which devolved budgetary responsibility within a strengthened managerial hierarchy (Bezes, 2010).

From about 2000 on, three reform movements, initially disconnected, seem to have developed in a converging and mutually strengthening direction (see also Bouckaert et al., 2010, Chapter 9). First, came the LOLF (2001), which revamped the financial steering, control, and potential evaluation from a vast number of single line items to a limited number of missions and programmes. Second, was the RGPP (2007) which combined a presidentially guided policy review agenda with tough savings, and ultimately also a ministerial restructuring focused on efficiency and productivity. Third, has come the territorial reform of the French state, where regions were created and the regional prefect has the leading and coordinating capacity for deconcentrated, regional, and departmental activities. Decrees from 1964 and 1982 were replaced by the decree of 2004 and the crucial one of 2010. This resulted in reshuffled regional prefectures that establish strategic plans, but also in one-stop-shops and multitasking administrations. Ultimately, the LOLF (missions/programmes and budget holders) facilitates the horizontal and vertical logic of restructuring organizations (merging ministries and regional prefectural departments) and their activities, which are then reviewed by the RGPP.

M. Implementation process

The French reforms have been implemented in a fairly piecemeal way, with different initiatives coming from different ministries at different times, and a good deal of successive 're-packaging' of some basically similar ideas (e.g. about being more responsive to citizen-users). For example, CDRs were pushed much further in some ministries than in others (Trosa, 1995). However, the *grands corps* appear to have remained in control of most of the changes (at least until very recently— see Eymeri-Douzans, 2009), and their central roles have not been seriously undermined (Corbett, 2010; Rouban, 1996, pp. 154–5).

Prime ministers have often played a leading role in reforms, especially Chirac, Rocard, Juppé, and Jospin. The procedural device of the circular has been much resorted to. The ministries most heavily involved have been the Ministry of Public Service (which has undergone several changes of name), the Ministry of Finance, and the Ministry of the Interior (patron ministry for the prefects, and heavily involved in decentralizatiuon and deconcentration reforms). From 2008 the merged and enlarged Ministry of Budget, Public Accounts, and Civil Administration, and the mega Ministry MEEDDAT (Environment, Energy, Sustainable Development, and Planning), have clearly become dominant forces.

In practice it seems that reform implementation has often moved more smoothly and quickly in technical ministries and field services than elsewhere (Cole and Jones, 2005).

N. Reforms actually achieved

Despite the construction, after 1989, of an elaborate network of evaluation institutions (Duran, Monnier, and Smith, 1995), there seems to have been no across-the-board systematic evaluation of French management reforms. There have, however, been some assessments of particular aspects, for example the 1996 *Cour des Comptes* report on CDRs, the 2002 Ministry of Public Service report on the Public Establishments (external agencies), and the 2002 Interministerial Delegation on the Reform of the State report on the contractualization, and the 2003 Court of Audit report on administrative deconcentration and the reform of the state (Cour des Comptes, 2003).

Less formal assessments have been made by some academics (e.g. Bezes, 2010; Clark, 1998; de Montricher, 1996; Flynn and Strehl, 1996; Rouban, 1996) and by some officials (Trosa, 1995, 1996). In general, it might be said that outcome data is hard to come by, but that, thematically,

French governments have held more closely to the values of a strong administrative state committed to some form of strategic planning than has Australia, New Zealand, or the UK. Significant modernization has taken place, and the decentralization reforms of 1982 seem to have been a genuine political and managerial watershed. The 2002 LOLF reforms aimed at bringing budgeting, accounting, and performance measurement within a single, programmatic framework were also undoubtedly an important step (Bezes, 2010; Corbett, 2010; Trosa, 2002—see below for details). However, much of the machinery of a centralized civil service remains fundamentally unaltered. In particular, centralized control of personnel still survives. Partly because of these constraints, the experiments with organizational diversity and user-responsiveness, though certainly substantial, have been somewhat less pervasive than in Australasia or the UK.

Key Events—France

	General	Organization	Personnel	Finance
1980–5	1981 Mitterand President (Socialist) 1981 Mauroy, PM (Socialist) 1984 Fabius PM (Socialist)	1981–2 Nationalization of 7 industrial groups, 39 banks, and 2 financial groups 1982 Decentralization Acts	1981–3 Creation of 82,000 new jobs in the public sector	
1986–90	1986 First elections of regional councils 1986 Chirac Prime Minister (Conservative) *co-habitation* till 1988. 1988 Mitterand President (Soc.) 1988 Rocard PM (Socialist)	1986–7 First privatization wave 1990 200 service projects 1990 60 centres of responsibility 1990 Reform of Post and Telecom starts	1984–6 Elimination of 12,000 public sector jobs. 1986–8 Elimination of 33,000 public sector jobs	1988 Circular on government working methods introducing cost-effectiveness
1991–5	1991 Cresson Prime Minister (Socialist) 1992 Bérégovoy PM (Socialist) 1992 Act on regional administration 1993 Balladur Prime Minister (Conservative) till 1995 1995 Chirac President (Conservative) 1995 Juppé PM (Conservative)	1990–3 Opening of public companies to private investors 1991 Interministerial Committee on Evaluation 1991 Interministerial Committee for Territorial Administration (CIATER) 1993 second wave of privatization 1991 470 service projects 1991 PTT transformed into two independent public companies 1992 Deconcentation Charter 1992 127 centres of responsibility 1993 Committee for Reorganization and Deconcentration 1995 Interministerial Committee for State Reform and State Reform Commission 1993 Report Picq on efficiency of the state	1991 Committee for Renewal of the Public Service 1994 Circular on management of state employees for deconcentrated services	1995 Pilot on deconcentration of financial control of deconcentrated spending
1996–2000	1997 Jospin PM (Socialist) *cohabitation* till 2002 1998 Santel report on deconcentration	1996 Cour des Comptes report on responsibility centres 1996 All prefectures become responsibility centres 1997 Balladur launches TQM 1998 State Reform Commissionreplaced by General Direction of the Administration and Civil Service 1998 Multiannual Programme of Modernization 1998 and 1999: Third privatization waves (by Jospin) 1999 Interministerial Delegation for State Reform (DIRE) replaces State Reform Commission and the Sub-Directorate for modernization of the General Directorate for Administration and Public Service (GDAFP) 2000 E-Gov is objective of State Reform	2000 Limited introduction of the 35-hour week in the public sector	2000 Failed attempt to merge tax assessment and tax collection

(continued)

Continued

	General	Organization	Personnel	Finance
2001–5	2001 Mauroy report on decentralization 2002 Chirac President (Conservative) 2002 Raffarin Prime Minister (Conservative) 2005 de Villepin Prime Minister (Conservative) 2002 proportion of cabinet members with ENA degrees has fallen from 33% (1960s) to 15%	2001 Establishment of the Institut de la Gestion Publique et du Développement Economique (Ministry of Economic Affairs, Finance, and Industry) 2001 Carcenac report on e-government 2003 Cour des Comptes report on mixed effects of performance contracts 2003 Health care reform 2005 Creation of a Directorate General for State Modernization within the Ministry of Finance. This merged the Directorate for Budgetary Reform with three offices previously attached to the Prime Minister—the Office for Modernization of Public Management and State Structures, the Office for Service Users and Administrative Simplification and the Electronic Administration Development Agency. This was therefore a strengthening of the hand of the Ministry of Finance (Bezes, 2007, p. 87). With 68 contract staff out of a total of 115 A grades it also became a channel for consultants from the private sector firms to get involved in state reform (Eymeri-Douzans, 2009)	2003 Strikes because of Raffarin's proposals for public retirement reforms 2003 ENA candidates 1705 for 100 positions (historical high) 2003 Pilot on performance bonuses for senior bureaucrats	2001 Loi Organique relative aux Lois de Finances (LOLF) 2001 Reform of Public Procurement Code
2006–10	2007 Sarkozy President (Conservative) 2007 Fillon PM (Conservative) 2010 Decree (16 February) establishing the authority of regional prefects over departmental ones	2007 RGPP General Review of Public Policies 2007 Merger of Directorate General of Taxation, and Directorate General of Public Accounts (merging also tax assessment and collection) 2008 Large mergers resulting in mega ministries: MINEFI (economy, finance, and industry) with Employment and Civil Servants: Minister of Budget, Public Accounts, and Civil Administration. Also, creation of a Ministry of Immigration, Integration, National Identity, and Co-Development; Creation of MEEDDAT (Ministry of Environment, Energy, Sustainable Development, and Planning) merging four ministries 2008 Dati Reform reducing number of courts from 1190 to 866	2008 Silicani White Paper on the future of the public service	2007 Merger of Directorate General of Taxation (DGI) with Directorate General of Public Accounts (DGCP). The accompanying measures to this large-scale merger of financial administrations were—for several million euros—contracted out to three major consultancy firms 2009 Audit Committee to look at budget reductions (consisting of the spending ministry, Budget and Public Accounts ministry, Presidential Staff, and consultants). 2010 New way of financing universities (activities and performance)

GERMANY

A. Socio-economic forces: general

Germany is by far the biggest and most populous, as well as one of the richest, of the eight European states in this book. See Appendix A.

B. Global economic forces

Again, see Appendix A. Germany is heavily engaged in international trade and is almost alone in Europe in maintaining a large export sector in manufactured goods. It was one of the hardest hit in the early stages of the GEC (see Table A.2) but was subsequently one of the EU economies to recover most rapidly (2009–10).

C. Sociodemographic forces

Although there were some pressures which affected all three levels of German administration (e.g. the huge challenge of integration with the former German Democratic Republic from 1990), many social problems are dealt with mainly by local authorities. These include high rates of unemployment with more people depending on social welfare benefits which are provided by local authorities. Citizens have also become more demanding and more self-confident in their relationship with public services, many of which are provided by local authorities. Local government is therefore under much greater pressure to introduce improved services for citizens. Furthermore, due to increasing competition for production facilities, local authorities are involved in policies of regional economic development, and have to provide new services for business communities (Röber, 1996, p. 175).

One problem for government at all levels has been the high rate of immigration and asylum seeking which Germany has experienced. This has led to racial tensions, especially in some parts of the east. Table A.8 shows that Germany has one of the highest percentages of foreign-born residents in our set of twelve countries.

D. National socio-economic policies

Compared to the EU norm, Germany still has a large manufacturing sector. This results in significant competition with the USA and the Asian countries. Prior to the introduction of the euro in 2001, the German currency, the DM, had been one of the strongest in the world. Monetary policy had been directed by the *Bundesbank* which developed its policy independently from the political executive, and which served as a model for the new European Central Bank. Germany is a country with a strong corporatist tradition, in which firms and banks and trade unions have tended to work closely together. However, Germany's poor economic performance since 2000 brought these arrangements into question. At the time of writing Germany appears to have made the strongest recovery from the GEC in the EU, but some analysts question whether this can be sustained—in which case the pressure for fundamental labour market reforms is likely to return.

E. The political system

The German system is a chancellor model (*Kanzlerdemokratie*), which means that the chancellor is above other ministers and is more than the *primus inter pares*. The president has a primarily symbolic function, unlike the French or even (to a lesser extent) the Finnish president.

At the federal level there are two major parties, the Christian Democratic Union of Germany (CDU/Christian Social Union CSU) and the Social Democratic Party (SPD). Except for the big coalition between CDU/CSU and the SPD from 1966 till 1969, federal politics were dominated by coalitions of CDU/CSU with the small free liberal party (FDP) from 1946 until 1966, and again from 1982 till 1998. There was also a coalition of the SPD with the FDP from 1969 until 1982. At the *Länder* level the SPD and the Greens have formed coalition governments, and in 1998 for the first time they became part of a federal coalition.

The smaller parties are:

• The FDP (Free Democratic Party) which never went beyond 10 per cent of the national vote but has always been important as a coalition partner for either the CDU or the SPD. After the unification of Germany its relative share of votes decreased, because of a lack of programme and leadership.

- The Greens started as a movement and turned into a political party. As a consequence they still have two major tendencies, 'fundamentalists' and 'realists'. The more it becomes feasible to join governments, the more influence the *'realos'* seem to have. The Greens are part of some *Länder* and of the post-1998 federal governments.
- The former communists, the Party of Democratic Socialism PDS (former SED) has gained momentum, especially in former East Germany.

To get into the federal Parliament (*Bundestag*) political parties have to have a minimum of 5 per cent of the votes. This eliminates the smaller parties and sometimes posed problems for the FDP and the Greens. The voting system is mixed. The first vote (*Erststimme*) is majoritarian, and the second vote (*Zweitstimme*) is proportional.

F. New management ideas

The German changes could be characterized more by administrative tightening up and modernization than by marketization or minimization (Derlien, 1998). The German trajectory has also been marked more by incrementalism ('permanent flexibility of institutional frameworks') than by fundamental change (Benz and Götz, 1996, p. 5), and more by improvement of the existing system than an import of other systems (König, 1997; Bach and Jann, 2010).

At the local level, where most management reforms have taken place, new management ideas were promoted by the Local Management Co-op or the 'Joint Local Government Agency for the Simplification of Administrative Procedures' (*Kommunale Gemeinschaftstelle für Verwaltungsvereinfachung*, KGSt). The KGSt is an independent consultancy agency organized by a voluntary membership of municipalities, counties, and local authorities with more than 10,000 inhabitants.

Following the Tilburg model from the Netherlands, the KGSt propagated a modern system of local government, which was labelled the 'New Steering Model' (*Das Neues Steuerungsmodell*). The main characteristics of this model are 'clear-cut responsibilities between politics and administration, a system of contract management, integrated departmental structures and an emphasis on output control' (Röber, 1996, p. 176; see also Klages and Löffler, 1996, p. 135). Elements of this 'New Steering Model' have been applied in a growing number of big cities and counties, and during the

1990s a variety of participatory innovations were also made at local levels, especially the use of local referenda (Wollmann, 2001).

On the whole, therefore, changes in Germany have been informed by ideas developed within the public sector, rather than by private sector managers or 'gurus'. One partial exception to this is the field of quality improvement, where TQM ideas have exerted a significant influence.

G. Pressure from citizens

The focus on democracy and citizen participation was always very present in Germany and was labelled as *Ausserparlamentarische Opposition* (APO—citizen opposition outside parliament). The fact that the CDU/CSU was in power for almost twenty years encouraged leftist intellectuals to organize themselves to fight government policies and to protect democracy outside the legislature. Since the SPD joined government, first as part of the Big Coalition, then as the ruling party in the 1970s, the APO was weakened. In the 1970s the pressure from citizens resulted in Citizen Initiatives (*Bürgerinitiativen*), where citizens gathered and tried to approach political parties, administrations, and institutions in a more positive way. Thousands of initiatives were taken in the fields of public infrastructures, environmental matters, housing, transport, or education. In the 1990s there was the important new development of local referenda, which became widely used (Wollmann, 2001). However, the vast majority of these initiatives have been pitched at a local level, and it has to be remembered that Germany is a highly decentralized country, in which most public services are provided by subnational authorities (see Table 3.2).

H. Party political ideas

There is little radical challenge to the *Rechtsstaat* and the basic functioning of the system. The concept of modernization does not embrace the kinds of radical reforms which have been attempted in New Zealand and the UK. It is usually the product of agreements made between management and the trade unions (Röber and Löffler, 1999). The talk of a 'slim state', which was popular at the end of the Kohl Chancellorship, did not in fact result in any major changes at the federal level (Sachverständigenrat 'Schlanker Staat', 1997).

In 1992 the then candidate Chancellor Engholm (SPD) released a managerialist public sector reform paper. In 1993 there was a similar party paper by the ruling Christian Democrats. In general, specifically party political 'lines' on administration seem to be absent. Party political ideas are not developed at the federal level but basically at the state and local levels since the electoral process is focused at these levels. This results in sometimes diverging visions and practices according to specific situations, which are then not translated in a common federal party line.

I. Chance events

At the end of the 1970s the Baader-Meinhof Group (Red Army Faction, RAF) carried out terrorist acts against representatives of the political, industrial, and administrative establishment. This resulted in a discussion on the presence and the removal of 'extremists' in the public service (*Berufsverbot*). This included a concern to neutralize civil servants who had been Nazis, or Communists, as well as sympathizers with the terrorist RAF.

From 1990 German unification caused serious pressure at all levels and aspects of society (though whether this can really be deemed a 'chance event' is debatable). Financially, there was the political decision to equate the eastern and western *Deutsch Mark*. The '*Treuhandanstalt*' organized the privatization of most of the East Germany economy and the resulting unemployment had to be absorbed by the social security system. The former DDR administrative system was reformed according to the BRD system, and even the location of the capital changed from Bonn to Berlin. The transformation of local government in East Germany was 'between imposed and innovative institutionalization' (Wollmann, 1997). However, the main thrust of unification was not to experiment with new forms of administration but was rather to extend the West German system to the East.

J. Elite decision-making

At present, the perspective of the state as a provider of services remains predominant in Germany. However, the 1993 federal plan for the elderly of 1993 was a first indication that the German state may increasingly act as facilitator rather than as a direct provider, and there have been a number of further moves in this direction. Nevertheless, the idea of local authorities as multifunctional providers has probably

remained more closely intact than in most other western European countries – certainly more than, for example, in the UK or the Netherlands.

The legal status of the civil service has always been a political issue of administrative reforms. The constitutionally guaranteed status of civil servants remains untouched and is unlikely to change fundamentally (partly because so many German MPs are themselves civil servants):

[T]he question whether to impose a national administrative reform program from above or whether to leave freedom for local and sectoral initiatives is only a theoretical one in the Federal Republic of Germany, where federal structure and tradition by nature forbid a centralized approach to administrative reforms.

(Klages and Löffler, 1996, p. 143)

K. The administrative system

The 'legal state' or *Rechtsstaat* is a key idea in the German system:

While the *Rechtsstaat* and federal principles constitute the essential formal parameters for policy making and public-sector change, the market economy and the welfare state establish substantial norms which delineate functions and responsibilities of the state... These complex arrangements between state and market economy, based on neo-corporatist linkages and intermediary organizations, allow the co-existence of market ideals such as free enterprise, individualism and subsidiarity, with a positive evaluation of the welfare state.   (Benz and Götz, 1996, p. 17)

Within this setting, the Federal Republic of Germany has sixteen *Länder*, of which three are city states (Berlin, Bremen, and Hamburg), plus hundreds of local governments. The size of the *Länder* varies from 17.7 million inhabitants (North Rhine-Westphalia) to 700,000 (Bremen), or from 70,000 km^2 (Bavaria) to 400 km^2 (Bremen). Local government consists of 329 counties (*Kreise*), 115 non-county municipalities (*Kreisefreie Städte*), and 14,915 municipalities (*Gemeinde*) which are governed according to different models.

The administrative structure in the Federal Republic of Germany is moulded by three principles. The first principle is 'separation of powers', which distributes legislative, executive, and judicial powers among separate institutions. A second principle is federalism, which defines *Länder* as 'members of the Federation yet retaining a sovereign state power of their own' (Röber, 1996,

p. 170). Local government is the last founding principle. Local government in Germany mainly operates on two levels, that of the local authorities and of the counties (Röber, 1996, p. 170). Local self-government has a long tradition in Germany. The Basic Law and all *Land* constitutions guarantee the right of every community to govern local affairs under its own responsibility (OECD country profiles, 1992, p. 126; OECD, 1997*d*).

The development of public management in Germany has not been uniform because German administration is extremely varied and complex. Central government only plays a modest part in the direct administration of public services. Many public duties, such as education and police, are administered by the states (*Länder*) which have considerable political and administrative power, whilst other public duties (e.g. social services) are administered by local authorities. As a consequence the impact of public management and public managers varies throughout Germany and at different levels of public administration (Röber, 1996, p. 169–70; Wollmann, 2001).

The role of federal administration is mainly limited to law-making and is not concerned with service delivery as such, which therefore reduces the need for administrative reform at that level. The concept of *Rechtsstaat* and the principle of legality are embedded in a negotiating and contracting state (Sommerman, 1998). The German system of public administration is characterized by the classical bureaucratic model with strong emphasis on legality and proper fulfilment of regulatory functions (*Ordnungsaufgaben*). This model is based on the Weberian ideal type of bureaucracy with a tall hierarchy of positions, functional specialization, strict rules, impersonal relationships, and a high degree of formalization (Röber, 1996, p. 170). However, the upper levels of the federal civil service are extensively politicized. It is common for many such senior officials to change jobs or take study leave when the political colour of the government changes (Götz, 1997). The federal ministries do, however, have a penumbra of agencies. The number of these increased from the 1950s until the 1990s, and then declined slightly into the 2000s (just when agencies were being increased in the UK and the Netherlands). The development of this agency system has been 'neither comprehensive nor planned; they are much more evolutionary than revolutionary, driven by sectoral policies and not by any overall agency policy' (Bach and Jann, 2010, p. 443).

L. Contents of the reform package

The modernization of public administration in Germany has to be understood in 'terms of a "bottom-up" revolution: there are few reform initiatives at the federal level, at least some German Länder show up as modernization pioneers, but the truly new entrepeneurs in the field of modernization are the local governments' (Klages and Löffler, 1996, p. 134).

The elements of the 'New Steering Model' that local governments and some *Länder* put into practice included:

- result-oriented budgeting;
- cost calculation of administrative products;
- introduction of commercial bookkeeping;
- decentralized resource accountability;
- definition of indicators for quality standards;
- customer orientation;
- outsourcing, contracting-out, and privatization;
- openness to 'competition'.

Faced with budgetary problems, some hospitals also adopted variants of the New Steering Model.

Klages and Löffler (1996, pp. 137–41) argue that there was an east-west division in the modernization approach of local government, due to the specific problems facing public administration in East Germany. The restructuring of the East German public sector was dramatic. The transformation encompassed changes in governmental competencies (from holistic planning authority to a balancing function, typical for a market economy), in the civil service (from political cadre administration to a civil service based on professional qualifications), in organization (from unity of powers to horizontal and vertical separation of powers), and in procedures (from the guidance principle of the party to legalistic administrative behaviour). Territorial restructuring of local authorities was necessary in the face of the enormous financial problems the local authorities faced. In the eastern part of Germany, the Weberian model was put in place, while, by contrast, the western part experimented with the New Steering Model and other innovations.

Major reforms at the federal level have been few and far between. There has been plenty of discussion and speech-making (e.g. over the idea of a 'slim state' in the late 1990s) but there has often been little tangible result. From 1999 the *Modern State: Modern Administration* programme focused on the idea of an 'enabling state', based on modern management, elimination of bureaucracy, and e-government. However, implementation was not easy, and the 'red–green' coalition ended up resuming some of the reform ideas of its CDU predecessor (Bach and Jann, 2010; Jann, 2003; Schröter, 2007). Certain themes appear repeatedly in reform documents—especially reducing unnecessary bureaucracy (which has featured three or four times since 1980) and 'modernization' (which can mean a variety of things in different contexts). Since 2000, recurrent themes have included integrated service delivery (shared service centres have been an ongoing project since 2005), e-government (Ministry of the Interior 2006*a*), and innovation (Ministry of the Interior, 2006*b*).

M. The implementation process

The initiation and implementation of changes in Germany is through pilot projects rather than by a comprehensive approach. At the federal level reforms are frequently tried out by one or a few ministries rather than (UK style) being imposed by the core executive on the whole of the government. This has advantages, but can also create problems of dual structures and isolated islands of reforms. The modernization pressure comes from the lower levels of government and is pushing through the *Länder* up to the federal level. The usual tempo of reform is a gradual one, with extensive consultation and a measured approach over a number of years.

One huge exception to this generalization was the unification with East Germany, which was definitely a top-down process, and was necessarily carried out quickly.

N. Reforms actually achieved

There are no recognizable official evaluations of the outcomes of federal reforms. There are surveys and academic analyses of the implementation of the New Steering Model, but these lie largely outside our focus on the federal level. Some academic treatments of the federal reforms go some way towards evaluating them (e.g. Schröter, 2007; Wollmann, 2001).

Key Events—Germany

Period	General	Organization	Personnel	Finance
1980–5	1980–2 Schmidt (Social Democrat) as Chancellor 1982–98 Kohl (Christian Democrat) as Chancellor	1983 Federal commission to simplify laws and administration		
1986–90	1990 German Re-unification	1986 Creation of Ministry of Environmental Affairs	1990 onwards: Large numbers of West German civil servants seconded to the east to set up a new administration in the eastern *Länder*	1986 Amendment to Federal budget code—uniform accounting system
1991–5	1991 Capital moved from Bonn to Berlin (although in 2010 more than 50% of federal employees still work in Bonn)	Steps towards privatization of mail and telecommunications. Massive privatization in the former East Germany 1995 Creation of a 'Lean State' Advisory Council		1993 Reform of financial distribution system between federal government and *Länder*
1996–2000	1998–2005 Schröder (Social Democrat) as Chancellor. Green Party part of the governing coalition for the first time 2000 Joint Procedural Act	1996 Reduction in the number of federal authorities 1999 Launch of programme *Modern state: Modern Administration* (renewed in 2004). Emphasis on efficiency 2000 onwards—Creation of a federal intranet. Also launch of programme to put federal services online for citizens	1998–2002 Reduction of 18,000 in total number of federal staff 1998 Introduction of new civil service competency system in some ministries (but faded out after 2002)	1998 Cost and results accounting system introduced to more than 20 ministries and agencies
2001–5	2005–9 Merkel (Christian Democrat) as Chancellor. Forms a 'Grand coalition'	2003 Initiative to reduce bureaucracy (set of 74 projects) 2005 Launch of shared service centre programme (a large project which continues to the end of our period) 2005 *Bundonline 2005* (succeeded by *eGovernment 2.0* a year later)	2003 Reform of the civil service law	2003 Introduction of activity costing to federal offices 2004 Pilot projects for product budgeting 2005 Online system for public procurement
2006–10	2009 CDU/CSU/FDP coalition wins the election. Merkel continues as Chancellor	2006 Ministry of Interior launches *Focused on the Future: Innovations for Administration.* 2006 Ministry of the Interior launches *eGovernment 2.0* 2010 (–13) Ministry of Interior launches *A Networked and Transparent Administration*	Continuing reduction in total number of federal staff	*Föderalismusreform* I and II—reforming financial relations between the federal government and the *Länder*

ITALY

A. Socio-economic forces: general

With a population of 60 million Italy is, together with Germany, France, and the UK, one of the big states of western Europe. See Appendix A.

B. Global economic forces

See Appendix A. Italy has a lower level of imports and exports as a percentage of GDP than Belgium, Germany, or the Netherlands, but a higher level than Australia or the USA.

C. Sociodemographic issues

Italy is experiencing the same growth in the elderly population as other EU and North American countries and, despite the stereotypical Italian image of the strong, extended family, this is putting significant strains on the social and health care services (see Appendix A, Figure A.1). Culturally (and politically) Italy exhibits strong contrasts between a poor and 'backward' south and an economically and socially more dynamic north. Italy has also been subject to sudden upsurges in the numbers of asylum seekers, in a country which has hitherto had quite a low percentage of foreign-born residents.

D. National socio-economic policies

There is a tradition of extensive state direction over the economy, including state ownership of banking and insurance, as well as industrial companies. Furthermore, industrial policy was traditionally oriented towards the support of the big Italian private firms. However, globalization and the opening of national markets within the EU have put strong pressures on this situation. There was widespread privatization of state firms during the 1990s.

During the 1990s the EU's 'convergence criteria' obliged governments to address the very high level of national debt, and propelled 'savings' to the top of the political agenda. This, in turn, impacted upon welfare state policies.

An important feature of the Italian economic and political situation is the long-standing contrast between the rich, industrialized and urbanized north and the much poorer, more rural south.

E. The political system

Until the political crisis of 1993–4 there were two main parties, the Christian Democrats (with vote shares of 33–40% during the 1980s) and the Communist Party (with around 30%). There was also a Socialist Party, and various other smaller parties of the right and left. Governments changed frequently and were often of the grand coalition type. The same individuals from the political elite tended to be in power for long periods. In the early and mid 1990s, however, a political and economic crisis (political bribery and other illegal activities, the need for large public expenditure cuts) led to changes in both the electoral system (from proportional towards more majoritarian arrangements) and the pattern of parties (the effective collapse of both the Christian Democrats and the Communists and their replacement by a shifting coterie of new parties).

After 1994 the Italian political system looked more majoritarian, but still displayed fragmented coalitions, anti-system parties (e.g. the Northern League, the refounded, smaller Communist Party) and parties identified principally with charismatic leaders (e.g. Prime Minister Berlusconi's *Forza Italia*, Di Pietro's Italy of Values Party). During these upheavals the position of the President of the Republic (previously a largely symbolic role) became somewhat more influential.

There was also a period where many senior civil servants began to be appointed to political positions, indeed, there were two 'technical' governments—the Ciampi administration of 1993 and the Dini administration of 1995—which were headed by former central bank executives.

There has also been a move away from centralization and towards federalism, with major constitutional reforms in 2001. However, the detailed implementation of this strategy has been quite slow. At the local level the influence of party machines has declined and there has been a trend towards elected mayors and provincial presidents.

F. New management ideas

In the 1980s there was a fashion for promoting a corporate, managerial culture in bodies such as regional and local authorities and hospitals and health care units. During the 1990s there was a strange melange of traditional, French-derived administrative doctrines and NPM ideas. The EU also had a distinct influence, particularly because of the reform of the structural funds from the late 1980s, which helped introduce new ideas about financial management, planning, and evaluation (mandatory evaluations became a feature of the reformed structural funds system). The Treasury was an important channel for these influences. However, the strong legal and cultural features of Italian administration have often meant that ideas from outside (e.g. performance-related pay) have been heavily adapted during implementation, so that their originally intended effects were lost (Ongaro and Valotti, 2008). As Italy moved into the twenty-first century, the intensification of international networking at regional and local levels facilitated the introduction of new ideas from the 'bottom-up'.

G. Pressures from citizens

Trust in the civil service is not high in Italy (in Table 5.7 it remained the lowest of the eight European countries). However, it did appear to increase somewhat between 1997 and 2002 (see Table 5.7). Trust in politicians tends to be very low. In general it might be said that there has been strong, if diffuse, public pressure for reform—a growing awareness (fuelled by the greater international traffic in ideas) that inefficiency and even corruption are not just 'part of the way things are', but are problems which can be tackled.

H. Party political ideas

The fragmentation and volatility of the party system during the recent period makes it hard to identify consistently 'leading' ideas. Rather, there have been certain groups of (sometimes contradictory) themes, for example:

- privatization (under pressure from EU institutions)
- downsizing and contracting out
- some 'governance' ideas, including, most obviously, decentralization and federalization, but sometimes also an enhanced emphasis on

public participation and third-sector partnership in service provision
- emphasis on the primacy of political control (often entailing a tightening of traditional, hierarchical controls, plus the introduction of a 'spoils system' in the mid 1990s)
- the continuing fight against corruption (on most measures a bigger problem in Italy than in any of our other eleven countries).

I. Chance events

Bribery is not a chance event, but its discovery, perhaps, may be so regarded! The 'clean hands' enquiry, which began in the winter of 1992, was something of a watershed. It discredited a large part of the political and business elite, and provided a catalyst for deep changes in the party system and the whole political class.

The monetary crisis of summer 1992 made a major impact. It led to a new approach to the national deficit and to tremendous pressure on public organizations to find savings. The later GEC (2008) also made an impact. Italy was seen as one of the weaker members of the eurozone, and was obliged to take strong budgetary measures during 2010—including, for example, a move to freeze civil service salaries for the next three years.

J. Elite decision-making

The crises of 1992–4 made it politically very important to be seen as a 'reformer', and provided a background to many proposals and ideas. Proposals to distance administrative responsibility from the political leadership (while leaving them with steering instruments) were understandably popular, and offered nodes for consensus. Privatization was one example of this, and one which also helped provide cash during a period of budgetary restraint. Decentralization was another rallying cry, expressed with particular vigour by the Northern League. The relative public popularity of the EU made it less difficult for politicians to carry through policies of privatization and downsizing, since these could be represented as being essential responses to EU convergence criteria. Public management reforms have probably been somewhat lower on the political agenda since the turn of the century (Ongaro, 2009, p. 77).

More recently the Minister for the Civil Service and Innovation, Brunetta, has conducted something of a populist campaign against 'loungers' in the civil service who, it is implied, are one reason why the Berlusconi government has not been able to make some of its policies work. The remedies, it is said, are more transparency in public service pay and a tighter regime of evaluation and performance pay.

K. The administrative system

The Italian administrative system is related to its French cousin, and has sometimes been described as 'Napoleonic'. Significant elements include:

- a tradition of state direction of the economy and society;
- the presence of an elite state cadre, including the *Consiglio di Stato* (Council of State), the *Corte dei Conti* (national audit office) and the *Ispettorato Generale* (a financial inspectorate);
- the strong presence of the central state at regional level, personified in the person of the *prefetto* (prefect);
- the importance of a special body of administrative law, based on the concept that the state occupies an autonomous domain (see discussion of the *Rechtsstaat* in Chapter 3). A public service culture which is hence strongly juridical;
- a four-tier system—state, region, province, municipality, with large central ministries that until recently managed many functions. Until the 1990s the provinces had only limited functions;
- strong regional and cultural differences, despite the detailed framework of national rules and regulations (Ongaro and Valotti, 2008).

Overall, the image is of a slow-moving and rather inefficient administration, although with great variation, including pockets of much more modern and innovative practice. Tables 5.1 and 5.4 show Italy as having by far the lowest score among our twelve countries on the World Governance Indicators, and also by far the lowest position on the IMD's government efficiency index.

L. Contents of the reform package

There was no single, defining 'package'. During the 1980s there was a good deal of innovation at local levels and in the health service, much of which was aimed at strengthening management and modernizing budgeting and planning procedures. However, it was not until the 1990s that major national reforms got under way. At the beginning of that decade local authorities were

given greater autonomy to organize their services in different ways, and an important law on transparency in public administration was introduced.

Then, during the crisis of 1992–4 various reform packages took shape:

- privatization and liberalization of banking and insurance; the dismantling of the state industrial conglomerate IRI; the partial liberalization of the mobile phone sector;
- changes to the basis of public employment, in an attempt to introduce more decentralized collective bargaining and more private-sector-like disciplines;
- clearer lines being drawn between the roles of elected officials and public managers, particularly at the local level. In practice this demarcation between setting priorities (political) and managing resources (managerial) proved very hard to implement;
- financial management reforms: more recourse to block budgeting (giving lower tier authorities greater discretion to sub-allocate) but simultaneously a tightening of cash management;
- introduction of a citizens' charter (Schiavo, 2000) and of 'offices for relations with the public';
- reform of the national audit office, reducing its administrative power and partly re-orienting it from *ex ante* controls towards *ex post* controls and performance audit.

A second wave of reform took place in 1997–9:

- major decentralization: invoking the principle of 'subsiduarity', many functions were transferred to the regional and local levels. This was reinforced by a new constitutional law in 2001;
- further employment reform: strengthening private sector disciplines and introducing performance-related pay;
- a broad package of administrative simplification, including the widespread introduction of 'one stop shops' for businesses (Ongaro, 2004);
- restructuring of central government, including mergers of ministries and the creation of executive agencies that were supposed to operate through performance contracts;
- reform of the general system of controls, distinguishing between administrative controls, management controls, and strategic controls;
- accounting reform, aggregating expenditures into larger 'units';
- increased autonomy given to schools, universities, and chambers of commerce.

Since 2000 there has been no single, consistent, prominent focus. However, the following elements have, from time to time, been highlighted:

- greater customer focus in public services, partly through e-government. Also (2009) citizens are to be given enhanced rights to take failing administrative authorities to the administrative courts;
- continuing budget reforms;
- continuing adjustment and readjustment of civil service personnel regulations;
- following the 2008 GEC, the need to make substantial cuts in public spending.

M. The implementation process

Those reforms that were directly driven by the financial pressures of the economic crisis in the early 1990s tended to be implemented relatively quickly. The intensity of implementation of other reforms was very varied, with long delays and 'dilutions' being quite common. There is a widespread perception that Italy is weak on implementation, and there are a variety of theories about why that should be so (Ongaro and Valotti, 2008; Ongaro, 2009, p. 126). 'The gap between the principles underlying the design of reforms and the actual utilisation of management tools seems to be especially wide in the area of personnel management' (Ongaro and Valotti, 2008, p. 186).

There has been a considerable debate within Italy as to whether the reforms of the 1990s were mainly 'top-down' or 'bottom-up'. The answer seems to be 'both'. Some reforms were clearly driven by national laws. But, on the other hand, the autonomization and decentralization processes released many innovatory experiments in municipalities and local hospitals. The spread of 'city managers' was also a largely bottom-up phenomenon.

N. Results achieved

No general evaluation is available. It is clear that considerable structural change has taken place, and it seems likely that, in many instances, the client-orientation has also increased. In the mid 1990s considerable reductions in public spending were achieved, although it may be debated how far this was due to any managerial skill. Some particular evaluations have been made of specific reforms, for example Pessina and Cantu, (2000—for health care) or Valotti (2000—for local government). Ongaro's academic overview concludes that real forces for change were released during the 1990s, but that public management reform became politically somewhat less prominent after 2001 (Ongaro, 2009, pp. 179–89).

Key Events—Italy

Period	General	Organization	Personnel	Finance
1980–5	'Business as usual'—constantly changing coalition governments, but usually with the same political elite in charge	1980–1 Reforms of local government. 1983 Establishment of Public Administration Department		
1986–90	6th and 7th Andreotti governments	1989–91 Higher education reform 1990 New rules on administrative transparency		
1991–5	1992 'Clean hands' inquiry 1992 Reforming 'technical' government of Amato 1993 Electoral reforms: powers of mayors strengthened and national electoral system moves from a proportional system to a semi-majoritarian hybrid 1993 Reforming government of Campi 1994 Centre-right coalition under Berlusconi wins election 1995 Dini becomes Prime Minister	Mergers of ministries 1993 Introduction of citizens' charters (not very successful—subsequently reintroduced)	1993 Decree states that public employment is subject to the same general rules as private employment	1991 Reform of Finance Ministry 1992 Monetary crisis 1994 Reform of the Court of Accounts. Shift away from ex ante controls 1995 Reform of pension system
1996–2000	1997 Prodi as Prime Minister. Leading a centre-left coalition 1997 Devolution of competencies to regional and local governments	Creation of independent administrative authorities 1997 Provision on the development of performance measures 1999 Launch of one-stop shops for businesses dealing with government 1999 Centralization of public procurement 1999 Merger of ministries	1998 Decree allowing the appointment of top public officials by political bodies (a 'spoils system'. Appointment of managers from outside the public service is also made easier 1999 Introduction of personnel evaluations	1997 Budget reform—aggregating lines into units and making each unit the responsibility of a director general
2001–5	2001 Centre-right coalition led by Berlusconi wins a large majority in both houses	2001 Creation of Ministry of Technological Innovation	2002 Extension of spoils system to all staff with a managerial role 2005 Law reintroduces a minimum length (3 years) to managers' contracts	
2006–10	2006 Prodi returns to power with a large and unwieldy centre-left coalition and a very small majority. 2008 Berlusconi returns to power with a substantial majority for his centre-right coalition	The Prodi coalition is weak and management reforms not as high on the agenda as during the 1990s 2009 'e-Gov 2012' action plan 2009 'Friendly networks' initiative to provide 'one-stop' access points for citizens 2009 The 'Brunetta Reform'—a decree embracing significant revisions to civil service law, aimed at improving public sector productivity and responsiveness to citizens (OECD, 2010c)	2009 Tightening of the personnel system to enforce the annual ranking of personnel and to focus performance bonuses on the top 25%. Claims greater transparency 2009 Decree enables citizens to take administrative authorities to court if they do not respect expected standards of service	2010 GEC obliges government to make cuts, including a 3-year freeze on civil service wages

Note A: Those seeking a more detailed account are recommended to consult Ongaro, 2009, which includes (pp. 32–49) a table similar in concept to this one, but much more detailed.
Note B: Unlike most of the other country files, we do not here give details of all the prime ministers and governments and their parties. The reason is one of simple practicality—both governments and parties have changed so often during the period under study. Ongaro (2009, chapter 2) is a good guide to this complexity.

THE NETHERLANDS

A. Socio-economic forces: general

The Netherlands has a population of 16.6 million citizens (2010). Demographically:

Population aging will reduce economic growth and increase resource transfers to the elderly. This will put pressure on the retirement-income and healthcare, insurance systems. The Netherlands is better placed than most OECD countries to meet these pressures because it has a large, funded occupational pension system. Even so, the government budget balance is projected to deteriorate when the baby boom generation passes into retirement. (OECD, 2002b, p. 3)

To safeguard the current position following the 2008 GEC, the new government (Rutte 1) will implement a savings programme of Euro 18 billion, which is about 6 per cent of total expenditure.

B. Global economic forces

The Netherlands is particularly exposed to international trading conditions, having one of the largest international trade sectors among our twelve countries (Table A.3).

Even though the Netherlands retains a strong economy under fiscal pressure, raising taxes is not on the agenda for the Rutte 1 government. Since additional expenditure for education, public security, infrastructure, and services for elderly are a priority, substantial savings may have to come from social expenditure.

C. Sociodemographic issues

Since the 1980s and even at the beginning of the 1990s the Netherlands were second only to Sweden (among the twelve countries reviewed), in respect of the high proportion of GDP devoted to social expenditure. During the 1990s and especially in the late 1990s the proportion stabilized and even decreased, relative to other countries (e.g. Sweden, Finland, France)

Even with a relatively low foreign population (4.2% of the total population), the Netherlands have a significant foreign-born population (10.7% of the total population in 2007) (see also Table A.8). This has resulted in the Rutte 1 government planning to restrict and limit access for foreign populations to the Netherlands. Over the past decade immigration has become a 'hot topic' in Dutch politics. The population aged 65 and over is currently 15.5 per cent of the total population and is predicted to increase to 23.5 per cent in 2050, placing the Netherlands in the middle of our twelve countries in this respect (see Table A.6).

D. National socio-economic policies

Until the recession of the 1970s the post-war history of the Dutch public sector had been one of more or less continuous expansion. Then, between 1974 and 1982 the budget situation deteriorated from surplus to a large deficit. Unsurprisingly, the 1980s were a period of sharp cutbacks in the public sector, combined with a series of measures to develop tighter control over state expenditures. Since 1989 the Dutch economy has performed better, although it shared in the international slowdown of the early 1990s. Employment growth since 1994 has been ahead of many other EU member states. Although the governments of the mid and late 1990s have enjoyed a less threatening position on public spending than their 1980s predecessors, the economic circumstances are changing:

These are undoubtedly testing times for the Netherlands, with the economy moving away from sustained non-inflationary growth, which had been the hallmark of the Dutch model for nearly two decades. (OECD, 2002b, p. 1)

The 2008 GEC forced the Dutch government to intervene in the banking system. Since the pension system relies on a capitalization system, substantial losses were taken. However, the Dutch system has the capacity to cut budgets drastically if necessary. The resignation of the Balkenende administration ushered in the current Rutte-Verhagen government (2010–), which is reducing total spending by 6 per cent.

E. The political system

The Netherlands are a unitary, but decentralized state: 'traditionally, the Dutch state . . . has always resisted centralisation of state authority' (Kickert and In 't Veld 1995, p. 45). The political system is consociational, consensual, multi-party, and corporatist (Lijphart, 1984). Elections take place according to a system of proportional representation. During the 1980–2000 period the main parties were Christian Democrat (a 1980s' merger of previously separate Christian parties), a Liberal Party (conservative), a Progressive Liberal Party, and a Social-Democrat party. The Christian parties were continuously in government from the First World War until 1994, allied to varying groupings of other parties. Through the 1970s the governing coalitions were centre left, in the 1980s centre right. Unusually, in 1994 and 1998, a *'purple'* (left–right) coalition was formed *without* Christian Democrat participation. After the elections of May 2002 and January 2003, the Christian Democrats returned to government.

In the Netherlands almost every sector of government policy consists of a myriad of consultative and advisory councils, which are deeply intertwined with government and form an 'iron ring' around the ministerial departments . . . Deliberation, consultation, and pursuit of compromise and consensus form the deeply rooted basic traits of Dutch political culture. (Kickert and In 't Veld 1995, p. 53)

The Socialist-led purple coalition (Kok, 1994–1998–2002) was succeeded by the Christian Democrat-led Balkenende governments (2002–3 and 2006–10).

The 2002 elections were affected by the murder of Fortuyn. He was a populist politician who gained a significant number of seats (17% of the votes) for his 'Lijst Pim Fortuyn' protest party and—as if from nowhere—became the second largest party in the Second Chamber. The three traditional parties represented almost 60 per cent of the votes. The political tensions resulted in new elections in 2003 where the Fortuyn listed seats dropped substantially (to 5.6% of the votes). It became clear that, without their charismatic leader, the party was composed of contradictory interests and attitudes. This period traumatized the political elite of the Netherlands. Whereas the three main political families once more represented almost 75 per cent of the votes in the 2003 elections, further fragmentation of the party-political system followed.

In the 2006 elections the three traditional parties (CDA, VVD, and PvdA) dropped back to about 60 per cent. Each party acquired a mirroring, radical fringe party that split the vote (religious, conservative, and left). The 2010 elections clearly demonstrated this. The three traditional

parties represented only 53.7 per cent of the vote, while the combined radical fringe parties gained 43.7 per cent of the votes, of which 15.4 per cent was for the far-right movement PVV of Wilders. This fragmentation of the political system, and the support of the far-right party of Wilders resulted in very difficult coalition negotiations for a conservative (Christian Democrats and conservatives) minority government (52 seats) with the support of the far-right movement (24 seats) to give them a 76/150 majority.

As a consequence, the Dutch political system is less consociational and consensual than it was in the 1990s. This has implications for its public policies and its public sector reform programmes.

F. New management ideas

Formerly, the system of consultative and advisory councils (see E, above) afforded many channels for both business-based and academic ideas to enter public administration:

the Dutch ministries are relatively open organisations. They are not only populated by career civil servants, but also by many external consultants and scientists who contribute enthusiastically to policy making in general. (Kickert and In 't Veld, 1995, p. 56)

In this respect, therefore, the Netherlands has been dissimilar to more closed, *Rechsstaat*-type regimes such as Germany or France. Following the Second World War there was a notieable 'de-juridification' of public administration. During the 1980s specific reform ideas came from a number of other countries, especially Sweden, the UK, and the USA (Roberts, 1997, p. 101).

As in many other countries, during the 1980s notions of comprehensive planning were in rapid retreat, and business-origin management ideas increasingly penetrated the public sector. However, in the Netherlands, the drive for efficiency and savings did not carry the same anti-government ideological edge as it did, for example, in the UK under Thatcher or in the USA under Reagan.

It should also be noted that the Netherlands, relative to its size, has one of the largest communities of public administration academics in Western Europe. Many professors played some part in advising government on administrative reform. During the 1980s open systems approaches and network theories provided alternative perspectives to business management approaches and, during the 1990s, the Dutch academic community played an important part in developing the 'new steering model' of governance (Kickert and In 't Veld 1995, pp. 59–60; Kickert, 2000, 2008).

A typical procedure for generating new management ideas in the Netherlands is to establish commissions which produce a report for debate in the Cabinet and in Parliament, and major evaluations which suggest corrective actions. The commissions consist of executive politicians, MPs, academics, or stakeholders. These commissions report on a range of issues varying from, for example, structures of government (Van Veen, Vonhoff, Wiegel, Scheltema), coordination (De Grave), responsibility (Scheltema), or communication (Wallage, Doctors van Leeuwen). Since about 2000, however, the academic channel has probably lost importance, and international sources (OECD, consultants, etc.) have gained.

Evaluations are also a key source for new management ideas. The 2004 VBTB evaluation on financial performance management resulted in a policy shift (Bouckaert and Halligan, 2008, p. 288), and the 2003 Programme Different Public Sector (*Een Andere Overheid*) was effectively abandoned (Luts et al., 2009).

From about 2005 on, there has been a shift towards a pragmatic approach to public sector reform. The 2007 *Renewal of the Central Government* focused on better policy, good implementation, fewer administrative burdens, better control, and more efficiency (Ministerie Binnenlandse Zaken, 2007, 2008; see also: Tweede Kamer der Staten Generaal, 2007). Increasingly there was also an awareness that the benefits of focusing on performance also have a cost. As a result two new themes to guide public sector reform seem to have emerged: 'Comply or explain' and 'trust'. Since the 2008 GEC the saving strategy obviously has also come to dominate the debate.

'Comply or explain' means that a degree of freedom has been created where it is possible not to comply if one can explain why it is not possible or desirable to provide performance information for strategic plans and budgets, or monitoring, or reporting. Also, and in the same line of thinking, 'trust' has become an increasing topic of debate in managing relationships within the public sector, for example between the Ministry of Interior and local government, even if there are official doubts (Ministerie van Binnenlandse Zaken, 2009*b*, p. 7). 'Comply or explain' and 'trust' also fit well into a strategy of cutting costs of public sector bureaucracies, and reducing administrative burdens.

G. Party political ideas

Whilst political parties undoubtedly developed broad notions about how Dutch government should be reformed it is necessary to remember that the significance of the ideas of any one party for practical action is likely to be less in a consensual, multiparty system than in the kind of one-party dominance which has usually characterized government in New Zealand and the UK. That having been said, one may note a number of party political themes which gained some salience.

First, it is clear that the first Lubbers government, which came to power as a centre-right coalition in 1982, was influenced by the right-wing Anglo-American neo-liberal governments of the time. It adopted a rhetoric which was pro-privatization and in favour of slimming the central state. Over time this emphasis became somewhat diluted, especially when the third Lubbers' administration (1989–94) included the Social Democrats as major partners (instead of the Liberals, as in the first and second Lubbers' governments). Simultaneously, however, the Social Democrats muted their previous ideological resistance to various forms of business-like practices being (selectively) introduced to the public sector. Additionally, the pressures to cut back public spending receded during the 1990s, so that the context for debate was less acute.

Later, during the 1990s, there was a certain disenchantment with some of the reforms. Following some critical analyses (e.g. *Algemene Rekenkamer*, 1995) of the many ZBOs (autonomous administrative bodies) created during the 1980s, the new 'purple coalition' government of the mid 1990s declared its intention of restoring the 'primacy of politics', meaning a greater measure of public accountability and transparency for non-ministerial public bodies (Roberts, 1997).

In general, there is a shift of solution strategies from coordination and solving the stovepipes system, to a debate on what the core business is and how to make (autonomous) administrations more responsible for results, costs, and quality (Ministerie van Binnenlandse Zaken, 2009*a*, 2009*b*). From there, debate has started on how not to lose control over these autonomous administrations, to reconnect the public sector and its policies to what citizens and society want, especially since the traditional parties were so successfully challenged electorally by radical fringe parties and movements that appealed to the electorate.

H. Pressure from citizens

Whilst there is a popular suspicion that 'the bureaucracy' is inefficient, and while public service seems to have become a less attractive career for young people, Dutch public opinion does not seem to support the strongly anti-government attitudes which have been quite popular in the USA and, to a lesser extent, in Australia, New Zealand, and the UK. But also in comparison to other European countries public opinion in the Netherlands has a positive attitude towards the government. Dutch public opinion also places a high value on institutions such as Parliament, social security, health care, and education. With specific reference to the civil service, it comes out as the second most trusting country after Sweden (Table 5.7).

I. Elite perceptions of what management reforms are desirable and feasible

Much elite attention has been focused on budgetary problems. The development of performance indicators, contractualization, and output budgeting were all seen as desirable and feasible. More recently, however, the Cost Benefit Analysis of performance information itself has become an issue. The concern to cut expenses was ever-present and frequently dominant. During the 1980s and early 1990s the political elite was most interested in strategies for achieving cutbacks. One can see from Table 5.5 that this seems to have had some effect—in 1980 the Netherlands had been one of the countries with the highest proportion of social expenditure in GDP, whereas by 2005 on this measure it was ranked seventh out of twelve.

Top officials, however, were also enthusiastic about the possibilities of management reforms per se. During the election campaign in May 2002, the populist candidate Fortuyn emphasized the malfunctioning of administrations and certain public policies. In 2010 the populist Wilders also emphasized maladministration. It could be said that the Dutch public administration elite are now on the defensive.

J. Chance events

Confidence in the administrative and political system has been under pressure. There was a fireworks factory that exploded in Enschede in 2000 (23 people killed, about 950 wounded). There was a heavy fire in Volendam in 2003 (14 people killed and 180 wounded). In 2005 there was a fire in the Schiphol 'prison' for illegal detainees (eleven people killed). With so many people killed and injured, questions on procedures related to permits and inspections were raised, and resulted in review and evaluation of inspection services. Investigations indicated a culture of 'cosiness' and slackness between the regulators and the regulatees.

Then there was the murder of Pim Fortuyn (2002) which led to a parliamentary commission to look for responsibilities and levels of accountability among the different administrative and political actors involved. Further, there was also the Theo Van Gogh murder (2004) which put pressure on the image of a pluralist, multicultural, and tolerant society, and the role of public policies in achieving this.

Finally, there was a large-scale public works fraud which raised the issue of ethical standards in the public sector.

The 2008 financial crisis certainly had effects on the public sector, but here, as elsewhere, we choose not to regard that as a 'chance event'.

K. The administrative system

'Ministerial responsibility is the cornerstone of our system' (Kickert and In 't Veld, 1995, p. 46). Ministers are responsible politically, in criminal and in civil law. Collective decision-making takes place in the weekly council of ministers. The prime minister is not as strong a coordinating and centralizing force as in the UK system—indeed, various attempts during the 1980s and 1990s to strengthen the prime minister's office have been rejected or dropped. S/he remains *primus inter pares*.

In the mid 1990s there were fourteen ministries (the number has varied over time, e.g. in 1982 the new government abolished the Ministry of Public Health and Environment and transferred its functions to two new ministries). The Rutte 1 cabinet has eleven ministries. There is a one-to-one relationship between ministers and ministries, except for the Ministry of the Interior where there is an additional minister for immigration and asylum. Because of the absence of a strong central power each has considerable autonomy—more so than would be the case in either New Zealand or the UK. The highest civil servant in each ministry is the secretary general, and ministries are generally divided into directorates general. In 1995 the ABD (Algemene Bestuursdienst) was created (Senior Executive Service) which included at the end of 2010 about 800 civil servants.

The civil service is not partisan, and civil service and political careers are separate. Ministries are fairly open organizations, at least in the sense that they frequently bring outside experts into the processes of policy deliberation (see F above).

The provincial and municipal levels are highly significant in terms of services, expenditure, and personnel. The number of municipalities evolved from 1.121 in 1900 to 483 in 2004 and to 430 currently (2010). There are twelve provinces, of which the last one, Flevoland, was added in 1986 as it was reclaimed from the sea. These subnational tiers are responsible for most of the expensive, labour-intensive welfare state services (municipalities account for roughly one-third of public expenditure, though much of this is financed by central government). Many of the cutbacks of the 1980s were directed at these levels.

L. Contents of the reform package

The contents of the reform package developed over time, with shifts in the coalition government, and with changes in the fortunes of the Dutch economy. In general terms it might be said that a more radical package appeared in the early part of our period, especially under the 'Lubbers 1' centre-right coalition of 1982–6. Privatization was a prominent theme, but the scope for returning state bodies to private ownership was less than in the UK or New Zealand, because the extent of pre-existing state ownership was more modest. Nevertheless the Postbank (10,500 staff), Posts and Telecommunications (95,000 staff), the Royal Mint, and the Fishery Port Authority—the four main state companies—were either corporatized or wholly or partly sold off.

Alongside privatization, the 'Lubbers 1' administration announced a series of 'great operations'. These comprised measures to trim central government spending, decentralize activities to lower levels of government, and simplify legal and bureaucratic procedures.

The 1980s was also a period in which many new ZBOs (autonomous (semi) public organizations) were created. A survey showed that, by 1992, 18 per cent of total state expenditure passed through these semi-autonomous bodies. Some were long-established (e.g De Nederlandse Bank) but more than 40 per cent dated from after 1980 (Algemene Rekenkamer, 1995). In 2005 one count numbered the population of ZBOs at well over 600 (see also Bouckaert et al., 2010, Chapter 10).

In the 1990s the departmental agency, rather than the ZBO, became the fashionable format for decentralizing administrative authority. These included (for example) agencies for Meteorology, Immigration and Naturalization, Defence Telematics, and the Government Buildings Service.

In HRM/personnel management there was a gradual shift towards the 'normalization' of the terms of public service, that is, bringing them more in line with private sector labour conditions. The Netherlands, along with most other countries in this study, experienced a tension between the desire to use HRM to build a more skilled and highly motivated workforce, and the desire to shed jobs and economize (Korsten and der Krogt, 1995). In 1995 a senior civil service (De Algemeen Bestuursdienst) was introduced.

Throughout the period there was a trend to develop and refine performance indicators for a widening range of public services. Initially there was a firm policy to have a high performance indicator coverage of the budget (VBTB), including efficiency and effectiveness, and to have developed monitoring systems, also for benchmarking purposes (De Kool, 2008), plus a rich cost-accounting system. This policy has been weakened by the 'comply or explain' and 'trust' guidelines which have a) reduced the indicator coverage in key documents, b) led to the redefinition of cost information as non-financial information which does not need to be audited, and c) emphasized trust-driven relationships for control, including municipalities (though how far this is rhetoric rather than reality is hard to tell).

Since the 1970s the Dutch government has been interested in performance-oriented budgeting and policy analysis. During the 1980s the need for stringent financial control dominated the performance agenda. As the government finances were again under control in the early 1990s, results-oriented budgeting and management regained attention. In 1991 internal agencies were set up within the departments. These internal agencies have an accrual budget and are managed by a results oriented steering model (Smullen, 2010). In the 1990s there was also an increasing trend to integrate performance measures into the budget documents. Finally, in 2001, performance budgeting was legally implemented (VBTB): the format of the budget bill became outcome-oriented and policy objectives and performance measures were integrated in the explanatory memorandum. Departmental accounting offices were transformed into departmental audit offices (2002) which were merged into the Central Audit Directorate (2008). This is part of a concern to reduce the administrative overload of inspection, checking, and auditing. Reducing the 'control tower' became a concern stemming from the doctrine that the benefits of measurement and regulation should be significantly more substantial than the costs (see also Bouckaert and Halligau, 2008, appendix V).

M. The implementation process

In many, perhaps most countries, the rhetoric of public management reform outdistances the actual changes in practice. This has certainly been true for the Netherlands. The implementation of decentralization is a good example:

the decentralisation process in the 1980s and 1990s became largely a power struggle. Spending departments often held out resolutely (and with success) against the transfer of power to provinces and municipalities. Decentralisation only began to asume any importance when spending cuts and decentralisation were brought together in a single context: municipalities were permitted to take over certain tasks if they were prepared to accept 90% funding; the 10% contraction was (without much evidence) justified as 'efficiency gains'. (Derksen and Korsten, 1995, p. 83)

More generally, implementation has been an incremental and selective process—much less of a series of dramatic 'waves' as in the UK or New Zealand. This is perhaps only to be expected of a politico-administrative system that prides itself on its consensual character. However, this is not to suggest that implementation has always been smooth. Waves of savings have affected implementation, and waves of political pressure by radical and populist parties have shifted the policy contents.

N. Reforms actually achieved

The Netherlands is a country where programme and policy evaluation has been fairly widely practised (even as early as 1991 a survey recorded 300 evaluations being undertaken across 14 ministries) but for a considerable time, relatively little of this effort has focused upon management reforms per se. For example, many ZBOs were created during the 1980s, but, writing in the mid 1990s, one Dutch expert considered that their performance was a blind spot (Leeuw, 1995). Certainly there does not seem to have been any overall evaluation of the reforms, such as the 'great operations' of the Lubbers 1 and 2 administrations. There have, however, been a few academic assessments (e.g. Ministerie van Binnenlandse Zaken, 2009*a*). There have also been partial evaluations by the administration, for example on VBTB, on quality in the public sector (Ministerie van Binnenlandse Zaken, 2009*c*), and by the Court of Audit (*Algemene Rekenkamer*), for example on the functionality of the agencies. In particular, the *Algemene Rekenkamer* published a 1995 report which was highly critical of the lack of public accountability of some ZBOs. The report indicated that only 22 per cent of the ZBOs surveyed produced performance indicator data for their parent ministries. Financial control procedures were often weak, and in some cases the legal basis for certain tasks was not clear (*Algemene Rekenkamer*, 1995). The Court of Audit has from time to time continued to produce critical reports of a number of the key public management reforms (see www. rekenkamer.nl).

Key Events—The Netherlands

	General	Organization	Personnel	Finance
1980–5	1981 Van Agt Prime Minister (CD, Soc.) 1981 Major Operations: deregulations, privatization, reconsideration 1982 Lubbers Prime Minister (CD, Lib.)	1982 Reorganization including decentralization	1984 Central Steering Committee for Personnel Policy	
1986–90	1986 Lubbers II Prime Minister (CD, Lib.) 1989 Lubbers III Prime Minister (CD, Soc.)	1990 Ministerial Committee for Major Efficiency Operations	1989 Pay differentials 1989 School of Public Administration (NSOB) 1990 Small-Scale Efficiency Operations	1986 Financial Accountability Operation (till 1991) 1990 Performance Indicators (PIs) in budget
1991–5	1991 Core Business Operation 1992 *Towards More Results-Oriented Management* (government report) 1994 Kok Prime Minister (Soc., Lib.) 1994 *Choices for the Future* 1994 Ministerial Committee for Political Reform (Interior) 1994 Ministerial Committee for Market Improvement, Deregulation, and Legislative Quality (PM) 1995 *Back to the Future* (Policy document on ICT and use of information)	1992 Interiors: Major Efficiency Operation (privatization and staff reduction) 1992 Agreement Central-Local: transfer of tasks 1993 Tailor-Made Advice: revision of advisory bodies 1993 Towards Core Ministries (small administrative centres 1994 Start Agencies (4) 1995 Government position on semi-privatized bodies; screening of 253 Autonomous Administrative Authorities (AAA)	1991 'Normalization' of status of government employees; evaluation of performance-related pay 1992 Agreement (with trade unions) to privatize General Pension Fund (by 1996) 1993 Organization and Working Methods of the Civil Service (core tasks) 1994 1st Annual Report on Personnel Management 1995 Senior Public Service (SPS) (database on top mobility)	1992 Ministries report on policy evaluation in budget memorandum 1992 Strengthen Accounting Law (1976): more PIs 1993 Policy Evaluation Programme 1994 'Reconsideration Procedure' replaced by Interdepartmental Policy Audit 1995 Double bookkeeping for agencies. 1995 Adjust Accounting Law
1996–2000	1996 Framework Act on Advisory System 1997 Cohen report: Market and Government 1998 Kok Prime Minister (Soc., Lib.)	1997 Evaluation of Agencies 1998 Total of 19 agencies	1997 36-hour week in public service 1998 extension of SPS to all 1,500 management positions 2000 Review of SPS 2000 Reform of employment guidance system	1996 Financial Relations Act (municipalities) 1996 Commission for Finance audits PIs (Parliament) 1997–8 PIs in budget (second stage): outputs; third stage: link cost/expenses–output (efficiency) 1998. Interdepartmental Management Audit 1999 VBTB: policy goals structure budget. 2000 Government Governance 2000 ZBO new regulation on budget and accounts

Period				
2001–5	2002 Balkenende I (Prime Minister) (CDA/ Fortuyn) 2003 Balkenende II Prime Minister (CDA, Lib.) 2003 Programme *A Different Government*: rethinking central government tasks, reducing bureaucracy and administrative burden, improving organization, establishing e-government 2005 Committee on governmental overload	2001 Total of 23 agencies 2001 New rules for establishing ZBO 2002 Framework Law ZBO (total of 340 ZBOs; some are reduced to agency)	2002 Reorganization of public employment organization, including marketization 2003 Creation of a Shared Service Center HRM	2001 RPE Regulation on Performance Measurement and Policy Evaluation 2001–2 Public Finance Act 2002 Report on PPP financial instruments 2002 Reform of Departmental Accounting Offices into Departmental Audit Offices (DAD) 2003 Overregulation and Overcontrol (Interdepartemental policy review) 2004 Audit Function Quality Plan (final report to improve the performance of central government audit departments) 2004–5 Report Interdepartmental investigation (IBO) on regulation pressure and control pyramid 2004 Evaluation of VBTB (linking PIs to budget)
2006–10	2006 Balkenende III Prime Minister (CDA, Lib.) 2007 Balkenende IV Prime Minister (CDA, Soc.) *Renewal of Central Government* (Vernieuwing Rijksdienst): downsizing government's workforce, de-compartmentalizing the ministries, improving organization, improving quality of public services, reducing administrative burden 2007 *Government for the Future* (gathering knowledge and building expertise)	2006 Total of agencies is 40, total of ZBOs is about 430 2006 Charter Law on ZBOs 2007 Regulation for cost accounting in agencies and ZBO 2008 DG Central Government Organization and Operational Management 2008 Inspection Reform Programme (modernization of central government inspectorates) 2009 BLDs stabilized around 40; total of (clustered) ZBOs is 125	2007 Mobility Organization. 2008–11 Downsizing the public employment by 12,800 FTEs (7. 5% of total central government workforce)	2006 RPE new Regulation on Performance Measurement and Policy Evaluation 2008 Merger of different departmental audit services into one Central Audit Directorate
2010	2010 Government Rutte-Verhagen Prime Minister (Lib., CDA, with support from far right)			

NEW ZEALAND

A. Socio-economic forces: general

New Zealand is a small country (estimated population 4.4 million in 2010) in a peripheral geographical location (2,000 km from Australia). GNP per capita fell from 90 in 1985 to 76 in 1992 (where OECD average = 100). In 2007 it remained the lowest of our twelve countries (see Appendix A). There used to be very close economic and cultural ties to the UK, but these began to dwindle after the UK joined the European Community in 1973, and the favoured arrangements for NZ agricultural exports to the UK market were dismantled. There are two main population groups—whites and Maoris. The latter (12% of the population) have been increasingly politically active in insisting on their rights and pointing to inequalities—a process sometimes described as 'internal decolonization' (Castles et al., 1996, chapter 7).

See Appendix A for details of New Zealand's comparative position.

B. Global economic forces

The system of protectionism which had been in place since the Second World War was close to the point of collapse by the early 1980s. In 1952, 65 per cent of exports had gone to the UK and only 1.7 per cent to Asia. By 1982 the first figure had fallen to 14.7 per cent and the second had risen to 31.8 per cent (Castles et al., 1996, p. 25).

When the new Labour government led by David Lange came to power in July 1984 the economy was stagnant and the national debt was large. The NZ Reserve Bank suspended trading in the NZ dollar and a 20 per cent devaluation quickly followed. The government's first priorities were tax reform, financial deregulation, and privatization. The comprehensive (and subsequently world-famous) public management reforms of 1984–90 flowed directly from this financial and economic crisis. There are alternative interpretations concerning the extent to which the exchange rate crisis was also the symptom of a deeper economic crisis—critics say the new government exploited the situation to push through its radical agenda.

Restructuring the economy was undertaken at high speed, but the beneficial impacts took more than five years to show through. The interim period was very tough. In 1985 inflation reached 13 per cent. Overseas firms were prominent beneficiaries of the privatization programme, being mainly responsible for the purchase of the railways, the telephone system, and (thanks to financial deregulation) most of the major banks. Between 1985 and 1992 the economy actually shrank by 1 per cent. Between 1995 and 2008, however, respectable growth rates returned (see Table A.1).

C. Sociodemographic change

Prior to 1984 unemployment had usually been low (less than 5 per cent) in NZ. It rose rapidly between 1985 and the early 1990s, reaching more than 10 per cent in 1992/3. The social effects of this were widespread and harsh. This was partly because many social benefits were linked to employment status but also because from 1990 the National Government initiated the rapid dismantling of much of the previous welfare state system. Speaking of the 1980s, Castles et al. (1996, p. 101) refer to:

a very substantial decline in real wages over the latter half of the period was accompanied by distributional effects . . . These included an increased incidence of low pay for men, a decline in the share of real gross income of wage and salary earners accruing to each of the bottom three quintiles and a marked increase in the share of the top quintile.

As might be expected, women and ethnic minorities were particularly hard hit by the simultaneous worsening of employment conditions and slimming down of welfare provision.

During the twenty-first century New Zealand faces the same problems of ageing populations as all our other countries. At the moment it enjoys a somewhat younger population than most, but it is projected to experience a big growth in the elderly share after 2020 (Table A.6). In income terms it is a relatively egalitarian country (Table A.7).

D. National socio-economic policies

After 1984 there was a very clear commitment to a comprehensive economic restructuring (see above): tax reform (to lower the tax burdens on business);

financial deregulation (to attract foreign capital); and privatization (to promote efficiency and relieve pressures on public spending). The generous NZ welfare state was left largely intact at first, but major reforms aimed at reducing welfare and social security expenditure were instituted by the incoming National Party government of 1990. An Employment Equity Act introduced by the Labour Government in 1990 was soon repealed by its National successor. The Employment Contracts Act significantly deregulated the labour market. Since the mid 1990s, and the return of economic growth, governments have been able somewhat to soften their mix of economic policies.

E. The political system

The political executive is drawn exclusively from a small legislature, organized on Westminster principles. There is no upper house. There is no single written constitutional document nor any other major constraint on the government in power.

Until 1996 the electoral system was based on a single-constituency-member, 'first-past-the-post' system, which usually delivered a single party to power. Once in power: 'Public servants and their managers have long operated in a context in which the Prime Minister and cabinet could, if they wished, ride roughshod over any opposition' (Boston et al., 1996, p. 68). However, following a constitutional referendum in 1993 the electoral system was changed (1996) to one based on mixed member proportional representation (MMP). Subsequently, coalition governments have become the norm, and there has been considerable re-arrangement of the political parties.

Unlike other small countries in our set (Finland, the Netherlands), New Zealand has traditionally been fairly centralized. There has been: 'A preference for retaining key governmental powers and responsibilities at the central government level, with only limited devolution to sub-national government, despite considerable rhetoric about devolution in the 1980s' (Boston et al., 1996, p. 5).

F. New management ideas

The public management reforms in NZ were unusual both in their comprehensiveness and in the relatively high degree to which they were based on explicitly theoretical ideas about management. The then Central Financial Controller to the Treasury wrote: 'A number of literatures contributed ... The sources included public choice theory,

managerialism, transaction cost economics, public policy, public sector financial management and accounting' (Ball, 1993, p. 5).

There was a shared intellectual background within the quite small group of key ministers, senior civil servants, and businessmen who drove through the reforms: 'there were a series of quite close relationships set up, from about 1982 on, by a group that encompassed the corporate business sector, the senior Labour parliamentary group' (Canadian Broadcasting Corporation, 1994, p. 3). The highly theoretical character of much of this thinking was novel:

Like their British counterparts, senior New Zealand public servants had not been known in the past for their interest in theory. The emphasis on using theory to guide policy was, therefore, a novelty. It seems to have been due, at least in part, to the growing influence of economists and the particular kind of higher education which many of these economists, especially those in the Treasury, received. (Boston, 1995, p. 168)

The content of this thinking, in institutional terms, may be expressed as follows (borrowing from Boston et al., 1996, pp. 81–2):

- prefer private sector over state sector organizations wherever possible, especially for commercial functions;
- prefer non-departmental organizations over ministerial departments, especially for policy implementation;
- prefer small to large organizations;
- prefer single-purpose to multi-purpose organizations;
- allow pluriform administrative structures rather than seeking uniformity ('horses for courses');
- separate policy from operations;
- separate funding from purchasing and purchasing from providing;
- separate operations from regulation;
- separate provision from review and audit;
- prefer multi-source to single-source supply;
- place like with like (primarily on the basis of the purpose or the type of activity);
- aim for short ('flat') rather than long hierarchies;
- aim for 'straight-line' accountability/avoid 'multiple principals';
- decentralize wherever possible.

Since the late 1990s a rather different set of ideas has gained circulation. Drawing on international debates, but adapting them to the particular national circumstances, governments have stressed the potential of e-government, the need for 'joining-up', and the value of a unified, ethically committed public service.

G. Pressure from citizens

The rush of reforms from 1984 to 1994 could not be described as a response to direct pressure from citizens, in fact at first they were controversial and widely unpopular. They were a package pushed through quickly by an elite which took the window of opportunity for radical reform (Aberbach and Christensen, 2001). Since the 1996 shift to a system of proportional representation, such untrammelled elite actions have been rather more difficult, and the pace and scope of reform has been reduced.

H. Party political ideas

Until the advent of proportional representation in 1996 the main electoral competition had taken place between the Labour Party (broadly social democratic) and the National Party (broadly conservative). It is noticeable that the NZ Labour and Australian Labor governments were the only Labor/Social Democrat executives in the OECD to respond to the global economic pressures of the 1980s by actively embracing market-oriented reforms (Castles et al., 1996, p. 2). Labour had been in power from 1935 until 1949, and during that time had established what was arguably the world's first comprehensive welfare state. After this, however, Labour enjoyed only brief periods in power (1957–60 and 1972–5) before their coming to office in 1984.

Specifically *party* political ideas do not appear to have had much influence on the NZ reforms of 1984–90. The policies which were put in place were developed rapidly and without much external consultation by the governing elite (Castles et al., 1996). Unlike the Australian Labor Party, the NZ Party did not have particularly close links with the trade union movement, and its relatively unrestrained constitutional position allowed it to choose its policies with few major constraints. The ideas which have become more prominent since the late 1990s (see Section F above) do not seem to be strongly party-related: rather they have been drawn from the wider international circulation of ideas.

I. Chance events

It is not obvious that any chance events had a major and direct influence on the course and content of the public management reforms. However, it might be said that the Cave Creek disaster (in which, in 1993, fourteen young people died when an observation platform collapsed in a Department of Conservation nature reserve) provided a focus for much public unease about the changes which had been implemented over the previous decade. One theme in the media treatment of the Cave Creek tragedy was the lack of individual responsibility in the decentralized public service (Gregory, 1998).

J. Elite decision-making

The small, elite group of Labour Party ministers and civil servants who drove the NZ reforms from 1984 to 1990 were, in the main, enthusiasts for the new management ideas spelled out in Section F above. When the National Party returned to power in 1990 there was no great change to this 'menu', other, perhaps, than a willingness to apply these concepts even more vigorously than before to the social protection system. Nevertheless, it would be mistaken to see the NZ example as the pure and undiluted application of a set of tightly knit theoretical ideas. To begin with, the ideas do not all fit together perfectly—sometimes different principles or guidelines seem to point in different directions. Furthermore, many detailed, practical compromises had to be made (Boston et al., 1996, pp. 82–6). For example:

despite the substantial privatisation programme during the late 1980s, a number of important commercial organisations remain in public ownership, and there has been little public or political support for privatisation in areas like education, health care, and scientific research.   (Boston et al., 1996, p. 82)

By the turn of the century the mood had shifted somewhat and, without favouring any fundamental reversal of the great changes of 1984–94, governments became more concerned with issues of better institutional coordination, restoring morale and leadership within the public service, and more community involvement in policymaking and service design and delivery (Chapman and Duncan, 2007; State Services Commission, 2001, 2002)

K. The administrative system

At the outset of the reforms the NZ public service was a unified, non-party political, career service.

Senior public servants 'tended to take a broad service-wide perspective at least as much as a narrow departmental focus' (Boston et al., 1996, p. 56). It was heavily rule-bound (especially in matters of personnel and industrial relations), and by the early 1980s was widely regarded as inefficient.

Much of this was changed by the 1988 State Sector Act (see below) and other reforms. Personnel powers were decentralized and senior civil servants were henceforth employed on performance-related contracts. Large departmental structures were broken up into a larger number of smaller agencies, each with a more closely defined set of objectives and targets. The turnover of chief executives was quite rapid—over 80 per cent of those initially appointed had gone by 1995. Nevertheless, the State Services Commission has retained effective control of senior appointments—the system has not become as politicized as in Australia (Halligan, 2002). Furthermore, although more fragmented than formerly, it remains a highly centralized system in comparison with countries such as Finland, Germany, Sweden, or the USA (see Table 3.2).

When concerns arose concerning the fragmentation and loss of *esprit de corp* induced by the reforms the role of the State Services Commission (SSC) was revived somewhat. The 2004 State Sector Amendment Act enhanced its authority, and it subsequently promulgated a set of key state service development goals, which were themselves revised in 2007. The SSC also supported improved coordination between agencies (State Services Commission, 2008; Bouckaert et al., 2010, Chapter 5).

L. The contents of the reform package

The key management changes from the period of radical reform were embodied in four pieces of legislation:

- *The State Owned Enterprises Act, 1986*. This provided the basis for converting the old trading departments and corporations into businesses along private sector lines.
- *The State Sector Act, 1988*. Chief executives became fully accountable for managing their departments efficiently and effectively. The role of the State Services Commissioner shifted from that of employer and manager of the public service to that of employer of the chief executives and adviser to the government on

general management and personnel issues. Chief executives became the managers of their own departmental staff.
- *The Public Finance Act, 1989*. Introduced accruals accounting and insisted on a focus on outputs and outcomes rather than inputs and activities.
- *The Fiscal Responsibility Act, 1994*. Obliged the government to set out its fiscal objectives and explain how these were related to stated principles of responsible fiscal management.

After 1994 the pace of reform slowed. There were (understandably) signs of 'reform fatigue', and there were modest retreats and readjustments where the purity of the original doctrines seemed to have led to obviously negative consequences. Significantly, a major report in 2001 (the *Review of the Centre*, see State Services Commission, 2001 2002) emphasized the following problems:

- the need for better co-ordination in what had become a fragmented system of state sector organizations;
- the need to concentrate more on the formulation and pursuit of desired outcomes, rather than simply mechanically pursuing outputs;
- the need to involve citizens and communities more with policymaking, service design, and service delivery;
- the need to strengthen the public service culture, encourage the public service ethos, and invest in public service leadership.

In addition to these issues (each of which provoked certain particular reforms, such as strengthening the State Services Commission—see Table of Key Events), there were also (as in most other countries) a series of initiatives to develop and extend e-government.

M. The implementation process

The implementation process was vigorous—at times harsh—and fairly continuous for the eight years following the 1984 election. The key civil servants at the Treasury and the State Services Commission played central roles. Much use was also made of management consultants and other experts brought in from outside. The human relations climate was often poor—formally a fairly humanist model of Human Resource Management was adopted during the 1980s, but in practice there were many job losses, large restructurings, great pressures, and many upheavals (Boston et al., 1996, p. 213).

By the early twenty-first century it seemed that one of the longer-term results of the reforms—especially the budget and financial management reforms—had been a serious running down of the capability of government departments (Newberry, 2002). Resource starvation and short-termism appears to have been built in (intentionally or otherwise) to the procedures through which the Fiscal Responsibility Act and the Public Finance Act have been implemented.

The new issues and themes that arose from the late 1990s (see Section L above) brought with them a softer and less doctrinally charged manner of implementation than had obtained 1984–94.

N. Reforms actually achieved

The NZ government achieved what was probably the most comprehensive and radical set of public management reforms of any OECD country. For example, between 1988 and 1994 employment in the public service declined from 88,000 to 37,000 (though this includes civil servants who were transferred 'off books' to Crown Entities or State Owned Enterprises).

Unlike many other countries, New Zealand governments have commissioned at least two broad-scope evaluations of the reforms (Steering Group, 1991; Schick, 1996). Both came to positive conclusions, while identifying some areas of continuing concern. The Steering Group believed that: 'In the view of most people we spoke to or heard from, the framework is sound and substantial benefits

are being realized' (Steering Group, 1991, p. 11). Allen Schick, the American expert, concluded that 'the reforms have lived up to most of the lofty expectations held for them' (Schick, 1996, Executive Summary). Major productivity and quality improvements have been won in the state trading sector. The range of policy advice to ministers seems to have broadened. There is much greater flexibility of employment, and operational managers wield genuinely decentralized powers. There is much more performance information in the public domain (Boston et al., 1996, pp. 359–61).

Less positive results included:

- The costs of reform have not been closely estimated but seem very likely to have been high. These include extensive disruption, loss of continuity and of 'institutional memory'.
- A greater focus on outputs has been achieved, but sometimes at the expense of some loss of attention to *outcomes* (see State Services Commission, 2001, 2002).
- The accountability and monitoring arrangements for the somewhat diverse 'crown entity' category of institutions are unclear.
- It seems that there has been a gradual erosion of both the financial and the human resources of government departments (Whitcombe and Gregory, 2008; Newberry, 2002). However, although the size of the NZ public service was at first radically reduced (88,000 in 1984, fewer than 35,000 in 1995), it thereafter grew again, and by 2007 had reached 44,300.

Key Events—New Zealand

Period	General	Organization	Personnel	Finance
1980–5	1975–84 series of National Party governments with Muldoon as Prime Minister 1984 Labour Party form a government in the middle of an economic and currency crisis. Lange as Prime Minister			
1986–90	1989 After internal Cabinet strife, Lange is replaced as PM by Palmer. Then, in 1990, with an election approaching and the Labour government deeply unpopular, Palmer was in turn replaced by Moore 1990 National Party wins election by a landslide and forms a new government. Bolger Prime Minister (until 1997)	1986 The State Owned Enterprises Act. Converted the old trading departments and corporations into businesses along private sector lines 1988. The State Sector Act: Chief executives became fully accountable for managing their departments efficiently and effectively. The role of the State Services Commissioner shifted to that of employer of the chief executives and adviser to the government on general management and personnel issues. Chief executives became the managers of their own departmental staff		1989 The Public Finance Act: Introduced accruals accounting and insisted on a focus on outputs and outcomes rather than inputs and activities 1990 New National Government forced to bail out NZ National Bank
1991–5		1991 Steering Group Review of State Sector Reforms		1994 The Fiscal Responsibility Act: Obliged the government to set out its fiscal objectives and explain how these were related to stated principles of responsible fiscal management
1996–2000	1996 Legislation introducing new proportional electoral system (MMP) 1997 Shipley replaces Bolger as Prime Minister (and leader of the Nationalist Party) 1999 Labour-led coalition government comes to power Clark as Prime Minister (until 2008)	1996 The Schick Review (The Spirit of Reform) gives the NZ reforms a generally positive evaluation but draws attention to some emerging weaknesses		

continued

Continued

Period	General	Organization	Personnel	Finance
2001–5	Continuation of Labour-led coalition under Clark. Labour Coalition with Progressive Party renewed after their victory in the 2005 election	2001 Development and Crown Entity reform 2002 *Review of the Centre* report. Highlighted fragmentation and the unhelpful seperation of policy and operations 2004 State Services Amendment Act. Attempt to strengthen coordination and revive the authority of the State Services Commission 2005 State Services Commission publishes development goals for key state services (revised in 2007)		
2006–10	2008 Labour (Clark) loses election. Key (National Party) becomes Prime Minister	2008 State Services Commission publishes *Factors for Successful Co-ordination*	2007. New Standards of Integrity and Conduct come into force	

SWEDEN

A. Socio-economic forces: general

See Appendix A. Sweden is a relatively egalitarian society, with a high proportion of over 65s, and a middling proportion of foreign-born inhabitants.

B. Global economic forces

Sweden is a small country with an open economy. For economic details, see Appendix A. Its growth rate 2006–8 was fractionally above the OECD average and its international trade is proportionately large—half of GDP in 2008.

C. Sociodemographic issues

According to political scientists Lane and Ersson, who surveyed data on a number of social cleavages (1991, chapter 2), Sweden was among the most homogenous, least socially and/or ethnically divided countries in Western Europe. Nevertheless, it has experienced the same difficulties of an ageing population and increasing rates of family break-up as most other Western European and North American states. In the late 1980s and early 1990s the growth in the elderly population was particularly fast, and the over 65 population is predicted to increase rapidly again between 2010 and 2020 (see Table A.6). Also, large-scale immigration for the fifteen years is beginning to lessen the homogeneity.

D. National socio-economic policies

Throughout the period under study, Sweden maintained the largest (as a proportion of GDP) public sector in the Western world. It built and has maintained one of the world's most generous and egalitarian welfare states (Esping-Andersen, 1990). This was already giving rise to fiscal problems in the late 1970s, and the budget deficit peaked at 13 per cent of GDP in 1982. Although the budget moved briefly into surplus in 1987, Sweden subsequently experienced a further—and spectacular—deterioration in its budget balance. Some expert commentators began to see this as a virtually insoluble problem within the existing political and administrative system (Lane, 1995). Certainly, the late 1980s and early 1990s were a

particularly difficult time. A Conservative government came to power in 1991, and the early and mid 1990s were dominated by the acute necessity of making cuts and efficiency savings. However, by the late 1990s, budget balance had been restored (OECD, 1998). A considerable reduction in governmental financial liabilities was achieved from 1995 on (see Table A.5), but the high expenditure on sickness and disability benefits remained a major political issue, and was targeted for reductions by the Conservative coalitions that gained power in 2006 and renewed their mandate in 2010. Sweden continues to experience a difficult economic situation, as a small but open economy, sustaining the largest public sector in Western Europe.

E. The political system

Sweden is a unitary, but highly decentralized state. It has had a constitutional monarch since 1866, but the monarch's role is almost exclusively ceremonial. Executive power rests with the prime minister and the Cabinet (*Regering*). Almost all decisions are made collectively, not by individual ministers. The legislature (*Riksdag*) is a unicameral body with 349 seats. Part of its work goes on in a relatively non-partisan spirit unlike, say, the UK House of Commons or the Australian Parliament. Nevertheless, the significance of party is pervasive. The process of forming a government is initiated by the Speaker of the *Riksdag* (who plays a non-partisan role). S/he nominates a candidate for prime minister, but if more than 50 per cent of the members vote against, then another name must be put forward. The prime minister then appoints the rest of the ministers (normally about twenty), and s/he also decides on the number of government departments.

Elections to the *Riksdag* and to local governments take place every four years under a system of proportional representation. However, since the 1970s:

Not only has power been transferred from the *Riksdag* to the Cabinet, but public power appears to have become more diffused among several groups of actors, among which may be mentioned various bureaucracies that have grown from the exceptional expansion of the Swedish public sector, different organised interests, regional and local groups of actors. (Lane and Ersson, 1991, p. 262)

Since the 1920s, the Social Democratic Party has become the 'establishment' party in Sweden. It was continuously in government (once in coalition, between 1951 and 1957) from 1932 to 1976. Lane and Ersson (1991, p. 262) write that:

The strong position of the Social Democratic Party in state and society opened the way for the participation of organised interests in policy-making, exercising influence at various stages of the policy process. The major interest organisations include: the LO (*Lands-organisationen*), the TCO (white collar workers), the SACO-SR (academics), the SAF (employers' associa-tion), and the LRF (farmers' association).

In this context the 2010 election victory of the conservative Alliance for Sweden may have marked a significant threshold. For the first time since 1980 a right of centre grouping has won two successive elections, and remained in power for a long period. Nevertheless, the Social Democrats remain the largest single party in parliament.

F. New management ideas

The new management ideas which were circulating so vigorously in the Anglo-Saxon world during the 1980s and 1990s also reached Sweden. The Swed-ish system is a very 'open' one, in the sense that Swedish officials and academics play an active role in many international *fora* (probably dispropor-tionately so for a country of Sweden's modest pop-ulation) and educated Swedes can usually speak English. However, the Swedish governing elite did not embrace fashionable management ideas as enthusiastically as did their counterparts in some other countries. 'Marketization' ideas, although briefly in official favour from 1991 to 1994, never achieved the penetration which they enjoyed in New Zealand and the UK during the 1980s. Other new management concepts were more readily as-similated—for example, TQM was quite widely adopted, in various forms. And performance man-agement and Management by Objectives (MbO), based on a shift from an orientation to input and procedural controls to a system based on the achievement of measured results, became a central philosophy of the public management reforms from the late 1980s onwards. However, in 2006 the government launched a Commission to

evaluate the MbO approach, and its report levelled serious criticism against the MbO model (SOU:75). In 2009 the government decided to roll back MbO somewhat, reshaping it at a more realistic level.

From the late 1990s e-government provided a focus for a number of government initiatives, and in the 2000s transparency and accountability were prominent themes. In general one might say that Swedes have a well-developed sense of their own version of democracy, and that management ideas have to be adapted and repackaged to fit in with this 'Swedish way'.

G. Pressure from citizens

According to Premfors (1998), Swedish public atti-tudes towards their governments have been quite fickle. For example, the public sector, together with the Social Democrat leadership, fell rapidly from favour in the late 1980s and early 1990s, but as soon as 1992 there were signs that confidence in public sector institutions was increasing, and that the electorate feared any radical dismantling of the generous Swedish welfare state. In general it might be said that, during the period under consider-ation, most Swedes were impatient of the more bureaucratic aspects of the large government machine, but were protective of most of their wel-fare provisions, and were certainly not enamoured of the kind of 'new right', pro-market doctrines that were fashionable in the UK and the USA during the 1980s. Nevertheless, although they sup-ported another lengthy spell of Social Democrat-led government from 1994 to 2006, they then elected two successive centre-right coalitions. Culturally, more and more Swedes appear to be accepting 'individualistic' values and developing a more critical attitude to the apparent generosity of certain aspects of their welfare state.

H. Party political ideas

Premfors (1991) explains the internal political debate during the first half of the 1980s as a strug-gle between three camps—the decentralists, the traditionalists, and the economizers. The 1985 programme favoured decentralist ideas (which were also a means of off-loading fiscal responsibil-ities) but, quite quickly thereafter, the minister most concerned was heavily criticized on the grounds that he was more talk than action. In any case, by the late 1980s, with a fiscal crisis fully in process, decentralization and participation tended to seem less pressing than cutting expenditures. The economizers took over as the dominant group. Management by results became one of the most salient themes in administrative reform.

At the 1991 elections Sweden acquired its first Conservative Prime Minister since 1930. Neo-liberal ideas such as privatization and market testing, extensively borrowed from New Zealand and the UK, had been introduced by the Social Democrat government in 1989, but now became even more in favour among the political elite (Premfors, 1998, pp. 151–2). However, this was a relatively brief phase, and when the Social Democrats were voted back into power in September 1994 the 'reform talk' soon lost its high emphasis on the power of markets to solve problems. Nevertheless, the Social Democrat government did not introduce a new public management policy—they continued with elements of the previous one. The stress on economy and efficiency continued—and still continues—as budget problems are too deep to be solved overnight. After 2006 Reinfeldt's centre-right coalition focused on tightening eligibility for welfare benefits and on liberalizing the labour market so as to try to reduce unemployment. It would be a mistake, however, to see this as Thatcher or Reagan-style neo-liberalism: rather it is an incremental adjustment to what will still be an unusually comprehensive welfare system.

I. Chance events

None of particular prominence.

J. Elite decision-making

Policymaking is typically an open process, with extensive participation by experts and interested groups. Commissions play an important role in preparing new policies. Freedom of information legislation gives the public access to almost all official papers, even including most of the prime minister's correspondence.

One Swedish expert has suggested that, during the period covered by this study, there were three main schools of thought and opinion as to how the Swedish government should respond to its problems (Premfors, 1991—see Section H above). Decentralizers wanted to relax the detailed grip of the central state, and push out both operational management decisions and some increasingly uncomfortable resource allocation decisions to other levels of government, and even down to individual institutions, such as schools and hospitals. Economizers were mainly concerned with the looming deficit, and the inbuilt tendencies for welfare expenditures to expand. They sought to weaken the 'distributional coalitions' in Swedish policymaking. Traditionalists concentrated on preserving as much as they could of both the substance and the process of the Swedish state, as it had existed during its 'golden age' in the 1960s and early 1970s. From the late 1980s the economizers appeared to gain the upper hand, but Premfors (1998) suggests that, by the late 1990s, the decentralizers were once more gaining ground.

Issues of feasibility have tended to be determined partly by the strongly entrenched *process* by which government decisions were usually arrived at in Sweden. Typically, agencies planned with the aid of boards on which trade unions, employers associations, and other interest groups were strongly represented. Thus, feasibility questions were soon aired with those who would have to 'live' with any proposed reform, unlike the policymaking systems in, for example, the UK and New Zealand (where some reforms were conceived and promulgated by quite small groups of politicians and senior officials). The consensualist and corporatist ways of doing things remain strong in Sweden, even if the advent of centre-right administrations since 2006 has probably seen some shift in favour of organized business interests as opposed to organized labour. In 2007 the government decided to abolish the boards across a range of agencies. Nowadays agencies tend to have more decentralized and informal networks than, say, twenty years ago.

K. The administrative system

In 2009 only about 18 per cent of public servants worked for central government (one of the four lowest among our twelve countries—see Table 3.2). This reflects the importance of the county and municipal levels in the Swedish administrative system. There are 20 counties and 290 municipalities. The counties are responsible for most health care and are entitled to raise an income tax. Municipalities are responsible for housing, education, and social welfare.

Central government is also very decentralized by international standards (again, see Table 3.2). Swedish central government agencies have their operational autonomy protected by the constitution, and are responsible to the Cabinet collectively, not to individual ministers. In 2009 there were around 400 of them, and they employed over 234,500 staff (compared to the ministries, which employed around 4,800, of which 1,300 were within the ministry of Foreign Affairs); 61 per cent were women and 31 per cent men. Thus the ministries themselves tend to be small and largely devoted to policy advice and the preparation of legislation. Doubts have frequently been expressed concerning their capacity to guide or control the agencies (Molander et al., 2002; OECD, 1997a, p. 94, 1998 (Wilks, 1996)). However, recent scholarship on how governments steer the agencies gives a somewhat more positive picture (Jacobsson and Sundström, 2009).

The Swedish civil service is non-partisan, and minister/mandarin career paths are normally separate (see Table 3.1). The culture has been one of meritocracy and neutral competence. The top three officials in ministries are the state secretary, the director general for administrative affairs and the director general for legal affairs. Of these only the state secretary is a political appointment (although the minister will also appoint a political adviser and press secretary). It is also said that senior appointments to the powerful agencies (which are responsible for most implementation activities) have tended to become more party political in recent years (Molander et al., 2002). However, when the right-wing government came to power in 2006, they reformed the recruitment process in the direction of making it less party political.

L. Contents of the reform package

Following its 1976 ousting from government, the Social Democratic Party rethought its policies. One factor in their defeat appeared to be the way in which many people associated it, as the 'establishment' party, with bureaucratic inertia. When the Social Democrats returned to power in 1982 they were therefore determined to change their image in this respect, and to make the state machine more responsive and accessible to the ordinary citizen. They created a Ministry of Public Administration as a symbol of their reforming intent. In 1985 a Government Modernization Programme laid considerable stress on decentralization from the centre to counties and municipalities. Increased choice and user responsiveness were also emphasized. Deregulation and de-bureaucratization were further themes. Personnel authority was decentralized, so that agencies could now hire their own staff and set their own salary ranges, within national frameworks.

At that stage, privatization was not favoured. As one senior civil servant put it in 1987: 'The Swedish government in principle rejects privatisation as a means of solving the problems of the [public] sector. The main objection is that this would lead to distributive injustices' (Gustafsson, 1987, p. 180).

In the late 1980s a second phase of reform began, overshadowed by the growing fiscal crisis. The need to make efficiency gains and savings was paramount. In 1990 an Administration Programme was announced which aimed to generate a 10 per cent reduction in the size of the public sector. This was supposed to be achieved through a combination of measures: abolishing or merging agencies, increased delegation, and various productivity improvement initiatives. The focus on economy intensified with the arrival of a conservative (Bildt) government in 1991. At this point there was considerable rhetoric in favour of privatization, but in practice the government soon had to compromise on its original (and quite extensive) privatization schemes. In any case, the Social Democrats returned to power in 1994, though by that time they had abandoned their opposition in principle to privatization, and were prepared to accept it on a selective and pragmatic basis. Between 1990 and 1996 thirteen agencies did become public companies (the Swedes, like the Finns, tended to prefer a combination of the corporate format with state ownership rather than outright privatization like New Zealand and the UK). During the 1990s there was a good deal of thinking about what principles should govern each of the different main types of organizations in the Swedish public sector—legal and regulatory agencies, agencies providing public services, state enterprises, state companies, and so on.

From 1988 to 1993 a series of strong financial management reforms were implemented, including results-oriented budgeting, frame appropriations, and accruals accounting. Results-oriented management was officially adopted for all state organizations from 1988. The rise of this form of output- and outcome-oriented approach was accompanied by a parallel decline in the previously formidable machinery of Swedish planning (Wilks, 1996). Since 1993 each agency has been required to publish an annual report which includes performance data, an income statement, a balance sheet, an appropriation account, and a financial analysis (OECD, 1997a, p. 90). In 1996 the budget process itself was reformed, with a better defined first stage to the process in which firm ceilings to overall expenditure were fixed (OECD,

1998). On into the twenty-first century, further budget modernization remained a central plank of Swedish reform efforts. Proposals emerging from the VESTA workgroup aimed at putting central government and the national accounts on the same performance-oriented, accruals-accounted basis as the agencies (Gustafsson, 2000). A new management philosophy, which is being gradually phased in as a replacement to management by results, is management focused on activities or *verksamhetsstyrning*. The new model draws on a huge number of performance indicators and could thus be seen as a path-dependent continuation of previous management reforms.

Limiting public expenditure was never off the agenda. In 1993 a new system of central government grants to the municipalities strengthened the latter's autonomy (fewer detailed regulations from the centre) but also permitted central government to fix tight frame budgets and leave the local authorities to sort out how they would divide their circumscribed allocations.

Over the whole period from the mid 1980s, a variety of service quality improvement schemes were adopted, often based on TQM or ISO 9000 principles. These were implemented at all levels of government but there was no central plan or framework equivalent to, say, the UK *Citizen's Charter* (OECD, 1997a, p. 91). There was, however, a Swedish Institute for Quality (SIQ) model which has been quite widely adopted in the public sector, and the EFQM model has also been used.

During the 2000s, themes coming to the fore have included e-government as a means for strengthening a citizen-focus and offering 24/7 public services, and greater transparency, especially in the management of agencies (although it has to be said that Sweden already possessed one of the most open systems in the world). The Reinfeldt government has stressed the principle that activities that can be handled by the private market should not be provided by the state, yet it would also be fair to say that the period since 2000 has not been one marked by any high-profile, large-scale programmes for public management reform (see also Bouckaert et al., 2010, chapter 7; Bouckaert and Halligan, 2008, appendix).

M. The implementation process

Sweden has tended to avoid the sometimes strident or harsh styles of implementation favoured by Mrs Thatcher's administration in the UK, Mr Lange's in New Zealand, or Mr Howard's in Australia. The traditional Swedish processes of intensive, corporatist discussions between the main interested parties prior to action has, with a few exceptions, persisted. However, the employers' association, SAF, walked out of the agency boards in the early 1990s, which has meant a significant blow to the corporatist arrangements. Informal discussions are important, not only in the evolution of new policies, but also in the continuous steering of agencies (Pierre, 2003). As in Finland, extensive use has been made of pilot projects to test out key innovations (e.g. results-oriented budgeting) before they were 'rolled out' to the government more generally. An example would be the 1984 'Free municipalities' experiment, in which nine municipalities and three county councils piloted a system of greater freedom from central state regulation. Strenuous efforts were also made to minimize compulsory redundancies among public servants.

N. Reforms actually achieved

There is no doubt that substantial decentralization of powers to counties and municipalities was achieved during the 1980s and 1990s (and that this contributed to subsequent coordination problems). It is also clear that budgeting systems have been extensively modernized, and that a much more output-oriented set of arrangements has been firmly put in place since the late 1980s. Productivity studies, after showing a large overall deterioration in public sector productivity during the 1970s, and a smaller one even during the 1980s, indicated a productivity gain for the early 1990s.

While a superficial reading of Swedish reform documents might lead one to suppose that there had been steady progress with certain themes (e.g. performance management, agency accountability) over a long time period, some academic analysis is more sceptical. In a study of forty years of Swedish performance management Sundström (2006) concluded that there were systematic and serious problems with the approach, but that these were never openly recognized and confronted.

Sweden has developed a strong interest in evaluation, and a variety of evaluation bodies. The National Audit Office (*Riksrevisionsverket*, later *Riksrevisionen*) has long had an extensive role in evaluation and performance auditing, and has taken an interest in a number of public management reforms (Pollitt et al., 1999). There is also an

Expert Group on Public Finance, which has conducted large-scale studies of public productivity, and a Swedish Agency for Administrative Development. Yet, despite the existence of these units, no overall evaluation of the main reforms appears to have been undertaken.

Against these substantial achievements must be set the continuing concern that the central ministries lack the capability to set a really well-informed yet demanding set of performance targets for the agencies (Molander et al., 2002; OECD, 1997a, 1998). Furthermore, it is by no means clear that the members of the *Riksdag* are overwhelmingly interested in making use of the increased flow of performance data that is now available.

Key Events—Sweden

Period	General	Organization	Personnel	Finance
1980–5	Fälldin (Agrarian Liberal) Prime Minister 1979–82 Palme (Social democrat) Prime Minister 1982–6			1985 Experiment with three-year budgeting framework
1986–90	Carlsson (Social Democrat) prime Minister 1986–91	1988 Increased autonomy and management discretion for agencies 1990 Plan to slim administration by 10% through deregulation and decentralization	1988 Modernization of Public Employment Act	1988 Introduction of results-based management 1990 Budgets must also include statements on results
1991–5	Bildt (Conservative) Prime Minister 1991–4	1991 Ministry of Finance takes over most of the responsibility for central government administration	1991 Job Security System	1991 Privatization of a number of state enterprises
	Carlsson (Social Democrat) Prime Minister 1994–6	1992 Dissolution of SIPU (National Institute for Civil Service Training) 1995 Commission on Administrative Policy	1991 Public pension system made more similar to private sector systems	1992 Introduction of flexible frame budgets 1992 Agencies present accruals style financial reports (more or less continual changes in financial management rules for agencies through this period)
1996–2000	Persson (Social Democrat) Prime Minister 1996–2006	Further corporatization of various activities 1999 Creation of National Council for Quality and Development 2000 Commissions set up for a) the promotion of democracy and b) openness and transparency		1998 Creation of National Financial Management Authority
2001–5	2003 Referendum on joining the euro currency zone—rejected	2003 HERMES information system for government agencies. 2004 Creation of two new departments: Employer Policy and Employee Relations, and Human Resources Development 2004 Series of initiatives to promote e-government, including creation of an	2004 Plan for Gender Mainstreaming in Government Offices	2002 New government budgeting system (VESTA) 2003 National Audit Office is reconstituted as an independent entity reporting to parliament 2004–8 Restructuring of Swedish Military Defence aimed at radically cutting expenditure

continued

Continued

Period	General	Organization	Personnel	Finance
		ICT Strategic Advisory Board and a 24/7 Commission 2005 Ministry of Culture merged with Ministry of Education and Science 2005 Social Insurance Agency reformed into New Social Insurance Agency		
2006–10	2006–? Reinfeldt (Moderate Party) Prime Minister. He won a further term as leader of the Conservative Alliance for Sweden from 2010– but as a minority administration. 2008 Working Committee on Constitutional Reform presents its final report, which includes a variety of proposals for improving democratic participation	2006 e-invoicing introduced in agencies 2007 Ministry of Education, Research, and Culture divided into two ministries again. Also, creation of two new ministries: Integration, and Gender Equality. 2008 State enterprises henceforth subject to Global Reporting Intiative (increasing transparency) 2008 Government agencies ordinance — strengthening agency accountability and clarifying their governance structures	A series of measures during this period aimed at reducing Sweden's very high sickness and disability expenditures (the Conservative government criticized the existence of a 'working free class')	

UNITED KINGDOM

A. Socio-economic forces: general

See Appendix A.2 (above). The UK was one of the countries hardest hit by the 2008 GEC, mainly because the two most affected sectors—finance and housing—are both proportionately large in the UK economy. The end result was that the Conservative/Liberal Democrat government which came to power in 2010 felt obliged to make very large cuts in public spending (see more details below).

B. Global economic forces

See Appendix A. Although Table A.3 shows that the UK's international trade as a percentage of GDP is below the halfway point in our group of twelve countries, the UK is far more exposed to global forces than that figure alone would suggest, not least because of the enormous importance of the City of London as a global financial centre. Over the past thirty years Europe has gradually replaced the old British empire as the principal trading partner (the UK became a member of the EU in 1973).

C. Sociodemographic issues

See Appendix A. The UK has quite a high proportion of foreign-born residents (Table A.8), and experienced rapid immigration during the long boom from the mid 1990s to 2008. Its elderly population is (2010) about halfway down the 'league table' of our twelve countries but, as everywhere else, is increasing (Table A.6).

D. National socio-economic policies

The advent of Mrs Thatcher's Conservative government in 1979 marked the final abandonment of Keynesian policies of macro-economic management and the beginning of an era of vigorous monetarism. The general view was that the Public Sector Borrowing Requirement (PSBR) was a key variable that a responsible government should seek to minimize. This, in turn, implied a tight fiscal policy. So did the government's continuing determination to control inflation (which had reached frighteningly high levels during the 1970s and which was still running faster than that of most of the UK's main economic competitors). Thus the Conservative governments were committed to reducing the proportion of GDP that was represented by public spending. In practice, however, they were not tremendously successful at first (see Thain and Wright, 1995 for the details). Public sector borrowing fluctuated widely during the period of Conservative rule. At the beginning it had been 5 per cent of GDP. In 1987/8 it had fallen to –0.5 per cent (i.e. there was a surplus), but by 1993/4 it was up to 7.3 per cent.

The incoming 1997 Labour government inherited a fairly healthy economic situation, but committed itself to maintaining the previous government's tough spending plans for at least two years. However, it introduced important new principles and procedures for public expenditure planning and control, including periodic 'comprehensive spending reviews' (the first of these came in 1998, the second in 2000—see Chancellor of the Exchequer, 1998). The 2000 review resulted in substantial increases in spending on health care and education. An important innovation that came with the spending reviews was a system of Public Service Agreements (PSAs) where each department was obliged to make an agreement with the Treasury to the effect that, for a given level of funding, it would pursue a defined set of objectives, each of which had one or more targets attached. The increased spending seemed sustainable so long as the economy continued to grow, but when the GEC arrived in 2008—and initially vastly *increased* spending (to rescue banks etc.)—large public deficits soon ensued. By 2009 it was obvious that substantial spending cuts were all but inevitable, and the arguments between the main political parties were mainly about where and when rather than about the required direction, which almost all were forced, reluctantly, to acknowledge. In October 2010 the new coalition government finally introduced a harsh spending review which projected very large cuts in public spending over the following four years. It was estimated that these would cause roughly 0.5 million job losses in the public sector, plus a further 0.5 milion in that part of the private sector that relies on the public sector for work and income.

E. The political system

The UK is a unitary and highly centralized state. The political system is majoritarian and adversarial, with a first-past-the-post electoral basis. There are two major parties (Conservative, Labour) and a number of minor parties, the most important of which is the Liberal Democrat party. All governments after the Second World War were Labour or Conservative until the formal Conservative/Liberal Democrat coalition created after the inconclusive 2010 general election. The Cabinet is mainly concerned with enforcing collective responsibility among ministers and with endorsing new policies. Most policies, however, are developed outside Cabinet, in departments or cabinet committees. The executive is powerful, reinforced by tight party discipline in the lower house of the legislature (the Commons). In normal times it can almost always get its legislation through. The upper house, for most of the period a mixture of a heriditary aristocracy, bishops, and appointed 'life peers', underwent major reform in 1999 to remove most of the hereditary element (only 92 out of the 740 or so peers were henceforth hereditary). The upper house basically only has the power to delay, not to reject, government legislation.

Another important constitutional change has been the creation of separate parliaments/assemblies for Scotland and Wales. The significance of these for public administration is still unfolding but there are certainly some effects—for example, some executive agencies being broken up into separate English, Scottish, and Welsh bodies. At first all three countries had the same party in power (Labour), but after the 2010 general election this was no longer the case, so new tensions may arise.

F. New management ideas

The UK has been very much part of the Anglophone, US-dominated world of managerialism, management consultants, and management gurus (Pollitt, 1993; Saint Martin, 2005). The Conservative governments of 1979–97 were particularly open to generic management thinking, and

to ideas injected into government by the private sector. Mrs Thatcher's first efficiency adviser, Derek Rayner, was a businessman, and many other managers were subsequently brought into government in various advisory capacities (Metcalfe and Richards, 1990). The succeeding Labour administration continued to use high-profile business people for important public roles, as did the Conservative/Liberal Democrat coalition from 2010. Government spending on management consultancy rose to very high levels (National Audit Office, 2006). Top government advisers usually seemed to favour generic management theory (see, e.g. Barber, 2007).

G. Pressure from citizens

There was no single, citizen-inspired movement for reform. Management changes came from political, business, and administrative elites. Nevertheless, public opinion played a part. The popularity of early measures of privatization (selling public housing to the tenants, issuing shares for British Telecom) helped convince the government that this was a policy that could be pursued much further. The public was also receptive to the government's message that the quality of public services should be raised although, ironically, the 1991 *Citizen's Charter* was launched very much as a top-down exercise, with little consultation of public opinion (Prime Minister, 1991). The general 'decline of deference' was also a significant background influence on a number of user-oriented reforms.

During the New Labour administrations after 1997, public opinion tended to focus on the performance of the major welfare state services, health care, and education. The government made these its top domestic priorities, and substantially increased expenditure in both sectors. Much use was made of focus groups and public opinion surveys. Results, however, were slow in coming, and the government failed to achieve some of its (many) targets, whilst fulfilling others. Even where they had success, however, there was the question of whether the public would believe that services really were improved. The vast majority of citizens were not aware of the detailed performance information that was available, or, even if they were aware of it, did not necessarily trust it. At the beginning of the Conservative/Liberal Democrat government a majority of the public accepted that there needed to be substantial cuts in public spending, but that did not mean that they accepted the particular cuts that were actually made.

H. Party political ideas

The decisive shift towards managerialism came in 1979, when a neo-conservative government was elected in place of a centre-left administration (see also Canada and the USA—but note that managerialist reforms in Australia and New Zealand were launched principally by centre-left parties—Castles et al., 1996). However, that is not to say that, at the beginning, Conservative politicians necessarily had very precise ideas about management reform. Rather it was a case of certain broad beliefs and doctrines which inclined the government in a particular direction. Among these were beliefs that the private sector was inherently more efficient than the public sector, that the civil service was too privileged and complacent, and that the state was too big and too interventionist (Pollitt, 1993). However, more detailed ideas evolved during the long period in office.

The New Labour government which took over from 1997 contained many traditional supporters of public services. Party policy stressed 'partnerships', 'modernization', and (later) 'joined-up government' rather than private sector solutions. The internal market mechanisms in the National Health Service were much disliked, and were partly dismantled, as was the compulsoriness of contracting out local services. Never-theless, behind these surface shifts away from marketization, many elements of NPM thinking continued—not least performance measurement, which was further intensified. More generally, the Blair government's early identification with a 'third way' in politics, translated into a 'third way' in public administration also—more public–private partnerships, extension of the Private Finance Initiative, more benchmarking, and so on. From about 2003 there came a strong emphasis on 'choice', which frequently implied MTMs of one kind or another. When Cameron became prime minister in 2010 he strongly promoted the idea of a 'big society' rather than a 'big government'. The precise implications of this were far from clear, but the general direction seemed to be towards decentralizing services and seeking to enlist both commercial companies and civil society associations to take over, or at least share in, activities previously performed by public authorities.

I. Chance events

There is only one which stands out as having a large and direct effect on management reform, and that was the GEC of 2008 (unless one counts the Falklands War as a chance, with its tonic effect on the Conservative government's electoral ratings and subsequent success in the 1983 general election—though even this would have to be seen as an indirect influence).

On the other hand, there have been particular events in particular organizations or sectors which have had significant local influences. Examples would include a series of tragic failures in child protection (which obliged governments to address the reform of social services departments), and the behaviour of certain left-wing local councils which provided central government (under Mrs Thatcher) with one of its pretexts for abolishing certain large, urban councils and instituting various additional controls on the remainder. Under New Labour a series of fatal train accidents led directly to a reconsideration of the organizational arrangements for the privatized railway system, and some strengthening of the public presence on the regulating body. The National Health Service continued under Labour, as under the Conservatives, to supply the media with a steady trickle of tragic and unfortunate episodes which were inevitably used as political ammunition in the ongoing struggle to reform that huge and complex set of organizations (e.g. Francis, 2010; Healthcare Commission, 2009).

J. Elite decision-making

The boldness of Mrs Thatcher's Conservative government grew as its political confidence was boosted by the election victories of 1983 and 1987. By the late 1980s some members of the Cabinet, including Mrs Thatcher herself, advocated the return of many hitherto public functions and activities to the private sector, combined with the introduction of market-type mechanisms to much of the remaining, 'rump' public sector. This general orientation continued into the Major administration (1990–7), as evidenced by the further privatizations of the railways and British Coal, the selling-off of some Next Steps executive agencies and the expansion of the Private Finance Initiative. The aspirations of the incoming Labour government of 1997 were different, but not enormously so. The urge to privatize disappeared, but there was no countervailing desire to take organizations or functions back into public ownership. The Private Finance Initiative was retained and expanded. Even if the tone was more sympathetic to public sector staff, the general belief in the scope for using business ideas to improve public management and to provide more efficient and high quality services persisted.

The unusual dominance of a single party form of executive within the British system gives governments an equally unusual ability to realize their reform desires, even when these are controversial in Parliament or unpopular in the country (e.g. the 1989 reform of the National Health Service was hugely unpopular, both among NHS staff and the wider public, but the 'provider market' was forced through all the same, see Pollitt, Birchall, and Putman, 1998). It is clear that, since 1979, governments of both major parties have regarded continuing and deep administrative change as perfectly feasible. In the UK the barriers to (and political costs of) this kind of reform are considerably lower than in many other countries. However, while reforms can be forced through again and again, the consequences for those who run public services can easily become negative. By the time New Labour won its second election in 2001, there were signs of 'reform fatigue' and 'measurement fatigue' in several major public services. By the end of the Brown administration (2010) the unceasing flood of reports, reforms, and initiatives was widely perceived as one of the government's weaknesses rather than as a strength (Pollitt, 2007).

K. The administrative system

The permanent civil service is still the main source of advice and support for ministers, though it is almost certainly less dominant in this role than it was thirty years ago, and the use of substantial numbers of partisan political advisers is now firmly entrenched (Peters and Pierre, 2004). The civil service is neutral in party political terms, right up to the most senior level (permanent secretary). The culture of the upper civil service is generalist (and non-legalist). The single most important constitutional doctrine for senior civil servants remains that of 'ministerial responsibility' which means (roughly) that ministers must answer to the House of Commons for all the doings of their ministries, and that civil servants normally remain anonymous but have a prime duty to support and protect 'their' minister. Therefore civil servants are *not* held to have any higher duty towards 'the state' (not a concept much in use), the legislature, or the citizenry.

Central government is organized into departments, most of which are headed by a Cabinet minister. The majority of civil servants now work in semi-autonomous executive agencies, which are still, constitutionally, part of their 'parent' departments (Pollitt et al., 2004).

Local government is less protected from central government interventions than in most other European states. The period of Conservative government from 1979 to 1997 was one of considerable tension between the centre and local authorities. Central government both passed many new pieces of legislation restricting the discretion of local authorities (especially in relation to finance) and gave many functions to local quangos and other non-elected bodies (Cochrane, 1993; Painter et al., 1996; Stoker, 1988). Relations between central and local government were easier after the New Labour government came to power in 1997, but the habit of close central regulation and supervision of local authorities has continued. Thus from the late 1990s local authorities were enmeshed in an elaborate, if regularly changing system of performance measurement devised by central government (Boyne and Law, 2005). The Cameron coalition government came to power promising greater freedom for local authorities, but it also made very large cuts in their levels of financial support. At the time of writing it remains to be seen how these alleged new freedoms will work out.

L. The contents of the reform package

With the advantage of hindsight, the period of Conservative government could be said to have three broad phases of development in respect to management reform. From 1979 until 1982–3 there was a fierce drive for economies and the elimination of waste. Civil service numbers were cut, first by 14 per cent and then, subsequently, by a further 6 per cent. Rayner scrutinies (see Metcalfe and Richards, 1990) sought to find more efficient ways of undertaking tasks, and usually concluded that staffing reductions were possible.

In the early 1980s, however, the emphasis shifted to improving financial and general management, and increasing efficiency. The Financial Management Initiative was launched in 1982 and embraced the whole of central government with its philosophy of more decentralized management, more decentralized budgets, more targets, and more professionalism (Zifcak, 1994). The National Audit Office and Audit Commission were brought into being (the relevant legislation being passed in 1983 and 1982, respectively), and each was given a mandate that stressed the '3Es'—economy, efficiency, and effectiveness. In the National Health Service central government insisted on the introduction of general managers to every health authority (Harrison et al., 1992). Performance indicator systems began to sprout for most public services, central and local (Pollitt, 1986).

During the mid 1980s the privatization programme gathered momentum, with the sales of British Telecom (1984), British Gas (1986), the British Airports Authority (1987), and water supply and sewerage (1989). Between 1979 and 1990 about 800,000 employees were transferred from the public sector to the private.

The third phase of Conservative reform was the most radical. Following their convincing victory in the 1987 election, Mrs Thatcher's administration launched a series of fundamental restructurings. Market-type mechanisms were introduced on a large scale—in health care, community care, and education. The 'purchaser/provider split' was imposed by central government as a basic model for most locally provided services (Pollitt, Birchall, and Putman, 1998). Performance measurement systems were sharpened, and the annual publication of national league tables for schools and hospitals became significant media events. Privatization continued (electricity, 1990–3; railways 1994). In central government the Next Steps report of 1988 led to the creation, within ten years, of more than 140 executive agencies which employed in excess of 70 per cent of the non-industrial civil service (Chancellor of the Duchy of Lancaster, 1997; O'Toole and Jordan, 1995). During the mid 1990s a number of central ministries were significantly downsized, following a programme of management reviews (e.g. HM Treasury, 1994). In 1991 both the *Citizen's Charter* (Prime Minister, 1991) and ambitious programmes of contracting out and market-testing were launched (*Competing for Quality*—HM Treasury, 1991). These two well represented the main tendencies of the 1990s: a huge emphasis on 'customer service' (Clarke and Newman, 1997) and an equally intense concern to keep up the pace of contracting out and marketization.

The new Labour government of 1997 reversed very little of what had gone before. Although ideologically more sympathetic to the public sector they did not reverse the privatizations or the purchaser/provider splits, although they took some steps to ameliorate the least popular consequences of the latter. If anything, they intensified the 'league table' system still further, and 're-branded' the *Citizen's Charter* programme as the 'Service First' initiative. Many of their proposals shared the underlying assumptions about the transformatory capacity of better, more professional public management which had been characteristic of their Conservative predecessors (e.g. the idea of a benchmarked Procurement Excellence model or the 'Best value' initiative in local government—see Chancellor of the Exchequer, 1998). In 1999 the prime minister issued a White Paper, *Modernizing Government*, which offered a slightly curious mixture of old themes (e.g. greater responsiveness and quality) with faintly millenarial visions of the government's role in the 'Information Age' (Prime Minister and the Minister for the Cabinet Office, 1999). Subsequently the increases in public spending, particularly in health care and education, were accompanied by further intensification of central target-setting and performance measurement, continuing the trend towards 're-regulation' of the public sector which had begun under the Conservatives (Hood et al., 1999). As Mr Blair famously said, his second term of office came to be about 'delivery, delivery, delivery' (see Barber, 2007).

It is hard to summarize developments between the *Modernizing Government* White Paper (1999) and the end of the New Labour administration just over a decade later, partly because there were so many of them! New initiatives, reports, and reorganizations flooded out from Whitehall. Major public services such as health care, education, and the police were repeatedly reorganized and required to adopt new central government initiatives (Pollitt, 2007; Pollitt and Bouckaert, 2009). Recurrent themes included a continuing emphasis on performance measurement, multiple attempts at 'joined-up government', great rhetorical stress on partnerships, and much talk of increasing citizens' 'choice' of public services (see, e.g. Cabinet Office, 2000, 2008; HM Government, 2009; HM Treasury, 2010; National Audit Office, 2009, 2010). On the financial side, the whole of central government moved to accruals accounting. These reform themes involved various potentially conflicting instruments. Thus, the Blair and Brown governments both continued to develop a massive, top-down architecture of performance measurement, often—but not always—linked to the Treasury's Public Service Agreements (PSAs). This embraced local as well as central government. Yet at the same time there was much talk (and action) around partnership and decentralization. The latter themes were also in some tension with the parallel calls for greater joining-up. Certainly market-type mechanisms continued to be widely used, alongside strong hierarchical instructions. During the Brown administration (2008–10) there were signs that the government was retreating from some of its centralized command-and-control activities (Cabinet Office, 2008; HM Government, 2009), but this retreat (if that is what is was) had not gone very far before Labour fell from power in the 2010 election (see also Bouckaert and Halligan, 2008, appendix and Bouckaert et al., 2010 chapter 6)

It is too soon to say much about the Cameron's Conservative/Liberal Democrat coalition government. At the level of rhetoric it strongly emphasizes decentralization and 'returning' power and initiative to local communities and, wherever possible, to civil society and the private sector. At the same time it needs to make major cuts in public expenditure. The first real clues as to how this might work came with the Comprehensive Spending Review decisions announced in October 2010: £83 billion of cuts were announced, including reductions of 20 per cent in police spending, 8 per cent in defence, 7 per cent in local government funding and 25 per cent in the Department of Justice. Health care and education were given priority, but, in the former case, the tiny increase (0.1% per year over four years) will be swamped by demographic and technological changes. Education was cut by only 1 per cent, but nevertheless spending on school building was reduced by almost two-thirds, and funding for university tuition virtually disappeared (students instead faced a big rise in fees). It will be interesting to see how and how far these plans are implemented—the past historical record suggests that the government is likely to encounter severe practical and political problems in carrying these plans through (Pollitt, 2010*a*).

The government also announced the dismantling of several elements of the New Labour management architecture. There was to be a 'bonfire of targets', including the system of Departmental Strategic Objectives which had been introduced in 2007, and the pivotal Public Service Agreements which had formed the basis of the system since 1998. Some key indicators will be kept, but, again, the detail is not clear at the time of writing.

M. The implementation process

In the UK, reform has been continual, often intense, and sometimes harsh. Public sector employees have become accustomed to constant restructurings, downsizings and new 'initiatives'. Much of the change has been strongly driven from the top. The Treasury and the Cabinet Office have been the main actors, though most departments have been heavily involved, especially Health (for the NHS), Environment (for local government), Education (the reform of schools, colleges, and universities) and Social Security. Under New Labour No. 10 Downing Street itself became a significant reform 'player', housing, inter alia, the Strategy Unit, the Prime Minister's Delivery Unit (Barber, 2007), and the Office of Public Services Reform.

N. Reforms actually achieved

As noted above, British central government is relatively unfettered in its ability to make administrative changes (Pollitt, 2007). So when it determines to carry something through, it usually can. As Section L made clear, many large-scale reforms have been put in place. That is not to say that all have achieved the results forecast or claimed for them. Sometimes one can 'take a horse to water but not make him drink' (see Pollitt, Birchall, and Putman, 1998, for an assessment of this factor in health care, education, and housing reforms).

The Conservative governments of 1979–97 were not enthusiastic about mounting large-scale evaluations of their management reforms. Ministers tended to take the line that reform was essential, and self-evidently desirable, and that formal, public evaluation might prove a delay and distraction. Internal management reviews were more common. The 1997–2010 Labour governments were more committed to formal evaluation, but often found it politically expedient to move on to new reforms before the full evaluations of their previous efforts were available (Walker, 2001).

There have, however, been a number of specific evaluations of particular initiatives, and some of these were made available within the public domain. For example, there was a useful series of assessments of the Next Steps programme, which were basically positive in tone (e.g. Trosa, 1994) although acknowledging the danger of fragmentation and loss of departmental control (Office of Public Services Reform, 2002). There has also been a series of very useful performance audits, addressed to different reforms, from the National Audit Office (e.g. National Audit Office, 1999, 2006, 2009, 2010). For example, as reported in Chapter 5, one study found that the departmental Capability Review programme had apparently led to improvements in capacity and leadership, but that these could not be connected either to PSA performance achievements or to outcomes (National Audit Office, 2009).

Some academic evaluations have begun to appear. One of the most thorough of these suggests that there have probably been substantial, though not spectacular efficiency gains, increased responsiveness to service users, but significant loss of equity (Boyne et al., 2003). Another has concluded that the programme for reforming the civil service, while falling well short of its claims for 'transformation' and radical step-change, has nevertheless achieved more incremental/less spectacular continuous improvement (Bovaird and Russell, 2007).

Key Events—United Kingdom

Period	General	Organization	Personnel	Finance
1980–5	1979–90 Thatcher (Conservative) prime Minister	From 1979 Rayner Scrutinies (efficiency studies led by a businessman) 1983 First set of performance indicators for the National Health Service Major privatizations begin, including British Aerospace (1981) and Telecom (1984)	1981 Civil Service Department abolished 1981 Management and Personnel office (MPO) created within the Cabinet Office	1982 Financial Management Initiative (Zifcak, 1994)
1986–90	1990–7 Major (Conservative) Prime Minister	1988 Next Steps initiative to establish executive agencies. By 1996 there were 127 agencies employing 375,000 civil servants 1989 White Paper *Working for Patients* introduces market mechanisms to the National Health Service		1990 Trading Fund Act extends range of government agencies able to use trading funds
1991–5	1992 Maastricht Treaty (EU)	1991 *Citizen's Charter* 1993 Programme of Fundamental Reviews of ministries (leads to downsizings averaging 20%)	1991 Treasury allows departments new flexibilities on personnel management, pay, and allowances 1992 13 agencies introduce group bonus schemes 1994 White Paper *Continuity and Change* on civil service reform 1995 Further White Paper, *Taking Forward Continuity and Change*	1994 Private Finance Initiative launched (later developed further by Labour Government and becomes a major instrument for public sector investment)
1996–2000	1997 Labour wins election, Blair becomes Prime Minister (1997–2007) 1999 House of Lords Act, drastically reduces the hereditary element in the House of Lords	1999 White Paper *Modernising Government* 1999 e-government strategy paper 1999 Freedom of Information Act	1996 Creation of Senior Civil Service (SES) 1999 Launch of Civil Service Reform Programme (Bovaird and Russell, 2007)	1998 Introduction of Public Service Agreements (PSAs), in which departments agree with the Treasury to achieve certain targets in exchange for their resource allocations 1998 First Comprehensive Spending Review
2001–5		2002 Further e-government strategy. 2004 Gershon Review of the efficiency of the public sector 2004 Launch of DirectGov website 2005 Cabinet Office launches departmental Capability Reviews (National Audit Office, 2009); 17 departments are reviewed in less than two years	2004 Civil service reform: delivery and values (Cabinet Office, 2004) 2004 *Well-Placed to Deliver* (Lyons Review, 2004) proposes major deconcentration of civil servants from London and the South East 2005 Launch of Professional Skills for Government training programme	2001 Introduction of Resource Accounting and Budgeting
2006–10	2007 Green Paper *The Governance of Britain* 2007 Brown takes over from Blair as Prime Minister 2010 general election: Conservative/Liberal Democrat coalition government formed. Cameron Prime Minister	2008 *Excellence and Fairness: Achieving World Class Public Services* (Cabinet Office, 2008) 2009 *Putting the Frontline First: Smarter Government* (HM Government, 2009) 2010 New government abolishes Public Service Agreements, Departmental Strategic Objectives, and a number of other performance indicators		2010 Comprehensive Spending Review: new coalition government announces major cuts over the following four years right across the public sector

UNITED STATES OF AMERICA

A. Socio-economic forces: general

The USA is unique among the twelve countries in this study in its status as a military and economic 'superpower'. It is rich and powerful (see Table A.1). Thus it is probably in a better position than other states to influence the course of global trends. Nevertheless, there are limits to its power, and it, too, is subject to the challenges of an ageing society, changing social values and norms, and mass immigration—plus the growing economic rivalry with China.

B. Global economic forces

Imports and exports form a considerably smaller proportion of the US economy than for any of the other eleven countries reviewed in this book. Yet, as with social trends, the US is far from immune to international economic trends. See Appendix A for key statistics.

C. Sociodemographic issues

Although rich on the basis of average per capita incomes (Table A.1) the USA spends a surprisingly small amount of government money on social expenditure (Table A.2). By comparison with most European countries it has only a 'thin' welfare state.

D. National socio-economic policies

The 1980s was a period during which political and popular awareness of the federal deficit grew—alongside the growth of the deficit itself. High levels of defence spending under the Reagan administration, together with its failure to cut back on social programmes as sharply as had originally been intended, contributed to this problem (Stockman, 1986). These increases dwarfed the savings and cuts that flowed from managerial efficiency improvements (see Section M below). Under Clinton, from 1992, however, more effective measures were taken to control the deficit, and at the same time the economy entered a long boom. In 1997 President Clinton and the Republican dominated Congress agreed a five-year plan to balance the budget, and by the time President Clinton made

his 1999 State of the Union address, a political debate was building up on the question of what to do with the anticipated budget surpluses. George W. Bush inherited a rapidly changing economic situation, and after the 11 September, 2001 terrorist attacks, it became abundantly clear that the US economy was slowing down. By background and conviction, the new President was fiscally conservative, pro-big business and pro-market, but (like Reagan) his increased military and security spending, along with a series of tax cuts, soon threatened the federal fiscal balance. 'Ironically, despite Bush's campaign rhetoric about smaller government and more efficient management, his tactical decisions to pursue an unpopular war, cut domestic programmes, and increase the size of the bureaucracy, have created the largest public debit in history' (Milakovitch, 2006, p. 476). Towards the end of the 2000–8 Bush Presidency the renewed deficit was further amplified by the impacts of the global economic crisis of 2008–9. Famously, soon after assuming office, President Obama launched a $787 billion dollar spending package designed to prop up a reeling American economy—the American Recovery and Reinvestment Act. The long-run deficit picture remains grim as the generation of children born shortly after the Second World War (the 'baby boomers') enter retirement, leading to increased consumption of federal retirement and medical services.

E. The political system

The USA possesses a unique political system among our twelve countries. It is a federal state, with a constitutionally entrenched division of powers between the executive, legislature, and judiciary. From the 'founding fathers' on, there has been an ideological commitment to maintain a system of 'checks and balances' to ensure that no one of the three main branches of government can dominate.

There is a two-party system (Republican and Democrat) but the parties are each 'broad churches', and, by European standards, there is little party discipline within the legislature, each Congressman/woman or Senator being free to vote and act according to his/her own dictates, though in recent decades party discipline has increased (Hetherington, 2009). Individual committees within the legislature also enjoy high independence, and the chairs of the senior committees are major political figures in their own right. Specific constituency interests have a strong influence on voting patterns. There is no equivalent to the Christian Democrat, Social Democrat or Socialist Parties which are such a familiar presence in Western European politics. The president is directly elected every four years and cannot serve more than two successive terms.

The legislature is bicameral and, relative to the executive, unusually powerful by European standards. The president and the executive cannot rely on getting their way—certainly not in matters of administrative reform. The agencies of the executive may be partly or wholly 'captured' by interest groups represented within the legislature. Many expert commentators have remarked on the legislature's predilection for 'micro-managing' the federal bureaucracy and its lack of interest in management reform (e.g. Kettl, 2009). 'No recent president has been able to garner much interest or support from Congress for his management initiatives' (Breul and Kamensky, 2008, p. 1023).

Washington politics is also characterized by a 'spoils system', in which an incoming administration hands out large numbers of senior administrative posts to political sympathizers (nowadays up to 4,000, including many posts which in most of our other countries would go to career civil servants—Peters, 2010). These (often short-term) political appointees then work alongside career civil servants (Heclo, 1977—he memorably called it a 'government of strangers'). The spoils system has grown in size since 1980, and the 'intensity of politicization has been increasing markedly, especially in the second Bush administration' (Peters, 2010, p. 119). Finally, it should be remembered that the American legislature frequently indulges in 'pork barrel' politics—where the benefits of public programmes are carefully calculated to appeal to particular constituencies and regions. Contracting out—which has grown significantly over the past three decades—is one example of this: 'the allure to members of Congress of bringing contracts and jobs back to their districts is insatiable' (Durant et al., 2009, p. 214).

Finally, it must not be forgotten that, although the main focus of this book is on national-level governments, the USA has an extensively decentralized and democratized system of governance. Of approximately 22 million public servants holding office in 2006, only about 2.7 million were at the federal level, and only about 15 per cent of those employees are based in Washington DC. Of this 2.7 million, 800,000 were in the postal service, 700,000 in the Department of Defense and 250,000 in the Veterans Administration, leaving fewer than 1 million staffing the whole of the remainder of the federal machine. 'Most of the service delivery, including that for many federal programs, is done by state and local governments' (Peters, 2010, p. 118). The contracting out of public services also contributes to this relatively small centre—by 2002 contract employees represented 62 per cent of the combined total of contractees, the civil service, and military positions (Durant et al., 2009, p. 208).

F. New management ideas

The USA is characterized by a 'business-oriented', 'free enterprise' culture. Its system of government is also very open and fragmented. These factors have meant that it has been very easy for private sector management concepts to enter the public sector. At various times the federal administration has expressed enthusiasm towards most of the contemporary management techniques and approaches, including management by objectives, downsizing, TQM, benchmarking, and re-engineering.

A historical perspective indicates that there is nothing particularly new in this openness to business techniques. For example, in the 1960s the federal government famously adopted a Planning, Programming, and Budgeting System (PPBS), and in the 1970s other techniques with private sector conceptual origins, such as Zero-Based Budgeting (ZBB) and organizational development, were also enthusiastically embraced. As far back as the start of the twentieth century, progressive reformers were looking to the private sector for models of efficient management.

The second Bush administrations from 2001 to 2009 were exceptionally favourable to approaches of private sector origin. A month after his inauguration, the President made a speech in which he said that reforms must be a) citizen-centred, b) results-centred and c) market-based (Breul and Kamnesky, 2008, p. 1015). His administration aggressively pursued both a new performance pay system and massive contracting out. Most notoriously, it contracted out so much of the war effort in Iraq that by the end of 2006 there were almost 100,000 private contractors in the country—almost as many as there were US combat troops (Scahill, 2007). Two major new performance pay systems were introduced—in the Departments of Homeland Security and Defense (Perry et al., 2009).

G. Pressure from citizens

Since the 1970s, US public opinion has tended to become increasingly critical of both the motives and the competence of federal government (Bok, 1997; Kaufman, 1981). Most Americans believe that the federal bureaucracy wastes huge sums of money. However, the accuracy of popular perceptions of its federal government can be questioned; for example, while a majority believed that the administrative overheads ate up more than 50 per cent of the social security programme, the true figure was actually less than 2 per cent (Bok, 1997, p. 56). Nevertheless, US presidents and their colleagues have to operate against a background in which the proportion of Americans who believe that public officials don't care what people think has grew from 36 per cent in 1964 to 66 per cent in 1996, and the proportion who thought that quite a few people in government are crooked has rose (over the same period) from 29 per cent to 51 per cent (Orren, 1997). This set of attitudes does not so much point towards specific management reforms as it handicaps all reformers, insofar as their efforts and motives are likely to be regarded with widespread scepticism by the public. It is one manifestation of the strong populist (Jeffersonian) theme in American politics, with its mixture of fear of and suspicion for any kind of technocratic, Washington-based elite (Peters, 2010, pp. 118–19).

At the same time, however, citizen approval of particular services co-exists with their generalized mistrust of 'the feds'. Major institutions such as the Social Security Administration, the Internal Revenue Service and the Postal Service regularly score highly on customer satisfaction, and at least equal private sector satisfaction scores. A contemporary example is the 'tea-party' movement that has been sharply critical of the scope of government, but at the same time is largely supportive of social security programmes (Moynihan and Ingraham, 2010).

H. Party political ideas

These, too, were influenced by the general 'free enterprise' culture, and by the absence of a Social Democratic or Socialist Party of any size or salience. Thus a majority of both Republicans and Democrats have been willing to sign up to notions of more 'businesslike' government. Since the late 1970s, however, a substantial group of right-wing Republicans have taken a more radical stance. Deeply sceptical of the efficacy of federal actions, they have argued for fundamental downsizing of the civil service and a general reduction in 'government interference'. At the time of writing, the anti-federal bureaucracy theme is being propounded as vigorously as ever, despite the fact that an activist, Democratic presidency is installed in the White House. One example of this would be the way that the Obama administration's idea of having a government-run health insurance scheme to run alongside private schemes (one part of the health reform bill) led straight to the bitterest ideological attacks, including the (to Europeans laughable) suggestion that President Obama was some kind of socialist, or even communist.

I. Chance events

Some events had an impact on specific aspects or sectors of the federal administration. Two examples would be the 1986 Challenger space shuttle explosion (which had a big impact on the National Aeronautics and Space Administration, one of the largest federal agencies) and the 1994 Oklahoma City bombing, which starkly illustrated the depths of hatred for the federal authorities felt by some groups on the radical right of the American political spectrum.

However, the clearest example of event-driven policymaking was the range of measures adopted following the Al Quaeda terrorist attacks of 11 September, 2001. These led directly to a major federal reorganization, with the creation of the Department of Homeland Security as its centrepiece. Other reorganizations stemmed from the huge damage caused in 2005 by Hurricane Katrina, when it came ashore close to New Orleans. This was a national disaster, but also a public relations disaster for the Bush presidency, which therefore led to considerable reorganization of federal emergency services (Sylves, 2006; Waugh, 2006). At the time of writing the Obama administration has been struggling to address the huge oil spill following an explosion of a BP drilling rig in the Gulf of Mexico. It seems likely that, as with previous natural and technological disasters, this will lead to reforms of various kinds, including new regulatory powers being given to public authorities, and reorganization within the Interior Department.

J. Elite decision-making

It is less appropriate to speak of a (singular) elite perception in the USA than in some more centralized and homogenous European countries. Traditionally, in the USA, executive perceptions of what was needed tended to be somewhat at variance with the perceptions of leading groups within the legislature. Whilst it may have been relatively easy to secure consensus on the proposition that the federal government needs to be more flexible, efficient, customer-friendly, and coordinated, it has been much more difficult to build a broad coalition of support for a package of specific and concrete measures to achieve this. As George W. Bush's *President's Management Agenda* document put it, 'All too often, Congress is part of the government's managerial problems' (Office of Management and Budget, 2001, p. 6).

As indicated above, reformers had to contend with a general loss of trust in the federal machine, a tendency which was frequently encouraged by presidents themselves. Since Lyndon Johnson, all successful presidential candidates (with the partial exception of the George H. W. Bush) have presented themselves as outside critics determined to fix the problems of the federal government. From the 1930s to the 1980s presidents frequently pursued ambitious reorganizations of government, as Congress was largely content to delegate such powers to the executive. However, a combination of a Supreme Court decision that such legislative deference was excessive, and a growing reluctance on the part of Congress to cede such powers has seen less attention to reorganization.

Instead of moving boxes around, presidents turned to changes in technique—budgetary and accounting systems, privatization, customer service systems, performance management—have been regarded as more feasible/less politically controversial than wholesale redesign of the government's other aspects of public management. More ambitious reforms that sought to make personnel policies more flexible, sometimes by reducing civil service protections, failed to win legislative support amidst strong lobbying by public sector unions (e.g. Reagan's 1986 Civil Service Simplification Act, Clinton's Personnel System Reinvention and Omnibus Civil Service Reform Acts, and Bush's Freedom to Manage Act).

The most notable exception to these trends was the passage of the 2002 Homeland Security Act, which created the Department of Homeland Security. The Act allowed President Bush to move twenty-two agencies from across government into a single department, while giving the Secretary of the Department significant new personnel authority. But the unusual politics of the Act—in the aftermath of 9/11 an enormously popular President Bush was able to link management issues to national security—emphasizes the difficulties of pursuing large-scale reform (Moynihan, 2005), and President Obama has shown little intent to pursue reform via legislation. Nevertheless, one ongoing clear dividing line between the parties has been a Republican desire to eliminate many traditional civil service protections, and future policy windows may be exploited for this purpose.

By the end of the 1980s there were signs of a real collapse of morale within the federal service (Volcker, 1989). This was in hardly anyone's interest, and provided the incoming Clinton administration with a base on which to build support for a new attempt at reform. This took the form of the National Performance Review and the Government Performance and Results Act (see Section N below). The George W. Bush Presidency, from 2000, declared three aims for the federal machine, 'actively promoting...innovation through competition', being 'citizen-centered', and 'results-oriented' (Office of Management and Budget, 2001, p. 4). The Obama administration maintained some of the same priorities—continuing to emphasize performance and citizen engagement for example—but interpreted these terms somewhat differently.

K. The administrative system

The US administrative system is quite fragmented and highly permeable to influences from outside the executive itself. Unlike many European countries, the USA never developed a unified and powerful central state apparatus. It democratized before it industrialized, and industrialized before the main era of state-building (Amenta and Skocpol, 1989). During the twentieth century a patchwork of departments and agencies grew up, which successive attempts at reform (especially the Brownlow Committee of 1936 and the Hoover Commissions of 1949 and 1955) only partly succeeded in rationalizing (Savoie, 1994).

By the mid 1990s the federal machine consisted of a wide variety of organizational forms (Peters, 1995). These included fourteen cabinet departments, a large number of independent executive organizations (e.g. the National Aeronautics and Space Administration), independent regulatory commissions (e.g. the Federal Trade Commission), and public corporations (e.g. the Tenessee Valley Authority, the Federal Deposit Insurance Corporation). There are also organizations within the sphere of the legislature which are important players in financial and management issues—especially the Congressional Budget Office (CBO) and the General Accounting Office (GAO).

While a modest employer in terms of its proportion of the total labour force (2.4%) or of the total public labour force (only 15%), the federal government is still a big employer in absolute terms.

In summary, the American public bureaucracy is a mixture of a highly professionalized and depoliticized civil service at its lowest levels, and a highly politicized and transient set of officials at the top of public organizations. (Peters, 2010, p. 120)

L. Contents of the reform package

Of the twelve countries in this study the USA is probably the one which has been home to the strongest anti-government rhetoric, and the lowest public trust of government (it is not clear which is the cart and which is the horse). Five of the last six presidents (Carter in 1976, Reagan in 1980 and Clinton and Bush Snr in 1992, Bush Jnr in 2000) felt it politically advantageous to include criticism of the federal bureaucracy as a significant element in their electoral campaigns. In practice, however, their actions have varied from attempts at sympathetic modernization of the federal departments and agencies (Carter and Clinton) to attacks on alleged bureaucratic 'waste' and duplication, combined with the introduction of more and more political appointees (Reagan, G. W. Bush). Ever-expanding contracting out seems to have been a feature of administrations of both political colours. This has grown steadily from the (always existing) contracting out for products (computers, military hardware), through contracting for general services (office cleaning, prison management) to contracting for what many would regard as core government functions (including policy-making and monitoring contracts), and contracting for HRM functions such as recruitment and workforce planning (Durant et al., 2009).

One reform which took place just before the period covered by this book, but which needs to be mentioned, was President Carter's 1978 Civil Service Reform Act (CSRA—see Ban and Ingraham, 1984). This created a Senior Executive Service (SES) of about 8,000, and introduced performance appraisal and merit pay. The SES provision had been designed partly to cater for growing public/private pay differentials (in favour of the latter), but Congress soon cut the share of SES positions that were eligible for bonuses from 50 per cent to 20 per cent. One rueful contemporary comment on the implementation of the CSRA was that Congressional support for it was 'a mile wide but an inch deep'. President Reagan was subsequently able to make good use of the 1978 Act to dominate personnel administration to a greater extent than his predecessors had been able to. A quarter of a century later George W. Bush was promising to 'establish a meaningful system to measure performance. Create awards for employees who surpass expectations', as though this were a new idea (Office of Management and Budget, 2001, p. 11).

The Reagan administration introduced a welter of reforms, many of them designed to bring 'business disciplines' to the federal civil service. It was also systematic in exploiting the Presidency's huge power of patronage to appoint Conservatives to key positions throughout Washington. Some of the principal initiatives were:

- Appointing Donald Devine, an arch-conservative and virulent critic of the federal bureaucracy, to be head of the Office of Personnel Management (OPM). 'Career officials were shocked and demoralized by Devine's hostility to them' (Savoie, 1994, p. 222).
- The President's Council on Integrity and Efficiency (founded 1981). 'It questioned many practices, identified billions of savings as a result of audits, launched civil and criminal actions, and introduced many sanctions against government agencies or employees' (Savoie, 1994, p. 189).
- Reform 88 (launched in 1982). This was a broad-scope programme, somewhat lacking in focus. Actions under its umbrella included upgrading computer systems and improving financial management and accountability.
- The Council on Management and Administration (1982).
- The President's Private Sector Survey on Cost Control (PPSSCC, better known as the 'Grace Commission', 1982).

- The Council on Management Improvement (1984). This was a council of assistant secretaries from across federal departments and agencies, tasked to develop long-range management improvement plans and reinforce the implementation of Reform 88.
- The President's Productivity Program (from 1985). This was aimed at increasing the productivity of government agencies by 20 per cent by 1992. Measures included the widespread adoption of TQM.
- 'Although not nearly as successful as he would have liked, Reagan promoted privatisation, contracting out, and user fees at every opportunity' (Savoie, 1994, p. 215).

The Grace Commission was one of the most publicized of these initiatives, and in some ways typified the Reagan administration's approach. It involved bringing in large numbers of business people (2,000, supported by 859 companies) with a brief to identify bureaucratic 'waste'. Over a two-year period it generated forty-seven reports containing 2,478 recommendations. It claimed potential savings of $298 billion, though a General Accounting Office analysis suggested that the true figure was more like $98 billion. Some of its recommendations were partly or wholly implemented, but many were not (Pollitt, 1993, pp. 91–5). In proportion to the size of the effort (and of the fanfare—see Grace, 1984) it left only a small trace. The much less widely publicized Council on Integrity and Efficiency probably had a considerably greater impact.

President Bush (1988–92) was less overtly antibureaucrat than Reagan—possibly because he had a lifetime of public service behind him. He presided over a growing crisis in the morale of the federal service, but was seemingly unable to take any particularly strong action to counter it. In 1989 a task force identified serious weaknesses in the public service (including pay, performance appraisal, and career development systems and morale—Volcker, 1989). In 1990 a General Accounting Office study came to broadly similar conclusions (US General Accounting Office, 1990). Yet no major reforms were undertaken. As one observer wrote at the time: 'America's flame of managerial reform seems to have died down to a glowing ember' (Hede, 1991, pp. 507–8). President Bush's main interests seem to have lain with high policy issues rather than management reform.

By contrast, the incoming Clinton administration of 1992 was keen to restore status to the federal machine, and to do so by pursuing a high-profile reform which would lead to a government that 'works better and costs less'. The centrepiece of their programme, entrusted to Vice President Gore, was the National Performance Review (NPR—see Gore, 1996, 1997; National Performance Review, 1997; and countless other publications). This package included proposals for savings (promises of $108 billion worth) and downsizing (by 252,000, subsequently raised by Congress to 272,900), as well as for 'empowerment' and 'reinvention'. Different stakeholders have stressed different aspects, and from the start it was clear that there were tensions between, for example, the 'savings and downsizing' theme and the 'empowerment and reinvention' theme. 'In practice NPR has been a messy and sometimes disorganised multi-front war against the government's performance problems' (Kettl, 1994, p. 5).

A second major management reform proceeded alongside the NPR. The 1993 Government Performance and Results Act (GPRA) mandated the development of strategic planning and performance measurement throughout the federal government (National Academy of Public Administration, 1994). Its origins went back to draft Congressional legislation from the Bush era (Radin, 1998, p. 308). Three years of pilot projects were planned before the reporting requirements were 'rolled out' to the rest of the federal government in 1997.

After 2000, the approach of George W. Bush in some ways echoed that of Reagan. He placed great emphasis on competitive outsourcing and the advantages of competition. He 're-invented' the idea of performance budgeting, and made a results orientation one of his central themes. He also re-invented performance-related pay, and installed it in two major federal departments (Perry et al., 2009). Like almost every other Western government, he lauded the potential of e-government. Without referring to the Clinton–Gore NPR (which, in rhetorical terms at least, quickly disappeared from view), he discovered that federal managers lacked discretion, and headlined 'freedom to manage' as a goal (Office of Management and Budget, 2001, p. 5). However, in the aftermath of 9/11 he also set up a Department of Homeland Security, and used this as a vehicle for achieving greater managerial flexibility and freedom from

Congressional control (see also Bouckaert et al., 2010, chapter 11).

In contrast with his two immediate predecessors, President Obama's tenure has not been marked by high-profile reform packages designed to garner political attention. There is no equivalent to the National Performance Review, or the Presidents Management Agenda. Nevertheless, the Office of Management and Budget (OMB) and the OPM have quietly pursued reforms, largely using executive authority, that they hope will have a significant impact on public management. Since there is no central reform blueprint, understanding the specific goals of the Obama White House requires looking to statements of White House officials before Congress, budget documents, or internal memorandum. A 2010 memo from the OMB to Senior Executive Service officials offers perhaps the best summary of Obama's goals:

1. Driving agency top priorities: As part of the budget process, agency heads were asked to identify three to eight performance goals that they will be held publicly accountable for. Legislation in Congress has proposed to make this process permanent. The White House also has pushed agencies that interact with the public to develop transparent service standards that can be used as dashboards to summarize citizen experience of government.
2. Cutting waste: The Obama White House has sought to cut programmes deemed as duplicative, out-of-date, or underperforming.
3. Reforming contracting: In a marked contrast with previous administrations, the Obama administration sought to limit, and in some cases reverse, contracting out.
4. Closing the IT gap: As with Bush and Clinton, the Obama White House argues that technology can significantly improve performance, but poor implementation of IT projects has limited that potential.
5. Promoting accountability and innovation through open government: Obama promised to clearly communicate how well they were doing, in the hope that it would improve public understanding of government, but also provide a spur to better performance by agencies. Performance metrics and goals have been made publicly available, and the White House has sought to emphasize transparency in both

programmes and special initiatives, creating websites that track spending of stimulus funds, for example. The White House also promised to create 'problem-solving networks' that capture the input of citizens and practitioners inside and outside of government.
6. Attracting and motivating top talent: The Office of Personnel Management was directed by the President to find ways of using executive authority to make government attractive to younger people, and to make simpler the confusing and slow recruitment process.

M. The implementation process

Implementing management reform has always been difficult for US presidents. As noted above, the powers of Congress to intervene in organizational restructurings are as extensive as its powers to reshape budgets. Nor are the agencies themselves under such clear and unequivocal hierarchical authority as would be usual in the case of, say, a British or French agency. Many exist as one corner in an 'iron triangle', with Congress as a second corner, and one or more major interest groups as a third (e.g. farmers, or the oil companies, or the defence industries). These links can give agencies the capacity to resist unwelcome changes through political channels.

Furthermore, implementation of some important reforms has been entrusted mainly to political appointees (rather than career civil servants). For example, the 'reinvention' teams established under the NPR were usually led by Clinton appointees. Sometimes this helps give impetus, but at other times it produces oscillations and discontinuities, as political appointees find their attentions are drawn away to other issues of current political salience, or, indeed, they themselves leave their posts (the turnover among political appointees can be brisk).

A further complication is the highly legalistic nature of much US management reform. Even when a president gets a reform through Congress s/he must then see what the courts make of it. An interesting case is the way the process of contracting out has become a vehicle for extending the reach of legislative and judicial values deep into the 'contract state'. For example, legal obligations for transparency can be placed on any body that uses government funds. 'Due to the growth and persistence of the contract state, Congress and the

U.S. Supreme Court have begun to extend the reach of the American state into the private and nonprofit sectors in an effort to maintain the constitutional character of the polity' (Bumgarner and Newswander, 2009, p. 203). De-regulating federal human resource management (an objective of the second Bush administration) was another area in which legal advice and legal capacity seems to have been crucial (Riccucci and Thompson, 2008).

Unsurprisingly, therefore, the record of implementation of reforms has been patchy. Organizationally the key player in management changes would normally be the OMB. In practice, however, this has not always been a substantial force for management reform. Within OMB the emphasis on management has varied, and for considerable periods the bulk of their effort has been directed to short-term budgetary issues, with management improvement taking a poor second place (see Savoie, 1994, for an account of the changing role of OMB under Reagan). Under Clinton, OMB took a lead role in implementing the GPRA, but, by contrast, made only limited inputs to the NPR reinvention activities. Even with the GPRA, however, the nature of the US governmental system led to implementation difficulties:

Although the aims of GPRA suggest that the information produced under the Act will support more rational decisionmaking, both the structure of the US government and current developments in other areas make this extremely difficult. The structure creates a disconnect between budget functions, agency organisation, and the jurisdictions of appropriations committees. The fragmented nature of decisionmaking, including budget decisionmaking, limits the ability of any institution of government in either the executive or the legislative branch to look at crosscutting issues and the government as a whole. (Radin, 1998, p. 311)

Under G. W. Bush the OMB played a crucial role in administering the Program Assessment Rating Tool (PART) and, more generally, in regularly checking departments and agencies' progress in implementing the President's Management Agenda (Breul and Kamensky, 2008). This was a break with the Clinton and Reagan era reliance on special commissions to lead reform efforts, and restored the institutional primacy of the OMB. PART, in particular, gave a mechanism by which the OMB could not only evaluate the performance of agencies, but redirect their goals where it found them wanting (Moynihan 2008).

Thus far, President Obama has maintained a strong emphasis on performance management (Moynihan 2009). Obama fulfilled a campaign promise by appointing a Chief Performance Officer, who is also the Deputy Director for the OMB, and the most visible representative of the President's reform agenda. In terms of tone, Obama appointees want to project a style distinct from previous presidencies. Obama officials suggested that Clinton and Gore's Reinventing Government was too decentralized ('let a thousand flowers bloom'), while the Bush OMB was overly controlling in its interaction with agencies, resulting in a good deal of agency resistance. 'By contrast, the Obama OMB declares that it wants to create a "focused collaboration" with agencies, characterized by principles of prioritization, transparency, engagement, and rapid results' (Moynihan, 2009, p. 6; see also Bouckaert and Halligan, 2008, appendix).

N. Reforms actually achieved

Despite the existence of a flourishing evaluation culture in the US public sector, it is extremely difficult to come to any sure assessment of the impact of the reforms since 1980. At a micro-level there have clearly been many examples and cases of efficiency gains, modernization of systems, and increased attention to customer responsiveness. Some of the NPR publications are spattered with up-beat examples of such performance improvements (e.g. Gore, 1997). However, broad-scope evaluations seem thin on the ground. An academic review of NPR reinvention laboratories identifies some successes (especially where there has been 'stubborn' leadership) but also some failures and continuing problems (Ingraham, Thompson, and Sanders, 1998). Certainly most of the reforms of the Reagan administration were not subject to scientific evaluation—the mood of the times was somewhat against evaluation, as being itself a further symptom of bureaucratic empire-building and obfuscation. Assessments of GPRA by the GAO indicate a mixed picture, with some performance plans following well short of what the act seems to require (e.g. General Accounting Office, 1998, 2001). As for the NPR, one authoritative academic assessment is mixed—in the main, federal agencies technically complied with NPR, but effectively dampened much of its intended force. Cultural change has been patchy (Thompson, 2000). Subsequently, in his incoming management agenda,

George W. Bush laid great stress on the fact that 'What matters in the end is completion. Performance. Results.' (Office of Management and Budget, 2001, p. 1). However, although setting targets for most of its initiatives, the President's agenda was largely silent about arrangements for evaluation and accountability. Perhaps, this is 'business as usual', since, as the Agenda itself notes:

Congress, the Executive Branch, and the media have all shown far greater interest in the launch of new initiatives than in following up to see if anything useful ever occurred. (Office of Management and Budget, 2001, p. 3)

Most academic commentaries on the success or otherwise of the G. W. Bush management reforms seem to give them a mixed bill of health. Performance budgeting and performance pay have both been problematic (Gilmour and Lewis, 2006; Perry et al., 2009; Riccucci and Thompson, 2008), and the structural innovation of the Department of Homeland Security is itself exceptionally difficult to evaluate in terms of 'results'. The Bush-era PART process consumed enormous amounts of time and attention as almost every federal programme was assessed. But outside of the executive branch, it had limited influence, and did not seem to alter appropriations decisions in Congress (Moynihan 2008). Efforts to institutionalize PART via legisla-

tion also drew little support, and the Obama administration has shown little inclination to continue with the tool, preferring instead to invite agencies to compete for funds for evaluations that promise a clear impact. Obama officials criticized PART as too broad in its focus, failing to pay close enough attention to important programmes. Obama's first Chief Performance Officer also criticized the Bush administration for generating a great deal of performance information, but rarely using it, promising that the Obama White House would actively use data to manage agencies, and encourage agency leaders to learn from data.

It is relatively early to assess the Obama administration, although the President's emphasis on transparency and publicly available metrics may make such assessments easier (and are, in themselves, evidence of implementation of the transparency goal). At the same time, the reliance on limited and specific reform goals has kept muted expectations, so that any progress may be regarded as a success. In cutting waste, the White House has pointed to initial success, claiming that 60 per cent of proposed cuts were accepted by Congress, which is about three times the rate of success of previous administrations. In the area of performance management, the long-run test will be whether agency heads, and Congress, take seriously the performance goals they promise to achieve.

Key Events—USA

Period	General	Organization	Personnel	Finance
1980–5	1980–8 Reagan Presidency (Republican)	1981 Council on Integrity and Efficiency 1982 Council on Management and Administration 1984 Council of Management Improvement 1985 President's Productivity Program—aimed to increase agency productivity by 20% by 1992	1983–8 Number of separate federal payroll systems reduced from 132 to 53	1982 Launch of Reform 88 1982 President's Private Sector Survey on Cost Control (the 'Grace Commission'). Produced many reports and recommendations, but frequently not implemented 1984–8 Number of separate financial systems reduced from 370 to 253
1986–90	1988–92 G.Bush Presidency (Republican)	1989 Management by Objectives system allows White House to monitor key programmes. Discontinued in 1991	1990 Federal Employees Pay Comparability Act	
1991–5	1992–2000 Clinton Presidency (Democrat) 1992 National Performance Review (NPR) announced as a headline reform programme 1993 Government Performance and Results Act (GPRA). See Radin 2006 for critique	1995 Government-wide electronic contracting system	1994 Federal Workforce Restructuring Act cuts federal workforce by 272,000 full-time equivalents	1991 Chief Financial Officers Act 1991 Office of Federal Financial Management set up within OMB
1996–2000	2000–8 G. W. Bush Presidency (Republican)	1996 Information Technology Management Act: created a Chief Information Officer for each agency		
2001–5	2001 9/11 terrorist attack on New York and Washington	2001 G. W. Bush's President's Management Agenda 2001 Launch of Results.gov, a web portal for the President's Management Agenda 2002 Introduction of Programme Assessment Rating Tool (PART—see Milakovich, 2006; Moynihan 2008) 2002 Creation of Department of Homeland Security, which fuses 22 previous	2002 Homeland Security legislation includes provisions permitting the Secretary to relax the usual personnel regulations 2004 OMB and the Office of Personnel Management (OPM) set out the rules for a new performance-related pay system for senior executives (see Perry et al., 2009)	Having inherited a fairly sound fiscal position from the Clinton Presidency, the G. W. Bush Presidency oversaw an increasing deficit, thanks to increased military expenditure and tax cuts for the wealthy

2006–10	2008 Global economic crisis. 2008– Obama Presidency (Democrat)	departments and agencies, and is focused on preventing further terrorist attacks. 2007 President G. W. Bush issues an Executive Order requiring all agencies to appoint performance improvement officers	Initial White House emphasis on performance management, transparency, and citizen engagement, but no 'headline' programme for public management	Federal deficit worsens dramatically with onset of Global Economic Crisis, and huge federal expenditures to prop up financial institutions and US carmakers

■ BIBLIOGRAPHY

6, P. (2004) 'Joined-Up Government in the Western World in Comparative Perspective: A Preliminary Literature Review and Exploration', *Journal of Public Administration Research and Theory*, 14:1, pp. 103–38.

Aberbach, J. and Christensen, T. (2001) 'Radical Reform in New Zealand: Crisis, Windows of Opportunity, and Rational Actors', *Public Administration*, 79:2, pp. 403–22.

Accenture (2008) *An International Comparison of the United Kingdom's Public Administration*, London, Accenture.

Advisory Group on Reform of Australian Government Administration (2009) *The Reform of Australian Government Administration: Building the World's Best Public Service*, Canberra, Commonwealth of Australia, October.

—— (2010) *Ahead of the Game: Blueprint for the Reform of the Australian Government Administration*, Canberra, Commonwealth of Australia, October.

Agranoff, R. (2007) *Managing within Networks: Adding Value to Public Organizations*, Washington DC, Georgetown University Press.

—— and McGuire, M. (2001) 'Big Questions in Public Network Management Research', *Journal of Public Administration Research and Theory*, 11:3, pp. 295–326.

Albertini, J.-B. (1998) *Contribution à une théorie de l'Etat déconcentré*, Bruxelles, Bruylant.

Alford, J. (2009) *Engaging Public Sector Clients: From Service-Delivery to Co-Production*, Basingstoke and New York, Palgrave/Macmillan.

Algemene Rekenkamer (1995) *Tweede Kamer*, 1994/5, 24120, no. 3.

—— (2002) *Verantwoording en toezicht bij rechtspersonen met een wettelijke taak deel 3*, 's-Gravenhage, Sdu Uitgevers.

Andrews, M. (2008) 'The Good Governance Agenda: Beyond Indicators without Theory', *Oxford Development Studies*, 36:4, pp. 379–407.

—— (2010) 'Good Government Means Different Things in Different Countries', *Governance*, 23:1, pp. 7–35.

Arndt, C. (2008) 'The Politics of Governance Ratings', *International Public Management Journal*, 11:3, pp. 275–97.

Aucoin, P. and Savoie, D. (1998) *Program Review: Lessons for Strategic Change in Governance*, Ottawa, Canadian Centre for Management Development.

—— —— (2009) 'The Politics–Administration Dichotomy: Democracy Versus Bureaucracy?', pp. 97–117 in O. Dwivendi, T. Mau, and B. Sheldrick (eds.) *The Evolving Physiology of Government: Canadian Public Administration in Transition*, Ottawa, University of Ottawa.

Auditor General of Canada (1993) 'Canada's Public Service Reform, and Lessons Learned from Selective Jurisdictions', *Report, 1993,* chapter 6, Ottawa, Auditor General of Canada.

—— (1997) *Annual report*, Ottawa, Auditor General of Canada.

—— (2001) *Reflections on a Decade of Serving Parliament*, February, Ottawa, Office of the Auditor General.

Australian Public Service Commission (2004) *A History in Three Acts: Evolution of the Public Service Act 1999*, Canberra, Commonwealth of Australia.

—— (2007) *Building Better Governance*, Canberra, ACT, Commonwealth of Australia.

—— (2009) *Challenges of Evidence-Based Policymaking*, Canberra, ACT, Commonwealth of Australia.

Bach, T., Fleischer, J., and Hustedt, T. (2010) *Organisation und steuerung zentralstaatlicher behörden*, Berlin, Edition Sigma.

Bach, T. and Jann, W. (2010) 'Animals in the Administrative Zoo: Organizational Change and Administrative Autonomy in Germany', *International Review of Administrative Sciences*, 76:3, pp. 443–68.

Baker, R. and Rennie, M. (2006) 'Forces leading to the Adoption of Accrual Accounting by the Canadian Federal Government: An Institutional Perspective', *Canadian Accounting Perspectives*, 5:1, pp. 83–112.

Balk, W. (1996) *Managerial Reform and Professional Empowerment in the Public Service*, Westport, Quorum Books.

Ball, I. (1993) 'New Zealand Public Sector Management', paper presented to the 1993 National Accountants in Government Convention, Hobart, 26–8 May.

Ban, C. (2010*a*) 'Reforming the Staffing Process in the European Union Institutions: Moving the Sacred Cow out of the Road', *International Review of Administrative Sciences*, 76:1, pp. 5–24.

—— (2010*b*) 'Intégrer la "maison" communautaire: L'arrivé au sein de la Commission des directeurs issus des nouveaux Etats membres', *Revue française d'administration publique*.

—— and Ingraham, P. (1984) *Legislating Bureaucratic Change: The Civil Service Reform Act of 1978*, New York, SUNY Press.

Barber, J. (2007) *Instruction to Deliver: Tony Blair, Public Services and the Challenge of Achieving Targets*, London, Politicos.

Barberis, P. (1998) 'The New Public Management and a New Accountability', *Public Administration*, 76:3, pp. 451–70, Autumn.

Barbier, J.-C. and Simonin, B. (1997) 'European Social Programmes: Can Evaluation of Implementation Increase the Appropriateness of Findings?', *Evaluation*, 3:4, October, pp. 391–407.

Bartoli, A. (2008) 'The Study of Public Management in France: La spécificité du modèle français d'administration', pp. 14–41 in W. Kickert (ed.) *The Study of Public Management in Europe and the US: A Comparative Analysis of National Distinctiveness*, Abingdon, Routledge.

Barzelay, M. and Gallego, R. (2010*a*) 'The Comparative Historical Analyses of Public Management Policy Cycles in France, Italy and Spain: Symposium Introduction', *Governance*, 23:2, pp. 297–307.

—— —— (2010*b*) 'The Comparative Historical Analyses of Public Management Policy Cycles in France, Italy and Spain: Symposium Conclusion', *Governance*, 23:2, pp. 209–23.

Batley, R. and Larbi, G. (2004) *The Changing Role of Government: The Reform of Public Services in Developing Countries*, Basingstoke, Palgrave/Macmillan.

BBC News (1999) 'UK Politics: Government Puts a Gloss on its Goals', 26 July <http://bbc.co.uk/1/ hi/uk_politics/403993.stm>, accessed 13 October 2004).

—— 'Annual Report: A Hostage to Fortune?', 13 July <http://bbc.co.uk/1/hi/uk_politics/831585. stm>, accessed 13 October 2004).

BBK NESS Site (2009) *National Evaluation of Sure Start* <http://www.ness.bbk.ac.uk>, accessed 18 May.

Beale, V. and Pollitt, C. (1994) 'Charters at the Grass Roots: A First Report', *Local Government Studies*, 20:2, Summer, pp. 202–25.

Behn, R. (2001) *Re-Thinking Democratic Accountability*, Washington, DC, Brookings Institution.

Bekkers, V. And Homburg, V. (2005) 'E-Government as an Information Ecology: Background and Concepts', pp. 1–19 in V. Bekkers, and V. Homburg (eds.) *The Information Ecology of E-Government*, Amsterdam, IOS Press.

Bellamy, C. and Taylor, J. (1998) *Governing in the Information Age*, Buckingham, Open University Press.

Bellamy, R. and Palumbo, R. (2010) *From Government to Governance*, London, Ashgate.

Benz, A. and Götz, K. (1996) 'The German Public Sector: National Priorities and the International Reform Agenda', pp. 1–26 in A. Benz and K. Götz (eds.) *A New German Public Sector? Reform, Adaptation and Stability*, Aldershot, Dartmouth.

Berg, A.-M. (2010) 'Lean And Mean or Fat And Nice? On The Importance Of Organizational Redundancies and Diversity', paper presented to the annual conference of the European group for Public Administration, Toulouse, September.

Bevan, G. and Hood, C. (2006) 'What's Measured is What Matters: Targets and Gaming in the English Public Healthcare System', *Public Administration*, 84:3, pp. 517–38.

Bevir, M. and Rhodes, R. (2006) *Governance Stories*, London, Routledge.

Bezes, P. (2007) 'The "Steering State" Model: The Emergence of a New Organizational Form in the French Public Administration', *Sociologie du Travail*, 49S, e67–e89.

—— (2010) 'Path Dependent and Path-Breaking Changes in the French Administrative System: The Weight of Legacy Explanations' pp. 158–73 in M. Painter and G. B. Peters (eds.) *Tradition and Public Administration*, Basingstoke, Palgrave/Macmillan.

Bilodeau, N., Laurin, C., and Vining, A. (2007) '"Choice of Organizational Form Makes a Real Difference": The Impact of Corporatization on Government Agencies in Canada', *Journal of Public Administration Research and Theory*, 17, pp. 119–47.

Blöndal, J. et al. (2008) 'Budgeting in Australia', *OECD Journal on Budgeting*, 8:2, pp. 1–64.

Bogdanor, V. (ed.) (2005) *Joined-Up Government*, Oxford, Oxford University Press.

Boje, D., Gephart, R., and Thatchenkey, T. (eds.) (1996) *Postmodern Management and Organization Theory*, London, Sage.

Bok, D. (1997) 'Measuring the Performance of Government', pp. 55–76 in J. Nye, P. Zelikow, and D. King (eds.) *Why People Don't Trust Government*, Cambridge, Mass., Harvard University Press.

Boorsma, P. and Mol, N. (1995) 'The Dutch Public Financial Revolution', pp. 219–32 in W. Kickert and F. van Vught (eds.) *Public Policy and Administration Sciences in the Netherlands*, London, Prentice Hall/Harvester Wheatsheaf.

Borins, S. (1995) 'Public Sector Innovation: The Implications of New Forms of Organisation and Work', pp. 260–87 in G. Peters and D. Savoie (eds.) *Governance in a Changing Environment*, Montreal and Kingston, Canadian Centre for Management Development and McGill-Queen's University Press.

—— (ed.) (2008) *Innovations in Government: Research, Recognition and Replication*, Washington, DC, Brookings Institute.

Boston, J. (1995) 'Lessons from the Antipodes', pp. 161–77, in B. O'Toole and G. Jordan (eds.) *Next Steps: Improving Management in Government?*, Aldershot, Dartmouth.

—— et al. (1996) *Public Management: The New Zealand Model*, Auckland, Oxford University Press.

Bouckaert, G. (1995a) 'Charters as Frameworks for Awarding Quality: The Belgian, British and French Experience', pp. 185–200, in H. Hill and H. Klages (eds.) *Trends in Public Sector Renewal: Recent Developments and Concepts of Awarding Excellence*, Europäischer Verlag der Wissenschaften, Beiträge zur Politikwissenschaft, Band 58, Frankfurt am Main, Peter Lang.

—— (1995b) 'Improving Performance Measurement', pp. 379–412, in A. Halachmi and G. Bouckaert (eds.) *The Enduring Challenges of Public Management: Surviving and Excelling in a Changing World*, San Francisco, Jossey-Bass.

—— (1996a) 'Informing the Clients: The Role of Public Service Standards Statements', pp. 109–116, in OECD, *Responsive Government, Service Quality Initiatives*, Paris, OECD, PUMA.

—— (1996b) 'Measurement of Public Sector Performance: Some European Perspectives', pp. 223–37 in A. Halachmi and G. Bouckaert (eds.) *Organisational Performance and Measurement in the Public Sector*, London, Quorum Books.

—— (2000) 'Techniques de modernisation et modernisation des techniques: Evaluer la modernisation de la gestion publique', pp. 107–28, in L. Rouban (ed.) *Le Service Public en Devenir*, Paris, L'Harmattan.

—— (2001) 'Pride and Performance in Public Service: Some Patterns of Analysis', *International Review of Administrative Sciences*, 67, pp. 9–20.

—— (2002a) 'Modernising the Rechtsstaat: Paradoxes of the Management Agenda', pp. 71–83, in K-P. Sommermann and J. Ziekow (eds.) *Perspectiven der Verwaltungsforschung*, Berlin, Duncker & Humblot.

—— (2002b) 'Administrative Convergence in the EU: Some Conclusions for CEEC's', pp. 59–68, in F. Van den Berg, G. Jenei, and L. T. LeLoup (eds.) *East-West Co-Operation in Public Sector Reform: Cases and Results in Central and Eastern Europe*, Amsterdam, International Institute of Administrative Sciences Monographs (Vol. 18), IOS Press.

—— (2002c) 'Reform of Budgetary Systems in the Public Sector', pp. 17–42, in M. Högye (ed.) *Local Government Budgeting*, Budapest, OSI/LGI, Open Society Institute (Local Government and Public Service Reform Initiative).

—— (2007) 'Cultural Characteristics from Public Management Reforms Worldwide', pp. 29–64, in K. Schedler and I. Proeller (eds.) *Cultural Aspects of Public Management Reform*, Amsterdam, Elsvier.

—— (2010) 'New Public Leadership for Public Service Reform', pp. 51–67, in J. Pierre and P. Ingraham (eds.) *Comparative Administrative Change and Reform: Lessons Learned*, Montreal and Kingston, McGill-Queen's University Press.

—— and Ulens, W. (1998) *Mesure de la performance dans le service public: exemples étrangers pour les pouvoirs publics Belges*, Bruxelles, Service Fédereaux des Affaires Scientifiques, Techniques et Culturelles.

—— and François A. (1999) *Modernisation de l'administration les questions de recherche*, Bruxelles, SSTC.

—— and Verhoest, K. (1999) 'A Comparative Perspective on Decentralisation as a Context for Contracting in the Public Sector, Practice and Theory', pp. 199–239 in Y. Fortin (ed.) *La Contractualisation dans le Secteur Public dans des Pays Industrialisés depuis 1980*, Paris, L'Harmattan.

—— Ormond, D., and Peters, G. (2000) *A Potential Governance Agenda for Finland*, Research Report No. 8, Helsinki, Ministry of Finance.

—— and Peters, B. G. (2002) 'Performance Measurement and Management: The Achilles' Heel in Administrative Modernization', *Public Performance & Management Review*, London, Sage, 25:4, pp. 359–62.

—— et al. (2002) 'Trajectories for Modernizing Local Governance, Revisiting the Flanders Case', *Public Management Review: An International Journal of Research and Theory*, Routledge, 4:3, pp. 309–42.

—— and Thijs, N. (2003) *Kwaliteit in de publieke sector: Een handboek voor kwaliteitsmanagement in de publieke sector o.b.v. een internationaal comparatieve studie*, Gent, Academia Press.

—— and Halligan, J. (2008) *Managing Performance: International Comparisons*, London, Routledge/ Taylor and Francis.

—— et al. (eds.) (2008) *Public Management Reforms in Central and Eastern Europe*, Bratislava, NISPAcee Press.

—— Peters, G. B., and Verhoest, K. (2010) *The Co-ordination of Public Sector Organizations: Shifting Patterns of Public Management*, Basingstoke, Palgrave/Macmillan.

Bourgault, J. and Carroll, B. (1997) 'The Canadian Senior Public Service: The Last Vestiges of the Whitehall Model?', pp. 91–100, in J. Bougault, M. Demers, and C. Williams (eds.) *Public Administration and Public Management in Canada*, Quebec, Les Publications du Quebec.

—— Dion, S., and Lemay, M. (1993) 'Creating Corporate Culture: Lessons from the Canadian Federal Government', *Public Administration Review*, 53:1, pp. 73–80.

—— and Savoie, D. (1998) 'Managing at the Top', paper for the authors' roundtable, Revitalising the Public Service, Ottawa, Canadian Centre for Management Development, 12–14 November.

Bourgon, J. (1998) *Fifth Annual Report to the Prime Minister on the Public Service of Canada*, Ottawa, Privy Council Office.

Bovaird, T. and Löffler, E. (2003) 'Evaluating the Quality of Public Governance: Indicators, Models and Methodologies', *International Review of Administrative Sciences*, 69:3, pp. 313–28.

—— and Russell, K. (2007) 'Civil Service Reform in the UK, 1999–2005: Revolutionary Failure or Evolutionary Success?', *Public Administration*, 85:2, pp. 301–28.

—— and Tizzard, J. (2009) 'Partnership Working in the Public Domain', pp. 233–47 in T. Bovaird and E. Löffler (eds.) *Public Management and Governance* (2nd edn.), London and New York, Routledge.

Bovens, M. (1998) *The Quest for Responsibility: Accountability and Citizenship in Complex Organizations*, Cambridge, Cambridge University Press.

—— and Zouridis, S. (2002) 'From Street-Level to System-Level Bureaucracies: How Information and Communication Technology is Transforming Administrative Discretion and Constitutional Control', *Public Administration Review*, 62:2, pp. 174–84.

Bowen, C. (2009) 'Service Delivery Reform: Designing a System that Works for You', Address to the National Press Club, Canberra, 16 December.

Boyne, G. (1998) 'Bureaucratic Theory Meets Reality: Public Choice and Service Contracting in US Local Government', *Public Administration Review*, 58:6, November/December.

—— et al. (2003) *Evaluating Public Management Reforms*, Buckingham, Open University Press.

—— et al. (eds.) (2006) *Public Service Performance: Perspectives on Measurement and Management*, Cambridge, Cambridge University Press.

Brans, M. and Hondeghem, A. (1999), 'The Senior Civil Service in Belgium' pp. 121–46, in E. C. Page and V. Wright (ed.), *Bureaucratic Elites in Western European States*, London, Oxford University Press.

—— —— (2005) 'Competency Frameworks in Belgian Governments: Causes, Construction and Content', *Public Administration*, 83:4, pp. 823–37.

Breul, J. and Kamensky, J. (2008) 'Federal Government Reform: Lessons from Clinton's "Reinventing Government" and Bush's "Management Agenda" Initiatives', *Public Administration Review*, November/December, pp. 1009–26.

Broucker, B., Depré, R., and Hondeghem, A. (2010) 'Les propositions de réformes', *La Revue Nouvelle*, 65:1, pp. 31–9.

Bruijn, H. de (2002) *Managing Performance in the Public Sector*, London, Routledge.

Bruning, E. (2010) 'A Methodological Assessment of Ten Years of Canada's *Citizens First* Satisfaction Survey Research', *International Review of Administrative Sciences*, 76:1, pp. 85–91.

Brunsson, N. (1989) *The Organisation of Hypocrisy: Talk, Decisions and Actions in Organisations*, Chichester, John Wiley.

—— (2006) *Mechanisms Of Hope: Maintaining the Dream of the Rational Organization*, Copenhagen, Copenhagen Business School Press.

—— and Olsen, J. (1993) *The Reforming Organization*, London and New York, Routledge.

Budget Department (1997) *Public Sector Productivity in Sweden*, Stockholm, Swedish Ministry of Finance.

Bumgarner, J. and Newswander, C. (2009) 'The Irony of NPM: the Inevitable Extension of the Role of the American State', *American Review of Public Administration*, 39:2, pp. 189–207.

Bureau of Transport and Communications (1995) *Evaluation of the Black Spot Program*, Canberra, Australia Government Publishing Service.

Burrell, G. (1997) *Pandemonium: Towards a Retro-Organization Theory*, London, Sage.

Business and Enterprise Committee (2009) *Eighth Report, Session 2008–09: Post Offices—Securing their Future*, 23 June. <http://www.publications.parliament.uk/pa/cm200809/cmberr/371/37102.htm>, accessed 11 September, 2009.

Cabinet Office (2008) *Excellence and Fairness: Achieving World Class Public Services*, London, HMSO.

Caiden, N. (1988) 'Shaping Things to Come', pp. 43–58, in I. Rubin (ed.) *New Directions in Budget Theory*, Albany, SUNY Press.

Cameron, D. and Simeon, R. (1998) 'Intergovernmental Relations and Democratic Citizenship', paper presented to the authors'

roundtable, Revitalising the Public Service, Ottawa, Canadian Centre for Management Development, 12–14 November.

Canadian Broadcasting Corporation (1994) *The Remaking of New Zealand*, Toronto, CBC Radio Works.

Canadian Centre for Management Development (1998a) *Citizen/Client Surveys: Dispelling Myths and Redrawing Maps*, Ottawa, CCMD.

—— (1998b) *Government at your Service: A Progress Report from the Citizen-Centred Service Network*, Ottawa, CCMD.

Carlitz, R. et al. (2009) 'Budget Transparency Around the World: Results from the 2008 Open Budget Survey', *OECD Journal on Budgeting*, 9:2, pp. 1–17.

Carter, N. (1998) 'On the Performance of Performance Indicators', pp. 177–94, in M-C. Kesler, P. Lascoumbes, M. Setbon, and J.-C. Thoenig (eds.) *Évaluation des politiques publiques*, Paris, L'Harmattan.

Castells, M. (2001) *The Internet Galaxy: Reflections on the Internet, Business, and Society*, Oxford, Oxford University Press.

—— (2010) *The Rise of the Network Society* (2nd edn.), Chichester, West Sussex, Wiley-Blackwell.

Castles, F. (ed.) (2007) *The Disappearing State: Retrenchment Realities in an Age of Globalisation*, Cheltenham, Edward Elgar.

—— Gerritsen, R., and Vowles, J. (eds.) (1996) *The Great Experiment: Labour Parties and Public Policy Transformation in Australia and New Zealand*, St Leonards, NSW, Allen and Unwin.

Centre for Finnish Business and Policy Studies (1996) *Not Revolution But Re-Evaluation: A Report of Political Decision-Making in Finland*, April, Helsinki (translated by the Public Management Department, Ministry of Finance).

Chancellor of the Duchy of Lancaster (1997) *Next Steps: Agencies in Government: Review, 1996*, Cm3579, London, The Stationery Office.

Chancellor of the Exchequer (1998) *Modern Public Services For Britain: Investing In Reform*, Cm4011, London, The Stationery Office.

Chapman, G. and Duncan, J. (2010) 'New Millennium, New Public Management and the New Zealand Model', *Australian Journal of Public Administration*, 69:3, pp. 301–13.

Chapman, R. (1998) 'Problems of Ethics in Public Sector Management', *Public Money and Management*, 18:1, January/March, pp. 9–13.

Christensen, T. and Lægreid, P. (eds.) (2001) *New Public Management: The Transformation of Ideas and Practice*, Aldershot, Ashgate.

—— —— (eds.) (2007*a*) *Transcending New Public Management: The Transformations of Public Sector Reforms*, Aldershot and Burlington VA, Ashgate.

—— —— (2007*b*) 'The Whole of Government Approach to Public Sector Reforms', *Public Administration Review*, November/December, pp. 1059–66.

—— Lie, A., and Lægreid, P. (2007) 'Still Fragmented Government or Reassertion of the Centre?', pp. 17–41, in T. Christensen and P. Lægreid (eds.) *Transcending New Public Management: The Transformations of Public Sector Reforms*, Aldershot and Burlington, VA, Ashgate.

Christiaens, J., Reyniers, B., and Rollé, C. (2010) 'Impact of IPSAS on Reforming Governmental Financial Information Systems: A Comparative Study', *International Review of Administrative Sciences*, 76:3, pp. 537–54.

Christiansen, T. (2001) 'The European Commission: Administration in Turbulent Times', pp. 95–114 in J. Richardson (ed.) *European Union: Power and Policy-making* (2nd edn.) London, Routledge.

Clark, D. (1997) 'The Civil Service and New Government', speech by the Rt. Hon. Dr David Clark, MP, Chancellor of the Duchy of Lancaster, QE11 Centre, London, 17 June.

—— (1998) 'The Modernization of the French Civil Service: Crisis, Change and Continuity', *Public Administration*, 76:1, Spring, pp. 97–115.

Clarke, J. and Newman, J. (1997) *The Managerial State*, London, Sage.

Cole, A. and Jones, G. (2005) 'Reshaping the State: Administrative Reform and New Public Management In France', *Governance*, 18:4, pp. 567–88.

—— and Eymeri-Douzans, J-M. (2010) 'Introduction: Administrative Reforms and Mergers in Europe—Research Questions and Empirical Challenges', *International Review of Administrative Sciences*, 76:3, pp. 395–406.

Committee of Independent Experts (1999) *First Report on Allegations Regrading Fraud, Mismanagement and Nepotism in The European Commission*, Brussels, 15 March.

Committee of Public Accounts (2000) *Improving the Delivery of Government IT Projects*, 1st Report, Session 1999–2000, London, House of Commons.

Commonwealth (1983) *RAPS/Reforming the Australian Public Service: A Statement of the Government's Intentions*, Canberra, AGPS.

Commonwealth Secretariat (1993) *Administrative and Managerial Reform: A Commonwealth Portfolio of Current Good Practice*, London, Management Development Programme, Commonwealth Secretariat.

Corbett, A. (2010) 'Public Management Policymaking in France: Legislating the Organic Law on Laws of Finance (LOLF), 1998–2001', *Governance*, 23:2, pp. 225–49.

Cour des Comptes (2003) *La déconcentration des administrations et la réforme de l'État*, special public report, Paris, Cour des Comptes, November.

Crosby, P. (1979) *Quality is Free*, New York, McGraw Hill.

Curristine, T. (2005) 'Performance Information in the Budget Process: Results of the OECD 2005 Questionnaire' *OECD Journal on Budgeting*, 2, pp. 87–131

Czarniawska, B. and Sevón, G. (eds.) (1996) *Translating Organizational Change*, de Gruyter, New York.

Davies, J. (2009) 'The Limits of Joined-Up Government: Towards a Political Analysis', *Public Administration*, 87:1, pp. 80–96.

Davis, G. et al. (1999) 'What Drives the Machinery of Government Change? Australia, Canada and the United Kingdom, 1950–1997', *Public Administration*, 77:1, pp. 7–50.

De Jong, M., Lalenis, K., and Mamadouh, V. (eds.) (2002) *The Theory and Practice of Institutional Transplantation: Experience with the Transfer of Policy Institutions*, Dordrecht, Kluwer.

De Kool, Denis (2008) *Inventarisatie Rijksmonitors 2008 en administratieve lasten*, Center for Public Innovation, July 2008.

Demmke, C. and Moilanen, T. (2010) *Civil Services in the EU of 27: Reform Outcomes and the Future of the Civil Service*, Bern, Peter Lang.

Denham, A. and Garnett, M. (1998) *British Think-Tanks and the Climate of Opinion*, London, UCL Press.

Department of Finance (1996) *Measuring up: A Primer for Benchmarking in the Australian Public Service*, Discussion Paper No. 4, Canberra, Resource Management Improvement Branch.

—— (1998*a*) *The Performance Improvement Cycle: Guidance for Managers*, Canberra, Department of Finance and Administration.

——(1998*b*) *Lessons Learned from Others: International Experience on the Identification and Monitoring of Outputs and Outcomes*, Discussion Paper 2, Canberra, Department of Administration and Finance.

Derksen, W. and Kortsen, A. (1995) 'Local Government: A Survey', pp. 63–86, in W. Kickert and F. van Vught (eds.) *Public Policy and Administration Sciences in The Netherlands*, London, Prentice Hall/Harvester Wheatsheaf.

Derlien, H.-U. (1998) *From Administrative Reform to Administrative Modernization*, Bamberg, Verwaltungswissenschaftliche Beitrage 33.

Development Team (1998) *International Experience on the Identification and Monitoring of Outputs and Outcomes*, Canberra, Department of Finance and Administration, March.

Dixon, R., Hood, C., and Jones, L. (2008) 'Ratings and Rankings of Public Service Performance: Special Issue Introduction', *International Public Management Journal*, 11:3, pp. 253–5.

Donahue, J. (2008) 'The Unaccustomed Inventiveness of the Labor Department' pp. 93–112, in S. Borins (ed.) *Innovations in Government: Research, Recognition and Replication*, Washington, DC, Brookings Institute.

Dorrell, S. (1993) *Public Sector Change is A World-Wide Movement*, speech by the Financial Secretary to the Treasury, Stephen Dorrell, to the Chartered Institute of Public Finance and Accountancy, London, 23 September.

Drechsler, W. and Kattel, R. (2008) 'Towards the Neo-Weberian State? Perhaps, but Certainly, Adieu, NPM!', *NISPAcee Journal of Public Administration and Policy*, Special issue: 'A Distinctive European Model? The Neo-Weberian State, 1:2, pp. 95–9.

Driscoll, A. and Morris, J. (2001) 'Stepping Out: Rhetorical Devices and Culture Change in Management in the UK Civil Service', *Public Administration*, 79:4, pp. 803–24.

Dror, Y. (1971) *Design for Policy Sciences*, New York, Elsvier.

Dryzek, J. (1996) 'The Informal Logic of Institutional Design', pp. 103–25, in R. Goodin (ed.) *The Theory of Institutional Design*, Cambridge, Cambridge University Press.

Du Gay, P. (2000) *In Praise of Bureaucracy*, London, Sage.

——(ed.) *The Values of Bureaucracy*, Oxford, Oxford University Press.

Duhamel, R. (1996) *Evaluation Report: Improved Reporting to Parliament Project on Performance Indicators*, A Report of the Parliamentary Working Group, Ottawa, December.

Dunleavy, P. (1991) *Democracy, Bureaucracy and Public Choice: Economic Explanations in Political Science*, Hemel Hempstead, Harvester/Wheatsheaf.

——(1994) 'The Globalisation of Public Service Production: Can Government be the "Best in the World"?', *Public Policy and Administration*, 9:2, Summer, pp. 36–65.

—— (2010) *The Future of Joined-Up Public Services*, London, 2020 Public Services Trust.

—— and Hood, C. (1994) 'From Old Public Administration To New Public Management', *Public Money and Management*, 14:3, July/September, pp. 9–16.

—— et al. (2006*a*) *Digital Era Governance: IT Corporations, the State and E-Government*, Oxford, Oxford University Press.

—— et al. (2006*b*) 'New Public Management is Dead—Long Live Digital-Era Governance', *Journal of Public Administration Research and Theory*, 16:3, pp. 467–94.

Dunn, C. (ed.) (2002) *The Handbook of Canadian Public Administration*, Don Mills, Ontario, Oxford University Press.

Dunn, W. (1993) 'Policy Reforms as Arguments', pp. 254–90 in F. Fischer and J. Forester (eds.) *The Argumentative Turn in Policy Analysis and Planning*, London, UCL Press.

Dunsire, A. (1973) *Administration: The Word and The Science*, London, Martin Robertson.

—— (1993) 'Modes of governance', pp. 21–34, in J. Kooiman (ed.) *Modern Governance: New Government–Society Interactions*, London, Sage.

—— and Hood, C. (1989) *Cutback Management in Public Bureaucracies*, Cambridge, Cambridge University Press.

Duran, P., Monnier, E., and Smith, A. (1995) 'Evaluation à la française', *Evaluation*, 1:1, July, pp. 45–63.

Durant, R., Girth, A., and Johnston, J. (2009) 'American Exceptionalism, Human Resource Management and the Contract State', *Review of Public Personnel Administration*, 29:3, pp. 207–29.

Dwivendi, O., Mau, T., and Sheldrick, B. (eds.) (2009) *The Evolving Physiology of Government: Canadian Public Administration in Transition*, Ottawa, University of Ottawa Press.

East, P. (1997) 'Opening Address to Public Service Senior Management Conference', Wellington, NZ, 9 October.

Efficiency Unit (1988) *Improving Management in Government: The Next Steps*, London, HMSO.

Eichenbaum, C. and Shaw, R. (2007) 'Ministerial Advisers and the Politics of Policy-Making: Bureaucratic Permanence and Popular Control', *Australian Journal of Public Administration*, 66:4, pp. 453–67.

Ellinas, A. and Suleiman, E. (2008) 'Reforming the Commission: Between Modernization and Bureaucratization', *Journal of European Public Policy*, 15:5, pp. 708–25.

Erin Research Inc. (1998) *Citizens First*, Ottawa, Canadian Centre for Management Development.

—— (2005) *Citizens First 4* Toronto, Institute for Citizen Centred Service and the Institute of Public Administration of Canada.

—— (2008) *Citizens First 5* Toronto, Institute for Citizen Centred Service.

Esping-Andersen, G. (1990) *The Three Worlds of Welfare Capitalism*, Cambridge, Polity.

European Commission (1995) *Eurobarometer: Trends, 1974–94*, Brussels, European Commission.

—— (1997a) *Evaluating EU Expenditure Programmes: A Guide* (1st edn.), Brussels, DGXIX/02, European Commission.

—— (1997b) *MAP 2000: Modernisation of Administration and Personnel Policy for the Year 2000* (draft memorandum from Mr Liikanen in agreement with the President: doc.IX/486/97), Brussels, DGIX.

—— (1998) *SEM 2000: Implementation by the Services: Information Note from the President, Mrs Gradin and Mr Liikanen*, SEC(98)760 final, Brussels, Secretariat General, 14 May.

—— (2000) *Reforming The Commission: A White Paper (Parts 1 And 2): Communication from Mr Kinnock, in Agreement with the President and Mrs Schreyer*, Brussels, European Commission, 1 March.

—— (2001a) *European Governance: A White Paper*, COM2001/408, Brussels, European Commission.

——(2001b) *Implementing Activity Based Management in the Commission: Communication from the President in Agreement with Mr Kinnock and Mrs Schreyer to the Commission*, SEC92001 1197/6&7, Brussels, European Commission.

—— (2003) *European Commission—Progress Review of Reform* (COM(2003) 40 final/2), Brussels, European Commission.

European Court of Auditors (2010) *Impact Assessments in the EU Institutions: Do They Support Decision-Making?*, Special Report 3/2010, Luxembourg, European Court of Auditors.

European Foundation for Quality Management (1996) *Self-Assessment, 1997: Guidelines for the Public Sector*, Brussels, EFQM.

Eurostat (2010) *Eurostat Yearbook 2010: Europe in Figures*, Luxembourg, Eurostat/European Commission.

Evaluation Partnership (1999) *Evaluation of the Implementation and Results of SEM2000 and its Contribution to the Overall Management Reform of the Commission*, Brussels, European Commission.

Evers, A. et al. (1997) *Developing Quality in Personal Social Services: Concepts, Cases and Comments*, Aldershot, Ashgate.

Executive Office of the President of the United States (1995) *Budget of the United States Government, Fiscal Year 1995*, Washington, DC.

Eymeri-Douzans, J.-M. (2009) 'French Administrative "Co-Governors" as a Policymaking Elite: Permanence and Changes', paper presented at the European Consortium for Political Research Conference, Potsdam, September.

Farnham, D., Horton, S., Barlow, J., and Hondeghem, A. (eds.) (1996) *New Public Managers in Europe: Public Servants in Transition*, Basingstoke, Macmillan.

Federal Ministry of the Interior (2006) *Focused on the Future: Innovations for Administration*, Berlin: Federal Ministry of the Interior.

Federal Ministry of the Interior (2009) *The Federal Public Service*, Berlin, Federal Ministry of the Interior <http://www.bmi.bund.de>.

Ferlie, E. and Geraghty, J. (2005) 'Professionals in Public Service Organizations: Implications for Public Sector Reforming', pp. 422–5, in E. Ferlie, L. Lynn Jnr, and C. Pollitt (eds.) *The Oxford Handbook of Public Management*, Oxford, Oxford University Press.

Fischer, F. and Forester, J. (eds.) (1993) *The Argumentative Turn in Policy Analysis and Planning*, London, UCL Press.

Flynn, N. and Strehl, F. (eds.) (1996) *Public Sector Management in Europe*, London, Prentice Hall/Harvester Wheatsheaf.

Foster, C. (1992) *Privatization, Public Ownership and the Regulation of Natural Monopolies*, Oxford, Blackwell.

—— and Plowden, F. (1996) *The State Under Stress*, Buckingham, Open University Press.

Francis, R. (2010) *Independent Inquiry into Care Provided by Mid Staffordshire NHS Foundation Trust, January 2005–March 2009*, HC375-1, London, The Stationery Office.

Franks, C. (2009) 'The Unfortunate Experience of Dueling Protocols: A Chapter in the Continuing Quest for Responsible Government in Canada', pp. 118–50 in O. Dwivendi, T. Mau, and B. Sheldrick (eds.) *The Evolving Physiology of Government: Canadian Public Administration in Transition*, Ottawa, University of Ottawa Press.

Fountain, J. (2001) *Building the Virtual State: Information Technology and Institutional Change*, Washington, DC, Brookings Institution.

Gaertner, K. and Gaertner, G. (1985) 'Performance-Contingent Pay for Federal Managers', *Administration and Society*, 17:1, pp. 7–20.

Geertz, C. (1973) *The Interpretation of Culture*, London, Hutchinson.

General Accounting Office (1990) *Why and How the GAO is Reviewing Federal College Recruiting*, Washington, DC, US House of Representatives.

—— (1994) *Deficit Reduction: Experiences of Other Nations*, Washington, DC, GAO/ AIMD–95–30, December.

—— (1995) *Managing for Results: Experiences Abroad Suggest Insights for Federal Management Reforms*, Washington, DC, GAO/GGD-95–120.

—— (1997) *Performance Budgeting: Past Initiatives Offer Insight For GPRA Implementation*, Washington, DC, GAO/AIMD-97–46, March.

—— (1998) *The Results Act: Observations on the Department of State's Fiscal Year 1999 Annual Performance Plan*, Washington, DC, GAO/NSIAD-98-210R, June.

—— (2001) *Managing for Results: Federal Managers' Views On Key Management Issues Vary Widely Across Agencies*, Washington, DC, GAO-01-592

Giddens, A. (1990) *The Consequences of Modernity*, Cambridge, Polity Press.

Gilmour, J. and Lewis, D. (2006) 'Does Performance Budgeting Work? An Examination of the Office of Management and Budget's PART Scores', *Public Administration Review*, September/October, pp. 742–52.

Goldstein, H. (2004) 'International Comparisons of Student Attainment: Some Issues Arising from the PISA Study', *Assessment in Education*, 11:3, pp. 319–30.

Good, D. (2007) *The Politics of Public Money: Spenders, Guardians, Priority Setters, and Financial Watchdogs inside the Canadian Government*, Toronto, University of Toronto Press.

Goodin, R. (1996) *The Theory of Institutional Design*, Cambridge, Cambridge University Press.

Gore, A. (1993) *From Red Tape to Results: Creating a Government that Works Better and Costs Less: Report of the National Performance Review*, Washington, DC, US Government Printing Office.

—— (1996) *The Best-Kept Secrets in Government: A Report to President Bill Clinton*, Washington, DC, US Government Printing Office, National Performance Review.

——(1997) *Businesslike Government: Lessons Learned from America's Best Companies*, Washington, DC, National Performance Review.

Götz, K. (1997) 'Acquiring Political Craft: Training Grounds for Top Officials in the German Core Executive', *Public Administration*, 75:4, Winter, pp. 753–75.

Gould, S. (1988) *Time's Arrow, Time's Cycle*, Harmondsworth, Penguin Books.

Government Decision in Principle on Reforms in Central and Regional Government (1993) Helsinki, Council of State.

Gow, I. (2004) *A Canadian Model of Public Administration?* Ottawa, Canada School of Public Administration.

Grace, P. (1984) *Burning Money: The Waste of Your Tax Dollars*, New York, Macmillan.

Green-Pederson, C. (2002) 'New Public Management Reforms of the Danish and Swedish Welfare States: The Role of Different Social Democratic Responses' *Governance*, 15:2, pp. 271–84.

Gregory, R. (1998) 'Political Responsibility For Bureaucratic Incompetence: Tragedy at Cave Creek', *Public Administration*, 76:3, Autumn, pp. 519–38.

——(2006) 'Theoretical Faith and Practical Works: De-Autonomising and Joining-Up in the New Zealand State Sector', pp. 137–61, in T. Christensen and P. Lægreid (eds.) *Autonomy and Regulation: Coping with Agencies in the Modern State*, Cheltenham, Edward Elgar.

Grek, S. (2008) *PISA in the British Media: Leaning Tower or Robust Testing Tool?*, Centre for Educational Sociology, University of Edinburgh.

Greve, C., Flinders, M., and van Thiel, S. (1999) 'Quangos—What's in a Name: Defining Quangos from a Comparative Perspective', *Governance*, 12:1.

Grossi, G. and Newberry, S. (2009) 'Theme: Whole of Government Accounting—International Trends', *Public Money and Management*, 29:4, pp. 209–13.

Gualmini, E. (2008) 'Restructuring Weberian Bureaucracy: Comparing Managerial Reforms in Europe and the United States', *Public Administration*, 86:1, pp. 75–94.

Gustafsson, A. (2000) *Performance Budgeting In Sweden: Outline of a Reform Programme*, paper presented to an International Symposium on Accruals Accounting and Budgeting, Paris, 13/14 November, Stockholm, Ministry of Finance.

Gustafsson, L. (1987) 'Renewal of the Public Sector in Sweden', *Public Administration*, 65:2, pp. 179–92.

Guyomarch, A. (1999) 'Public Service, Public Management and the Modernization of French Public Administration', *Public Administration*, 77:1, pp. 171–93.

Habermas, J. (1976) *Legitimation Crisis*, London, Heinemann.

Hacque, S. (2001) 'The Diminishing Publicness of Public Service under the Current Mode of Governance', *Public Administration Review*, 61:1, January/February, pp. 65–82.

Halachmi, A. and Bouckaert, G. (1995) *The Enduring Challenges of Public Management*, San Francisco, Jossey-Bass.

Halligan, J. (1996a) 'The Diffusion of Civil Service Reform', pp. 288–317, in H. Bekke, J. Perry, and T. Toonen (eds.) *Civil Service Systems In Comparative Perspective*, Bloomington and Indiana, Indiana University Press.

—— (1996b) 'Australia: Balancing Principles and Pragmatism', pp. 71–112, in J. Olsen and B. Peters (eds.) *Lessons from Experience: Experiential Learning in Administrative Reforms in Eight Democracies*, Oslo, Scandinavian University Press.

—— (1997) 'New Public Sector Models: Reform in Australia and New Zealand', pp. 17–46 in J.-E. Lane (ed.) *Public Sector Reform: Rationale, Trends and Problems*, London, Sage.

—— (2002) 'Politicians, Bureaucrats and Public Sector Reform in Australia and New Zealand', pp. 157–168 in G. Peters and J. Pierre (eds.) *Politicians, Bureaucrats and Administrative Reform*, London, Routledge.

—— (2008) 'Australian Public service: Combining the Search for Balance and Effectiveness with Deviations on Fundamentals', pp. 13–30, in C. Aulich and R. Wettenhall (eds.) *Howard's Fourth Government*, Sydney, University of New South Wales Press.

—— and Power, J. (1992) *Political Management in the 1990s*, Melbourne, Oxford University Press.

Hammer, M. and Champy, J. (1995) *Reengineering the Corporation: A Manifesto for a Business Revolution* (rev. edn.), London, Nicholas Brealey.

Hammond, K. (1996) *Human Judgement and Social Policy: Irreducible Uncertainty, Inevitable Error, Unavoidable Injustice*, New York, Oxford University Press.

Handy, C. (1993) *Understanding Organizations*, Harmondsworth, Penguin.

Harden, I. (1992) *The Contracting State*, Buckingham, Open University Press.

Harder, P. and Lindquist, E. (1997) 'Expenditure Management and Reporting in the Government of Canada: Recent Development and Backgrounds', pp. 71–89, in J. Bougault, M. Demers, and C. Williams (eds.) *Public Administration and Public Management: Experiences in Canada*, Québec, Les Publications de Québec.

Harrison, S. and Pollitt, C. (1994) *Controlling Health Professionals: The Future of Work and*

Organisation in the NHS, Buckingham, Open University Press.

Harrison, S., Hunter, D. J., and Pollitt, C. (1990) *The Dynamics Of British Health Policy*, London, Unwin Hyman.

—— Marnoch, G., and Pollitt, C. (1992) *Just Managing: Power and Culture in the National Health Service*, Basingstoke, Macmillan.

Hartley, J. (1983) 'Ideology and Organizational Behaviour', *International Studies of Management and Organization*, 13:3.

—— et al. (eds.) (2008) *Managing to Improve Public Services*, Cambridge, Cambridge University Press.

Hauner, D. and Kyobe, A. (2008) *Determinants of Government Efficiency*, IMF Working Paper 08/228, Washington, DC, International Monetary Fund.

Hautamäki, J. et al. (2008) *PISA06 Finland: Analyses, Reflections, Explanations*, Helsinki, Ministry of Education.

Hawke, L. (2007) 'Performance Budgeting in Australia', *OECD Journal on Budgeting*, 7:3, pp. 1–15.

—— (2008) 'The Politics of Public Money: Spenders, Guardians, Priority Setters, and Financial Watchdogs inside the Canadian Government', *Australian Journal of Public Administration*, 67:3, pp. 373–4.

Healthcare Commission (2009) *Investigation into Mid Staffordshire NHS Foundation Trust*, London, Healthcare Commission, March.

Hetherington, M. (2009) 'Putting Polarization in Perspective', *British Journal of Political Science*, 39:2, pp. 413–48.

Heclo, H. (1977) *A Government of Strangers*, Washington, DC, Brookings Institution.

Heintzman, R. (1997) 'Canada and Public Administration', pp. 1–12, in J. Bourgault, M. Demers, and C. Williams (eds.) *Public Administration and Public Management: Experiences in Canada*, Québec, Les Publications du Québec.

Held, D. (1984) 'Power and Legitimacy in Contemporary Britain', pp. 299–369, in G. McLennan, D. Held, and S. Hall (eds.) *State and Society in Contemporary Britain: A Critical Introduction*, Cambridge, Polity.

—— et al. (1998) *Global Transformation*, Cambridge, Polity Press.

—— (2004) 'Political Globalization', pp. 73–88 in D. Held, *Global Covenant: The Social Democratic Alternative to the Washington Consensus*, Cambridge, Polity Press.

Heseltine, M. (1980) 'Ministers and Management in Whitehall', *Management Services in Government*, 35.

High Quality Services, Good Governance and a Responsible Civic Society (1998) The Government Resolution, Helsinki, Oy Edita Ab.

Hill, H. and Klages, H. (1995) 'Verbindung mit dem Deutschen Landkreistag' in H. Hill and H. Klages (eds.) *Kreisverwaltung der zukunft. Vergleichende untersuchung aktueller modernisierungsansätze in ausgewählten Kreisverwaltungen*, Düsseldorf, Raabe Fachverlag.

—— —— (eds.) (1993) *Qualitäts- und erfolgsorientiertes verwaltungsmanagement. Aktuelle tendenzen und entwurfe*, Berlin, Duncker and Humblot.

Hill, M. and Hupe, P. (2002) *Implementing Public Policy*, London, Sage.

—— —— (2009) *Implementing Public Policy: An Introduction to the Study of Operational Governance* (2nd ed.), London: Sage.

Hirst, P. (2000) 'Democracy and Governance', in J. Pierre (ed.) *Debating Governance*, Oxford: Oxford University Press, pp. 13–35.

HM Government (2009) *Putting the Frontline First: Smarter Government*, Cm7753, London, The Stationery Office.

HM Treasury (1998) *Whole of Government Accounts*, July, London, HM Treasury.

—— (2010) *Total Place: A Whole Area Approach to Public Services*, March, London, HM Treasury

Hofstede, G. (2001) *Culture's Consequences: Comparing Values, Behaviors, Institutions and Organizations Across Nations*, Thousand Oaks, Calif., Sage.

Hojnacki, W. (1996) 'Politicization as a Civil Service Dilemma', pp. 137–64, in H. Bekke, J. Perry, and T. Toonen (eds.) *Civil Service Systems In Comparative Perspective*, Bloomington and Indiana, Indiana University Press.

Holkeri, K. and Summa, H. (1996) *Contemporary Developments in Performance Management: Evaluation of Public Management Reforms in Finland: from Ad Hoc Studies to a Programmatic Approach*, paper presented to PUMA/OECD, 4–5 November, Paris.

—— and Nurmi, J. (2002) 'Quality, Satisfaction and Trust in Government: The Finnish Case', paper presented to the Conference of the European Group of Public Administration, 4–7 September, Potsdam.

Holmes, M. and Shand, D. (1995) 'Management Reform: Some Practitioner Perspectives on the Past Ten Years', *Governance*, 8:4, October, pp. 551–78.

Homburg, V. (2008) 'Red Tape and Reforms: Trajectories of Technological and Managerial Reforms in Public Administration', *International Journal of Public Administration*, 31, pp. 749–70.

Hondeghem, A. (2000) 'The National Civil Service in Belgium', pp. 120–8, in H. J. G. M. Bekke and F. Van der Meer (eds.), *Civil Service Systems in Western Europe*, Cheltenham Edward Elgar.

—— and Nelen, S. (2002) *L'égalité des sexes et la politique du personnel dans le secteur public*, Paris, L'Harmattan.

—— and Depré, R. (2005) *De Copernicushervorming in perspectief: veranderingsmanagement in de federale overhead*, Vanden Broele, Brugge.

—— and Vandermeulen, F. (2000) 'Competency Management in the Flemish and Dutch Civil Service', *International Journal of Public Sector Management*, 13:4, pp. 342–53.

—— (2010) 'The National Civil Service in Belgium' in H. Bekke and F. Van Der Meer (eds.) *Civil Service Systems in Western Europe*, Cheltenham, Edward Elgar.

—— et al. (eds.) (2010) *Een decennium justitiële hervormingen in België: Octopus Revisited*, Vanden Boele, Brugge.

Hood, C. (1976) *The Limits of Administration*, London, Wiley.

—— (1991) 'A Public Management for all Seasons', *Public Administration*, 69:1, Spring, pp. 3–19.

—— (1995) 'Contemporary Public Management: A New Global Paradigm?', *Public Policy and Administration*, 10:2, Summer, pp. 104–17.

—— (1996) 'Exploring Variations in Public Management Reform of the 1980s', pp. 268–317, in H. Bekke, J. Perry, and T. Toonen (eds.) *Civil Service Systems in Comparative Perspective*, Bloomington and Indianapolis, Indiana University Press.

—— (1998) *The Art of the State: Culture, Rhetoric and Public Management*, Oxford, Oxford University Press.

—— (2002) 'Control, Bargains, and Cheating: The Politics of Public-Service Reform', *Journal of Public Administration Research and Theory (J-Part)*, 12:3, pp. 309–32.

—— (2005) 'Public Management: The Word, the Movement, the Science', pp. 7–26 in E. Ferlie, L. Lynn Jnr, and C. Pollitt (eds.) *The Oxford Handbook of Public Management*, Oxford, Oxford University Press.

—— and Jackson, M. (1991) *Administrative Argument*, Aldershot, Dartmouth.

—— et al. (1999) *Regulation Inside Government: Waste Watchers, Quality Police and Sleaze-Busters*, Oxford, Oxford University Press.

—— and Peters, G. B. (2004) 'The Middle Aging of New Public Management: Into the Age of Paradox?', *Journal of Public Administration Research and Theory*, 14:3, pp. 267–82.

—— and Lodge, M. (2006) *The Politics of Public Service Bargains*, Oxford, Oxford University Press.

Horton, S., Hondeghem, A., and Farnham, D. (eds.) (2002) *Competency Management in the Public Sector*, IOS, IIAS.

Howard, D. (1998) 'The French Strikes of 1995 and their Political Aftermath', *Government and Opposition*, 33:2, Spring, pp. 199–220.

Hudson, J. (1999) 'Informatization and the Delivery of Government Services: A Political Science Perspective', Ph.D. thesis, Uxbridge, Department of Government, Brunel University.

Hughes, O. (2003) *Public Management and Administration: An Introduction* (3rd edn.) Basingstoke, Palgrave/Macmillan.

Hupe, P. L. and Meijs, L. C. P. M. (2000) *Hybrid Governance: The Impact of the Nonprofit Sector in The Netherlands*. The Hague/Rotterdam/Baltimore: Social and Cultural Planning Office/Erasmus University/Johns Hopkins University.

Huxham, C. and Vangen, S. (2000) 'What Makes Partnerships Work?' in S. Osborne (ed.) *Public-Private Partnerships*, London, Routledge.

ICM (1993) *Citizen's Charter Customer Survey* (conducted for the Citizen's Charter Unit), London, ICM Research.

Immergut, E. (1992) *Health Politics: Interests and Institutions in Western Europe*, Cambridge, Cambridge University Press.

Ingraham, P. (1996) 'The Reform Agenda for National Civil Service Systems: External Stress and Internal Strains', pp. 247–67, in H. Bekke, J. Perry, and T. Toonen (eds.) *Civil Service Systems in Comparative Perspective*, Bloomington and Indiana, Indiana University Press.

Ingraham, P. (1997) 'Play it Again Sam: It's Still Not Right: Searching for the Right Notes in Administrative Reform', *Public Administration Review*, 57:4, July/August, pp. 325–31.

—— Peters, G. and Moynihan, D. (1998) *Public Employment and the Future of the Public Service*, paper presented to the authors' roundtable, Revitalising the Public Service, Ottawa, Canadian Centre for Management Development, 12–14 November.

—— Thompson, J., and Sanders, P., (eds.) (1998) *Transforming Government: Lessons from the Reinvention Laboratories*, San Francisco, Josey-Boss.

Innovative Public Services Group (2002) 'Survey Regarding Quality Activities in the Public Administrations of the European Union Member States', Madrid, Subdireccion General de Gestion de Calidad (unpublished).

Inter-American Development Bank (IADB) (2007) *Datagob: Governance Indicator Database* <http://www.iadb.org/datagob/> accessed 01/09/2008.

Jackson, P. (2001) "Public Sector Value-Added: Can the Public Sector Deliver?', *Public Administration*, 79:1, pp. 5–28.

Jacobsson, B. and Sundström, G. (2009) 'Between Autonomy and Control: Transformation of the Swedish Administrative Model', pp. 103–26 in, P. Roness and H. Saetren (eds.) *Change and Continuity in Public Sector Organizations*, Bergen, Fagbokforlaget.

James, O. (2003) *The Executive Agency Revolution in Whitehall: Public Interest Versus Bureau-Shaping Perspectives*, Basingstoke, Palgrave/Macmillan.

Jann, W. (2003) 'State Administration and Governance in Germany: Competing Traditions and Dominant Narratives', *Public Administration*, 81:1, pp. 95–118.

—— Röber, M., and Wollmann, H. (2006) *Public Management: grundlagen, wirkungen und kritik*, Berlin, Edition Sigma.

Jauvin, N. (1997) 'Government, Ministers, Macro-Organisation Chart and Networks', pp. 45–58, in J. Bourgault, M. Demers, and C. Williams (eds.) *Public Administration and Public Management: Experiences in Canada*, Quebec, Les Publications du Québec.

Jobert, B. and Muller, P. (1987) *L'État en action*, Paris, Presses Universitaires de France.

Johnson, C. and Talbot, C. (2007) 'The UK Parliament and Performance: Challenging or Challenged?' *International Review of Administrative Sciences*, 73:1, pp. 113–31.

Johnson, J. (1998) 'Strategy, Planning, Leadership and the Financial Management Improvement Plan: The Australian Public Service 1983 to 1996', *Public Productivity and Management Review*, 21:4, June, pp. 352–68.

Joss, R. and Kogan, M. (1995) *Advancing Quality: Total Quality Management in the National Health Service*, Buckingham, Open University Press.

Joustie, H. (2001) 'Performance Management in Finnish State Administration', pp. 18–19, in *Public Management in Finland*, Helsinki, Ministry of Finance.

Kaufman, H. (1981) 'Fear of Bureaucracy: A Raging Pandemic', *Public Administration Review*, 41:1, January/February, pp. 1–9.

Kaufmann, F., Majone, G., and Ostrom, V. (eds.) (1986) *Guidance, Control and Evaluation in the Public Sector*, Berlin, de Gruyter.

Kaufmann, D., Kraay, A., and Mastruzzi, M. (2007) *Governance Matters VI: Governance Indicators for 1996–2006*, World Bank Policy Research Working Paper 4280.

—— —— —— (2009) *Governance Matters VIII: Governance Indicators for 1996-2008*, World Bank Policy Research Working Paper 4978.

Keeling, D. (1972) *Management in Government*, London, Allen and Unwin.

Kelman, S. (2005) *Unleashing Change: A Study of Organizational Renewal in Government*, Washington, DC, Brookings Institution

—— (2007) 'Public Administration and Organizational Studies', *Academy of Management Annals*, 1:1, pp. 225–67.

—— (2008) 'The "Kennedy School School" of Research on Innovation in Government', pp. 28–51, in S. Borins (ed.) *Innovations in Government: Research, Recognition and Replication*, Washington, DC, Brookings Institute.

—— and Friedman, J. (2009) 'Performance Improvement and Performance Dysfunction: An Empirical Examination of the Distortionary Impacts of the Emergency Room Wait-Time Target in the English National Health Service', *Journal of Public Administration Research and Theory*, 19, pp. 917–46.

Keohane, R. and Nye, J. (eds.) (2001) *Governance in a Globalization World*, Washington, DC, Brookings Institution.

Kernaghan, K. (1997) 'Values, Ethics and Public Service', pp. 101–11, in J. Bourgault, M. Demers, and C. Williams (eds.) *Public Administration and Public Management: Experiences in Canada*, Québec, Les Publications du Québec.

—— (2009*a*) 'Moving towards Integrated Public Governance: Improving Service Delivery through Community Engagement', *International Review of Administrative Sciences*, 75:2, pp. 239–54.

—— (2009*b*) 'Putting Citizens First: Service Delivery and Integrated Public Governance', pp. 249–69, in O. Dwivendi, T. Mau, and B. Sheldrick, (eds.) *The Evolving Physiology of Government: Canadian Public Administration in Transition*, Ottawa, University of Ottawa.

Kettl, D. (1994) *Reinventing Government? Appraising the National Performance Review*, Washington, DC, The Brookings Institution.

—— (2000) *The Global Public Management Revolution: A Report on* the *Transformation Of Governance*, Washington, DC, The Brookings Institution.

—— (2005) *The Global Public Management Revolution* (2nd edn.), Washington, DC, The Brookings Institution.

—— (2009) *The Next Government of the United States: Why Our Institutions Fail Us and How to Fix Them*, New York and London: W. W. Norton.

—— et al. (1996) *Civil Service Reform: Building a Government that Works*, Washington, DC, The Brookings Institution.

—— Pollitt, C., and Svara, J. (2004) *Towards a Danish Concept Of Public Governance: An International Perspective*, Forum for Offetlig Topeldelse, Copenhagen.

—— and Kelman, S. (2007) *Reflections on 21st Century Government Management*, Washington, DC, IBM Center for the Business of Government.

Khan, A. and Mayes, S. (2009) *Transition to Accrual Accounting*, Washington, DC, International Monetary Fund.

Kickert, W. (ed.) (1997) *Public Management and Administrative Reform in Western Europe*, Cheltenham, Edward Elgar.

—— (2000) *Public Management Reforms in the Netherlands: Social Reconstruction of Reform Ideas and Underlying Frames of Reference*, Delft, Eburon.

—— (2007) 'Public Management Reforms in Countries with a Napoleonic State Model', pp. 26–51, in C. Pollitt, S. van Thiel, and

V. Homberg (eds.) *New Public Management in Europe: Adaptation and Alternatives*, Basingstoke, Palgrave/Macmillan.

—— (ed.) (2008) *The Study Of Public Management in Europe and the US*, London and New York, Routledge and Taylor Francis.

—— and In 't Veld, R. (1995) 'National Government, Governance and Administration', pp. 45–62, in W. Kickert and F. van Vught (eds.) *Public Policy and Administration Sciences in the Netherlands*, London, Prentice Hall/Harvester Wheatsheaf.

—— Klijn, E.H., and Koppenjan, J. (eds.) (1997) *Managing Complex Networks: Strategies for the Public Sector*, London, Sage.

King, A. (1976) *Why is Britain Becoming Harder to Govern?*, London, BBC.

King, G., Keohane, R. and Verber, S. (1994) *Designing Social Enquiry: Scientific Inference in Qualitative Research*, New Jersey, Princeton University Press.

Klages, H. (1998) 'New Public Management in Germany: The Implementation Process of the New Steering Model', *International Review of Administrative Sciences*, 64, pp. 41–54.

—— and Löffler, E. (1996) 'Public Sector Modernisation in Germany: Recent Trends and Emerging Strategies', pp. 132–45, in N. Flynn and F. Strehl (eds.) *Public Sector Management in Europe*, London, Prentice Hall/Harvester Wheatsheaf.

Klein, R. and Plowden, W. (2005) 'JASP Meets JUG: Lessons of the 1975 Joint Approach to Social Policy for Joined-Up Government', pp. 107–13, in V. Bogdanor, (ed.) *Joined-Up Government*, Oxford, Oxford University Press.

Klijn, E-H. (2005) 'Networks and Inter-Organizational Management: Challenging, Steering, Evaluation and the Role of Public Actors in Public Management', pp. 257–81, in E. Ferlie, L. E. Lynn Jr, and C. Pollitt (eds.) (2005) *The Oxford Handbook of Public Management*, Oxford: Oxford University Press.

——(2008) 'Governance and Governance Networks in Europe: an Assessment of Ten Years of Research on the Theme', *Public Management Review*, 10:4, pp. 505–25.

Klijn, E.-H. and Koppenjan, J. (eds.) (1997) *Managing Complex Networks: Strategies for the Public Sector*, London, Sage.

Klijn, E.-H. (2000) 'Politicians and Inter-Active Decision-Making: Institutional Spoilsprts or Playmakers?' *Public Administration*, 78:2, pp. 365–87.

Knill, C. and Balint, T. (2008) 'Explaining Variation in Organizational Change: The Reform of Human Resource Management in the European Commission and the OECD', *Journal of European Public Policy*, 15:5, pp. 669–90.

König, K. (1996) *On the Critique of New Public Management*, Speyer, 155, Speyer Forschungsberichte.

—— (1997) 'Entrepreneurial Management or Executive Administration: The Perspective of Classical Administration', pp. 217–36, in W. Kickert (ed.) *Public Management and Administrative Reform in Western Europe*, Cheltenham, Edward Elgar.

—— and Siedentopf, H. (eds.) (2001) *Public Administration in Germany*, Baden-Baden, Nomos.

Koppenjan, J. and Klijn, E.-H. (2004) *Managing Uncertainties in Networks*, London: Routledge.

Korsten, A. and van der Krogt, T. (1995) 'Human Resources Management', pp. 233–48, in W. Kickert and F. van Vught (eds.) *Public Policy and Administration Sciences in the Netherlands*, London, Prentice Hall/Harvester Wheatsheaf.

Kotter, J. (1996) *Leading Change*, Boston, Harvard Business School.

Küchen, T. and Nordman, P. (2008) 'Performance Budgeting in Sweden', *OECD Journal on Budgeting*, 8:1, pp. 1–11.

Lane, J.-E. (1995) 'The Decline of the Swedish Model', *Governance*, 8:4, pp. 579–90.

—— (ed.) (1997) *Public Sector Reform: Rationale, Trends and Problems*, London, Sage.

—— (2000) *New Public Management*, London, Routledge.

—— and Ersson, S. (2002) *Culture and Politics: A Comparative Approach*, Aldershot, Ashgate.

Lawrence, R. (1997) 'Is it Really the Economy, Stupid?', pp. 11–132, in J. Nye, P. Zelikow, and D. King (eds.) *Why People Don't Trust Government*, Cambridge, Mass., Harvard University Press.

Leeuw, F. (1995) 'The Dutch Perspective: Trends in Performance Measurement', paper presented at the International Evaluation Conference, Vancouver, 1–5 November.

Leftwich, A. (ed.) (1984) *What is Politics? The Activity and its Study*, Oxford, Blackwell.

Le Grand, J. and Bartlett, W. (1993) *Quasi Markets and Social Policy*, Basingstoke, Macmillan.

Lehtoranta, O. and Niemi, M. (1997) *Measuring Public Sector Productivity in Finland: Progress Report*, paper presented to OECD/UNECE/EUROSTAT Meeting of National Accounts Experts, June, Paris.

Leicht, K. et al. (2008) 'New Public Management and New Professionalism across Nations and Contexts', *Current Sociology*, 57:4, pp. 581–605.

Le Loup, L. (1988) 'From Micro-Budgeting to Macro-Budgeting', pp. 19–42, in I. Rubin (ed.) *New Directions in Budget Theory*, Albany, SUNY Press.

Leon, L. de (1997) 'Administrative Reform and Democratic Accountability', pp. 237–54, in W. Kickert (ed.) *Public Management and Administrative Reform in Western Europe*, Cheltenham, Edward Elgar.

Levy, R. (2004) 'Between Rhetoric and Reality: Implementing Management Reform in the European Commission', *International Journal of Public Sector Management*, 17:2, pp. 166–77.

Light, P. (1995) *Thickening Government: Federal Hierarchy and the Diffusion of Accountability*, Washington, DC, Brookings Institution.

—— (1997) *The Tides of Reform: Making Government Work 1945–1995*, New Haven, Yale University Press.

Lijphart, A. (1984) *Democracies: Patterns of Majoritarian and Consensus Government in Twenty-One Countries*, London, Yale University Press.

—— (1999) *Patterns of Democracy: Governance Forms and Performance in 36 Countries*, New Haven, Yale University Press.

Likierman, A. (1995) 'Performance Indicators: Twenty Lessons From Early Managerial Use', pp. 57–66, in P. Jackson (ed.) *Measures for Success in the Public Sector*, London, Public Finance Foundation/Chartered Institute of Public Finance and Accountancy.

—— (1998a) 'Resource Accounting and Budgeting: Where are we Now?', *Public Money and Management*, 18:2, April/June, pp. 17–20.

Lindblom, C. (1959) 'The Science of Muddling Through' *Public Administration Review*, 19:3, pp. 79–88.

—— (1979) 'Still Muddling, Not Yet Through', *Public Administration Review*, 39:6, pp. 517–26.

Lindquist, E. (2006) *A Critical Moment: Capturing and Conveying the Evolution of the Canadian Public Service*, Ottawa, Canadian School of Public Service.

Listhaug, O. and Wiberg, M. (1995) 'Confidence in Public and Private Institutions', pp. 298–322, in H.-D. Klingemann and D. Fuchs (eds.) *Citizens and the State: Beliefs in Government*, vol. 1, Oxford, Oxford University Press.

Lodge, M. (2010) 'Public Service Bargains in British Central Government: Multiplication, Diversification and Reassertion?', pp. 99–113, in M. Painter and G. B. Peters (eds.) *Tradition and Public Administration*, Basingstoke, Palgrave/Macmillan.

Löffler, E. (1995) *The Modernisation of the Public Sector in an International Perspective: Concepts and Methods of Awarding and Assessing Quality in the Public Sector in OECD Countries*, Speyer Forschungsberichte 151, Speyer, Forschungsinstitut für Öffentliche Verwaltung.

—— (1999) *Accountability Management in Intergovernmental Partnerships*, OECD.

—— and Vintar, M. (eds.) (2004) *Improving the Quality of East and West European Public Services*, Aldershot, Ashgate.

Lomas, K. (1991) *Contemporary Finnish Poetry*, Newcastle-upon-Tyne, Bloodaxe Books.

Lowndes, V. and Skelcher, C. (1998) 'The Dynamics of Multi-Organisational Partnerships: An Analysis of Changing Modes of Governance', *Public Administration*, 76:2, Summer, pp. 313–33.

Luts, M., Hondeghem A., and Bouckaert, G. (2009) *De efficiënte overheid geanalyseerd. Naar een kleinere en betere Nederlandse overheid*, Leuven, SBOV.

Lynn, L., Heinrich, C., and Hill, C. (2001) *Improving Governance: A New Logic for Empirical Research*, Washington, DC, Georgetown University Press.

Lynn, L., Jnr (2006) *Public Management: Old and New*, New York and London, Routledge/Taylor and Francis.

—— (2008) 'What is a Neo-Weberian State? Reflections on a Concept and its Implications', *NISPAcee Journal of Public Administration and Policy*, Special issue: 'A distinctive European model? The Neo-Weberian State', 1:2, pp. 17–30.

Maas, G. and van Nispen, F. (1999) 'The Quest for a Leaner, Not a Meaner Government', *Research in Public Administration*, 5, pp. 63–86.

McCormack, L. (2007) 'Performance budgeting in Canada', *OECD Journal on Budgeting*, 7:4, pp. 49–66.

Machiavelli, N. (2005) [*c*.1516] *The Prince*, London, Penguin.

Mahon, R. and McBride, S. (eds.) (2008) *The OECD and Transnational Governance*, Vancouver, University of British Columbia Press.

Majone, G. (1996) *Regulating Europe*, London, Routledge.

Mallory, J. (1997) 'Particularities and Systems of Government', pp. 15–23, in J. Bourgault, M. Demers, and C. Williams (eds.) *Public Administration and Public Management: Experiences in Canada*, Québec, Les Publications du Québec.

Management Advisory Board (1993*a*) *Accountability in the Commonwealth Public Sector*, Canberra, MAB/MIAC, No. 11, June.

—— (1993*b*) *Building a Better Public Service*, Canberra, MAB/MIAC No.12, June.

—— (1994) *On-Going Reform in the Australian Public Service: An Occasional Paper to the Prime Minister*, Canberra, MAB/MIAC No. 15, October.

—— (2003) *Organizational Renewal*, Canberra, ACT, Commonwealth of Australia.

—— (2004) *Connecting Government: Whole Of Government Responses to Australia's Priority Challenges*, Canberra, ACT, Commonwealth of Australia.

Manning, N. (2001) 'The Legacy of the New Public Management in Developing Countries', *International Review of Administrative Sciences*, 76:2, pp. 297–312.

March, J. and Olsen, J. (1995) *Democratic Governance*, New York, Free Press.

Margetts, H. (1998) *Information Technology in Government: Britain and America*, London, Routledge.

—— 6, P., and Hood, C. (2010) *Paradoxes of Modernization: Unintended Consequences of Public Policy Reform*, Oxford, Oxford University Press.

Marmor, T., Mashaw, J., and Harvey, P. (1990) *America's Misunderstood Welfare State*, New York, Basic Books.

Mayne, J. (1996) *Implementing Results-Based Management and Performance-Based Budgeting: Lessons from the Literature*, Discussion Paper No. 73, Ottawa, Office of the Auditor General of Canada.

Mazel, V. (1998) 'Supporting Managerial Growth of Top Dutch Civil Servants', *Public Management Forum*, 4:6, November/December, pp. 4–5.

Meier, K. and O'Toole, L. (2009) 'The Dog That Didn't Bark: How Public Managers Handle Environmental Shocks', *Public Administration* 87:3, pp. 485–502.

Metcalfe, L. (1993) 'Public Management: From Imitation to Innovation', pp. 173–89, in J. Kooiman (ed.) *Modern Governance: New Government–Society Interactions*, London, Sage.

—— (1996) 'The European Commission as a Network Organisation', *Journal of Federalism*, 26:4, Fall, pp. 43–62.

—— and Richards, S. (1987) 'Evolving Public Management Cultures', pp. 65–86 in J. Kooiman and K. Eliassen (eds.) *Managing Public Organizations*, London, Sage.

—— —— (1990) *Improving Public Management* (enlarged edn.), London, Sage/European Institute of Public Administration.

Meyer, J. and Rowan, B. (1991) 'Institutionalised Organisations: Formal Structure as Myth and Ceremony', in W. Powell and P. DiMaggio (eds.) *The New Institutionalism in Organisational Analysis*, Chicago, University of Chicago Press.

—— and Gupta, V. (1994) 'The Performance Paradox', *Research in Organizational Behavior*, 16, pp. 309–69.

Micheletti, M. (2000) 'The End of Big Government: Is it Happening in the Nordic Countries?', *Governance*, 13:2, pp. 265–78.

Middlemas, K. (1995) *Orchestrating Europe: The Informal Politics of European Union, 1973–1995*, London, Fontana.

Mihm, C. J. (2001) 'Implementing GPRA: Progress and Challenges', pp. 101–12, in D. W. Forsythe, *Quicker, Better, Cheaper? Managing Performance in American Government*, New York, The Rockefeller Institute Press.

Milakovitch, M. (2006) 'Comparing Bush-Cheney and Clinton-Gore Performance Management Strategies: Are They More Alike Than Different?', *Public Administration*, 84:2, pp. 461–478.

Milward, H. B. and Provan, K. (2000) 'Governing the Hollow State' *Journal of Public Administration Research and Theory*, 10:2, pp. 359–80.

Ministère de la Fonction Publique et des Réformes Administratives (1992) *La charte des services publiques*, Paris, Ministère de la Fonction Publique.

—— (1994a) *L'accueil dans les services publiques*, Paris, Ministère de la Fonction Publique.

Ministerie van Financiën (1998) *Verder met resultat: Het agentschapsmodel 1991–1997*, Den Haag, Dutch Ministry of Finance.

Ministerie van Binnenlandse Zaken en Koninkrijksrelaties (2007) *Nota Vernieuwing Rijksdienst*, Den Haag, BZK, September.

—— (2008) *Eerste Voortgangsrapportage, Programma Vernieuwing Rijksdienst*, Den Haag, BZK, May.

—— (Van Twist, M., van der Steen M., Karré, P., Peeters, R., and Van Ostaijen, M.) (2009a) *Programma Vernieuwing Rijksdiesnt, Overheid voor de Toekomst, Vernieuwende verandering: Continuïteit en discontinuïteit van vernieuwing van de Rijksdienst*, Den Haag, BZK.

—— (2009b) *Programma Vernieuwing Rijksdienst, Overheid voor de Toekomst, Kwaliteitsontwikkelingen van de Rijksoverheid*, Den Haag, BZK.

—— (2009c) *Programma Vernieuwing Rijksdienst, Overheid voor de Toekomst, New Public Management voorbij?*, Den Haag, BZK.

Ministry of Finance (1993) *Government Decision in Principle on Reforms in Central and Regional Government*, Helsinki, Ministry of Finance.

—— (1995) *The Public Sector in Finland*, Helsinki (document prepared for a meeting of EU Directors General).

—— (1997) *Public Management Reforms: Five Country Studies*, Helsinki, Ministry of Finance.

—— (2004) *Values to be Part of the Daily Job*, Helsinki, Ministry of Finance.

—— (2010) *Finnish Public Governance: A Background Report*, Helsinki, Ministry of Finance, March.

Modell, S., Jacobs, K., and Wiesel, F. (2007) 'A Process (Re)Turn? Path Dependencies, Institutions and Performance Management in Swedish Central Government', *Management Accounting Research*, 18, pp. 453–75.

Mol, N. (1995) 'Quality Improvement in the Dutch Department of Defence', pp. 103–28, in C. Pollitt and G. Bouckaert (eds.) *Quality Improvement In European Public Services: Concepts, Cases and Commentary*, London, Sage.

Molander, P., Nilsson, J-E. and Schick, A. (2002) *Does Anyone Govern? The Relationship between the Government Office and the Agencies in Sweden*, report from the SNS Constitutional Project, Stockholm, SNS.

Montricher, N. de (1996) 'France: in Search of Relevant Changes', pp. 243–71, in J. Olsen and B. Peters (eds.) *Lessons From Experience: Experiential Learning in Administrative Reforms in Eight Democracies*, Oslo, Scandinavian University Press.

—— (1998) 'Public Sector Values and Administrative Reforms', pp. 108–36, in B. G. Peters and D. Savoie (eds.) *Taking Stock: Assessing Public Sector Reforms*, Montreal and Kingston, McGill-Queen's University Press and Canadian Centre for Management Development.

Moore-Wilson, M. (1997) 'Challenges Facing the Australian Public Service', *Canberra Bulletin of Public Administration*, 85, August, pp. 38–47.

Morgan, B. (1999) 'Regulating the Regulators: Meta-Regulation as a Strategy for Re-Inventing Government in Australia', *Public Management*, 1:1, pp. 49–65.

Moynihan, Donald P. (2005) 'Homeland Security and the U.S. Public Management Policy Agenda', *Governance*, 18:2 171–96.

—— (2008) *The Dynamics of Performance Management*, Washington, DC, Georgetown University Press.

—— (2009) 'The Politics Measurement Makes: Performance Management in the Obama Era', *The Forum*, 7(4): article 7.

—— and Patricia W. Ingraham (2010) 'The Suspect Handmaiden: The Evolution of Politics and Administration in the American State', *Public Administration Review*, 70:S1.

Murray, R. (1998) *Productivity as a Tool for Evaluation of Public Management Reform*, paper presented to the European Evaluation Society Conference, October, 29–31 Rome.

National Academy of Public Administration (1994) *Towards Useful Performance Measurement: Lessons Learned from Initial Pilot Performance Plans Prepared under the Government Performance and Results Act*, November, Washington, DC, National Academy of Public Administration.

National Audit Office (1995) *The Meteorological Office: Evaluation of Performance*, HC693, 25 August, London, HMSO.

—— (1996) *State Audit in the European Union*, London, National Audit Office.

—— (1997) *Annual Report, 1997*, London, National Audit Office.

—— (1999) *Government on the Web*, HC87, London, The Stationery Office.

—— (2006) *Central Government's Use of Consultants*, HC 128, Session 2006–7, London, The Stationary Office.

—— (2009) *Assessment of the Capability Review Programme*, HC123, Session 2008–9, London, National Audit Office.

—— (2010) *Reorganising Central Government*, HC452, Session 2009–10, London, National Audit Office, 18 March.

National Performance Review (1997a) *Blair House Papers*, January, Washington, DC, National Performance Review (see also NPR website, <http://www.npr.gov>).

—— (1997b) *Serving the American Publics: Best Practices in Customer-Driven Strategic Planning*, Federal Benchmarking Consortium Study Report, Washington, DC, National Performance Review.

Newberry, S. (2002) 'New Zealand's Public Sector Financial Management System: Resource Erosion in Government Departments', Ph.D. thesis, University of Canterbury, NZ.

—— and Pallot, J. (2006) 'New Zealand's Financial Management System: Implications for Democracy', *Public Money and Management*, 26:4, pp. 221–7.

Next Steps Team (1998) *Towards Best Practice: An Evaluation of the First Two Years of the Public Sector Benchmarking Project, 1996–98*, London, Efficiency and Effectiveness Group, Cabinet Office.

Niemi, M. (1998) 'Measuring Public Sector Productivity: Productivity Change between Years 1995 and 1996 in Central Government', Helsinki, Statistics Finland (unpublished paper).

The NISPAcee Journal of Public Administration and Policy (2008), 1:2, Special issue: 'A distinctive European model? The Neo-Weberian State'.

Nispen, F. K. M. van and Possetth, J. (2006) 'Performance Budgeting in the Netherlands: Beyond Arithmetic', *OECD Journal on Budgeting*, 6:4, pp. 37–62.

Nivette, N. (1996) *The Decline of Deference*, Peterborough, Broadview Press.

Norris, P. (2001) *Digital Divide: Civic Engagement, Information Poverty, and the Internet Worldwide*, Cambridge, Cambridge University Press.

Nye, J. Jnr, Zelikow, P., and King, D. (eds.) (1997) *Why People Don't Trust Government*, Cambridge, Mass., Harvard University Press.

O'Connor, J. (1973) *The Fiscal Crisis of the State*, New York, St Martin's Press.

OECD (1992) *OECD Country Profiles*, Paris, OECD.

—— (1993a) *Managing with Market-Type Mechanisms*, Paris, PUMA/OECD.

—— (1993b) *Private Pay For Public Work: Performance-Related Pay for Public Service Managers*, Paris, PUMA/OECD.

—— (1994) *Public Management Developments: Survey 1993*, Paris, PUMA/OECD.

—— (1995) *Governance in Transition: Public Management Reforms in OECD Countries*, Paris, PUMA/OECD.

—— (1996) *Responsive Government: Service Quality Initiatives*, Paris, PUMA/OECD.

—— (1997a) *In Search of Results: Performance Management Practices*, Paris, PUMA/OECD.

—— (1997b) *The Changing Role of the Central Budget Office*, OCDE/GD(97)109, Paris, PUMA/OECD.

—— (1997c) *Family, Market and Community: Equity and Efficiency in Social Policy*, Social Policy Studies No. 21, Paris, OECD.

—— (1997d) *OECD Country Profiles*, Paris, OECD.

—— (1998) *Budgeting in Sweden*, Paris, PUMA/OECD.

—— (2001) *Managing Cross-Cutting Issues*, Paris, PUMA/OECD <http://www.oecd.org/puma/strat/managing.htm>.

—— (2002a) *Public Sector Modernisation: A New Agenda*, CCNM/GF/GOV/PUBG(2002)1, paper presented at the OECD Global Forum on Governance seminar at the London School of Economics, 2–3 December, Paris, OECD.

—— (2002b) *Economic Survey of the Netherlands*, Paris, OECD.

—— (2005a) *E-government for a Better Government*, Paris, OECD.

—— (2005b) *Modernising Government: The Way Forward*, Paris, OECD.

—— (2007) *The Programme for International Student Assessment (PISA): Executive Summary*, Paris, OECD.

—— (2009a) *Government at a Glance 2009*, Paris, OECD.

—— (2009b) *Measuring Government Activity*, Paris, OECD.

—— (2010a) *OECD Factbook 2010*, Paris OECD.

—— (2010b) *OECD Public Governance Reviews: Finland: Working Together to Sustain Success: Assessment and Recommendations*, Paris, OECD.

—— (2010c) *Modernizing the Public Administration: A Study on Italy*, Paris, OECD.

Office of Management and Budget (2002) *The President's Management Agenda*, Washington, DC, Government Printing Office <http://www.whitehouse.gov/omb/>.

Office of Public Services Reform (2002) *Better Government Services: Executive Agencies in the 21st Century*, London, Cabinet Office <http://www.civilservice.gov.uk/agencies.

Office of the US President (1993) *Budget Baselines, Historical Data and Alternatives for the Future*, Washington, DC, January.

Olsen, J. and Peters, B. (eds.) (1996) *Lessons from Experience: Experiential Learning in Administrative Reforms in Eight Democracies*, Oslo, Scandinavian University Press.

Ongaro, E. (2004) 'Process Management in the Public Sector: The Experience of One-Stop Shops in Italy', *International Journal of Public Administration*, 17:1, pp. 81–107.

—— (2009) *Public Management Reform and Modernization: Trajectories of Administrative Change in Italy, France, Greece, Portugal and Spain*, Cheltenham and Northampton, Mass, Edward Elgar.

—— and Valotti, G. (2008) 'Public Management Reform in Italy: Explaining the Implementation Gap', *International Journal of Public Sector Management*, 21:2, pp. 174–204.

Osborne, D. and Gaebler, T. (1992) *Reinventing Government: How The Entrepreneurial Spirit is Transforming the Public Sector*, Reading, Mass., Adison Wesley.

Osborne, S. (ed.) (2000) *Public–Private Partnerships: Theory and Practice in International Perspective*, London, Routledge.

—— (ed.) (2010) *The New Public Governance: Emerging Perspectives on the Theory and Practice of Public Governance*, London and New York, Routledge/Taylor and Francis.

O'Toole, B. and Jordan, G. (eds.) (1995) *Next Steps: Improving Management in Government*, Dartmouth, Aldershot.

Packwood, T., Pollitt, C., and Roberts, S. (1998) 'Good Medicine? A Case Study of Business

Re-Engineering in a Hospital', *Policy and Politics*, 26:4, pp. 401–15.

Page, E. (1997) *People Who Run Europe*, Oxford, Clarendon Press.

—— (2005) 'Joined-Up Government and the Civil Service', pp. 139–55, in V. Bogdanor (ed.) *Joined-Up Government*, Oxford, Oxford University Press.

Painter, M. and Peters, G. B. (eds.) (2010) *Tradition and Public Administration*, Basingstoke, Palgrave/Macmillan.

Pandey, S. (2010) 'Cutback Management and the Paradox of Publicness', *Public Administration Review*, July/August, pp. 564–71.

Parker, D. (1999) 'Regulating Public Utilities: What Other Countries Can Learn from the UK Experience', *Public Management*, 1:1, pp. 93–120.

——(ed.) (2000) *Privatisation and Corporate Performance*, Cheltenham, Elgar.

Pawson, R. and Tilley, N. (1997) *Realistic Evaluation*, London, Sage.

Pederson, T. (2002) 'Consumer Power Will Transform the Public Sector', *2QConference* (newspaper of the 2nd Quality Conference for Public Administrations in the EU, Copenhagen, October), pp. 2–3.

Pemberton, H. (2000) 'Policy Networks and Policy Learning: UK Economic Policy in the 1960s and 1970s', *Public Administration*, 78: 4 pp. 771–92.

Perrow, C. (1972) *Complex Organisations*, Glenview, Scott Foreman.

Perry, J. and Kraemer, K. (eds.) (1983) *Public Management: Public and Private Perspectives*, California, Mayfield.

—— and Pearce, J. (1985) 'Civil Service Reform and the Politics of Performance Appraisal', pp. 140–60 in D. Rosenbloom (ed.) *Public Personnel Policy: The Politics of Civil Service*, London, Associated Faculty Press.

—— and Hondeghem, A. (eds.) (2008) *Motivation in Public Management: The Call of Public Service*, Oxford, Oxford University Press.

—— Engbers, T., and Jun, S. (2009) 'Back to the Future? Performance-Related Pay, Empirical Research, and the Perils of Persistence', *Public Administration Review*, January/February, pp. 39–51.

Peters, G. (1995) 'Bureaucracy in a Divided Regime: the United States', pp. 18–38, in J. Pierre (ed.) *Bureaucracy in the Modern State: An Introduction to Comparative Public Administration*, Aldershot, Edward Elgar.

—— (1996a) 'Theory and Methodology', pp. 13–41, in H. Bekke, J. Perry, and T. Toonen (eds.) *Civil Service Systems in Comparative Perspective*, Bloomington and Indiana, Indiana University Press.

—— (1996b) *The Future of Governing: Four Emerging Models*, Kansas, University Press of Kansas.

—— (1997) 'A North American Perspective on Administrative Modernisation in Europe', pp. 255–70, in W. Kickert (ed.) *Public Management and Administrative Reform in Western Europe*, Cheltenham, Edward Elgar.

—— (1998a) 'What Works? The Antiphons of Administrative Reform', pp. 78–107, in B. G. Peters and D. Savoie (eds.) *Taking Stock: Assessing Public Sector Reforms*, Montreal and Kingston, Canadian Centre for Management Development and McGill-Queen's University Press.

—— (1998b) 'Managing Horizontal Government: The Politics of Co-Ordination', *Public Administration*, 76:2, Summer, pp. 295–311.

—— (2010) 'Public Administration in the United States: Anglo-American, Just American, or Which American?' pp. 114–28 in M. Painter and G. B. Peters (eds.) *Tradition and Public Administration*, Basingstoke, Palgrave/Macmillan.

—— and Savoie, D. (1998) 'Introduction', pp. 3–19, in B. G. Peters and D. Savoie (eds.) *Taking Stock: Assessing Public Sector Reforms*, Montreal and Kingston, Canadian Centre for Management Development and McGill-Queen's University Press.

—— and Pierre, J. (eds.) (2001) *Politicians, Bureaucrats and Administrative Reform*, London, Routledge.

—— and Bouckaert, G. (2003) 'What is Available and what is Missing in the Study of Quangos?', in C. Pollitt, and C. Talbot, (eds.) *Unbundled Government*, London, Taylor and Francis.

—— and Pierre, J. (eds.) 2004) *Politicization of the Civil Service in Comparative Perspective*, London, Routledge.

Peters, T. (1987) *Thriving on Chaos: Handbook for a Management Revolution*, London, Pan.

Peterson, J. and Shackleton, M. (2002) *The Institutions of the European Union*, Oxford, Oxford University Press.

Peterson, M. (2000) 'The Fate of "Big Government" in the United States: Not Over, But Undermined', *Governance*, 13:2, pp. 251–64.

Pew Research Centre (1998) *Deconstructing Distrust: How Americans View Government*, <http://www.people-press.org/trustrpt.htm>.

Pierre, J. (1998) *Externalities and Relationships: Rethinking the Boundaries of the Public Service*, paper for the authors' roundtable, Revitalising the Public Service, Ottawa, Canadian Centre for Management Development, 12–14 November.

—— (ed.) (1995) *Bureaucracy in the Modern State: An Introduction to Comparative Public Administration*, Aldershot, Edward Elgar.

—— (ed.) (2000) *Debating Governance*, Oxford: Oxford University Press.

—— (2003) 'Central Agencies in Sweden: A Report from Utopia', in C. Pollitt and C. Talbot (eds.) *Unbundled Government*, London, Taylor and Francis.

—— (2010) 'Administrative Reform in Sweden: The Resilience of Administrative Tradition', pp. 191–202, in M. Painter and G. B. Peters (eds.) *Tradition and Public Administration*, Basingstoke, Palgrave/Macmillan.

Pierson, P. (2000) 'Increasing Returns, Path Dependence and the Study of Politics', *American Political Science Review*, 94:2, pp. 251–67.

Pollitt, C. (1984) *Manipulating the Machine: Changing the Pattern of Ministerial Departments, 1960–83*, London, Allen and Unwin.

—— (1986) 'Beyond the Managerial Model: The Case for Broadening Performance Assessment in Government and the Public Services', *Financial Accountability and Management*, 2:3, Autumn, pp. 155–70.

—— (1990) 'Performance Indicators: Root And Branch', pp. 167–78, in M. Cave, M. Kogan, and R. Smith (eds.) *Output and Performance Measurement in Government: The State of the Art*, London, Jessica Kingsley.

—— (1993) *Managerialism and the Public Services* (2nd edn.), Oxford, Blackwell.

—— (1995) 'Justification by Works or by Faith? Evaluating the New Public Management', *Evaluation*, 1:2, October, pp. 133–54.

—— (1996a) 'Anti-statist Reforms and New Administrative Directions: Public Administration in the United Kingdom', *Public Administration Review*, 56:1, January/February, pp. 81–7.

—— (1998) 'Managerialism Revisited', pp. 45–77 in B. G. Peters and D. Savoie (eds.) *Taking Stock: Assessing Public Sector Reforms*, Montreal and Kingston, McGill-Queen's University Press and Canadian Centre for Management Development.

—— (2000) 'Institutional Amnesia: A Paradox of the "Information Age"?', *Prometheus*, 18:1, pp. 5–16.

—— (2001a) 'Integrating Financial and Performance Management', *OECD Journal on Budgeting*, 1:2, pp. 7–37.

—— (2001b) 'Integrating Financial Management and Performance Management' *OECD Journal on Budgeting*, 1:2, pp. 7–38.

—— (2002) 'Clarifying Convergence: Striking Similarities and Durable Differences in Public Management Reform', *Public Management Review*, 4:1, pp. 471–92.

—— (2003a) *The Essential Public Manager*, Buckingham, Open University Press/McGraw Hill.

—— (2003b) 'Joined-Up Government: A Survey', *Political Studies Review*, 1:1, pp. 34–49.

—— (2005) 'Decentralization: A Central Concept in Contemporary Public Management', pp. 371–97, in E. Ferlie, L. E., Lyn Jnr, and C. Pollitt, (eds.) *The Oxford Handbook of Public Management*, Oxford, Oxford University Press.

—— (2006a) 'Performance Management in Practice: A Comparative Study of Executive Agencies', *Journal of Public Administration Research and Theory*, 16:1, pp. 25–44.

—— (2006b) 'Performance Information for Democracy: The Missing Link?', *Evaluation*, 12:1, pp. 38–55.

—— (2007) 'New Labour's Re-Disorganization: Hyper-Modernism and the Costs of Reform—A Cautionary Tale', *Public Management Review*, 9:4, pp. 529–43.

—— (2008) *Time, Policy, Management: Governing with the Past*, Oxford, Oxford University Press.

—— (2009) 'Structural Change and Public Service Performance', *Public Money and Management*, 29:5, pp. 285–91.

—— (2010a) 'Cuts and Reforms: Public Services as We Move into a New Era', *Society and Economy*, 32:1, pp. 17–31.

—— (2010b) 'Simply the Best? The International Benchmarking of Reform and Good Governance', pp. 91–113, in J. Pierre and P. Ingraham (eds.) *Comparative Administrative*

Change And Reform: Lessons Learned (Festschrift for Guy B. Peters), Montreal and Kingston, McGill-Queens University Press.

—— (2011) 'Not Odious but Onerous? Comparative Public Administration', *Public Administration*, 89:1, pp. 114–127.

—— and Bouckaert, G. (eds.) (1995) *Quality Improvement in European Public Services: Concepts, Cases and Commentary*, London, Sage.

—— et al. (1997) *Trajectories And Options: An International Perspective on the Implementation of Finnish Public Management Reforms*, Helsinki, Ministry of Finance.

—— and Summa, H. (1997) 'Reflexive Watchdogs? How Supreme Audit Institutions Account for Themselves', *Public Administration*, 75:2, Summer, pp. 313–36.

—— Birchall, J., and Putman, K. (1998) *Decentralising Public Service Management The British Experience*, Basingstoke, Macmillan.

—— et al. (1999) *Performance or Compliance? Performance Audit and Public Management in Five Countries*, Oxford, Clarendon Press.

—— et al. (2001) 'Agency Fever? Analysis of an International Fashion', *Journal of Comparative Policy Analysis: Research and Practice*, 3, pp. 271–90.

—— and Bouckaert, G. (2003) 'Evaluating Public Management Reforms: An International Perspective', in H. Wollman (ed.) *Evaluating Public Sector Reforms*, Aldershot, Edward Elgar.

—— and Talbot, C. (eds.) (2004) *Unbundled Government: A Critical Analysis of the Global Trend to Agencies, Quangos and Contractualisation*, London and New York, Routledge/Taylor and Francis.

—— et al. (2004) *Agencies: How Governments Do Things Through Semi-Autonomous Organizations*, Basingstoke, Palgrave/Macmillan.

—— Van Thiel, S., and Homburg, V. (eds.) (2007) *New Public Management in Europe: Adaptations and Alternatives*, Basingstoke, Palgrave/Macmillan.

—— and Bouckaert, G. (2009) *Continuity and Change in Public Policy and Management*, Cheltenham, Edward Elgar.

—— and Op de Beeck, L. (2010) *Training Top Civil Servants: A Comparative Analysis*, Leuven, Public Management Institute, Katholieke Universiteit Leuven.

—— et al. (2010) 'Performance Regimes in Health Care: Institutions, Critical Junctures and the Logic of Escalation in England and the Netherlands', *Evaluation*, 16:1, pp. 13–29.

—— and Hupe, P. (2011) 'Talking about Government: The Role of Magic Concepts', *Public Management Review*, 89:1, pp. 114–27.

Power, M. (1997) *The Audit Society: Rituals of Verification*, Oxford, Oxford University Press.

Premchand, A. (1983) *Government Budgeting and Expenditure Controls: Theory and Practice*, Washington, DC, International Monetary Fund.

Premfors, R. (1991) 'The "Swedish Model" and Public Sector Reform', *Western European Politics*, 14:3, July.

—— (1998) 'Reshaping the Democratic State: Swedish Experiences in a Comparative Perspective', *Public Administration*, 76:1, Spring, pp. 141–59.

President of the Treasury Board (1997) *Accounting for Results, 1997*, Ottawa, Treasury Board Secretariat.

Pressman, J. and Wildavsky, A. (1973) *Implementation*, Berkeley, University of California Press.

Prime Minister (1988) *Civil Service Management Reform: The Next Steps*, Cm.542, London, HMSO.

——(1991) *The Citizen's Charter: Raising The Standard*, Cm.1599, London, HMSO.

—— Chancellor of the Exchequer, and Chancellor of the Duchy of Lancaster (1994) *The Civil Service: Continuity and Change*, Cm.2627, London, HMSO.

—— and the Minister for the Cabinet Office (1999) *Modernising Government*, Cm.413, London, The Stationery Office.

Puoskari, P. (1996) *Transformation of the Public Sector*, Helsinki, Ministry of Finance.

Pöysti, T. (2010) *OECD Public Governance Review of Finland Gives a Good Basis for the Public Management Agenda of the Next Electoral Period*, Helsinki, National Audit Office, 31 May.

Put, V. and Bouckaert, G. (2010) 'Managing Performance and Auditing Performance', pp, 223–36 in T. Christensen and P. Lægreid (eds.) *The Ashgate Research Companion to New Public Management*, Farnham, Ashgate.

Radin, B. (1998) 'The Government Performance and Results Act (GPRA): Hydra-Headed Monster or Flexible Management Tool?', *Public Administration Review*, 58:4, July/August, pp. 307–16.

Radin, B. (2000) 'The Government Performance and Results Act and the Tradition of Federal Management Reform: Square Pegs in Round Holes', *Journal of Public Administration and Research Theory*, 10:1, pp. 111–35.

—— (2006) *Challenging the Performance Movement: Accountability, Complexity and Democratic Values*, Washington, DC, Georgetown University Press.

—— (2009) 'Overhead Agencies and Permanent Government: The Office of Management and Budget in the Obama Administration', *The Forum*, 7:4, article 8, pp. 1–15.

Rainey, H. and Steinbauer, P. (1999) 'Galloping Elephants: Developing Elements of a Theory of Effective Government Organizations', *Journal of Public Administration Research and Theory*, J. Part, 9:1, pp. 1–32.

Rambøll/Euréval/Matrix (2009) *Evaluation of the EU De-Centralised Agencies*, Copenhagen, Rambøll.

Regulation (EC) no 1049/2001 of the European Parliament and of the Council of 30 May 2001 Regarding Public Access to European Parliament, Council and Commission Documents, Official Journal of the European Communities L145/43, 31 May 2001.

Reichard, C. (2008) 'The Study of Public Management in Germany: Poorly Institutionalized and Fragmented', pp. 42–69, in W. Kickert (ed.) *The Study of Public Management in Europe and the US*, London and New York, Routledge and Taylor Francis.

The Reorganization of Central Government (1970) Cmnd 4506, London, HMSO.

Rhodes, R. (1997) 'Re-inventing Whitehall, 1979–1995', pp. 43–60, in W. Kickert (ed.) *Public Management and Administrative Reform in Western Europe*, Cheltenham, Edward Elgar.

—— (2000) 'Governance and Public Administration', in Pierre, J. (ed.) *Debating Governance*, Oxford: Oxford University Press, pp. 54–90.

Riccucci, N. and Thompson, F. (2008) 'The New Public Management, Homeland Security, and the Politics of Civil Service Reform', *Public Administration Review*, September/October, pp. 877–90.

Ridley, F. (1996) 'The New Public Management in Europe: Comparative Perspectives', *Public Policy and Administration*, 11:1, Spring, pp. 16–29.

Röber, M. (1996) 'Germany', pp. 169–94, in D. Farnham, S. Horton, J. Barlow, and A.

Hondeghem (eds.) *New Public Managers in Europe*, Macmillan, Basingstoke.

—— and Löffler, E. (1999) 'Flexibilities in the German Civil Service', in S. Horton and D. Farnham (eds.) *Human Resource Flexibilities in the Public Services: International Comparisons*, Basingstoke, Macmillan.

Roberts, A. (2006) *Blacked Out: Government Secrecy in the Information Age*, Cambridge, Cambridge University Press.

—— (2010) *The Limits of Discipline: Global Capitalism and the Architecture of Government*, Oxford, Oxford University Press.

Rockman, B. (1998) 'The Changing Role of the State', pp. 20–44, in B. G. Peters and D. Savoie (eds.) *Taking Stock: Assessing Public Sector Reforms*, Montreal and Kingston, Canadian Centre for Management Development and McGill-Queen's University Press.

Romakkaniemi, P. (2001) 'Access to Finnish Public Sector Information and its Services', pp. 4–7 in *Public Management in Finland*, Helsinki, Ministry of Finance.

Rosenau, P. (ed.) (2000) *Public–Private Policy Partnerships*, Westwood, Mass., Massachusetts Institute of Technology.

Rouban, L. (1995) 'The Civil Service Culture and Administrative Reform', pp. 23–54 in B. G. Peters and D. Savoie (eds.) *Governance in a Changing Environment*, Montreal and Kingston, Canadian Centre for Management Development and McGill-Queen's University Press.

—— (1997) 'The Administrative Modernisation Policy in France', pp. 143–58, in W. Kickert (ed.) *Public Management and Administrative Reform in Western Europe*, Cheltenham, Edward Elgar.

—— (2007) 'Public Management and Politics: Senior Bureaucrats in France', *Public Administration*, 85:2, pp. 473–501.

Rubin, I. (1992) 'Budgeting: Theory, Concepts, Methods and Issues', pp. 3–22, in J. Rabin (ed.) *Handbook of Public Budgeting*, New York, Marcel Dekker.

Rudd, K. (2008) *Address to Heads of Agencies and Members of the Senior Executive Service*, Canberra, 30 April <http://www.apsc.gov.au/media/rudd300408.htm>, accessed 5 May 2010.

Sachverständigenrat 'Schlanker Staat' (1997) *Abschlussbericht, Band 1*, Bonn, Sachverständigenrat Schlanker Staat im Bundesministerium des Innern.

Sahlin-Andersson, K. (2001) 'National, International and Transnational Constructions of New Public Management', pp. 43–72, in T. Christensen and P. Lægreid (eds.) *New Public Management: The Transformation of Ideas and Practice*, Aldershot, Ashgate.

—— and Engwall, L. (eds.) (2002) *The Expansion of Management Knowledge: Carriers, Flows and Sources*, Stanford, Calif. Stanford Business Books.

Saint Martin, D. (2005) 'Management Consultancy', pp. 671–94, in E. Ferlie, L. Lynn Jnr, and C. Pollitt (eds.) *The Oxford Handbook of Public Management*, Oxford, Oxford University Press.

Savoie, D. (1994) *Thatcher, Reagan, Mulroney: In Search of a New Bureaucracy*, Toronto, University of Toronto Press.

—— (1997) 'Central Agencies: A Government of Canada Perspective', pp. 59–69, in J. Bourgault, M. Demers, and C. Williams (eds.) *Public Administration and Public Management: Experiences in Canada*, Quebec, Les Publications du Québec.

Scahill, J. (2007) *Blackwater: The Rise of the World's Most Powerful Mercenary Army*, London, Serpent's Tail.

Schedler, K. and Proeller, I. (eds.) (2007) *Cultural Aspects of Public Management Reform*, Amsterdam, Elsvier.

Schiavo, L. (2000) 'Quality Standards in the Public Sector: Differences between Italy and the UK in the Citizen's Charter Initiative', *Public Administration*, 78:3, pp. 679–98.

Schick, A. (1996) *The Spirit of Reform: Managing the New Zealand State Sector in a Time of Change*, Wellington, State Services Commission.

—— (2001) 'Getting Performance Measures to Measure Up', pp. 39–60, in D. W. Forsythe *Quicker, Better, Cheaper? Managing Performance in American Government*, New York, The Rockefeller Institute Press.

Scholte, J. (2000) *Globalization: A Critical Introduction*, Basingstoke, Macmillan.

Schröter, E. (2007) 'Reforming the Machinery of Government: The Case of the German Federal Bureaucracy', pp. 251–71 in R. Koch and J. Dixon (eds.) *Public Governance and Leadership*, Wiesbaden, Universitäts-Verlag.

and Wollmann, H. (1997) 'Public Sector Reforms in Germany: Whence and Where? A Case of Ambivalence', *Administrative Studies/Hallinnon Tutkimus*, 3, pp. 184–200.

Select Committee on a Certain Maritime Incident (2002) *Report*, Canberra, Senate Printing unit, October.

Shergold, P. (1997) 'A New Public Service Act: The End of the Westminster Tradition?', edited text of an address, *Canberra Bulletin of Public Administration*, No. 85, August, pp. 32–7.

Simon, H. (1946) 'The Proverbs of Administration', *Public Administration Review*, 6, pp. 53–67.

Smullen, A. (2010) *Translating Agency Reforms: Rhetoric and Culture in Comparative Perspective*, Basingstoke, Palgrave/Macmillan.

Sommerman, K.-P. (1998) 'Autorité et contrat dans l'administration moderne en Allemagne', *Annuaire Européen d'Administration Publique*, 20, Aix-Marseilles.

Sorber, B. (1996) 'Experiences with Performance Measurement in the Central Government: The Case of the Netherlands', pp. 309–18, in A. Halachmi and G. Bouckaert (eds.) *Organisational Performance and Measurement in the Public Sector: Towards Service, Effort and Accomplishment Reporting*, Westport, Conn., Quorum Books.

Sørensen, E. and Torfing, J. (2009) 'Making Governance Networks Effective and Democratic through Metagovernance', *Public Administration* 87:2, pp. 234–58.

SOU 2007:75 (2007) *Att styra staten: Regeringens styring av sin förvaltning*, Stockholm, Statens Offentliga Utredningen.

Spierenberg, D. (1979) 'Proposals for Reform of the Commission of the European Communities and its Services', Brussels, Commission of the European Communities.

State Services Commission (2001) *Review of the Centre*, Wellington (NZ) <http://www.ssc.govt.nz/roc>.

—— (2002) *Current Problems in Public Management*, Wellington (NZ) <http://www.ssc.govt.nz/current-problems-public-management>.

Statistics Canada (1995) *Canada: A Portrait*, Ottawa, Minister of Industry.

Steane, P. (2008) 'Public Management Reforms in Australia and New Zealand', *Public Management Review*, 10:4, pp. 453–65.

Steering Group (1991) *Review of State Sector Reforms*, Auckland, State Service Commission.

Steunenberg, B. and Mol, N. (1997) 'Fiscal and Financial Decentralization: A Comparative

Analysis of Six West European Countries', pp. 235–56, in J.-E. Lane (ed.) *Public Sector Reform: Rationale, Trends and Problems*, London, Sage.

Stevens, A. and Stevens, H. (2001) *Brussels Bureaucracts? The Administration of the European Union*, Basingstoke, Palgrave.

Stewart, J. (1994) 'The Rebuilding of Public Accountability', pp. 75–9, in N. Flynn (ed.) *Reader: Change in the Civil Service*, London, Public Finance Foundations.

Stivers, C. (2009) 'The Ontology of Public Space: Grounding Governance in Social Reality', *American Behavioural Scientist*, 52:7, 1095–108.

Stockman, D. (1986) *The Triumph of Politics*, London, Bodley Head.

Stone, B. (1995) 'Administrative Accountability in the "Westminster" Democracies: Towards a New Conceptual Framework', *Governance*, 8:4, pp. 505–26.

Stone, D. (1996) *Capturing the Political Imagination: Think Tanks and the Policy Process*, London, Frank Cass.

Straw, J. (1998) 'Resource Accounting and NHS Trusts', *Public Money and Management*, 18:2, April/June, pp. 35–8.

Summa, H. (1995) 'Old and New Techniques for Productivity Promotion: From Cheese-Slicing to a Quest for Quality', pp. 155–65, in A. Halachmi and G. Bouckaert (eds.) *Public Productivity through Quality and Strategic Management*, Amsterdam, IOS Press.

Sundström, G. (2006) 'Management by Results: Its Origin and Development in the Case of the Swedish State' *International Public Management Journal*, 9:4, pp. 399–427.

Swedish Ministry of Finance (1997) *Public Sector Productivity in Sweden*, Stockholm, Budget Department/Swedish Ministry of Finance.

Sylves, R. (2006) 'President Bush and Hurricane Katrina: A Presidential Leadership Study', *Annals of the American Academy of Political and Social Science*, March 604, pp. 26–56.

Talbot, C. (1994) *Re-Inventing Public Management: A Survey of Public Sector Managers' Reactions to Change*, Northants, Institute of Management.

—— (1996) *Ministers and Agencies: Control, Performance and Accountability*, London, CIPFA.

—— (1997) 'Public Performance: Towards a Public Service Excellence Model', Discussion Paper No. 1, Monmouthshire, Public Futures.

—— and Johnson, C. (2007) 'Seasonal Cycles in Public Management: Disaggregation and Re-Aggregation', *Public Money and Management*, 27:1, pp. 53–60.

Task Force on Management Improvement (1992) *The Australian Public Service Reformed: An Evaluation of a Decade of Management Reform*, Canberra, Management Advisory Board, AGPS.

Thain, C. and Wright, M. (1995) *The Treasury and Whitehall: The Planning and Control of Public Expenditure, 1976–1993*, Oxford, Clarendon Press.

Thiel, S. van (2001) *Quangos: Trends, Causes and Consequences*, Aldershot, Ashgate

Thomas, P. (2009) 'Trust, Leadership, and Accountability in Canada's Public Sector', pp. 215–48, in O. Dwivendi T. Mau and B. Sheldrick, (eds.) *The Evolving Physiology of Government: Canadian Public Administration in Transition*, Ottawa, University of Ottawa.

Thompson, G. et al. (eds.) (1991) *Markets, Hierarchies and Networks: The Co-ordination of Social Life*, London, Sage.

Thompson, J. (2000) 'Reinvention as Reform: Assessing the National Performance Review', *Public Administration Review*, 60:6, November/December, pp. 508–21.

Thompson, J. R. and Rainey, H. (2003) *Modernizing Human Resource Management in the Federal Government: The IRS Model*, Washington, DC, IBM Endowment for the Business of Government.

Tiihonen, S. (1996) 'The Administration of the Summit in Finland', unpublished conference paper.

Toulemonde, J. (1997) 'Europe and the Member States: Cooperating and Competing on Evaluation Grounds', pp. 117–32 in O. Rieper and J. Toulemonde (eds.) *Politics and Practices of Intergovernmental Evaluation*, London, Transaction.

Treasury Board of Canada (1996) *Getting Government Right: Improving Results Measurement and Accountability*, Ottawa, Ministry of Public Works and Government Services.

Trosa, S. (1994) *Moving on: Next Steps*, London, Efficiency Unit, Cabinet Office.

—— (1995) *Moderniser l'administration: Comment font les autres?*, Paris, Les Éditions d'Organisation.

—— (1996) 'Quality Strategies in Three Countries: France, the United Kingdom and Australia', pp. 265–97 in OECD, *Responsive Government: Service Quality Initiatives*, Paris, PUMA/OECD.

—— (1997) 'Chairman's summary', pp. 5–9 in OECD, *Benchmarking, Evaluation and Strategic Management in the Public Sector*, Paris, PUMA/OECD.

—— (2002) *Le guide de la gestion par programmes: Vers une culture du résultat*, Paris, Éditions d'Organisation.

Tweede Kamer der Staten-Generaal (2007) *Trendnota Arbeidszaken Overheid 2008*. Tweede Kamer, vergaderjaar 2007–2008, 31201, nrs.1–2. Sdu Uitgevers, 's Gravenhage.

United Nations (2001) *World Public Sector Report: Globalization and the State*, New York, Department of Economic and Social Affairs, UN.

Vancoppenolle, D. and Legrain, A. (2003) 'Le New Public Management en Belgique: Comparaison des réformes en Flandres et en Wallonie', *Administration Publique*.

Van de Walle, S (2006) 'The State of the World's Bureaucracies' *Journal of Comparative Policy Analysis* 8:4, pp. 437–48.

—— Van Roosbroek, S., and Bouckaert, G. (2008) 'Trust in the Public Sector: is there any Evidence for a Long Term Decline?', *International Review of Administrative Sciences*, 74:1, pp. 47–64.

Van Dooren, W. and Van de Walle, S. (eds.) (2008) *Performance Information in the Public Sector: How it is Used*, London, Palgrave/Macmillan.

—— W., Bouckaert, G., and Halligan, J. (2010) *Performance Management in the Public Sector*, London and New York, Routledge/Taylor and Francis.

Veggeland, N. (2007) *Paths of Public Innovation in the Global Age: Lessons from Scandinavia*, Cheltenham and Northampton, Mass., Edward Elgar.

Verschuere, B. and Barbieri, D. (2009) 'Investigating the "NPM-ness" of Agencies in Italy and Flanders: The Effects of Place, Age and Task', *Public Management Review* 11:3, pp. 345–73.

Volcker, P. (1989) 'Leadership for America: Rebuilding the Public Service', task force report to the National Commission on the Public Service, Washington, DC, National Commission on the Public Service.

Vowles, J. et al. (1995) *Towards Consensus: The 1993 Election in New Zealand and the Transition to Proportional Representation*, Auckland, Auckland University Press.

Wagschal, U. (2007) 'A Mortgage on the Future? Public Debt Expenditure and its Determinants, 1981–2001', pp. 215–44, in F. Castles (ed.) *The Disappearing State: Retrenchment Realities in an Age of Globalisation*, Cheltenham, Edward Elgar.

Walker, R. (2001) 'Great Expectations: Can Social Science Evaluate New Labour's Policies?' *Evaluation*, 7:3, pp. 305–30.

Wanna, J.; Jensen, L., and De Vries, J. (eds.) (2003) *Controlling Public Expenditure: The Changing Roles of Central Budget Agencies—Better Guardians?*, Cheltenham, Edward Elgar.

Waugh, W. (2006) 'The Political Costs of Failure in the Katrina and Rita Disasters' *Annals of the American Academy of Political and Social Science*, March 604, pp. 10–25.

Weber, M. (1947) *The Theory of Social and Economic Organisation* (translated by A. M. Henderson and Talcott Parsons), Glencoe, Ill., The Free Press.

Weiss, C. (1992) *Organisations for Policy Analysis: Helping Government Think*, London, Sage.

Whitcombe, J. and Gregory, R. (2008) 'Assessing the Quality of Government in Post-NPM New Zealand: Mediating Social Science with Social Criticism', paper presented to the Structure and Organization of Government (SOG) Conference, Gothenburg, 13–15 November.

White, A. and Dunleavy, P. (2010) *Making and Breaking Whitehall Departments: A Guide to Machinery of Government Changes*, London, Institute of Government/London School of Economics.

Wildavsky, A. (1979) *Speaking Truth to Power: The Art and Craft of Policy Analysis*, Boston, Little, Brown and Co.

Wilkinson, R. and Pickett, K. (2010) *The Spirit Level: Why Equality is Better for Everyone*, London, Penguin.

Williams, D. (2000) 'Reinventing the Proverbs of Government', *Public Administration Review*, 60:6, November/December, pp. 522–34.

Williamson, O. (1975) *Markets and Hierarchies: Analysis and Anti-Trust Implications*, New York, Free Press.

Wilson, J. Q. (1989) *Bureaucracy*, New York, Basic Books.

Wise, C. (1990) 'Public Service Configurations and Public Organizations: Public Organizational Design in the Post-Privatization Era', *Public Administration Review*, 50:2, pp. 141–55.

Wollmann, H. (1997) 'Modernization of the Public Sector and Public Administration in the Federal Republic of Germany: (Mostly) a Story of Fragmented Incrementalism', pp. 79–103, in M. Muramatsu and F. Naschold (eds.) *State and Administration in Japan and Germany: A*

Comparative Perspective on Continuity and Change, Berlin, de Gruyter.

Wollmann, H. (2001) 'Germany's Trajectory of Public Sector Modernization: Continuities and Discontinuities', *Policy and Politics*, 29:2, pp. 151–69.

—— (ed.) (2003) *Evaluation of Public Sector Reform: Concepts and Practice in International Perspective*, Cheltenham and Northampton, Mass., Edward Elgar.

World Bank (Latin America and the Caribbean) (2008) 'Review of the Policy Utility of the worldwide Governance Indicators for the Central American Countries', working paper 0108, June 11, Washington DC, World Bank.

Worthy, B. (2010) 'More Open but Not More Trusted? The Effect of the Freedom of Information Act 2000 on the United Kingdom Central Government', *Governance*, 23:4, pp. 561–82.

Wright, V. (1989) *The Government and Politics of France* (3rd edn.), London, Unwin Hyman.

—— (1997) 'The Paradoxes of Administrative Reform', pp. 7–13, in W. Kickert (ed.) *Public Management and Administrative Reform in Western Europe*, Cheltenham, Edward Elgar.

Yesilkagit, K. and De Vries, J. (2004) 'Reform Styles of Political and Administrative Elites in Majoritarian and Consensus Democracies: Public Management Reforms in New Zealand and the Netherlands', *Public Administration*, 82:4, pp. 951–74.

Yin, R. (1994) *Case Study Research: Design and Methods* (2nd edn.), London, Sage.

Younge, G. (2003) 'Shades of Grey' (an interview with Hans Blix), *Guardian G2*, 28 March, pp. 2–3.

Zifcak, S. (1994) *New Managerialism: Administrative Reform in Whitehall and Canberra*, Buckingham, Open University Press.

■ INDEX

A

aboriginal peoples 231, 247
accountability 7, 110, 180
  management 197–8, 199–201,
    204
  politicians 168–74
accounting systems 83–6, 308–9
  accruals 85, 317
  cash 84, 85
  double-entry book-keeping 84
  FABRIC 83
  Whole-of Government
    Accounting (WGA) 85–6
  see also auditing
administration:
  development 6
  vs management 184
  see also bureaucracy; civil service;
    management; political-
    administrative systems
administrative factors 34
administrative systems:
  resistance to change 42–3
  see also European Commission;
    individual countries
advice 107, 302, 308, 316, 328
  Australia 233, 234
  consultants 4, 6, 14, 29, 66, 156
  European Commission 68, 70
  source of 66–7
  see also ideas
advisers, political 175–6, 212
Afghanistan 1
agencies 40–3, 132
  central 77, 79, 81, 83, 103–6,
    113, 116, 250, 252–3
  created 99, 103, 261, 282, 287
  executive 2, 14, 140, 163, 165,
    187, 198, 218, 314–17, 322
  international 13, 97
  merged 308, 324
Anglo-Saxon-model 19
attribution problem 134–5, 144
auditing 156, 252, 273, 294–5
  central 165
  explosion of 204
  internal 244, 260–1
  performance 86–7, 197–8, 287,
    309, 319

reforms 71, 86–7
  see also accounting systems
Australia 210, 231–7
  administrative system 55, 66,
    233–4
  centralization 53
  citizen pressure 232
  downsizing 232, 233, 236
  economic growth 231
  elite decision-making 233
  elite relationships 60, 65–6, 171,
    175–6, 187
  Government Business
    Enterprises 234
  immigration 231
  international trade 231
  key events 237
  new management ideas 232
  Outcome Framework 83
  party politics 232–3
  personnel management 88, 91
  policy advice 66
  political system 55, 66, 232
  population 231
  privatization 234
  public private partnerships 232
  Public Service Act 90
  Public Service (APS) 151
  public spending 231
  reform:
    implementation 235
    package 234–5
    results 130, 136, 138, 152–3,
      235–6
    trajectory 80, 82, 84, 86–7, 89,
      92–3, 96–7, 100–1, 103,
      107–8, 110, 116–17
    types of 6, 11, 12, 38, 40
  socio-economic indicators 224,
    225, 226, 228
  socio-economic policies 231–2
  state structure 51, 52

B

Belgium 238–46
  administrative system 48, 51,
    56, 65, 66, 241–3
  centralization 52–3

civil service 243
Conseil d'Etat 62
Copernicus Reforms 18, 88, 149,
    151, 167, 240, 241, 243, 244
DNA database 202
downsizing 238, 240
elites 241–2
Flemish and Walloon
  communities 103
international trade 238
key events 245–6
new management ideas 239–40
party politics 240–1
personnel management 88, 91
political system 48, 56, 65, 66,
    238–9
population 238
public debt 238
public sector employment 242
reform:
  implementation 244
  package 243–4
  results 130, 147–9, 151, 154,
    244
  trajectory 80, 82, 84, 93–4, 97,
    101–2, 114, 116–17, 167–8,
    170–1
  types of 12, 37, 43
socio-economic indicators 224,
    225, 227
socio-economic policies 238
welfare state 238
benchmarking 38, 81, 108, 117,
    216, 217, 232, 235, 294,
    315, 322
Brazil 13, 78
bribery 286
  see also corruption
British Coal 140
British Steel 140
budget monitoring 83
budgetary restraint 286
budgeting 115–16
  frame- or block- 79, 266
  performance 80, 83, 116, 294,
    326
  a political process 82
  programme 275
  results-oriented 266

budgeting (*cont.*)
  super 78
  VBTB 107
  zero-based 322
bureau-professionalism 72
bureaucracy:
  downsizing 195–6
  political control of 101, 187–90
  traditional 48, 71–3
  see also administration; civil
    service; management;
    personnel management;
    political-administrative
    systems
business model 23

C

Canada 171, 247–55
  administrative system 55, 61,
    64, 66, 67, 249–50
  advisers 175
  centralization 52
  citizen pressure 248
  corruption 249, 251
  downsizing 249, 250, 252
  elite decision-making 249–50
  elite relationships 60
  Expenditure Management
    System (EMS) 81, 251
  Federal Accountability Act 81
  immigration 247
  Increased Ministerial Authority
    and Accountability 250
  key events 254–5
  'La Rèleve' 18
  Management Accountability
    Framework (MAF) 83
  migration 247
  new management ideas 248
  party politics 248–9
  personnel management 88
  political system 55, 61, 64, 66,
    67, 171, 247–8
  population 247
  reform:
    implementation 252–3
    package 248, 250–2
    results 130, 137, 144–5,
      151–2, 253
    trajectory 82, 87, 92–4, 97–8,
      100, 103, 106, 110, 112,
      117, 121
    types of 6, 40, 45
  socio-economic indicators 224,
    225, 226, 227, 229

socio-economic policies 247
state structure 51
trade offs 195–6
Treasury 157
welfare state 247
capacity 132, 153, 154
capital mobility 35
centralization 52, 86, 96, 104, 165,
  184, 210, 250, 261
  see also decentralization
chance events 40–1
  see also European Commission;
    individual countries
China 13, 78, 256
citizens:
  empowerment 167, 217
  participation 267
  pressure from 39
  satisfaction 144–8
  see also customers; European
    Commission; *individual
    countries*; public attitudes;
    public opinion
citizens' charters 2, 113, 151, 156,
  159, 167, 177, 287, 314, 317
civil servants 62
  difficult role 164
  long-serving 185
  motivation 195–6, 204
  political activities 162
  politicization 60–1
  public attitude towards 162,
    176–80
  relationship with ministers 49,
    59–61, 69
  role 168–74, 180
  tenure 89, 195–6, 204
  typical 90–1
civil service:
  Belgium 243
  decentralized 93–4, 301
  Finland 265–6
  France 42, 153, 273
  modernization 243–4
  morale 324
  Netherlands 294
  performance-related pay 4,
    92–3
  promotion 92–3
  senior executive service
    (SES) 92, 151, 234, 325
  staffing 227–8
  Sweden 308
  tenure 91–2
  trust in 167–8
  United Kingdom 316

USA 322
  see also administration;
    bureaucracy; management;
    personnel management;
    political-administrative
    systems
civil society 3–4
collectivism 64
Commonwealth 156
competition 116
constitutional law 6, 37
consultants 6, 14, 29, 66, 156
context 41–3, 47
contracting out 2, 3, 198–9, 204,
  233, 322, 325
contractualization 100, 271, 275,
  292
contradictions 186–7
convergence, cultural 11–15, 49
cooperation, voluntary 23, 99
coordination 96–7, 99–101, 152,
  208, 213
  failure 153–4
  horizontal 51, 53–4, 68, 97, 105,
    187, 198–9, 204, 259, 265,
    267
  see also joined-up government
corruption 28, 46, 86, 121, 183,
  185
  Canada 249, 251
  France 272
  Italy 286
cost cutting *see* public expenditure
  savings
culture 38, 48–9
  administrative 49
  convergence 11–15, 49
  European Commission 69
  elements of 64
  governance 61–6
customers 10
  empowerment 187–90, 203–4
  see also citizens

D

data:
  need for 206–7
  performance 157, 158
decentralization 96–7, 101–4, 116
  Finland 266–7
  France 52, 271, 274
  Italy 79, 286, 287
  and regime type 164
  Sweden 308
  see also centralization

Denmark 44, 79, 130, 172
deregulation 150, 308
digital divide 194
Digital Era Governance (DEG) 19, 97, 122–3
DNA databases 201–2
downsizing 186, 196
  Australia 232, 233, 236
  Belgium 238, 240
  of bureaucracies 89, 97, 101, 104–5, 182
  Canada 249, 250, 252
  Italy 286
  UK 113, 318
  USA 322, 323, 326

E

e-government 7, 212, 283, 306, 309, 326
economic factors 34–6
  see also global economic crisis (GEC)
economic growth 222–4, 231, 256
economic indicators 222–5
economies *see* public expenditure saving
education 226, 229
  Belgium 244
  enrolment rates 141
  Finland 268
  France 272
  Germany 280
  Netherlands 290
  New Zealand 299
  UK 18, 102, 104, 114, 129, 135, 313, 314, 317, 318
  universities 108
effectiveness 128
  definition 15, 129, 133, 200
  improvement in 143–4
  measurement of 108
  scores 129–30
  versus accountability 199–201, 204
efficiency 7, 134, 316–17
  definition 15, 133, 140, 200
  improvement in 140–3
  measurement of 108
elites 49, 59–61
  decision-making 32–4, 45
  see also civil servants; European Commission; politicians; *individual countries*
employment:
  Belgium 242

government 138
  public sector 242
empowerment 99, 150, 190, 326
  citizens 167, 217
  customers 187–9, 203–4
European administrative space 120
European Commission (EC) 2, 67–71, 256–62
  Activity-Based Management (ABM) 260
  administration system 259
  agency system 68
  chance events 258
  citizen pressure 258
  College of Commissioners 259
  Common Agricultural Policy (CAP) 257
  coordination 68, 143
  culture 69–70
  Directors General 69, 259
  economic forces 256
  economic policy 257
  elite decision-making 258–9
  elite relationship 69
  key events 262
  Kinnock reforms 68, 92, 94, 101, 126, 143, 157, 259, 260
  management reform 257–8, 259–60
  migration 256
  new management ideas 257–8
  party politics 258
  personnel management 88, 91
  policy advice 66
  political system 257
  population 256
  reform:
    implementation 260
    package 259–60
    results 260–1
    trajectory 84, 93, 97, 99, 101, 105, 115
    types of 10, 43, 190
  Santer Commission 70, 87, 257, 258, 260
  SEM 2000 and MAP 2000 70, 94, 122, 157, 260, 261
  social policy 257
  transparency 202
  vertical authority 68
European Council of Ministers 69, 258
European Court of Auditors 87, 261

European Foundation for Public Administration 258
European Parliament 69, 87, 258
European social model 120
European Union:
  convergence criteria 37, 136, 263, 285
  downsizing 249, 250, 252
  monetary union 238, 263
evaluation problems 15–17
evidence 13–14
expectations 146, 151
exports *see* international trade

F

financial management trajectories 77–87
Finland 263–70
  administrative system 55, 58, 64, 67, 265–6
  centralization 52
  citizen pressure 264
  civil service 265–6
  decentralization 266–7
  economy 263
  elite decision-making 264–5
  elite relationships 60, 166–7, 172, 177
  governance culture 63
  immigration 263
  key events 269–70
  Ministry of Finance 104
  new management ideas 264
  party politics 264
  personnel management 88
  political system 55, 58, 64, 67, 263–4
  population 263
  post offices 193–4
  public debt 263
  Public Management Department 14
  reform:
    implementation 267
    package 266–7
    results 128, 137, 149, 150–2, 267–8
    trajectory 78, 80, 82, 84, 87, 89, 91, 93–4, 97–8, 101–5, 112–13, 116–17
    type of 2, 14, 37
  socio-economic indicators 225, 227, 229, 230
  structural factors 42

flexibility 132, 150, 153, 193–5, 204
France 187, 271–8
  administrative system 51–2, 54, 57, 65, 166–7, 175, 273
  citizen pressure 272
  civil service 42, 153, 273
  Conseil d'Etat 62
  Directorate General for State Modernization 14
  elite decision-making 272–3
  fiscal deficit 271
  governance culture 63
  grands corps 60, 67, 91–2, 95, 275
  key events 277–8
  new management ideas 271–2
  party politics 272
  personnel management 88, 91
  political system 54, 65, 166–7, 175, 271
  population 271
  reform:
    implementation 275
    package 273–5
    results 136, 150, 151, 275–6
    trajectory 82–3, 89, 93–4, 98, 101–4, 106, 108–9, 112, 114, 116–17, 210
    type of 6, 10, 13, 19, 38, 40, 43
  socio-economic indicators 224, 226, 227
  unemployment 271
freedom of information (FoI) 8, 110–11
function 48–9

G

Germany 279–84
  administrative system 54, 58, 64, 66–7, 72, 166–7, 281–2
  Bundesverwaltungsgericht 62
  centralization 52–3
  citizen pressure 279, 280
  civil service 42, 49
  constitutional law 37
  economy 279
  elite decision-making 281
  elite relationships 60, 61
  governance culture 63
  immigration 279
  international trade 279
  key events 284
  legal system 281
  local government 38

new management ideas 280
party politics 280–1
personnel management 88
political system 54, 58, 64, 66–7, 72, 166–7, 279–80
reform:
  implementation 283
  package 282–3
  results 130, 137–8, 149–50, 283
  trajectory 78, 80, 82, 84, 87, 91, 94–5, 97–103, 105, 108, 110, 112–13, 115–17, 121
  type of 2, 12, 19
'slim state' 18
socio-economic indicators 223, 227, 228, 230
state structure 51
terrorism 281
unification 281
welfare state 281
global economic crisis (GEC) 8, 26–8, 77, 89, 104, 106, 121, 222, 231
  Belgium 241
  Finland 263, 267
  France 91
  Germany 279
  post- 190, 191, 215
  UK 54, 91, 313, 315
  USA 91
globalization 8, 36, 271
governance 7
  concept significance 21–3
  culture 61–6
  definition 21–2
  digital era 97, 122–3
  integrated public 152–3
  networks 21
  in NPG model 122–4
government:
  central 2, 25–6
  coalition 54
  debt 225
  employment 138
  entrepreneurial 9
  joined-up 7, 151, 152–3, 198–9, 204, 212, 235, 267, 317, 318
  legitimacy 163, 177–9, 241, 243
  local 2, 102, 105, 114, 136, 152, 162, 264, 279, 280–2, 292, 316–18
  minority 54
  nature of 48–9, 54–9
  open 110–11

single-party 54
  see also state
government effectiveness *see* effectiveness
government expenditure 136–9, 224, 225
  see also public expenditure
Greece 27

H

healthcare 226–7
  National Health Service (NHS) 17, 78, 85, 100, 107, 109, 114, 121, 142–3, 315, 317
hierarchies 10, 16, 99
Hong Kong 130
human resource management (HRM) *see* personnel management

I

ICT 107, 184, 192
ideas, sources of 38, 39–40, 49
  see also advice
immigration 228, 229–30
  Australia 231
  Canada 247
  European Commission (EC) 256
  Finland 263
  Germany 279
  Netherlands 290
  Sweden 305
  United Kingdom 313
implementation networks 44–5
imports *see* international trade
income inequality 228–9
inflation 144, 313
information, lack of 176–7
innovation 10, 113, 193–5, 204
  Germany 283
  Italy 287
  United Kingdom 313
  United States 324, 327, 329
  see also outcomes
inputs and outputs 15, 101, 131, 134–6, 140–3, 165, 200, 222, 301
institutional memory loss 182–3
integration 153, 232
  public governance 152–3
  service provision 198–9, 204, 212
intellectual factors 34

intentionality, degree of 34
internal scrutiny 197–8, 204
International Monetary Fund
	(IMF) 156
	Determinants of Government
		Efficiency 140–1
international networks 4, 8, 163
international organizations 264
international trade 224–5
	Australia 231
	Belgium 238
	Germany 279
	Netherlands 290
	Sweden 305
	UK 313
	USA 321
Italy 13, 43, 285–9
	administrative system 55, 57–8,
		64–5, 287
	centralization 52
	citizen pressure 286
	citizen's charter 177
	downsizing 286
	economy 285
	elite decision-making 286–7
	elite relationships 60
	international trade 285
	key events 289
	new management ideas 286
	party politics 286
	personnel management 88, 91
	political system 55, 57–8, 64–5,
		285
	population 285
	reform:
		implementation 288
		package 287–8
		results 128, 136, 151, 288
		trajectory 79, 80, 84, 95,
			100–1, 103, 109, 115–18
	socio-economic indicators 226,
		229
	trust in civil service 167–8
	welfare state 285

J

Japan 13
joined-up government 198–9,
	204, 212, 235, 267, 317, 318
	see also cooperation

K

knowledge 30, 218–20, 233
	bureaucratic 71–2, 185

citizens' 177, 179, 181
Korea 13

L

law 6, 37, 88
	Belgium 243, 244
	European Commission 256, 257
	Finland 266
	France 273, 275
	Germany 73, 282
	Italy 287
	Netherlands 292
	role of 6, 37, 217
	training in 42, 62–3
leadership 10, 169
legitimacy 193–5, 204
local detail 23

M

management:
	autonomy 187–90, 203–4, 274
	consultants 6, 14, 29, 66, 156
	financial 77–87
	macro-economic 35
	and politics 4, 161–81
	processes 131–2, 134
	versus administration 184
	see also administration;
		bureaucracy; civil service;
		personnel management;
		political-administrative
		systems
Management Accountability
	Framework (MAF),
	Canada 83
management reform see public
	management reform (PMR)
managerialism 166, 232
market model 150, 151
market-type mechanisms
	(MTMs) 10, 99, 114, 116
marketization 100, 117
mass media 5, 8, 40, 109, 163, 259
Mexico 13, 79, 249
micro-economic theories 39
ministers:
	difficult role 164
	relationship with mandarins 49,
		59–61, 69
	see also politicians
modernization 166, 271, 274, 280
Modernizing (managerial and
	participatory) 116
monetarism 313

moral standards 178
multiplier effect 14

N

Napoleonic model 19
Neo-Weberian State (NWS)
		model 19, 114, 127, 150,
			168, 212
	choice of model 22–3, 76
	customer empowerment 188
	described 118–22
	elements of 118–19
	evidence fit 82, 169, 172
	hierarchy 99
	and HRM 95
	as a normative vision 119
	performance measures 109
	pros and cons 208–10
	trade-offs 196, 198–9, 201, 203
	trust 195
Netherlands 211, 290–7
	administrative system 48, 54–6,
		64–5, 67, 293–4
	citizen pressure 293
	civil service 294
	economy 290
	elite decision-making 293
	fires 293
	fireworks explosion 39, 41
	governance culture 63
	immigration 290
	international trade 290
	key events 296–7
	ministerial responsibility 293
	new management ideas 291–2
	party politics 292
	personnel management 88, 91
	political system 48, 54–6, 64–5,
		67, 290–1
	population 290
	reform:
		implementation 295
		package 294–5
		results 130, 137, 150–1, 155,
			295
		trajectory 79–80, 82–3, 87,
			97–8, 100–1, 103, 106–7,
			109, 111–12, 116–17, 121
		type 6, 14, 38, 40
	socio-economic indicators 224,
		225, 226, 227, 228, 229
	state structure 52
	trade offs 170–1, 175
	ZBOs 294
networking 162, 172–4, 190, 212

networks:
  governance 21
  implementation 44–5
  international 4, 8, 163
  model 20, 99, 168–9
new management ideas *see*
  European Commission;
  ideas; *individual countries*
New Public Governance (NPG)
  model 24, 95, 99, 109, 111,
  127, 212
  customer empowerment 188
  evidence fit 105–6, 122–4, 169,
  172–4
  implementation 114
  implications for politicians
  168–74
  model choice 22–3, 76
  pros and cons 208–10
  trade-offs 189, 192–3, 196,
  198–9, 201, 203
New Public Management (NPM)
  model 6, 24, 95, 99, 109,
  117, 120, 166, 212–13
  anglophone literature 12–13
  definition 9–11
  evaluation 15–18, 82, 105–6,
  155, 169, 170–2
  hard and soft versions 10
  implementation 114
  implication for politicians
  168–74
  methodology 25–6
  model choice 22–3, 76
  package 113
  pros and cons 207–10
  trade-offs 187, 189, 192–3, 196,
  198–9, 201, 203
  trust 195
New Public Management (NPM)
  countries 91, 93, 103, 107,
  108, 111, 112, 116, 150
New Zealand 40, 207, 209, 210,
  298–304
  administrative system 53–7, 65,
  72, 300–1
  Cave Creek 41, 300
  citizen pressure 300
  civil service, decentralized 301
  economy 298–9
  elite decision-making 300
  elite relationships 60, 61
  key events 303–4
  Key Results Area (KRAs) 97, 107
  new management ideas
  299–300

party politics 300
personnel management 88, 91
political system 53–7, 65, 72,
  299
politics/administration
  border 165–6, 171, 175–6,
  178
population 298
reform:
  implementation 301–2
  package 301
  results 138, 143–4, 151–2,
  154, 301–2
  trajectory 78–9, 81–7, 89, 92,
  96–8, 100–3, 105–8, 110,
  114, 116–17
  type 2, 6, 11–12, 34, 39–40
Senior Public Managers
  Conference 45
socio-economic indicators 224,
  225, 229, 230
State Services Act 93
state structure 51–2
Treasury 104
unemployment 298
welfare state 298, 299, 300
New Zealand model 18
non-governmental organizations
  (NGOs) 2
Nordic model 19
Norway 13, 14, 77–8, 165

O

OECD 222, 226, 227
  on budgeting 78, 80–1
  Government at a Glance 86,
  141–2
  influence of 13, 49, 66, 156, 171
  PISA 129, 130–1
  Public Management
  Committee 6, 9
  PUMA 38, 39, 113, 207
official publications 216–17
organization:
  coordination 96–7, 99–101
  decentralization 96–7, 101–4
  departmental mergers 100
  economizing 140
  new 112
  performance indictors 101
  reform trajectories 95–106
  scale 96–7, 104–5
  specialization 96–7, 98–9, 100
organizational cultures 154
organizational forms 10

outcomes 13–15, 17, 18, 19–20
  see also performance; public
  management reform
outsourcing 38, 233

P

paradigm 75, 149
paradoxes 186, 191
participatory model 150, 151
partnerships 7, 162, 190, 198–9,
  204, 212, 317
  Public Private Partnerships 3,
  24, 110, 232
party politics *see* European
  Commission; *individual
  countries*; politics
path dependency 42, 120, 124,
  213
pensions 194, 226
performance 10
  attribution 158–9
  auditing 86–7, 197–8, 287, 309,
  319
  budgeting 80, 83, 116, 326
  conceptual framework 133–4
  data 157, 158
  improvement 78, 121
  indicators 18, 101, 165, 275,
  294
  information on 148
  international comparisons 109,
  127–30
  measurement 106–10, 234, 267,
  317, 318
  and results 126–7
  target 134, 317, 318
personnel management 151
  reform trajectories 87–95
  see also civil service
personnel regulation 42–3
planning, strategic 97
policies, conflicting objectives
  15–16
policy advice *see* advice
political advisers 175–6, 212
political control 101, 187–90,
  203–4
  arm's length 7
political factors 34
political-administrative
  systems 37–8, 47–74
  borderline shift 162, 163–8
  existing 41–3, 47, 71–3
  features 48–9
  see also administration;

administrative systems;
bureaucracy; civil service;
European Commission;
individual countries
politicians:
public attitude towards 162,
176–80
training 181
view of results 156–7
see also ministers
politics:
definition 162
and management 4, 161–81
party ideas 39–40
party loyalty 163
pork barrel 322
population:
age structure 226–7
see also European Commission;
individual countries
Portugal 151
poverty 226
power distance 64
priorities 2, 79, 189
privacy 201–3, 204–5
privatization 40, 117, 234, 314
productivity 219
Canada 253
Finland 267
France 275
improvement 9, 133, 140–3,
158
and innovation 195
New Zealand 302
Sweden 308–10
and technology 7, 192, 204
USA 326
see also efficiency
professionalism 172
public attitudes 162, 176–80
see also citizen pressure; public
opinion
public choice school 40
public debt 238
public expenditure 155
increases 37
priorities 27–8, 79–80
restrained 77
savings 9, 35–7
cheese slicing 27–8, 78–80
European Commission 261
Finland 267
France 275
Italy 286
meanings of 135–6
methodology 137

Netherlands 290, 295
scale 104
Sweden 305, 308
UK 313–14, 318
USA 321, 325, 326
versus quality 187, 191–3, 204
social 37, 138–9
see also government expenditure
public interest model 62–3, 181
public knowledge 176–7
public management reform
(PMR) 32–45
adaptation 216
announcing 13, 44
capacity 121
contradictory 45
costs 41–2
countervailing factors 41–2
the debate 1–30
defined 2
dilemmas 185–6
direction of 9–11
evaluation 309–10
focus of 52
future of 215–18
global convergence 11–15
increasing prominence 5–9
intensity 112
legalistic 327
limitations of 46, 183, 185
not a vote-catcher 171
objectives 132, 134
optimism about 182–3
politics/administration
borderline 162, 163–8
recommendations 44
timescale 41–2, 217–18
top-down or bottom-up 112,
113–14
public management reform (PMR)
implementation 3, 44–5,
111–15, 121
see also European Commission;
individual countries
public management reform (PMR)
packages:
content 43–4
piecemeal 34
see also European Commission;
individual countries
public management reform (PMR)
results 45, 76, 214–15
academics' viewpoint 149, 156,
157–8
assessment problems 131–5
criteria for 158–9

economies 135–40
effectiveness 143–4
efficiency 140–3
management processes 131–2, 134
operational 131, 134
and performance 136–7
politicians' viewpoint 156–7
value of 159
views of 155–8
see also European Commission;
individual countries
public management reform (PMR)
trajectories 75–125, 211–13
definition 75–6
financial management 77–87
implications for politicians 162,
168–74
organizational 95–106
performance
measurement 106–10
personnel management/
HRM 87–95
and regime type 159–60
transparency and open
government 110–11
see also European Commission;
individual countries
public opinion 70, 126, 154, 171,
181
see also citizen pressure; public
attitudes
public private partnerships
(PPPs) 3, 24, 110, 232
public service bargains 162, 174–6
public-private borderzone 3–4

Q

quality 7, 204
versus saving 191–3

R

Rechtsstaat model 62, 72, 94, 108,
167
reform *see* public management
reform (PMR)
regime type, and reform
trajectories 159–60
reorganization reversal 17
research, future 218–21

S

scenario 75–6
Singapore 130

socio-demographic factors 34, 36–7
  see also European Commission;
    individual countries
socio-demographic
  indicators 226–30
socio-economic policies 37
  see also European Commission;
    individual countries
source criticism 29
Soviet Union 264
Spain 13
specialization 71, 86, 96, 97, 98,
  100, 104
state:
  federal 51, 232, 238, 247, 279, 313
  hollow 3
  minimal 117
  participatory 150
  unitary 51–3
  see also government
state structure 49–54
  centralization 51–3
  horizontal 51, 68
  vertical 49–51, 68
  see also decentralization
structural factors 35, 38, 42
structure 2, 17, 48–9, 112
Sweden 187, 305–12
  administrative system 64–5, 67,
    307–8
  citizen pressure 306
  civil service 308
  elite decision-making 307
  governance culture 63
  immigration 305
  international trade 305
  key events 311–12
  new management ideas 306
  party politics 306–7
  personnel management 88
  political system 64–5, 67, 305–6
  political/administrative
    border 165–6, 172, 177
  population 305
  reform:
    implementation 309
    package 308–9
    results 128, 130, 136–7, 142,
      150, 155, 309–10
    trajectory 79, 82–4, 87, 91,
      93–4, 97–8, 100–5, 109–11,
      116–17
    type of 6, 14, 38, 40
  socio-economic indicators 226,
    227, 229
  state structure 51

structural factors 42
trust in civil service 167
welfare state 305, 306

T
Talk-Decision-Practice-Results
  framework 14
targets 134, 165, 189, 317, 318
  see also performance
tax:
  competition 35
  payroll 226
technology 192, 232
  digital divide 194
  ICT 107, 184, 192
tools and techniques 25–6
trade unions 89, 93, 233
trade-offs 184–5, 186–205, 218
transparency 7, 83, 110–11,
  201–5, 212, 234
trust 7, 10, 324, 325
  in the civil service 167
  decreasing 146–8, 177–8
  promotion of 193–5, 204
  public 8

U
unemployment 144, 271, 298
United Kingdom 207, 210, 216,
  313–20
  administrative system 47–8, 55,
    57, 59, 65–7, 316
  adversarial system 38
  auditing 114, 154, 165
  bureau-professionalism 72
  Capability Reviews 154
  centralization 53
  chance events 315
  citizen pressure 314–15
  Citizen's Charter 151, 167, 177,
    314, 317
  civil service 42, 316
  consultants 14
  Department of Social
    Security 43
  downsizing 113, 318
  driving on the right 42
  economy 313–14
  education system 18, 102, 104,
    114, 129, 135, 313, 314,
    317, 318
  efficiency gains 143
  elite decision-making 315–16
  elite relationships 61

executive agencies 187
FABRIC 83
Geddes Axe 27
governance culture 63
immigration 313
international trade 313
key events 320
National Audit Office 154, 317, 319
new management ideas 314
Next Steps 98, 113, 139–40, 199,
  214, 315, 317, 319
NHS 17, 78, 85, 100, 107, 109,
  114, 121, 142–3, 315, 317
party politics 315
personnel management 88, 90–1
political system 47–8, 55–7, 59,
  65–7, 314, 316
political/administrative
  border 170–1, 175–6
population 313
post offices 193–4
Prime Minister's Public Service
  Delivery Unit 14
public spending 28, 155
reform:
  implementation 318
  package 316–18
  results 10, 137–8, 152, 318
  trajectory 78–80, 82–4, 87,
    92–3, 106, 108–14, 116–17,
    98, 101–3
  types 2, 6, 11, 12, 14, 38, 40
Rolling back the state 149
secondary legislation 37
social security 191
socio-economic indicators 224,
  225, 226, 229
socio-economic policies 313–14
state structure 51–2
'Total Place' 174
trade offs 192, 197–8, 202
Treasury 104
trust in civil service 167
welfare state 314
Welsh and Scottish
  assemblies 102
United Nations, Public
  Administration Network
  (UNPAN) 6
United States 175, 178, 197, 210,
  214, 321–31
  administrative system 51, 64,
    72, 324–5
  centralization 52–3
  chance events 323–4
  citizen pressure 323

civil service 120–1, 322
Department of Homeland
    Security 17
downsizing 322, 323, 326
economic growth 256
economic indicators 223
economy 321
elite decision-making 324
federal public procurement 18
General Accounting Office 79
Grace Commission 67
international trade 321
key events 330–1
NASA 41
National Performance Review
    (NPR) 42–3, 61, 132, 149,
    151, 177, 326, 328
new management ideas 322–3
Occupational Safety and Health
    Administration (OSHA) 144
party politics 323
personnel management 89, 91
political system 64, 72, 321–2, 325
population 321

public spending 155
reform:
    implementation 327–8
    package 325–7
    results 130, 136, 138, 328–9
    trajectory 80, 82, 84, 89, 92–4,
        97, 100–1, 103, 106–8,
        110–12, 117, 121
    type of 2, 6, 11–12, 40, 44, 47, 54
socio-economic indicators 224,
    225, 226, 227, 229, 230
state structure 51, 58–9
trade offs 187–8, 195
welfare state 321
utopia 75

_____

V

visions 148–55

_____

W

waste 9, 121, 316, 326

Weber, Max 71
welfare service 190
welfare state 190, 226, 227
    Belgium 238
    benefits-claiming system 43
    Canada 247
    costs of 6, 35, 52, 138–9
    Italy 285
    New Zealand 298, 299, 300
    public attitude towards 133,
        163, 178
    Sweden 305, 306
    UK 314
    USA 321
    see also government
        expenditure; public
        expenditure
World Bank 13, 38, 49, 66, 156
    Worldwide Governance
        Indicators (WGIs)
        127–30
World Competitiveness
    Yearbook 141